GRAMMAR

of the

CHURCH
SLAVONIC
LANGUAGE

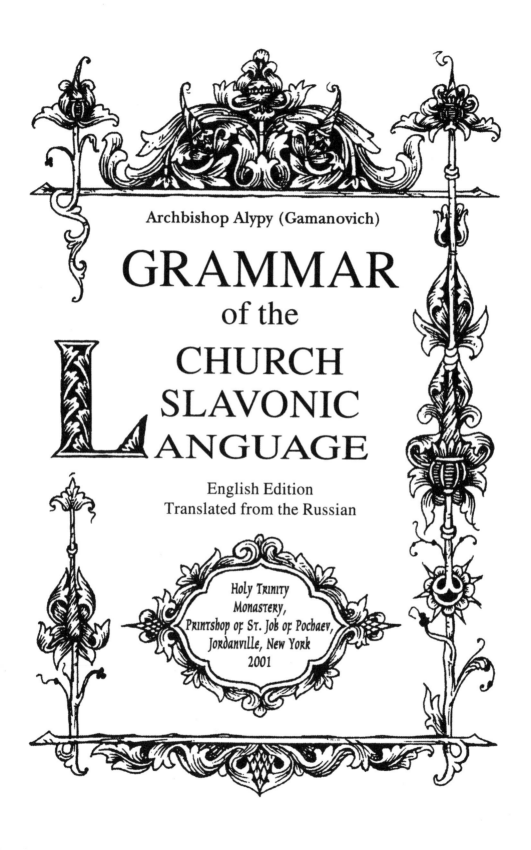

Archbishop Alypy (Gamanovich)

GRAMMAR

of the

CHURCH
SLAVONIC
LANGUAGE

English Edition
Translated from the Russian

Holy Trinity
Monastery,
Printshop of St. Job of Pochaev,
Jordanville, New York
2001

Grammar of the Church Slavonic Language © 2001 Holy Trinity Monastery

Translated from the Russian original by Archpriest John Shaw

Second Printing 2016

PRINTSHOP OF
SAINT JOB OF POCHAEV

An imprint of

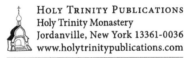

HOLY TRINITY PUBLICATIONS
Holy Trinity Monastery
Jordanville, New York 13361-0036
www.holytrinitypublications.com

ISBN 978-0-88465-064-5 (paper)

Library of Congress Control Number: 201131583 200

Introduction

CHURCH SLAVONIC, as the name itself indicates, is a language meant for a special purpose. The word "Church" shows its use in church services, and the term "Slavonic" points to the fact that it is employed by Slavic peoples, for the most part the Russians, Serbs and Bulgarians.

The beginning of Church Slavonic writing goes back to the second half of the 9th century. The entire system of Slavonic writing — its characters, sounds and spelling — was the work of the brothers Ss. Constantine and Methodius. They were born in Thessalonica, where their father was an assistant to the city prefect, or mayor. There is a theory that their father was a Slav. Many Slavs lived in the area around Thessalonica, and therefore many of the city's inhabitants knew the Slavonic tongue. So too did Constantine and Methodius. It was upon Constantine that the main part of the burden fell, in working out the grammatical system of Slavonic. He had received an excellent education at the Court, where a high post awaited him; but he chose, instead, to serve God in the monastic calling, and withdrew to a monastery on the "Narrow Sea" [Sea of Marmora]. Soon, however, he was asked to return, and was appointed teacher of philosophy[1] at the court school of the Emperor Bardas. Even in his early years, Constantine attracted attention as an outstanding philosopher and polemicist, and therefore in all difficult theological matters the Emperor and his entourage turned to him. When in 862 A.D. the Moravian prince Rostislav sent legates to the Emperor Michael to ask for missionaries that could preach the Christian faith to his people in their own language, the choice fell upon Constantine. His brother Methodius was at first an officer in the Strum district of Macedonia. Having served 10 years in this capacity and come to know the vanity of worldly life, he withdrew

---

[1]St. Constantine is also known by the name of Constantine the Philosopher.

to a monastery on Mt. Olympus. In Constantine's work of enlightening the Slavs, Methodius became his indispensable assistant. At that time there was as yet no written Slavonic language, although there had been attempts to write it using Latin or Greek characters, or the "marks and slashes" referred to by the 10th century Bulgarian writer, the monk Khrabr ["the Bold"]: Пр҃ѣжде оубо словѣне не имѣхѫ кънигъ, нѫ чрьтами и рѣзами чьтѣхѫ и и гатаахѹ, погани сѫще[2].

    The holy brothers began by composing an alphabet, translated several books, and, together with certain other helpers, set off for Moravia. Their preaching, in a language understood by the people, proceeded with good result; but the German clergy saw the Slavic populace slipping out of their influence, and began creating every manner of obstacle. They slandered the holy brothers before Pope Nicholas I of Rome, under whose jurisdiction Moravia fell. The brothers were forced to make a trip to Rome to defend themselves. Their path lay through Pannonia, where for a time they preached at the request of Prince Kocel. In Rome, the holy brothers found that Pope Nicholas I was no longer among the living; and his successor, Pope Adrian II, being of a milder disposition, received them cordially and gave his blessing to preach in Slavonic. While in Rome, Constantine took ill and died, tonsured before his repose into the great schema with the name of Cyril. His passing was on Feb. 14, 869 A.D. St. Methodius was consecrated a bishop, and resumed his earlier preaching, first in Pannonia, and then in Moravia, where, despite great obstacles including even imprisonment, he preached the word of God in the Slavonic language until his repose, in Velehrad on April 6, 885 A.D. The memory of the two brothers is observed on May 11. The Popes sometimes approved and sometimes forbade the use of Slavonic. This unstable policy depended on Papal relations

---

[2] "For previously the Slavs had no books, but by means of marks and slashes they read and divined, being pagans".

Глаголица и уставъ кириллицы.
(Указанныя числа относятся къ глаголицѣ)

Глаг.	№	Кир.		Глаг.	№	Кир.		Глаг.	Кир.	
✝	1	А	а	Э	80	О	о		Ѣ	ѣ
Ⱎ	2	Б	б	Ⱂ	90	П	п		Ю	ю
Ⰲ	3	В	в	Ⱃ	100	Р	р	(△)	ІА	я
Ⰳ	4	Г	г	Ⱄ	200	С	с	Ⰵ	Ѧ юсъ малый	
Ⰴ	5	Д	д	ꙋ	300	Т	т	Ⰶ	ІѦ юсъ мал. йотир.	
Э	6	Е э, Ѥ е		ЭЭ	400	ОУ, Ꙋ	у	Ⰼ	Ѫ юсъ большой	
Ⰶ	7	Ж	ж'	Ⱇ	500	Ф	ф	Ⰼ	ІѪ юсъ бол. йотир.	
Ⰵ	8	Ѕ Ꙁ	дз'	Ⱖ	600	Х	х		Ѯ	кс
Ⰹ	9	З	з	Ⱉ	700	Ѡ	о		Ѱ	пс
Ⰺ, Ⰻ	10	І	і	Ⱋ	800	Щ	щ'	Ⱚ	Ѳ	ѳ
Ⰻ	20	И	и	Ⱆ	900	Ц	ц'			
Ⰾ	30	(ћ)	г'	Ⱜ	1000	Ч	ч'	Ⰸ, Ⱚ	Ѵ ижица	
ꙗ	40	К	к	Ш		Ш	ш'			
Ⰾ	50	Л	л	Ⱚ		Ъ	ъ			
Ⱀ	60	М	м	ЭꙊ		Ы	ы			
Ⱁ	70	N	н	Ⰱ(э)		Ь	ь			

Числовое значеніе кириллицы указано въ курсѣ грамматики.

Буквы кириллицы начертаны по Остромирову Евангелію.

Кириллическій знакъ числа Ҁ –90 (съ греческаго) былъ позже замѣненъ буквой Ч.

with the Western and Eastern Carolingians as well as with the Byzantine Emperor. After the death of Methodius, his disciples were expelled from Moravia, and the center of their missionary work was moved to the confines of Bulgaria and Serbia. Noted disciples of the holy brothers were their followers Gorazd, Clement and Naum, who developed a widespread activity in Bulgaria.

The alphabet currently used in Church Slavonic is known as the Cyrillic, named after its composer St. Cyril [Constantine]. But at the outset of Slavonic letters there was also another alphabet, called the Glagolitic. The phonetic systems of both are equally well worked out, and almost coincide. The Glagolitic alphabet is distinguished by the highly involved convolution of its characters, and this no doubt is why it was displaced by the simpler and more easily written Cyrillic. "Glagolitsa" remained in use only in the liturgical books of the Croatian Roman Catholics.

Among linguistic scholars there are various opinions as to which alphabet is the older and which was in fact invented by St. Constantine [Cyrill]. Most scholars lean towards the view that Constantine invented the Glagolitic, and that the Cyrillic alphabet came into use somwhat later. Those who consider Cyrillic to be of later origin are of the view that it came into use in eastern Bulgaria, under the rule of Tsar Simeon (893-927 A.D.), who tried to imitate Byzantium in all things. Some, though, tend to think that both alphabets were the work of Constantine.

The basis of the Cyrillic alphabet is the Greek uncial script, with the addition of letters derived from various sources for the purely Slavic sounds. The source of the Glagolitic alphabet, according to the view of certain scholars, was the Greek minuscule hand. Be that as it may, many of the Glagolitic characters are so far removed from their source that linguistic scholars were long at a loss to determine what the source had originally been. Some of the letters, for example, seem to be derived from ancient Hebrew, Samaritan, even Coptic prototypes. (See Selischev's *Staroslavianskii iazyk*).

The Old Church Slavonic language is based on Old Bulgarian, as spoken by the Slavs of the Macedonian district. In those days the linguistic differences between the various Slavic peoples were far less than they are today, and Old Church Slavonic quickly gained a pan-Slavic significance. Yet Old Slavonic had its own grammatical and phonetic peculiarities that set it apart from the speech of non-Bulgarian Slavs. As a result, the scribes who copied over the sacred texts inadvertently gave them characteristics of their own dialect. In this manner, manuscripts of various traditions arose: Bulgarian, Serbian, Russian, and so forth.

Old Church Slavonic was also a literary language, that is, a language used in chronicles, lives of Saints, various legends and homilies; and since a language such as this reflected the influence of the spoken tongue, Old Church Slavonic, especially in its phonetics and spelling, did not have a frozen form, but gradually changed. In various places, these changes took place along the lines of the local speech. If one takes an early Serbian printed text (for example, one of Bozhidar Vukovich's editions published in 16th century Venice) and compares it with an early Russian printed text (e.g. those of Ivan Feodorov from the 16th century), one can see a notable difference in spelling and grammar, while the underlying text itself remains the same. But because Serbia and Bulgaria were under the Turkish yoke, the printing of books was not easy. Russia was in a special position. Soon printing was widespread in southern, southwestern, and Muscovite Rus', and these printed editions found their way to Serbia and Bulgaria. In this way, Russian versions of the Slavonic texts displaced the other national variants.

At the outset, Cyrillic texts were written in sharply-defined characters standing straight: this hand is known as "Ustav". Ustav texts were written with a reed pen, as can be seen in the depitcions of the Evangelists in the Ostromirovo Gospel, and indeed the very contour of the letters reflects their being written with a reed. In the

Glagolitic writing in the Zographou Gospel, end of the 9th century (page 1).

late 14th century, another hand appeared with the letters somewhat at a slant and more freely delineated: this form is called "Polu-ustav" or "Semi-Ustav". At first this hand was used for everyday needs, but later the liturgical books began also to be written in Semi-ustav, but inscribed with greater care and neatness. Soon, Semi-ustav altogether displaced the Ustav hand. In the 16th century a script appeared with a free, loose shape, known as "Skoropis'" or "Rapid hand"; but this was not used in ecclesiastical texts. Like Semi-ustav, Skoropis' was written with a quill pen, which gave them both their distinctive style.

Church Slavonic, as used in Russia, took on various orthographic peculiarities over the centuries, gradually evolving under the influence of Russian.

In Church Slavonic texts one might note the following points of orthography and phonetics, as having undergone change:

In an ancient text, the sign ˮ or ˆ was used to show the softness [palatalization or iotation] of the 'liquid' consonants р̓, л̓, н̓ [r', l', n']:

    мор̓е /mor'e/—"sea",

    волꙗ /vol'a/—"will, volition",

    н̓ивꙗ /n'iva/—"meadow".

Similar signs to show "softness" were placed over gutturals in foreign words:

    к̓есарь /k'esar'/—"Caesar",

    хитонъ /h'iton/—white baptismal garment.

Sometimes, in the manner of Greek texts, breathings were placed over vowels at the beginning of a word. However, this was not the practice in all manuscripts; for example, in the Ostromirovo Gospel book, such breathings are only found now and then. Here are some examples from the Ostromirovo Gospel:

    исплꙑнитьсѧ /ispəlnit'sja [ispolnitsja]/—"will be filled";

    съвьршени /səv'rʃeny [soversheny]/—"perfect" (p. 278 retro);

е не · з҃ · по · н҃ · е ва :

є отъ матѳеа гла ѳ҃е ⸖—

Лъ врѣмѧ оно

прѣходѧщоу

н(і)сусоу · по

нюмь н до

ста дъва

слѣпьца · зо

вѫщанглѭ ща

помилоунны

с(ы)ноу двдовъ при

шъдшоу жен

моу въдомъ · при

Ustav writing in the Ostromirovo Gospel, 1057 A.D. (page 68).

отъвьрⷢзінса /otv'rgyisja [otvergiysja]/—"turning away" (p. 235 retro);

костаⷩтиноу, лавⷬеⷩтию /kostantinu, lavrentiyu/—"to Constantine, to Lawrence" (p. 286).

In Polu-ustav writing, which appeared at the end of the 14th century, breathing and accent marks already become a part of the text. The breathing signs appeared not only over vowels at the beginning of a word, but over any vowel without a consonant before it: for example:

іѡа́ннъ /ioann/—"John".

The writer of the late 14th and early 15th centuries, Konstantin Kostencheskii, in order to aid the memory in using the marks called *dasía* (smooth breathing) and *apostróf* (breathing combined with accent) offers the following analogy: vowls are wives, consonants are husbands. Wives may go with uncovered head only in the presence of their husbands; thus a vowel preceded by a consonant has no *dasia* or *apostrof*. If a wife goes out into the street or into society, she should have her head covered, otherwise she disgraces her honor:

и̏ к томоу нѐ до̑ина быти въ домоу моу́жа ıеⷷ [га] нь [но] съ влоу́ннцами /i k tomou nest' dostoina byti v domou mouzha jeja, no s bloudnitsami/—("and is no longer fit to be in her husband's house, but with the harlots")—Thus the vowel without a preceding consonant should have its head covering: the *dasia* or *apostrof*. But over a consonant, one should not put these markings, since a hat for a man is a disgrace to him: срамлꙗеⷮ сиⷯ гꙗкоже и̏ моу́жа же́ⷩска оу́тваⷬь /sraml'ajet' sikh jakozhe i mouzha zhenska utvar'/—("It shames these, as does women's raiment a man").

If two consonants, belonging to separate syllables, meet, then the mark called *yerok* [ꙵ] should be placed as a custodian or witness, so as to "avoid collision". In the Ostromirovo Gospel book, the sign ˘ , as a substitute for the *yerok*, stands only between two identical consonants:

а̏сⷬарии /assarii/—"farthing" (Matth. 10:29); a Hebrew coin, the *as* or *assarion*. (p. 234).

варавв꙼ꙗ/varavvǫ/—"Barabbas" [accusative case], (p. 164

Greek uncial writing from the 9th century.

Greek minuscule writing, about 986 A.D. (from the Menologian of Basil II).

retro);

сарєф,о̑,оу сидоньскѫ /sareftu or sareffu sidon'sky /—Sarephtha in Sidon (p. 276 retro).

Another of the marks written about the text in Slavonic is the "titlo". These "titla" could be either simple, or combined with a [miniature] letter. The omission of letters under the titlo-sign followed a different pattern than the one customary in later Slavonic texts—thus "God" [Bog] was written б҃ъ (the modern form is бг҃ъ); "Lord" [Gospod'] appeared as г҃ь (modern form: гд҃ь); "Christ" [Christos] was х҃с (modern хр҃то́съ). Titla were used less often in Ustav writing than later became the practice in Polu-ustav and in the first printed books.

As marks of punctuation in ancient texts, a dot or cross ( ) was often put between phrases, or several dots in a decorative form ( ), sometimes adding a comma or a dash—this last form especially at the end of a paragraph.

The authentic pronunciation of the greater and lesser *yus* (ѫ, ѧ) seems to have been lost in the Russian language even in the 10th century, since Russian scribes often used these letters incorrectly. However, in Old Church Slavonic ecclesiastical texts, a more or less etymologically correct use of these characters is found down to the 16th century.

The semi-vocalic *yer* (ъ) and *yer'* (ь), which had lost their short pronunciation, became o and є respectively when the accent fell upon them in the middle of a word; if they were unaccented, the ъ disappeared, and in some cases ь disappeared as well, for example:

съньмъ — со́нмъ /sonml: "throng"

отьць, отьца — О҆те́цъ, О҆тца̀ /otets, ottsa/: "father, father's"; in this way the "fleeing *o* and *e*" were formed:

со́нъ, сна̀ /son, sna/: "sleep, dream";

го́рєкъ, го́рькїй /gorek, gor'kii/: "bitter".

The configuration ъı was, in Polu-ustav writing, replaced by ы.

ьі after the guttural consonants (г, к, х) began to disappear by
the 16th century, and was replaced by the letter и.

Some letters could be written in more than one way (for
example, *u* could be written оу, ꙋ:

o could be о, Ꙫ, ѡ &c.). The secondary forms were at first
purely decorative or practical, i.e. when space was limited, оу́ might
be replaced by ꙋ; but later, in printed books, these forms began to
have a special orthographical role.

The vowel /i/ could, in early texts, be written either и or ї,
and ї was the less commonly used, mostly at the end of a line when
there was little space left. In cases where two /i/ occurred together,
the second was often written ї: и҃іс҃ (*i-i-[su]-s*, = "Jesus"), for
example, is found in the Ostromirovo Gospel. In Polu-ustav
writing, ї is much more frequent, and the tradition arises of writing
it before vowels.

И with a short mark over it [for semivocalic *y*] (й) came into
use in the 14th century, but in the long-form endings of adjectives for
the masculine singular it remained without the short mark until the
reforms of Patriarch Nikon, and in the texts used by the Old
Believers it retains this form even today: e.g. с҃тыи б҃же (*s-[vja-]ty-i
b-[o-]zhe*, = "Holy God").

The vowel /o/ was expressed by the letters о, ѡ and in Polu-
ustav also by Ꙫ. The form ѡ (omega) was introduced into Slavonic
in writing Greek words. In Ustav script, ѡ is only rarely met with,
and is often lacking even in words that came through Greek: for
example, иоанъ [*ioan*, ="John"] in the Ostromirovo Gospel. In Polu-
ustav, ѡ is much more common, and is often used in a purely
decorative manner at that—not for any spelling need. Ꙫ also had a
decorative function, although in some manuscripts and printed texts
(e.g. certain editions of Ivan Feodorov), there was a tendency to use
it where the stress fell on that syllable.

The vowel /u/ could be written in the forms оу and ꙋ. The
latter form was used in Ustav writing for the most part at the end of
a line, if space was short. In Polu-ustav the two were

interchangeable, the choice being purely decorative. But in printed books, an effort can be seen to give these forms an orthographical significance. Here is an excerpt from a postscript to a Martyrology [Prolog], published by the Edinovertsy [Old Believers who were in communion with the rest of the Orthodox Church], as concerns how to use оу and ꙋ:

Та́кѡ же и ѡ ꙋ, и оу, разсꙋжде́нїе ѿ дре́внихъ прїа́хомъ. идѣже рѣчь ѿтѧжча́етсѧ, или изостра́етсѧ, тоу полага́хꙋ, оу, дре́внїи писцы̀. та́кѡ прїидоу́, принесоу́, везоу́, идоу́, лꙋкоу́, лоукꙋ́. развѣ идѣже, о, предварѧ́етъ за є҆ди́ною бꙋ́квою. та́кѡ, томꙋ, тꙋ, ꙋ, полага́етсѧ: или, златоꙋстъ: или поꙋче́нїе...

(From the *Prolog* reprinted in 1875 from the first edition under Patriarch Joseph in 1644—"Thus also concerning whether to write ꙋ or оу, this view has come down to us from the ancients: where the grave accent is placed, or the acute with a breathing mark, the ancient scribes used оу, as in [the words] *priidou, prinesou, vezou, idou; lukou, louku;* except if *o* should occur in the preceding syllable, as in *tomu, komu, tu*—[in that case] ꙋ is prescribed, as in *Zlatoust*, or *poucheniye*..."). Be that as it may, this rule of orthography was not always observed: under the same Patriarch Joseph there were books published in which the use of оу and ꙋ was somewhat different.

The vowel /e/ was conveyed in two different ways, according to its pronunciation: the character є was pronounced like modern Russian "э" [like English "e" in "net"], and another character, ю, was pronounced like modern Russian "e" [as in English "*yet*"; or as in "vignette", vs. "net" above]. This latter character, ю, was written at the beginning of words, as well as after vowels and in certain other cases (e.g. ХВАЛЮНЪ, /hval'en/, ="praiseworthy"). In Polu-ustav writing, there was no distinction made between the "hard" and "soft" *e*; only in certain manuscripts (for example, in a manuscript of Pozharsky's) was the ancient "soft" ю represented by the large ҫ; but in most manuscripts, the choice was purely decorative. In printed books, the large form Ⲥ was generally used at the beginning of a word. Sometimes it is to be met with in the middle of a word, but apparently without any orthographic value. The hard and soft pronunciations of є survived up to the 18th century, and the Old Believers maintain a similar pronunciation to this day.

The letter Ѕ in Old Slavonic stood for the sound "dz" [as in English "ad<u>z</u>e"], derived from a palatalized [iotated] г: ботн, мно́ѕн ("gods", "many"). Subsequently, this sound lost its original pronunciation and came to be sounded simply "z", because of which, in later texts, Ѕ was often used incorrectly.

In the beginning of book printing, the printers were at one and the same time the editors of the text, so that spelling depended on them; therefore every printer had his own idiosyncracies on how to spell. Understandably enough, when the book trade became more widespread, efforts were made to standardize the orthography.

In the South and Southwest of Rus', there were local peculiarities in print. Printing was more developed there than in Muscovy. The struggle with Roman Catholicism and the Unia obliged the Orthodox not to lag behind the West culturally. There were several large printeries in the South and Southwest: in Kiev, Lvov, Ostrog and Vilno, along with a number of other smaller printeries. Several seminaries were in this area. Epsecially noted was the Moghila Academy in Kiev, which sent forth educated defenders of the faith. It appears that the Slavonic language as a whole received its "polished" form there, in the South and Southwest. It was there that the first Slavonic-Russian lexicon and grammars appeared. The southwestern scholar Lavrenty Zizany, in 1596, published a primer and a Church Slavonic grammar. The learned philologian Melety Smotritsky published a grammar of the Church Slavonic language in 1619 which, somewhat revised and expanded, was reprinted in Moscow in 1648. In the mid-18th century, Smotritsky's grammar was republished in Moldavia for the Bulgarians and Serbs. But despite all this, in the South and the Southwest, the text of the liturgical books was not the best.

And so, Slavonic continued to evolve in its spelling and pronunciation till the 17th century. At that time, under Patriarch Nikon, a correction of the service books, or rather a new translation of them, was carried out. At the same time, the orthography of Church Slavonic was definitively established. In the correction of the books, the Kievan scholars played a major role, and no doubt for that reason it was the grammar that had been worked out in the South that became the basis for determining grammatical forms and spelling; though to be sure, the peculiarities of the Moscow editions were also taken into account. Thus the Slavonic language of the liturgical books took on its final form in the 17th century.

After that, the grammatical side of Church Slavonic did not change, but the text of the liturgical books sometimes was subjected to revisions even after the Niconian reform. Thus, under Empress Elizaveta Petrovna, the Bible was examined and corrected, though it had not been under Patriarch Nikon. It would appear that later, too, the texts underwent correction—certain words or phrases were replaced by other, more easily understood, expressions. By comparing the liturgical text of the Slavonic Gospel with the edition meant for private reading, one can find a number of differences in the words and phrases used. The Niconian translation proved to be far from above reproach. Its shortcoming lies in a narrowly literal rendering of the Greek text, often producing passages that are hard to understand. At the beginning of the 20th century, before the revolution, an effort was made to overcome this drawback. There was, in 1915, an edition of the Lenten Triodion with a newly revised text. But one cannot say that this new edition achieved its purpose too well. There were many changes in places where the old text could have been left as it was. We can show some comparisons of the text of the Lenten Triodion as it was before and after this revision: in the earlier editions, where the word бла́гоу́тро́бїе ("mercy, compassion") had stood, it was replaced everywhere in the

Polu-ustav writing from a 15th century Gospel.

new edition by блꙉгосⷫ҇рдїе ("kind-heartedness"). In the previous editions, in the service of the 6th Hour for Good Friday, мꙋжа сꙋща на Ѻдрѣ возставихъ ("I raised up the man who lay on his bed") was so changed that the last word became исправихъ ("I made straight"). The previous editions had used the phrase оу҆мнаѧ вѡиистѣ҇ва ("bodiless hosts" [i.e. of Angels]), which was changed to невеществеⷩ҇наѧ вѡиистⷵва (same sense). The new revision completely eliminated the Slavonic forms и҆же, ꙗ҆же, е҆же ("which", or in some cases not to be translated): in place of the old text за е҆же любити мѧ ("instead of loving Me"), we find in the new version вмѣстⷲ любве ко мнѣ (6th Hour on Good Friday—"instead of love for Me"). Many other examples could be brought forth, but our task is not to do research on the text; merely to examine it from a grammatical point of view.

And so, this book is a grammar of Church Slavonic as it had taken shape by the middle of the 17th century.

Since Slavonic is a liturgical language, it follows that any Orthodox Christian who desires to take part in Slavonic services should know the language used in them. Therefore this grammar is meant not only for use as a seminary textbook, but also for wider use. Bearing in mind the fact that the Russian emigré community was educated in foreign schools, we have included, for the sake of fullness, a number of grammatical points that would normally be known from Russian.

ETYMOLOGY.

—

Concerning the Characters and Signs
Used in Church Slavonic.

§1. The Slavonic Alphabet.

In Church Slavonic, there are 40 characters:

А, а—az [a]
Б, б—búki [b]
В, в—védi [v]
Г, г—glagól' [g, gh]
Д, д—dobró [d]
Е, е, є—yest' [e, ye]
Ж, ж—zhivéte [zh, = s in pleasure]
Ѕ, ѕ—zeló [z]
З, з—zeml'á [z]
И, и—ízhe [i in 'machine']
I, ï—i [i]
К, к—káko [k]
Л, л—liúdi [l]
М, м—mysléte [m]
Н, н—nash [n]
О, о, о—on [Eng. 'more']
Ѡ, ѡ—omega [o]
П, п—pokóy [p]
Р, р—rtsý [r trilled]
С, с—slóvo [s]

Т, т—tverdo [t]
Оӱ, ꙋ, ȣ—uk [u]
Ф, ф—fert [f]
Х, х—kher [kh—cf. 'loch']
Ѽ, ѽ—ot [o + t]
Ц, ц—tsy [ts]
Ч, ч—cherv' [ch in church]
Ш, ш—sha [sh]
Щ, щ—shcha [shch]
Ъ, ъ—yer [hard mark; silent]
Ы, ы—yerý [similar to i in 'bit']
Ь, ь—yer' [soft mark; silent]
Ѣ, ѣ—yat' [ye]
Ю, ю—yu [yu; Eng. u in use]
Ꙗ, ꙗ—ya [ya]
Ѧ, ѧ—mály yus [ya]
Ѯ, ѯ—ksi [x in express]
Ѱ, ѱ—psi [ps]
Ѳ, ѳ—fitá (i.e. Greek theta) [f]
Ѵ, ѵ—ízhitsa [i]

The following letters have gone out of use:
    Ѫ, ѫ—yus bol'shóy
    Ꙛ, ꙛ—yus bol'shóy iotírovanny
    Ѩ, ѩ—yus mály iotírovanny

Note: The "great *yus*" [Ѫ] is used now only in the Paschalia tables to signify a year when Easter falls on April 24; the "lesser *yus*" [Ѧ], although still in use, has become merely a variant form of ꙗ.

§2. The Use and Pronunciation of the Letters.

1) Г.

Г where it occurs in foreign [i.e. Greek-orthography] words is pronounced like *n* before the gutturals—г, к, х: сѷгклн́тъ [*sinklít*, "senate, higher state assembly or council"], а́гг҃лъ [angel] (from σύγκλητος, ἄγγελος respectively). Only two words present exceptions: а́ггє́й [name of the Old Testament prophet Haggai or Aggæos, Aggeus], and а́ггєлъ —when it means "an evil spirit"—is written without the "titlo".

Note: It must be borne in mind that "foreign expressions" can be of various origins (Greek, Latin, Hebrew, Syriac, &c.); but they came into Church Slavonic via Greek, and therefore keep their Greek spelling so far as possible.

2) є, є.

є̀ is written at the beginning of words, while є is written in the middle and at the end of words; e.g. є́зєро [*yézero*, "lake"]. Besides that, the form є̀ is also used to distinguish cases of the dual and plural from singular forms that would otherwise be identical to them: thus, фарїсє́й [*fariséy*, "Pharisee"] is the nominative singular ["a Pharisee, the Pharisee"], while the spelling фарїсє̀й represents the genitive [possessive] plural ["of the Pharisees"].

3) ѕ

The consonant ѕ is written in the following words (and words derived from them):

ѕвѣзда̀	[*zvezdá*]	star
ѕвѣ́рь	[*zver'*]	beast
ѕє́лїє	[*zélie*]	greenery

ѕлакъ	[zlak]	herb
ѕло̀	[zlo]	evil
ѕмі́й	[zmiy]	serpent
ѕѣлѡ̀	[zeló]	greatly, very much

and is also used as the Slavonic numeral 6—ѕ̄.

4) и, ї.

и is written before consonants; ї is written:

a) before vowels[3]

b) before consonants, in foreign words, in place of the Greek letter *iota* (ι) and the diphthongs ει, οι: і́дωлъ (from εἴδωλον—"idol"), і́косъ (from οἶκος, "house")[4]

5) Оӱ, Ꙋ.

Оӱ is placed at the beginning of a word, while Ꙋ is written in the middle or at the end: e.g. оӱче́нїе [*uchéniye*, "teaching, doctrine"], рꙋкꙋ [*rúku*, "hand/arm", accusative case].

6) ꙗ, ѧ.

ꙗ is written at the beginning of words, but ѧ in the middle or at the end of words: ꙗ́кѡ [*jáko* —"like, as"], царѧ̀ [*tsarjá*—"of the king (genitive case), the king (accusative)"].

---

[3] One exception is сиѡ́на царѧ̀ ӓморре́йска (Ps. 135:9—"Sehon king of the Amorrhites"), perhaps in contradistinction to сїѡ́нъ [Sion, Zion] the holy mountain [cf. *Eng.* Sehon vs. Sion].

[4] The term "oikos" for a type of liturgical text is based on the tradition [according to St. Mark of Ephesus] that these chants were sung in the houses where St. Roman prayed (Diachenko's *Complete Slavonic Dictionary*, Moscow, repr. 1993, p. 220).—*Tr.*

An exception: а҆зы́ка [*jazýk*], when it means "tongue", is spelled with а to distinguish it from ꙗзы́ка in the sense of "nation, people" [often "heathen nation"—cf. Russ. "язычникъ"="pagan"]. "а҆" is also used for the pronoun "them", accusative plural.

7) Ѻ, o, ѡ.

Ѻ is written in the middle and at the end of words: село̀ [*seló*—"plot of land", "village"], по́ле [*póle*—"field"]; Ѻ is written, usually, at the beginning of words: Ѻц҃а [*otéts*—"father"], Ѻ́трока [*ótrok*—"lad, boy"]; in a medial position in the words і҆ѻрда́на [*iordán*—"Jordan"], і҆ѻппі́а [*ioppía*— "Joppa, Jaffa"], as well as in words with prefixes or compound words: пра́Ѻц҃а [*práotets*—"forefather" or "of the forefathers"], Ѿѻнꙋ́дꙋже [*ot-onúdu-zhe*—"from whence"], первоѻбра́зное [*pervo-obráznoye*—"pristine"] and the like. Ѡ is written *a)* where [*o*] is a prefix, in words such as ѡ҆кропле́нї́е [*o-kroplénie*—"aspersion, sprinkling"], *b)* to distinguish dual and plural case-endings from otherwise identical cases of the singular: e.g. рабо́ма [*rabóm*] is the instrumental singular and means "by a servant", "as a servant", while the spelling рабѡ́ма indicates the dative plural and means "*to* the servants"; *c)* in foreign words: і҆ѡа́нна [*ioánn*—"John"] from Greek Ἰωάννης, гео́ргїй [*geórgiy*— "George"] from Gk. Γεώργιος.

8) Ѳ, ѯ, and ѱ.

The letters ҄ѳ, ѯ, and ѱ are used exclusively in foreign words: ѳео́дѡра [*feódor*—"Theodore"] from Gk. Θεόδωρος, а҆леѯа́ндра [*aleksándr*—"Alexander"] from the Greek Ἀλέξανδρος (gen.— Ἀλεξάνδρου), самѱѡ́на ["Sampson"] from Gk. Σαμψών.

9) ѵ, ѷ.

The letter ѵ is used in foreign words and has two values: as "v" and as "i".

After а and є, ѵ is pronounced "v", since these combinations stand for the Greek diphthongs αὐ [*av*] and εὐ [*ev*]: ла́ѵра [*lavr*—"Laurus"], from the Greek Λαῦρος, полѷе́нктъ [*poliévkt* —"Polyeuctus"] from Gk. Πολύευκτος (gen. Πολυεύκτου), є҆ѵа́ггеліе [*evángeliye*—"Gospel"] from Gk. 'Ευαγγέλιον.

In the remaining cases, ѷ is pronounced as "i", and some sign is placed over it—ѷ, ѵ́, ѷ: ѵакі́н, ѳъ [*i-a-kínf*—"Hyacinth"], мѵ́ро [*míro*—"myrrh"], асѷгкрі́тъ [*asinkrít*—"one privy to secrets" (secretary of state, master of ceremonies—from Hellenized Latin *a secretis*)], мѡѷсе́й [*mo-i-séy*— "Moses"].

10) ѫ, ꙗ, ѧ, ꙗ

The group of *yus* letters, ѫ, ꙗ, ѧ, ꙗ, represented nasalized vowels in Old Church Slavonic writing: ę, ǫ —these were pronounced through the nose with a suggestion of an "n", as follows: the great yus (ѫ) was like the *on* in French *coton*; the iotated great yus (ꙗ) like the *yon* in Fr. *soyons*; the lesser yus (ѧ) like the *in* in Fr. *fin*; and the iotated lesser yus (ꙗ) represented this last sound preceded by a y-glide (somewhat as Fr. *moyen*).

Such a manner of pronouncing the group of *yus* letters according to their ancient sounds has been partly preserved in Polish. They usually occurred either before a consonant or at the end of a word; if, on the other hand, a vowel came after them, then they broke up into two sounds: a vowel and a consonant; and the nasal pronunciation was lost: ѫ resolved itself into ън or ъм, он or ом: ѧ = ьн [м], ен [м], нн [м], for example: дѫти [*dǫti*—"to blow"] gave надъменънїй [*nadménnyi* — "haughty, arrogant (inflated)"], звѫкъ [*zvǫk*—"sound"] gave звонъ [*zvon*—"a peal, ringing sound"]; начѧти [*nachęti*—"to begin"] gives начьнѫ [*nachnǫ*—"I will begin"], and начѣнъшїн [*nachenshi*— "beginning"].

In modern Church Slavonic writing (as also in Russian), the *yus* characters are not employed, since the sounds they stand for have long since been lost. They were replaced by the following vowels: ѫ = ѹ [*u*], ꙗ = ю [*yu*], ѧ, ꙗ = а, ꙗ [*ya*] and (after the "hushing" sibilants [see § 7, b) 4]) а [*a*]. For example: рѫка = рѹка́ [*ruká*

—"hand"], голѫбь = го́лꙋбь [*gólub'*—"dove, pigeon"], имѧ = и́мѧ [*ímja* — "name"], позна́ѭ = позна́ю [*poznajú*—"I become acquainted"]. However, traces of the Old Slavonic *yus* are to be found in the New Church Slavonic and Russian languages. They can be seen where the *yus* breaks up into two sounds (vowel and consonant); the *yer* (ъ) is dropped if it occurs in the middle of a word, and sometimes the *yer'* (ь) also is dropped, so that the "resolved" *yus* for the most part takes the form of an "n" or "m", for example: дꙋ́ти—надме́нный [*dúti*: to blow, *nadménny*: arrogant], нача́ти—начнꙋ́, взѧ́ти —возьмꙋ́ [*vzjati*: to take, *voz'mú*: I will take], во́нмемъ [*vónmem*: Let us attend] from внѧ́ти (ꙗ-ти — вън-ꙗ-ти—вон-ьм-емъ) [*vnjáti*: to be attentive].

§3. Signs Written Above the Letters.
a) Accents.

In Church Slavonic, the following "superscript" signs [i.e. diacritical marks written above the letters] are used: accents, breathings, and *titla*.

The accents marks are: the acute (´) (also called the *oksía*), the grave (`) (or *varía*), and the circumflex (^) (also called the *kamóra*). The acute accent is placed over a vowel at the begiining or middle of a word: e.g. ана́нїа [*anánia*—Ananias], а́гг҃лъ [Angel]. The grave accent is placed over a vowel that is the last letter of the word: распнѝ є҆го̀ [*raspní egó*—"Crucify him"]. But if, after the word ending in an accented vowel, the next word is one of the unaccented conjunctions же [*zhe* — but, and, whereas], бо [*bo*—for, because], ли [*li*—sign of a question] or the short forms of the 1st and 2nd person pronouns ми [*mi*—to me], ти [*ti*—to thee] &c., then the vowel at the end of the word has the acute accent, and the pronoun is without an accent: спаси́ мѧ [*spasí mja*—save me].

There are several pronouns that have a grave accent together with a breathing over a vowel, even though it stands at the beginning of the word, so as to make a distinction between case forms, for example: и́же [*ízhe*—"which", masculine], я́же [*jázhe*—"which", fem.], &c., as well as the conjunction у́бо [*úbo*—for, because, indeed].

The circumflex accent is placed over case-forms of the dual and plural, if they would otherwise be identical to singular forms of the same word, for example: ра́бъ [*rab*—"a servant"] is singular, but ра̂бъ ["of servants, of the servants"] is plural.

b) Breathings.

In Church Slavonic, following the model of Greek, a breathing mark is put over any vowel that comes at the beginning of a word (but only the "smooth" breathing: there is no rough breathing in Slavonic): Ѻ́цъ [*otéts*—"father"], и҆мѣ́нїе [*iménie*—"property, estate"]. The breathing mark may be combined with an accent, acute (῎—called *íso*) or grave (῍—called *apostróf*): я́кѡ [*jáko*—"like, as"], а҆ [*ja*—"them"].

c) Titla.

Certain words in Church Slavonic are purposefully abbreviated, or written with some of the letters left out, and in place of the omitted letters, either a simple mark (҃) is placed over the word, or else a mark with a miniature of one of the omitted letters (҇). Such marks are known as "titla" [from the Greek *títlos*, which in turn comes from the Latin *titulus*, meaning "title, superscription"].

The titlo-mark by itself is called a "simple titlo"; the second form shown above, with the included miniature letter, is called a *búkvennoje títlo* or "lettered titlo". The letters that can appear as part of such a combination are, usually, the following: с, г, д, о, р, and the combinations are designated by the Slavonic names of these letters: "slovo-titlo" (҇), "glagol'-titlo" (҇), "dobro-titlo" (҇), "on-titlo" (҇), and "rtsy-titlo" (҇).

Note: Not any word is written with a titlo, but only words indicating the object of special respect or veneration, for example: гд҃ь

[*Gospod'* —Lord], а́гг҃лъ [Angel], (but а́ггелъ *without* the titlo means "an evil spirit"), бг҃ъ [*Bog*—"God"] (but бо́гъ with no titlo means "idol", "pagan deity"); or else words that are very frequently met with, such as гаго́ла [*glagola* — "said"], чл҃в ҄҃бкъ [*chelovek* —"man"].

The following are common words written with a titlo:

а́гг҃лъ [*angel*—angel]
ап҃лъ [*apóstol*—apostle]
бг҃ъ [*Bog* — God]
бж҃твенный [*bozhéstvenny* — divine]
бла́гъ [*blag* — good]
бл҃же́нъ [*blazhén*—blessed, blissful]
бл҃гослове́нъ [*blagoslovén* — blessed]
бл҃гоче́тнѡ [*blagochéstno* — devoutly]
бл҃гть [*blagodát'* — grace]
бц҃а [*Bogoróditsa*— Theotokos]
воскр҃нїе [*voskresénie*—resurrection]
вл҃ка [*Vladýka* — Master]
вл҃чца [*Vladýchitsa* — Lady]
гд҃ь [*Gospód'* — Lord]
дв҃а [*Déva* — Virgin]
дх҃ъ [*Dukh* — Spirit]
є҃пископъ [*epískop* — bishop]
єѵ҃лїе [*Evángelie* — Gospel]
и́мⷬекъ [*ímjarek* — "supply proper name"]

їер҃лимъ [*Ierusalím* — Jerusalem]
ї҃иⷭъ [*Iisús* — Jesus]
кр҃тъ [*krest* — Cross]
кр҃титель [*Krestítel'*— the Baptist]

Мрі́а [María — Mary]

Мти [Máti — Mother]

Млтва [molítva — prayer]

Млть [mílost' — mercy]

Млрдї [milosérdie — kindheartedness]

Мланцх [mladénets—Infant]

Мчннкх [múchenik — martyr]

Нбо [nébo — heaven]

Нла [nedélja—Sunday]

Оцх [Otéts — Father]

Првнникх [právednik — righteous man]

Прпбнх [prepodóben — venerable]

Прстолх [prestól — Throne; Holy Table]

Прркх [prorók — prophet]

Стх [svjat — holy]

Стнтель [svjatítel' — hierarch]

Спсх [Spas — Saviour]

Снх [syn — Son]

Трца [Tróitsa — Trinity]

Хртосх [Hristós — Christ]

Цртво [tsárstvo — kingdom]

Црь [tsar' — king]

Црковь [tsérkov — church]

Чтный[chestnýj — honourable]

Чтый [chístyj [clean, pure]

and others.

Inscriptions on icons:

Мр̃ .ѳ.ѵ̃ (Greek: Μήτηρ τοῦ Θεοῦ — Мти бж̃іа [Máti Bózhija, Mother of God];

On the Saviour's halo: о̀ ѡ̃нх (Greek: ὁ Ὤν—"I am that I am" [Ex. 3:14]. Slavonic: сый [Sy, "He that existeth"; Russ. Сущій].

Besides the "superscript" signs mentioned above, the following are also used: the *yerók* (´) — used as a substitute for the hard sign (ъ—"*yer*"), and in old editions it may sometimes also replace the soft sign (ь—"*yer'*"); the *kavýka* (˘) used to indicate a footnote, for example: въ зáповѣдехъ твои́хъ поглꙋмлю́сѧ (Ps. 118:15—*v zápovedekh · tvoíkh poglumljúsja*— "I will meditate on thy commandments" [here there is a footnote to show that the Slavonic *poglumljúsja* must not be confused with a Russian word meaning "mock", "deride"]. Also used are brackets [ ], known in Slavonic as вмѣсти́тєльнаѧ.

§4. Punctuation Marks.

The following marks of punctuation are used in Church Slavonic (for convenient reference, they are lined up with the forms used in English and modern Russian, along with the Russian names).

Russian/English:	*Church Slavonic:*
, запятáя (comma)	—, comma
. тóчка (period)	—. period
: двоетóчіе (colon)	—: colon
; тóчка съ запятóй (semicolon)	—.(мáлая тóчка/lesser period[5])
. . . многотóчіе (dots)	—: colon
? вопроси́тельный знакъ (question mark)	—; вопроси́тєльнаѧ [*voprosítel'naja*] !
восклицáтельный знакъ (exclamation point)	—! ꙋди́в8́тєльнаѧ [*udivítel'naya*—exclamation point]

---

[5])A "lesser period" or "мáлая точка" is one after which the next sentence begins with a small letter.

Example: И вопросиша є̈го: что оӱбо; и̇лїа̇ ли є̈сѝ ты̀; и̇ глаго́ла: нѣ́смь. пррⷪ҇о́къ ли є̈сѝ; и̇ ѿвѣща̀: нѝ (John 1:21—"And they asked him, What then? Art thou Elias? And he said, I am not. Art thou that prophet? And he answered, No").

§5. How Numbers are Represented in Slavonic.

Church Slavonic numerals are indicated by letters, placed under the "titlo" sign. Single digits are shown by a titlo over the letter that stands for the given number, and if there are two or more digits, then the titlo is over the second from the last letter; thousands are shown by a slanted bar with two short cross-strokes:

а̃ — 1	є̃і — 15	р̃ — 100
в̃ — 2	ѕ̃і — 16	с̃ — 200
г̃ — 3	з̃і — 17	т̃ — 300
д̃ — 4	и̃і — 18	у̃ — 400
є̃ — 5	ѳ̃і — 19	ф̃ — 500
ѕ̃ — 6	к̃ — 20	х̃ — 600
з̃ — 7	к̃а — 21	ѱ̃ — 700
и̃ — 8	л̃ — 30	ѡ̃ — 800
ѳ̃ — 9	м̃ — 40	ц̃ — 900
і̃ — 10	н̃ — 50	҂а̃ — 1,000
а̃і — 11	ѯ̃ — 60	҂в̃ — 2,000
в̃і — 12	о̃ — 70	҂ацѯ̃д — 1964
г̃і — 13	п̃ — 80	҂зуо̃в — 7472
д̃і — 14	ч̃ — 90	҂р̃ — 100,000
		҂҂а̃ — 1,000,000

Note: The Slavonic numerals in Cyrillic writing are based on the Greek, and therefore follow the order of the Greek alphabet. In Glagolitic writing, they followed the order of the Glagolitic alphabet (see above, p. 4).

There were also special forms and names for larger numbers, but at present these are no longer in use. However, some of the names have survived:

Ა — ᲢᲛᲀ *[tma]* (10,000)

Ა — ᲛᲔᲑᲔᲬᲜ *[legeon]* or ᲜᲔᲥᲕᲑᲐᲖ *[nesved']* (100,000)

Ა — ᲚᲔᲬᲐᲠ *[leodr]* (1,000,000)

Ა — ᲕᲠᲐᲜ *[vran]* (10 *leodr*)

Ა — ᲙᲝᲚᲝᲓᲐ *[koloda]* (10 *vran*)

Ა — ᲢᲛᲀ ᲢᲔᲛ *[tma tem]* (10 *koloda*)

§6. Instructions for Reading in Church.

1) Reading aloud in church is done to a special recitative melody, reverently, distinctly, with careful observance of the marks of punctuation.

This reading ought not to be like a declamation of secular literary works. In reading during divine services, there is no place for theatrical pathos or the display of personal emotion, which always has an unpleasant effect on those who have come to worship.

2) One must constantly pay attention to the accented, or stressed, syllables, since they do not necessarily coincide with those of modern Russian: we should read ᲙᲠᲐᲡᲔᲜ ᲓᲝᲑᲠᲝᲢᲝᲘ [*krasén dobrótoju*—"fair in beauty", Ps. 44:2], and not *ᲙᲠᲐᲡᲔᲜ ᲓᲝᲑᲠᲝᲢᲝᲘ [which would be the modern Russian, as opposed to the Church Slavonic, pronunciation].

3) Slavonic words should be pronounced as they are written, i.e. it is incorrect to pronounce an unstressed Ო the same as ᲀ, and Ე must never be rendered like Russian ё [*jo*]; the endings ᲀᲒᲬ, ᲔᲒᲬ must be pronounced as *-ago, -ego* and not *-ava, -eva* as they are in modern Russian. Thus we read ᲝᲢᲪᲀ as [*ottsá*] and not as [*attsá*], ᲠᲝᲟᲓᲔᲜᲜᲀᲒᲬ as [*rozhdénnago*], not [*razhdjónnava*].

Note 1: When the letters ы and ѧ occur after the "hushing" sibilants [see §7, b) 4 below], one ought not to attempt to pronounce their ususl sound, since in this position they are used merelyto distinguish one noun case from another (see §8).

Note 2: When the prefixes под [pod-], и҆з [iz-], ѿ [ot-], ѡ҆б [ob-] and the like are attached to words beginning with и҆, there is no reason for trying to articulate the hard mark[6]) separately from the и҆; it is perfectly correct here to pronounce ы [ʐi], which is actually so written in some words, for example: ѡ҆бышє́дшє ѡ҆быдо́ша мѧ̀, и҆ и҆́менемъ гдⷭ҇нимъ противлѧ́хсѧ и҆̀мъ (Matins, Verse at "God is the Lord" [from Ps. 117:11] —"Having surrounded, they [all nations] compassed me about, and in the name of the Lord I resisted them"). Ї҆и҃съ же скры́сѧ, и҆ и҆зы́де и҆з цр҃кве (John 8:59—"But Jesus hid himself, and went out of the temple").

4) One should pronounce the Slavonic г [g, gh] not as an occlusive stop [i.e. like English g], but as a fricative [as in Modern Greek, or in Spanish between two vowels—or like a voiced h]. It is believed that in Old Church Slavonic, the г was an occlusive [as sounded by the Serbs and Bulgarians] (cf. Smirnovsky's Old Church Slavonic grammar [see Bibliography at end of this book]), but in New Church Slavonic it is customary to pronounce it as a fricative, as in Ukrainian.

THE SOUNDS OF CHURCH SLAVONIC.

§7. The Division of Sounds.

The sounds of Church Slavonic are divided into vowels and consonants.

---

[6]) The *yerok* (ˊ) stands for the hard sign (ъ).

a) Vowels.

The vowels are either "hard" [i.e. plain] or "soft" [i.e. causing palatalization of a preceding consonant]:

Hard: а [a]   о [o]   оӱ, ꙋ [u]   ы [y]   ѣ - н

Soft: ꙗ [ѧ] є   ю   и [ї, v̈]

Note: The sound of ѣ is of itself "soft", but in the declension endings of nouns it appears only in the "hard" declension [see §33], whereas its counterpart in the "soft" declension is и.

Note: The letter є in Church Slavonic never has the sound *yo* of the modern Russian ë.

й is a *semivowel:* that is, it is pronounced like English *y* in words like *yellow*.

The letters *yer* (ъ) and *yer'* (ь) are not really sounds at all, but rather signs showing the softness [palatization, iotation] or hardness of a preceding consonant, or else marking a separation in pronunciation.

In Old Church Slavonic, ъ and ь represented reduced vowels with unclear articulation (pronunciation): ъ was pronounced like a short slurred "o", and ь like a short slurred "e". In Old Church Slavonic, ъ and ь could form syllables, and were written in the middle of words in those positions where, in New Church Slavonic and in Russian, the "fleeting o and є" occur, for example: Old Slavonic съна [sъn—"sleep", "dream"]: New Slavonic со́нъ, genitive case: сна̀ [son, sna]; OCS дьнь [dъnь—"day"], NCS де́нь, днѐ [den', dne].

In New Church Slavonic, as in Russian, the characters ъ, ь have lost their old syllabic value, and have come to indicate only the hardness or softness of consonants: e.g. кро́въ [krov—shelter], кро́вь [krov'—blood], тьма̀ [t'ma—"darkness" or "multitude, swarm"], ѡбъѧ̂тїѧ [objátiya—embraces, warm reception].

Ъ is written, usually, at the end of words after a hard consonant; after prepositions; and also to set apart prefixes when the word to which they are attached begins with a vowel. However, in this last case it is more often replaced by the *yerok* (ʼ), and in some editions the *yerok* is also placed after [attached] prepositions: thus ѡбъѧвити as well as ѡ҆ѧвити [*objavíti*—"to make known, announce"], и҆зѡбразити [*izobrazíti*—"to represent", "depict"].

b. Consonants.

Consonant sounds are subdivided according to the speech organs by which they are produced, or the place of their articulation, as follows:

1) labials [produced with the lips]: б [b], п [p], в [v], ф [f], (ѳ[=f]), м [m];

2) velars or gutturals [produced with the back part of the tongue raised towards the soft palate]: г [g], к [k], х [kh or strongly aspirated h];

3) dentals [produced with the tongue touching the teeth]: д [d], т [t], з [z], с [s], ц [ts];

4) palatals [produced with the surface of the tongue arching towards the hard palate], or "hushing" sibilants: ж [zh], ч [ch], ш [sh], щ [shch];

5) linguals [produced by the tongue]: р [r], л [l];

6) nasals [produced using the nasal cavity as a resonator]: м [m], н [n];

7) sibilants [fricative consonants produced on the hard palate]: з [z], с [s], ц [ts];

8) liquids [characterized by a smooth flow without friction]: м [m], н [n], р [r], л [l].

The sounds of the letters ѯ [ks, x] and ѱ [ps] are combinations, and therefore could be classified as "mixed".

The sound of ѳ is a dental in Greek (*th*), but since in Church Slavonic [in the Russian tradition] it is pronounced "f", it would be more appropriate to class it as a labial.

Consonant sounds are further divided into voiced and voiceless:

Voiceless: к, п, с, т, ф, ш: х, ц, ч, щ.

Voiced: р, л, м, н: г, б, з, д, в, ж.

§8. How Consonants Combine With Vowels.

Consonants join together with vowels and with the hard and soft signs ъ and ь according to the same rules as in Russian [that is, a consonant is hard or soft depending on whether it is followed by a hard or soft vowel, or by the hard or soft sign], except for the following peculiarities:

a) The "hushing" sibilants [or palatals—ж, ч, ш, щ] are considered soft by origin, and therefore they are followed by the *soft* vowels е and и, and not with the corresponding hard vowels о, ы and ѣ [see the first note to §7-a above]; as concerns the custom of writing а and ѹ after the "hushing" consonants, this is due to the fact that these consonants appeared as a result of palatalization [iotation] of the gutturals (ж from гj, ч from кj, ш from хj), while the soft vowels ѧ and ю also contain the element -j- (ѧ represents ja, ю stands for ju), so that writing these soft vowels after the already-softened "hushing" consonants would have produced a double iotation within the word. Thus, for example: тѹча [dark cloud] (instead of *тѹкjа), дѹша [soul] (in place of *дѹхjа).

In the plural and dual, a spelling with ы and ѧ after the "hushing" consonants is admitted; however, this serves only to distinguish case forms from otherwise-identical forms of the singular, and the "hushing" letters, written with these vowels, are to be pronounced as if they were written with и and а.

Note 1: In some editions, no doubt simply on the basis of old tradition, one sometimes meets with ѧ after the "hushing" consonants even in the singular (e.g. о̓трочѧ̀ [lad, boy], оу̓чѧ̀ [teaching] in those cases where this letter was used in Old Church Slavonic spelling.

Note 2: In Old Church Slavonic, the letterѧ represented a nasalized, and not an iotated vowel (see §2, 10), and for this reason could be combined with the "hushing" ["шипящіе"] consonants.

Sometimes, after the "hushing" letters, in case-endings, о and ѣ are written by way of exception: о in participles and adjectives in the neuter singular, and ѣ in nouns and the short form of participles in the nominative dual feminine and neuter, for example: Разбо́йничо покла́ніе ра́й ѡ҆кра́де (Hypakoé, from the Sunday Octoechos, T. 1—"The thief's repentance stole Paradise"); да бꙋ́дꙋтъ ѻ҆́ꙋши твои̂ внє́млющѣ гла́сꙋ моле́нїѧ моегѡ̀ (Verse at "Lord I have Cried", from Ps. 129:2—"Let Thine ears be attentive unto the voice of my supplication").

The sounds of ж and ш are considered to be hard "hushing" consonants in New Church Slavonic[7]), while щ and ч are soft. As in Russian, ъ is written after the "hushing" palatals at the end of masculine nouns, while ь is written after these letters at the end of feminine nouns: e.g. мꙋ́жъ ["man"]; и̂ возопѝ ѻ҆́трочнцъ (III Kings 17:22—"and the child cried out"); но́щь ["night"—*fem.*]; по́мощь ["help"—*f.*]; but in the case of masculine nouns that end in ч, the soft sign (ь) is always written: клю́чь ["key"], вра́чь ["physician"], ме́чь ["sword"]. The short form of masculine adjectives [cf. §53] is usually spelled with ъ: ло́жъ [= ло́женъ] ко́нь во спасе́нїе (Ps. 32:17—"Vain is the horse for salvation"); то́щъ ["empty"]; but in possessive adjectives [cf. §49], and from the short forms of participles of i-stem verbs (e.g. сотвори́ти [to make]—сотво́рь [having made]), ь is written, and here the ь is an inflection ending, which causes the softening or alternation of preceding consonants:

---

[7]) In certain other languages, ж and ш have retained their original softness, and therefore, in loan words, the writing of an iotated vowel is admitted in Russian in order to convey this "soft" pronounciation: e.g. жюри ["jury"], парашютъ ["parachute"].

Оте́цъ [father] — Оте́чь [father's, of the father], люби́ти [to love] — возлю́бль [having loved].

In the short form of particles, in the masculine gender, ъ or ь are used equally: творѧ́щъ [doing, making] or творѧ́щь (see the section on the declension of participles).

b) The combination жд is soft by its origin (see §11, b), but as a result of its having become hard, a certain vacillation is to be seen as to whether soft or hard vowels are used after it: thus наде́жда [hope], but the genitive case is either наде́жди or наде́жды, the instrumental— наде́ждею, the prepositional—ѡ наде́жди: во́ждь [leader], вожда́ [*gen.:* of the leader], вождо́мъ [*instr.:* by the leader], ѡ вожди́ [*prep.:* about the leader] and so on.

c) The sound of ц had been soft in Old Church Slavonic, and therefore was not followed by the hard vowels ы, ъ, о, but became hard in New Church Slavonic and in case-endings is combined with ы and ъ, in place of the old spellings with и and ь, for example: Оте́цъ, Отцы̀ [father, fathers] instead of the old forms отьць, отьци. New Church Slavonic does not admit of the combination of ц with о, any more than Old Slavonic did: лице́ [face, person; cf. Russ. " лицо"], Отце́мъ [*instr.:* by the father—in Russian this would be "отцомъ"].

Note: As an exception to the above rule, we find жерцѡ́въ (I Maccabees 11:23—"[certain of the elders of Israel and]*of the priests...*"), although the form жерце́въ also occurs.

d) The guttural consonants г, к, х were, in Old Slavonic, followed only by hard vowels (а, о, ꙋ, ы), and when they fell before soft vowels (и, е, ѣ), then they were softened into the "hushing" palatals and into sibilants[8]) according to the pattern indicated in §11.

---

[8]) An exception is formed by foreign words, in which the gutturals, even though they occur before soft vowels, are not subject to this

In New Church Slavonic, under the influence of Russian, the gutturals came to be joined with the soft и in place of the older spelling with ы [ʒɪ]; however, in those cases where ы had been replaced by и, no permutation of the gutturals before this latter character took place; for example: дꙋси [souls] is the nominative plural; but дꙋхи instead of дꙋхы is the accusative and instrumental plural.

e) In word roots, the letter ѣ is written in the same words as in Russian [old orthography], with the exception of the following: кꙋпѣль [baptismal font], прилѣжный [assiduous], прѣнїе [in both senses: "decay" and "argument"]; the name є҆лїссе́й [Elisseus, Elisha] is written without ѣ.

f) In the word тьма̀ [darkness, multitude] and in the soft declension ending ‿ьми (беззако́ньми [by means of iniquities], дверьмѝ [by or through the doors]) in certain editions, for the most part the Kievo-Pechersky editions, the ь is omitted: тма̀, беззако́нми, двермѝ.

§9. Capitalization.

The following are capitalized:

The first word of a sentence that begins a new section of the text, or follows a period.

Note: After a "lesser period" ("малая точка"), which is equivalent to a semicolon in Russian and English, the first word of a sentence is not capitalized (see §4).

The first word of each verse in some editions of the New Testament and the Psalter.

However, the names of the Three Persons of the Divinity, and of higher beings venerated in the Christian religion, proper names and proper geographical desiagnations — none of these are set

---

permutation: ке́дръ (cedar), ке́сарь (Caesar), ки́тъ (whale), а҆́гг҃лъ (angel), хїтѡ́нъ (tunic, baptismal garment).

apart with capital letters. However, in the Kievo-Pechersky editions from the 17th to the end of the 19th centuries, these words were capitalized. A similar use of capitals has been practiced in some non-Kievan editions in the 20th century as well.

Note: In Church Slavonic, capitalization is partly replaced by the use of the "titlo" sign. Thus for example бг҃ъ [God] vs. бо́гъ [a god, i.e. an idol], or а́гг҃лъ [Angel] vs. а́ггелъ [an evil spirit, angel of Satan]. In order to make it easier for people to read them, there have been recent editions printed without the titlo-abbreviations. In such cases, one should follow the usual rules of capitalization as in Russian and English, and write names relating to God and to the Theotokos, and all proper names of people and places, with a capital letter.

§10. Vowel Alternations.

In Church Slavonic, there is an alternation of vowels both in the roots of words and in the endings, and this is an important factor both in word-building and in changes of word meaning. The reasons for this alternation go back to a distant antiquity, to the Indo-European and Common Slavonic past.

The vowel alternations in Church Slavonic are basically the same as in Russian[9]):

1) Two vowels alternate:
е — о: вел_ю̀ [I command]—во́л_ѧ [will]; вез_у̀ [I carry, transport]—во́з_ъ [cart, load];
о — а: твор_и́ти [make, create]—тва́рь [creation];
ѣ — а: лѣ́з_у̀ [I climb, make my way]—лаз_и́ти [to clamber];
[ь]—и: жд_у̀ [I wait]— ѡ_жид_а́ти [to await, expect];

------

[9]) However, in modern Russian, in many forms this alternation has undergone a morphological process whereby it has been "evened out": for example, in Slavonic we find клену̀, кла́ти [to swear, curse] but in Russian the corresponding forms are кляну, проклясть.

о—оу̑: глóх-нꙋти [to go deaf]—глꙋх-ъ [deaf]; крóх-а [crumb]—со-
кр꙼ш-а́ти [to destroy];

оу̑—ы: оу̑ч-и́ти [teach, learn]—на-вык-а́ти [gain experience].

Three or more vowels alternate:

ѥ—о—а: веꙋ-ꙋ [I lead]—вод-и́ти [to lead]—ва́ꙿ-ити [accuse, take
to court];

[ъ]—о—ы—ꙋ: зв-а́ти [to call]—зов-ꙋ [I call]—при-зыв-а́ти [to
call, invoke];

о—[ъ]—ы—ꙋ: воз-дох-нꙋти [to sigh]—д[ъ]х-нꙋти [breathe,
perfective]—дыш-а́ти [breathe, imperfective aspect]—дꙋхъ
[spirit];

ѥ—[ь]—и—о—ѣ: рек-ꙋ [I say]—рцы̀ [say thou!]—на-рицꙿ-а́ти [to
give a name to, call]—про-рóк-ъ [prophet]—рѣч-ь [speech];

[ь]—ѥ—и—о: бр-а́ти [to take]—бер-ꙋ [I take]—со-бир-а́ти [to
gather]—со-бóр-ъ [gathering, council, cathedral]
And many other similar alternations of root vowels.

2) Alternations resulting from the loss of the semivowels ъ
and ь.

The Old Slavonic semivowels (or silent letters) ъ nd ь
underwent a change in New Church Slavonic: in some cases they
were strengthened to о and ѥ respectively, while in others the ъ
disappeared altogether and is written only at the end of a word after
hard, or hardened, consonants (for example, нóжъ [knife] instead of
the O.S. ножь), and ь either vanished, or else survived merely as an
indicator that the preceding consonant is soft; thus we arrive at the
"fleeting" о and ѥ:

о — (alternates with no sound): сóнъ—снà [sleep; *of* sleep];
и̑зсóхнꙋти—и̑схóхъ [become dry];

ѥ — (alternates with no sound): Ѻ̑тéцъ—Ѻ̑тцà [father; *of* the father];
гóрѥкъ—гóрькїй [bitter].

3) Alternations in vowel + consonant combinations.

Inherited from the ancient period of the Slavonic language are the alternations that take place in root vowels before the consonants н, м, в and j, with the following peculiarity: if the combi-nation of vowel + consonant (н, м, в, j) comes before a consonant (or at the end of a word), then it becomes a vowel as follows: єн[м]—ѧ (lesser yus); он[м]—ѫ[ѫ][10], ов—ѫ, єв—ю, [ъ]в—ы, оj— ѣ or и.

In these combinations, the following alternations can be noted:

єн—он—[ь]н; [ъ]н—ын

} ѧ, ѧ (=lesser yus) — ѫ [ѫ]

єм—ом—[ь]м—нм: [ъ]м—ым

и́мѧ—и́мєнє [name];
на-ч[ь]н-ѫ—на-чнн-а́ю [begin]—на-ча́-ло [beginning];
в[ъ]з-є́мл-ю [I will take away, remove]—воз-ьм-ѫ [I will take]—в[ъ]з-нм-а́ю [I take away]—в[ъ]з-ѧ́-ти [to take];
д[ъ]мѫ [I inflate]—воз-дым-а́ю [I fill with smoke]—дѫ-ти [to blow];
про-п[ь]н-ѫ [I nail to wood] —о̄-по́н-а [veil, curtain]—про-пѧ́-ти [nail, crucify]—пѫ-то [fetters, hobble, manacle];
трѫ-съ [shaking, earthquake]—трѧс-ти́ [to shake];
вѧз-а́ти [to bind]—ѹ́з-ы [bonds].

ов — ѫ — ав — ы:
сло́в-о [word]—слѫ-х-ъ [hearing, thing heard]—сла́в-а [glory] — слы́-шати [to hear];
ков-а́ти [to forge]—кѫ-ю̀ [I forge, hammer metal];

[ъ]в—ов—ы:

р[ъ]вáти [to tear]—ровъ [ditch, moat]—рьі_ти [to dig]; крóвъ
[cover, roof]— крьі_ти [to cover, to roof];

ев—ю:
плев_áти [to spit]—плю_ю̀ [I spit]; клев_áти [to peck, bite]—клю_ю̀
[I peck];

оj—ѣ:
по_ю̀ [=поj-ȣ— I sing]—пѣ_ти [to sing];

оj—аj—и:
напою̀ [напоj-ȣ—I give to drink]—напаá_ти [to give to
    drink]—пи́_ти [to drink];
раз_бóй [robbery, brigandage]—би́_ти [to beat];

и—ѣ:
вид_ѣти [to see]—вѣд_ѣти [to know, to wit]; вис_ѣти [to hang,
weigh]—вѣсъ [weight].

   This alternation may take place even in those situations
where the vowel occurs after в and the resulting combination (в +
vowel) falls between consonants: ва — ьі: квáсъ [leaven]— кис_
нȣти [to sour] (Old Slavonic къі_); хва_тáти [to seize]—хи́_титити [to
snatch, swipe] (OS хъі_).
   Similar changes take place in the alternation of vowels before
the liquids р, л, only with this difference: if the combination of a
vowel + р or л is followed by a consonant, then the liquid changes
place with the preceding vowel, and the vowel is strengthened (for
example: беρ_ȣ [I take]—брé_мѧ [burden], Old Slavonic брѣ_мѧ;
кол_ю̀ [I pierce, stab]—клá_ти [to stab]; however, in New Church
Slavonic this rule is often broken (for example: Old Slavonic
ѿврѣсти [to open]—ѿврьзѫ [I will open]; in New Church Slavonic
the corresponding forms are ѿвéрсти — ѿвéрзȣ).
   Examples of alternation:
ер—ор—[ь]р—ир—ре (OS рѣ):

ɓɛρ-ȣ [I take]—ɛο-ɓόρ-ȥ [gathering]—ɓ[ь]ρά-ти [to take]—ɛο-
ɓнρ-άти [to gather]—ɓρέ-мѧ [burden]; мόρ-ȥ
[pestilence]—οỹ-мнρ-άти [to be dying, near death]—οỹм[ь]ρ-
ȣ [I shall die]—ɛмέρ-ть [death]—οỹмρέ-ти [to die];
ɓρɛцни̇ (OS ɓρѣ̇цни̇)[to cast, fling]—ɓράгȥ [enemy]—поɓέргȥ
(participle)[having cast];
ɓορ-ю́ɛѧ [I battle]—ɓρά-тнɛѧ [to do battle];
Ȯρ-ю̇ [I plow]—ρά-ло [plowshare];

ɛλ—αλ—λλ:

пέ-пɛλ-ȥ [ashes]—пαλ-и̇ти [to burn]—пλά-мѧ [flame];

λɛ—λλ:

ɓλɛ-цни̇ [to pull]—ɓλαч-и̇ти [to draw, drag]—Ȯɓ-λακ-ȥ
[cloud, throng].

Note: The peculiarities noted above, which took place in Old Church
Slavonic in the combinations ɛн[м], он[м], оɓ, ɛɓ and oj, i.e. their change
into vowels before a consonant, and also the exchange of positions of a vowel
with a liquid (ρ,λ) before a consonant, came from the so-called "law of open
syllables" that goes back to the Proto-Slavonic period. According to this law,
a syllable was supposed to end only with a vowel, i.e. it was not permitted for
two consonants to come together if the first belonged to one syllable and the
second to the next, even though certain combinations of consonants were
permissible at the beginning of any syllable (for example: пρά-ɓь-дα [truth,
righteousness], н-ɛκρα [spark], ɛ-ɛ́ть-ɛ́тɓо [essence, nature] and so on).

Changes in Consonants.

§11. The Softening of Consonants.

a) The gutturals г, к, х before the soft vowels ɛ, н, ѣ, ь, ѧ
[lesser *yus*] and **j** , as a result of being softened, alternate with the
"hushing" palatals and sibilants (with the **j** absorbed by the palatal).

The origin of this changing of gutturals into "hushing" palatals
goes back to a more ancient epoch of the Slavonic language, while the
change of gutturals into sibilants belongs to a later one.

Changes of gutturals into palatals:

г	+	ѥ, н, ѣ, ь, ѧ (lesser *yus*)	>	ж
к		"	>	ч
х		"	>	ш

Examples:

бг҃ъ [God]—бж҃е [O God]; человѣкъ [man]—человѣче [O man]; дх҃ъ [Spirit]—дш҃е [O Spirit];

бѣг-ꙋ [I run]—бѣжиши [thou runnest]; книга [book]—книжникъ [scribe] (from кънижьникъ, ь not being written after "hushing" palatals), ѻ҃трокъ [boy]—ѻ҃трочѧ [child](ѧ instead of ѧ);

дꙋхъ [spirit]—дꙋшѧ [soul](from *дꙋхjѧ);

г, к, х + ѣ result in жа, ча, ша (ѣ changes into а after the "hushing" palatals):

крик-нꙋти [to cry out, *perfective*]—крнчати (from крикѣти> крнчѣти > крнчати [to cry out, *imperfective*]);

возаыхати [to sigh]—аышати [to breathe].

The change of gutturals into sibilants occurs only before н (from *oi*) and ѣ (from *oi, ai*[11]). Usually these changes of gutturals to sibilants take place in declension endings and in the endings of the imperative mood, for example:

г + н, ѣ >		з	бг҃ъ [God, *nominative case*]—бз҃ѣ [*prepositional case*]—бо́зн [gods]
к	"	ц	ѻ҃трокъ[boy, *nom.*]—ѻ҃троцѣ[*prep.*]—ѻ҃троцꙑ [-н] [boys]
х	"	с	дꙋхъ [spirit]—дꙋсѣ [*prep.*]—дꙋсн [spirits].

---

[11]) The diphthongs *oi, ai* changed into н, ѣ long before there was any written form of Old Slavonic.

Note: When the letter к comes between a guttural consonant and a soft vowel, it does not prevent the softening of guttural sounds: e.g. вóлхвъ [sorcerer, magus]—волсви [the Magi].

The change of gutturals into sibilants also takes place after ь, н, ѧ (lesser *yus*):

е[ь], н, ѧ +г+vowel >з   кнагѝна[princess]—кнѧ́зь [prince]
                               стóгна [street]—стезà [path, way]

" к"   ц   ли́къ [choir]—лицѐ [face, person]
                               восклѝкнȣти[exclaim, *perfective*]—
                               восклицáти[exclaim,   *imperfective aspect*]

" х "   с

b) The dentals д, т, з, с, ц are softened into "hushing" consonants before **j**; and then the **j** is swallowed up by the "hushing" letters:

д — жд [12]): сȣди́ти [to judge]—сȣждȣ [I judge](instead of сȣд-j-ȣ).

т— щ: хотѣ́ти [to want]—хощȣ [I want, I will]

ст—щ: мости́ти [to pave, lay a floor]—мощȣ [I pave]

з— ж: лизáти [to lick]—лижȣ [I lick]

---

[12]) In Old Russian, the letter д was softened into ж, which has survived in many instances in modern Russian as well (e.g. вид-ѣти—виж-у); Church Slavonic texts in pre-Niconian books abounded with this form of softening: исхожéнïе [a going out], преждеwсвѧщéннаѧ [Presanctified Liturgy]. In modern Church Slavonic texts, sometimes 'Russisms' such as these are encountered as a rarity: Та́инство стрáнное вѝжȣ, instead of вѝждȣ (From the 9th Eirmos of the Canon of Christmas Matins—"A strange mystery do I see..."). Хвали́те є҆го̀ во оу҆твержéнïи си́лы є҆гẁ (Verse at the Praises—"Praise Him in the firmament of His power", Ps. 150:1).

с — ш: пнса́_тн [to write]—пншꙋ̆ [I write]

ц — ч: Ѻ҆те́ц_ъ [father]—Ѻ҆те́ч_е_скїй [fatherly, paternal]

The combination ск becomes ст before a soft vowel; before j, it becomes щ: галїле́йскъ [Galilean, pertaining to Galilee]—ѡ҆ галїле́йстѣ [about the Galilean...], и҆ск_а́тн [to seek]— и҆щ_ꙋ̆ [I seek].

A similar permutation takes place in the following combinations:

зг — жд: ро́зга [vine, birch]—ро́ждїе [branch]

зд — жд: прнгвозди́_тн [to nail, perf.]—прнгвожда́_тн [impf.]

здн—ждн: ѹ҆празднн́_тн [abolish, pf.]—ѹ҆пражднꙗ́_тн [impf.]

зн—жн: соблазни́_тн [to entice, pf.]—соблажнꙗ́_тн [impf.]

тв—щвл: ѹ҆мертвн́_тн [deaden, mortify, pf.]—ѹ҆мерщвлꙗ́_тн [impf.]

сл—шл: мы́слн_тн [to think]—помышлꙗ́_тн [to reflect, think about]

c) The labials б, п, в, ф and м, if followed by j, are softened by adding л, and in this case the j does not disappear:

люби́_тн [to love]—любл_ю̀ [I love]

лови́_тн [to try to catch]—ловл_ю̀ [I seek to catch]

топи́_тн [to sink]—топл_ю̀ [I sink]

а҆враа́м_ъ [Abraham]—а҆враа́мл_ь [Abraham's].

§12. Changes of Consonants In Combinations.

When consonants come together, certain sounds change into others:

a) The groups дт, тт change into ст:

клад_ꙋ̆ [I put, set]—клас_тн (instead of *клад_тн—to put)

плет_ꙋ̆ [I plait, weave]—плес_тн̀ [to plait](instead of *плет_тн̀).

b) г, к joined with т before н become щ: мог_ꙋ̆ [I can]—мощн̀ [to be able], пек_ꙋ̆ [I bake] —пещн̀ [to bake].

c) Sometimes the combination зж is replaced by жд, as in Old Slavonic: вождєлѣ́ти, вождєлѣ́нїє (instead of возжєла́ти, "to yearn, long for"). Всегда̀ ꙗдо́мый и҆ никогда́же и҆жднва́ємый (Liturgy, Prayer of the Fraction—"ever eaten, and never consumed")—instead of и҆зжнва́ємый, hence the Russian иждивеніе [living expenditures]; ражднза́ємый [inflamed with passions] instead of разжнза́ємый.

d) The prefixes воз, и҆з, раз change their final з to с before the voiceless consonants к, п, т, х, ц and ч: раскопа́ти [to dig up], воспѣ́ти [to extol, sing praises of], расто́ргнꙋти [brek forth, tear apart], и҆схо́дъ [exodus, going-out], и҆сцѣли́ти [to heal], и҆счеза́ти [to vanish].

Note: The prefix низ does not change its final з before the above-mentioned voiceless consonants: e.g низпосла́ти [to send down]. Before ш, these prefixes do not change their letter з: возше́лъ є҆сѝ ["thou didst ascend"]. As to the spelling that would be used before ф and щ, it is difficult to say, as such combinations are not likely to occur in Church Slavonic.

§13. Elimination of Consonants.

a) The labials б and п drop out before н, while в drops out after б: с_гиб_а́ти [to bend, *impf.*]— г_нꙋ_ти [*pf.*] (instead of *гб_нꙋ_ти), сп_а́ти [to sleep]—со́_нъ [sleep (*noun*), a dream] instead of со́п_нъ), вла́сть [power, authority]—о̑б_ласть [rule over a specific district, realm](instead of *о̑б_вла́сть).

b) The dentals д, т drop out before the liquids л, м, н and с:
па́д_ати [to fall]—па́_лъ [fell] (instead of *па́д_лъ)
плес_ти́ (плет_тѝ) [to plait, braid, weave]—пле́_лъ [plaited] (instead of *пле́т_лъ)
вѣ́д_ати [to wit, to know]—вѣ́_мъ [I know] (instead of *вѣ́д_мъ),
вѣ́_си (for *вѣ́д_си) [thou knowest]
оу҆_вад_а́ти [to weaken]—ва́_нꙋ_ти (for *вад_нꙋ_ти) [to wilt].

Note: The final ѧ in the indeclinable participle (used only in compound verb tenses) is never dropped in Church Slavonic: нє́слѧ є҆сѝ [thou haste borne, carried](but not *нє́сѧ as in modern Russian).

§14. Sound Patterns in Slavonic.

1) While Russian has the fully-vocalized syllables оро, оло, ере—to these correspond the syllables ра, ла, ре, ле in Church Slavonic:

Russian:	Church Slavonic:
борода (beard)	брада̀
колосъ (ear of corn)	кла́съ
серебро (silver)	сребро̀
молоко (milk)	млеко̀

Note: The word "пелена [swaddling clothes]" in New Church Slavonic has the same vowel combination as in Russian: пелена̀ (instead of the Old Church Slavonic пла́на): пеленами повѝта (Christmas Matins, Ode 1—"wrapped in swaddling clothes").

2) Where there is an initial "o" in Russian words, this often corresponds to an initial є in Church Slavonic:

Russian:	Slavonic:
олень	є҆ле́нь [deer]
одинъ	є҆ди́нъ [one]

§15. Word Structure.

In Church Slavonic, the morphological makeup of words is the same as in Russian.

We distinguish the following word-parts: root, ending and prefix.

That part of the word that remains unchanged in all forms, declensions or conjugations, is called the *root*; the part of the word that comes after the root is known as the *ending*; the part of the word that stands before the root, is called a *prefix*. For example: in the word оу҄-вѣр-ов-а-ти [to come to believe (in)], оу҄- is a prefix, -вѣр- is the root, and -ов-а-ти is the ending.

In endings, one must further make the distinction between *suffixes* and *inflections*. An inflection is the part of the ending that changes when the word is declined [in nouns, adjectives and participles] or conjugated [in verbs]. A suffix is an unchangeable part of the ending, located between the root and the inflection. Thus in the preceding example, -ти is the inflection ending that shows this is the infinitive of a verb, while -ов-а- consists of two verb suffixes.

A suffix serves to form various parts of speech from the root, or else to change the meaning; an inflection shows that the word belongs to one or another part of speech, and shows how it is related to other words in the sentence, for example: мꙋж-ъ [man], мꙋж-е-ств-о [courage, fortitude], мꙋж-е-ств-енн-ый [manly, steadfast], мꙋж-е-ств-енн-ѣйш-ій [most or outstandingly courageous, steadfast].

The root together with the suffix or prefix, but without the inflection endings, is called the *stem*. Thus in the word оу҄вѣрова-ти, the stem would be оу҄вѣрова-.

§16. Primary vs. Derivative Words.

Words that consist of a root and an inflection ending, are called *primary* [not derived from other words]: вод-а̀ [water], нес-тѝ [to bear, carry, *pf.*].

Words that include suffixes in their makeup, are called *derivative:* вод-н-ый [watery, pertaining to water], нос-и́-ти [to carry, *impf.*].

§17. Simple vs. Compound Forms.

Words that consist of only one root are known as *simple*. Words that contain two or more roots are called *compound:* славо-словіе [doxology], дре́во благо-сѣнно-ли́ственнное (from the Akathist to the Theotokos—"Tree whose leaves offer good shade", i.e. under which one can seek refuge without danger).

If words are combined by means of the linking vowels o, є, then this is called a *proper* [собственное сложеніе] compound word: ꙁемлѧ-трѧсе́нїе [earthquake].

The combining of words without these connecting vowels is called *improper* [несобственное]: ца́рь-гра́дъ [Constantinople], трн-дне́вєнъ [of three days, "He that rose on the third day"].

§18. Words Classified by Meaning.

Words seen in all their variety, since they are a reflection of reality, express various kinds of meaning. They may signify an entity, a quality, an action, a quantity, or else express the connection between concepts, and so on; and depending on their meaning, all words are divided into special categories, which are called the *parts of speech.*

There are nine parts of speech:

> nouns,
> adjectives,
> pronouns,
> numerals,
> verbs,
> adverbs,
> prepositions,
> conjunctions,
> interjections.

The first six parts of speech have an independant lexical and grammatical meaning in a sentence, and they make up its primary and secondary members. They are called *significant* (or *independant*) parts of speech.

Prepositions and conjunctions serve to show the relationship between the words in a sentence. They are called *auxiliary* parts of speech.

Interjections are an expression of emotions, and do not form part of the syntactical structure of a sentence, but they adjoin it.

§19. The Forms of Words.

The first five parts of speech change their forms, and therefore are known as variable. The remaining four are invariable parts of speech.

The changes take place according to case, person, gender and number.

Changes according to case are known as *declension*.

Changes according to person are known as *conjugation*.

Besides the singular and plural numbers, in Church Slavonic there also exists a *dual number*, which is used to refer to two persons or two objects, especially when they form a pair (e.g. eyes, feet, hands).

In Church Slavonic, as in Russian, there are seven cases:

nominative [a noun standing alone, or the subject of a sentence];

genitive [possessive—"of"];

dative [indirect object—"to"];

accusative [direct object, recipient of the action];

instrumental [denotes agent or means];

prepositional [used after certain prepositions; "locative"];

vocative [used for direct address].

They serve to answer the same questions in Church Slavonic as they do in Russian. The vocative case has its own proper endings, for example: ра́бе [O servant!], же́но [O woman!].

Parts of Speech.

THE NOUN [SUBSTANTIVE].

§20. A *noun* is the name we give to any word that signifies an entity [person, being, object, thing, &c.], or has a substantive sense, in the world of reality or of thought: а҆́гг҃лъ [angel], ра́дость [joy], вода̀ [water].

§21. Nouns are either *concrete* or *abstract*. Concrete nouns are those that represent a physically real or perceptible entity: вода̀ [water], землѧ̀ [earth, land], бг҃ъ [God], а҆́гг҃лъ [angel]. Abstract nouns are those that relate to the world of invisible, mental concepts, and have a generalized quality: бж҃ество̀ [divinity], добро̀ [good in general; a good thing], ѕло̀ [evil in general, an evil], терпѣ́нїе [patience].

A grammatical characteristic of abstract nouns is that they are used mostly in the singular.

§22. All nouns are either *animate* or *inanimate*.

Animate nouns are the names of living beings, whether they belong to the visible world or the invisible: а҆́гг҃лъ [angel], человѣ́къ [man, human], ко́нь [horse].

The grammatical characteristic of these nouns is that, in the masculine singular, their accusative case is the same as the genitive: ви́ждꙋ человѣ́ка, конѧ̀ [I see a man, a horse].

In the plural, the accusative case for all genders is often the same as the nominative, but it may also take the form of the genitive, for example: помѧнѝ на́съ грѣ́шныхъ и҆ непотре́бныхъ ра́бъ твои́хъ (Vespers, 3rd Prayer of Light—"Remember us sinners and unprofitable servants of Thine").

When inanimate nouns are used figuratively to refer to animate beings, they take on the same peculiarity: церко́внаго ка́менѧ, всехва́льнаго петра̀... досто́йнѡ восхва́лимъ (Sedalen [Sessional Hymn] at Matins for June 29—"The rock of the Church, the all-laudable Peter... let us worthily praise").

Inanimate nouns are the names of objects that do not constitute living beings: стóлъ [table], дóмъ [house, home], нóжъ [knife].

§23. Depending on their characteristics and composition, nouns are classified as *proper nouns, common nouns, collective nouns* and *material nouns*.

1) Proper nouns—any name of a specific individual person or entity, that sets it apart from a general class or type: їордáнъ [the Jordan], їудéа [Judea].

Note: In Church Slavonic, proper nouns are not capitalized (see §9).

2) Common nouns—generalized names for homogeneous entities, which may designate either the whole class or type, or any member of the group taken individually: стóлъ [table, a table, the table], дóмъ [house, a house, the house], нóжъ [knife, a knife, &c.].

3) Collective nouns—those indicating a group of like objects, taken as a whole: пóлкъ [regiment], стáдо [flock, herd], кáменїе [a cliff or stony place].

4) Material nouns—these indicate homogeneous materials as such, where a part of the material has all the qualities of the whole: мукá [flour], вїнó [wine], водá [water], жѝто [grain].

Material nouns are used mostly in the singular. They cannot be joined to numerals, but are counted by measures and weights: пѧ́ть мѣ́ръ пшенѝцы [five measures of wheat].

The Formation of Nouns.

§24. Nouns, depending on their structure, are either *primary [prototypical]* or *derivative.*

Primary nouns are those that have their declension endings attached directly to the root: вод-á [water], дóм-ъ [house], кóн-ь [horse].

Derivative nouns are those that contain suffixes: рыб-áрь [fisherman], цáр-ств-ї-е [kingdom].

In Church Slavonic, as in Russian, there are many suffixes by means of which various words with different meanings and nuances can be formed from one root.

§25. Suffixes used to form nouns denoting an agent— one who performs an action:

a) _др_ь —builds from the stems of nouns and verbs:

рыб_а́р_ь [fisherman, from рыб_а, fish];

звон_а́р_ь [bell-ringer, from звони́_ти, to ring];

врат_а́р_ь [gate-keeper, from врат_а̀, gates];

пе́к_др_ь [baker, from пещѝ, to bake].

_ец_ъ —builds on verbal stems:

плов_е́ц_ъ [one who swims or sails, from плы́_ти, to go by water];

ќуп_ец_ъ [merchant, from ќупи́_ти, to buy];

твор_е́ц_ъ [Creator: твори́_ти, to make, create, do];

—from adjectival stems, often preceded by an additional suffix:

ста́р_ец_ъ [elder, from ста́р_ый, old];

хи́тр_ец_ъ [cunning person, from хи́тр_ый, cunning, sly];

млад_е́н_ец_ъ [infant, from млад_ый, young];

пе́рв_ен_ец_ъ [first-born, from пе́рв_ый, first];

_ник_ъ — builds from stems of nouns, adjectives and verbs, often preceded by the suffixes _н, _ен_ and others:

кни́ж_н_ик_ъ [scribe, from кни́г_а, book];

пл҄ѣн_н_ик_ъ [prisoner, from пл҄ѣн_ъ, captivity];

ср́од_н_ик_ъ [kinsman, from ср́од_н_ый, related, akin];

избра́н_н_ик_ъ [elect, chosen one; from избра́н_н_ый, chosen];

споспѣ́ш_н_ик_ъ [companion in monastic life, from споспѣ́ш_ств_ов_а́ти, aid or encourage];

о҆у́ч_ен_и́к_ъ [disciple, from о҆у҆чи́_ти, to teach or learn].

_ач_ь — builds from verbal stems:

тк_а́ч_ь [weaver, from тк_а́_ти, to weave];

ков_а́ч_ь [blacksmith, from ков_а́_ти, to forge];
-тел_ь — from verbal stems:
спаси́_тел_ь [Saviour, from спас_а́_ти, to save];
наказа́_тел_ь [mentor, instructor, from наказ_а́_ти, to instruct, educate];
оу҆чи́_тел_ь [teacher, from оу҆чи́_ти, to teach];
-[й]ц_а —with verbal stems:
вїнопі́_йц_а [wine-drinker, wine-bibber: пи́_ти, to drink];
ꙗ҆́д_ц_а [eater, glutton: ꙗ҆́с_ти, to eat];
оу҆бі́_йц_а [murderer: оу҆би́_ти, to kill].
-ты́р_ь — with verbal stems:
па́с_тыр_ь [shepherd, pastor, from пас_тѝ, to tend a flock];
-та_й — with verbal stems:
хода́_та_й [intercessor, from ходи́_ти, to go (and ask on behalf of another)];
глаша́_та_й [herald, crier, from глаша́_ти, to proclaim, to voice];
соглада́_та_й [spy, observer, from согла́д_а_ти, to watch, investigate];
-ꙋн_ъ — with verbal stems:
пѣ́ст_ꙋн_ъ [guardian, pedagogue, from пѣ́ст_ов_а_ти, to have care over s.o.];
-ок_ъ — і҆́н_ок_ъ [monk, one who must live "otherwise" or "apart": і҆́н_ый, other];
-ин_ъ —gives noun stems a singular sense:
граждан_и́н_ъ [a citizen]—гражда́н_е [citizens].
Suffixes denoting children or the young of animals:
-нщ_ъ : дѣ́тищ_ъ [child, offspring];
ѻ҆́троч_нщ_ъ [child—boy or girl];
ко́зл_нщ_ъ [kid, young goat].
-ѧт- (note that in the nominative singular the -т- drops out)—

Ѻ҆трочѧ̀ [child, infant]—Ѻ҆троч_ѧ́т_е [children];

Ѻ҆рлѧ̀ [eaglet]—Ѻ҆рл_ѧ́т_е [eaglets, baby eagles].

b) Suffixes used to denote persons according to origin, location or religion; note that _ин_ъ drops out in the plural:

_ан[ан]_ин_ъ: сѵ́р_ан_ин_ъ [a Syrian: сѵрі́а, Syria];

хрїстї_а́н_ин_ъ [a Chistian: хр̑то́съ, Christ];

самар_ан_и́н_ъ [Samaritan: самарі́а, Samaria];

гражд_ан_и́н_ъ [citizen: гра́д_ъ, city].

_ец_ъ: тꙋ́зе́м_ец_ъ [local person, native of those parts: зем_лѧ̀, land]; combined with the suffix _ин_ъ: нѣ́м_ч_и́н_ъ [Teuton, German: ец permutated to ьч].

_ич_ь (masc.), _н_а (fem.)—to denote "child of"; these suffixes are added to the possessive adjectives [see §49]: цар_е́в_ич_ь, цар_е́в_на [king's son/daughter: цар_е́в_ъ, the king's];

кнѧ́ж_ич_ь, кнѧж_н_а̀ [prince's son/daughter: кнѧ́ж_ь, the prince's];

крал_е́в_ич_ь, крал_е́в_на [child of a king: кра́л_ев_ъ, king's];

брата́н_ич_ь [brother's son—cf. Genesis 14:14].

These suffixes are much used in Russian patronymics.

c) To indicate persons of the female sex, nouns are generally formed from the parallel masculine forms, using the following suffixes:

_иц_а:

спꙋ́т_н_ик_ъ [travelling companion, *m.*], спꙋ́т_н_иц_а [travelling companion, *f.*];

оу҆ч_ен_и́к_ъ—оу҆ч_ен_и́ц_а [disciple, student];

ца́р_ь—цар_и́ц_а [king, queen];

врат_а́р_ь—врат_а́р_н_иц_а [gate-keeper];

_ын_а (_ин_а):

ра́б_ъ—раб_ы́н_а [servant, handmaid];

кнѧ́з_ь—кнаг_и́н_а [prince/princess];

болѧ́р_ин_ъ—болѧ́р_ын_а [boyar/boyaress];

и҆н_ок_ъ—и҆н_ок_ин_а [monk/nun];

This suffix can also be used to denote persons of female gender according to location, origin or religion:

мѡавı́т-ꙗн-ин-ъ—мѡавı́т-ꙗн-ы́н-ꙗ [Moabite/Moabitess];

самар-ꙗн-и́н-ъ—самар-ꙗн-ы́н-ꙗ [Samaritan];

_ы— (Thus in the nominative singular, but in the other cases this radical separates into _ов [_ъв_]: свекр-ы̀—свекр-о́в-е [mother-in-law]; Also in abstract nouns—

> непло́д-ы—непло́д-ов-е [barrenness, inability to bear
> children];
>
> лю̈в-ы̀—лю̈в-[ъ]в-е̇ [love, charity].

_ер— (in all cases except the nominative singular):

> ма́т-и—ма́т-ер-е [mother];
>
> дꙟ-ѝ—дꙟ-е́р-е [daughter].

d) The names for animals do not have their own suffixes, but for the most part use the same ones as in the case of people:

> _тел-ь — пѣ́-тел-ь [rooster, from пѣ́-ти, to sing];
>
> _иц-а — лев-ъ—льв-и́ц-а [lion, lioness].

§26. Suffixes used to form nouns denoting objects:

a) Nouns denoting the instrument used for an action:

_л-о —with verbal stems:

> ра́-л-о [ploughshare, from ѡра́-ти, to plough];
>
> писа́-л-о [writing instrument, from писа́-ти, to write];
>
> би́-л-о [gong, eggbeater, from би́-ти, to beat].

b) Nouns denoting the place of some object or action, and sometimes the entity or action connected with a given place. They are formed from noun or verb stems:

_иꙟ-е—то́рж-иꙟ-е [market place, from то́рг-ъ, trade];

> пожа́р-иꙟ-е [site of a fire, incendiary; from пожа́р-ъ,
> fire].

_аниꙟ-е—сватѝ-лиꙟ-е [sanctuary, from свати́-ти, to hallow, sanctify];

> ѡбита́-лиꙟ-е [habitation, from ѡбита́-ти, to dwell,
> inhabit].

_ЕНЦЕ—КЛА́Д_ЕНЦЕ [cemetery, from КЛА́С_ТН, to lay aside].

c) Suffixes to denote various items:

_Н_НК_Ъ: (from noun stems):

       ПОДСВѢ́ЦІ_Н_НК_Ъ [candlestick, from СВѢЦІ_А́, candle].

_ЛЬННК_Ъ: (from verbal stems):

       СВѢТН́_ЛЬННК_Ъ [lamp, from СВѢТН́_ТН, to shine].

_Н_НЦ_А: (from adjective stems):

       БОЛЬ_Н_Н́Ц_А [hospital, from БОЛЬ_Н_ЫЙ, sick];

       ТЕ́М_Н_Н́Ц_А [dungeon, from ТЕ́М_Н_ЫЙ, dark].

    —(from noun stems):

       РН́З_Н_НЦ_А [sacristy, from РН́З_А, robe or vestment];

       ЖН́Т_Н_НЦ_А [granary, from ЖН́Т_О, grain].

Nouns from a verbal stem having this suffix, can denote the place or instrument of the action:

       МѴ̈РОВА́Р_Н_НЦ_А [place where Holy Oil is prepared, from ВАРН́_ТН, to boil];

       МЕ́ЛЬ_Н_НЦ_А [(wind-)mill, from МОЛО́_ТН, to mill or grind];

       КАДН́ЛЬ_Н_НЦ_А [censer, thurible, from КАДН́_ТН, to cense].

_ЕЛ_Ь [_ѢЛ_Ь]: (from verbal stems):

       КѴ̈П_ѢЛ_Ь [baptismal font, from КѴПА́_ТН, to bathe];

       СВНР_ѢЛ_Ь [reed-pipe, as in Isaiah 5:12, from СВНРА́_ТН, to play a wind instrument];

_Н_А: (from noun stems; usually denotes the place for some activity or profession):

       ПОВА́Р_Н_А [kitchen, place for cooking, from ПО́ВАР_Ъ, cook];

       ПЕКА́Р_Н_А [bakery, from ПЕКА́Р_Ь, baker].

_В_О: (from verbal stems):

       ПН́_В_О [beverage, from ПН́_ТН, to drink];

       СО́ЧН_В_О [sauce, from СОЧН́_ТН, to give juice].

-х-ъ: (verbal stems):

смѣ́-х-ъ [laughter, from смѣ́а-ти-сѧ, to laugh];

слꙋ-х-ъ [hearing, thing heard, from слꙑ́-ти, be heard of, known].

-нн-а: (noun or verb stems):

паꙋ́ч-и́н-а [cobweb, from паꙋ́к-ъ, spider];

блевот-и́н-а [vomit, from блева́-ти, to regurgitate];

лич-и́н-а [mask, from лиц-ѐ, face, person];

ма́сл-ин-а [olive, from ма́сл-о, oil].

-ок-ъ: (from verbal stems, with both a concrete and an abstract meaning):

ѡста́н-ок-ъ [remnant, from ѡставла́-ти, to leave];

свит-ок-ъ [scroll, from свит-и, to wind, roll up];

нача́т-ок-ъ [beginning, first-fruit, from нача́-ти, to begin].

-ес-: (in neuter nouns ending in -о; in all cases except the nominative/accusative singular):

тѣ́л-о—тѣ́л-ес-ѐ [body—of-the-body];

дре́в-о—дре́в-ес-ѐ [tree, wood; of-the-tree/wood].

-мѧ [-мен]: (in neuter nouns):

пле́-мѧ—пле́-мен-е [tribe];

бре́-мѧ—бре́-мен-е [burden].

-н-: (in concrete as well as abstract nouns):

ста́-н-ъ [station, position, encampment, from стоа́-ти, to stand];

со́-н-ъ [sleep, dream, from спа́-ти, to sleep];

рꙋ-н-о̀ [fleece; mowed grass, meadow; from рва́-ти, to tear (something out)];

стра-н-а̀ [side, district, cf. просто́р-ъ, expanse, scope, range].

§27. Abstract nouns are for the most part formed from adjectives or verbs, and only an insignificant number are from other nouns.

Abstract nouns derived from adjectives show some abstract quality, peculiarity or characteristic:

ꙮ_оⷭт_ь: мꙊдр_оⷭт_ь [wisdom, from мꙊдр_ъ, wise];

    крѡ́т_оⷭт_ь [meekness, from крѡ́т_ок_ъ, meek];

    щедр_оⷭт_ь [compassion, from щедр_ъ, compassionate];

    крѣп_оⷭт_ь [victory, might, from крѣп_ок_ъ, mighty].

_от_а: наг_от_а̀ [nakedness, from наг_ъ, naked];

    добр_от_а̀ [goodness, from добр_ъ, good];

    крас_от_а̀ [beauty, from крас_ен_ъ, beautiful, splendid].

_ин_а: глꙊб_ин_а̀ [depth, from глꙊб_ок_ъ, deep];

    дол_и́н_а [dale, valley, from доль_н_ый, "of the valley, lower"];

    сѣд_ин_а̀ [grayness, gray hair, from сѣд_ъ, gray];

    йст_ин_а [truth, from йст_ый, true];

    Долина and сѣдина took on a concrete meaning.

_ї_е: весел_ї_е [joy, from весел_ъ, joyous];

    оўсерд_ї_е [eagerness, endearment, diligence, from оўсерд_н_ый, sincere];

By means of this suffix, nouns with a concrete sense are formed from substantives having a prefix:

—indicating extended area: помѡ́р_ї_е [sea coast], распꙊт_ї_е [cross-roads];

—denoting a thing: поднѡ́ж_ї_е [footstool].

_ын_а: горд_ы́н_а [pride, from гѡ́рд_ъ, proud];

    свѧт_ы́н_а [object of veneration, from свѧ́т_ъ, holy];

    пꙊст_ы́н_а [desert, wasteland, from пꙊст_ъ, empty, desolate (concrete meaning)].

_ств_о: лꙊкав_ств_о [craftiness, deception, from лꙊкав_ъ, sly, wicked, evil];

    богат_ств_о [riches, wealth, from богат_ый, rich].

With this suffix, abstract nouns denoting a quality or essence are formed from substantives:

    человѣ́ч_е_ств_о [humanity, from человѣ́к_ъ, man,

human being];

бж҃_є_ство̀ [divinity, from бг҃_ъ, God];

дѣв_ство_о [virginity, from дѣв_а, virgin];

оте́ч_є_ство_о [fatherland, from оте́ц_ъ, father];

ца́р_ство_о [kingdom, from ца́р_ь, king];

Some of these nouns can also take the suffix _ї_є:

ца́р_ств_ї_є [kingdom], оте́ч_є_ств_ї_є [fatherland].

Nouns formed from verb stems express an action or a condition:

_ї_є: (with the stems of past passive participles [§§99-100]):

ѡсꙋжде́н_ї_є [condemnation, from ѡсꙋжде́н_ъ, condemned];

оу҆че́н_ї_є [teaching, cf. наꙋче́н_ъ, taught];

моле́н_ї_є [prayer, cf. оу҆моле́н_ъ, moved by entreaties];

распꙗ́т_ї_є [crucifixion, from распꙗ́т_ъ, crucified];

жит_ї_є̀ [life, cf. и҆зжи́т_ъ, (gradually) overcome, obsolete, outlived].

_от_а [_єт_а]:

раб_о́т_а [servitude, cf. ра́б_ъ, servant, рабо́та_ти, to serve];

сꙋ_ет_а̀ [vanity, cf. сꙋети́_ти_сꙗ, to strive in vain];

таг_от_а̀ [weight, burden, cf. таготи́_ти_сꙗ, to be weighed down, oppressed].

_б_а: борь_б_а̀ [warfare, battle, from боро́_ти_сꙗ, to battle];

слꙋж_б_а [service, from слꙋжи́_ти, to serve];

а҆лч_б_а [hunger, from а҆лка́_ти, to be hungry];

сꙋдь_б_а̀ [destiny, from сꙋди́_ти, to deem, judge].

_єж_ъ: мꙗт_е́ж_ъ [uprising, from мꙗс_тѝ, to trouble, disturb];

пад_е́ж_ъ [pit, downfall, from па́да_ти, to fall].

_н_ь, _сн_ь, _зн_ь:

да́_н_ь [tribute, from да́_ти, to give];

пѣ́_сн_ь [song, from пѣ_ти, to sing];

жи҃_зн_ь [life, from жи́_ти, to live];

болѣ҃_зн_ь [illness, from болѣ́_ти, to hurt, be sick];

боѧ́_зн_ь [fear, from боѧ́_ти_сѧ, to be afraid].

_тв_а: моли́_тв_а [prayer, from моли́_ти_сѧ, to pray];

    жа́_тв_а [harvest, from жа́_ти, to reap];

    клѧ́_тв_а [oath, curse, from клѧ́_ти, to swear].

_т_ь: вла́с_т_ь [power, from владѣ́_ти, to have sway, be

    master];

    напа́с_т_ь [assault, trial, from напада́_ти, to attack].

_изн_а:

    оу҆кор_и́зн_а [insult, dishonor, from оу҆корѧ́_ти, to

      reproach];

    глав_и́зн_а [book, chapter, scroll with decorated top;

      from глав_а̀, head].

§28. Collective nouns are formed by means of the suffix _ï_е:

    ка́мен_ï_е [stony area, crag, cliff];

    ве́рб_ï_е [patch of willows, willowy area];

    рѣ́п_ï_е [turnips, turnip patch];

    бра́т_ï_е [brethren, brothers as a group].

§29. Nouns with a diminutive or augmentative connotation:

_ин_а: год_и́н_а [time, hour, year; from го́д_ъ, in sense of

    "time"];

    хи́ж_ин_а [hut, from хи́ж_а, older хъ̏із_ъ, cognate

      with Old English *hus*, "house"];

    хра́м_ин_а [house, sometimes in a figurative sense,

      ="body"; from хра́м_ъ, house, temple].

§30. To make diminutives or forms of endearment, the
suffix _к (or, with softening/ palatization, _ц) is used, and often
preceded by е, и, о:

    о҆ко́н_ц_е [a little window];

    ча́д_ц_е [little or dear child];

    стꙋ́ч_ец_ъ [little twig or shoot—term for brushes used

      in administering Holy Oils];

вдов҃ница [a "little" or poor widow];

вѣно́къ [a "little crown" of flowers, i.e. a wreath].

§31. The suffix -ницѣ, besides the meaning given above (§26, c), can also have a pejorative sense: Пагубное соборнище, богомѐрзкихъ лукавнующихъ богоубийцъ со́нмище, преста̀ хрⷭ҇тѐ тебѣ̀ (Matins of Good Friday, Ode 9—"The destructive band of evil men, hateful to Heaven, the council of the murderers of God, drew near to Thee, O Christ").

§32. The Gender of Nouns.

Nouns can be of one of three grammatical genders: masculine, feminine, and neuter.

The gender of nouns is determined: 1) by the ending, or 2) by the meaning.

1) If nouns denote inanimate objects, their gender is determined by the ending:

The endings of masculine nouns are -ъ, -ь, -й:

сто́лъ	[table];
о҆́гнь	[fire];
ка́мень	[stone];
кра́й	[edge, region].

Feminine nouns end in -а, -ѧ, -ь, -ы:

рука̀	[hand, arm];
земла̀	[land, earth];
ве́сь	[village];
люб̀ы	[love].

Neuter nouns in in -о, -е, -мѧ:

село̀	[plot of land, field; town, (larger) village;]
мо́ре	[sea];
и҆́мѧ	[name].

2) If nouns denote animate beings, their gender is according to their meaning, for example:

воево́да	[commander]—masculine;

ЖЕН_а̀	[woman, wife]—feminine;

The above nouns have the same inflection endings, but different genders.

Nouns denoting animate beings have (besides those indicated above in point 1) the following endings as well: masculine in _а, _а̀, feminine in _н, neuter in _а, _а̀. For example:

Masculines:

ра́бъ	[servant, slave];
ко́нь	[horse];
іере́й	[priest];
ю́ноша	[young man, youth];
су́дїа̀	[judge].

Feminines:

дѣ́ва	[virgin];
рабы́на̀	[handmaid, female servant, slave];
марїа́мь	[Mariam, Miriam, Mary];
непло́ды	[barrenness, inability to give birth];
ма́ти	[mother].

Neuter:

пле́ма̀	[tribe];
о́вча̀	[sheep];
а́гна̀	[lamb];
ча́до	[child].

Some feminine proper names are spelled with _ъ: марїа́м_ъ, єлїсаве́т_ъ [Elizabeth]. However, in older editions they are spelled with _ь: марїа́м_ь, єлїсаве́т_ь. These nouns are declined according to the 3rd declension (on the model of за́повѣдь, see §41), which shows that it is correct to spell them with the ending _ь (Luke 1:57—єлїсаве́ти, "Elizabeth's"; Numbers 12:4: in the Russian Bible, Маріами; in the Church Slavonic—марїа́мѣ, "unto Miriam").

On the other hand, марїа́мъ can be treated as an indeclinable word, taking its oblique cases from марі́а (compare Luke 2:19: марїа́мъ, with v. 34 of the same chapter, where we find и̑ речѐ къ мαρі́н—"And he said to Mary").

Some nouns can be either masculine or feminine, depending on the sex they refer to. Nouns of this type are said to be of common gender: млαдέнєцъ [infant], сиротὰ [orphan].

The gender of nouns that exist only in the plural can be determined by comparing the general characteristics of their declension endings with those of other words, for example: the ending _ɑ in the plural belongs to neuter nouns:

        оу́стὰ   [lips, mouth—neuter plural];

        врαтὰ   [gates, gateway—neuter plural];

Feminine:

        но́жницы—но́жницъ [scissors, declined like жєны̀—жέнъ, women];

Masculine:

        лю́дїє—людє́й [people, declined like пꙋтї̈—пꙋтє́й, paths].

The form мо́щи—мощє́й [relics] is declined like зάповѣдь—зάповѣдє́й, which shows that it is feminine, and so on.

§33. The Declension of Nouns.

Nouns may be divided into four declensions, according to the ways they are declined.

To the first declension belong masculine nouns ending in _ъ, _ь, _й: рάв_ъ [servant], ко́н_ь [horse], крά_й [district, edge], as well as neuters that end in _o, _є: сєл_о̀ [field, town], мо́р_є [sea].

The first declension is subdivided into *hard* and *soft* [declension-variants] on the basis of its inflection endings: the *hard* declension comprises the nouns that end in a hard letter: _ъ, _o — рάв_ъ, сєл_о̀; the *soft* declension consists of the nouns ending in a soft letter: _ь, _й, _є — цάр_ь, крά_й, мо́р_є.

Nouns whose stem ends in a palatal letter [the "hushing" sibilants] and ц belong to a *mixed* declension, since they have both hard and soft inflection endings (see §8, a): мꙋ́жъ, мꙋ́жɑ, мꙋ́жємъ.

§34. Models of the 1st Declension.

Singular.

Hard Declension.   *Soft Declension.*

Nom. ра́бъ [slave] село̀ [field] ца́рь [king] мо́ре [sea] кра́й [edge]
иере́й [priest]

Gen.	раба̀	села̀	цара̀	мо́ря	кра́я	иере́я
Dat.	рабу̀	селу̀	царю̀	мо́рю	кра́ю	иере́ю
Acc.	раба̀	село̀	цара̀	мо́ре	кра́й	иере́а
Instr.	рабо́мъ	село́мъ	царе́мъ	мо́ремъ	кра́емъ	иере́емъ
Prep.	рабѣ̀	селѣ̀	цара̀и	мо́ри	кра́и	иере́и
Voc.	ра́бе	село̀	царю̀	мо́ре	кра́ю	иере́ю [-е]

Dual (="*two, a pair of...*").

N.A.V.	раба̂,	села̂, -ѣ̀	цара̂	мю́ра, -н	кра̂я	иере̂а
G. P.	рабу̀	селу̀	царю̂	мю́рю	кра́ю	иере́ю
D.Ins.	рабо́ма	село́ма	царе́ма	мо́рема		кра́ема	иере́ема [-ома]

Plural.

N.V.	рабѝ	села̀	царѝ [ца́рїе]	мора̀	кра̂и	иере́є
Gen.	рабѡ́въ[ра̂бъ]	се́лъ	царе́й	море́й	кра́євъ	иере́й
Dat.	рабѡ́мъ	селѡ́мъ	царе́мъ	море́мъ	кра́емъ	иере́емъ, -ѡмъ]
Acc.	рабы̀ [-ѡ́въ]	села̀	царѝ[-е́й]	мора̀	кра̂и	иере́и
Instr.	рабы̀	се́лы	царѝ [-ьмѝ]	мю́рн	кра̂и	иере́и
Prep.	рабѣ́хъ	селѣ́хъ	царе́хъ	мора́хъ	кра́ехъ	иере́ехъ

Singular:

Hard, ending in Guttural: *Mixed:*   *Soft, ending in -ïе:*

Nom.	ду́хъ [spirit]	о̂трокъ [boy]	му́жъ [man]	зна́менїе [sign]
Gen.	ду́ха	о̂трока	му́жа	зна́менїа
Dat.	ду́ху	о̂троку	му́жу	зна́менїю
Acc.	ду́хъ [-а]	о̂трока	му́жа	зна́менїе
Instr.	ду́хомъ	о̂троко́мъ	му́жемъ	зна́менїемъ
Prep.	ду́сѣ	о̂троцѣ̀	му́жн	зна́менїн

Voc.	а́ш_є	о́троч_є	м́ж_ъ	зна́мені_є

Dual.

N.A.V.	а́х_а	о́трѡк_а	м́ж_а	зна́мені_а
G. P.	а́х_ъ	о́трѡк_ъ	м́ж_ъ	зна́мені_ю
D. I.	а́х_ома	о́трок_ома	м́ж_ема	зна́мені_ема

Plural:

N. V.	а́є_н	о́троц_ы¹)	м́ж_н [_їє]	зна́мені_а
Gen.	а́х_ѡ́въ	о́трок_ѡ́въ	м́ж_ѐй	зна́мені_й
Dat.	а́х_ѡ́мъ	о́трок_ѡ́мъ	м́ж_е́мъ	зна́мені_е́мъ
Acc.	а́х_н²)	о́трок_н	м́ж_ы³)	зна́мені_а
Instr.	а́х_н	о́трок_н	м́ж_ы	зна́мені_н
				or: зна́мен_[ь]_мн
Prep.	а́є_ѣ́хъ	о́троц_ѣ́хъ	м́ж_а́хъ	зна́мені_нхъ

When guttural consonants are followed by soft vowels, they are modified according to the following scheme:

г + н, ѣ >з	г + є >ж	_бѓъ	_бз́ѣ	_бо́зн	_бж́є
к " >ц	к " > ч	_о́трокъ	_о́троцѣ	_о́троцы[н]	_о́трочє
х " >с	х " > ш	_а́хъ	_а́сѣ	_а́сн	_а́шє

§35. Notes on the Cases.

1) The accusative singular of animate nouns is usually the same as the genitive (§22), but there are also cases where it is the same as the nominative: Прїнми́те д̃хъ ст̃ъ (John 20:22—"Receive ye the Holy Ghost"); Всади́ м́жа на ко́нь (IV Kings 9:17—"Set a man on a horse"). In the plural, the accusative of animate nouns usually is the

---

¹) In Old Church Slavonic: отроц_н, see §8, c, d).

²) In Old Church Slavonic: доух_ꙁі [ы], see §8, d).

³) _ы is used after palatals ("hushing" sibilants) only to distinguish one case from another (§8, a).

same as the nominative, but it may also be the same as the genitive: й вы́шлите всѣ́хъ рабѡ́въ гд҃ннхъ (IV Kings 10:23—"And send forth all the servants of the Lord").

2) In the prepositional singular of the soft declension, the ending _ѣ is sometimes found: й сы́нове сїѡ́нн возра́дꙋютса ѡ цар҃ѣ своє́мъ (Ps. 149:2—"And let the children of Sion exult in their King"); in nouns whose stem ends in a palatal, _ѣ may also occur: въ мꙋж҃ѣ (Acts 17:31; 25:5—"by the man..."); nouns whose stem ends in _ц may have _ѣ or _ы: въ се́рдцы своє́мъ (Matth. 5:28— "in his heart").

3) In the nominative plural, the ending _ы may be met with in place of _н: да ка́менїѐ сїѐ хлѣ́бы бꙋ́дꙋтъ (Matth. 4:3—"let these stones become bread"); хлѣ́бы ѡскꙋдѣ́ша (I Kings [Samuel] 9:7—"the bread is spent").

4) The instrumental plural, besides the usual ending _ы, _н (рабы̀, цари̑) may also have the very common ending _[ь]мн: сынмн, царьмн, but not all nouns can take this ending. Sometimes, no doubt under the influence of Russian, an ending _амн is also found: e.g. грѣха́мн (Isaiah 14:21 —"for sins"); скорпїѡ́намн (III Kings 12:11—"with scorpions"); Ѻрꙋ́жїамн бо вѣ́ры (Tropar for July 8—"for, by the weapons of faith...").

5) In the prepositional case (under Russian influence) the endings _ахъ, _ѧхъ are to be met with: въ слѣ́дахъ же бє́зданы ходи́лъ лн є҆сѝ; (Job 38:16—"Hast thou walked in the tracks of the deep?"); neuter nouns in particular tend to form this ending: въ сердца́хъ (Eccles. 9:3—"in the hearts"); въ предста́тельствахъ (Tropar of the Dormition of the Theotokos—"by [thy] intercessions"), while, in the neuter nouns of the *soft* declension, _ѧхъ seems to have displaced the normal ending _єхъ entirely: то́й на мора́хъ ѡснова́лъ ю̀ є҆́сть (Ps. 23:2—"He hath founded it upon the seas"); возра́дꙋютса на ло́жахъ свои́хъ (Prokeimenon—"[The Saints] shall rejoice upon their beds"); въ пола́хъ дꙋбра́вы (Ps. 131:6—"in the fields of the wood").

6) The word гдь [the Lord] is declined according to the hard declension in the oblique cases of the singular; the vocative case has the ending _и: гди [O Lord]; in the plural, it is declined according to the soft declension.

A Note on the Neuter Dual.

Neuter nouns (of the 1st and 4th declensions, see §34 above) in the dual number had, in Old Church Slavonic, endings according to the feminine forms in the nominative and accusative cases: _ѣ, _и.

In New Church Slavonic (since the 17th century), the practice has become established of writing the dual number of neuter nouns with endings on the pattern of masculine forms also: _а, _ѧ. Nouns that denote the paired parts of the body, for the most part, kept their ancient endings, i.e like those of the feminine. For example, *with feminine-like endings:* на рамѣ свои (Luke 15:5—"[he layeth it] on his shoulders"); на ѻбѣ рамѣ свои (Gen. 9:23—"upon both their shoulders"); на плещи єѧ (Gen. 21:14—"putting it on her shoulder"); кто́ дастх мнѣ крилѣ, ꙗкѡ голꙋбинѣ (Ps. 54:7— "Who will give me wings like a dove's?"); да бꙋдꙋтх оуши твои внемлющѣ гласꙋ... (Ps. 129:2— "Let thine ears be attentive to the voice [of my supplication]"); ꙗкѡ видѣстѣ ѻчи мои (Luke 2:30-31—"For mine eyes have seen..."); двѣ ѻцѣ имꙋщꙋ (Matth. 18:9—"having two eyes"). *With masculine-like endings:* два кѡльца злата (Exodus 36:27 [Septuagint version]—"two golden rings"); на ѻба рамена (Ex. 36:27ff. [in a section of the Septuagint without numbered verses]—"on both shoulders"); даны бышъ женѣ два крила (Rev. 12:14—"And to the woman were given two wings"); за два ѻка моѧ (Judges 16:28—"for my two eyes"). With the numerals два, ѻба the endings are usually of the masculine type.

When neuter nouns have masculine-type endings in the dual, the form they take coincides with the plural. The dual number may be evidenced by the numerals два [two], ѻба [both]; by a verb in the dual number; and, it would appear, the position of the accent, for example: кѡлѣна моѧ изнемого́ста (Ps. 108:24—"my knees are weakened"); на чресла своѧ (Gen. 37:34—"[sackcloth] upon his loins"); и стегнѣ чресла своѧ (III Kings 18:46—"and he girt up his loins"); чресла ваша препоѧсана (Ex. 12:11—"your loins girded"); чресла ваша (Luke 12:35—"[Let] your loins [be girded about]"). The examples with the word чресла show a distinction by means of the accent: in the first two examples, as can be seen, the number is dual, since чресла [loins] refers to one person. In the last two, we have the plural number, since many persons are had in mind—"ваша" ["your"—plural].

§36. Orthographical Peculiarities of the Cases.

In the case endings of the dual and plural, in order to set them apart from like-sounding forms of the singular, ѡ is written in place of о in the word-stems or inflections, є in place of є, and where these vowels are not present, then the circumflex accent (ˆ) is used; for example, рабо́мъ is the instrumental singular ["by a servant"], while рабѡ́мъ is the dative plural ["to the servants"]; царе́мъ ["by the king"] is the instrumental singular, while царє́мъ ["to the kings"] is the dative plural; ра́бъ is the nominative singular [a/the servant], while ра̂бъ [of the servants] is the genitive plural.

If a word contains both о and є, preference is usually given to ѡ, though much depends on the copyist, who can pick either ѡ, є or the circumflex (ˆ) depending on which symbol is the most convenient to use.

In the genitive plural endings _ѡвъ and _євъ, and in the dative plural endings _ѡмъ and _ємъ, the letters ѡ and є must be written.

In words whose root ends in a palatal ["hushing" sibilant], in order to set apart the cases of the dual and plural, _ы is written in place of и: in the plural, _ы is usually written in the accusative and instrumental cases, and while this is met with in the nominative and vocative, more common in these cases is the use of the circumflex accent (ˆ), ѡ or є: мꙋжи [men] is the nominative and vocative form, while мꙋжы̂ is the spelling of the accusative and instrumental.

The spelling rules are followed in all other declinable parts of speech.

§ 37. Peculiarities of the 1st Declension.
I. In the Sigular.

1) The dative case, instead of having the usual endings _ꙋ and _ю, may in some words have the endings _ови, _єви: сы́нови [to the son], царе́ви [to the king].

Proper names and foreign words in particular tend towards this form of the dative; and they are more likely to have the hard ending _овн, even when they belong to the soft declension: петро́вн [to Peter], мѡѵсе́овн [to Moses], а҆рхїере́овн [to the high priest].

2) Some nouns of the primary [prototypical, non-derived] class have the following:

In the genitive singular, the ending _у̀: ѿ до́му рабо́ты (Exodus 20:2—"from the house of servitude"); съ ѻ҆́нагѡ по́лу і҆ѻрда́на (Matth. 4:25—"from the far [*lit.* yon] side of the Jordan"); му́жеска по́лу (Luke 2:23—"of the male sex"); до ни́зу (Mark 15:38—"to the bottom").

They also take the ending _у̀ in the prepositional case, when it denotes location: въ до́му ѻ҆ц҃а̀ моегѡ̀ (John 14:2—"in My Father's house"); ста̀ верху̀ (Matth. 2:9—"it... stood over...").

3) Masculine nouns of foreign origin with the ending _ей, and neuters with the ending _їе, have the ending _а in the genitive singular: а҆рхїере́а [of the hierarch, high priest], є҆ѵа́їа [of the Gospel].

4) Words with the ending _ъ, _їй in the nominative singular, take the ending _е in the vocative: ѻ҆́тче [O father], сла́вїе [O nightingale]; those whose nominative ends in _ей can have either _е or _ю in the vocative: фарїсе́е (Matth. 23:26—"thou Pharisee"); а҆рхїере́ю (Jan. 30, Doxasticon at the Litiya—"O hierarch"); those that end in ь, have _ю in the vocative: царю̀ [O king]; those with a palatal followed by _ъ, _ь, have _у̀ in the vocative: му́жъ—му́жу, вра́чь—врачу̀ [O physician].

II. In the Plural.

5) Some words have _ове, _еве as a nominative plural ending: врче́ве [physicians], сы́нове [sons].

6) In nouns denoting a calling or position and having the ending _ей, the nominative plural has the ending _е, and in the case of nouns that end in _рь, the plural takes the ending _їе: фарїсе́й—фарїсе́е [Pharisee, Pharisees], па́стырь—па́стырїе [pastor, pastors].

7) Nouns denoting the performer of an action, and having the ending _тель, may end in either _е or _їе in the nominative plural: преда́телє (Acts 7:52—"betrayers"); свидѣ́телїе (Acts 7:58 —"witnesses").

8) Nouns signifying the names of tribes or peoples and ending in _нннъ, form their nominative plural by replacing this ending with _е: галїлеаннннъ [a Galilean], галїлеане [Galileans].

9) In the genitive and dative, and less often in the prepositional case, some words have a suffix inserted: _ов_ in the hard declension and _ев_ in the soft: сынѡ́въ [of sons], сыновѡ́мъ [unto the sons], ѡ сынов҄ѣхъ [concerning the sons].

10) The dative case of foreign nouns ending in _еи has not only the form _ємъ, but _ѡмъ as well: архїереємъ [to the high priests], і̓Удеѡмъ [to the Jews, Judæans].

11) Neuter nouns ending in _нце may have _ахъ, _нхъ, or _ехъ in the prepositional plural: на собо́рнцахъ (Matth. 10:17—"in the congregations"); при и̓схо́днцнхъ (Ps. 1:3—"by the sources [of waters]"); на со́нмнцехъ (Luke 11:43—"in the synagogues").

12) The word бра́тъ [brother] is declined in the plural as follows:

Nom. бра́тїа   Acc. бра́тїй
Gen. бра́тїй   Inst. бра́тїамн
Dat. бра́тїамъ Prep. ѡ бра́тїахъ

Note: Instead of the forms of the plural, the collective form бра́тїа (genitive бра́тїй, vocative бра́тїе) is more often used: бра́тїе моа̀, не клени́теса... (James 5:12—"My brethren, swear not..."). In view of the fact that when collective nouns are used, the predicate [verb] is usually in the plural, and the collective form бра́тїа is the same as the бра́тїа which is the nominative plural [of бра́тъ], it is often hard to tell when this word is used as a collective noun, and when it is used as a plural: и̓ ѡ̓блобызавъ всю̀ бра́тїю свою̀, пла́каса надъ нн́мн: и̓ по си́хъ глаго́лаша къ нему̀ бра́тїа є̓гѡ̀ (Gen. 45:15—"Moreover he [Joseph] kissed all his brethren, and wept upon them: and after that his brethren talked with him"). In the following two

examples, a distinction is made by the possessive adjective: пріидоша братїѧ
іѡсифова (Gen. 45:16—"Joseph's brethren are come"); и идоша же
братїѧ іѡсифовы десѧть (Gen. 42:3—"And Joseph's ten brethren
went...")): here we see the collective form in the first example, but the plural in
the second.

13) Nouns taken from the Hebrew—адѡнаі [Adonai, "Lord",
used as a substitute for the Hebrew radicals sometimes rendered as
"Jehovah"], ёлѡі [Eloi, "my God"], саддаі [Shaddai, "the Mighty"],
равві [Rabbi, "master, teacher"] &c. are not declined at all;
sometimes, too, the name іисъ [Jesus] is undeclined, when it stands
together with хртосъ [Christ]: іисъ хртомъ [Gal. 1:1—"By Jesus
Christ"].

Note: Sometimes these words may have declension endings: рука
адѡнаѧ гда (Ezek. 8:1—"The hand of the Lord God"); ѽ лютѣ мнѣ,
адѡнаю гди (Ezek. 9:8—"Ah, woe is me, O Lord God").

14) The word кормчїй [helmsman, pilot] in New Church
Slavonic is a noun declined on the model of іерей, славій: кормчїю
всемудру (Octoechos T. 4, Sunday Canon to the Trinity, Ode 5
—"to the All-Wise Shipmaster"). In Old Slavonic, it had the form
кормчии and was declined on the pattern of feminine nouns ending
in _а, _ѧ: землѧ, hence, as a survival, the form seen in кормчїю
рождшаѧ гда (Supplicatory Canon to the Theotokos, Ode 4—"O
thou who didst bear the Lord, the Pilot").

§38. A General Note on the 1st Declension.

The reason the first declension has such a variety of different forms is
that it has absorbed nouns that once belonged to other declensions. This took
place in the earliest times. It was for the most part masculine and neuter nouns
with an o-stem that formed the mainstay of the 1st declension. This thematic
vowel, as a result of weakening and softening, gave rise to the following vowels

o — ŏ = ъ.

jo (е) — jь (= ь), but after vowels — ь (jь) = й.

o — мѣсто [place];

jo = ѥ — мо́рѥ [sea];
ŏ = ъ — бо́гъ [god, deity];
jь = ь — во́ждь [leader];
jь = й — кра́й [edge, region].

To this declension consisting of o-stem nouns, other nouns were added whose stem-vowel was a short *u*: ŭ = ъ: сы́нъ [son; compare the Old English **sunu**, son], до́мъ [house, home; cf. Latin **domu-s**], which used to have their own declension; and then to these there was further added a class of masculine nouns which had a short *i* as a stem-vowel: ῐ = ь: го́сть [guest], госпо́дь [lord].

Although they had taken on the declension endings of the o-stem nouns, the ŭ-stem and ῐ-stem nouns nevertheless contributed peculiarities of their own. Characteristic of the ŭ-stem nouns are these endings: _ȣ in the genitive and prepositional singular: въ до́мȣ [in the house]; the dative singular ending _ови, _еви; the nominative plural in _ове; the genitive plural ending _овъ; the insturmental plural _[ъ]ми: сы́нми [by sons].

Peculiarities of the i-stem nouns are the nominative plural ending _їе: госпо́дїе [lords]; the instrumental plural _ьми: госпо́дьми [by the lords], and the vocative singular ending _и in the word го́споди [O Lord].

These peculiarities were taken on by analogy by many nouns of other stems, which had gone into the 1st declension; although the tendency toward them is found mostly in nouns to which they are proper: thus o-stem nouns often have the endings _ови, _еви on the model of the u-stems: ми́р_ови [unto peace], со́тник_ови [to the centurion], мȣж_еви [to the man], вра́ч_еви [to the physician], and so on.

§39. The 2nd Declension.

The 2nd declension includes nouns of both masculine and feminine gender that end in _а, _ѧ: жена̀ [woman], воево́да [commander], ꙁемлѧ̀ [land, earth], сꙋдїѧ̀ [judge].

Models of the 2nd Declension.
Singular.

	Hard Declension.		Soft Declension.		Mixed Declension.
Nom.	жен-а̀	рꙋк-а̀	ꙁемл-ѧ̀	сꙋдї-ѧ̀	ю̆нош-а
Gen.	жен-ы̀	рꙋк-ѝ	ꙁемл-ѝ	сꙋдї-ѝ	ю̆нош-и
Dat.	жен-ѣ̀	рꙋц-ѣ̀	ꙁемл-ѝ	сꙋдї-ѝ	ю̆нош-и [ѣ]4

	Hard Declension.		Soft Declension.		Mixed Declension.
Acc.	жен-ꙋ	рꙋк-ꙋ	ꙁе́мл-ю	сꙋдї-ю̀	ю̆нош-ꙋ
Instr.	жен-о́ю	рꙋк-о́ю	ꙁемл-е́ю	сꙋдї-е́ю	ю̆нош-ею
Prep.	жен-ѣ̀	рꙋц-ѣ̀	ꙁемл-ѝ	сꙋдї-ѝ	ю̆нош-и
Voc.	же́н-о	рꙋк-о̀	ꙁемл-ѐ	сꙋдї-ѐ	ю̆нош-е

Dual Number.

	Hard Declension.		Soft Declension.		Mixed Declension.
N.A.V.	жен-ѣ̑	рꙋц-ѣ̑	ꙁе́мл-ѝ	сꙋдї-ѝ̑	ю̆нѡш-и
G. P.	жен-ꙋ̑	рꙋк-ꙋ̑	ꙁе́мл-ю	сꙋдї-ю̑	ю̆нѡш-ꙋ
D. I.	жен-а́ма	рꙋк-а́ма	ꙁе́мл-ама	сꙋдї-а́ма	ю̆ношама

Plural.

	Hard Declension.		Soft Declension.		Mixed Declension.
N. V.	жен-ы̑	рꙋк-и̑5	ꙁе́мл-и	сꙋдї-и̑	ю̆нѡш-и
Gen.	же́н-ъ	рꙋк-ъ	ꙁеме́л-ь	сꙋдї-й[е́й	ю̆нош-ъ
Dat.	жен-а́мъ	рꙋк-а́мъ	ꙁемл-а́мъ	сꙋдї-а́мъ	ю̆нош-амъ

---

4) Under the influence of Russian, -ѣ may be found after palatals in place of -и: ю̆ношѣ (II Mac- cabees 7:25—"[to give counsel] unto the young man").

5) There is no softening, since -ы used to be written here (See §8, d).

Acc.	жєн_ы̀	рꙋк_и	зємл_и	сꙋдї_и̂ [_е́й]	ю̑нош_ы[6] [_ъ]
Instr.	жєн_а́ми	рꙋк_а́ми	зємл_а́ми	сꙋдї_а́ми	ю̑нош_а́ми
Prep.	жєн_а́хъ	рꙋк_а́хъ	зємл_а́хъ	сꙋдї_а́хъ	ю̑нош_ахъ

§40. Peculiarities of the 2nd Declension.

1) Masculine nouns that end in _їѧ take the ending _ємъ in the instrumental singular: ѓсаїемъ [by Isaias, Isaiah], іеремі́емъ [by Jeremias/Jeremiah].

2) Nouns whose stem ends in a palatal ["hushing" sibilant] may sometimes have, alongside of the usual form of the accusative plural, the ancient form as well: thus мрє́жи [nets] in Mark 1:16, 18, but мрє́жа, the ancient form, in Mark 1:19; дꙋшы ва́ша [your souls], but in some editions дꙋша̀ ва́ша (Luke 21:19—"[possess ye] your souls").

Nouns ending in _ѧ after a vowel (вы́ѧ, neck; мо́лнїѧ, lightning; ѕмі́ѧ, viper; and others) have kept the ancient forms of the nominative and accusative plural: ѕмїѧ̂ во́змꙋтъ (Mark 16:18 —"they shall take up serpents"); лꙋчезарнаѧ твоѧ̂ мѡ́лнїѧ (Sunday Mesonycticon, Trinitarian doxologies—"Thy resplendent lightnings"); своѧ̂ же покори́ша вы̑ѧ (Vespers, in the Prayer of Bowed Heads—"they have humbled [bowed] their necks"); but стрꙋѧ̀ [stream, flow, current], plural стрꙋѝ (compare the Old Slavonic forms: singular вы́ѧ, мо́лнїѧ, ѕмі́ѧ, and the nominative and accusative plural: вы́ѩ, мо́лнїѩ, ѕмі́ѩ).

3) Before ѣ in the dative and prepositional singular, and in the nominative, accusative and vocative dual, the softening of gutturals occurs (see §34).

4) The accusative plural of animate nouns is usually the same as the nominative, but it may also coincide with the genitive: ѿпꙋсти́лъ є҆сѝ ѻ҆трокови́цъ (Daniel 13:21—"thou didst send away the maids").

---

6) After palatals, _ы is written only to distinguish one case from another.

§41. The 3rd Declension.

The 3rd declension consists of nouns, for the most part feminine, and only a few masculine, that end in _ь: болѣ́знь [disease, f.], ми́лость [mercy, f.], мꙋ́дрость [wisdom, f.]; of the masculine gender are горт́а́нь [larynx, palate, throat], пꙋ́ть [path, way].

At a very early time, numerous masculine nouns that had belonged to the 3rd declension passed over into the 1st declension (for example, го́лꙋбь [dove, pigeon], та́ть [thief], госпо́дь [lord], го́сть [guest] and many others.

The 3rd declension also includes several words declined only in the plural: гꙋ́сли [cithara, a stringed instrument], ꙗ́сли [manger, crib, creche], пе́рси [chest], мо́щи [relics], лю́дїе [people], and others. Госпо́дїе [lords], in the plural, retains the endings of the 3rd declension.

Model Nouns of the 3rd Declension.
Singular.

	Feminine	Masculine.
Nom.	за́повѣ́д_ь [commandment]	пꙋ́т_ь [path]
Gen.	за́повѣ́д_и	пꙋ́т_и́
Dat.	за́повѣ́д_и	пꙋ́т_и́
Acc.	за́повѣ́д_ь	пꙋ́т_ь
Instr.	за́повѣ́д_їю	пꙋ́т_е́мъ
Prep.	за́повѣ́д_и	пꙋ́т_и́
Voc.	за́повѣ́д_е	пꙋ́т_ь [_и]

Dual.

N.A.V.	за́пωвѣ́д_и	пꙋ́т_и́
G., P.	за́пωвѣ́д_їю	пꙋ́т_їю̀
D., I.	за́повѣ́д_ема [_ьма]	пꙋ́т_ьма̀

Plural.

N., V.	за́пωвѣ́д_и	пꙋ́т_и́
Gen.	за́повѣ́д_ей	пꙋ́т_и́й [_е́й]
Dat.	за́повѣ́д_емъ	пꙋ́т_е́мъ

Acc.	ӡа́пѡⷡ҇ѣ́д҇-и		пꙋ́т҇-и̑
Instr.	ӡа́повѣ́д҇-ьми		пꙋ́т҇-ьми̑
Prep.	ӡа́повѣ́д҇-ехъ		пꙋ́т҇-е́хъ

§42. The 4th Declension.

The 4th declension consists of masculine, feminine and neuter nouns whose stem is longer in the oblique cases than it is in the nominative. A characteristic peculiarity of this declension is the ending _е in the genitive singular.

The endings of the nominative, and of the stem in the other cases:

Neuter nouns:

_ѧ — _ен: и́м_ѧ, и́м_ен_е [name]; пле́м_ѧ, пле́м_ен_е [tribe];

_ѧ [а]—ѧт [ат]: о̑троч_а̀, о̑троч_а́т_е [boy]; о̑сл_а̀, о̑сл_а́т_е [ass];

_о—ес: не́б_о, неб_ес_ѐ [sky, heaven]; чꙋ́д_о, чꙋ́д_ес_ѐ [miracle];

Feminine nouns:

_и — ер: ма́т_и, ма́т_ер_е [mother]; дщ_ѝ, дщ_е́р_е [daughter];

_ы—ов [ꙋв]: свекр_ы̀, свекр_о́в_е [mother-in-law]; люб_ы̀, люб_в_ѐ [love].

Masculine nouns:

_ь [ы] — ен: ка́м_ен_ь (from ка́м_ы—ка́м_ен_е, [rock, stone]); де́н_ь —дн_ѐ [day], ко́рен_ь—ко́рен_е [root] (no change in stem).

This difference between the stems of the nominative and oblique cases came about as follows:

1) In neuter nouns inding in мѧ: he final _ѧ (yus maly) resolved itself into _ен_ before the inflection endings of the oblique cases (see §2, 10): и́м_ѧ — йм_ен_е.

2) In feminine nouns ending in _ы, the final _ы resolved itself into _ов_ [ꙋв] before the case endings: люб_ы̀—люб_в_ѐ—люб_о́в_ь (see §10, III-2).

3) In masculine nouns inding in _ь (where the stem ends in _ мєн_): these nouns originally had the ending _ы: камы [rock], пламы [flame], sometimes adding a suffix _к_ъ: камыкъ [1]).

The final _ы of these nouns had a nasalized pronunciation. Before the endings, the _ы resolved itself into _єн_. In New Church Slavonic, the nominative of these nouns is used only with the _єн_ and the inflection _ь: камєнь, пламєнь, кремєнь [flint], рємєнь [strap].

4) In the nominative singular of the following nouns, there has been an abbreviation of the stem. Neuter nouns ending in _о: нєбо — нєбєсє: here the с of the stem has disappeared, and the є was replaced by о. Neuter nouns ending in _ат: Орла̀ — Орл_а́т_є [eaglet]: т has been dropped from the stem. Something similar is to be seen in Greek neuter nouns: πνεῦμα—πνεύματ-ος [spirit]. In feminine nouns ending in _и: ма́ти — ма́т_єр_є, р has been dropped from the stem, while є has been replaced by н (in other languages this root is the same: Latin *mater*, German *Mutter*, Greek μήτηρ, Doric μάτηρ).

The nouns стєпєнь [degree, step], ко́рєнь [root], дєнь [day] have not undergone stem changes.

---

[1]) These old forms can still be met with: ѡдождѝ камыкъ гора́щъ (Luke 17:29—"It rained fire and brimstone"); камыкъ тьмы̀ (Job 28:3—"the stones of darkness"); разсы́пашаса камы́цы (Lam. 4:1—"the stones are poured out"); камы́квъ ѻ́гнєнныхъ (Ezek. 28:16—"of the stones of fire"); я́кѡ ѻ́гнь пла́мы (Lam. 2:3—"like a flaming fire").

§43. Models of the 4th Declension.

Neuter nouns.

Singular.

Nom., Voc. [heaven, sky]	и҆́мѧ [name]	ѻ҆троча̀ [boy]	не́бо
Gen.	и҆́мен_е	ѻ҆троча́т_е	небес_ѐ
Dat.	и҆́мен_и	ѻ҆троча́т_и	небес_ѝ
Acc.	и҆́мѧ	ѻ҆троча̀	не́бо
Instr.	и҆́мен_емъ	ѻ҆троча́т_емъ	небес_е́мъ
Prep.	и҆́мен_и	ѻ҆троча́т_и	небес_ѝ

Dual.

N., A., V.	и҆мен_и	ѻ҆трѡча́т_и	небес_и̑
Gen., Prep.	и҆мен_у̀	ѻ҆троча́т_у̀	небес_у̀
Dat., Instr.	и҆мен_е́ма [_ама]	ѻ҆троча́т_ема [_ама]	небес_е́ма

Plural.

Nom., Voc.	и҆мен_а̀	ѻ҆троча́т_а	небес_а̀
Gen.	и҆ме́н_ъ	ѻ҆троча́т_ъ	небе́с_ъ
Dat.	и҆мен_е́мъ [_ѡмъ]	ѻ҆троча́т_емъ[_ѡмъ]	небес_е́мъ
Acc.	и҆мен_а̀	ѻ҆троча́т_а	небес_а̀
Instr.	и҆мен_ы̀	ѻ҆троча́т_ы	небес_ы̀
Prep.	и҆мен_ѣ́хъ	ѻ҆троча́т_ѣхъ	небес_ѣ́хъ

Masculine nouns.

Singular.

Nom., Voc.	степе́н_ь [degree]	де́н_ь [day]	ка́мен_ь [stone]
Gen.	степе́н_е	дн_ѐ	ка́мен_е
Dat.	степе́н_и	дн_ѝ, дн_е́ви	ка́мен_и
Acc.	степе́н_ь	де́н_ь	ка́мен_ь
Instr.	степе́н_емъ	дн_е́мъ	ка́мен_емъ
Prep.	степе́н_и	дн_ѝ	ка́мен_и

Dual.

N., A., V.	стєпе́н_и	дн_и̂	ка́мєн_и
Gen., Prep.	стєпе́н_ꙋ	дн_і́ю, дн_ю̀	ка́мєн_ꙋ
Dat., Instr.	стєпе́н_ема	дєн_ьма̀	ка́мєн_ьма[_ема]

Plural.

Nom., Voc.	стєпе́н_и	дн_іє, дн_и̂	ка́мєн_и [_їѧ]
Gen.	стєпе́н_єй [_їй]	дн_ій [_е́й]	ка́мєн_їй
Dat.	стєпе́н_ємꙁ	дн_е́мꙁ	ка́мєн_ємꙁ
Acc.	стєпе́н_и	дн_и̂	ка́мєн_и
Instr.	стєпе́н_ьми	дєн_ьми	ка́мєн_ьми
Prep.	стєпе́н_єхꙁ	дн_е́хꙁ	ка́мєн_єхꙁ

Feminine nouns.

Singular.

Nom., Voc.	ма́ти [mother]	свєкры̀ [mother-in-law] цє́рковь [church; ancient form: цє́ркы]
Gen.	ма́тєр_є	свєкро́в_є	цє́ркв_є
Dat.	ма́тєр_и	свєкро́в_и	цє́ркв_и
Acc.	ма́тєр_ь	свєкро́в_ь	цє́рков_ь
Instr.	ма́тєр_їю	свєкро́в_їю	цє́рков_їю
Prep.	ма́тєр_и	свєкро́в_и	цє́ркв_и

Dual.

N., A., V.	ма́тєр_и	свєкрѡ́в_и	цє́ркв_и
Gen., Prep.	ма́тєр_їю	свєкрѡ́в_їю	цє́рков_їю
Dat., Instr.	ма́тєр_ема	свєкро́в_ама	цє́ркв_ама

Plural.

Nom., Voc.	ма́тєр_и	свєкрш́в_и	цє́ркв_и
Gen.	ма́тєр_їй [_єй]	свєкро́в_єй	цє́ркв_є́й
Dat.	ма́тєр_ємъ	свєкро́в_амъ	цє́ркв_амъ
Acc.	ма́тєр_єй [_и]	свєкро́в_єй [_и]	цє́ркв_и
Instr.	ма́тєр_ьми	свєкро́в_ами	цє́ркв_ами
Prep.	ма́тєр_єхъ	свєкро́в_ахъ	цє́ркв_ахъ
Voc.			цє́ркв_є (Palm

Sunday Vespers, at the Aposticha).

Notes on the Cases.

In place of the plural forms of ка́мєнь, very often the collective form of this word is used: да ка́мєнїє сїѐ хлѣ́бы бꙋ́дꙋтъ (Matth. 4:3—"that these stones be made bread"); ка́мєнїємъ побива́хꙋ стєфа́на (Acts 7:59—"And they stoned Stephen").

The plural form is also used, although less often: ка́мєнїа (IV Kings, 19:18); ка́мєнїй (III Kings, 18:31); ка́мєньми (II Cor. 11:25); на ка́мєнїахъ (Jeremiah 14:6—"upon the rocks"); на ка́мєнєхъ (Jer. 18:3—"[making a vessel] on the stones").

Note: The plural forms ка́мєнїа, на ка́мєнїахъ, are, it would seem, inter-related with the collective form ка́мєнїє.

There sometimes occur forms of ка́мєнь that are declined according to the 1st declension: къ ка́мєню рєммш́ню (Judges 20:47—"[they fled] to the rock of Remmon"); ка́мєню вѣ́ры (June 29, at the Litiya—"Thou rock of faith"); цєрко́внаго ка́мєна (June 29, Sedalen at Matins—"the Church's rock").

Neuter nouns in the prepositional plural have the spelling _ ѣхъ: ѡ̑ врємєнѣхъ ("concerning the times"), ѡ̑ ѻ̑сла́тѣхъ ("about the asses"), на нєбєсѣхъ ("in heaven").

The nouns свєкры̀ and цє́рковь, in the endings of the dative, instrumental and prepositional plura, as well as the dative and instrumental dual, have the vowel а: _ама, _амъ, _ами, _ахъ.

§44. Peculiarities of the 4th Declension.

The nouns Óко [eye] and оýхо [ear] are declined in the singular and plural on the pattern of нéбо, but in the dual they are declined without the suffix _ес:

Nom., Acc., Voc.	Óчи [Óцѣ] eyes	оýши [ears]
Gen., Prep.	Óчїю	оýшїю
Dat., Instrum.	Óчи́ма	оýши́ма

Neuter nouns ending in _о, due to the likeness of their nominative case to that of the 1st declension, often take forms without the suffix _ес, along the pattern of first declension nouns: слóвомъ (Matth. 8:16—"with his word"); во Óцѣ твоéмъ (Matth. 7:4—"[a beam is] in thine own eye").

Слóво [word], when it refers to the Person of the Son, does not take the suffix _ес in the oblique cases: безъ истлѣнїѧ бга слóва рóждшꙋю (in the acclamation to the Theotokos sung after the Consecration and elsewhere, beginning *It is truly meet and right*,—"thou who without defilement barest God the Word").

On the model of мáти [mother] is declined дщѝ [daughter]; the model of свекры̀ is followed by любы̀ [love], неплóды [sterility], крóвь [blood], цéрковь [church, formerly цéркы]; declined like кáмень are плáмень [flame], реме́нь [strap], креме́нь [flint], and кóрень [root].

The word оýдъ [limb, member, body part], besides the usual forms of the 1st declension, sometimes takes the endings of the 4th declension, on the model of neuter nouns ending in _о: благодáрными оýдесы̀ мои́ми (Prayer of St. Simeon the New Theologian before Communion— "with thankfulness in all my members").

Texts for Practice.

1) Никто́же мо́жетъ двѣма̀ господи́нома рабо́тати. 2) Й видѣвше фарїсе́е, глаго́лахꙋ ѹ҆ченикѡ́мъ є҆гѡ̀: почто̀ съ мытари̂ й грѣ́шники ѹ҆чи́тель ва́шъ ꙗ҆́стъ й пїе́тъ; 3) Не стяжи́те зла́та, ни сребра̀, ни мѣ́ди при поясѣ́хъ ва́шихъ, ни пиры̀ въ пꙋ́ть, ни двою̀ ри̂зꙋ, ни сапѡ́гъ, ни жезла̀: досто́инъ бо є҆́сть дѣ́латель мзды̀ своеѧ̀. 4) Не скрыва́йте себѣ̀ сокро́вищъ на землѝ, и҆дѣ́же че́рвь й тлѧ̀ тли́тъ, й и҆дѣ́же та́тїе подко́пываютъ й кра́дꙋтъ. 5) Й слы́шавше а҆рдїере́е й фарїсе́е при̂тчи є҆гѡ̀, разꙋмѣ́ша, ꙗ҆́кѡ ѡ҆ ни́хъ глаго́летъ. 6) Возда́дите ѹ҆́бо ке́сарева ке́сареви: й бж҃їѧ бг҃ови. 7) І҆ерꙋсали́ме, і҆ерꙋсали́ме, и҆зби́вый прⷪ҇о́ки й ка́менїемъ побива́яй пѡ́сланныѧ къ тебѣ̀, коль́краты восхотѣ́хъ собра́ти ча̂да твоѧ̀, ꙗ҆́коже собира́етъ ко́кошъ птенцы̀ своѧ̀ под крилѣ̀, й не восхотѣ́сте; 8) Ходѧ̀ же при мо́ри галїле́йстѣмъ, ви́дѣ сі́мѡна й а҆ндре́а бра́та тогѡ̀ сі́мѡна, вмета́юща мре́жи въ мо́ре: бѣ́ста бо рыба́рѧ. 9) Го́ре ва́мъ фарїсе́ѡмъ, ꙗ҆́кѡ лю́бите предсѣда̂нїѧ на со́нмищихъ й цѣлова̂нїѧ на то́ржищихъ. 10) Не́бо мнѣ̀ престо́лъ є҆́сть, землѧ̀ же подно́жїе нога́ма мои́ма. 11) Гдѣ́ ти, сме́рте, жа́ло; гдѣ̀ ти, а́де, побѣ́да; 12) Премꙋ́дрость мꙋ́жеви ражда́етъ ра́зꙋмъ. 13) До́мове беззако́нныхъ требꙋ́ютъ ѡ҆чище́нїѧ. 14) Ме́рзость гдⷭ҇еви пꙋ̂тїе нечести́выхъ. 15) Тогда̀ і҆и҃съ нача́тъ поноша́ти градовѡ́мъ. 16) Нѣ́сть на́ша бра́нь къ кро́ви й пло́ти, но къ нача́лѡмъ, й ко власте́мъ, й къ мїродержи́телемъ тьмы̀ вѣ́ка сегѡ̀, къ дꙋхѡ́мъ ѕло́бы поднебе́снымъ. 17) Разлꙋчи́тся ѻ҆те́цъ на сы́на, й сы́нъ на ѻ҆тца̀: ма́ти на дще́рь, й дщѝ на ма́терь: свекры̀ на невѣ́стꙋ [свою̀], й невѣ́ста на свекро́вь. 18) Да не свари́ши ꙗ҆гнѧ́те во млецѣ̀ ма́тере.

Key to the Exercise.

1) No man can serve two masters [Matth. 6:24]. 2) And when the Pharisees saw, they said unto His disciples, Why eateth

your Master with publicans and sinners? [Matth. 9:11]. 3) Provide neither gold, nor silver, nor brass in your purses, Nor scrip for your journey, neither two coats, neither shoes, nor yet staves: for the workman is worthy of his meat [Matth. 10:9-10]. 4) Lay not up for yourselves treasures upon earth, where moth and rust corrupt, and where thieves break through and steal [Matth. 6:19]. 5) And when the chief priests and Pharisees had heard his parables, they perceived that he spake of them [Matth. 21:45]. 6) Render therefore unto Cæsar the things that are Cæsar's, and unto God the things that are God's [Matth. 22:21]. 7) O Jerusalem, Jerusalem, that killest the prophets and stonest them which are sent unto thee, how often would I have gathered thy children together, even as a hen gathereth her chicks under her wings, and ye would not! [Matth. 23:37]. 8) Now as he walked by the sea of Galilee, he saw Simon and Andrew his brother casting a net into the sea: for they were fishers [Mark 1:16]. 9) Woe unto you, Pharisees! for ye love the uppermost seats in the synagogues, and greetings in the markets [Luke 11:43]. 10) Heaven is My throne, and earth is My footstool [Acts 7:49]. 11) O death, where is thy sting? O grave, where is thy victory? [I Cor. 15:55]. 12) Wisdom is prudence to a man [Prov. 10:23]. 13) The houses of the transgressors need purification [Prov. 14:9, *Septuagint*]. 14) The ways of the wicked are an abomination to the Lord [Prov. 15:9]. 15) Then Jesus began to upbraid the cities [Matth. 11:20]. 16) For we wrestle not against flesh and blood, but against principalities, against powers, against the rulers of the darkness of this world, against spiritual wickedness in high places [Eph. 6:12]. 17) The father shall be divided against the son, and the son against the father; the mother against the daughter, and the daughter against the mother; the mother-in-law against her daughter-in-law [Luke 12:53]. 18) Thou shalt not seethe a kid in his mother's milk [Exodus 23:19].

PRONOUNS.

§45. Pronouns are words that replace nouns, adjectives or numbers, e.g. Поими Отрочà й мáтерь є̓гѡ̀ (Matth. 2:13—"Take the young child and *his* mother"). Ꙗ҆ко́въ пе́рстный, таковѝ й пе́рстнїи (I Cor. 15:48—"*Such* as is the earthly, *such* also are the earthly"). Долготà Опо́ны є̓ди́ныѧ двáдесѧть й О̓смь лакте́й... мѣ́ра тáѧжде да бꙋ́детъ всѣ̑мъ Опо́намъ (Ex. 26:2—"The length of one curtain shall be eight and twenty cubits... *the same* measure shall be for all the curtains").

According to their meaning, pronouns are divided into the same classes as in Russian [and English]:

1) personal—
   а҆́зъ, I
   ты̀, thou
   О̓́нъ [й], he [him]
   О̓нà [ю], she [her]
   О̓но̀ [є], it.

2) reflexive—
   себѐ, self [myself, thyself, himself, herself, itself, &c.].

3) demonstrative—
   то́й: тà, тáѧ: то̀, то́е: that
   се́й [сі́й], сїà, сїѐ: this
   О̓́нъ, О̓́на, О̓́но: О̓́ный, _аѧ, _ое: yon, that
   О̓́въ, _а, _о: О̓́вый, _аѧ, _ое: this [near at hand]
   такі́й, _áѧ, о́е: such
   таковы́й, _áѧ, _о́е: such, of such nature
   толи́кїй, _аѧ, _ое: so great, such a great
   сицевы́й, _áѧ, _ое: such as this.

4) possessive—
   мо́й, моѧ̀, моѐ: my, mine.
   тво́й, твоѧ̀, твоѐ: thy, thine.

свой, своѧ, своє: one's own [the which belongs to the
    subject].

нашъ, _а, _є: our, ours

вашъ, _а, _є: your [plural], yours.

5) interrogative—

    кто̀, что̀; who? what?

    кі́й, ка́ѧ, ко́є; which?

    чі́й, чїѧ̀, чїє̀; whose?

    какі́й, кака́ѧ, како́є; what kind of?

    како́въ, _а̀, _о̀; каковы́й, _а́ѧ, _о́є; of what nature?

    та̑ко́въ, _а̀, о̀; таковы́й, _а́ѧ, _о́є; of such nature

    коли́къ, _а, _о; how great?

    кото́рый, _аѧ, _оє; which one [of several]?

6) relative—

    и́же, ꙗ́же, е̑́же: which, the one that...

    е̑ли́къ, _а, _о: е̑ли́кїй, _аѧ, _оє: as many as, as much
        as...

    та̑́къ, _а, _о: та̑кі́й, _а́ѧ, _о́є: such as

    As well as those listed above as interrogative: коли́кїй,
    кто̀, что̀, &c.

7) definite [emphatic]—

    ве́сь, всѧ̀, всє̀: all, all of...

    всѧ́къ, _а, _о: всѧ́кїй, _аѧ, _оє: every, any

    са́мый, _аѧ, _оє: the same, the very

    кі́йждо, ка́аждо, ко́єждо or ко́ждо: each, every

    всѧ́чєскїй, _аѧ, _оє: any, every, all

    и̑нъ, _а, _о: и̑ны́й, _а́ѧ, _о́є: another

8) indefinite—

    нѣ́кто, нѣ́что: someone, something

    нѣ́кїй, нѣ́каѧ, нѣ́коє: some, a certain

9) negative—

    никто̀, ничто̀: no one, nothing

ннктóже, нчтóже: nobody, nothing whatever
нкíй, _áа, _óе: нкотóрый, _áа, _óе: no, not a...

§46. The Formation of Pronouns.

Many pronouns have lost the vowel of their root, and therefore in such cases the root takes the form of a consonant.

Personal pronouns. The 1st person has several roots:
а̀з — ӑзъ (from this, through the softened form язъ, comes the Russian я): "I";

м — м_ене, м_а: "me"; м_ы: "we";

н — н_ы, н_асъ: "us" [cf. German u*n*s, Latin *n*os].

The 2nd person is shown by the letters т and в:
т — т_ы̀ [thou], т_об_ою [thee, instrumental case];
в — в_ы̀ [ye], в_áсъ [you], &c.

The 3rd person is expressed by means of the following pronouns:
о̆нъ, о̀на̀, о̀но̀ [he, she, it] and й, а̀, е̂ [him, her, it].

The 3rd person pronoun о̆нъ, о̀на̀, о̀но̀ was borrowed from the demonstrative pronoun о̆нъ, о̆н_ый: these forms, however, are used only in the nominative; for the oblique cases of the 3rd person, the pronouns й, а̀, е̂, which do not have a nominative case, are used. Joined to the conjunction же, the pronouns й, а̀, е̂ [йже, я̀же, е̂же] do have a nominative form, as relative pronouns.

Note: The pronouns й, а̀, е̂ were originally demonstrative, and showed definiteness. At some time in the ancient period, and as late as the beginning of Slavonic writing, these pronouns were used as definite articles [i.e. equivalent to the English article "the"], attached to the end of adjectives, and later they became part of the adjective, resulting in the longer, or "full" adjective endings.

In Church Slavonic, the demonstrative pronouns сі́й, то́й are often used as pronouns of the 3rd person, for example: Сі́й (οὗτος) прїи́де во свидѣ́тельство (John 1:7—"This man came for a witness"); Не бѣ̀ то́й (ἐκεῖνος) свѣ́тъ (John 1:8—"He was not that light"); the Russian version of the Bible uses онъ ["he"] in both verses [as does the King James Version in the second case].

Demonstrative pronouns are derived from the following roots:
From с— сі_й [сі́й], сі_а̀, сі_è: and with the suffixes _иц_ев_ —с_иц_ев_ы́й, _а́а, _óе ["this kind of..."].

From т— то́й, та̀, та́_а, то̀, то́_е [that]; from the same root, with the suffix _ак_: т_ак_і́й, _а́а, _óе [such]; with _ак_ов_: т_ак_о́в_ъ, _а̀, _о̀, and with the long endings таков_ы́й, _а́а, _óе. With the suffixes _ол_ик_: т_ол_и́к_ъ, _а, _о, толи́к_і́й, _а́а_ _óе [so great, so much].

From Он_ and Ов_: Он — о̆н_ъ, о̆н_а, о̆н_о and the long forms о̆н_ы́й, _а́а, _óе [yon, that]; Ов_— о̆в_ъ, о̆в_а, о̆в_о and the long forms о̆в_ы́й, _а́а, _óе [this one; the one/the other].

From the demonstrative с_ was derived the *reflexive* pronoun с_еб_è.

Possessive pronouns are formed from the roots of the personal pronouns of the 1st and 2nd persons: м — м_о́й [my],
ты̀ — тв_о́й [thy],
н — н_а́шъ [our],
в — в_а́шъ [your],
and from the reflexive с (св = сб) — св_о́й.

Interrogative pronouns are formed from the roots к and ч (the latter derived from к): кі́_й, ка́_а, ко́_е [what]; чі́_й, чї_а̀, чї_è [whose]; к_то̀ [who], ч_то̀ [what]; and from the same roots by means of suffixes:

_ак_ — к_ак_і́й, _а́а, _о́є; (which, what?)

_ак_ов_ — к_ак_о́в_ъ, _а̀, _о̀; к_ак_ов_ы́й, _а́а, _оє; (what kind of?)

_о_лнк_ — к_олнк_ї́й, _аа, _оє; (how great, how many?)

_о_тор_ — к_о_тор_ый, _аа, _оє; (which?)

The pronouns кто̀, что̀ were formed by joining the demonstrative то́й [тъ] to к_, ч_.

Interrogative pronouns, when used in the absence of a question, take on a *relative* meaning. From the root є́л and the suffix _нк_, the relative pronoun є́л_нк_ъ, є́л_нк_ї́й (as much as, as many as) is formed. The relative pronouns йже, йа́же, є́же are treated above.

Definite (emphatic) pronouns are formed from the following roots:
сам — сам_ъ, _а̀, _о̀ [self]: сам_ый, _аа, _оє [same, selfsame, very]; в[є]с — вєс_ь, вс_а̀, вс_є̀ [all, whole]; with the suffix _ак_ — вс_а́к_ъ, _а, _о: вс_а́к_ї́й, _аа, _оє [each, every]; with the suffix _ач_є_ск_ — вс_а́ч_є_ск_ї́й, _аа, _оє [every, any, all]; нн — йн_ъ, _а, _о: нн_ы́й, _аа, _о́є [another].

The pronouns кі́й_ждо, ко́_ждо [every] consist of of the interrogative pronoun кі́й [къ] and the particle _ждо.

Indefinite and *negative* pronouns are formed by means of the prefixes нѣ and нн, which are attached to the interrogative pronouns: нѣ_кто [someone], нн_кто̀ [no one], нѣ_кі́й [a certain], нн_кото́рый [any], &c.

The Declension of Pronouns.

§47. The pronouns а́зъ [I], ты̀ [thou], сєбє̀ [self], кто̀ [who], что̀ [what], нѣкто [someone], нѣчто [something], ннкто̀ [no one], ннчто̀ [nothing] do not change according to gender; all the others change. Certain of the pronouns also add й, а, є to their gender endings: о́н_ъ — о́ны_й, о́н_а — о́на_а, о́н_о — о́но_є.

According to their declension, the pronouns in Church Slavonic are divided into two groups: to the *first* group belong the personal pronouns а́зъ and ты̀ and the reflexive себѐ — they have like endings and are declined differently from other pronouns; to the *second* group belong all other pronouns, and they are declined on the model of the 3rd person pronoun, and either the endings of these pronouns are soft like those of the 3rd person pronoun, or else the soft vowels and their signs are replaced by the corresponding hard ones. In the first case the declension is called *soft*, and in the second case, *hard*.

	1st Group			**2nd Group (Soft Declension)**		
				Singular.		
				Masculine	Neuter	Feminine.
Nom.	а́зъ	ты̀		о́нъ [й]	о́но̀ [є̈]	о́на̀ [ѧ̈]
Gen.	менѐ	тебѐ	себѐ	є҆гẁ	є҆гẁ	є҆ѧ̀
Dat.	мнѣ̀,	тебѣ̀,	себѣ̀, си	є҆мꙋ̀	є҆мꙋ̀	є҆́й
	мѝ	тѝ				
Acc.	менѐ,	тебѐ, себѐ, сѧ̀		є҆го̀, й	є҆̀	ю̀
	мѧ̀	тѧ̀				
Instr.	мно́ю	тобо́ю	собо́ю	и́мъ	и́мъ	є҆́ю
Prep.	мнѣ̀	тебѣ̀	себѣ̀	[н]є́мъ	[н]є́мъ	[н]є́й
				Dual.		
Nom.	мы̀	вы̀		о́на	о́на	о́нѣ
Acc.	ны̀	вы̀		ѧ̀	ѧ̀	ѧ̀
G., Pr.	на́ю	ва́ю		є҆ю̀	є҆ю̀	є҆ю̀
D., Ins.	на́ма	ва́ма		и́ма	и́ма	и́ма

Plural.

	Masculine.		Neuter.	Feminine.
Nom.	мы̀	вы̀	ѻ҆нѝ	ѻ҆нѝ	ѻ҆нѣ̀
Gen.	на́съ	ва́съ	и҆́хъ	и҆́хъ	и҆́хъ
Dat.	на́мъ	ва́мъ	и҆̃мъ	и҆̃мъ	и҆̃мъ
Acc.	ны̀, на́съ вы̀, ва́съ		а҆̃, и҆́хъ	а҆̃	а҆̃, и҆́хъ
Instr.	на́ми	ва́ми	и҆́ми	и҆́ми	и҆́ми
Prep.	на́съ	ва́съ	[н]и́хъ	[н]и́хъ	[н]и́хъ

Soft Declension.

Singular.

	Masculine.	Neuter.	Feminine.
Nom.	мо́й	моѐ	моѧ̀
Gen.	моегѡ̀	моегѡ̀	моеѧ̀
Dat.	моем꙼	моем꙼	мое́й
Acc.	мо́й, моего̀	моѐ	мою̀
Instr.	мои́мъ	мои́мъ	мое́ю
Prep.	мое́мъ	мое́мъ	мое́й

Dual.

	Masculine.	Neuter.	Feminine.
Nom., Acc.	моѧ̂	моѧ̂, моѝ	моѝ
Gen., Prep.	моє́ю	моє́ю	моє́ю
Dat., Instr.	мои́ма	мои́ма	мои́ма

Plural.

	Masculine.	Neuter.	Feminine.
Nom.	моѝ	моѧ̂	моѝ
Gen.	мои́хъ	мои́хъ	мои́хъ
Dat.	мои̂мъ	мои̂мъ	мои̂мъ
Acc.	моѧ̂, мои́хъ	моѧ̂	моѧ̂, мои́хъ
Instr.	мои́ми	мои́ми	мои́ми
Prep.	мои́хъ	мои́хъ	мои́хъ

Hard Declension.

Singular.

	Masculine.	Neuter.	Feminine.
Nom.	то́й	то́е, то̀	та́а, та̀
Gen.	тогѡ̀	тогѡ̀	тоѧ̀
Dat.	тому̀	тому̀	то́й
Acc.	то́й, того̀	то́е, то̀	ту̀, ту̀ю
Instr.	тѣ́мъ	тѣ́мъ	то́ю
Prep.	то́мъ	то́мъ	то́й

Dual.

	Masculine.	Neuter.	Feminine.
Nom., Voc.	та̂	тѣ̂, та̂	тѣ̂
Gen., Prep.	тѡ̀ю	тѡ̀ю	тѡ̀ю
Dat., Instr.	тѣ́ма	тѣ́ма	тѣ́ма

Plural.

	Masculine.	Neuter.	Feminine.
Nom.	ті́и [ти]	та̂а, та̂	ты́а, ты̂
Gen.	тѣ́хъ	тѣ́хъ	тѣ́хъ
Dat.	тѣ́мъ	тѣ́мъ	тѣ́мъ
Acc.	ты́а, тѣ́хъ	та̂а, та̂	ты́а, ты̂, тѣ́хъ
Instr.	тѣ́ми	тѣ́ми	тѣ́ми
Prep.	тѣ́хъ	тѣ́хъ	тѣ́хъ

Notes on the Cases.

1) After prepositions, the oblique cases of the personal pronouns о́нъ [й], она̀ [а], оно̀ [є], which begin with vowels, take the prefix н: ѡ не́мъ, за ню̀ [about him, for her], and in the accusative case the masculine pronoun й is reduced to ь: на́нь [=на (н)й]: Се́й де́нь, є̀го́же сотвори́ гд҃ь, возра́дуемсѧ ѝ возвесели́мсѧ во́нь (Ps. 117:24—"This is the day which the Lord hath made, let us rejoice and be glad therein").

Note 1: In place of во́нь, the Kiev editions have въ Ѻ́нь. This form was adopted in error, as if derived from the demonstrative pronoun Ѻ́нъ (ѡ́бъ Ѻ́нъ по́лъ і҆Ѻрда́на, "on the far side of the Jordan").

Note 2: Originally, in Old Church Slavonic, the consonant н was part of the prepositions въ, съ, къ (вън, сън, кън—in, with, to), but subsequently the н was felt as the beginning of the 3rd person pronoun, and then it came to be used, not only after these prepositions, but after others as well (на [on], по́д [under], за [for], &c.).

2) The short oblique forms of the pronouns а҆́зъ, ты̀ and себѐ (мѝ, тѝ, сѝ, мѧ̀, тѧ̀, сѧ̀, ны̀, вы̀) lose their own accent if they stand after a word accented on a final vowel, and then the preceding word is written with an acute accent on the last letter instead of a grave, e.g. спасѝ мѧ, вонмѝ мн, бл҃гословѝ ны and so on: тѣ́мже молю̀ вы (II Cor. 2:8—"Wherefore I beseech you"). Such pronouns are called *enclitic*. However, if the logical accent falls on one of these words, then they do not lose their own accent: и҆ прїимꙋ̀ вы̀ къ себѣ̀ (John 14:3—"and I will receive you unto Myself"); никто́же своегѡ̀ сѝ да и҆́щетъ (I Cor. 10:24—"Let no man seek his own").

3) The relative pronouns и҆́же, ꙗ҆́же, е҆́же and the determinatives кі́йждо, ко́ждо, ка́аждо, ко́ждо decline only the first part, while the particles _же, _ждо remain unchanged: е҆гѡ́же, е҆мꙋ́же, коегѡ́ждо, коемꙋ́ждо, and so on.

4) The reflexive pronoun себѐ is declined only in the singular and has no nominative.

5) In the pronouns of the 2nd group, the ending of the genitive singular is expressed by ѡ to distinguish it from the similar forms of the accusative: є҆гѡ̀ [his] is the genitive case, while є҆го̀ [him] is the accusative. In the Kievan editions, the pronouns of the 1st group have the "large" є҆ in the genitive singular to distinguish them from the accusative: мене́, тебе́, себе́ are used for the genitive and мене́, тебе́, себе́ for the accusative.

Plural forms that are otherwise identical to singular forms are customarily marked with a circumflex accent (ˆ): thus твоѧ̀ is the feminine singular, and твоѧ̑ is the plural. But in the 3rd person and relative pronouns [о́нъ (и҆), и҆же], to distinguish the cases, the initial "iso" accent [breathing + acute] is replaced by the "apostroph" [breathing plus grave]: и́мъ is the instrumental singular, while и̑мъ is the dative plural; и́же, ꙗ҆же are singular, while и̑же, ꙗ̑же are plural.

By this same method the accusative plural is marked to distinguish it from the genitive plural of the same pronouns: и́хъ, и́хже are genitive plural, while и̑хъ, и̑хже are accusative plural.

§48. On the model of мо́й and тво́й are declined all the other pronouns: some according to the soft declension, others according to the hard:

1) According to the *soft* declension: тво́й, сво́й, кі́й, чі́й, се́й, что̀, нⷤкі́й, нⷤчто, ничто̀, на́шъ,

ва́шъ:

2) According to the *hard* declension: и́нъ, о́нъ, о́въ, са́мъ, всѧ́къ, какі́й [ка́къ], такі́й [та́къ],

є҆ли́къ, толи́къ, коли́къ, кто̀, нⷤкто, никто̀.

Peculiarities in the Declension of Pronouns.

1) The interrogative pronouns кто̀, что̀ are declined only in the singular, and the oblique cases are formed directly from the stem

(кⷮ, чь), without the syllable _то: ко_гѡ̀, че_гѡ̀.

In the same manner are declined the pronouns formed from them: the indefinite нѣ́кто, нѣ́что [someone, something] and the negative никто̀, ничто̀, никто́же, ничто́же [no one, none, nothing], and if the negative pronoun is joined with a preposition, then the preposition is put between ни_ and the pronoun: не ра́диши ни ѡ ко́мже [neither carest Thou for anyone--Matthew 22:16]; ни сварѧ́тсѧ ни съ ки́мъ, ни возненави́дитъ вса́каго человѣ́ка [neither will he argue with anyone, nor hate anyone--Prologue for July 3, Homily of Isaiah the Monk]; є҆ди́нъ нѣ́кто ю҆́ноша и҆де по не́мъ [And there followed Him a certain young man--Mark 14:51]; си́мѡне, и҆́мамъ ти̑ нѣ́что рещѝ [Simon, I have somewhat to say unto thee--Luke 7:40]; ѹ҆ма́лилъ є҆сѝ є҆го̀ ма́лымъ чи́мъ ѿ а҆́гглъ [Thou madest him a little lower than the Angels--Heb. 2:7].

2) The interrogative pronoun кі́й, ка́ѧ, ко́е derives its forms from the two stems кі́й and ко́е, and its case endings are like those in the declension of the personal pronoun и̑, ѧ̀, є̀.

In like manner are declined: the indefinite нѣ́кій, the determinative кі́йждо and the negative никі́й; in which last pronoun, in the prepositional case, the preposition is put between the syllable ни and the pronoun: да ни въ ко́емъ грѣсѣ̀ прогнѣ́ваю бга̀ [lest by any sin I anger God--Morning Prayers, Prayer to the guardian Angel].

Note: In the forms: ѿ нѣ́кихъ ([it was said] by some--Luke 9:7), не прїити̑ нѣ́кимъ ([before] that certain were come--Gal. 2:12) an elision has taken place (instead of нѣ́кїихъ, нѣ́кїимъ).

3) The pronouns на́шъ, ва́шъ belong to the mixed declension, i.e., for the most part they are declined according to the soft declension, only the iotated vowels are replaced by the hard ones. In the plural, ѧ appears in the endings merely to distinguish cases.

Singular

	Masculine	Neuter	Feminine
Nom.	кі́й	ко́е	ка́ѧ
Gen.	ко́егѡ	ко́егѡ	ко́еѧ̀
Dat.	ко́емꙋ	ко́емꙋ	ко́ей
Acc.	кі́й, ко́его	ко́е	кꙋ́ю
Instr.	кі́имъ	кі́имъ	ко́ею
Prep.	ко́емъ	ко́емъ	ко́ей

Dual.

	Masculine	Neuter	Feminine
Nom., Acc.	ка̑ѧ	ка̑ѧ/ кі́и	кі́и
Gen., Prep.	ко́ею	ко́ею	ко́ею
Dat., Instr.	кі́има	кі́има	кі́има

Plural.

	Masculine	Neuter	Feminine
Nom.	кі́и[1]	ка̑ѧ	кі́ѧ
Gen.	кі́ихъ	кі́ихъ	кі́ихъ
Dat.	кі́имъ	кі́имъ	кі́имъ
Acc.	кі́ѧ, кі́ихъ	ка̑ѧ	кі́ѧ, кі́ихъ
Instr.	кі́ими	кі́ими	кі́ими
Prep.	кі́ихъ	кі́ихъ	кі́ихъ

With Stem Ending in a "Hushing" Sibilant:
Singular.

	Masculine	Neuter	Feminine
Nom.	на́шъ	на́ше	на́ша
Gen.	на́шегѡ	на́шегѡ	на́шеѧ
Dat.	на́шемꙋ	на́шемꙋ	на́шей

---

[1]) The ancient form ці́и has been kept in the indefinite pronoun нѣ́кці́и.

Acc.	на́шꙁ, на́шего	на́ше	на́шꙋ
Instr.	на́шнмꙁ	на́шнмꙁ	на́шею
Prep.	на́шемꙁ	на́шемꙁ	на́шей

Dual.

Nom., Acc.	на̂ша	на̂ша / на́шн	на́шн
Gen., Prep.	на̂шею	на̂шею	на́шею
Dat., Instr.	на́шнма	на́шнма	на́шнма

Plural.

	Masculine	Neuter
Feminine		
Nom.	на́шн	на̂ша	на́шѧ
Gen.	на́шнхꙁ	на́шнхꙁ	на́шнхꙁ
Dat.	на́шымꙁ	на́шымꙁ	на́шымꙁ
Acc.	на́шѧ, на́шнхꙁ	на̂ша	на́шѧ, ₋нхꙁ
Instr.	на́шнмн	на́шнмн	на́шнмн
Prep.	на́шнхꙁ	на́шнхꙁ	на́шнхꙁ

кто̀, что̀: Who, what?

Nom.	кто̀	что̀	
Gen.	когѡ̀	чегѡ̀	чесѡ̀, чесогѡ̀
Dat.	комꙋ̀	чемꙋ̀	чесомꙋ̀
Acc.	кого̀	что̀	чесо̀
Instr.	кн́мꙁ	чн́мꙁ	
Prep.	ко́мꙁ	че́мꙁ	чесо́мꙁ

4) In pronouns a final guttural is softened before a soft vowel: всѧ́цѣмꙁ, толнцѣмꙁ.

In pronouns with a final guttural (всѧ́кꙁ, е҆лн́кꙁ, толн́кꙁ &c.) the prepositional masculine and neuter may be formed either with ѣ or with о: ѡ толнцѣмꙁ and ѡ толн́комꙁ, e.g.: во всѧ́цѣмꙁ терпѣ́нїн [in all patience--Ephes. 6:18], which could also be во вѣ́комъ терпѣ́нїн, and so forth. Similar double forms are to be encountered in the feminine dative and prepositional: всѧ́кой and всѧцѣ́й.

5) The pronouns є҆ли́къ, коли́къ, толи́къ have noun-type inflections in some cases, e.g. the genitive, толи́ка, the dative толи́кꙋ, the prepositional--а҆ще на толи́цѣ село ѿда́ста; ([tell me] whether ye sold the land for so much?--Acts 5:8). Other forms Other forms (usually with inflection endings beginning with _ѣ) of these pronouns are properly pronominal: the instrumental толи́цѣмъ, the instrumental form толи́цѣмъ (and also -комъ) and all the forms of the plural:

Nom.	толи́цы	Acc.	толи́ки
Gen.	толи́цѣхъ	Instr.	толи́цѣми
Dat.	толи́цѣмъ	Prep.	толи́цѣхъ

Example: ви́дите, коли́цѣми кни́гами писа́хъ ва́мъ мое́ю рꙋко́ю (Gal. 6:11--"See how long a letter I have written you by mine own hand").

In a like manner, compound pronouns with _ов_: како́въ, тако́въ, ꙗ҆ко́въ--have some forms on the pattern of the short adjectival declension, fro example, the genitive ꙗ҆кова̀, the dative case ꙗ҆ковꙋ̀, while the other forms are of the pronominal declension.

6) A characteristic peculiarity of the short pronouns (such as и́нъ, ѻ҆́нъ, ѻ҆́въ, са́мъ and others) is to be seen in the following inflection endings: in the masculine and neuter genitive singular, _огѡ, in the feminine, _оѧ, for example: и҆но́гѡ, и҆но́ѧ, само́гѡ̀, само́ѧ̀: in the instrumental singular, masculine and neuter, and in all the plural oblique cases (except the accusative)--ѣ appears in the inflections: instrumental singular--ѻ҆́нѣмъ: genitive plural--ѻ҆́нѣхъ, dative plural--ѻ҆́нѣмъ, instrumental plural--ѻ҆́нѣми, prepositional--ѡ̀ ѻ҆́нѣхъ.

Ѻ҆́въ--*this:*
Short Form:
Singular.

	Masculine	Neuter	Feminine
Nom.	Ѻ҆́въ	Ѻ҆́во	Ѻ҆́ва
Gen.	Ѻ҆́вогѡ	Ѻ҆́вогѡ	Ѻ҆́воѧ
Dat.	Ѻ҆́вомꙋ	Ѻ҆́вомꙋ	Ѻ҆́вой
Acc.	Ѻ҆́въ, Ѻ҆́вогѡ	Ѻ҆́во	Ѻ҆́вꙋ
Instr.	Ѻ҆́вѣмъ	Ѻ҆́вѣмъ	Ѻ҆́вою
Prep.	Ѻ҆́вомъ	Ѻ҆́вомъ	Ѻ҆́вой

Dual.

Nom., Acc.	Ѻ҆́ва	Ѻ҆́ва /Ѻ҆́вѣ	Ѻ҆́вѣ
Gen., Prep.	Ѻ҆́вою	Ѻ҆́вою	Ѻ҆́вою
Dat., Instr.	Ѻ҆́вѣма	Ѻ҆́вѣма	Ѻ҆́вѣма

Plural.

Nom.	Ѻ҆́ви	Ѻ҆́ва	Ѻ҆́вы
Gen.	Ѻ҆́вѣхъ	Ѻ҆́вѣхъ	Ѻ҆́вѣхъ
Dat.	Ѻ҆́вѣмъ	Ѻ҆́вѣмъ	Ѻ҆́вѣмъ
Acc.	Ѻ҆́вы, Ѻ҆́вѣхъ	Ѻ҆́ва	Ѻ҆́вы, Ѻ҆́вѣхъ
Instr.	Ѻ҆́вѣми	Ѻ҆́вѣми	Ѻ҆́вѣми
Prep.	Ѻ҆́вѣхъ	Ѻ҆́вѣхъ	Ѻ҆́вѣхъ

Full Form.
Singular.

Nom.	Ѻ҆́вый	Ѻ҆́вое	Ѻ҆́ваѧ
Gen.	Ѻ҆́вагѡ	Ѻ҆́вагѡ	Ѻ҆́выѧ
Dat.	Ѻ҆́вомꙋ	Ѻ҆́вомꙋ	Ѻ҆́вой
Acc.	Ѻ҆́вый, Ѻ҆́ваго	Ѻ҆́вое	Ѻ҆́вꙋю
Instr.	Ѻ҆́вымъ	Ѻ҆́вымъ	Ѻ҆́вою
Prep.	Ѻ҆́вомъ	Ѻ҆́вомъ	Ѻ҆́вой

	Masculine	Neuter	Feminine
		Dual.	
Nom., Acc.	ѻ҆́бла	ѻ҆́бла /ѻ҆́вѣн	ѻ҆́вѣн
Gen., Prep.	ѻ҆́вюю	ѻ҆́вюю	ѻ҆́вюю
Dat., Instr.	ѻ҆́выма	ѻ҆́выма	ѻ҆́выма

	Masculine	Neuter	Feminine
		Plural.	
Nom.	ѻ҆́вїн	ѻ҆́вла	ѻ҆́выла
Gen.	ѻ҆́выхъ	ѻ҆́выхъ	ѻ҆́выхъ
Dat.	ѻ҆́вымъ	ѻ҆́вымъ	ѻ҆́вымъ
Acc.	ѻ҆́выла, ѻ҆́выхъ	ѻ҆́вла	ѻ҆́выла, ѻ҆́выхъ
Instr.	ѻ҆́вымн	ѻ҆́вымн	ѻ҆́вымн
Prep.	ѻ҆́выхъ	ѻ҆́выхъ	ѻ҆́выхъ

7) The pronoun ве́сь [all] has forms according to the soft declension and according to the hard. A dual number, on account of the meaning, is absent. There is also no dual number for the pronoun вся́къ, derived from ве́сь.

8) The full or long pronouns, i.e. those which have й, ѧ, ѥ attached to their gender endings (и́ный, ѻ҆́вый, ѥли́кїй, кото́рый and so forth), are declined on the model of the full or long declension of adjectives.

9) The numeral ѥди́нъ is used as an indefinite pronoun [ѥди́нъ челове́къ (one man) = нѣ́кїй челове́къ (a certain man)]. It is declined on the model of the pronoun то́й. The numerals ѻ҆́ба, ѻ҆́бѣ can also be used as pronouns, in the sense of "both"--"one and the other", as can the ordinal number дрꙋ́гїй [second, next] in the sense of "another", and the combinations ѥди́нъ дрꙋ́гаго or дрꙋ́гъ дрꙋ́га have the sense of reciprocal pronouns, "each other", "one another": и дрꙋ́га ко дрꙋ́зѣй вопїѧхꙋ [and they cried out to each other--Paschal Oikos], дрꙋ́гъ дрꙋ́га [each other, in the Litany of Peace].

Texts for Practice.

1) И҆ сѐ два̀ ѿ ни́хъ бѣ́ста и҆ду́ща въ то́йже де́нь въ ве́сь ѿстоѧ́щу ста́дїй шестьдесѧ́тъ ѿ і҆ерусали́ма, є҆́йже и҆́мѧ є҆ммау́съ. И҆ та̑ бесѣ́доваста къ себѣ̀ ѡ҆ всѣ́хъ си́хъ приключшихсѧ. И҆ бы́сть бесѣ́дующема и҆́ма и҆ совопроша́ющемасѧ, и҆ са́мъ і҆и҃съ прибли́живсѧ, и҆дѧ́ше съ ни́ма: ѻ҆́чи же є҆ю̀ держа́стасѧ, да є҆гѡ̀ не позна́ета. Рече́ же къ ни́ма: что̀ су́ть словеса̀ сїѧ̑, ѡ҆ ни́хже стѧза́етасѧ къ себѣ̀ и҆ду́ще, и҆ є҆ста̀ дра́хла; Ѿвѣща́въ же є҆ди́нъ, є҆му́же и҆́мѧ клеѡ́па, рече́ къ нему̀: ты̀ ли є҆ди́нъ пришле́цъ є҆сѝ во і҆ерусали́мъ, и҆ не оу҆вѣ́дѣлъ є҆сѝ бы́вшихъ въ не́мъ во дни̑ сїѧ̑; И҆ речѐ и҆́ма: кі́ихъ; Ѻ҆на́ же рѣ́ста є҆му̀: ꙗ҆́же ѡ҆ і҆и҃сѣ назарѧни́нѣ, и҆́же бы́сть му́жъ проро́къ, си́ленъ дѣ́ломъ и҆ сло́вомъ пред̾ бг҃омъ и҆ всѣ́ми людьми́: ка́кѡ преда́ша є҆го̀ а҆рхїере́й и҆ кнѧ̑зи на́ши на ѡ҆сужде́нїе сме́рти, и҆ распѧ́ша є҆го̀: мы́ же надѣ́ѧхомсѧ, ꙗ҆́кѡ се́й є҆́сть хотѧ̀ и҆зба́вити і҆и҃ла: но и҆ над̾ всѣ́ми си́ми, тре́тїй се́й де́нь є҆́сть дне́сь, ѿне́лиже сїѧ̑ бы́ша. Но и҆ жены̀ нѣ̑кїѧ ѿ на́съ оу҆жаси́ша ны̀, бы́вшыѧ ра́нѡ оу҆ гро́ба. 2) Ѻ҆нѣ́ма же ѿверзо́стѣсѧ ѻ҆́чи, и҆ позна́ста є҆го̀: и҆ то́й неви́димь бы́сть и҆́ма. 3) Сїѐ да помышлѧ́етъ таковы́й, ꙗ҆́кѡ ꙗ҆́цы же є҆смы̀ сло́вомъ посла́нїй, ѿстоѧ́ще, такови́и и҆ ту̀ су́ще є҆смы̀ дѣ́ломъ. 4) Бою́сѧ же, є҆гда̀ ка́кѡ прише́дъ, не ꙗ҆́цѣхъ же хощу̀, ѡ҆брѧ́щу ва́съ, и҆ а҆́зъ ѡ҆брѧ́щусѧ ва́мъ, ꙗ҆кова́ же не хо́щете. 5) Ка́кѡ мы̀ оу҆бѣжи́мъ ѡ҆ толи́цѣмъ неради́вше спасе́нїи; 6) И҆зми́те ѕла́го ѿ ва́съ сами́хъ. 7) Ка́цѣмъ подоба́етъ бы́ти ва́мъ во ст҃ы́хъ пребыва́нїихъ и҆ бл҃гоче́стїихъ. 8) Всѧ́цѣмъ хране́нїемъ блюди́ твоѐ се́рдце: ѿ си́хъ бо и҆схѡ́дища живота̀. 9) Ѿку́ду на́мъ въ пу́стыни хлѣ́би толи́цы, ꙗ҆́кѡ да насы́титсѧ толи́къ наро́дъ;

Key.

1) And, behold, two of them went that same day to a village called Emmaus, which was from Jerusalem about threescore furlongs. And they talked together of all these things which had happened. And it

came to pass, that, while they communed together and reasoned, Jesus himself drew near, and went with them. But their eyes were holden that they should not know him. And he said unto them, What manner of communications are these that ye have one to another, as ye walk, and are sad? And one of them, whose name was Cleopas, answering said unto him, Art thou only a stranger [1] in Jerusalem, and hast not known the things which are come to pass there in these days? And he said unto them, What things? And they said unto him, Concerning Jesus of Nazareth, which was a prophet mighty in deed and word before God and all the people: And how the chief priests and our rulers[2] delivered him to be condemned to death, and have crucified him. But we trusted that it had been he which should have redeemed Israel: and beside all this, today is the third day since these things were done. Yea, and certain women also of our company made us astonished, which were early at the sepulchre [Luke 24:13-22]. 2) And their eyes were opened, and they knew him: and he vanished out of their sight [Luke 24:31]. 3) Let such an one think this: that, such as we are in word by letters when we are absent, such will we be also in deed when we are present [II Cor. 10:11]. 4) For I fear, lest, when I come, I shall not find you such as I would; and that I shall be found unto you such as ye would not [II Cor. 12:20]. 5) How shall we escape, if we neglect so great a salvation? [Heb. 2:3]. 6) Therefore put away from among yourselves that wicked person [I Cor. 5:13]. 7) What manner of persons ought ye to be, in all holy conversation and godliness [II Peter 3:11]. 8) Keep thy heart with all diligence; for out of it are the issues of life [Prov. 4:23]. 9) Whence should we have so much bread in the wilderness, as to fill so great a multitude? [Matth. 15:33].

---

[1]This can also be translated, "Art thou *the only* stranger?"

[2]Or: How *our chief priests and rulers...*

THE ADJECTIVE.

§49. Adjectives are words that indicate a quality of an object and answer the question "What kind of... ?" or "Whose?"

Adjectives, since they express a quality of an object, are always used with nouns and agree with them in gender, number and case.

According to their meaning, adjectives are classed as qualitative, relative, and possessive.

Adjectives that characterize objects without relation to other objects, are known as *qualitative:* до́брый ра́бъ [the good servant].

Adjectives giving characteristics that relate one object to another on the basis of place, time, material and the like, are called *relative:* геє́нна ѻ҆́гненнаѧ [fiery Gehenna].

Adjectives that indicate belonging are known as *possessive:* сн҃ъ бж҃їй [Son of God].

According to their endings, adjectives are classed as short or long.

The short endings of adjectives:

	Hard:			Soft:		
Masculine:	ъ	до́бр_ъ	ь	человѣ́ч_ь, си́н_ь	й	бу̑й
Feminine:	а	до́бр_а̀	ѧ	человѣ́ч_а, си́н_ѧ		бу̑_ѧ
Neuter:	о	до́бр_о̀	е	человѣ́ч_е, си́н_е		бу̑_е

Adjectives with full or long endings add to the gender endings of the short forms the pronouns и҆̂, ѧ̂, є҆̂:

Masculine: до́бръ+и=до́брый си́нь+и=си́нїй бу̑й+и=бу̑їй
Feminine: добра̀+ѧ=до́браѧ си́нѧ+ѧ=си́нѧѧ бу̑ѧ+ѧ=бу̑ѧѧ
Neuter: добро̀+е=до́брое си́не+е=си́нее бу̑е+е=бу̑ее

In like manner there arose the oblique case endings of the full or long adjectives. This process of formation of full adjectives came about while the language was still in the Old Slavonic period. To the short (noun) endings of the oblique cases were attached the oblique forms of the pronouns и, ꙗ, ѥ, and furthermore in the long forms thus arrived at, the following changes took place: with the loss of **j** between vowels, there took place an assimilation of vowels, and at a later period an elision:

добра + кго > добрааго > добраго > до́брагѡ

добро‍ + кмо‍ > добро‍о‍мо‍ > добро‍мо‍ > до́бромѹ --and so on.

In ancient times the pronouns и̑, а̑, е̑ (demonstratives) had the value of definite articles when joined with adjectives; afterwards, they merged with the adjectives, giving rise to the long forms. The long adjectives have a "definite" significance, while the short adjectives have an "indefinite"; however, in New Church Slavonic the definite vs. indefinite categories are not fully adhered to. If one compares Church Slavonic texts with the Greek, the Greek adjectives with the definite article almost always correspond to the long adjectives in Slavonic.

§50. Formation of Adjectives.

Adjectives are either primitive or derived.

Primitive adjectives are those whose endings are joined directly to the stem. Only qualitative adjectives can belong to this category: до́бръ [good], стра́ръ [old], бѹ́й [rowdy, senseless], си́нь [blue].

Derivative adjectives are those whose endings are joined to the stem with the aid of suffixes, one or several; in this category we find all types of adjectives--qualitative, relative, and possessive: ги́бокъ [tractable], ѹ́зокъ [narrow], го́рекъ [bitter].

§51. The most important suffixes used to form adjectives are the following:

    1) Qualitative:

_к_ (ок, к; ек, ьк, к; нк): высо́к_ъ, высо́к_їй [high]; оу́з-ок_ъ, оу́з-к_їй [narrow]; го́р_ек_ъ, го́р_ьк_їй [bitter]; вел_и́к_ъ [great].

_л_ (ел, л): свѣ́т_ел_ъ, свѣ́т_л_ый [bright, filled with light].

_н_ (ен, ьн, н): сıл_ен_ъ, сıл_ьн_ый [strong]; ıа̋с_ен_ъ, ıа̋с_н_ый [clear].

_ав_, _ив_: велич_а́в_ъ [grand, magnificent]; лѹк_а́в_ъ [crafty, evil]; мѵ́роточ_и́в_ый [myrrh-flowing]; послѹшл_и́в_ъ [obedient].

_ат_, _ит_: бог_а́т_ый [rich]; пери_а́т_ый [feathered]; знамен_и́т_ый [noted, famed]; домов_и́т_ъ [one who possesses a house, takes pleasure in it].

ист: рѣ́ч_и́ст_ъ [talkative, eloquent].

    2) Relative:

_н_: желѣ́з_н_ый [made of iron], го́р_н_їй [upper, higher, on high].

_ан_, _ян_: пло́т_ан_ый [fleshly]; древ_ян_ъ [wooden]; ко́ж_ан_ый [of leather]; ро́ж_ан_ый [horned].

_ш_: дне́_ш_н_їй [today's]; кромѣ́_ш_н_їй [that which is outside].

    3) Possessive:

_ь: кнѧ́ж_ь [the prince's]; человѣ́ч_ь [man's, of man]; ıа́кwвл_ь [of Jacob].

_ї_: бж҃_ї_й [God's, of God]; ра́б_ї_й [servant's, pertaining to a servant].

_ев_, _ов_: ı̇з҃ра́ил_ев_ъ [of Israel]; ı̇ẃсиф_ов_ъ [of Joseph].

_ин_: голѹ́_ин_ый [a dove's]; марı́_ин_ъ [of Mary].

_ск_: ı̇ѹде́й_ск_ъ [Judean, of Judea]; человѣ́ч_е_ск_їй [human, of men, mankind's].

_ен_ (ьн): владьı́ч_ен_ь, владьı́ч_н_а [the master's]; бг҃оро́дич_ен_ъ [pertaining to theTheotokos]; мѹ́ченич_ен_ъ [martyricon, pertaining to the martyrs].

Possessive adjectives have only the short form, with the exception of those in _ск_ and _нн_, which can have either the short or the long form: і҆ꙋде́йскъ and і҆ꙋде́йскїй, голꙋби́нъ and голꙋби́нный.

Adjectives having the suffix -ь (jь), as a result of softening, show an alternation of the final consonants of the stems before this suffix (see §11): человѣ́къ, человѣ́чь: кнѧ́зь, кнѧ́жь: і҆а́ковъ, і҆а́ковль and so on.

Some adjectives can have equally the suffixes _ь and _ї_: кнѧ́жь and кнѧ́жїй, дѣви́чь and дѣви́чїй [a/the girl's, maiden's].

Adjectives with the suffix _ск_ express, not individual possession, but a sense of belonging or being proper to a group or kind; thus человѣ́че_ск_їй means "belonging to, or proper to humans".

Adjectives with the suffix _нн_, if they are expressed with the long endings, signify belonging or being proper to a group or kind: ѕвѣри́нный нра́въ --the morals of animals, wild beasts.

§52. If adjectives with the full ending have a doubled н, then in all of the short gender and case endings except for the masculine nominative, the doubled н [нн] is retained.

This occurs in the following qualitative adjectives:

1) *a)* In adjectives formed from noun and verb stems in _н:
и҆́стинный [и҆́стина]: и҆́стиненъ, и҆́стинна [true];
неи҆змѣ́нный [и҆змѣн_ѧ́ти]: неи҆змѣ́ненъ,
        неи҆змѣ́нна [unchanged];
бг҃а и҆́стинна ѿ бг҃а и҆́стинна [True God of True God--Nicene Creed].

b) In adjectives formed from nouns with their stem ending in _н preceded by a consonant:
болѣ́зненный [болѣ́зн_ь]: болѣ́зненъ, болѣ́зненна
        [diseased];

БЕЗБОѧ́ЗНЕННЫЙ [БОѧ́ЗН_Ь]: БЕЗБОѧ́ЗНЕНЪ, БЕЗБОѧ́ЗНЕННА
[fearless];
Хрⷭ҇ТІА́НСКІА КОНЧИ́НЫ... БЕЗБОЛѣ́ЗНЕННЫ ["A Christian
ending...painless"--Litany of Fervent Supplication].

c) In adjectives formed from nouns with the ending _Α_НІ́Е, _Е_
НІ́Е, in the masculine there can be the endings _НЕН_ and _ЕНЪ:
БЕЗДЫХА́ННЫЙ [ДЫХА́НІЕ]: БЕЗДЫХА́НЕНЪ, БЕЗДЫХА́ННА [without
breath, not breathing]
НЕПРИКОСНОВЕ́ННЫЙ [ПРИКОСНОВЕ́НІЕ]: НЕПРИКОСНОВЕ́НЪ,
НЕПРИКОСНОВЕ́ННА [untouched];
ВИ́ДИМЪ ПЛО́ТІЮ БЕЗДЫХА́НЕНЪ МЕ́РТВЪ ["Seen in the flesh, a
lifeless corpse"--Holy Saturday Matins, First Stasis, v. 36].

2) In adjectives with the ending _ЕННЫЙ, formed from noun
stems with two or more preceding consonants:
Е҆СТЕ́СТВЕННЫЙ: Е҆СТЕ́СТВЕНЪ, Е҆СТЕ́СТВЕННА [natural, of nature];
БЕЗЧИ́СЛЕННЫЙ: БЕЗЧИ́СЛЕНЪ, БЕЗЧИ́СЛЕННА [countless,
innumerable].
СОЕСТЕ́СТВЕННО БЖⷭ҇ТВО̀ ["the Divinity of One Essence"--
Matins for Jan. 30, Ode 6].

3) In adjectives formed from past passive participles; in the
masculine nominative they have the ending _ЕН, and sometimes _
НЕНЪ:
СОВЕРШЕ́НЪ, СОВЕРШЕ́ННА [perfect, complete];
БЛАЖЕ́НЪ, БЛАЖЕ́ННА [blessed, blissful];
НЕИЗРЕЧЕ́НЕНЪ, НЕИЗРЕЧЕ́ННА [ineffable, beyond description].
ТЫ̀ БО Е҆СЍ БГЪ НЕИЗРЕЧЕ́НЕНЪ ["For Thou art God ineffable"--
Divine Liturgy of St. John Chrysostom, Anaphora].
ДНЀ ВСЕГѡ̀ СОВЕРШЕ́ННА ["A day all perfect"--i.e. that the whole
day be perfect--Litany of Fervent Supplication].

Adjectives in _ный that are formed from verbs of the imperfective aspect do not double the н: варе́наѧ пшени́ца [boiled wheat], сꙋшено́е ѻ҆во́щїе [dried fruit].

§53. Declension of Adjectives.

Like nouns, adjectives are grouped into hard and soft declensions.

The short adjectives are, in their gender endings, comparable with the nouns of the 1st and 2nd declensions, and and are declined on the same pattern: adjectives of the masculine and neuter genders according to the 1st declension, while those of the feminine gender are declined according to the 2nd declension.

Declension of Adjectives with the Short endings.

Hard Declension:
Singular.

	Masculine	Neuter	Feminine
Nom.	мꙋдр_ъ [wise]	мꙋдр_о	мꙋдр_а
Gen.	мꙋдр_а	мꙋдр_а	мꙋдр_ы
Dat.	мꙋдр_ꙋ	мꙋдр_ꙋ	мꙋдр_ѣ
Acc.	мꙋдр_ъ [_а]	мꙋдр_о	мꙋдр_ꙋ
Instr.	мꙋдр_ымъ	мꙋдр_ымъ	мꙋдр_ою
Prep.	мꙋдр_ѣ	мꙋдр_ѣ	мꙋдр_ѣ
Voc.	мꙋдр_е	мꙋдр_о	мꙋдр_а

Dual.

	Masculine	Neuter	Feminine
N., A., V.	мꙋдр_а	мꙋдр_а, _ѣ	мꙋдр_ѣ
G., P.	мꙋдр_ꙋ	мꙋдр_ꙋ	мꙋдр_ꙋ
D., I.	мꙋдр_ыма	мꙋдр_ыма	мꙋдр_ыма

Plural.

Nom., Voc.	мꙋдр҃и	мꙋдр҃а	мꙋдр҃ы
Gen.	мꙋдр҃ыхъ	мꙋдр҃ыхъ	мꙋдр҃ыхъ
Dat.	мꙋдр҃ымъ	мꙋдр҃ымъ	мꙋдр҃ымъ
Acc.	мꙋдр҃ы [-ыхъ]	мꙋдр҃а	мꙋдр҃ы
Instr.	мꙋдр҃ы[-ыми]	мꙋдр҃ы[-ыми]	мꙋдр҃ыми
Prep.	мꙋдр҃ыхъ	мꙋдр҃ыхъ	мꙋдр҃ыхъ

Soft Declension:

Singular.

	Masculine	Neuter	Feminine
Nom.	госпо́день-ь (the Lord's)	госпо́дн-е	госпо́дн-ѧ
Gen.	госпо́дн-ѧ	госпо́дн-ѧ	госпо́дн-и
Dat.	госпо́дн-ю	госпо́дн-ю	госпо́дн-и
Acc.	госпо́день-ь[-ѧ]	госпо́дн-е	госпо́дн-ю
Instr.	госпо́дн-имъ	госпо́дн-имъ	госпо́дн-ею
Prep.	госпо́дн-и	госпо́дн-и	госпо́дн-и
Voc.	госпо́день-ь	госпо́дне	госпо́дн-ѧ

Dual.

N., A., V.	госпѡ́дн-ѧ	госпѡ́дн-ѧ,-и	госпѡ́дн-и
G., P.	госпѡ́дн-ю	госпѡ́дн-ю	госпѡ́дн-ю
D., I.	госпо́дн-има	госпо́дн-има	госпо́дн-има

Plural.

N., V.	госпѡ́дн-и	госпѡ́дн-ѧ	госпѡ́дн-и
Gen.	госпо́дн-ихъ	госпо́дн-ихъ	госпо́дн-ихъ
Dat.	госпѡ́дн-имъ	госпѡ́дн-имъ	госпѡ́дн-имъ
Acc.	госпѡ́дн-и[-ихъ]	госпо́дн-ѧ	госпѡ́дн-и[-ихъ]
Instr.	госпѡ́дн-и[-ими]	госпѡ́дн-и[-ими]	госпѡ́дн-ими
Prep.	госпо́дн-ихъ	госпо́дн-ихъ	госпо́дн-ихъ

§54. Concerning the Vocative Case of Adjectives.

When adjectives are used as nouns, in the vocative case the short endings are always used: e.g. Безꙋмне, въ сїю́ но́щь дꙋшꙋ твою̀ и҆стꙗ́жꙋтъ ѿ тебѐ [Thou fool, this night thy soul shall be required of thee--Luke 12:20).

When adjectives of definition are used with nouns in the vocative case, the adjectives usually have the long endings, but the short also occur: лꙋка́вый ра́бе [thou wicked servant--Luke 19:22]; ра́бе бла́гі́й и҆ вѣ́рный [thou good and faithful servant--Matth. 25:21]; требла́же́нне васі́лїе, григо́рїе всемꙋ́дре, всезла́те и҆ всечⷭ҇тне їѡа́нне [O thrice-blessed Basil, Gregory most wise, John most golden and most honourable--Vespers for Jan. 30, Aposticha].

§55. Differences of Declension between Nouns and Short Adjectives.

Although the short adjectives are declined on the pattern of nouns, nevertheless their declensions do not fully coincide. The divergences are as follows:

1) Singular: the masculine and neuter instrumental have the long adjectival endings -ымъ, -нмъ: мꙋ́дрымъ, госпо́днимъ.

2) Dual: the dative and instrumental cases have the full adjectival endings -ыма, -нма: мꙋ́дрыма, госпо́днима, although endings of ancient origin are to be met with according to the noun declension, for example: колѣ́нома їи҃левома (the [twelve] tribes of Israel--Matth. 19:28).

3) Plural: all the cases except the nominative and accusative have endings according to the long declension; the instrumental masculine and neuter can have the short or the long form (with the sense of the short), for example: пре́д ста́рѣйшины їи҃левы и҆ пре́д лю́дьми́ мои́ми (before the elders of Israel and before my people—I Kings[I Samuel] 15:30 [*Septuagint version*]; и҆ сни́де съ мꙋ́жми́

і҃8дннымн (and went down with the men of Judah--II Kings [Samuel] 19:16); пред Ѻ҃трокн давідовыми (before the servants of David--II Kings [Samuel] 18:7).

§56. Possessive adjectives in _їй [ра́бїй, of a servant] are short adjectives (their final _й is not a pronoun, but a gender ending), and therefore they are declined for the most part as short adjectives, on the model of 1st-declension nouns in _й: кра́й [district, territory], like the other short adjectives, although they sometimes do take on the long endings: бж҃їа сннзхожде́нїа Ѻ҃гнь оу҃стыдѣ́са въ вавѷло́нѣ инога́ (By God's coming down, the fire was put to shame in Babylon once--Eirmos, Sunday Canon of the 8th Tone); ра́дУйса, а҃гннце, ро́ждшаа бж҃їаго а҃гнца (Rejoice, thou ewe that bare the Lamb of God--Akathistos Canon, Ode 3).

Declension of Short Adjectives Ending in -й.
Singular.

	Masculine	Neuter	Feminine
Nom.	бж҃їй кра́й *God's land*	бж҃ї_е знáменï_е *God's sign*	бж҃ï_а мн́лостын_а *God's mercy*
Gen.	бж҃ї_а крá_а	бж҃ï_а знáменï_а	бж҃ï_а мн́лостын_н
Dat.	бж҃ï_ю крá_ю	бж҃ï_ю знáменï_ю	бж҃ï_н мн́лостын_н
Acc.	бж҃ï_й крá_й	бж҃ï_е знáменï_е	бж҃ï_ю мн́лостын_ю
Instr.	бж҃ï_нмъ крá_емъ	бж҃ï_нмъ знáменï_емъ	бж҃ï_ею мн́лостын_ею
Voc.	бж҃ï_й крá_ю	бж҃ï_е знáменï_е	бж҃ï_а мн́лостын_е

Dual.

	Masculine	Neuter	Feminine
N., A., V.	бж҃ï_а крá_а	бж҃ï_а,_н знáменï_а,_н	бж҃ï_н мн́лωстын_н
G., P.	бж҃ï_ю крá_ю	бж҃ï_ю знáменï_ю	бж҃ï_ю мн́лωстын_ю
D., I.	бж҃ï_нма крá_ема	бж҃ï_нма знáменï_ема	бж҃ï_нма мн́лостын_ама

Plural.

	Masculine	Neuter	Feminine
N., V.	бж҃ï_н крá_н	бж҃ï_а знáменï_а	бж҃ï_а мн́лωстын_н
Gen.	бж҃ï_нхъ крá_ёвъ	бж҃ï_нхъ знáменï_й	бж҃ï_нхъ мн́лостын_ь

Dat.	бжї_нмъ кра́_емъ	бжї_нмъ зна́менї_емъ	бжї_нмъ ми́лостын_амъ
Acc.	бжї_н кра́_н	бжї_а зна́менї_а	бжї_а ми́лшстын_н
Instr.	бжї_н кра́_н	бжї_н зна́менї_н	бжї_нмн ми́лостын_амн
Prep.	бжї_нхъ кра́_ехъ	бжї_нхъ зна́менї_нхъ	бжї_нхъ ми́лостын_а хъ

§57. The Declension of Full Adjectives.

Hard Declension:
Singular.

	Masculine	Neuter	Feminine
N., V.	мꙋ́др_ый *(wise)*	мꙋ́др_ое	мꙋ́др_аа
Gen.	мꙋ́др_агѡ	мꙋ́др_агѡ	мꙋ́др_ыа
Dat.	мꙋ́др_омꙋ	мꙋ́др_омꙋ	мꙋ́др_ѣй [_ой]
Acc.	мꙋ́др_ый[_аго]	мꙋ́др_ое	мꙋ́др_ꙋю
Instr.	мꙋ́др_ымъ	мꙋ́др_ымъ	мꙋ́др_ою
Prep.	мꙋ́др_ѣмъ	мꙋ́др_ѣмъ	мꙋ́др_ѣй[_ой]

Dual.

N., A., V.	мꙋ́др_аа	мꙋ́др_аа,_ѣн	мꙋ́др_ѣн
G., P.	мꙋ́др_ꙋю	мꙋ́др_ꙋю	мꙋ́др_ꙋю
D., I.	мꙋ́др_ыма	мꙋ́др_ыма	мꙋ́др_ыма

Plural.

N., V.	мꙋ́др_їн	мꙋ́др_аа	мꙋ́др_ыа
Gen.	мꙋ́др_ыхъ	мꙋ́др_ыхъ	мꙋ́др_ыхъ
Dat.	мꙋ́др_ымъ	мꙋ́др_ымъ	мꙋ́др_ымъ
Acc.	мꙋ́др_ыа[_ыхъ]	мꙋ́др_аа	мꙋ́др_ыа[_ыхъ]
Instr.	мꙋ́др_ымн	мꙋ́др_ымн	мꙋ́др_ымн
Prep.	мꙋ́др_ыхъ	мꙋ́др_ыхъ	мꙋ́др_ыхъ

Soft Declension:

Singular.

	Masculine	Neuter	Feminine
N., V.	си́н‑їй *(blue)*	си́н‑ее	си́н‑яя
Gen.	си́н‑ягѡ	си́н‑ягѡ	си́н‑їѧ
Dat.	си́н‑емꙋ	си́н‑емꙋ	си́н‑ей
Acc.	си́н‑їй[‑яго]	си́н‑ее	си́н‑юю
Instr.	си́н‑имъ	си́н‑имъ	си́н‑ею
Prep.	си́н‑емъ	си́н‑емъ	си́н‑ей

Dual.

N., A., V.	си̂н‑яя	си̂н‑яя, ‑їй	си̂н‑їй
G., P.	си̂н‑юю	си̂н‑юю	си̂н‑юю
D., I.	си̂н‑има	си̂н‑има	си̂н‑има

Plural.

	Masculine	Neuter	Feminine
N., V.	си́н‑їй	си̂н‑яя	си̂н‑їѧ
Gen.	си́н‑ихъ	си́н‑ихъ	си́н‑ихъ
Dat.	си̂н‑имъ	си̂н‑имъ	си́н‑имъ
Acc.	си̂н‑їѧ[‑ихъ]	си̂н‑яя	си̂н‑їѧ[‑ихъ]
Instr.	си́н‑ими	си́н‑ими	си́н‑ими
Prep.	си́н‑ихъ	си́н‑ихъ	си́н‑ихъ

Declension of Adjectives with Guttural Stems.

Singular.

	Masculine	Neuter	Feminine
N., V.	благ‑і́й *(good)*	благ‑о́е	благ‑а́ѧ
Gen.	благ‑а́гѡ	благ‑а́гѡ	благ‑і́ѧ
Dat.	благ‑о́мꙋ	благ‑о́мꙋ	блаз‑ѣ́й
Acc.	благ‑і́й [‑а́го]	благ‑о́е	благ‑ꙋ́ю
Instr.	благ‑и́мъ	благ‑и́мъ	благ‑о́ю
Prep.	блаз‑ѣ́мъ	блаз‑ѣ́мъ	блаз‑ѣ́й

Dual.

N., A., V.	бла҃гаѧ	благаѧ, блаꙁ-ѣ́н	блаꙁ-ѣ́н
G., P.	благ-Ꙋю	благ-Ꙋю	благ-Ꙋю
D., I.	благ-и́ма	благ-и́ма	благ-и́ма

Plural.

N., V.	блаꙁ-і́н	благ-а́ѧ	благ-і́ѧ
Gen.	благ-и́хъ	благ-и́хъ	благ-и́хъ
Dat.	благ-и́мъ	благ-и́мъ	благ-и́мъ
Acc.	благ-і́ѧ [-и́хъ]	благ-а́ѧ	благ-і́ѧ
Instr.	благ-и́ми	благ-и́ми	благ-и́ми
Prep.	благ-и́хъ	благ-и́хъ	благ-и́хъ

Note: The adjective мно́гъ has the following peculiarities: instrumental singular, masculine and neuter: мно́ꙁѣмъ, and in the plural for all genders, genitive мно́ꙁѣхъ, dative: мнѡ́ꙁѣмъ, prepositional: мно́ꙁѣхъ. In Old Church Slavonic, this adjective was among the pronouns, from which it retained the forms noted.

Declension of Adjectives with Stems in a "Hushing" Sibilant.

Singular.

N., V.	ни́щ-їй (poor, needy)	ни́щ-ее	ни́щ-аѧ
Gen.	ни́щ-агѡ	ни́щ-агѡ	ни́щ-їѧ
Dat.	ни́щ-емꙋ	ни́щ-емꙋ	ни́щ-ей
Acc.	ни́щ-їй [-аго]	ни́щ-ее	ни́щ-Ꙋю
Instr.	ни́щ-имъ	ни́щ-имъ	ни́щ-ею
Prep.	ни́щ-емъ	ни́щ-емъ	ни́щ-ей

Dual.

N., A., V.	ни́щ-аѧ	ни́щаѧ, -їй	ни́щ-їй
G., P.	ни́щ-Ꙋю	ни́щ-Ꙋю	ни́щ-Ꙋю
D., I.	ни́щ-има	ни́щ-има	ни́щ-има

Plural.

N., V.	нн҃щ_їн	нн҃щ_аѧ	нн҃щ_ыѧ
Gen.	нн҃щ_нхъ	нн҃щ_нхъ	нн҃щ_нхъ
Dat.	нн҃щ_ымъ	нн҃щ_ымъ	нн҃щ_ымъ
Acc.	нн҃щ_ыѧ[_нхъ]	нн҃щ_аѧ	нн҃щ_ыѧ[_нхъ]
Instr.	нн҃щ_нмн	нн҃щ_нмн	нн҃щ_нмн
Prep.	нн҃щ_нхъ	нн҃щ_нхъ	нн҃щ_нхъ

Notes on the Adjectives.

1) In adjectives whose stem ends in a guttural, softening occurs according to the general rule before soft vowels: благі́й --- блазі́н (see §11).

2) Before soft vowels, the combination _ск_ changes to _ст_: сы́нъ человѣ́ческїй, ѡ҆ сы́нѣ человѣ́честѣмъ (the Son of Man, about/concerning the Son of Man).

3) Adjectives whose stem ends in a "hushing" sibilant, as in the case of nouns, have a mixed declension.

4) The adjectives и҆спо́лнь [full], свобо́дь [free, left to oneself, cast off], ѹ҆до́бь [easy, fearless] and several others like them, are not declined: и҆спо́лнь не́бо и҆ землѧ̀ сла́вы твоеѧ̀ ["Heaven and earth are full of Thy glory"--Liturgy].

5) Forms of the dual and plural that coincide with singular forms are distinguished by the same means as in nouns: i.e. by the use of ѡ, є, the circumflex accent (ˆ) and ы after the hushing sibilants.

In the singular, the genitive case is written with the ending _агѡ, _ѧгѡ to distinguish it from the accusative ending _аго, ѧго.

§58. Formation of the Degrees of Comparison.

In Church Slavonic, as in Russian [and English], there are three degrees of comparison: the positive, comparative and superlative.

The comparative degree is formed by means of suffixes:

1) the most ancient: _ьш, and

2) the late form _ѣйш_, or _айш_ after the "hushing" sibilants.

The Short Form.

In forming the stem for the comparative degree, the ancient and later suffixes are used differently. The ancient suffix (_ьш_) is used, in forming the stem, in adjectives with the suffix _к (ок, ѥк) and in certain primitive stems in _ъ, _л, _о (e.g. χȣд_ъ, scant, *bad*) joined directly to the stem: the stem consonant is softened, and the suffix _к (if it was in the stem of the positive degree) dropped.

In the use of the later suffix (_ѣйш_), the suffix of the positive degree stem is retained.

In the nominative singular masculine, the ш in the suffixes _ ьш, _ѣйш, _айш is dropped; in the nominative singular neuter, the ending occurs with as well as without the ш.

Positive degree:	Root:	Stem for the comparative degree:
		With ьш:
вꙑс_óк_ъ *high*	вꙑс	вꙑш_ш
глȣб_óк_ъ *deep*	глȣб	глȣбл_ьш
слáд_ок_ъ *sweet*	слад	слажд_ш
		With ѣйш, айш:
бог_áт_ъ *rich*	бог	бог_ат_ѣйш
крас_éн_ъ *splendid*	крас	крас_н_ѣйш
вꙑс_óк_ъ	вꙑс	вꙑс_оч_айш

The endings of comparative short adjectives are as follows:

a) In adjectives with the suffix _ьш:

masculine: _ій, feminine: _[ь]ш_и, neuter: _ѥ or _[ь]ш_ѥ:

вы́ш_їй, вы́ш_ши, вы́ш_є or вы́ш_шє: higher;
глꙋбл_їй, глꙋбл_ьш_н, глꙋбл_є or глꙋбл_ьш_н: deeper;
сла́жд_їй, сла́жд_ш_н, сла́жд_є or сла́жд_ш_є: sweeter.
Primitive stems: хꙋжд_їй, хꙋжд_ш_н, хꙋжд_є [хꙋжд_ш_є]:
worse.

b) In adjectives with the suffix _ѣйш [_айш]:
masculine: _ѣй, feminine: _ѣйш_н, neuter: _ѣє, _ѣйш_є, in addition
to which there is a softening of gutturals (permutation into the
"hushing" sibilants), and _ѣ is changed into _а, final _д (in primitive
stems--хꙋд_ꙁ) and final _ꙃ (in adjectives with the suffix _к [ок, єк])
change to _ж (and the suffix _к is dropped).
бог_ат_ѣй, бог_ат_ѣйш_н, бог_ат_ѣє [бог_ат_ѣйш_є]: richer.
крас_н_ѣй, крас_н_ѣйш_н, крас_н_ѣє [крас_н_ѣйш_є]: more
beautiful, splendid.
выс_оч_а́й, выс_оч_а́йш_н, выс_оч_а́є [выс_оч_а́йш_є]: higher.
(хꙋд_ꙁ): хꙋж_а́й, хꙋж_а́йш_н, хꙋж_а́є [хꙋж_а́йш_є]: worse.

(бли́ꙃ_ок_ꙁ) ближ_а́й, ближ_а́йш_н, ближ_а́є [ближ_а́йш_є]: nearer.

The Full Form.

The full endings for adjectives in the comparative degree are
the following:
a) In adjectives with the suffix -ьш: -(ь)ш-їй, -(ь)ш-ꙗꙗ, -
(ь)ш_єє:
вы́ш-шїй, вы́ш-шꙗꙗ, вы́ш-шєє: higher;
глꙋбл_ьшїй, глꙋбл_ьшꙗꙗ, глꙋбл_ьшєє: deeper;
b) In adjectives with the suffix _ѣйш (айш): ѣйш_їй, ѣйш_
ꙗꙗ, ѣйш_єє:
бог_ат_ѣйш_їй, бог_ат_ѣйш_ꙗꙗ, бог_ат_ѣйш_єє: richer;
выс_оч_а́йш_їй, выс_оч_а́йш_ꙗꙗ, выс_оч_а́йш_єє: higher.

In Church Slavonic, there are several adjectives that form their degrees of comparison from other stems:

Masculine:	Neuter:	Feminine:
ВЕЛИ́КІЙ (great)—БО́Л_ІЙ (greater)	БО́Л_Е, БО́Л_ЬШЕ	БО́Л_ЬШИ
БО́Л_ЬШІЙ	БО́Л_ЬШЕЕ	БО́Л_ЬШАѦ
ВА́Щ_ІЙ (greater)	ВА́Щ_Е, ВА́Щ_ШЕ	ВА́Щ_ШИ
ВА́Щ_ШІЙ	ВА́Щ_ШЕЕ	ВА́Щ_ШАѦ
ДО́БРЫЙ (good) ЛУ́Ч_ІЙ (better)	ЛУ́Ч_ШЕ	ЛУ́Ч_ШИ
ЛУ́Ч_ШІЙ	ЛУ́Ч_ШЕЕ	ЛУ́Ч_ШАѦ
БЛАГІ́Й (good) ОУ́Н_ІЙ (better)	ОУ́Н_Е, ОУ́Н_ШЕ	ОУ́Н_ШИ
ОУ́Н_ШІЙ	ОУ́Н_ЕЕ[1], ОУ́Н_ШЕЕ	ОУ́Н_ШАѦ
МА́ЛЫЙ (small) МН_І́Й (lesser, less)	МЕ́Н_ЬШЕ	МЕ́Н_ЬШИ
МЕ́Н_ЬШІЙ	МЕ́Н_ЬШЕЕ	МЕ́Н_ЬШАѦ
ЅЛЫЙ́ (evil, ill) ГО́Р_ІЙ (worse)	ГО́Р_ШЕ, ГОР_Ѣ́Е[2]	ГО́Р_ШИ
ГО́Р_ШІЙ	ГО́Р_ШЕЕ	ГО́Р_ШАѦ

Note 1: The adjectives ЛУ́ЧІЙ and ГО́РІЙ appear not to have short forms of the neuter without the suffix ш (ЛУ́Ч_е, ГО́Р_е). ОУ́Нее seems to be a full form without a suffix. Горѣе was formed by means of the later suffix.

Note 2: Sometimes these adjectives also form comparatives regularly, from their own stems: ДОБРѢ́ЙШІЙ, ЅЛѢ́ЙШІЙ.

---

[1]Luke 17:2--"It were *better* for him that a millstone..."

[2](Private) Evening Prayer 3: "Sins I have committed...*worse* than a beast".

§59. The Use of the Comparative and Superlative Degrees in Church Slavonic.

The superlative degree has no special suffixes; it generally makes use of the suffix of the comparative degree _ѣйш_ and less often _[ь]ш_, and the distinction between the comparative and superlative consists mainly in the different senses in which they are used.

In the comparative, the degree of a quality in some object is compared with the same quality in another object: не дꙋша́ ли бо́льшн є҆́сть пн́щн (Matth. 6:25--Is not the life more than meat?). The comparative degree can also indicate the greater or lesser degree of a quality in one and the same object by comparison to another of its states: да́ждь премꙋдромꙋ внн́ꙋ, и҆ премꙋдрѣйшїй бꙋдетъ (Give a wise man occasion, and he will be yet wiser--Prov. 9:9 [Septuagint]).

In the superlative degree, what occurs is not comparison, but rather an object is set apart by reason of the highest quality in a series of other objects (not less than three) of the same kind or type, for example: Ꙁмі́й же бѣ мꙋдрѣйшїй всѣхъ ꙃвѣре́й ("Now the serpent was the most crafty of all the beasts"--Gen. 3:1). A formal sign of the superlative may be seen in the presence of the word всѣхъ, ѿ всѣхъ ("of all") with the degree of comparison; in the use of nouns with the prepositions ѿ, въ, междꙋ [from/of, in, among] or the use of nouns with the genitive plural so as to indicate the realm of objects from which something is set apart. When it is difficult to make the distinction, the Russian preposition изъ may be inserted. For example: і҆и҃се, свѣте, превы́шшїй всѣхъ свѣтлосте́й ("Jesus, the Light above all Lights"--Akathistos Hymn to the Saviour, Oikos 6). But in the text, Превы́шшаѧ а҆́гг҃лъ, мїрска́гѡ мѧ̀ превы́шша сли́тїѧ сотвори́ ("O thou who art above the Angels, raise me above the world's confusion"--Midnight Song to the Mother of God, from the

Morning Prayers)--we are dealing with the comparative degree, since this could not be translated "O thou who are the highest *of* the Angels", the Mother of God not being an Angel. Consequently, She is being compared to them, and not set apart from among them. Other examples: є҆́же малѣ́йше ѹ҆́бо є҆́сть ѿ всѣ́хъ сѣ́менъ: є҆гда́ же возрасте́тъ, бо́лѣе всѣ́хъ ѕе́лїй є҆́сть (Matth. 13:32—"Which indeed is the least of all seeds: but when it is grown, it is the greatest among herbs"). Дне́сь въ бо́льшаго ѿ прⷪро́къ рожде́нїи і҆ѡа́нна и҆спо́лнися ("Today [the word of Isaiah] is fulfilled in the Nativity of John, the greatest of the Prophets"—Vespers for June 24, Doxasticon at the Aposticha). Ѹ҆чи́телю, ка́я за́повѣдь бо́льши є҆́сть въ зако́нѣ; (Matth. 22:36—"Master, which is the great commandment in the law?"). Кто̀ ѹ҆́бо бо́лїй є҆́сть въ црⷭтвїи нбⷭнѣмъ; (Matthew 18:1—"Who is the greatest in the kingdom of heaven?"). а҆́зъ бо є҆́смь мнїй а҆пⷭтолѡвъ (I Cor. 15:9—"For I am the least of the Apostles"). Кі́й мни́тся и҆́хъ бы́ти бо́лїй; (Luke 22:24—"which of them should be accounted the greatest").

When the superlative degree is expressed, there may not be words indicating the range of objects from which someone or something stands out, e.g. поне́же ѡ҆брѣ́тенъ є҆сѝ мꙋдрѣ́йшїй ("because thou art found wisest"—I Esdras 4:42 [II Esdras in the Slavonic Bible]—wisest one of three, as seen in the context).

The form of comparative degree may show the especially high quality of the object without relation to other objects, i.e., without comparison or setting apart, for example: ѽ сладча́йшая моѐ весно̀, сладча́йшее моѐ ча́до (Holy Saturday Matins, 3rd Stasis, verse 17: "O my sweet springtime, my sweetest child"). Къ преспѣ́янїю же и҆ ѹ҆множе́нїю добродѣ́тели бжⷭтвеннѣ́йшїя (Canon of Preparation for Holy Communion, Ode 7: "unto furtherance and increase of Divine virtue"). Древесє́мъ безслове́снымъ не принесо́сте че́сти (Octoechos T. 5, Wednesday at Matins, Ode 7--"Ye showed no honors to [utterly] dumb [figures of] wood..."). This absolute form of comparison is formally assigned to the superlative, but in contradistinction to the principal superlative, it is called the *absolute superlative*, or the *elative* (from the Latin term *elativus*). Such an elative superlative usually bears an emotional-stylistic character.

Note: In grammars of Old Church Slavonic, also indicated is a form of the superlative made by means of the prefix нан_, joined to the comparative degree: e.g. нанстарѣн[й], "oldest". However, in Church Slavonic liturgical books it is difficult to find such forms of the superlative, except for наипаче (adverb). In his monumental Church Slavonic dictionary (Полный церковно-славянскій словарь), Fr. G. Diachenko does not list a single word beginning нан_ except for наипаче.

Adjectives in the positive degree with the prefixes все_, веле_, тре_, три_, пре_ merely show a high degree of some quality without any sense of comparison or setting something apart from a group; for this reason, such forms are not part of the system of degrees of comparison.

§60. Declension of Short Comparative Adjectives.

Singular.

	Masculine	Neuter	Feminine
N., V.	мудр-ѣй (wiser)	мудр-ѣе [_ѣйше]	мудр-ѣйши
Gen.	мудр-ѣйша	мудр-ѣйша	мудр-ѣйши
Dat.	мудр-ѣйшу	мудр-ѣйшу	мудр-ѣйши
Acc.	мудр-ѣйш-з [_а]	мудр-ѣе [_ѣйше]	мудр-ѣйшу
Instr.	мудр-ѣйшимз	мудр-ѣйшимз	мудр-ѣйшею
Prep.	мудр-ѣйши	мудр-ѣйши	мудр-ѣйши

Dual.

	Masculine	Neuter	Feminine
N., A., V.	мудр-ѣйша	мудр-ѣйша, _ѣйши	мудр-ѣйши
G., P.	мудр-ѣйшу	мудр-ѣйшу	мудр-ѣйшу
D., I.	мудр-ѣйшима	мудр-ѣйшима	мудр-ѣйшима

Plural.

N., V.	мꙋдр-ѣйше [-н]	мꙋдр-ѣйша	мꙋдр-ѣйша
Gen.	мꙋдр-ѣйшихъ	мꙋдр-ѣйшихъ	мꙋдр-ѣйшихъ
Dat.	мꙋдр-ѣйшымъ	мꙋдр-ѣйшымъ	мꙋдр-ѣйшымъ
Acc.	мꙋдр-ѣйша	мꙋдр-ѣйша	мꙋдр-ѣйша
Instr.	мꙋдр-ѣйшими	мꙋдр-ѣйшими	мꙋдр-ѣйшими

The full forms of the comparative and superlative degree are declined regularly, on the pattern of long adjectives with the stem in a "hushing" sibilant.

Texts for Practice.

1) Никто́же приставля́етъ приставле́нїѧ пла́та небѣле́на ри́зѣ ве́тсѣ…ниже́ влива́ютъ вїна̀ но́ва въ мѣхи ве́тхи. 2) Во мно́зѣ ꙗзы́цѣ сла́ва царю̀: во ѡскꙋдѣ́нїи же люде́й сокрꙋше́нїе. 3) Ра́бъ смы́слень ѡблада́етъ влады́ки безꙋмными. 4) Подоба́етъ ꙋ́бо є̓пⷭ҇копꙋ бы́ти непоро́чнꙋ… тре́звенꙋ, цѣломꙋ́дрꙋ, бл҃гоговѣ́йнꙋ, честнꙋ̀, страннолюби́вꙋ, ꙋ̓чи́тельнꙋ. 5) Всѧ̑ ꙋ́бо чи́ста чи́стымъ: ѡскверне́нымъ же и̓ невѣ́рнымъ ничто́же чи́сто. 6) Кри́тѧне при́снѡ лжи́ви, ѕли́й ѕвѣ́рїе, ꙋ̓тро́бы пра́здныѧ. 7) Бꙋ́ихъ же и̓ ненака́занныхъ стѧза́нїй ѿрица́йсѧ, вѣ́дый, ꙗ́кѡ ражда́ютъ сва́ры. 8) Є̓ли́цы ꙋ́бо соверше́нни, сїѐ да мꙋдрствꙋ́имъ. 9) Превы́шшаѧ а̓́гг҃лъ, мїрскі́агѡ мѧ̀ превы́шша сли́тїѧ сотворѝ. 10) Тѣ́мже блаже́нна є̓сѝ въ ро́дѣхъ родѡ́въ, бг҃облаже́ннаѧ, херꙋві́мѡвъ свѣтлѣ́йши, и̓ серафі́мѡвъ честнѣ́йши сꙋ́щаѧ. 11) Лꙋ́чша себѐ не и̓щѝ, и̓ крѣпльша себѐ не пыта́й. 12) Бре́мене па́че себѐ не воздвижѝ, и̓ крѣпльшꙋ̀ и̓ богатѣ́йшꙋ себѐ не прїѡбща́йсѧ. 13) Ꙗ̓́ннсе, свѣ́те, превы́шшїй всѣ́хъ свѣтлостей. 14) Ꙗ̓́нсе, крѣпосте высо-ча́йшаѧ. 15) Ра́дꙋйсѧ, всѣ́хъ небе́сныхъ чинѡ́въ превы́шшаѧ безъ разсꙋжде́нїѧ. 16) И ꙗ́коже не возгнꙋша́лсѧ є̓сѝ скве́рныхъ є̓ѧ̀

оу́стъ[1] и нечи́стыхъ, цѣлꙋ́ющихъ та̀, нижѐ мои́хъ возгнꙋша́йса
скве́ршихъ ѻ҆ны́а оу́стъ и нечи́стшихъ, нижѐ ме́рзкихъ мои́хъ и
нечи́стыхъ оу́стѣнъ, и скве́рнагѡ и нечисте́йшагѡ моегѡ̀ ꙗ҆зы́ка.

Key.

1) No man putteth a piece of new cloth unto an old garment...neither do men put new wine into old bottles [Matth. 9:16-17]. 2) In a populous nation is the glory of a king: but in the failure [lack] of people is ruin [Prov. 14:28--*Septuagint*]. 3) A wise servant shall have rule over foolish masters [Prov. 17:2--*Septuagint*]. 4) A bishop then must be blameless...vigilant, sober, devout, honest, given to hospitality, apt to teach [I Tim. 3:2]. 5) Unto the pure all things are pure: but unto them that are defiled and unbelieving, nothing is pure [Tit. 1:15]. 6) The Cretans are alway liars, evil beasts, slow bellies [Tit. 1:12]. 7) But foolish and unlearned questions avoid, knowing that they do gender strifes [II Tim. 2:23]. 8) Let us, therefore, as many as be perfect, be thus minded [Philippians 3:15]. 9) O thou who art above the Angels, raise me above the world's confusion [Morning Prayer, Midnight Song to the Thetokos]. 10) Therefore thou art blessed for all generations, thou who art blessed of God: more radiant than the Cherubim, and more honourable than the Seraphim [Prayer following the Canon to the Mother of God]. 11) Seek not one better than thyself, and test not one more powerful than thyself [Prologue for June 28]. 12) Burden not thyself above thy power, and have no fellowship with one that is mightier and richer than thyself [Ecclus. 13:2]. 13) Jesus, the Light above all Lights [Akathist Hymn to the Saviour, Oikos 6]. 14) Jesus, Supreme Strength! [Akathist to the Saviour, Oikos 7]. 15) Rejoice, thou who art higher without question than all the host of heaven [Theotokion at "Lord I have cried" for June 30]. 16) And as Thou didst not spurn her foul and

---

[1]) оу́ста means "mouth" (Greek στόμα), while оу́стнѣ (with the н) means "lips" (Greek χείλη).

unclean lips, kissing Thee, neither spurn Thou my fouller lips than those, and more unclean; nor yet my vile and impure mouth, and my foul and unclean tongue [2nd Prayer of Preparation for Holy Communion, of St. John Chrysostom].

NUMERALS.

§61. *Numerals* are the name we give words that indicate the quantity or order of objects.

Numerals that indicate quantity (answering the question "how many?") are called *cardinal* numbers.

Numerals that indicate the order in which objects are arranged (answering the question "which?") are called *ordinals*.

Besides these, there also exist the following categories of numerals: collective (e.g. ѻбоѐ, троѐ [both, a set of three]); multiple numbers (e.g. є҆динокра́тный, двокра́тный, сꙋгꙋбый--onefold, twofold, reiterated]); and fractions (по́лъ, четве́рть, десѧти́на--half, quarter, tenth part).

Slavonic numerals, like Russian, are based on the decimal system, and therefore independant names exist only for the basic numbers, the rest being derived from them. Thus, numerals can have the following structure: *a)* basic or simple numbers, the first ten, as well as сто̀, ты́сѧща, тьма̀, легеѡ́нъ, леѡ́дръ [100, 1,000, 10,000, 100,000, 1,000,000] and the like; and *b)* compound: those consisting of combinations of simple numbers: трина́десѧть, три́десѧть и҆ пѧ́ть [13, 35] and so on.

The numerals in Church Slavonic, when they indicate the number of people, can be used with much greater freedom than is the case in Russian, for example: и҆ призва̀ ѻ҆бана́десѧть, и҆ нача́тъ и҆́хъ посыла́ти два̀ два̀ (Mark 6:7--"And he called unto him the twelve, and began to send them forth by two and two"). The same freedom of use can be seen in the Greek text: Καὶ προσκαλεῖται τοὺς δώδεκα, καὶ ἤρξατο αὐτοὺς ἀποστέλλειν δύο δύο. ВОЗВРАТЍШАСѦ ЖЕ СЕ́ДМЬДЕСѦТⷯ Сⷯ РА́ДОСТЇЮ (Luke 10:17—"And the seventy returned again with joy"): Ὑπέστρεψαν δε οἱ ἑβδομήκοντα μετὰ χαρᾶς.

§62. The Declension of Simple Quantitative Nume rals.

The numerals є҆ди́нⷯ, два̀, трѝ, четы́ре [1, 2, 3, 4] are adjectives, while пѧ́ть [5] and the rest are nouns. This is reflected in the character of their declension and the way they are joined with nouns, whose number they indicate.

The characteristic features of the numeral adjectives are their gender endings and their agreement with the nouns. To be sure, as regards трѝ, четы́ре [3, 4] it can be said that they have lost the distinction of gender, even though the forms трѝ, трѝ, четы́ре, четы́ри are used.

The numeral є҆ди́нⷯ is declined on the model of то́й, in the singular, dual and plural, and can have several senses:

1) As a numeral; the plural form in this case is not a contradiction, since certain nouns have only the plural form, e.g. «врата̀ є҆ди́на га́дова» (Ezek. 48:34-35—"One gate of Gad") and the numeral agrees with its noun in number and gender.

2) As an adjective, in the sense of "only": «є҆ди́не вѣ́дый человѣ́ческагѡ сꙋ́щества не́мощь» ["Thou Who alone knowest the frailty of human nature"—Eirmos of the 1st Tone]; in the sense of "without others": «и҆ и҆до́ша въ мѣ́сто пꙋ́сто корабле́мъ є҆ди́ни» (Mark 6:32—"And they departed into a desert place by ship privately").

3) To indicate an abstract unity, the neuter singular is used: «а҆́зъ и҆ Оц҃ъ є҆ди́но є҆сма̀» (John 10:30—"I and My Father are one").

The numeral є҆ди́нⷯ can also have long endings on the model of the full adjectives.

Singular.

	Masculine	Neuter	Feminine
Nom.	є҆ди́н_ъ *one*	є҆ди́н_о	є҆ди́н_а
Gen.	є҆ди́н_огѡ	є҆ди́н_огѡ	є҆ди́н_ оѧ[1]
Dat.	є҆ди́н_омꙋ	є҆ди́н_омꙋ	є҆ди́н_ой
Acc.	є҆ди́н_ъ [_ого]	є҆ди́н_о	є҆ди́н_ꙋю
Instr.	є҆ди́н_ѣмъ	є҆ди́н_ѣмъ	є҆ди́н_ою
Prep.	є҆ди́н_омъ	є҆ди́н_омъ	є҆ди́н_ой

Dual.

N., A.	є҆ди̑н_а	є҆ди̑н_а,_ѣ	є҆ди́н_ѣ
G., P.	є҆ди́н_ою	є҆ди́н_ою	є҆ди́н_ою
D., I.	є҆ди́н_ѣма	є҆ди́н_ѣма	є҆ди́н_ѣма

Plural.

Nom.	є҆ди́н_и	є҆ди́н_ы	є҆ди̑н_а
Gen.	є҆ди́н_ѣхъ	є҆ди́н_ѣхъ	є҆ди́н_ѣхъ
Dat.	є҆ди́н_ѣмъ	є҆ди́н_ѣмъ	є҆ди́н_ѣмъ
Acc.	є҆ди́н_ы	є҆ди́н_ы	є҆ди̑н_а
Instr.	є҆ди́н_ѣми	є҆ди́н_ѣми	є҆ди́н_ѣми
Prep.	є҆ди́н_ѣхъ	є҆ди́н_ѣхъ	є҆ди́н_ѣхъ

Dual.

N., A.	два̀, ѻ҆́ба *two, both*	два̀, двѣ̀; ѻ҆́ба, ѻ҆́бѣ	двѣ̀, ѻ҆́бѣ
G., P.	двою̀ [двꙋ̀], ѻ҆бою̀	двою̀[двꙋ̀],ѻ҆бою̀	двою̀[двꙋ̀], ѻ҆бою̀
D., P.	двѣма̀, ѻ҆бѣ́ма	двѣ́ма, ѻ҆бѣ́ма	двѣма̀, ѻ҆бѣ́ма

The numerals два̀, ѻ҆́ба are declined only in the dual, on the pattern of the pronoun то́й.

The numerals ѻ҆́ба, ѻ҆́бѣ ["both"] are of like quantitative meaning with два̀, двѣ̀, but signify the two or their action as a unit,

---

[1] є҆ди́нꙋ проти́вꙋ є҆ди́ноѧ (I Maccabees 13:28--"one against another").

and in sense come close to the pronouns "the one and the other". Ѻба, Ѻбѣ in combination with деѧть has the value of a number and is equivalent to the numeral два, e.g. Ѻбанадесѧте колѣна (Acts 26:7-- "[our] twelve tribes"), сꙋдѧще Ѻбѣманадесѧте колѣнома і҆и҃левома (Matth. 19:28--"judging the twelve tribes of Israel").

The numerals трі҆е[3], четыре[4] are declined only in the plural.

трі҆ѐ, трѝ (three)

Plural.

	Masculine	Neuter and Feminine
(Common)		
Nom.	трі҆ѐ, трѝ	трѝ
Gen.	трі҆е́хъ, тре́хъ	тре́хъ
Dat.	трі҆е́мъ, тре́мъ	тре́мъ
Acc.	трі҆е́хъ, тре́хъ, трѝ	трѝ
Instr.	трі҆е́мн, тре́мн	тре́мн
Prep.	трі҆е́хъ, тре́хъ	тре́хъ

четыре, четырн (four)

	Masculine	Neuter and Feminine
Nom.	четыре [_н]	четырн
Gen.	четырехъ	четырехъ
Dat.	четыремъ	четыремъ
Acc.	четырн [_е]	четырн
Instr.	четырьмн	четырьмн
Prep.	четырехъ	четырехъ

The numbers from пѧть (5) to десѧть (10) are declined on the model of substantives of the 3rd declension (e.g. ко́сть, *bone*), usually only in the singular.

The numeral ді́слть is also declined like the 3rd declension
nouns (except for certain forms) in all three numbers. Besides the
usual forms of the declension, in the plural this numeral has forms
built on the pattern of the soft-declension adjectives as well. The
numbers from пѧ́ть to де́влть (9) can also have similar plural
endings: нє погꙋблю̀ дєсѧти́хꙁ ра́ди (Gen. 18:32--"I will not destroy
it for ten's sake"); четы́редесѧти пѧти́хꙁ ра́ди (Gen. 18:28--"for the
sake of forty-five").

	Singular	Plural	Dual
Nom.	де́слт_ь *(ten)*	де́слт_и[_є]	де́слт_и[_ѣ]
Gen.	де́слт_и	де́слт_ꙁ, _и́хꙁ *(adjectival form)*	де́слт_ꙋ
Dat.	де́слт_и	де́слт_ємꙁ, _и́мꙁ *(adj.)*	де́слт_ьма̀
Acc.	де́слт_ь[_є]	де́слт_и[_є]	де́слт_и [_ѣ]
Instr.	де́слт_їю	де́слт_ьми́	де́слт_ьма̀
Prep.	де́слт_и	де́слт_єхꙁ, _и́хꙁ *(adj.)*	де́слт_ꙋ

	Singular	Plural	Dual
Nom.	сто̀ *(hundred)*	стꙿа̀	стѣ̀
Gen.	стꙿа̀	сꙋ́тꙁ	стꙋ̀
Dat.	стꙋ̀	стꙿꙋ́мꙁ	стома̀
Acc.	сто̀	стꙿа̀	стѣ̀
Instr.	стꙿо́мꙁ	стꙿы̀	стома̀
Prep.	стꙿѣ̀	стꙿѣ́хꙁ	стꙋ̀

Numerals ending in -а [ты́слща, тьма̀] are declined
according to the 2nd declension; those in _ꙁ, _о (лєгєю́нꙁ[100,000],
лєꙋа́рꙁ[1,000,000], сто̀ [100]) follow the 1st declension; the numeral
нєсвѣ́дь (100,000) follows the 3rd.

The numerals тьма̀ [10,000], нєсвѣ́дь [100,000], besides their
normal significance as num- bers, have also a more general meaning,
an unspecified "great number".

Note: The numerals нєсвѣ́дь and лєꙋа́рꙁ do not occur in
liturgical books.

§63. Formation of Compound Numerals.

Compund numbers are formed as follows:

a) The numbers from 11 to 19 are formed by joining the figures from 1-9 to дєсать by means of the preposition на, and дєсать which is the object of the preposition, is in the accusative case (на́ дєсать or на́ дєса́тє): є҆ди́н҃-на́-дєсать[є]--є҆диннона́дєсать[є]; in New Church Slavonic, this numeral is used only with the connecting vowel о: є҆диннона́дєсать сынѡ́въ свои́хъ (Gen. 32:22-- "his eleven sons"); двана́дєсать[є], пать҃на́дєсать[є] and so on.

Note: По растри́гѣ́ же въ лѣ́то то́а́же ѻ҆смы́а ты́са́щи, второ́агѡ ста҃ чєтвє́рица на дєса́тицꙋ (Prolog, May 15, the life of St. Dimitri the Crown Prince--"And after the deposition, in the same year 7114 [*anno creationis*]")--this example shows clearly the use of the accusative case after на in the formation of numerals.

b) Numbers signifiying the tens from 20 to 90 are formed from the units showing the number of tens, and дєсать, which is joined with them in the manner of nouns, by agreement or government. The numbers два̀, трѝ, чєты́рє agree with дєсать in case and number, and in this combination дєсать has no distinctions of gender: (два̀ дєса́ти and not *двѣ̀ дєса́ти) = двадєсать, трѝ дєса́ти = тридєсать, чєты́рє дєса́ти=чєты́рєдєсать. The final -и of these numerals has been shortened to -ь. (But: пать҃дєса́тъ).

The numbers from пать to дєвать are joined with дєсать by government, i.e. they are followed by the genitive plural: пать дєса́тъ ["five tens"]= пать҃дєса́тъ [50], шєсть дєса́тъ [6 tens] = шєсть҃дєса́тъ [60] and so forth.

In like manner are formed the numerals for hundreds: by agreement--двѣ́стѣ́ [=200](in the dual number) or двѣ́сти (under the influence of Russian), три́ста [300], чєты́рєста [400]; or by government--пать҃сѡ́тъ [500], шєсть҃сѡ́тъ [600], and so on. The numbers from 200 to 400 are almost always written as one word in the nominative case, although now and then they can be met with written as two words; those from 500 to 900, on the contrary, are mostly written separately in the nominative, though forms written as a single word are also used.

The remaining numbers, expressing larger figures--ты́сѧща, тьма̀, легеѡ́нъ, лео́дръ &c. are joined with the units expressing their quantity in the same manner as are those for the tens and hundreds, but they are written separately: двѣ̀ ты́сѧщы, двѣ̀ тьмѣ̀: три̑ ты́сѧщы, три̑ тьмы̑: пѧ́ть ты́сѧщъ, пѧ́ть те́мъ and so on.

c) Complex numbers are always written as separate words. The last figure is usually joined by means of the conjunction и̑, but all the other figures can be joined by и̑ as well; and complex numbers without и̑ are also to be encountered: и̑ проро́ницати бꙋ́дꙋтъ дні́и ты́сѧщꙋ двѣ́стѣ и̑ ше́стьдесѧ́тъ (Rev. 11:3--"And they shall prophesy a thousand two hundred and threescore days"); и̑ размѣ́ри стѣ́нꙋ є̑гѡ̀ во сто̀ и̑ четы́редесѧть и̑ четы́ри ла́кти (Rev. 21:17-- "And he measured the wall thereof, an hundred and forty and four cubits"); и̑ поживе́ є̑ве́ръ лѣ́тъ сто̀ три́десѧть четы́ри, и̑ роди̑ фале́ка (Gen. 11:16--[*Septuagint version*] "And Heber lived an hundred and thirty-four years, and begat Phaleg").

§64. Declension of Compound Quantitative Numerals.

The component parts of compound numbers in Church Slavonic have not yet lost their independent meaning, and therefore when the number is declined the parts are declined like separate words, even though they make up one word. This has resulted in the fact that various forms can be used to indicate one and the same case of a given compound number.

a) The compound numbers from 11 to 19, formed with the preposition на, are declined as follows: either—

1) the first part [the unit] is declined: и̑ до́мъ сво́й созда̀ соломѡ́нъ тремина́десѧть лѣ́ты (III Kings 7:1--"But Solomon was building his own house thirteen years"); or—

2) only the second part is declined, in which case it takes endings on the model of adjectives of the soft declension: мѣра єгѡ̀ четыренадесѧтихъ лакѡ́тъ (III Kings 7:15--[*Septuagint*]"a circumference of fourteen cubits encompassed it"). Or else—

3) Both parts are declined: по пѧтинадесѧти ря́дъ (III Kings 7:4--"fifteen [pillars] in each row").

In the numeral єдиннона́десѧть the second part is usually declined, rarely the first: єдиному̀на́десѧть ꙗви́сѧ (Mark 16:14; Luke 24:9--"He appeared unto the eleven").

The conjunctions же, бо, ѹ̑бо usually break up these compound numbers and are written after the first part: єди́нїй же на́десѧте ѹ̑чениць̀ (Matth. 28:16--"Then the eleven disciples").

Note: In the oblique cases, the component parts of these numerals are sometimes written separately: по тре́хъ на́десѧтихъ дне́хъ (Prolog for March 5: "After thirteen days").

Possible combinations for the declension of два̑на́десѧть[_є]:

1) First part in the Dual: 2) Both parts in Dual:
Nom., Acc. два̑на́десѧть[_є]
Gen., Prep. дво̑юна́десѧте [_ь]   дво̑юна́десѧту́
Dat., Instr. дв҄ѣмана́десѧте[_ь]   дв҄ѣмана́десѧтьма

3) 2nd part in the Sing.: 4) 2nd part in the Pl.: 5) 1st part in Dual, 2nd in Singular:

Nom.	два̑на́десѧть[є]		
Gen.	два̑на́десѧти	_нхъ	дво̑юна́десѧти
Dat.	два̑на́десѧти	_нмъ	дв҄ѣмана́десѧти
Acc.	два̑на́десѧть[є]		
Instr.	два̑на́десѧтїю	_ьми	дв҄ѣмана́десѧтїю
Prep.	два̑на́десѧти	_нхъ	дво̑юна́десѧти

Slavonic Numerals:

	Cardinal:		Ordinal:	
1:	а̃	є҆ди́нъ, _а, _о	1st:	пе́рвый, _аѧ, _ое
2:	в̃	два̀, _ѣ̑, _ѣ̑	2nd:	вторы́й, _аѧ, _о́е
3:	г̃	трїѐ, трѝ, _н̑	3rd:	тре́тїй, _їѧ, ї̈е
4:	д̃	четы́ре, _н, _н	4th:	четве́ртый, _аѧ, _ое
5:	є̃	пѧ́ть	5th:	пѧ́тый, _аѧ, _ое
6:	ѕ̃	ше́сть	6th:	шесты́й, _а́ѧ, _ое
7:	з̃	се́дмь	7th:	седмы́й, _аѧ, _ое
8:	и̃	о́смь	8th:	о́смый, _а́ѧ, _о́е
9:	ѳ̃	де́вѧть	9th:	девѧ́тый, _аѧ, _ое
10:	і̃	де́сѧть	10th:	десѧ́тый, _аѧ, _ое
11:	а̃і	є҆диннома́десѧть	11th:	пе́рвыйнаде́сѧть, є҆диннодесѧ́тый
12:	в̃і	двана́десѧть[е]	12th:	вторы́йнаде́сѧть, дванадесѧ́тый
13:	г̃і	трина́десѧть[е]	13th:	тре́тїйна́десѧть, триннадесѧ́тый
14:	д̃і	четырена́десѧть[е]	14th:	четве́ртыйна́десѧть, четыренадесѧ́тый
15:	є̃і	пѧтьна́десѧть[е]	15th:	пѧтыйна́десѧтый, пѧтьнадесѧ́тый
16:	ѕ̃і	шестьна́десѧть[е]	16th:	шесты́йна́десѧть, шестьнадесѧ́тый
17:	з̃і	седмьна́десѧть[е]	17th:	се́дмыйна́десѧть, седмьнадесѧ́тый
18:	и̃і	о́смьна́десѧть[е]	18th:	о́смыйна́десѧть, о́смьнадесѧ́тый
19:	ѳ̃і	девѧтьна́десѧть[е]	19th:	девѧ́тыйна́десѧть, девѧтьнадесѧ́тый
20:	к̃	два́десѧть	20th:	двадесѧ́тый

30:	а҃	тридесатъ[е]	30th:	тридесѧ́тый
40:	м҃	четыредесатъ[е]	40th:	четыредесѧ́тый
50:	н҃	пѧтьдесѧ́тъ	50th:	пѧтьдесѧ́тый
60:	ѕ҃	шестьдесѧ́тъ	60th:	шестьдесѧ́тый
70:	о҃	седмьдесѧ́тъ	70th:	седмьдесѧ́тый
80:	п҃	о҆смьдесѧ́тъ	80th:	о҆смьдесѧ́тый
90:	ч҃	девѧтьдесѧ́тъ	90th:	девѧтьдесѧ́тый
100:	р҃	сто̀	100th:	со́тный
200:	с҃	двѣстѣ̀	200th:	двосо́тный, второсо́тный
300:	т҃	триста	300th:	трисо́тный
400:	у҃	четыреста	400th:	четвертосо́тный
500:	ф҃	пѧтьсѡ́тъ	500th:	пѧтьсо́тный
600:	х҃	шестьсѡ́тъ	600th:	шестьсо́тный
700:	ѱ҃	седмьсѡ́тъ	700th:	седмьсо́тный
800:	ѿ҃	о҆смьсѡ́тъ	800th:	о҆смьсо́тный
900:	ц҃	девѧтьсѡ́тъ	900th:	девѧтьсо́тный
1,000:	҂а҃	тысѧща	1,000th:	тысѧщный
2,000:	҂в҃	двѣ тысѧщы	2,000th:	двотысѧщный, второтысѧщный
8,000:	҂н҃	о҆смь тысѧщъ	8,000th:	о҆смаѧ тысѧща
10,000:	҂і҃	тьма̀	100,000:	҂р҃ : легеѡ́нъ
		1,000,000:	҂҂а҃ :	лею́дръ

b) The numbers дванадесѧтъ[е] and о҆банадесѧтъ[е] can have five different combinations in their declension [see tables above on p. 82]:

1) the first part is declined in the dual number: на двоюнадесѧте престо́лу (Matth. 19:28—"upon twelve thrones");

2) both parts are declined in the dual: двѣманадесѧтьма супру́гома волѡ́въ (III Kings 19:19—"with twelve yoke of oxen");

3) the 2nd part is declined in the singular: дванадесѧти лѣ́тъ (III Kings 2:12—"Then sat Solomon upon the throne of David his father] for twelve years");

4) the second part is declined in the plural, with the endings of soft-declension adjectives: дванадесатихъ же апостоловъ (Matth. 10:2—"[the names] of the twelve Apostles");

5) both parts are declined: the first part in the dual, the second in the singular: по двоюнадесати супругъ (III Kings 19:19--"[plowing] with twelve yoke of oxen before him"—*lit.* "behind twelve yoke of oxen").

c) The compound numbers from 20 to 40 decline only the second part in the singular or plural (in the genitive, dative, and prepositional cases for the most part, taking the adjectival endings): e.g. двадесати и пати лѣтъ (Numbers 4:3—"from twenty-five years old [and upward]"); не погублю тридесатихъ ради (Gen. 18:30—"I will not destroy [the city] for the sake of thirty"); четыредесатемъ (March 9, 3rd Ode of the 2nd Canon—"[we flee for refuge] unto [you] the 40 [warriors of Christ]").

d) The compound numbers from 50 to 90 are declined in the following manner:

1) The first part is declined, while the second part remains in all cases in the genitive, according to the law of government, on which this construction is based: по патидесатъ (Luke 9:14—"[for they were] about five thousand [men]"); патїюдесатъ (Luke 7:41—"[one owed five hundred pence, and the other] fifty");

2) or else both parts are declined, with the second part taking the forms of the singular or plural (soft adjectival declension): девятидесати и трехъ (Prolog for Aug. 19th—"of 93"); ѡ девятидесатихъ и девати праведникъ (Luke 15:7—"[more than over] ninety and nine just persons"); съ патїюдесатьми ихъ (IV Kings 1:14—"with their fifties [i.e. their military detachments of 50 men]")

e) Numbers from 200 to 400 decline both parts (by the law of agreement)[1]; those from 500 to 900 decline, it would appear, only the first part (by the law of government)[2]. In the oblique cases the component parts of these numerals usually are written separately, but joined forms are also to be encountered. For example: на трéхъ стѣхъ пѣназь (John 12:5—"for three hundred pence"); и гна̀ съ четыⷬьми сты̀ мꙋжéй, двѣсти же мꙋжéй ѡстáшаса (I Kings [I Samuel] 30:10—"But [David] pursued, [he] and four hundred men, for two hundred abode behind"); предварѝ же пришéствїе хрⷭто́во лѣты ѡсмїюсώтъ (Prolog for July 20, Prophet Elias—"He preceded the birth of Christ by [about] 800 years"); є҆дѝнъ бѣ̀ до́лженъ пати́юсώтъ дннáрїй (Luke 7:41—"the one owed five hundred pence").

f) Compounds of multiple numbers decline all parts: двꙋ̀ ты́саⷳъ пати́сώтъ девати́десати и̂ трéхъ (Prolog for Aug. 19—"[of] two thousand five hundred and ninety-three").

§65. Numerals used with Nouns.

The numerals from є҆дѝнъ to четы́ре, like adjectives, when used with nouns function as modifiers and agree with their noun in gender, number and case: бѣ̀ і҆ѡ́на во чрéвѣ ки́товѣ трѝ днѝ и̂ трѝ нώщи (Matth. 12:40--"Jonah was three days and three nights in the whale's belly"); четы́ри царѝ на па́ть (Gen. 14:9--"four kings with [against] five").

---

[1] The "law of agreement" means that the number is used like an adjective and agrees with the noun in gender, number and case.-- *Tr.*

[2] The "law of government" means that the number is used like a noun, followed by the noun in the genitive: e.g 1,000 men = "a thousand *of* men".

The numerals from 5 and up are treated grammatically as nouns, but logically as abstract numbers, defining the quantity of nouns, and therefore in these numerals there is a certain wavering in their connection with nouns: in some declension cases, like nouns, they govern nouns in the genitive plural, while in other cases they agree with the nouns in the manner of adjectives of definition or apposition. Thus in the nominative, genitive and accusative cases they always govern their nouns: nom., acc.—пѧ́ть ѻве́цъ [five sheep], gen.—пѧти́ ѻве́цъ (just as па́стырь ѻве́цъ [shepherd, pastor of sheep], па́стырѧ ѻве́цъ), while in the dative, instrumental and prepositional cases they are joined either by agreement or, less often, by government: dative:—пѧти́ ѻвца́мъ, instrumental:.—пѧті́ю ѻвца́ми, prep.—ѡ пѧти́ ѻвца́хъ. Examples of agreement: въ седми́ лѣ́тѣхъ (Gen. 41:47—"in the seven [plenteous] years"); стома̀ а́гнцы (Gen. 33:19—"[he bought] for a hundred lambs" ; седмі́ю та́тивами (Judges 16:7—"[if they bind me] with seven moist cords"). Examples of government: по пѧти́ сі́кль на главу́ (Numbers 3:47—"five shekels apiece"); стома̀ сі́клей (Deut. 22:19—"[they shall fine him] an hundred shekels"); по стꙋ́ тала́нтъ (II Chronicles 27:5—"[And the children of Ammon paid him] an hundred talents [of silver]").

The numerals ты́сѧща, тьма̀ and легеѡ́нъ are usually joined to nouns in all cases by government: ты́сѧща человѣ́къ, ты́сѧщи человѣ́къ, ты́сѧщію человѣ́къ and so on, but one may also encounter a connection by means of agreement: сотвори́ ве́черю ве́лію вельмо́жамъ свои́мъ ты́сѧщи му́жемъ (Dan. 5:1—"made a great feast to a thousand of his lords").

§66. Peculiarities in the use of Compound Numbers with Nouns.

Numerals consisting of two figures and more, since they are made up of simple figures, are joined with nouns on the same principle as simple numerals.

a) Nouns that stand with the numbers from 11 to 14 are joined either with the first part of the number or the second (in the nominative, if the number ends in -є, the noun usually is joined with the first part)—for example, with the first part: є҆ди́нїи же на́десѧте ѹ҆ченицы̀ (Matth. 28:16—"Then the eleven disciples..."); Ѻ҆бана́десѧте ѹ҆ченика̀ (Matth. 20:17—"[Jesus...took] the twelve disciples"); на двоюна́десѧте престѡ́лꙋ (Matth. 19:28—"upon twelve thrones"); ро́дове четырена́десѧте (Matth. 1:17—"fourteen generations"). With the second part: двана́десѧть и҆сто́чникѡвъ (Exodus 15:27—"twelve wells"); двꙋна́десѧти сынѡ́въ (Ex. 28:21—"[the names of the] children [of Israel], twelve").

In the numbers from 15 to 19, the figures of the first part are of the same [declensional] character as десѧть [the second part], and therefore regardless of whether the noun is joined with the first or second part of the numeral [i.e. regardless of which part of the numeral has the declension endings] , the result is the same: съ патїюна́десѧть сы́ны or съ патьна́десѧтїю сы́ны [with fifteen sons].

b) Nouns that stand with numbers consisting of tens, are joined with them as with десѧть (§65), by agreement and sometimes by government, e.g. седмина́десѧти мꙋже́мъ (Judges 9:2--"[is it better that] seventy men [should reign over you, or that...]"); на седмина́десѧти ѻ҆слѧ́хъ (Judges 12:14 --"on threescore and ten ass colts").

c) With numerals of two figures, consisting of hundreds, nouns are usually joined by government, but sometimes forms of joining by agreement are to be met with, e.g. съ четы́рьми сты̀ мꙋже́й (I Kings [Samuel] 30:10—"with four hundred men"); на тре́хъ стѣ́хъ пѣ́нѧзь (John 12:5—"for three hundred pence"); патїюсѡ́тъ дина́рїй (Luke 7:41—"[owing] five hundred pence"); agreement: ꙗ҆ви́сѧ бо́ле патѝ сѡ́тъ бра́тїамъ (I Cor. 15:6—"He was seen of above five hundred brethren").

d) Nouns that stand with numerals of multiple figures are joined to the last figure; but if the noun comes before the numeral, it is joined with the first figure: сынъ тридесѧть и двою лѣтъ (IV Kings 8:17—"Thirty and two years old was he when he began to reign"); четыредесѧть и шестїю лѣтъ (John 2:20—"Forty and six years [was this temple in building]"); съ шестїюдесѧтъ и шестїю хрⷭ҇то́выми оуго́дники (Jan. 4, 9th Ode at Matins: "With the sixty-six Saints of Christ"); лѣтъ о́смьдесѧтъ и четы́ре (Luke 2:37—"[a widow] of about fourscore and four years"); лѣ́ты о́смїю сѡ́тъ (Prolog for June 20—"eight hundred years").

§67. Exceptions in the Use of Nouns with Numerals.

The following cases may be noted, where the noun joined with numerals from 5 and up, as the subject of a sentence, can be in the nominative case (instead of the usual genitive):

a) When the noun seems to bear the main emphasis, and the number is used merely as a modifier or apposition, e.g. in the service for the 7 Youths of Ephesus (Aug. 4): ꙗ́коже ѿ сна́ а́бїе воста́ша, вкꙋ́пѣ се́дмь о́троцы бжⷭ҇твеннїи (Vespers, at *Lord I have cried*—"As if from sleep they woke at once, together, the seven divine youths"); честны́ѧ дѣ́ти се́дмь (Matins, Ode 1—"the honourable seven children"); ѕвѣ́зды неꙋкло́нны се́дмь (Ode 3—"seven steadfast stars"); да восхва́лѧтсѧ стїи о́троцы се́дмь (Ode 6—"Let the holy seven youths be praised") and elsewhere; in the service for the 40 Martyrs (March 9): бга на́мъ, мꙋ́ченницы четыредесѧте, нынѣ бл҃гопрем҃ѣнна сотвори́те ва́шими моли́твами (Ode 1—"Now render God well-disposed towards us by your prayers, ye Forty Martyrs"); четыредесѧте хрⷭ҇то́вы мꙋ́ченницы (Ode 5—"the Forty Martyrs of Christ").

b) Especially characteristic in this regard are examples in which the subject precedes the numeral: и идо́ша же бра́тїѧ ї҆ѡ́сифовы де́сать (Gen. 42:3—"And Joseph's ten brethren went"); бы́ша же є҆мꙋ̀ сы́нове се́дмь (Job 1:2—"And there were [born] unto him seven sons"); мосе́ллемі́ю же сы́нове и҆ бра́тїа ѻ҆смьна́десать, си́льнїи (I Chronicles 26:9—"And Meshellemiah [Mosellemia] had eighteen sons and brethren, mighty men").

c) With the verb бы́ти [to be], indicating possession: и҆ а҆ха́вꙋ бѣ́ша се́дмьдесать сы́ны въ самарі́и (IV Kings 10:1—"And Ahab had seventy sons in Samaria"); и҆ бы́ша є҆мꙋ̀ трида́сать сы́ны и҆ трида́сать дще́ри (Judges 12:9—"And he had thirty sons, and thirty daughters"). But in such expressions the usual method of joining is also possible: и҆ геде́ѡнꙋ бы́ша се́дмьдесать сынѡ́въ (Jd. 8:30—"And Gideon had threescore and ten sons").

d) When the numeral is a nominal part of the predicate: и҆ да бꙋ́дꙋтъ ѻ҆смь столпы̀, и҆ стѡ́ала и҆́хъ сре́брана шестьна́десать (Ex. 26:25—"And there shall be eight posts, and their sixteen silver sockets").

Note: It may well be that such a formulation of the subject reflects the influence of the Greek original, in which the subject with a numeral always is put in the nominative plural (beginning with the number 2), e.g. Gen. 42:3: κατέβησαν δὲ οἱ ἀδελφοὶ Ἰωσὴφ οἱ δέκα—Job 1:2: ἐγένοντο δὲ αὐτῷ υἱοὶ ἑπτά.

§68. Formation and Declension of Ordinal Numerals.

Ordinal numerals are formed from the cardinals (except for є҆ди́нъ[1] and два̀) by adding the full adjectival endings to the stem, either directly or with the aid of a suffix: пе́рвый, в_тор_ы́й, тр_е́_тїй, четве́р_т_ый, пѧ́т_ый and so on.

---

[1] As part of є҆диннона́десать, є҆ди́нъ can have an ordinal form: во є҆ди́ный же на́десать ча́съ (Matth. 20: 6--"And about the eleventh hour").

The ordinals from 11 to 19 usually join the full adjectival endings to the stem of the first part, but the endings can also be joined to the second part: въ третїйна́десать де́нь (II Maccabees 15:37: "[to celebrate] the thirteenth day"); є҆диннона́десА́тоє лѣ́то (III Kings 6:38—"In the eleventh year").

The same endings are joined to the ordinals from 20 to 90, and also from 200 to 900, attached to the second part either directly or by means of the suffix _н_: двадеса́тый, пАтьдеса́тый, седмьдеса́тый, со́тный, двосо́тный and so on.

Note: The suffix _н_ is taken primarily by the hundreds and only sometimes by the tens: пАтьдеса́тоє лѣ́то (Leviticus 25:10-11—"[And he shall hallow] the fiftieth year"); въ шестьсо́тноє лѣ́то въ житїи҆ но́евѣ (Gen. 7:11—"In the six hundredth year of Noah's life"); въ четыредеса́тноє и҆ четвертосо́тноє лѣ́то (III Kings 6:1—"[And it came to pass] in the four hundredth and fortieth year" [*literally:* in the fortieth and four hundredth year].

In numerals of multiple figures, the last figure [only] is put in the ordinal form: въ лѣ́то сто̀ седмьдеса́тъ второ́е (I Maccabees 14:1—"in the hundred threescore and twelfth [172th] year").

Note: In numbers of multiple figures, sometimes several figures can be in the ordinal form, but then the manner of expressing the multiple-digit ordinal is somewhat different: По растри́гѣ же въ лѣ́то то́же ѻ҆смы́А ты́сАщн, втора́гѡ ста̀ четверица на деса́тицꙋ (7114—see §63-a, Note). (Prolog for May 15, life of St. Dimitri the Crown Prince).

The component parts of multiple numbers are sometimes conjoined by the connecting vowel о: въ лѣ́то ѻ҆смона́десА́тоє (Dan.

3:1—"In his eighteenth year"); оу҆ченникώмъ сочетавшагw седмодесѧ́тнымъ (Nov. 22, Apostle Philemon, Ode 6— "[proclaiming the glory] of Him who counted thee as the seventeenth Apostle").

Alongside of the ordinal вторы́й [2nd], дрꙋгі́й can also be used with the same meaning, although it has the additional significance of a pronoun meaning "another").

Ordinal numerals are declined regularly on the pattern of full adjectives: пе́рвыйнадесѧ́ть, пе́рвагwнадесѧ́ть, пе́рвомꙋ́надесѧ́ть and so on.

§69. Collective Numerals.

In Church Slavonic, collective numerals are far less common than in Russian; in those places where collective numerals are used in the Russian version of the Holy Scriptures, in the Slavonic we find for the most part the quantitative [cardinal] numbers, for example: и҆дѣ́же бо є҆ста̀ два̀, и҆лѝ трїѐ со́брани во и҆́мѧ моѐ... (Matth. 18:—"For where two or three are gathered together in My name..."), but in the Russian the words "двое", "трое" are used here.
In Church Slavonic the following collective numerals are used:

двóи (masculine and feminine), двóѧ (neuter) and двóе["a twosome"],
трóи (m. & f.), трóѧ (n.) and трóе ["a threesome"],
ѻ҆бóи (m. & f.), ѻ҆бóѧ (n.) and ѻ҆бóе ["both"],
четверы̀, патеры̀, шестеры̀ are for all genders.

The plural collective numerals двóи, двóѧ, трóи, трóѧ, ѻ҆бóи, ѻ҆бóѧ had also forms for the singular in Old Church Slavonic: двои(й), двоꙗ, двок, трои(й), троꙗ, трок, обои, обоꙗ, обок, which had forms of the oblique cases in the singular: двокго, двокмоу, and so forth, e.g.: кдино отъ двокго прѣдложимь вамь (*Suprasl' MS.*,

53—"We offer you one of two things"). From these forms only
двоѐ, троѐ, обоѐ survived, and came to be parallel to the plural
forms, with only this difference, that the plural forms seem to be used
with nouns having no singular.

The numerals двоѐ, троѐ acquired the sense of the plural, and
nouns are used with them in the genitive plural. The numerals двои,
двоѧ, трои, троѧ agree with their nouns [in gender and case]. Their
oblique cases are in common; they are declined as plurals.

Examples: а́зъ да́мъ тебѣ̀ сребренникѡвъ де́сѧть въ го́дъ, и̇
двои ри́зы (Judges 17:10—"I will give thee ten pieces of silver a year,
and a pair of garments"); ѿ восто́ка врата̀ тро́ѧ (Rev., 21:13—"on the
east, three gates"); съ ни́мъ двоѐ осля́тъ съ бре́мены (Judges
19:10—"and there were with him two asses, saddled"); двоѐ прошꙋ̀ ѹ҆
тебѐ (Prov. 30:7—"Two things I have required of thee"); то́й ѹ҆би̇
двои́хъ (I Chronicles 11:22—"he slew two [lionlike] men"); троѐ а́зъ
наведꙋ̀ на тѧ̀ (II Kings [II Samuel} 24:12—"I will bring [one of] three
things down upon thee"); двоѧ̑ сїѧ̑ слы́шахъ (Ps. 61 [62]:12—"I have
heard these two things").

The collective numeral обоѐ has the sense of the singular.
Forms of this numeral in the singular (e.g. обо́егѡ по́лꙋ) have
remained in use. обои, обоѧ are declined in the plural and agree
with the noun they modify.

Besides having the value of a numeral, обоѐ also means "the
one and the other"; обои--"the ones and the others", i.e. "both".

Examples: ѡ҆ста́вите расти̑ обоѐ кꙋ́пнѡ до жа́твы (Matth.
13:30—"Let both grow together until the harvest"); томꙋ̀ во обое́мъ
зра́цѣ: и̇бо обоѐ є҆стество̀ въ не́мъ є҆сть вои́стиннꙋ (Octoechos:
Tone 8, Saturday at Little Vespers, Theotokion--"[we adore] Him in
both forms: for both natures are truly present in Him"); чꙋ́жде
ма́теремъ дѣ́вство, и̇ стра́нно дѣва́мъ дѣторожде́нїе: на тебѣ̀ бцⷣе
обоѧ̑ ѹ҆стро́ишасѧ (Eirmos, T. 8, Ode 9—"Foreign to mothers is

virginity, and strange to virgins is childbearing: in thee, O Theotokos, both have found their place"); ѿ ѻбои́хъ сынѡ́въ є҆ѧ̀ (Ruth 1:5—"[bereft] of her two sons"); на ѻбои́хъ кра́ехъ є҆гѡ̀ (Exodus 26:19--"[two sockets to one post] on both its sides"); кла́тва да бꙋ́детъ бж҃їѧ междꙋ̀ ѻбои́ми (Ex. 22:11—"an oath of God shall be between them both"); сотвори́вый ѻбоѧ̀ є҆ди́но (Ephesians 2:14—"who hath made both one"); ѻбоѝ во є҆ди́номъ дꙋ́сѣ (Eph. 2:18—"we both [have access] by one Spirit").

The collective numerals четверы̀, патеры̀ and the like are declined as plurals and agree with their nouns in all cases: патеры̀ ри́зы (Gen. 45:22—"five changes of raiment"); патеры́хъ ри́зъ and so on.

§70. Multiple and Fractional Numerals.

Multiple and fractional numerals usually consist of the cardinal or ordinal numbers and the words кра́тъ ["times"] and ча́сть ["part"].

Multiples: пѧ́ть кра́тъ [five times], ше́сть кра́тъ [six times]; є҆диннокра́тный [single, unique, that which took place only once], двократный [twofold], троекра́тный [threefold, triple], пѧтикра́тный [five-fold] and so on; "doubled" and "tripled" can also be expressed by сꙋгꙋ́бый, трегꙋ́бый.

Fractions: є҆ди́на ча́сть [one part], двѣ̀ ча́сти [two parts], трѝ ча́сти [three parts]; пе́рваѧ ча́сть [first part], втора́ѧ ча́сть [second part], деса́таѧ ча́сть [tenth part], and so on; and also по́лъ [half], че́тверть [quarter], деса́тина [a tenth].

In short multiple numbers only the figure itself is declined, while the word кра́тъ remains unchanged: се́дмь кра́тъ, седми́ кра́тъ: however, the entire expression can be used, as it appears, without change: не глаго́лю тебѣ̀, до се́дмь кра́тъ, но до се́дмьдесѧтъ кра́тъ седмери́цею (Matth. 18:22—"I say not unto thee, Until seven times: but, Until seventy times seven"). Short numerals with adjectival endings are declined on the model of adjectives.

In fractional numbers, the figure is declined along with "ча́сть", while по́лъ, че́тверть, десяти́на decline as nouns.

Examples: десяти́нꙋ даю̀ всегѡ̀, є҆ли́кѡ притяжꙋ̀ (Luke 18:12—"I give tithes of all that I possess"); деся́тꙋю ча́сть є҆фі̀ [мѣ́ры], вмѣ́шены въ є҆ле́й четве́ртыѧ ча́сти и́на [мѣ́ры] (Numbers 15:4—"A tenth part of an ephah [a measure], mingled with oil, even with the fourth part of a hin [a measure]").

Texts for Practice.

1) Ше́дъ же прїе́мый пѧ́ть тала́нтъ, дѣ́ла въ ни́хъ, и҆ сотвори́ дрꙋга̑ѧ пѧ́ть тала́нтъ. Та́кожде и҆ и́же два̀, прїѡбрѣ́те и҆ то́й дрꙋга̑ѧ два̀. 2) Тогда̀ оу҆подо́бися ца́рствїе нбⷭ҇ное десѧти́мъ дѣ́вамъ... Пѧ́ть же ѿ ни́хъ мꙋ́дры, и҆ пѧ́ть ю҆ро́дивы. 3) Двѣ̀ ме́люще въ же́рновахъ: є҆ди́на пое́млетсѧ, и҆ є҆ди́на ѡ҆ставлѧ́етсѧ. 4) Не оу҆́ ли разꙋмѣ́ете, ниже́ по́мните пѧ́ть хлѣ́бы пѧти́мъ ты́сѧщамъ, и҆ коли́кѡ кѡ́шъ взѧ́сте; Ни ли се́дмь хлѣ́бы четы́ремъ ты́сѧщамъ, и҆ коли́кѡ ко́шницъ взѧ́сте; 5) И҆ прїе́мъ пѧ́ть хлѣ́бъ и҆ двѣ̀ ры̑бѣ, воззрѣ́въ на нбо бл҃гослови́. 6) По двоюна́десѧти мⷭ҇ѧцѣхъ въ домꙋ̀ ца́рства своегѡ̀, въ вавꙋлѡ́нѣ бѣ̀ хода̀, ѿвѣща̀ ца́рь, и҆ рече́: нѣ́сть ли се́й вавꙋлѡ́нъ вели́кїй... 7) А҆ми́нь глаго́лю ва́мъ, ꙗ҆́кѡ вы̀ ше́дшїи по мнѣ̀, въ пакибытїѐ, є҆гда̀ сѧ́детъ сн҃ъ чл҃вѣ́ческїй на престо́лѣ сла́вы своеѧ̀, сѧ́дете и҆ вы̀ на двоюна́десѧте престѡ́лъ, сꙋдѧ́ще ѻ҆бѣмана́десѧте колѣ́нома і҆и҃левома. 8) И҆ ꙗ҆́же къ мо́рю четы́ре ты́сѧщи и҆ пѧ́ть сѡ́тъ мѣ́рою: врата̀ тро́ѧ, врата̀ є҆ди́на га́дова: и҆ врата̀ а҆си́рова: и҆ врата̀ нефѳали́мова є҆ди́на. Ѡ҆крꙋ́глость же ѻ҆смина́десѧти ты́сѧщъ: и҆́мѧ же гра́дꙋ, ѿ негѡ́же днѐ бꙋ́детъ, гдⷭ҇ь та́мѡ, бꙋ́детъ и҆́мѧ є҆мꙋ̀. 9) И҆ число̀ вѡ́инѡвъ ко́нныхъ двѣ̀ тьмѣ̀ те́мъ: и҆ слы́шахъ число̀ и́хъ. 10) И҆ напо́лнисѧ хра́мъ ды́ма ѿ сла́вы бж҃їѧ и҆ ѿ си́лы є҆гѡ̀: и҆ никто́же можа́ше вни́ти во хра́мъ, до́ндеже сконча́ютсѧ се́дмь ꙗ҆́звъ седми́хъ а҆́гг҃лъ. 11) И҆ слы́шахъ гла́съ ве́лїй ѿ хра́ма глаго́лющъ седми́мъ а҆́гг҃лѡмъ.

12) И҆ бы́сть въ четыредеся́тное и҆ въ четвертосо́тное лѣ́то и҆схо́да сынѡ́въ і҆сра́илевыхъ и҆з̾ є҆гѵ́пта, въ лѣ́то четве́ртое, въ мѣ́сяцъ вторы́й, ца́рствꙋющꙋ царю̀ соломѡ́нꙋ над̾ і҆сра́илемъ, и҆ созда̀ хра́мъ гдⷭ҇еви. 13) Въ лѣ́то седмоенадеся́ть факе́а сы́на ромелі́инна, воцари́ся а҆ха́зъ сы́нъ і҆ѡа҆д҄а́ма царя̀ і҆ꙋ́дина. 14) И҆ да бꙋ́детъ разстоѧ́нїе гра́дꙋ къ сѣ́верꙋ двꙋ́стꙋ и҆ пѧти́десѧти, и҆ къ ю҆́гꙋ двꙋ́стꙋ и҆ пѧти́десѧти... 15) И҆ въ лѣ́то сто̀ шестьдеся́тое взы́де а҆леѯа́ндръ сы́нъ а҆нтїо́ховъ є҆пїфа́нъ, и҆ ѡ҆держа̀ птолемаі́дꙋ, и҆ прїѧ́ша є҆го̀, и҆ ца́рствова та́мѡ.

Key:

1) [Matth. 25:16-17]: The he that had received the five talents went and traded with them, and made other five talents. And likewise he that had received two, he also gained other two. 2) [Matth. 25:1-2]: Then shall the kingdom of heaven be likened unto ten virgins... And five of them were wise, and five foolish. 3) [Matth. 24:41]: Two women shall be grinding at the mill; the one shall be taken, and the other left. 4) [Matth. 16;9-10]: Do ye not yet understand, neither remember the five loaves of the five thousand, and how many baskets ye took up? Neither the seven loaves of the four thousand, and how many baskets ye took up? 5) [Mark 6:41]: And when he had taken the five loaves and two fishes, he looked up to heaven, and blessed. 6) [Dan. 4:29-30]: At the end of twelve months he walked in his palace of the kingdom of Babylon. The king spake, and said: Is not this the great Babylon... 7) [Matth. 19:28]: Verily I say unto you, That ye which have followed me, in the regeneration when the Son of man shall sit in the throne of his glory, ye also shall sit upon twelve thrones, judging the twelve tribes of Israel. 8) [Ezek. 48:34-35]: And towards the sea four thousand and five hundred, with their three gates: one gate of Gad, one gate of Asher, one gate of Naphtali. It was round about eighteen thousnd measures: and the name of the city from that day shall be, The Lord is there. 9) [Rev. 9:16]: And the number of the army of the horsemen was two hundred thousand thousand: and I heard the number of them. 10) [Rev. 15:8]: And the

temple was filled with smoke from the glory of God, and from his power; and no man was able to enter into the temple, till the seven plagues of the seven angels were fulfilled. 11) [Rev. 16:1]: And I heard a great voice out of the temple speaking to the seven angels. 12) [III Kings 6:1]: And it came to pass in the four hundred and fortieth year after the children of Israel were come out of Egypt, in the fourth year and the second month of the rule of King Solomon over Israel, that he built the temple of the Lord. 13) [IV Kings 16:1]: In the seventeenth year of Phakee son of Romelias, began Achaz the son of Joatham king of Juda to reign. 14) [Ezek. 48:17]: And there shall be a space to the city northward two hundred and fifty, and southward two hundred and fifty... 15) [I Maccabees 10:1]: In the hundred and sixtieth year Alexander, the son of Antiochus *surnamed* Epiphanes, went up and took Ptolemais: for the people had received him, by means whereof he reigned there.[1]

VERBS.

§71. The Verb in General.

Verbs are what we call words that express some action or state of being. Examples: є҆́же ѹ҆́бо бг҃ъ сочета̀, чл҃вѣ́къ да не разлꙋча́етъ (Mark 10:9:—"What God *hath joined together*, let not man *put asunder*"). Воздрема́ша вси̑, и҆ спа́хꙋ (Matth. 25:5—"They all slumbered and slept").

The basic, initial form of a verb is known as the *infinitive mood:* твори́ти [to make], писа́ти [to write], and so on. In this respect the infinitive has the same relation to all the other forms of the verb as the nominative case of a noun does to the other cases.

---

[1]) *literally:* And they received him, and he reigned there.

The inifinitive ending ⸗ти is joined to the stem of the verb either directly or by means of suffixes. In the first case a verb is known as *primitive,* in the second case it is known as *derivative.*

Primitive verbs whose stem ends in г, к have the infinitive ending -щи (from г, к + т = щ, --see §12, *b*): мог⸗ти = мощѝ, пек⸗ти = пещѝ.

Derivative verbs make use of the following suffixes to form their infinitives:

⸗а⸗	плáк⸗а⸗ти[to weep]	⸗ва⸗	оу̑мы⸗вá⸗ти[to wash]
⸗а̑⸗	да⸗а̑⸗ти[to give]	⸗ева⸗	врач⸗евá⸗ти[to heal]
⸗ѣ⸗	бол⸗ѣ̑⸗ти[to be sick]	⸗ова⸗	бесѣ́д⸗ова⸗ти [to talk, converse]
⸗и⸗	хвал⸗и́⸗ти[to praise]	⸗нва⸗	сдéрж⸗нва⸗ти [to restrain]
⸗нꙋ⸗	гнв⸗нꙋ⸗ти[to perish]	⸗ыва⸗	спѝс⸗ыва⸗ти [to copy]

Verbs have certain states or categories: voice, aspect, mood, tense, person, number and, in some cases gender (in the dual number).

The changes a verb undergoes according to mood, tense, number and person are called its *conjugation.*

Besides conjugation forms, verbs also have participles, which while expressing the categories of aspect, voice and tense, which are signs of a verb, at the same time have characteristics of adjectives and like them change according to case and gender.

The infinitive is an unchanging form of the verb.

The congjugated forms of a verb in a sentence constitute the predicate.

All verbal forms have the syntactical ability to govern (with or without a preposition) the cases of nouns, e.g. благовѣ́стихъ слóвомъ, благовѣ́стивый слóвомъ ("I evangelized by word"; "having evangelized by word"); and to be modified by adverbs: дóбрѣ благовѣ́стихъ, дóбрѣ благовѣ́стивый ("I have evangelized well"; "having evangelized well").

Verbal forms can add the preposition ⸗ся to their usual endings, and in that case they are called *reflexive*[1] : моли́тися [to pray--cf. Lat. *precor*, Gk. εὔχομαι "I pray"], прибли́житися [to draw near--cf. Fr. *s'approcher de*, "to near oneself to..."], прибли́жвыйся [having drawn nigh], and so on.

The preposition -ся in verb forms, although it is a component part of the word, nevertheless in Church Slavonic is still felt to be to some extent an independent word: this is shown by the fact that between the verb and -ся other words can be inserted: the pronouns ми, ти or the conjunction же: мо́лимтися (or мо́лим ти ся [we pray Thee]), кла́няемтися [we worship Thee], поклони́шижеся ["but thou wilt adore"]; and also two reflexive verbs can sometimes share a single -ся: возвесели́тижеся и возра́довати подоба́ше (Luke 15:32—"It was meet that we should make merry and be glad"); да не смуща́ется се́рдце ва́ше, ни ѹстраша́етъ (John 14:27—"Let not your heart be troubled, neither let it be afraid").

Sometimes the -ся precedes its verb, and is attached to the preceding word: ра́венся творя̀ бгу (John 5:18—"making himself equal with God"); и ми́лися дѣемъ (Eucharistic Anaphora of St. John Chrysostom—"and we implore Thee"), but also: тебѣ̀ ми́ли дѣемся (Matins, 11th Prayer of Light).

§72. Transitive and Intransitive Verbs.

All verbs, based on their sense, are divided into two groups: transitive and intransitive. *Transitive* verbs are those that express the action of someone or something that affects another (its object), and the object is then put in the accusative case without a preposition: ю́ноша чте́тъ кни́гу (the youth reads a book), наста́вникъ глаго́лаше

---

[1]) The term "**reflexive verb**" should not be confused with the term "verb of the medio-passive mood". [In Russian the terms are "возвратный глаголъ" versus "глаголъ возвратнаго залога"--*Tr.*]

поꙋченїе (the teacher gave a lecture, lesson) and so on. The object of a transitive verb is called the *direct object*.

The *intransitive* verbs are those that either call for no object at all, or else that take an object in some oblique case (with or without a preposition), but not in the accusative case without a preposition: и́ти [to go], стоѧ́ти [to stand], оу҆гожда́ти царю̀ [to seek favor with the king], and so on.

Intransitive verbs include those expressing movement or position in space, as well as a physical or moral state, such as: ходи́ти [to go], плы́ти [travel by water], стоѧ́ти [to stand], бѣжа́ти [to flee], болѣ́ти [to be ill], дыша́ти [to breathe], молча́ти [to be silent] and so forth.

A mark of transitive verbs is the suffix _и_: жи́_ти [to live], жи_ви́_ти [to enliven, bring to life]; жена̀ [wife], жен_и́_ти [to give someone a wife]; мр_е́_ти [to die], мор_и́_ти [mortify, deaden] and so on.

A mark of intransitive verbs is the suffix _ѣ_ (or _а_ after the "hushing" sibilants) or _нꙋ_, whereas in the corresponding transitive verbs (when their formation is possible) this suffix corresponds to _и_: богат_ѣ_ти, богат_и́_ти [to grow rich, to make someone else rich]; ѡ҆слаб_ѣ_ти, ѡ҆сла́_и_ти [to grow weak, to cause to weaken]; бѣл_ѣ_ти, бѣл_и́_ти [to become white, to whiten something]; дрож_а́_ти [to tremble]; молч_а́_ти [to be silent]; глох_нꙋ_ти, глꙋш_и́_ти [to grow deaf, to deafen, muffle]; сох_нꙋ_ти, сꙋш_и́_ти [to become dry, to dry something out]; вѧ_нꙋ_ти, оу҆вѧд_и́_ти [to wilt, to cause to wither].

Note: The suffix _нꙋ_ signifying transitiveness should not be confused with the suffix _нꙋ_ in verbs showing an action occurring only once: ки́_нꙋ_ти [to fling *(a single action)*], дви́_нꙋ_ти [to move *(once)*].

In some cases, verbs verbs can be either transitive or intransitive, depending on their meaning: e. g. Пои́мъ пѣснь но́вꙋю бг҃у (Eirmos, T. 1:—"Let us sing a new song to God"); here поимz is a transitive verb; пою бг҃у моемꙋ (Ps. 145:2—"I will sing to my God"); here пою is intransitive.

Intransitive verbs (except for those with the suffixes _ѣ_ and _нꙋ_) can become transitive by taking a prefix: Ра́дꙋйса, ꙗкω многосвѣ́тлое возсїавла́ешн просвѣще́нїе (Akathistos Hymn to the Theotokos, Oikos 11—"Rejoice, for thou makest illumination of great brightness to shine!"); лꙋчезáрнаѧ твоѧ̂ мώлнїѧ возсїáй мн, бж҃е мóй, трϊѵпостáсне вседѣ́телю, (Sunday Mesonycticon, Trinitarian Hymns—"Thy resplendent lightnings do Thou shine upon me, O my God, Who in Three Persons art the Creator of All"); прозабáлй травꙋ скотώмz (Ps. 103:14—"Bringing forth grass for cattle"); истáала мѧ̀ е҆́сть ре́вность твоѧ̀ (Ps. 118:139—"Zeal for Thee hath made me pine away").

§73. Voices of the Verb.

Depending on the ability of verbs to take objects, and on the character of the objects taken, verbs are divided into special categories known as *voices*.

The voices of verbs can be the following: active, passive, reflexive, reciprocal and middle.

1) The active voice expresses action that passes on to another object; consequently, all transitive verbs belong to the active voice: ѹ҆чени́кz чте́тz кни́гꙋ [the student reads a book], по́варz сотвори̇ ꙗ҆́стїе [the cook made food], вѣ́ра спасáетz человѣ́ка [faith saves a man].

2) The passive voice expresses action opposite to that of the active voice, that is, with the passive voice the recipient of the action is in the nominative case, and the one who does the action is in the genitive case with the preposition ѿ (especially if the source of the action is a person) or else in the instrumental case: кни́га чте́тсѧ ѿ ѹ҆чени́ка [the book is read by the student], ꙗ҆́стїе сотворе́но е҆́сть ѿ повара [the food was made by the cook], хрїстїаннн спасаетса ѿ вѣры (or вѣрою) [a Christian is saved by faith].

The passive voice can be expressed two ways: either by adding the reflexive pronoun са to the active voice of the verb, or else by a compound form, consisting of the passive participle and a copula: спасаетса or спасаемъ есть [he is saved]; спасется or спасенъ будетъ [he will be saved].

Examples: вѣрою мѡѵсей родивса сокровенъ бысть три мѣсацы ѿ Отецъ своихъ (Heb. 11:23—"By faith Moses, when he was born, was hid three months of his parents"); ѡправдаеми туне благодатїю его (Rom. 3:24—"Being justified freely by his grace"); Мыслимъ оубо вѣрою ѡправдитиса человѣку (Rom. 3:28 —"Therefore we conclude that a man is justified by faith"); имже держими вѣхомъ (Rom. 7:6—"wherein we were held"); сердцемъ бо вѣруетса въ правду, оусты же исповѣдуетса во спасенїе (Rom. 10:10—"For with the heart man believeth unto righteousness, and with the mouth confession ismade unto salvation"); Авраамъ, Отецъ нашъ не ѿ дѣлъ ли ѡправдаса (James 2:21—"Was not Abraham our father justified by works?"); ѿ стагѡ дха просвѣщаеми (II Peter 1: 21—"as they were enlightened by the Holy Ghost").

3) To the *reflexive* voice belong transitive verbs to which the reflexive pronoun -са has been added. These verbs show the action as returning to the originator, and concentrated in him, e.g. мыти (to wash something or someone), мытиса (to wash oneself); ѡдѣати (to dress someone), ѡдѣатиса (to dress oneself); радовати (cause someone to rejoice), возрадоватиса (to rejoice); возвращати (to return someone, something), возвращатиса (to make one's return, go back). Example: Гдь воцариса, въ лѣпоту ѡблечеса (Prokeimenon for Saturday Vespers [Ps. 92:1]—"The Lord reigneth, He hath clothed Himself in splendor").

The pronoun сѧ used with the reflexive voice has the value of a direct object.

4) The *reciprocal* voice expresses mutual action between two or more subjects. The actual form of the reciprocal voice is reflexive (i.e. with -сѧ), usually derived from transitive verbs, but the -сѧ in this case does not have the role of a direct object: цѣловати [to kiss, greet someone], цѣловатисѧ [to exchange greetings with someone]; брати [to battle someone], братисѧ [to engage in battle *with* someone]; препрѣти [to convince, out-argue, defeat in argument], препиратисѧ [to argue with someone]: Мно́жицею бра́шасѧ со мно́ю ѿ ю́ности моеѧ̀ (Ps. 128:1—"Many a time have they afflicted me from my youth"); со ѕвѣ́ремъ бора́хсѧ во є̓фе́сѣ (I Cor. 15:32—"I have fought with beasts at Ephesus"); пра́хꙋсѧ же междꙋ̀ собо́ю жи́дове (John 6:52—"The Jews therefore strove among themselves"); Ѡзира́хꙋсѧ оу̓̀бо междꙋ̀ собо́ю оу̓ченицы̀ (John 13:22—"Then the disciples looked one upon another").

Some intransitive verbs (without -сѧ) can have the sense of a reciprocal voice; for example: бесѣ́довати [to converse, *i.e.* with someone]; и̓ совѣ́това съ людьми́ (II Chronicles 20:21—"And he consulted with the people").

5) To the *middle* voice belong all intransitive verbs, with or without -сѧ, for example: ходи́ти [to walk, go], спа́ти [to sleep], свѣти́тисѧ [to shine]. Verbs that are not used without -сѧ should also be assigned to the middle voice, for example: смѣ́ѧтисѧ [to laugh], боѧ́тисѧ [to be afraid], надѣ́ѧтисѧ [to hope], &c., and also the verbs сжа́лити си̑ [to take pity], стꙋжа́ти си̑ [to be discouraged], жа́лити си̑ [to be displeased], which are used only with the reflexive pronoun си̑ instead of _сѧ: сжа́лиша си̑ ѕѣлѡ̀ (Matth. 18:31--"they were very sorry"); не стꙋжа́ти [си̑], (Luke 18:1—"[men ought always to pray] and not to faint"); не стꙋжа́ти си̑ въ ско́рбехъ мои́хъ (Eph. 3:13—"[I desire that ye] faint not at my tribulations"); жа́лаше си̑ (Acts 4: 2—"Being grieved [that they taught the people]").

§74. Aspects of the Verb.

Verbs in Church Slavonic, as in Russian, differ according to aspect.

Verbs that represent their action as being in progress, are called verbs of the *imperfective aspect;* for example: пнса́ти: пишꙋ̀, пнса́хъ: твори́ти: творю̀, твори́хъ.

Verbs that emphasize the moment when the action is begun or completed, are called verbs of the *perfective aspect:* for exmple: н дрꙋгі́й ꙋ҆ченнкъ течѐ скорѣ́е петра̀, н прїнде пре́жде ко гробꙋ (John 20:4--"and the other disciple did outrun Peter, and came first to the sepulchre"); in прїнде the moment in which the action was concluded; се н҆зыде сѣѧй сѣѧти (Mark 4:3--"Behold, there went out a sower to sow"); here н҆зыде emphasizes the moment the action was begun.

Verbs of the perfective aspect with the suffix _нꙋ_ express instantaneous action, or action taking place a single time; in these verbs, the start and finish of the action coincide into one point, for example: посѣка́ти [to cut off in general]__ꙋ҆сѣкнꙋ́ти [to cut off on one specific occasion]: Слы́шавъ же н҆рода речѐ, ꙗ҆кω, е҆го́же а҆зъ ꙋ҆сѣкнꙋхъ і҆ѡа́нна, то́й е҆сть (Mark 6:16—"But when Herod heard thereof, he said: It is John, whom I beheaded"); разслабле́ннаѧ ва́шѧ стѧгнꙋхъ (Good Friday, Third Hour—"I made your paralysed ones to walk").

Verbs of the imperfective aspect do not emphasize the presence of this moment, i.e. the completion or the beginning of an action, even though sometimes the context does show an action as having been completed, e.g.: ѿвѣща̀ пїла́тъ: е҆же пнса́хъ, пнса́хъ (John 19:22—"Pilate answered: What I have written, I have written". Cf. in the Russian version: "что я написалъ, то написалъ".) Пнса́хъ ва́мъ въ посла́нїн, не прнмѣшáтнсѧ блꙋднккѡ́мъ (I Cor. 5:9—"I wrote to you in an epistle, not to company with fornicators". Here in the Russian version the aspect is the same: "Я писалъ вамъ въ послАнїи...") The epistle had been written and dispatched: consequently, in this case the action was completed.

From this we can see that the imperfect aspect by no means always signifies an incomplete action; rather, verbs in the imperfect aspect do not emphasize the crowning moment (beginning or end) of the action, but only the fact that it took place.

Perfective verbs have no present tense, but they have a simple future: пишȣ (present tense--"I write"), напишȣ (simple future--"I *will* write").

§75. Verbal Pairs.

Almost all verbs have corresponding, paired forms in the imperfective and perfective aspects.

Verbs of the perfective aspect are formed for the most part by adding prefixes to verbs of the imperfective aspect, e.g. писáти__напислти, ити__прїити, дѣлати__содѣлати, &c.

Imperfective and perfective verbs are also distinguished by opposing suffixes: perfective verbs have _и, _е, _нȣ or lack the suffixes of imperfective verbs--_а, _ѧ, _ва:

родити__раждати: to bear, give birth
погибнȣти__погибáти: to perish
рѣшити__рѣшáти: to resolve
засохнȣти__засыхáти: to become dry
простити__прощáти: to forgive
совлещи__совлекáти: to pull off, uncover
плѣнити__плѣнáти: take captive
влѣзти__влѣзáти: to climb in, aboard
оу́мрети__оу́мирáти: to die
оу́спѣти__оу́спѣвáти: to succeed
бы́ти__бывáти: to be

§76. Imperfective Verbs of Secondary Formation.

From perfective verbs that have been formed with prefixes, imperfective counterparts can be made by adding the suffixes _ываа_ [_ивaа_], _вaа_, _aа_, _ѧа_, and sometimes _ова_ [_ѣва_]. These can be called imperfective verbs of *secondary* formation, for example:

Imperfective	Perfective	Imperfective (2)
писа́ти (to write)	переписа́ти (to copy)	переписы́вати (to be copying over)
"	написа́ти (write down)	написова́ти (be writing down)
молча́ти (be silent)	помолча́ти (keep silent)	помолчева́ти (be keeping silent)

би́ти (to beat), разби́ти (to shatter) разбива́ти (to keep shattering)
грѣ́ти (to warm) согрѣ́ти (to warm up) согрѣва́ти (be, keep warming up);
грузи́ти (to load, lade) погрузи́ти (to immerse) погружа́ти (keep immersing);
зна́ти (to know) позна́ти (find out) познава́ти (be finding out);
ши́ти (to sew) сши́ти (make a garment) сшива́ти (be making garments).

Such verbs of the second imperfective, depending on how they are used, may express a sense of extended duration or of repeated action, for example: Написова́шеся иногда̀ со ста́рцемъ і҆ѡ́сифомъ (Troparion for Dec. 24—"[And it came to pass that Mary] was enrolled [*i.e.* written down in the census] with the elder Joseph"); сшива́ше ко́жныѧ ри́зы грѣхъ мнѣ̀ (Great Canon of St. Andrew of Crete, Ode 2—"Sin hath sewn for me garments of skin"); человѣ́къ же выразꙋмѣва́ше ю̀: и҆ помолчева́ше, да ѹ҆разꙋмѣ́етъ (Gen. 24:21—"And the man, wondering at her, kept his peace, to wit [whether the Lord had made his journey prosperous or not]").

§77. Definite and Indefinite Forms of the Imperfective.

Several verbs without prefixes, signifying motion, have two forms of the imperfective aspect:

вести_водити [to lead]
ити_ходити [to go]
нести_носити [to carry]
летѣти_летати [to fly]
плыти_плавати [to sail, swim]--and several others.

The first of each set of verbs signifies *definite* action, for example вести or нести something in a specific direction. The second verb of each pair signifies *indefinite* action, for instance водити and носити which express generalized action, without any indication of its direction.

With the addition of a prefix, the imperfective, definite verbs are changed to the perfective aspect [изыти, изыдꙋ: I will go out], while the verbs that show indefinite action remain imperfective [исходити, исхождꙋ: I am going out, *or* I keep going out]: ѿ дней до дней исхождаахꙋ дщери ісраилевы плакати ѡ дщери іефѳаа галаадітина четыри дни въ лѣтѣ (Judges 11:40—"The daughters of Israel went yearly to lament the daughter of Jephthah the Gileadite four days in a year").

§78. Moods and Tenses.

Mood is what we call the grammatical category that expresses the relationship of the verb's action to reality.

In Church Slavonic, there are five different moods: the infinitive, the indicative, the subjunctive, the imperative and the optative.

The *infinitive* mood is the abstract form of the verb, and merely signifies action irrespective of circumstances: творити, писати: to make, to write.

The *indicative* mood shows the action as fully real: it indicates it as taking place in a specific time frame (present, past or future), or by means of the negative particles не, ни it denies it: Хождаста родителѧ єго̀ на всѧко лѣто во іерꙋсалймъ (Luke 2:41—"[Now] his parents went to Jerusalem every year").

The *subjunctive* mood expresses proposed action or action that is conditioned by various circumstances, showing in some cases the action as potential, in others as unreal: а̑ще бысте вѣровали мѡѵсеови, вѣровали бысте ꙋбо и мнѣ (John 5:46—"For had ye believed Moses, ye would have believed me").

The *imperative* mood expresses the will of the speaker, who requests, commands or urges that something be done: Потщи́сѧ себѐ искꙋсна поста́вити преⷣ бгомъ (II Tim. 2:15—"Study to shew thyself approved unto God").

The *optative* mood expresses a desire, intention or goal of the person speaking: Да и̑сповѣдаатсѧ гдⷭ҇еви мйлости єго̀ (Ps. 106:15—"Let the mercies of the Lord give glory unto him").

The indicative mood has the following tenses:
1) The present tense.

2) Future tenses:
    simple (perfective aspect),
    compound (imperfective aspect).

3) Past tenses:
    the aorist,
    the imperfect (transient),
    the perfect (past perfect),
    pluperfect (remote past).

The Conjugation of Verbs.
§79. General Information.

Verb forms are built from two stems: the infinitive stem and the stem of the present tense. We find the infinitive stem by dropping the ending -ти: for example, дѣла-ти, люби́-ти, нес-тѝ --here the infinitive stems are дѣла-, люби́-, нес-[to do, to love, to bear]. We obtain the stem of the present by taking the 3rd person plural of the present tense [*i.e.* "they do, they love, they bear"] and dropping the 3rd person ending -ꙋтъ [-ютъ] or -атъ [-атъ], and if the endings -ютъ, -атъ follow a vowel, then the y-glide [j] which is part of the letters ю and ѧ, must be taken as part of the stem: for example-- дѣлаj-ꙋтъ, люб'-атъ[1], несꙋ̆тъ give as the stem of the present: дѣлаj-, лю́б'-, нес-.

Note: The infinitive stem and the present stem may coincide, for example: нес-тѝ and нес-ꙋтъ.

The infinitive stem serves as the base for building the forms of the past tenses and past participles; the present stem is the base for the present forms (including the simple future), for the imperative and the present participles.

§80. The Main Conjugations of Verbs.

Based on how they build the forms of the present tense (and simple future) and those based on them, verbs are divided into two conjugations: the *first conjugation*, which has the connecting vowel -е- before the personal endings (except the 1st person singular and 3rd person plural): for example, писа́-ти, пи́ш-е-шн, and the *second conjugation*, which has the connecting vowel -и- before the person endings, e.g. ходи́-ти, хо́д-и-шн.

---

[1] The apostrophe (') is used here to show softness of the preceding consonant.

The verbs of the 1st conjugation are subdivided into two groups:

a) *1st-conjugation unsoftened [non-iotated]:* Verbs whose stem in the 1st person singular and 3rd person plural ends in a hard consonant:

нес-ꙋ, нес-ꙋтъ [carry, bear],
вед-ꙋ, вед-ꙋтъ [lead],
тек-ꙋ, тек-ꙋтъ [run],
мог-ꙋ, мо́г-ꙋтъ [may, can],
двигн-ꙋ, двигн-ꙋтъ [move].

b) *1st-conjugation softened [iotated]:* Verbs, all of whose forms show -j- at the end of the stem; and if the -j- follows a consonant, as a result of this iotation there is an alternation of consonants [see §11]; in this alternation, the -j- is absorbed by the "hushing" sibilants:

писа́-ти, пиш-ꙋ (from* писj-ꙋ), пи́ш-ешн [to write];
пла́ка-ти, пла́ч-ꙋ (from *пла́кj-ꙋ), пла́ч-ешн [to weep];
глаго́ла-ти, глаго́л-ю (from *глаго́лj-ꙋ), глаго́л-ешн [to speak, say];
игра́-ти, игра́-ю (from *игра́j-ꙋ), игра́-ешн [to play];
дѣла-ти, дѣла-ю (from *дѣлаj-ꙋ), дѣла-ешн [to make, do].

In the 2nd conjugation, -j- always appears at the end of the 1st person singular present stem, resulting in the alternation of consonants:

носи́-ти, нош-ꙋ (from *носj-ꙋ), but но́с-ишн [carry, bear];
люби́-ти, любл-ю (from *любj-ꙋ), but лю́б-ишн [to love];
сꙋди́-ти, сꙋжд-ꙋ (from *сꙋдj-ꙋ), but сꙋд-ишн [to judge]

Person Endings of the Present Tense:

	1st Conjugation:	2nd Conjugation:
	Singular.	
1st Person ["I"]	_ȣ [ю]	_ȣ [ю]
2nd Person ["thou"]	_ѥ_ши	_и_ши
3rd Person ["he"]	_ѥ_тъ	_и_тъ
	Dual.	
1st ["we twain"]	_ѥ_ва[_вѣ]	_и_ва[_вѣ]
2nd ["ye twain"]	_ѥ_та[_тѣ]	_и_та[_тѣ]
3rd ["those twain"]	_ѥ_та[_тѣ]	_и_та [_тѣ]
	Plural.	
1st ["we"]	_ѥ_мъ	_и_мъ
2nd ["ye"]	_ѥ_те	_и_те
3rd ["they"]	_ȣтъ [_ютъ]	_атъ [_лтъ]

The 1st and 2nd conjugations have also this further distinction between them:

The 3rd person plural of the 1st conjugation has the ending _ȣтъ [ютъ], while the 3rd person plural of the 2nd conjugation has the ending _атъ [_лтъ].

Note: The characteristics given above are not always enough to determine precisely which conjugation a given verb may belong to, since the connecting vowels и and ѥ, when unstressed, are of unclear pronunciation; but the *infinitive stem* permits one to distinguish more exactly:

a) To the 2nd conjugation belong all verbs whose stem ends in:

1) и_ти: ходи́_ти, хо́ди_ши (but primitives [underived prototypal verbs] belong to the 1st conjugation: би́_ти, бї́е_ши).

2) ѣ_ти, if the ѣ drops out in the present tense: видѣ_ти, ви́жд_ȣ, ви́ди_ши [to see], (but красиѣ_ти [to blush, turn red],

красни́ѣ_ю, as well as primitives [пѣ_ти, to sing] belong to the 1st conjugation).

3) а_ти, when preceded by a "hushing" sibilant, if the а drops out in the present tense: стꙋча́_ти, стꙋчи́_ши [to strike]; (but велича́_ти, велича́_ю, велича́_еши [magnify, praise the greatness of] as well as primitives [жа́_ти, harvest] belong to the 1st conjugation).

Also of the 2nd conjugation are сто_а́_ти [stand] and бо_а́_тиса [fear].

b) All remaining verbs belong to the 1st conjugation; only a few depart from this rule and show some forms according to the 1st conjugation and other forms according to the 2nd. Such verbs are called "verbs of mixed conjugation".

The person endings of the dual number change by gender: _ва [1st person] and _та [2nd and 3rd person] are used for the masculine, while _вѣ, _тѣ are used for the feminine and neuter; however, the neuter can also take the same endings as the masculine. These endings have the same meaning in the present tense and in the past tenses (aorist and imperfect). Examples: Ѳавѡ́рх и е҆рмѡ́нх ѡ и́мени твое́мх возра́дꙋетаса (present tense—Ps. 88:13—"Thabor and Hermon shall rejoice in Thy name"); ꙗ҆кѡ ви́дѣстѣ [_та] о҆чи мои (Luke 2:30—"for mine eyes have seen": aorist); е҆гда́ же и҆да́сте [aorist] возвѣсти́ти ѹ҆ченикѡ́мх е҆гѡ̀, и се і҆и́сх срѣ́те ꙗ҆ глаго́ла: ра́дꙋйтеса. О҆нѣ же пристꙋпльше, ꙗ҆стеса [aorist] за но́зѣ е҆гѡ̀, и поклони́стеса [aorist] е҆мꙋ̀ (Matth. 28:9— "And as they went to tell His disciples, behold, Jesus met them, saying: Hail. And they, coming up, took hold of His feet, and adored Him").

§81. Verbs of the Archaic Conjugation.

Besides the main conjugations of verbs, there are several verbs belonging to the *archaic* conjugation. In the case of these verbs, the person endings are joined directly to the stem, without a connecting vowel. These verbs are the following: бы́_ти [to be], да́_ти [to give], ꙗс_ти [to eat], вѣ́дѣ_ти [to know], има́_ти [to have].

The verb бы́ти is used extensively, as it has the role of an auxiliary verb in forming the compound verbal tenses.

Conjugation of the Auxiliary Verb бы́ти, "To Be".

Indicative Mood.
Singular.

	Present.	Simple Future.	Compound Future.
1st Person:	є҆смь	бу́ду	хощу́ бы́ти
2nd Person:	є҆си	бу́деши	хо́щеши бы́ти
3rd Person:	є҆сть	бу́детъ	хо́щетъ бы́ти

Dual.

1st Person:	є҆сва, _ѣ	бу́дева, _ѣ	хо́щева, _ѣ бы́ти
2nd Person:	є҆ста, _ѣ	бу́дета, _ѣ	хо́щета, _ѣ бы́ти
3rd Person:	є҆ста, _ѣ	бу́дета, _ѣ	хо́щета, _ѣ бы́ти

Plural.

	Present	Simple Future	Compound Future
1st Person	є҆смы̀	бу́демъ	хо́щемъ бы́ти
2nd Person	є҆стѐ	бу́дете	хо́щете бы́ти
3rd Person	су́ть	бу́дутъ	хота́тъ бы́ти

Indicative Mood
Singular

	Aorist		Imperfect
	Imperfective (Transient)	Perfective	
1st Person	бы́хъ	бѣ́хъ	ба́хъ
2nd Person	бы́сть [бы̀]	бѣ̀	ба́ше
3rd Person	бы́сть [бы̀]	бѣ̀	ба́ше

Dual.

1st Person	БЫ́ХОВА, -ѣ	БѢ́ХОВА, -ѣ	БА́ХОВА, -ѣ
2nd Person	БЫ́СТА, -ѣ	БѢ́СТА, -ѣ	БА́СТА, -ѣ
3rd Person	БЫ́СТА, -ѣ	БѢ́СТА, -ѣ	БА́СТА, -ѣ

Plural.

1st Person	БЫ́ХОМЪ	БѢ́ХОМЪ	БА́ХОМЪ
2nd Person	БЫ́СТЕ	БѢ́СТЕ	БА́СТЕ
3rd Person	БЫ́ША	БѢ́ША	БА́ХУ

Indicative Mood.
Singular.

	Perfect (Action Completed in Past)[1]	Pluperfect (Distant Past)[2]
1st Person	БЫ́ЛЪ, -à, -о ҄ЕСМЬ	БЫ́ЛЪ, -à, -о БѢ́ХЪ [БА́ХЪ]
2nd Person	БЫ́ЛЪ, -à, -о ҄ЕСИ	БЫ́ЛЪ, -à, -о БѢ́
3rd Person	БЫ́ЛЪ, -à, -о ҄ЕСТЬ	БЫ́ЛЪ, -à, -о БѢ́

Dual.

1st Person	БЫ́ЛА, -И ҄ЕСВА, -ѣ	БЫ́ЛА, -И БѢ́ХОВА, -ѣ
2nd Person	БЫ́ЛА, -И ҄ЕСТА, -ѣ	БЫ́ЛА, -И БѢ́СТА, -ѣ
3rd Person	БЫ́ЛА, -И ҄ЕСТА, -ѣ	БЫ́ЛА, -И БѢ́СТА, -ѣ

Plural.

1st Person	БЫ́ЛИ ҄ЕСМЫ	БЫ́ЛИ БѢ́ХОМЪ
2nd Person	БЫ́ЛИ ҄ЕСТѢ	БЫ́ЛИ БѢ́СТЕ
3rd Person	БЫ́ЛИ СУ́ТЬ	БЫ́ЛИ БѢ́ША

---

[1] This is the tense that in English we call "present perfect"-- e.g. *I have been.--Tr.*

[2] Called in English the "past perfect"--e.g. *I had been.--Tr*

Imperative Mood	Subjunctive Mood	Optative Mood
	Singular.	
1st Person	бы́лъ, _а, _о бы́хъ	да бꙋ́дꙋ
2nd Person бꙋ́ди	бы́лъ, _а, _о бы̀	да бꙋ́дєши
3rd Person бꙋ́ди	бы́лъ, _а, _о бы̀	да бꙋ́детъ
	Dual.	
1st Person бꙋ́дива, _ѣ	бы́ла, _и бы́хова, _ѣ	да бꙋ́дева, _ѣ
2nd Person бꙋ́дита, _ѣ	бы́ла, _и бы́ста, _ѣ	да бꙋ́дета, _ѣ
3rd Person	бы́ла, _и бы́ста, _ѣ	да бꙋ́дета, _ѣ
	Plural.	
1st Person бꙋ́демъ	бы́ли бы́хомъ	да бꙋ́демъ
2nd Person бꙋ́дите	бы́ли бы́сте	да бꙋ́дете
3rd Person	бы́ли бы́ша	да бꙋ́дꙋтъ

Infinitive Mood: бы́ти.

Participles:

Present	Past
Short: сы́й[1], сꙋщи, сꙋще	Short: бы́въ, бы́вши, бы́вше
Full: сы́й, сꙋщаѧ, сꙋщее	Full: бы́вый, бы́вшаѧ, бы́вшее

Past in _лъ (not declined):

бы́лъ, былà, бы́ло.

Notes on the Conjugation Tables for бы́ти.

The 1st person dual for the present tense has also another ending in _ма [_мѣ], and it may have displaced the form in _ва [_вѣ], e.g. а́зъ и ѻ́цъ є҆ди́но є҆смà (John 10:30—"I and the Father are One"); мꙋ́жїе,

---

[1]) The short form сы̀ is no longer used in New Church Slavonic.

чтò сïѧ творитè; и мы̀ подобострáстна є҆смà вáмъ человѣ́ка (Acts 14:15—"Ye men, why do ye these things? We also are men of like passions with you").

If the forms of the present tense are negated by the particle не, it is merged with them, giving the elided forms нѣ́смь [I am not], нѣ́си [thou art not], нѣ́сть [he is not], &c. However, the 3rd person plural is not elided: не сꙋ́ть [they are not].

The forms є҆си̑, є҆сть, when the follow the interrogative pronouns кто̀, что̀ [who, what] and the adverb гдѣ́ [where] are fairly often enclitic[1], for example: Что́ є҆сть сïè; (Mark 1:27—"What [thing] is this?"); Кто́ є҆сть сéй цр҃ь слáвы; (Ps. 23/24, v. 8—"Who is this King of glory?"); ты̀ кто́ є҆си̑; (John 1:19—"Who art thou?"); гдѣ́ є҆сть ѻ҆би́тель; (Luke 22:11—"Where is the guest chamber?").

The conjugation forms of both бы́хъ nd бѣ́хъ are forms of the aorist, only those of бы́хъ are of the perfective aspect, while those of бѣ́хъ are of the imperfective. The forms for both the 2nd and 3rd person of бы́хъ are бы́сть: бы̀ is used only as a subjunctive. The forms of бы́хъ can have a prefix: пребы́хъ [I remained], пребы́сть, забы́хъ [I forgot, neglected] and so on.

The forms of the imperfect usually occur in the 3rd person: бѧ́ше, бѧ́ста [_тѣ], бѧ́хꙋ and the other forms are little met with if at all[2]. Sometimes forms of the imperfect are encountered with the stem бѣ_: бѣ́ше, бѣ́хꙋ, e.g. и҆ согнꙋ́въ кни́гꙋ, ѿдáвъ слꙋ́зѣ, сѣ́де: и҆ всѣ́мъ въ сóнмнщи ѻ҆́чи бѣ́хꙋ зрѧ́ще нáнь (Luke 4:20—"And he closed the book, and he gave it again to the minister, and sa down. And the eyes of all them that were in the synagogue were fastened on him").

---

[1]) *Enclitic* words are those that lack an accent of their own and are treated as though part of the preceding word.--*Tr.*

[2]) See Horace G. Lunt, *Old Church Slavonic Grammar,* Mouton & Co., The Hague, Netherlands, 1959: 9.6, p. 87.

The Indicative Mood.
§82. Present Indicative.

By comparison with the infinitive, in the stem of the present tense the following changes take place:

1) The final consonant of the stem of primitive verbs, if it had changed before the ending _ти, returns to its original form in the present stem: вес-тѝ (for *вед-ти): вед-ꙋ̀: течѝ (for *тек-ти): тек-ꙋ̀: мощѝ (for *мог-ти): мог-ꙋ̀.

2) If before the _ти there is a ѧ (or а before the "hushing" sibilants) with the value of *yus*[1], then before the endings of the present tense it resolves itself into a vowel and a consonant: ꙗ̃-ти, е̂мл-ю [to take]; клѧ́-ти, клен-ꙋ̀ [to swear]; жа́-ти, жн-ꙋ̀ [to mow, reap].

3) In verbs with the ending _ов-а-ти, _е-ва-ти: _ов_ and _ев_ become ꙋ/ю in the present stem: бесѣ́д-ов-а-ти, бесѣ́дꙋ̀-ю [to discuss, carry on a conversation]; оу̑трен-ев-а-ти, оу̑треню-ю, оу̑треню-еши [rise early, be vigilant].

4) In verbs with the suffix _нꙋ_, н is kept in the present stem: со́хнꙋ-ти, со́хн-ꙋ, со́хн-еши [to become dry].

Note: Some verbs can lack the _нꙋ_ in the infinitive, even though in the present and simple future, they retain the suffix _н_: дѣ́-ти [to do], ста́-ти [to stand], стꙑ́-ти [become cold]: дѣ́-н-ꙋ, ста́-н-ꙋ, стꙑ́-н-ꙋ.

Conjugation of the Present Tense.

нес-тѝ	пнс-а́-ти	люб-и́-ти	вел-ѣ́-ти	сꙋ́дⷣти
[to bear]	[to write]	[to love]	[to command]	
				[to judge]

---

[1]) That is, as opposed to ѧ when it simply stands for а preceded by a *y*-glide (**j**).

Singular.

1st	нес_ꙋ́	пиш_ꙋ́	лю́бл_ю̀	бѣл_ю̀	сꙋ́жд_ꙋ
2nd	нес_е́_ши	пи́ш_е_ши	лю́б_и_ши	бѣл_и́_ши	сꙋ́д_иши
3rd	нес_е́_тъ	пи́ш_е_тъ	лю́б_и_тъ	бѣл_и́_тъ	сꙋ́д_итъ

Dual.

1st	нес_е́_ва, _ѣ	пи́ш_е_ва,_ѣ	лю́б_и_ва,_ѣ	бѣл_и́_ва,_ѣ	сꙋ́д_и_ва, _ѣ
2nd	нес_е́_та,_ѣ	пи́ш_е_та,_ѣ	лю́б_и_та,_ѣ	бѣл_и́_та,_ѣ	сꙋ́д_и_та, _ѣ
3rd	нес_е́_та,_ѣ	пи́ш_е_та,_ѣ	лю́б_и_та,_ѣ	бѣл_и́_та,_ѣ	сꙋ́д_и_та, _ѣ

Plural.

1st	нес_е́_мъ	пи́ш_е_мъ	лю́б_и_мъ	бѣл_и́_мъ	сꙋ́д_и_мъ
2nd	нес_е́_те	пи́ш_е_те	лю́б_и_те	бѣл_и́_те	сꙋ́д_и_те
3rd	нес_ꙋ́тъ	пи́ш_ꙋтъ	лю́б_ятъ	бѣл_я́тъ	сꙋ́д_ятъ

§83. Change of the Final Consonants in the Stem.

The gutturals г and к are softened before the connecting vowel е in the 1st conjugation, and alternate with the "hushing" sibilants ж, ч (see §11): тек_ꙋ́, теч_е́_ши [run]; мог_ꙋ́, мо́ж_еши [can, be able]; лг_ꙋ́, лж_е́ши [lie, speak falsehood] (не лгꙋ̀, "I do not lie"--Gal. 1:20; но лгꙋ́тъ, "but they lie"--Rev. 3:9), while in the simple future the stem is softened: солж_ꙋ̀ "I will [not] lie [unto David]": Ps. 88:36), со́лж_ꙋтъ "[thine enemies] shall lie [to thee]"-- Ps. 65:3).

In the 1st softened conjugation in all forms, and in the 2nd conjugation in the 2nd person, as a result of the softening of the final consonant of the stem (see §80), the following alternations of consonants take place:

a) Labials: б becomes бл, п becomes пл, в becomes вл, м becomes мл:

(1st conjugation)

гнба́_ти [to perish]: гнблю,
  гнблешн

сы́па_ти [to strew, scatter]:
  сы́плю, сы́плешн

дрема́_ти [to doze]:
  дре́млю, дре́млешн

(2nd conjugation)

люби́_ти [to love]: люблю̀,
  лю́бншн

кꙋпи́_ти [to buy]:
  кꙋплю̀, кꙋпншн

лови́_ти [fish for sthg.]: ловлю̀,
  ло́вншн

ломи́_ти [to break ut]: ломлю̀,
  ло́мншн

b) Dentals: д becomes жд, т becomes щ, з becomes ж, с becomes ш:

страда́_ти [to suffer]:
  стражда́ꙋ, стра́ждешн

трепета́_ти [tremble]:
  трепе́щꙋ, трепе́щешн

ма́за_ти [anoint]: ма́жꙋ, ма́жешн

сꙋди́_ти [to judge]:
  сꙋжда́ꙋ, сꙋдншн

свѣти́_ти [to shine]:
  свѣщꙋ, свѣтншн

носи́_ти [to carry]: ношꙋ,
  но́сншн

вози́_ти [convey]:   вожꙋ,
  во́зншн

c) Gutturals: к becomes ч, г becomes ж, х becomes ш:

алка́_ти [to hunger]: а́лчꙋ, а́лчешн

строга́_ти [to plane, bevel]: стрꙋжꙋ, стрꙋжешн

изсыха́_ти [to wither]: изсы́шꙋ, изсы́шетъ (John 15:6—"he shall wither").

In the 2nd conjugation the gutturals in the end of the stem, having been softened into "hushing" sibilants in the infinitive (крнча́ти from *крнкѣ́ти, to shout), retain this softened state in all forms of the present tense, since they are softened both before j and н: крнча́_ти [крнк_], крнчꙋ, крнчншн: лежа́_ти [to lie, recline] from

*ЛЕГ_: ЛЕЖ&, ЛЕЖЙШН: СЛЫША_ТН [to hear, from *СЛЫХ_]: СЛЫШ&, СЛЫ́ШНШН.

    d) In the following combinations: СТ becomes Щ, СК becomes Щ, ЗД becomes ЖД, ЗДН becomes ЖДН, ЗН becomes ЖН, ТВ becomes ЩВЛ, СЛ becomes ШЛ:

1st conjugation:
РНСТА́_ТН [to contend, fight]: РНЩ&, РНЩЕШН
НСКА́_ТН [to seek]: НЩ&, НЩЕШН:

2nd conjugation:
ВОЗВѢСТН́_ТН [to proclaim]: ВОЗВѢЩ&, ВОЗВѢСТНШН
ПРНГВОЗДН́_ТН [to nail, attach by nailing]: ПРНГВОЖД&, ПРНГВОЗДНШН
ОӰПРАЗДНН́_ТН [to abolish]: ОӰПРАЖДНЮ, ОӰПРАЗДНЙШН
СОБЛАЗНН́_ТН [to tempt, seduce]: СОБЛАЖНЮ, СОБЛАЗНЙШН
ОӰМЕРТВН́_ТН [to mortify, deaden]: ОӰМЕРЩВЛЮ, ОӰМЕРТВНШН
МЫ́СЛН_ТН [to think]: МЫ́ШЛЮ, МЫ́СЛНШН

    Note: From the verb ПОСЛА́ТН, "to send", the forms do not show softening: ПОСЛЮ̀ ("I will send"—John 15:26), ПО́СЛЕТЪ ("he will send", John 14:26) since in Old Church Slavonic the spelling was ПОСЪЛА́ТН. But in Russian we find пошлю, пошлешь).

The Future Tense.
§84. The Simple Future.
    Morphologically, the simple future in no way differs from the present tense. The difference is merely in the aspects of the verb: verbs in the perfective aspect have a future meaning, e.g. ХВАЛН́ТН, ХВАЛЮ̀ ["to praise, I praise"—present tense]; ПОХВАЛН́ТН, ПОХВАЛЮ̀ [I *will* praise--future simple]; НЕСТН́, НЕС& [to bear, carry; I

bear—present tense]; понести, понесꙋ [I *will* bear—simple future].[1]

In Old Church Slavonic, the distinction between the present tense and the simple future depended not only on the verbal aspects, but also, as it would appear, on the context (especially in the use of certain verbs), and for this reason the aspect was not always used precisely. A certain lack of preciseness in the use of aspects has remained even in the present (corrected) text of the Slavonic Gospel, for example: востáвъ идꙋ [instead of the expected пойдꙋ] ко ѻ҆цꙋ моемꙋ, и҆ рекꙋ є҆мꙋ (Luke 17:8—"Arising I will go to my father, and say unto him"); є҆гдá же состарѣешиса, воздѣжеши рꙋцѣ твои, и҆ и҆нъ та поа́шетъ [instead of препоа́шетъ] и҆ ведетъ [instead of поведетъ], а҆може не хо́щеши (John 21:18—"But when thou shalt be old, thou shalt stretch forth thy hands, and another shall gird thee, and lead thee whither thou wouldst not").[2] оу҆готóвай, что вечера́ю [instead of повечера́ю] (Luke 17:8—"Make ready wherewith I may sup").

The accent in the 2nd person plural is often moved to the end: и҆мже ѿпꙋ́стите* грѣхи́, ѿпꙋ́статса и҆мъ: и҆ и҆мже держите́,* держа́тса (John 20:23—"Whose soever sins ye remit, they are remitted unto them; and whose soever sins ye retain, they are retained").

---

[1]) The system in English is actually quite similar. We have a *compound future*--"I *will* go", and the present can sometimes be used as a *simple future*--"when I go tomorrow". But because of the verb aspects, Slavonic has more freedom in the way it can show future action. --*Tr.*

[2]) In more contemporary English, as in the Slavonic here, the present would have been used with a future meaning.--*Tr.*

§85. The Compound Future.

The compound future tense consists of verbs in the infinitive mood combined with the personal forms of the auxiliary verbs и́мамъ, хощꙋ̀, начнꙋ̀: e.g. є҆гда̀ и҆мꙋ́тъ* всѧ̑ сїѧ̑ сконча́тисѧ* (Mark 13:4—"When shall these things be?"); что́ ми хо́щете* да́ти*, и҆ а҆́зъ ва́мъ преда́мъ є҆го̀; (Matth. 26:15—"What will ye give me, and I will deliver him unto you?"); вси̏ ви́дѧщїи начнꙋ́тъ* рꙋга́тисѧ* є҆мꙋ̀ (Luke 14:29—"And all that behold it [will] begin to mock him").

The compound future has the meaning of the imperfective aspect.

Conjugation of the Compound Future.

Singular	Dual	Plural
1st: и́мамъ нестѝ, хвали́ти	и҆ма́ва,-ѣ нестѝ	и́мамы нестѝ
2nd: и́маши нестѝ	и́мата, -ѣ нестѝ	и́мате нестѝ
3rd: и́мать нести	и́мата, -ѣ нестѝ	и҆мꙋ́тъ нестѝ

Note: The asterisk (*) is used to mark various forms examined in the paragraph.

The Past Tenses.
§86. The Aorist.

The aorist is formed from the infinitive stem in the following manner:

1) If the stem of the infinitive ends in a vowel, then the suffix -х- is joined directly to the vowel: e.g. би_ти [to beat]--би_х_ъ, глаго́ла_ти [to speak]--глаго́ла_х_ъ: and it should be noted that in the 2nd and 3rd person singular, the suffix -х- is absent and the ending is the "pure" stem of the infinitive.

2) If the infinitive stem ends in a consonant, then the suffix -х- is joined to it with the help of the connecting vowel o: нес_тѝ, нес_о́_х_ъ: мощ_ѝ, мог_о́_х_ъ. The form for the 2nd and 3rd person

singular is the ending _є, joined directly to the infinitive stem, with resulting softening of the gutturals (г, к, х): рєк_о́_х_ъ [I said], рє́ч_є [thou saidst, he/she said].

Endings of the Aorist:

Infinitive stem in vowel:	Infinitive stem in consonant:
Singular.	
1st p. _х_ъ	_о_х_ъ
2nd p. —	_є
3rd p. —	_є
Dual.	
1st p. _х_о_ва [в'ѣ]	_о_х_о_ва [в'ѣ]
2nd p. _є_та [_т'ѣ]	_о_є_та [_т'ѣ]
3rd p. _є_та [_т'ѣ]	_о_є_та [_т'ѣ]
Plural.	
1st p. _х_о_мъ	_о_х_о_мъ
2nd p. _є_тє	_о_є_тє
3rd p. _ш_а	_о_ш_а

The personal endings _ва [_в'ѣ] and _мъ are joined to the _х_ by means of о.

The suffix _х_ in the endings of the aorist alternates with _є_ and _ш_.

The formation of the aorist from verbs that have the suffix _нѫ_ has the following peculiarity: if the suffix _нѫ_ is preceded by a vowel, then the _нѫ_ is retained: e.g. мимѫ_ти [to pass by] мимѫ_хъ: if the suffix _нѫ_ is preceded by a consonant, then the aorist can be formed either with or without this suffix: двиг_нѫ_ти [to move], двигнѫ_хъ, двиг_о́_хъ.

The aorist can be formed from verbs of the perfective or imperfective aspect: твори́_ти [to create], твори́хъ: сотвори́_ти, сотворѝхъ: however, in the case of imperfective verbs of secondary formation (see §76), with a sense of repetition or prolongation, the aorist is not formed.

Concerning the meaning and use of the aorist and the other past tenses, see below in the section on Syntax.

Conjugation of the Aorist:

нес_тѝ *to bear*   писа́_ти *to write* люби́_ти *to love* велѣ́_ти *to command*

Singular.

1st p.	нес_о́_хъ	писа́_хъ	люби́_хъ	велѣ́_хъ
2 & 3.	нес_ѐ	писа̀	любѝ	велѣ́

Dual.

1st p.	нес_о́_х_о_ва, _ѣ	писа́_х_о_ва, _ѣ	люби́_х_о_ва, _ѣ
	велѣ́_х_о_ва, _ѣ		
2 & 3.	нес_о́_с_та, _ѣ	писа́_с_та, _ѣ	люби́_с_та, _ѣ
	велѣ́_с_та, _ѣ		

Plural.

1st p.	нес_о́_х_омъ	писа́_х_омъ	люби́_х_омъ
	велѣ́_х_омъ		
2nd p.	нес_о́_с_те	писа́_с_те	люби́_с_те
	велѣ́_с_те		
3rd p.	нес_о́_ш_а	писа́_ш_а	люби́_ш_а
	велѣ́_ш_а		

The verbs ꙗ_ти [to take], нача́_ти [to begin], ви́_ти [to wind, roll up], пи́_ти [to drink], and кла́_ти [to swear] take, in the 2nd and 3rd person singular of the aorist, the personal ending тъ: и прїа́тъ* и҆лїа̀ ми́лоть свою̀ и҆ сви́тъ* ю̀ (IV Kings 2:8--"And Elijah took his mantle, and wrapped it together"); и҆ воста̀, и҆ ꙗдѐ, и҆ пи́тъ* (III Kings 19:6--"And he arose, and did eat and drink"--the form пн́тх has been kept in the Paremia [Prophecy] read at Vespers for St. Elias the Prophet, but in this text as printed in the Slavonic Bible, it appears as и пн̀); ѿто́лѣ нача́тх* і҆и҃съ проповѣ́дати (Matth. 4:17—"From that time Jesus began to preach"); пришѐлъ є҆сѝ на зе́млю, ѿ дв҃ы вопло́щсѧ, ѝ распѧ́тїе прїа́тъ*, да на́съ свободи́ши ѿ рабо́ты вра́жїѧ: (Octoechos, T. 2, Friday morning Aposticha—"Thou didst come to earth, being incarnate of a Virgin, and acceptedst crucifixion[1], that Thou mightest deliver us from the enemy's servitude").

Note 1: The aorist of the verb рещѝ, alongside of forms of ancient origin [рѣ́хъ, "I spake, I said"; рѣ́ша, "they said"] has also forms of more recent origin: реко́хъ, реко́ша, e.g. тогда̀ рѣ́хъ: сѐ прїидꙋ̀ (Ps. 21:8—"Then I said: behold, I will come"); ꙗ҆́кw рѣ́ша вразѝ мои́ мнѣ̀ (Ps. 70:10—"For mine enemies said unto me"); реко́ша чи́стаѧ ѝ чⷮнꙗ̂ ꙋ҆ста̀ (Pentecost Matins, Ode 1—"There spake a pure and honorable mouth").

Note 2: The aorist ѡ҆жи́хъ has the 2nd and 3rd person ѡ҆живѐ (Luke 15:24—"came to life, is alive again").

§87. The Imperfect (Transient).

The forms of the imperfect are built from the infinitive stem, or from the present stem, with the aid of the suffixes ₋х₋, ₋ах₋, ₋ах₋, which were formed by elision from the Old Slavonic suffixes ₋ах₋, ₋ѣах₋ [₋аах₋], ₋ꙗах₋.

Endings of the Imperfect:
Singular.

1st Person:	₋хъ	₋ах₋ъ	₋ах₋ъ
2nd Person:	₋ш₋е	₋аш₋е	₋аш₋е
3rd Person:	₋ш₋е	₋аш₋е	₋аш₋е

---

[1]) This translation is clumsy, but its purpose is to help in understanding the Slavonic. --*Tr.*

Dual.

1st Person:	_χ_о_ва [вѣ]	_ах_о_ва [вѣ]	_ах_о_ва [вѣ]
2nd Person:	_с_та [тѣ]	_ас_та [тѣ]	_ас_та [тѣ]
3rd Person:	_с_та [тѣ]	_ас_та [тѣ]	_ас_та [тѣ]

Plural.

1st Person:	_χ_о_мъ	_ах_о_мъ	_ах_о_мъ
2nd Person:	_с_тє	_ас_тє	_ас_тє
3rd Person:	_χ_ꙋ	_ах_ꙋ	_ах_ꙋ

The forms of the imperfect are arrived at in the following
manner:

1) Verbs whose infinitive stem ends in the suffixes _а_, _ѧ_, -
ѣ_ or _и_ form their imperfect tense from the infinitive stem:

a) When the infinitive stem ends in _а_ or _ѧ_, the suffix _χ_
is added:

писа́_ти [to write], писа́_χ_ъ

вєлича́_ти [to magnify], вєлича́_χ_ъ

скончава́_ти [finish], скончава́_χ_ъ

пригвожда́_ти [to nail], пригвожда́χъ

оу̑трꙋжда́_ти [to cause difficulty], оу̑трꙋжда́_χ_ъ

оу̑мєрщвлѧ́_ти [to mortify], оу̑мєрщвлѧ́_χ_ъ

оу̑молѧ́_ти [to entreat], оу̑молѧ́_χ_ъ

оу̑пражднѧ́_ти [to abolish], оу̑пражднѧ́_χ_ъ[1])

сѣѧ_ти [to sow], сѣѧ_χ_ъ

---

[1]) This can occur either with softening (_жди_), or without
softening (_зди_): врагъ оу̑пражднѧ́шєсѧ (Octoechos, T. 6,
Wednesday at Matins, Ode 9—"The enemy was abolished");
и̑спраздни́хꙋ врє́тища своѧ̂ (Gen. 42:35—"They emptied their
sacks").

вопїѧ҃ти [to cry out], вопїѧ҃хъ

The forms of the imperfect in ѧ҃хъ, due to the truncated suffix (_х_ instead of _ах_), are very similar to those of the aorist (except for the 2nd and 3rd person singular and the 3rd person plural). The distinction between them can be made in the following manner: the imperfect can be recognized by the syntactical structure of the utterance (see the section on Syntax) and, in addition to that, from imperfective verbs of secondary formation (see §76), only the imperfect can be formed, e.g.:

напита́ти [to satiate], напита́хъ (aorist); — напитава́ти, напитава́хъ (imperfect);

закла́ти [to sacrifice], закла́хъ (aorist);—заклала́ти, заклала́хъ (imperfect):

и҆ приведо́ша но́щїю вси лю́дїе своѐ кі́йждо, є҆́же и҆мѧ́ше въ рꙋцѣ̀ свое́й, и҆ заклала́хꙋ та́мѡ (I Kings [Samuel], 14:34—"And at night the people brought each one that which was in his hand, and they sacrificed there").

b) Verbs whose infinitive stem ends in the suffix _ѣ_ add the suffix _ах_, and the ѣ and ах elide, forming ах:

болѣ́_ти [to hurt, be sick], [болѣ́_ах_ъ] болѧ́хъ

стыдѣ́_тисѧ [to be ashamed], [стыдѣ́_ахсѧ] стыда́хсѧ

щадѣ́_ти [to spare], [щадѣ́_ах_ъ] щада́хъ

хотѣ́_ти [to want, be about to] [хотѣ́_ах_ъ] хотѧ́хъ

c) When the infinitive stem ends in _н_, _ах_ is added, and then the _н_ of the stem becomes j, before which the usual alternation of consonants occurs, and if the j follows one of the "hushing" sibilants, it is absorbed by it:

моли́_ти [to entreat], мол_а́х_ъ (from *молj-а́х_ъ)
мы́сли_ти [to think], мы́шл_а́х_ъ[1])
блазни́_тися [to be enticed, to suspect], блажна́х_ся
ходи́_ти [to walk, to go], хожд_а́х_ъ
вози́_ти [to transport], вож_а́х_ъ
люби́_ти [to love], любл_а́х_ъ

Note: The verb суди́_ти [to judge], суд_а́х_ъ, without softening, is an exception: суда́ше (I Kings [Samuel] 7:6—"[and Samuel] judged [the children of Israel]").

2) The other verbs usually form the imperfect from the present stem by means of the suffixes _ах_ or _ах_; the gutturals к, г of the stem alternate with the "hushing" sibilants before the suffix _ах_ (from *_ѣахъ):

a) Verbs whose infinitive stem ends in a consonant:
вес_ти́ [to lead], вед_у́тъ: вед_а́х_ъ
плес_ти́ [to plait, braid], плет_у́тъ: плет_а́х_ъ
мощи́ [may, can], мог_у́тъ: мож_а́х_ъ
тещи́ [run, flow], тек_у́тъ: теч_а́х_ъ

b) Verbs whose infinitive stem, equivalent to the root, ends in a vowel:
кры́_ти [to cover, roof], кры́ютъ: кры́_а́х_ъ (from *кры̆j-а́х_ъ)
пи́_ти [to drink], пі_ю́тъ: пі_а́х_ъ
зна́_ти [to know], зна́_ютъ: зна́_ах_ъ
име́_ти [to have], име́_ютъ: име́_ах_ъ, a verb which has

---

[1]) Also: мы́слахъ (Mark 11:31--"And they reasoned with themselves"), but: помышла́хъ (Luke 20:5--"And they reasoned with themselves"). [Note a corresponding difference in the Greek: ἐλογίζοντο in Mark 11:31, συνελογίσαντο in Luke 20:5-- *Tr.*]

also elided forms: и҆мѧ́ше: и҆мѧ́хꙋ вса̑ ѻ҆́бща (Acts 2:44—"[they that believed] had all things common").

c) Certain verbs with the suffix _ꙗ_ in the infinitive:

гна́_ти [to urge, chase, persecute], го́н_ѧтъ: гон_ѧ́х_ъ[1]

ѣ҆́ха_ти [to ride], ѣ҆́д_ꙋтъ: ѣ҆́д_ах_ъ

зва́_ти [to call], зов_ꙋ́тъ: зов_ѧ́х_ъ

d) Verbs with alternation of ор/ра, ол/ла, ѧ[а]/ен[ем], ѣ/oj:

бра́_тисѧ [to strive, battle], бо́р_ѧтсѧ: бор_ѧ́хсѧ

кла́_ти [to pierce, slaughter], ко́л_ѧтъ: кол_ѧ́х_ъ

клѧ́_ти [to curse], клен_ꙋ́тъ: клен_ѧ́х_ъ

жа́_ти [to reap], жн_ꙋ́тъ: жн_ѧ́х_ъ

ꙗ҆́ти [to take], е҆мл_ю́тъ: е҆мл_ѧ́х_ъ

пѣ́_ти [to sing], по_ю́тъ: по_ѧ́х_ъ

e) Verbs with stems of various origins:

со́хнꙋ_ти [to become dry], со́хн_ꙋтъ: со́хн_ах_ъ

и҆_тѝ [to go], и҆д_ꙋ́тъ: и҆д_ѧ́х_ъ

плы́_ти [sail, swim, go by water], плов_ꙋ́тъ: плов_ѧ́х_ъ[2]

жи́_ти [to live], жив_ꙋ́тъ: жив_ѧ́х_ъ

Conjugation of the Imperfect:

писа́_ти *to write*   и҆збавлѧ́_ти *to deliver*   болѣ́_ти *to be sick*

Singular.

1st p.	писа́хъ	и҆збавлѧ́хъ	болѧ́хъ
2 & 3.	писа́ше	и҆збавлѧ́ше	болѧ́ше

---

[1]) Formation may also be from the infinitive: гони́_ти, гонj-ах_ъ, гонѧ́хъ.

[2]) Also from the infinitive stem: плы́_ти, плы́хъ (e.g. плы́хꙋ in Acts 27:13—"they sailed [close by Crete]").

Dual.

1st p.	пнса́хова [_вѣ]	и҆збавла́хова [_вѣ]	бола́хова [_вѣ]
2 & 3.	пнса́ста [_тѣ]	а҆збавла́ста [_тѣ]	бола́ста [_тѣ]

Plural.

1st p.	пнса́хомъ	и҆збавла́хомъ	бола́хомъ
2nd p.	пнса́сте	и҆збавла́сте	бола́сте
3rd p.	пнса́хꙋ	и҆збавла́хꙋ	бола́хꙋ

ходи́_ти *to go, wal* бра́_тнса [бо́р_атса] *to battle* кла́_ти [клен_ ꙋ́тъ] *to curse*

Singular.

1st p.	хожда́хъ	бора́хса	клена́хъ
2 & 3.	хожда́ше	бора́шеса	клена́ше

Dual.

1st p.	хожда́хова [_вѣ]	бора́ховаса [_вѣса]	клена́хова [_вѣ]
2 & 3.	хожда́ста [_тѣ]	бора́стаса [_тѣса]	клена́ста [_тѣ]

Plural.

1st p.	хожда́хомъ	бора́хомса	клена́хомъ
2nd p.	хожда́сте	бора́стеса	клена́сте
3rd p.	хожда́хꙋ	бора́хꙋса	клена́хꙋ

The forms of the imperfect are derived only from verbs of the imperfective aspect.

The forms of the 2nd person singular [i.e. "thou"] of the aorist and imperfect have almost been lost, and replaced by the corresponding forms of the perfect (see the Perfect in Syntax, §158-159). They have been preserved intact, as it would appear, only in the Gospel text used in divine services, for example: раввѝ, когда̀ здѣ̀ бы́сть; (aorist; John 6:25—"Rabbi, when camest thou hither?"); не бо́йса, марїа́мь, ѡ҆брѣ́те (aorist) бо благода́ть ѿ бга (Luke 1:30—"Fear not, Mary, for thou hast found favour with God");

глаго́ла є҆мꙋ і҆и҃съ: ты̀ речѐ (aorist; Matth. 26:64—"Jesus said unto him: Thou hast said [it]"); лꙋка́вый ра́бе и҆ лѣни́вый, вѣ́даше (imperfect) ꙗ҆́кѡ жнꙋ, и҆дѣ́же не сѣ́ахъ (Matth. 25:26—"Thou wicked and slothful servant, thou knewest that I reap where I sowed not."); взе́млеши є҆гѡ́же не положѝ (aorist; Luke 19:21—"thou takest up that thou layedst not down"); лꙋка́вый ра́бе: вѣ́даше (imperfect) ꙗ҆́кѡ а҆́зъ человѣ́къ ꙗ҆́ръ є҆́смь (Luke 19:22—"Thou wicked servant, thou knewest that I was an austere man").

§88. The Perfect (Completed Past).

The forms of the perfect tense are built with the past participle ending in _лъ and a copula, the present tense forms of the verb бы́ти [to be]. The participle in _лъ changes according to gender and number, while the copula changes according to person and number. Examples: мно́зи бо ѿ ни́хъ и҆здале́ча пришлѝ* сꙋ́ть* (Mark 8:3--"for many of them came from afar"); ѻ҆трокови́ца нѣ́сть* оу҆мерла̀*, но спи́тъ (Mark 5:39--"the damsel is not dead, but sleepeth"); что̀ є҆́смь* є҆щѐ не докончалъ*; (Matth. 19:20--"What lack I yet?").[1]

When two such participles stand together, usually only one copula is employed: ꙗ҆́коже восхотѣ́лъ, сотвори́лъ є҆сѝ (Jonah 1:14--"Thou hast done as it pleased thee"); сше́лъ и҆ воплоти́лса є҆сѝ, ꙗ҆́кѡ да спасе́ши всѣ́хъ (Morning Prayer 8, to the Lord Jesus Christ--"Thou didst come down and take flesh to save all").

---

[1] Note that in English, all three examples could have been rendered using the *present perfect:* "many *have come* from afar", "the damsel *hath not died*', and "What *have* I yet *left unfinished?" --Tr.

Conjugation of the Perfect:

Singular.

1st p. нє́слъ, -а̀, -о̏ є҆смь *I have borne*   хвали́лъ,-а, -о є҆смь *I have praised*   *[did praise]*

2nd p. нє́слъ, -а̀, -о̏ є҆сѝ   хвали́лъ, -а, -о є҆сѝ

3rd p. нє́слъ, -а̀, -о̏ є҆сть   хвали́лъ, -а, -о є҆сть

Dual.

1st p. нєсла̑, нєслѝ є҆сва̀, -ѣ̏   хвали́ла, -и є҆сва̀, -ѣ̏

2 & 3. нєсла̑, нєслѝ є҆ста̀, -ѣ̏   хвали́ла є҆ста̀, -ѣ̏

Plural.

1st p. нєслѝ є҆смы̀   хвали́ли є҆смы̀

2nd p. нєслѝ є҆стѐ   хвали́ли є҆стѐ

3rd p. нєслѝ сꙋ́ть   хвали́ли сꙋ́ть

In the 3rd person singular, the perfect sometimes is encountered without a copula, in the form of the _лъ participle alone, for example: но сєбѐ ѹ҆мали́лъ, зра́къ раба̀ прїи́мъ (Philippians 2:7—"But emptied himself, taking the form of a servant"); смири́лъ сєбѐ, послꙋшли́въ бы́въ да́же до смє́рти (Phil. 2:8—"He humbled himself, becoming obedient even unto death"); а҆́щє ли кто̀ ѡ҆скорби́лъ мєнѐ, нє мєнѐ ѡ҆скорби́ (II Cor. 2:5—"And if any one have caused grief, he hath not grieved me"); питаю́щаѧсѧ простра́ннѡ, жива̀ ѹ҆мєрла̀ (I Tim. 5:6—"For she that liveth in pleasures, hath died while yet living").

§89. The Pluperfect (Distant Past).

The pluperfect builds its forms from the past participle in _лъ and the aorist [бѣ́хъ] or imperfect [бѧ́хъ] of the verb бы́ти used as a copula. In conjugation, the forms of the _лъ-participle and the auxiliary verb change according to the same pattern as in the perfect tense. Examples: и҆зги́блъ* бѣ̀*, и҆ ѡ҆брѣ́тєсѧ (Luke 15:24--"he was lost, and is found"); мно́зи ѿ і҆ꙋдє́й бѧ́хꙋ* пришлѝ* къ ма́р,ѳѣ и҆ ма́рїи (John 11:19--"And many of the Jews were come to Martha and

Mary"); и҆ тьма̀ а҆́бїе бы́сть, и҆ не оу҆̀ в҃ѣ* прише́лъ* къ ни́мъ і҆и҃съ (John 6:17--"And it was now dark, and Jesus was not [yet] come to them").

Conjugation of the Pluperfect:

Singular.

1st p.	не́слъ, _а̀, _о̀ в҃ѣхъ [or ба́хъ] *I had borne*	хвали́лъ, _а, _о в҃ѣхъ [ба́хъ] *I had praised*
2 & 3.	не́слъ, _а̀, _о̀ в҃ѣ [ба́ше]	хвали́лъ, _а, _о в҃ѣ [ба́ше]

Dual.

1st p.	несла̂, _ѝ в҃ѣхова[_ѣ] or ба́хова[_ѣ]	хвали́ла, _и в҃ѣхова[_ѣ], or ба́хова[_ѣ]
2 & 3.	несла̂, _ѝ в҃ѣста [_ѣ], or ба́ста [_ѣ]	хвали́ла, _и в҃ѣста [_ѣ], or ба́ста[_ѣ]

Plural.

1st p.	неслѝ в҃ѣхомъ [ба́хомъ]	хвали́ли в҃ѣхомъ [ба́хомъ]
2nd p.	неслѝ в҃ѣсте [ба́сте]	хвали́ли в҃ѣсте [ба́сте]
3rd p.	неслѝ в҃ѣша [ба́хꙋ]	хвали́ли в҃ѣша [ба́хꙋ]

§90. The Descriptive (Periphrastic) Form of Tenses.

In Church Slavonic, there are rather frequently used descriptive forms of tenses, which consist of a copula (forms of the verb бы́ти, "to be") and the short form of the present active participle. In this combination, since it functions as a predicate, the participle is used only in the nominative case, its number and gender depend on the subject; the copula shows the tense or mood, for example:

Present tense: мꙋ́жїе, и҆̀хже вса́дисте въ темни́цꙋ, сꙋ́ть* въ цр҃кви стоѧ́ще* и҆ оу҆ча́ще* лю́ди (Acts 5:25—"the men whom ye put in prison are standing in the temple, and teaching the people").

Aorist: и҆ в҃ѣ* проповѣ́даѧ* на со́нмищахъ и҆́хъ, во все́й галїле́и, и҆ в҃ѣсы и҆згонѧ́* (Mark 1:39—"And he was preaching in their synagogues, and in all Galilee, and casting out demons"); и҆ в҃ѣ* сѣда̀* со слу́гами (Mark 14:54—"and he sat with the servants").

Imperfect: и бѧху* ученницы̀ іѡа́нновы и фарїсе́йстїи постѧщеса* (Mark 2:18—"And the disciples of John and the Pharisees used to fast").

Future: и ѕвѣ́зды бу́дутъ* съ небесè спада́юще* (Mark 13:25—"And the stars of heaven shall be falling down").

Imperative mood: бу́ди* оу҆вѣщава́аса* съ сопе́рникомъ твои́мъ (Matth. 5:25—"Be at agreement with thine adversary").

Rather frequently, especially in prayers and hymnody, the role of the copula in such constructions is taken by the verb не преставати [not to cease]: не преста́ю* благодара̀* ѡ̀ ва́съ (Ephesians 1:16—"I cease not to give thanks for you"); не преста́ахъ* оу҆ча̀ (Acts 20:31—"I ceased not to admonish"); не преста́аху* оу҆ча́ще* и благовѣ́ствующе* (Acts 5:42—"they ceased not to teach and preach"); не преста́й* мола́щиса* ѡ̀ на́съ (Akathistos Hymn to the Theotokos, Prayer 2— "Cease not to pray for us").

In a similar sense the following verbs also are used: пребыва́ти [to remain], прилѣжа́ти [to be diligent], не ѡскуд́ѣва́ти [to fail not]: Пе́тръ же пребыва́ше* толкíй*[in place of the Old Church Slavonic тлькы́i--see §95] (Acts 12:16—"But Peter continued knocking"); ꙗкоже прилѣжа́ху* вопроша́юще* е҆гò (John 8:7—"When therefore they continued asking him"); мола́щи* не ѡскуд́ѣва́й* ѡ̀ воспѣва́ющихъ... (Octoechos, Sunday dismissal hymn, Theotokion of the 5th Tone:—"Fail not to pray for those who hymn...").

The same applies to преста́ти [to cease], соверши́ти [to finish]: Преста́ните* свира́юще*, ꙗже над чреда́ми пасо́мыхъ старѣ́йшины (Dec. 24, 2nd Kathisma at Matins—"Cease from your piping, ye that are put over the flocks"); и бы́сть, е҆гда̀ соверши́* і҆и́съ заповѣ́даа* ѻ҆бѣмана́десате оу҆чеником́а свои́ма, пре́йде ѿуду оу҆чи́ти (Matth. 11:1—"And it came to pass, when Jesus had made an end of commanding his twelve disciples, he departed thence to teach").

With these periphrastic forms, one should probably list the combinations with ꙗви́тиса [to appear, seem] and ѡбрѣ́титса [to be found]: ꙗ́кѡ да ꙗвꙗ́тса* человѣ́кѡмꙁ постꙗ́цєса* (Matth. 6:16—"That they might be seen of men to fast"); ѡбрѣ́тєса* имꙋ́щи* во чрє́вѣ (Matth. 1:18—"she was found with child"); and the combination of пребыва́ти with the past participle: четырєнадєсꙗ́тый дне́сь де́нь жда́ꙋщє, не ꙗ́дшє* пребыва́єтє*, ничто́жє вкꙋси́вшє* (Acts 27:33— "This day is the fourteenth day that ye have tarried and continued fasting, having taken nothing").

§91. The Subjunctive Mood.

The subjunctive mood is built from the _лꙁ-participle and the copula, the aorist forms of the perfective aspect [бы́хꙁ] of the verb бы́ти [to be], for example: а́щє ѿ мі́ра бы́стє* бы́ли*, мі́рꙁ оу́бо своє̀ люби́лꙁ* бы̀* (John 15:19—"If ye were of the world, the world would love its own"); а́щє не бы́хꙁ* пришє́лꙁ* ѝ глаго́лалꙁ* и́мꙁ, грѣха̀ не бы́ша* имѣ́ли* (John 15:22—"If I had not come and spoken to them, they had not had sin").

Conjugation of the Subjunctive Mood:

Singular.

1st p. нє́слꙁ, _а̀, _о̀ бы́хꙁ *I would have borne* хвали́лꙁ, _а, _о бы́хꙁ *I would have praised*

2 & 3. нє́слꙁ, _а̀, _о̀ бы̀   хвали́лꙁ, _а, _о бы̀

Dual.

1st p. нєсла̂, _и бы́хова, _ѣ   хвали́ла, _и бы́хова, _ѣ

2 & 3. нєсла̂, _и бы́ста, _ѣ   хвали́ла, _и бы́ста, _ѣ

Plural.

1st p. нєслѝ бы́хомꙁ   хвали́ли бы́хомꙁ

2nd p. нєслѝ бы́стє   хвали́ли бы́стє

3rd p. нєслѝ бы́ша   хвали́ли бы́ша

Where there are two clauses in the subjunctive (the main and the subordinate clause), the subordinate subjunctive clause *sometimes* takes a perfect copula (that is, the present tense of the verb бы́ти), for example: а҆́ще бы̀* вѣ́дала* є҆сѝ* да́ръ бж҃їй... ты̀ бы проси́ла оу҆ негѡ̀, и҆ да́лъ бы ти во́дꙋ жи́вꙋ (John 4:10—"If thou knewest the gift of God... thou wouldest have asked of him, and he would have given thee living water"); гдⷭ҇и, а҆́ще бы̀* є҆сѝ* бы́лъ* здѣ̀, не бы оу҆́мерлъ мо́й бра́тъ (John 11:32—"Lord, if thou hadst been here, my brother had not died"); ѽ да бы̀* воцари́лисѧ* є҆стѐ*, да и҆ мы̀ бы́хомъ съ ва́ми ца́рствовали (I Cor. 4:8—"O, that ye did reign, that we might reign with you!"); ꙗ҆́кѡ а҆́ще бы̀* восхотѣ́лъ* є҆сѝ* же́ртвы, да́лъ бы́хъ оу҆́бо (Ps. 50—"For if Thou hadst desired sacrifice, I would have given it"). However, such subjunctive forms with a copula in the perfect are not found in the ancient texts (e.g. in the Ostromirovo Gospel and in the old [pre-Nikonian] Psalter).

With the conjunction да and the pronoun что, the subjunctive copula sometimes loses its person endings and takes the form бы, regardless of person: дабы̀* оу҆страни́лсѧ* ѿ страсте́й, и҆ твоеѧ̀ благода́ти и҆мѣ́лъ* бы* приложе́нїе (here бы is used in place of the 1st person бы́хъ: Canon of Preparation for Holy Communion, Ode 6—"So that [I] might be estranged from passions, and have an increase of Thy Grace"); ѽ да бы̀* воцари́лисѧ* є҆стѐ (I Cor. 4:8, as above); и҆ не ѡ҆брѣта́хꙋ, что̀ бы* сотвори́ли* є҆мꙋ̀ (Luke 19:48—"And they found not, what to do to him"); however, this practice is not always followed: ѽ да бы́сте* ма́лѡ претерпѣ́ли* безꙋ́мїю (II Cor. 11:1—"Oh, that ye might be patient a little with [my] folly").

The use of the copula is met with in other cases, outside of the norm, without personal endings (the copula becomes, as it were, a subjunctive particle): и҆ а҆́ще бы* ѻ҆́но по́мнили*... и҆мѣ́ли* бы* вре́мѧ возврати́тисѧ (Hebrews 11:15—"And if they had been mindful of that... they had doubtless time to return").

The imperfects подобаше [it was proper](with or without бы), достоаше [it was right], можаше [was possible], since these words express a modal sense of obligation or possibility, can have a subjunctive meaning, e.g.: подобаше* оу́бо, ѿ мꙋжїе, послꙋшавше менè не ѿвезтисѧ ѿ крнта (Acts 27:21—"Ye should indeed, O ye men, have hearkened unto me, and not have loosed from Crete"); понѐже подобаше* бы* є́мꙋ мно́жицею страдати (Hebrews 9:26—"For then he ought to have suffered often"); не достоаше* ли разрѣшнтисѧ є́н ѿ ю́зы сеѧ̀ въ де́нь сꙋббѡ́тный (Luke 13:16—"And ought not [she] be loosed from this bond on the Sabbath day?"); можаше* бо сїè мꙋ́ро про́дано бы́ти на мно́зѣ, и да́тисѧ ннщымъ (Matth. 26:9—"For this myrrh might have been sold for much, and given to the poor"). The infinitive in conjunction with бы can also have a subjunctive sense: оу негѡ́же бы* ѡбнта́ти* на́мъ (Acts 21:16—"[a disciple] with whom we should lodge").

§92. The Optative Mood.

The optative mood consists of forms of the present or simple future tenses, preceded by the particle да (which has the value of a conjunction in subordinate clauses): да несꙋ, да несе́шн, да несе́тъ: да прннесꙋ, да прннесе́шн, да прннесе́тъ (may I, thou, he bear; may I, thou, he bring), &c.

In main clauses the forms of the optative have the value of an imperative, and in this sense they are for the most part used in the 3rd person singular, plural, or dual: да сѷ́нтсѧ и́мѧ тво́е: да прїн́детъ црⷭ҇твїе тво́е: да бꙋ́детъ во́лѧ твоѧ̀ (Matth. 6:9-10—"hallowed be Thy name; Thy kingdom come; Thy will be done").

In subordinate clauses the optative mood is used to express desire or purpose: что̀ хо́щешн, да сотворю̀ тебѣ̀; ... оу́чн́телю, да прозрю̀ (Mark 10:51—"What wilt thou that I should do unto thee?... Rabboni, that I may see"); ꙗкоже хо́щете, да творѧ́тъ ва́мъ чело́вѣцы (Luke 6:31—"As ye would that men should do unto you").

§93. The Imperative Mood.

In Church Slavonic, the imperative mood has forms for all persons and numbers except for the 1st person singular and the 3rd person dual and plural.

The imperative mood is formed from the present stem (or that of the simple future) by means of the suffixes _н_ and _є_ (in place of the Old Church Slavonic _ѣ_).

Verbs of the 1st conjugation in the singular (2nd and 3rd person) and in the 2nd person of the dual and plural, have the suffix _н_, and after vowels this suffix _н_ becomes _й_ in both the singular and plural: по_ю́тъ [пѣ_тн, *to sing*], по́_й, по́й_тє (поj-н-). In the 1st person dual and plural, verbs of *a)* the 1st un-softened conjugation (see §80, *a*), including the verbs with the suffix _нꙋ_, have the suffix _є_, while verbs of *b)* the 1st softened conjugation (see §80, *b*) have the suffix _н_ after vowels, but after consonants they can have either _н_ or _є_ as a suffix. Examples:

    a) н̑д_ꙋ́тъ: н̑д_є_мъ, *let us go!*

    b) воспо_ю́тъ: воспо_н́_мъ, *let us sing!*

Пла́ч_ꙋтъ [пла́ка_тн, weep] can have either плач_н_мъ or плач_є_мъ as an imperative.

Note: Verbs of the 1st unsoftened conjugation, in Old Church Slavonic, had the suffix _ѣ_ for the imperative dual and plural. Forms with this suffix are still sometimes to be met with in the text of the Gospel used in divine services: по нє́мъ н̑дѣ́та въ до́мъ... н̑ рцѣ́та до́мꙋ вл҃цѣ (Luke 22: 10-11—"Follow him into the house... and say unto the goodman of the house").

The verbs of the 2nd conjugation take the suffix _н_ in all forms.

A small number of verbs of the 2nd conjugation have a stem ending in -j (after a vowel), for example: сто_я́тъ, бо_я́тсѧ, напо́_ѧтъ, та́_ѧтъ, поко́_ѧтъ (stand, fear, give drink, melt, rest) and certain others; in the 2nd and 3rd person singular and the 2nd person plural, the suffix _н_ changes to _й_: стó_й[те], бó_йса [бóй_теса], покó_й[те], напó_й[те]: жа́ждꙋщꙋю дꙋшꙋ мою̀ напóй водáмн (Troparion for Mid-Pentecost: "give my thirsting soul to drink of the waters").

The 2nd and 3rd persons singular do not have personal endings.

The endings of the imperative mood:

	1st Conjugation:		2nd Conjugation:
	a) unsoftened:	b) softened:	
Sing. 2nd:	_н ___	_н [_й]	_н [_й]
3rd:	_н	_н [_й]	_н [й]
Dual: 1st:	_е_ва[_вѣ]	_н[е]_ва [_вѣ]	_н_ва [_вѣ]
2nd:	_н_та[_тѣ]	_н_та [тѣ]	_н_та [_тѣ]
Plu. 1st:	_е_мꙋ	_н[е]мꙋ	_н_мꙋ
2nd:	_н_те	_н[й]_те	_т[й]те

In verbs of the 1st unsoftened conjugation with their stems ending in г, к, the alternation of consonants takes place before the suffixes _н_ and _е_ (see §11): помог_ꙋтꙋ, помоз_н [help], помóж_е_ мꙋ [let us help]; рек_ꙋтꙋ, р_цы̀ [say], рц_é_мꙋ [let us say]; ѿверг_ꙋтꙋ, ѿвéрж_н[1] [cast aside], ѿвéр_ж_е_мꙋ.

Conjugation of the Imperative Mood.
1st Conjugation
a) Unsoftened:

			Stem in a guttural:
		н_тн (to go)--нд_ꙋтꙋ	рещн̀ (to say)--рек_ꙋтꙋ
Sing.	2nd p.	нднѝ	рцы̀
	3rd p.	нднѝ	рцы̀

---

[1]) In Old Church Slavonic the form was ѿврьзн.

Dual:	1st p.	й́дєва [_в‑ѣ]	рцє́ва [_в‑ѣ]
	2nd p.	й́дн́та [_т‑ѣ]	рцы́та [_т‑ѣ]
Plural:	1st p.	й́дємъ	рцє́мъ
	2nd p.	й́дн́тє	рцы́тє

b) Softened:

With a soft consonant before _н_: With a vowel before the endings:

пла́ка_тн *(to weep)*--пла́ч_ꙋтъ   пѣ́_тн *(to sing)*--
по_ю́тъ

Sing.	2nd p.	пла́чн	по́й
	3rd p.	пла́чн	по́й

Dual:	1st p.	пла́чнва[_в‑ѣ], _єва[_‑ѣ]	по́йва[_в‑ѣ]
	2nd p.	пла́чнта[_т‑ѣ]	по́нта[_т‑ѣ]

Plural:	1st p.	пла́чнмъ, _ємъ	по́нмъ
	2nd p.	пла́чнтє	по́йтє

2nd Conjugation

любн́_тн *to love* [любн́_ѧтъ]   стꙋча́_тн *to knock* [стꙋч_а́тъ]

Sing.	2nd p.	любн̀	стꙋчн̀
	3rd p.	любн̀	стꙋчн̀

Dual:	1st p.	лю́бнва [_в‑ѣ]	стꙋчнва [_в‑ѣ]
	2nd p.	любн́та [_т‑ѣ]	стꙋчн́та [_т‑ѣ]

Plural:	1st p.	лю́бнмъ	стꙋчн́мъ
	2nd p.	любн́тє	стꙋчн́тє

Examples:

По не́мъ иди́та (1a)[1]: и и̂де́же а́ще вни́детъ, рцы́та (1a) господи́нꙋ до́мꙋ... (Mark 14:13-14—"Follow him; And whithersoever he shall go in, say to the master of the house..."). Глаго́ла и̂мъ і̂и҃съ: прїиди́те (1a), ѡ̂б(ѣ)дꙋ́йте (1b). (John 21:12—"Jesus said to them: Come and dine"). Ѿ дрꙋги́ни! прїиди́те (1a), вона́ми пома́жемъ (1b) тѣ́ло живоно́сное и̂ погребе́нное... и̂демъ (1a), потщи́мсѧ (2) і̂а́коже волсви́, и̂ поклони́мсѧ (2), и̂ принесе́мъ (1a) мѵ́ра і̂а́кѡ да́ры... и̂ пла́чимъ (1b), и̂ возопїи́мъ (1b)... (Paschal Oikos—"O friends, come, let us anoint with spices the Life-bearing and buried Body... Let us go, let us hasten like the Magi, and let us worship, and let us bring ointments as gifts... And let us weep, and cry out..."). а̂лчꙋ́щыѧ напита́имъ (1b), жа́ждꙋщыѧ напои́мъ (2), наги́ѧ ѡ̂блече́мъ (1a), стра́нныѧ введе́мъ (1a), боля́щыѧ и̂ въ темни́цѣ сꙋ́щыѧ посѣти́мъ (2) (Vespers on the Eve of Meat-Fare Sunday, at the Litiya—"Let us feed the hungry, let us give the thirsty drink, let us clothe the naked, let us welcome strangers, the sick and those in prison let us visit"). Поста̀ бж҃е́ственнымъ нача́ткомъ оу̂миле́нїѧ стѧжи́мъ (1b)—(Monday in the First Week of Lent, Sessional Hymn at Matins—"As God-given first fruits of the fast, let us acquire compunction"). Препоя́шимъ (1b) чре́сла на́ша оу̂мерщвле́нїемъ страсте́й (Thursday in the First Week of Lent, Aposticha Automelon at Vespers— "Let us gird our loins through the mortification of passions"). Моли́твами и̂ слеза́ми гд҃а спаса́ющаго на́съ взы́щемъ (1b) (Cheese-Fare Sunday at Forgiveness Vespers—"With prayers and tears let us seek the Lord Who saveth us").

(1a)—1st unsoftened conjugation, (1b)—1st softened conjugation, (2)—2nd conjugation.

---

[1] 1a = 1st conjugation, class "a", verbs with unsoftened stems.- -*Tr.*

The verbs да́мъ [give], ꙗ́мъ [eat], вѣ́мъ [know], all of which retain an archaic conjugation, as well as the verb ви́дѣти [to see], form the 2nd and 3rd person singular imperatives with the aid of the suffix _ь_(jь): да́ждь, ꙗ́ждь, вѣ́ждь, ви́ждь.

The 3rd person imperative appears to have gone completely out of use and to have been replaced by the optative (see §91), except for the form бу́ди (from the verb бы́ти, "to be"): бу́ди и́мѧ гдⷭ҇не блгⷭ҇ове́но ѿ нꙑ́нѣ и̇ до вѣ́ка (Ps. 112:2—"Blessed be the name of the Lord henceforth and forevermore"); бу́ди мнѣ̀ по глаго́лу тво́ему̀ (Luke 1:38—"Be it unto me according to thy word").

The 2nd person imperative and the 2nd person present tense (or simple future) often have different accents: the imperative usually has the accent on the suffix _и̇_, while the present indicative rather frequently is accented on the personal ending _тѐ: и̇ а́ще благотвори́тѐ (Luke 6:33—"And if ye do good"); а́ще не ѡ̇брати́тесѧ (Matth. 18:3—"except ye be converted").

§94. The Participle.

According to the way they are formed, participles are divided into two types: *active* participles, and *passive*.

Under the term "active participles" are grouped those formed from both transitive and intransitive verbs, having a like system of formation, although the voice [active, middle, passive] of the verb from which they are formed is kept by them, for example: и̇ти̇ [to go], и̇д-у́тъ: и̇ды́й ["going"--middle voice[1]]; твори́ти [to do, make, create], твор_ѧ́тъ: творѧ́й ["doing, making"—active voice].

Participles formed from reflexive verbs retain the reflexive pronoun _сѧ, as well as the characteristics of the reflexive voice: боѧ́тисѧ: боѧ́йсѧ ["fearing"].

---

[1]) The voices of Slavonic verbs are explained in §73.--*Tr.*

Passive participles are usually formed only from transitive verbs; however, there are cases when they are formed from intransitive verbs as well: твори́ти: твори́мый [made]; but быва́ти: быва́емый ["being", from an intransitive verb].

Participles can have short and long forms[1].

§95. Active Present Participles

Active participles of the *present tense* are formed from the present stem by means of the suffix _Ꙋщ_ [_ющ_] in the case of 1st conjugation verbs, and the suffix _ащ_ [_ящ_ after the "hushing" sibilants] in verbs of the 2nd conjugation:

Present stem: нес_[Ꙋтъ] дѣлаj-[Ꙋтъ] мо́л_[ятъ] молч_[а́тъ]

               [bear]   [do, make]   [entreat]   [keep silence]

Participial stem: несꙊщ_ дѣлающ_   мо́лящ_   молча́щ_

In verbs of the 1st softened conjugation, the suffix _Ꙋщ_, taking on the iotation (j) of the stem, changes to _ющ_: дѣлаj-[Ꙋтъ]=дѣлающ_, глаго́лj-[Ꙋтъ]=глаго́лющ_; if the stem ends in a "hushing" sibilant, then the -j- is swallowed by the latter: пла́ка_ти, пла́ч_Ꙋтъ [from *пла́кj-Ꙋтъ] =пла́чꙊщ_.

Case and gender endings are joined to the participle stem. In the masculine nominative case the participial suffix drops out (but in 2nd conjugation verbs, only the _щ_ drops out), although short forms of the participle are also met with having the suffix; the neuter nominative can be with or without the suffix, with forms like those of the masculine (e.g. зерно̀... сѣется со слеза́ми днесь: но прозя́бше, мíръ радостносотвори́тъ (Holy Saturday Matins, chants

---

[1]) For the distinction between short and long forms of adjectives, see §49.--*Tr.*

at the 118th Psalm, v. 87—"The seed... is sown with tears today: but having sprouted, will cause the world to rejoice"); и҆ не терпѧ̀ зрѣ́ти со́лнце поме́рче (*ibid.*—v. 106: "And the sun, not bearing to see, was darkened").

The endings of the short and long participles are the following:

	Masculine:	Neuter:	Feminine:
Short:	_ый, _ѧ, _Ꙋщ_ъ	_ый, _ѧ, _Ꙋщ_е	_Ꙋщ_и
Long:	_ый, _ѧй,	_Ꙋщ_ее	_Ꙋщ_ѧѧ

The Nominative Case of Short and Long Participles:

Participial Stem	Nominative Case		
	Masculine	Neuter	Feminine
несꙊщ_	нес_ый, _Ꙋщ_ь	нес_ый¹, _Ꙋщ_е	нес_Ꙋщ_и (*bearing*)
	нес_ый	нес_Ꙋщ_ее	нес_Ꙋщ_ѧѧ	
дѣла_ющ_	дѣла_ѧ, _ющ_ь	дѣла_ѧ, _ющ_е	дѣла_ющ_и (*doing*)
	дѣла_ѧй	дѣла_ющ_ее	дѣла_ющ_ѧѧ
мол_ѧщ_	мол_ѧ̀, _ѧ́щ_ь	мол_ѧ̀, _ѧ́щ_е	мол_ѧ́щ_и (*entreating*)
	мол_ѧ́й	мол_ѧ́щ_ее	мол_ѧ́щ_ѧѧ
молч_ѧ́щ_	молч_ѧ̀, _ѧ́щ_ь	молч_ѧ̀, _ѧ́щ_е	молч_ѧ́щ_и (*being silent*)
	молч_ѧ́й	молч_ѧ́щ_ее	молч_ѧ́щ_ѧѧ

The verbs of the 1st unsoftened conjugation (§80), in the nominative masculine (and neuter) have the ending _ый, in both the short and long forms: самарѧни́нъ нѣ́кїй грѧды́й, прїи́де на него̀ (Luke 10:33—"A certain Samaritan approaching, came upon him"). In this example the participle грѧды́й is an adverbial participle

---

¹) Cf. бѣ̀ грѧды́й (Luke 9:53 in the Gospel text used in divine services—"as though he would go", "of one going").

(equivalent to a gerund[1]) and therefore is to be viewed as the short form.

Note: In Old Church Slavonic, such short forms of the participle ended in -ъı: нєс-ъı, грѧд-ъı, but in New Church Slavonic such endings have gone out of use.

Present participles are formed only from verbs of the imperfect aspect.

§96. Active Participles (Past).

Active *past* participles are derived from the infinitive stem as follows: *a)* If the infinitive stem ends in a *consonant*, then it takes the suffix -ш- (in reality the suffix is -зш-, but the з is not expressed in writing); *b)* If the infinitive stem ends in a *vowel*, then it takes the suffix -вш- [-взш-]:

Infinitive stem: нєс-[ти]	вєс-[ти]	дѣла-[ти]	твори́[ти]
to bear	*to lead*	*to do*	*to create*
Participial stem: нєс-ш-	вєд-ш-	дѣла-вш-	твори́-вш-

The participle stem takes gender- and case-endings.

In the nominative masculine singular, the -ш- drops out; the neuter nominative can take forms with or without -ш-, on the model of the masculine.

The participles have the following short and long forms:

Masculine:	Neuter:	Feminine:
Short: -з, -вз -з, вз:	-ш-є, -вш-є	-ш-и, -вш-и
Long: -ъıй, -въıй	-ш-єє, -вш-єє	-ш-ая, -вш-ая

---

[1] A gerund is a kind of verbal noun expressing incomplete action. Examples of gerund-like constructions in English are "I have bread *to sell*", or "they are prepared *for reciting* the lesson".—*Tr.*

Nominative Case of Short and Long Participles:

Participle stem:	Nominative case:		
	Masculine:	Neuter:	Feminine:
нєс_ш_	нѣс_ъ, _ш_ъ	нѣс_ъ, нѣс_ш_є	нѣс_ш_и *(having borne)*
	нєс_ыꙵ	нєс_ш_єє	нєс_ш_ая
вєд_ш_	вѣд_ъ, _ш_ъ	вѣд_ъ,вѣд_ш_є	вѣд_ш_и *(having led)*
	вѣд_ыꙵ	вѣд_ш_єє	вѣд_ш_ая
дѣла_вш_	дѣла_въ, _вш_ъ дѣла_въ, дѣла_вш_є дѣла_вши *(having done)*		
	дѣла_выꙵ	дѣла_вш_єє	дѣла_вш_ая
твори_вш_	твори_въ, _вш_ъ твори_въ, твори_вш_є твори_вши *(having wrought)*		
	твори_выꙵ	твори_вш_єє	твори_вш_ая

Note: In verbs of the imperfective aspect, the long forms of the participles ending in _ыꙵ have past and present forms that coincide (although their derivation is different), and they can be distinguished only by the sense of the construction.

Verbs of the *perfective aspect* whose infinitive stem ends in _н_ build their forms with the aid of the suffix _ш_, while at the same time the _н_ of the stem becomes _ь (jь), before which as a result of softening, the alternation of consonants takes place (where possible)[1]: испроси_ти [to request], испрошь[ш]. As in the preceding formations, in the nominative masculine the _ш_ drops out (this applies also to the neuter as indicated above). The suffix _ь_ before ш or _ся is never omitted following л; in other cases, configurations with or without _ь_ may occur (especially after the "hushing" sibilants): возлюби_ти [to love, come to love, form an affection for], возлюбль, возлюбльши: сотвори_ти [make, fashion, create], сотворь, сотворши and also сотворьши: восклоньса, or восклонса (John 8:7--"he lifted up himself").

---

[1] See §11.

Participles of this formation have the following short and long endings:

Endings:	Masculine:	Neuter:	Feminine:
Short	_ь	_ь, _[ь]ш_е	_[ь]ш_н
Long	_ей	_[ь]ш_ее	_[ь]ш_аѧ

Short and Long Forms of the Participle:

Short	сотвор_ь	сотвор_ь, _[ь]ш_е	сотвор_[ь]ш_н
Long	сотвор_ей	сотвор_[ь]ш_ее	сотвор_[ь]ш_аѧ

[having wrought, made]

Verbs having a prefix, and also the suffix _нѹ_ after a consonant, for the most part form their participles without this suffix: по_двиг_нѹ_ти [to hasten, strive]: подвигъ [masc.], подвигши [fem.], e.g. а дрѹгое паде на камени, и прозѧбъ* оусше (Luke 8:6-- "And other fell upon a rock, and having sprung up, withered away")).

The verbs начати [to begin], ѧ_ти [to take], распѧ_ти [to crucify], take the suffix _ш_ [хш], and the *yus* [ѧ, or ѧ] resolves itselfbefore the х of the suffix into a vowel and consonant: начен_х, начен_[х]ши: пріем_х, пріем_[х]ши (also пріимх, пріимши "having received"); распенх, распен_[х]ши, but жати [to reap], пожабх.

§97. The Participle in -лх.

The active _лх_participle (or indeclinable participle) is formed from the infinitive stem by adding to it the suffix _л_: нес_ти, нес_лх: хвали_ти[to praise], хвалилх.

---

¹) прозѧбх from прозѧб_нѹ_ти, "to spring up".--*Tr.*

This participle is not declined by cases, by has gender and number:

Forms of the Participle in -ᴧ҂:

	Singular	Dual	Plural
Masc.	нє́ᴄᴧ҂	нєᴄᴧа̂	нєᴄᴧѝ
Fem.	нєᴄᴧа̀	нєᴄᴧѝ	нєᴄᴧѝ
Neut.	нєᴄᴧо̀	нєᴄᴧѝ	нєᴄᴧѝ

The consonants д, т drop out before the suffix _ᴧ_ (See §13b): вє́ᴧ҂ instead of *вє́д_ᴧ҂, ѡбрѣ́ᴧ҂ [found] instead of *ѡбрѣ́т_ᴧ҂.

Verbs with the suffix _нꙋ_ after a consonant omit, for the most part, this suffix in forming the participle: e.g. воᴄкрєᴄ_нꙋ_ти [to rise again, resurrect], воᴄкрє́ᴄᴧ҂.

The participle in _ᴧ҂ is not used independently, but only in the compound forms of verbs (see §88 and 89 above).

§98. Declension of the Active Participles.

The *short* forms of the active present and past participles are declined on the model of the short comparative adjectives (cf. §53).

Case Forms of the Short Participles:

Singular.	Masculine.	Neuter.	Feminine.
Nom.	твора̀, _а́щ_ь (1)	твора̀, _а́щ_є	твора́щ_и
Gen.	твора́щ_а	твора́щ_а	твора́щ_и
Dat.	твора́щ_ꙋ	твора́щ_ꙋ	твора́щ_и
Acc.	твора́щ_҂, _а	твора́щ_є	твора́щ_ꙋ
Instr.	твора́щ_имѕ	твора́щ_имѕ	твора́щ_єю
Prep.	твора́щ_ємѕ	твора́щ_ємѕ	твора́щ_и
Dual.			
N., A.	твѡра́щ_а	твора́щ_ѣ (2), _а	твѡра́щ_ѣ (3)
G., P.	твѡра́щ_ꙋ	твѡра́щ_ꙋ	твѡра́щ_ꙋ
D., I.	твора́щ_єма (4)	твора́щ_єма	твора́щ_єма

Plural.

Nom.	твоⷬ҇а́щ_е	твѡⷬ҇а́щ_а	твоⷬ҇а́щ_а[_е]
Gen.	твоⷬ҇а́щ_ихъ	твоⷬ҇а́щ_ихъ	твоⷬ҇а́щ_ихъ
Dat.	твоⷬ҇а́щ_ымъ (5)	твоⷬ҇а́щ_ымъ	твоⷬ҇а́щ_ымъ
Acc.	твоⷬ҇а́щ_а, _ихъ	твѡⷬ҇а́щ_а	твоⷬ҇а́щ_а, _ихъ
In.	твоⷬ҇а́щ_ими	твоⷬ҇а́щ_ими	твоⷬ҇а́щ_ими
Prep.	твоⷬ҇а́щ_ихъ	твоⷬ҇а́щ_ихъ	твоⷬ҇а́щ_ихъ

(1) Торжествꙋ́ющїй¹ свѣ́тлѡ желаⸯющъ* тѧ̀ гра́дъ, ѹ҆чрежда́емь быва́етъ, ꙗ҆́кѡ бога́тство ѡ҆брѣ́тшъ* та́йное, и҆ и҆сто́чникъ неѡскꙋ́денъ и҆сцѣле́нїй, пⷣте́че, главꙋ́ твою̀ (Feb. 24 at Matins, Ode 3—"Celebrating radiantly, the city that yearneth for thee is festive², as having found a secret treasure, and an inexhaustible source of healings, O Forerunner: thy head").

(2) Да бꙋ́дꙋтъ ѹ҆́ши твоѝ, внє́млющѣ* гла́съ моле́нїѧ моегѡ̀ (Ps. 129:2—"Let Thine ears be attentive to the voice of my supplication").

(3) Бѣ̀ же тꙋ̀ марі́а и҆ дрꙋга́ѧ марі́а, сѣдѧ́щѣ* пра́мѡ гро́ба (Matth. 27:61—"And there was Mary [Magdalene] and the other Mary, sitting over against the sepulchre").

(4) Ѡ҆нѣ́ же пристꙋ́пльше, ꙗ҆́стѣⷭ за но́зѣ є҆гѡ̀, и҆ поклони́стѣⷭ є҆мꙋ́... и҆дꙋ́щема* же и҆ма, сѐ нѣ́цыи ѿ кꙋстоді́и... (Matth. 28:9-11—"But they came up and took hold of His feet, and

---

¹) This form must be viewed as irregular, in place of торжествꙋ́ай.

²) Ѹ҆чрежда́тисѧ (εὐωχέω) means "to celebrate, to dine sumptuously, be nourished, filled with sweetness".

adored Him... And when they departed[1], behold, some of the guards...").

(5) Пристра́шнымъ же бы́вшымъ* и́мъ (мѵроносицамъ) и
поклоншымъ* ли́ца на зе́млю, реко́ста къ ни́мъ: что́ и́щете жива́го
съ ме́ртвыми; (Luke 24:5—"And as they [i.e. the Myrrhbearers] were
afraid, and bowed down their countenance towards the ground, they said
unto them: Why seek ye the Living with the dead?").

The past participles are also declined in the same manner.

Notes on the Cases:

1. After the participial suffix [ȣщ, ащ, ш], in the nominative
and accusative cases the spelling can be equally with ъ or ь, although in
some editions ь is used predominantly for the nominative case, while ъ is
counterposed to it as the spelling of the accusative.

2. Examples (4) and (5) above show that in the cases of the dual
and plural, except the nominative and accusative, the endings of the
feminine have been assimilated to those of the masculine (in Old Church
Slavonic, the feminine endings were distinctive).

3. Sometimes the short participles in the neuter singular have the
ending що[шо] instead of ще[ше]: непостоя́нныхъ и тле́нныхъ до́лȣ
влекȣщо... (Jan. 13, Matins, 3rd Canon, for the Venerable Fathers of
Sinai and Raitha, Ode 3—"[having cast aside] the downward pull[2] of
things temporary and corruptible..."); нынѣ ѿ земли́ изда́вшося
чȣде́съ заре́ю испȣща́етъ (July 5, St. Sergius of Radonezh, 4th sticheron
at "Lord I have cried"—"[Then, like a star, thou didst rise to the

---

[1]) Here the construction of идȣщема же и́ма is what is called
a "dative absolute" (in Russian "дательный самостоятельный"). It is
explained in §197.--Tr.

[2]) The Slavonic до́лȣ влекȣщо "pulling downward"
corresponds to the Greek τὸ χαμερπές, "that which creeps on the
ground".--Tr.

heavenly habitations, while thy body lay hidden; but--] now, relinquished by the earth, it giveth forth a dawn [new day] of miracles").

4. In the nominative masculine (and neuter) after the "hushing" sibilants, а is usually written (e.g. пишѧ̀ [writing], двнжѧ̀ [moving], but the ancient ending _ѧ is also to be met with.

5. The feminine participle in the nominative plural can have as an ending either _ѧ or _е (by parallel with the masculine): творѧ́щ_ѧ or творѧ́щ_е, сотво́рш_ѧ or сотво́рш_е.

The long forms of the participles are declined regularly on the model of the long adjectives with stem ending in a "hushing" sibilant (§57):

Sing.	Masculine	Neuter	Feminine
Nom.	творѧ́й *doing*	творѧ́щее	творѧ́щаѧ
Gen.	творѧ́щагw	творѧ́щагw	творѧ́щїѧ
Dat.	творѧ́щемꙋ	творѧ́щемꙋ	творѧ́щей
Acc.	творѧ́щїй [_аго]	творѧ́щее	творѧ́щꙋю
Instr.	творѧ́щнмъ	творѧ́щнмъ	творѧ́щею
Prep.	творѧ́щемъ	творѧ́щемъ	творѧ́щей
Dual			
N., A.	творѧ̂щаѧ	творѧ́щїн	творѧ́щїн
G., P.	творѧ̂щꙋю	творѧ̂щꙋю	творѧ̂щꙋю
D., I.	творѧ́щнма	творѧ́щнма	творѧ́щнма
Plural			
N.	творѧ́щїн	творѧ̂щаѧ	творѧ́щыѧ
Gen.	творѧ́щнхъ	творѧ́щнхъ	творѧ́щнхъ
Dat.	творѧ́щымъ	творѧ́щымъ	творѧ́щымъ
Acc.	творѧ́щыѧ [_нхъ]	творѧ̂щаѧ	творѧ́щыѧ [_нхъ]
In.	творѧ́щнмн	творѧ́щнмн	творѧ́щнмн
Prep.	творѧ́щнхъ	творѧ́щнхъ	творѧ́щнхъ

§99. Passive Participles (Present).

The passive participles of the *present tense* are formed from the present stem by means of the suffixes _ом_, _ем_, _им_:

1) Verbs of the 1st unsoftened conjugation take the suffix _ом_ : несу́тъ: нес_о́мъ, _а, _о [that which is carried]; зову́тъ: зов_о́мъ, _а, _о [that which is called].

This same suffix is taken by the verbs of archaic conjugation, вѣмъ and ꙗмъ: вѣд_омъ, _а, _о [that which is known]; ꙗд_о́мъ, _а, _о [that which is eaten].

2) Verbs of the 1st softened conjugation take the suffix _ем_: пи́шꙋтъ: пиш_ем_ь, _а, _о [that which is written]; зна́ютъ: зна́_ем_ь, _а, _о [that with which one is acquainted; known].

3) The verbs of the 2nd conjugation take the suffix _им_: хва́лѧтъ: хвал_и́м_ь, _а, _о [that which is praised]; лю́бѧтъ: люб_и́м_ь, _а, _о [that which is loved, liked].

Note: Verbs with the suffix _нꙋ_ have no present passive participle, since they are either verbs of the perfective aspect, or else transitive verbs : двигнꙋти [to strive], со́хнꙋти [to become dry].

Masculine participles with the suffixes _ем_, _им_ in the nominative and accusative cases are spelled with the ending _ь so as to distinguish them from the verb forms of the first person plural: e.g. велича́емь [magnified, praised, extolled], сꙋди́мь [judged], but: несо́мъ [carried]; e.g. Іерꙋсали́мъ бꙋдетъ попира́емь ꙗзы́ки (Luke 21:24—"Jerusalem shall be trodden down by the Gentiles"), but вѣдомъ во Іꙋде́и бг҃ъ (Ps. 75:2—"God is known in Judea").

§100. Passive Participles (Past).

Passive participles of the *past tense* are formed from the infinitive stem, by means of the suffixes _н_, _ен_, _т_:

) The suffix _н_ s used to form participles from verbs having an infinitive stem that ends in the suffixes _а_, _ѣ_: сдѣла_ти, сдѣла_ н_ъ, _а, _о [done]; вид‌ѣ_ти, вид‌ѣ_н_ъ, _а, _о [seen].[1]

2) The suffix _ен_ is used to form past participles from infinitive stems that end in:

a) a consonant: нес_ти̇, нес_е́н_ъ, _а, _о [borne, carried]; вес_ти̇, вед_е́н_ъ, _а, _о [led]; and if the gutturals г, к occur before the suffix, they are softened and replaced by ж, ч: рещи̇ [*рек_ти], реч_е́н_ъ, _а, _о [said, uttered]; возмощи̇ [*возмог_ти], возмо́ж_ен_ъ, _а, _о[possible].

b) _н_, which before the suffix becomes **j**, and then as a result of softening there occurs the alternation of consonants (where possible): оу̇моли̇_ти [to entreat], оу̇мол_е́н_ъ, _а, _о (from *оу̇молjенъ)[moved by entreaty]; возлюби̇_ти, возлюблен_ъ, _а, _о [beloved]; роди̇_ти [give birth, beget], рожде́н_ъ, _а, _о [born].

3) The suffix _т_ is used to form participles from infinitive stems, equivalent to roots, which end in a vowel:[2] би_ти [to beat], би_т_ъ, _а, _о [beaten]; ꙗ̃_ти [to take], ꙗ̃т_ъ, _а, _о [taken]; распа́_ти [to crucify], распа_т_ъ, _а, _о: простер_ти [to extend, spread out], простер_т_ъ, _а, _о: скры́_ти [to hide, conceal], скры́_т_ъ, _а, _о [hidden].

From verbs with the stem-root in _и_, _ы_, participles are also formed with the aid of the suffix _ен_, and before the suffix, _ы_ becomes _ов_ (see §10, 3): би_ти, бï_е́н_ъ, _а, _о [beaten]; испи̇_ти, испï_е́н_ъ, _а, _о[drink down, drain a cup]; оу̇мы́_ти, оу̇мов_е́н_ъ, _а, _о [washed]; скры́_ти, сокров_е́н_ъ, _а, _о [concealed].

---

[1]) Note that the corresponding English words use the same suffix -*n* to make the past participle: see, see*n*; do, do*n*e. --*Tr.*

[2]) Like -*n* and -*en*, -*t* is also used as a suffix to form past participles in English (e.g. *to mean, meant*), which can be a memory aid here.--*Tr.*

4) Some participles build their forms with the suffix _ЕН_ from the present stem: ЗАКЛА́_ТИ, ЗАКО́Л_ЮТЪ [sacrifice, slay], ЗАКОЛ_Е́Н_Ъ, _А, _О: but forms of the participle can also be derived from the infinitive stem: ЗАКЛА́_Н_Ъ, _А, _О [slain, sacrificed].

5) Verbs with their infinitive stem in _НУ_ have the following possibilities for forming their participles:

a) with the suffix _Т_: ПОДВИ́ГНУ_ТИ, ПОДВИ́ГНУ_Т_Ъ, _А, _О [roused, moved];

b) by means of the suffix _ЕН_: the suffix _НУ_, if it follows a vowel, usually is dropped: ПОСТИ́ГНУ_ТИ [to reach, attain], ПОСТИ́Ж_ЕН_Ъ, _А, _О: when the suffix _НУ_ is retained, then the У is lost, and the stem is compounded by the suffix _ОВ_: ПОСТИГНОВ_Е́Н_Ъ, _А, _О [attained]; ѼРИНУ_ТИ [to cast aside, reject], ѼРИНОВ_Е́Н_Ъ, _А, _О.

Past passive participles are formed for the most part from verbs of the perfective aspect.

The long forms of the passive participles are formed in the same manner as the long forms of adjectives: ЛЮБИ́М_Ь: ЛЮБИ́М_ЫЙ, _АА, _ОЕ [favorite, beloved]; НЕСО́М_Ъ: НЕСО́М_ЫЙ, _АА, _ОЕ [carried]; СОТВОРЕ́Н_Ъ: СОТВОРЕ́НН_ЫЙ, _АА, _ОЕ [created, made]; ОУ́МОВЕ́Н_Ъ: ОУ́МОВЕ́НН_ЫЙ, _АА, _ОЕ [washed].

The short and long passive participles are declined on the model of adjectives (see §53 and §57).

§101. Passive Forms of the Verb.

Passive verbal forms are expressed in two ways:

a) Either by means of the reflexive pronoun _СА, which is attached to transitive verbs;

b) Or by means of compound forms, consisting of passive participles and a copula (forms of the verb БЫ́ТИ, to be); the one who performs the action is then either in the instrumental case, or else in the genitive with the preposition Ѽ: И КРЕЩА́ХУСА* ВО ІѠРДА́НѢ Ѽ НЕГѠ, ИСПОВѢ́ДАЮЩЕ ГРѢХЍ СВОА̂ (Matth. 3:6—"And they were baptized in the Jordan by him, confessing their sins"); ПРЕ́ДАНИ* ЖЕ

ꙮ ꙮ (Luke 21:16—"And
ye shall be betrayed by your parents and brethren, and kinsmen and
friends"); тогда і́рѡдъ ви́дѣвъ, ꙗ́кѡ порꙋ́ганъ* бы́сть* ѿ
волхвѡ́въ, разгнѣ́васѧ ѕѣлѡ̀ (Matth. 2:16—"Then Herod,seeing
that he was mocked of the wise men, was exceeding wroth"). With
the compound passive forms, the performer of the action may not be
indicated at all: всѧ́ко ѹ́бо дре́во, є́же не твори́тъ плода̀ добра̀,
посѣка́емо* быва́етъ*, ѝ во ѻ́гнь вмета́емо* (Matth.
3:10—"Therefore every tree which bringeth not forth good fruit, is
hewn down, and cast into the fire").

The passive participle in compound forms is always in the
nominative case.

§102. Passive Forms of Tenses and Moods.

Compound passive forms, consisting of present participles, are
forms of the imperfective aspect; but those that consist of past
participles are forms of the perfective aspect; for example, несо́мъ
бꙋ́дꙋ (imperfective), принесе́нъ бꙋ́дꙋ (perfective aspect).

Infinitive : храни́мь бы́ти (imperfective aspect)
сохране́нъ бы́ти (perfective aspect)--*to be kept, preserved*
Present tense: храни́мь є́смь, є́сѝ, є́сть &c.
Future tense: храни́мь [сохране́нъ] бꙋ́дꙋ, бꙋ́деши, бꙋ́детъ &c.
Aorist: храни́мь [сохране́нъ] бы́хъ, бы́сть &c.
храни́мь бѣ́хъ, бѣ̀ &c.
Imperfect: храни́мь бѧ́хъ, бѧ́ше &c.
Perfect: сохране́нъ є́смь, є́сѝ, є́сть &c.
Pluperfect: сохране́нъ бѣ́хъ, бѣ̀ [бѧ́хъ, бѧ́ше] [бы́лъ є́смь, є́сѝ,
є́сть] &c.
Subjunctive: храни́мь [сохране́нъ] бы́лъ бы́хъ, бы̀ &c.
Imperative: храни́мь [сохране́нъ] бꙋ́ди, бꙋ́дева, бꙋ́дита &c.

Concerning the meaning and use of these forms, see below in Syntax (§154-169).

Examples:

РѢША ЖЕ СЛЫШАВШІИ: ТО КТО МОЖЕТЪ СПАСЕНЪ БЫ́ТИ; (Infinitive; Matth. 19:25—"Having heard, they said: Who then can be saved?"); можа́ше сіѐ мѵ́ро про́дано бы́ти (infinitive) на мно́зѣ, и да́тисѧ ни́щымъ (Matth. 26:9—"For this ointment might have been sold for much, and given to the poor"); на сіѐ бо и трꙋжда́емсѧ и поноша́еми ѐсмы̀ (present), ꙗ́кѡ ѹупова́хомъ на бга жи́ва (I Tim. 4:10—"For therefore we both labour and suffer reproach, because we trust[1] in the living God"); и бꙋ́дете ненави́дими (future) ѿ всѣ́хъ и́мене моегѡ̀ ра́ди (Luke 21:17—"And ye shall be hated of all men for my name's sake"); блюди́те, да не прельще́ни бꙋ́дете (future)—(Luke 21:8—"Take heed that ye be not deceived"); жива̀ вве́ржена бы́ста (aorist) ѻ́ба въ є҆́зеро ѻ҆́гненное, горѧ́щее жꙋ́пеломъ (Rev. 19:20—"Both were cast alive into a lake of fire, burning with brimstone"); не бо́йсѧ, ꙗ́кѡ посра́млена ѐси̇(perfect), ниже́ ѹусты́дисѧ, ꙗ́кѡ ѹукоре́на ѐси (perf.))Isaiah 54:4—"Fear not, because thou hast been put to shame, neither be confounded, because thou wast reproached); ѡ҆брѣ́те же та́мѡ человѣ́ка нѣ́коего и́менемъ ѐне́а, ѿ ѻ҆́сми лѣ́тъ лежа́ща на ѻ҆дрѣ́, и́же бѣ̀ разсла́бленъ (pluperfect) (Acts 9:33—"And there he found a certain man named Æneas, which had kept his bed eight years, and was sick of the palsy"); и жены̀ нѣ́кїѧ, ꙗ҆́же ба́хꙋ и҆сцѣле́ны (pluperfect) ѿ дꙋ́хѡвъ ѕлы́хъ и неду́гъ (Luke 8:2—"And certain women, which had been healed of evil spirits and infirmities"); а҆́ще бы̀ ѿ мі́ра сегѡ̀ бы́ло бы̀ ца́рство моѐ, слꙋги̇ мои̇ ѹ҆́бо подвиза́лисѧ бы́ша, да не пре́данъ бы́лъ бы́хъ (subjunctive mood) і҆ꙋде́ѡмъ (John 18:36—"If my kingdom were of

---

[1] The Slavonic uses the past tense, "We have put our trust"--
i.e. we still trust.--*Tr.*

this world, then would my servants fight, that I should not be delivered to the Jews").

§103. The Verbs of Archaic Conjugation.

The following verbs belong to the archaic conjugation: вы́ти: є҆́смь [to be], да́ти: да́мъ [to give], ꙗ҆́сти: ꙗ҆́мъ [to eat], вѣ́дѣти: вѣ́мъ [to know], и҆мѣ́ти or и҆ма́ти: и҆́мамъ [to have]--(see §81).

These verbs differ in their conjugation from the main conjugation of verbs only in the present tense (or in the simple future) and in the imperative; all their other forms are derived in the same manner as those of the main conjugations, with the exception of the aorist of the verb да́ти, which are of archaic formation: да́хъ (instead of *дадо́хъ), да́дѐ, да́хова &c. (Cf. рѣ́хъ: рѣ́ко́хъ, §86).

Note 1: The verb да́ти is of the perfective aspect, and therefore instead of the a present tense, it forms the simple future; the form даю̀ [I give] being derived from да-ꙗ́-ти.

Note 2: When the verb ꙗ҆́мъ takes the prefix с, the ꙗ becomes ѣ: с+ꙗ́мъ=снѣ́мъ (from съꙗ́-ѣмъ). [See §112 for an explanation of such prefixes].

Note 3: The verb и҆ма́ти takes its root from ꙗ́ти [to take] (Cf. прїꙗ́ти: прїима́ꙋ [to take, receive]).

Indicative Mood:

Simple Future.   Present.

Singular.

1st	да́-мъ *I will give*	ꙗ́-мъ *I eat*	вѣ́-мъ *I know*	и҆м-а-мъ *I have*
2nd	да́-си	ꙗ́-си	вѣ́-си	и҆м-а-ши
3rd	да́с-тъ	ꙗ́с-тъ	вѣ́с-ть	и҆м-а-ть

Dual.

1st	да́-ва, -вѣ	ꙗ́-ва, ѣ	вѣ́-ва, ѣ	и҆м-а-ва, ѣ
2 & 3	да́с-та, -ѣ	ꙗ́с-та, -ѣ	вѣ́с-та, ѣ	и҆м-а-та, ѣ

Plural.

1st	да́_мы	га́_мы	вѣ́_мы	йм_а_мы
2nd	да́є_тє	га́є_тє	вѣ́є_тє	йм_а_тє
3rd	дад_у́тъ, _а́тъ[1]	гад_а́тъ	вѣд_а_тъ	йм_у́тъ

Imperative Mood:

Singular

2 & 3	да́жд_ь	га́жд_ь	вѣ́жд_ь	йм_ѣ́_й
Dual I	дад_и́_ва, _ѣ	гад_и́_ва, _ѣ	вѣд_и_ва, _ѣ	йм_ѣ_и_ва, _ѣ
2 & 3	дад_и́_та, ѣ	гад_и́_та, ѣ	вѣд_и_та, ѣ	йм_ѣ_и_та, ѣ
Plu. I	дад_и́_мъ	гад_и́_мъ	вѣд_и_мъ	йм_ѣ_и_мъ
2	дад_и́_тє	гад_и́_тє	вѣд_и_тє	йм_ѣ_й_тє

Present Participle:

	Active.	Passive.
га́мъ:	гады́й[2], _у́цъ	гадо́мъ, _ый
	гаду́цн, _у́цаа	гадо́ма, _аа
	гаду́цє, _у́цєє	гадо́мо, _оє
вѣ́мъ:	вѣ́дый, _у́цъ	вѣ́домъ, _ый
	вѣ́дуцн, _у́цаа	вѣ́дома, _аа
	вѣ́дуцє, _у́цєє	вѣ́домо, _оє
йма́мъ:	ймы́й, _у́цъ	[Passive participles lacking]
	йму́цн, _у́цаа	
	йму́цє, _у́цєє	

---

[1]) Two forms are given, because дада́тъ is the traditional Old Church Slavonic form, while даду́тъ was introduced more recently under the influence of Russian.--*Tr.*

[2]) This is both the short and long form: see §95.

The verb да́мъ [*I will give*] is of the perfective aspect, and therefore has no present participle. Past participles are usually formed from the infinitive stem.

§104. Verbs Having Irregular Forms.

Only the main forms are shown, or those that present some difficulty in their formation (certain rare verb forms are omitted due to lack of documentation).

Б

блюсти́, [to observe, watch over; beware of] present tense блюдꙋ́тъ, aorist [со]блюдо́хъ, participle in _лъ [со]блю́лъ (§97).

[про]бости́, [to pierce, bore through] future прободꙋ́тъ, aorist прободо́хъ, _лъ-participle прободо́лъ (§97).

бра́ти, [to take] present берꙋ́тъ, imperfect бера́хъ (?).

бра́тися, [to battle], present бо́рѧтсѧ, aor. бра́хсѧ [бра́шасѧ, Ps. 128:1—"Often have they *fought against* me"), imperfect бора́хсѧ (I Cor. 15:32—"I *fought with* beasts"), _лъ-participle бра́лсѧ, past passive participle побо́ренъ.

бы́ти, [to be], pres. є̑́смь, future бꙋ́дꙋ, imperative бꙋ́ди, aorist бы́хъ, бѣ́хъ, imperfect бѧ́хъ, present participle сы́й, сꙋ́щи, past participle бы́въ, бы́вши, _лъ-participle бы́лъ (§81).

В

вести́ [to lead], pres. ведꙋ́тъ, _лъ-participle ве́лъ (§97).

ви́ти, [to wind, wrap], pres. вїю́тъ, aor. пови́хъ, 2nd, 3rd p. aor. пови́тъ, past passive participle пови́тъ.

ви́дѣти, [to see], imperative ви́ждь.

влещи́, [to drag, pull], pres. влекꙋ́тъ.

[ѿ]ве́рсти, [to open], (John 10:21—"*open* the eyes of the blind), future ѿве́рзꙋтъ, aorist ѿве́рзохъ, past participle ѿве́рзъ, _ шн, _лъ-participle ѿве́рзлъ, passive part. ѿве́ртъ [ѿве́рето, John 1:51—"ye shall see heaven *opened*").

[по]вре́щѝ [to cast], [воврещѝ, Luke 12:49—"to *cast* fire on the earth"], fut. пове́ргꙋ́тъ [пове́ргꙋ, Ezek. 6:4—"I will *cast down* your slain men."], imperative пове́ржи [не ѿве́ржи, Ps. 50—"*cast* me not away"], aorist повергѡ́хъ, active past participle пове́ргъ, _ши (Luke 4:35—"had *thrown* him in the midst"), _лъ-participle пове́рглъ, past passive part. пове́рженъ.

вѣ́дѣти, [to know], pres. вѣ́мъ, imperative вѣ́ждь, pres. active part. вѣ́дый, pres. passive part. вѣ́домъ.

[ꙋ́]вѧнꙋти, [to wilt], fut. ꙋ́вѧнꙋтъ, aor. ꙋ́вѧдѡ́хъ.

Г

гаснꙋти, [to go out (of a flame)], pres. гаснꙋтъ, aorist ꙋ́гасѡ́хъ.

[ꙋ́]глѣбнꙋти, [to be sunk, mired], fut. ꙋ́глѣбнꙋ, aorist ꙋ́глѣбѡ́хъ. [1]

[по]гребстѝ [to bury], fut. погребꙋ́тъ, aor. погребѡ́хъ: except for the infinitive, all forms are without the е in the stem.

гна́ти, [to chase, persecute, strive after], in the present stem гон_: гоню̀ (Philippians 3:12—"I follow after"); и̇згоню̀ (Luke 13:32—"I *cast out* devils"); imperative гони́те (I Thessalonians 5:15—"ever *follow* that which is good"); imperfect гонѧ́хъ (Ps. 37:21—"because I *strove after* goodness"); future stem жен_: пожене́те

---

[1]) This word is spelled ꙋ́глебнꙋти, ꙋ́глебнꙋ, ꙋ́глебѡ́хъ in the Russian edition of this book, but seems to be more usually written with ѣ. The Old Slavonic form given in Diachenko (p. 946) is ꙋ́гльбнꙋти.

(Leviticus 26:7--"Ye shall *pursue* your enemies"); и҆зженѝ (Gal. 4:30—"*Cast out* the bondwoman and her son"); infinitive stem гна̣: aorist и҆згна́хъ.

гибнꙋ́ти, [to perish], pres. ги́блю (Luke 15:17, from гиба́ти: "I here *perish* with hunger"); future with н: погѝбнетъ (Ps. 72:27—"they that go far from Thee shall *perish*"); active present participle гибнꙋ́щїѧ (I Peter 1:7—"gold *that perisheth*"); ги́блющее (John 6:27--"the meat *which perisheth*").

д

да́ти [to give], pres. да́мъ *I will give*, aorist да́хъ, 2nd & 3rd person дадѐ.

[воз]двигнꙋ́ти [to raise up], fut. воздвигнꙋ́, aor. воздвиго́хъ.

довлѣ́ти [to be enough, sufficient], use of which is attested only for the 3rd person singular and plural, present tense: довлѣ́етъ (Matth. 6:34—"*Sufficient* unto the day is the evil thereof").

досто́итъ [it is right, just, fitting]: (Mark 10:2—"*Is it lawful* for a man to put away his wife?"); used only in the 3rd p. singular. Imperf. досто́аше.

дра́ти [to tear, flay], pres. дерꙋ́тъ.

дѣ́ати [to do, put], besides the usual forms, has also parallel forms with the stem ̣дежд̣: воздежи́те (Ps. 133:2—"In the nights *lift up* your hands"), воздежꙋ́ (Ps. 62:5—"I will *lift up* my hands"), ѡ҆дежде́мсѧ (Matth. 6:31—"what clothing shall we *put on*?").

дꙋ́ти [to blow], (little used), present active participle дма́сѧ (Colossians 2:18--"in vain *puffed up*").

дхнꙋ́ти [to breathe], fut. дхнꙋ́тъ (дхне́тъ, Ps. 147:7--"His wind *shall blow*"), aor. дхнꙋ́хъ, 2nd & 3rd p. дхнꙋ́ (Pentecost Matins, Ode 9:—"To as many as the Grace *breathed*[cf.

"inspiration"] that issued forth from God"), and without _нꙋ_: и҆здахѻ́хъ, 2nd & 3rd p. и҆зды́ше (Mark 15:37—"gave up the ghost"); active past participle дхнꙋ́въ, _ши (Acts 27:13—"And the south wind gently *blowing*...); воздохнꙋ́ти, fut. воздохнꙋ́тъ, aor. воздохнꙋ́хъ, 2nd-3rd person воздохнꙋ́ (Mark 7:34—"he *sighed*"); active past participle воздохнꙋ́въ, _ши (Mark 8:12--"And he *sighed* deeply in his spirit").

Ж

жа́ти [to press], pres. жмꙋ́тъ.

жа́ти [to reap, harvest], pres. жнꙋ́тъ.

[ѹ҆]жаснꙋ́тисѧ [to wonder, be amazed], ѹ҆жаснꙋ́тсѧ (Isaiah 52:14—"As many have *been astonished at* thee"), aor. ѹ҆жасо́хсѧ.

жещѝ [to burn], pres. жгꙋ́тъ, сожже́тъ (Luke 3:17—"but the chaff he *will* burn"), aor. зажгѻ́хъ, зажже́ (Matth. 22:7—"*burned up* their city"), imperative разжзѝ, active pres. part. жгі́й, active past part. соже́гъ, _ши; passive present part. жгѻ́мъ (Nov. 19 at Vespers, at "Lord I have cried"—"*inflamed*"); passive past part. сожже́нъ.

жва́ти [to chew], pres. жꙋ́ютъ (?), aor. жва́хъ, impf. жва́хъ [жва́хꙋ, Rev. 16:10—"and they *gnawed* their tongues for pain"), present passive part. сожва́емъ (Job 20:18—"and he shall not be *consumed*").

жи́ти [to live], pres. живꙋ́тъ, aor. жи́хъ, и҆ждихъ (Sunday of the Prodigal Son, Sessional Hymn after the 3rd Ode—"I *have wasted*"[1]), 2nd-3rd p. ѡ҆живѐ (Luke 15:24—"For this my son was dead, and *is alive again*"); impf. жива́хъ.

---

[1]) Diachenko's Slavonic dictionary (p. 210) derives the form и҆ждити from Old Church Slavonic изджити, из-жити "to use up by living from".--*Tr.*

жре́ти [to offer sacrifice], (Old Church Slavonic жрьти, жьреши); pres. жру́тъ, aor. пожро́хъ, impf. жра́хъ, _лъ-participle пожерлъ, present passive part. жре́мъ, _ый, past pass. part. пожре́нъ.

жре́ти [to swallow up], (Old Church Slavonic жрѣти, жьреши) which has the same forms as the preceding verb except for the past passive participle: пожертъ (пожерты, Ps. 140:6—"Their judges, falling upon the rock, *have been swallowed up*").

З

зва́ти [to call], pres. зовутъ, aor. воз-зва́хъ, impf. зова́хъ and зва́ху (Matth. 21:9--"the multitudes...*cried*..."), active pres. part. зовый, _ущи, pres. pass. part. зово́мъ.

зда́ти [to build], pres. зижду́тъ, impf. зда́ху (Luke 17:28-- "they planted, they *builded*"); active part. зижда, _ущи (зиждай, Ps. 146:2--"The Lord *buildeth up* Jerusalem"), pass. part. зиждемь (Ps. 121:3--"Jerusalem, *which is built* as a city").

[про]за́бнути [to sprout, cause to bud], fut. про-за́бнутъ, aor. прозабо́хъ.

И

има́ти [имѣ́ти][to have], derived from я́ти (q.v.), pres. имамъ, active pres. part. имый, the other forms are from имѣти: aorist воз-нмѣхъ, impf. имѣ́ахъ, имѣ́аше [има́ше] &c.

исче́знути [to vanish], fut. исче́знутъ, aor. исчезо́хъ.

ити̇ [to go], pres. иду́тъ, after the prefixes по, пре and на the н is shortened to й: fut. пойду, прейду, по́йдеши, пре́йдеши, на́йдетъ; aor. идо́хъ, impf. ида́хъ; active past part. ше́дъ, _ши; _ лъ-participle ше́лъ, шли̇; after the prefixes и̇з, во̇з, ѡ̇б it has ы: и̇зы́де, взы́де, ѡ̇бы́де &c.

К

[въ]ки́снути [to become sour], fut. вски́снутъ, aor. вскисо́хъ, вски́се (Luke 13:21--"till the whole *was leavened*").

кла́ти [to stick, pierce], pres. ко́лютъ, impf. кола́хъ.

кла́ти [to curse], pres. кленꙋ́тъ, aor. кла́хъ, 2nd & 3rd p. кла́тъ, impf. клена́хъ,.

кова́ти [to forge, hammer], pres. кꙋю́тъ.

[при]коснꙋ́тисѧ [to touch], fut. прикоснꙋ́тсѧ, aor. прикоснꙋ́хсѧ, 2nd & 3rd p. прикоснꙋ́сѧ (Mark 5:27--"she...*touched* his garment").

кра́сти [to steal], pres. крадꙋ́тъ, aor. крадо́хъ, impf. крада́хъ, pres. act. part. крады́й, _ꙋщн, _лъ-participle кра́лъ.

[вос]креснꙋ́ти [to rise again], fut. воскреснꙋ́тъ, aor. воскресо́хъ, past active part. воскре́съ, _шн, _лъ-participle воскре́слъ.

кры́ти [to cover, conceal], pres. кры́ютъ, impf. кры́ахъ, past pass. part. сокрове́нъ, сокры́тъ.

Л

лга́ти [to lie, speak untruth], pres. лгꙋ́тъ (не лгꙋ̀, Galatians 1:20--"behold, I *lie* not"), fut. (with j in the stem): со́лжꙋ́тъ, солжꙋ̀ (Ps. 65:3--"thine enemies *shall lie* to thee"; Ps. 88:36--"I *will not lie* unto David"), present active participle лжꙋ́щїе (Matth. 5:11--"speak all manner of evil against you, *falsely*, for my sake"), (see §83).

лещѝ [to lie down, recline], fut. ла́гꙋтъ, aor. воз_лего́хъ.

лїа́ти [to pour], pres. лїю́тъ, imperative воз_ле́й.

[при]льпнꙋ́ти [to stick, adhere], fut. прильпнꙋ́тъ, aor. прильпо́хъ, прильпѐ (Ps. 21:16--"my tongue *hath cleaved* to my jaws").

влѣ́зти [to board, climb into], (Matth. 13:2—"he *went into* a ship"), fut. влѣзꙋ́тъ, aor. влѣзо́хъ.

М

мле́ти [to mill, grind], Old Church Slavonic млѣ́ти (сомле́тисѧ, Matins for Dec. 20, Ode 4, 2nd Canon: "I hasten *to be milled* like grain") pres. ме́лютъ, aorist ѝзмело́хъ (?), 2nd & 3rd p.

и҆зме́лѐ¹), impf. мела́хꙋ [мела́хꙋ, Num. 11:8--"and the people *ground* it in mills"], active present participle мела̀, _ющн (Luke 17:35 —"Two women shall be *milling*"), past passive part. и҆змеле́нъ).

[оу҆]мо́лкнꙋти [to be silent], fut. оу҆мо́лкнꙋтъ, aor. оу҆молко́хъ [и҆змо́лчѐ, Ps. 68:4—"my jaws *are become hoarse*"].

мощѝ [to be able], pres. мо́гꙋтъ, aorist мого́хъ, impf. можа́хъ, pres. act. part. могі́й, _ꙋщн.

мы́ти [to wash], pres. мы́ютъ, past passive part. оу҆мове́нъ (Matth. 15:20—"to eat with *unwashen* hands").

масти́са [to be troubled], fut. смꙋт̑ꙋтса (Ps. 67:6—"in like manner them that *provoke*"), aor. смато́хса (Ps. 76:5—"I *was troubled*, and spake not").

Н

небрещѝ [to neglect], pres. небрегꙋ́тъ, aor. небриго́хъ.

[оу҆]нзти́ [оу҆нза́ти], [to transfix, run through], fut. оу҆нзꙋ́тъ, aor. оу҆нзо́ша (Ps. 37:3—"For thy arrows *are fastened* in me"); past passive part. оу҆нзе́нъ (Christmas Matins, 2nd Canon, Ode 6, Eirmos—"but, I *pierced* by the tyrant's arrow").

[при]никнꙋ́ти [to bend over], fut. прннн́крꙋ́тъ, aor. при_нико́хъ, 2nd-3rd p. принн́че (Ps. 84:12—"justice *hath looked down* from heaven"), past part. принн́къ, _шн (John 20:5--"And he, *stooping down*, saw the linen clothes...").

Ѡ

ѡ҆блещѝ [to vest], fut. ѡ҆блекꙋ́тъ, active past part. ѡ҆бо́лкъ,

---

¹) Found in St. Dimitri of Rostov's *Lives of the Saints* (Четьи-Минеи), Aug. 11, lives of Ss. Theodore and Vassili of the Kievo-Pechersky Monastery.

_ШИ, ѡбле́къ, _ШИ, passive past part. ѡблече́на (Matth. 11:8—"a man *clothed* in soft raiment"), ѡболче́на (Mark 5:15—"sitting, and *clothed*, and in his right mind").[1]

П

па́сти [to fall], fut. паду́тъ.

[вос]перу́тъ [they will be elevated (in their thoughts)], occurs only in the future tense (but воспера́ти, воспера́ю: Matins for May 5, Ode 3—воспери́ся къ жела́нїю єгѡ "thou wast *inspired* [i.e. carried on high in thought] by the desire for this").[2]

пи́ти [to drink], pres. пїю́тъ, aor. пи́хъ, 2nd-3rd p. пи́тъ.

плева́ти [to spit], also плюва́ти (Mark 14:65—"And some began *to spit* on him"), pres. плюю́тъ.

пра́ти [to trample], fut. по_перу́тъ, imperfect not found (but попира́ти: попира́ше).

подоба́ти [to be proper, needful], has forms only in the 3rd p. singular: pres. подоба́етъ, impf. подоба́ше.

простере́ти [to spread out, extend], (Acts 27:30—кѡтвы простере́ти, "*to cast* anchors"), fut. простру́тъ, aor. простро́хъ, active past part. простеръ, _ШИ, _лъ-participle просте́рлъ, past passive part. просте́ртъ.

пѣ́ти [to sing], pres. пою́тъ, impf. поа́хъ, imperative по́й, past pass. part. пѣ́тъ.

---

[1] Note that both of these examples are in the *accusative case*, thus the form in _а. --*Tr.*

[2] This example, not in the Russian original, is provided to aid the student; also it is a rare case of the 2nd p. singular aorist occurring in post-Niconian editions aside from the Altar Gospel (Greek text has ἀνεπτερώθης). --*Tr.*

пѧ́ти [to stretch out], pres. пнѹ́тъ; active past part. распе́нъ, _шн (§97); past passive part. ра́спѧтъ (crucified).

Р

расти́ [to grow], pres. расту́тъ, aor. расто́хъ (Luke 8:7--"the thorns *sprang up*"), impf. растѧ́хъ (Luke 1:80--"And the child *grew*"), pres. part. расты́й, _ѹщн, past part. возра́стъ, _шн (?), _лъ-participle возра́слъ.

рещи́ [to say], fut. рекѹ́тъ (че́стнаѧ бо рекѹ́, Prov. 8:6--"For I *will speak* solemn [truths]"); aor. рѣ́хъ, реко́хъ, 2nd-3rd p. рече́; imperative рцы̀, рцы́те; active present part. реко́мъ, past passive part. рече́нъ.

[ѡб]рѣсти́ [to find], (this root occurs only with prefixes), fut. ѡбрѣтѹ́тъ, ѡбрѧщѹ́тъ: [с]рѣтѹ́тъ, [с]-рѧщѹ́тъ: aor. ѡбрѣто́хъ [found], срѣто́хъ [met].

С

[и̂з]-со́хнѹти [to dry out], fut. и̂схнѹ́тъ (и̂зсхне́тъ, Zacharias [Zechariah] 11:17--"his arm shall quite *wither away*"), и̂зсшѹ́тъ (Ps. 36:2--"For they shall soon *be withered* as the grass"); aor. и̂зсхо́хъ (Ps. 101:12--"I *am withered* like grass"); 2nd-3rd p. и̂зсше (Ps. 128:6--"which *withereth* afore it groweth up"); active past part. и̂зсо́хъ, _шн.

спа́ти [to sleep], pres. спѧ́тъ.

ста́ти [to arise, stand up, become], fut. ста́нѹ, imperative ста́ни, aor. ста́хъ.

стла́ти [to set out, spread], pres. сте́лютъ.

стрищи́ [to shear], (Gen. 31:19--"to *shear* his sheep"), pres. стригѹ́тъ.

строга́ти [to scrape, plane], pres. стрѹжѹ́тъ, impf. стрѹжа́хъ, pres. pass. part. стрѹжемь.

сѣсти [to sit down], fut. сѧдѹтъ, imperative сѧди, aor. сѣдохъ, act. pass. part. сѣдъ, _ши, _лъ-participle сѣлъ.

сѣщи [to hew, cut (stones)], pres. сѣкѹтъ.

[ѹ]_сѣкнѹти [to sever, cut off], fut. ѹсѣкнѹтъ, aor. ѹсѣкнѹхъ (Mark 6:16—"It is John, whom I *beheaded*").

[из]_сѧкнѹти [to run low, fail, be at end], fut. изсѧкнѹтъ, aor. изсѧкнѹхъ, 2nd-3rd p. изсѧкнѹ (Mark 5:29—"the fountain of her blood *was dried up*") and изсѧкохъ, 2nd & 3rd p. изсѧче (Gen. 8:13—"the waters *were lessened* upon the earth").

Т

тещи [to run], pres. текѹтъ, impf. течахъ, imperative тецы.

[по]_ткнѹтисѧ [to stumble], fut. поткнѹтсѧ (поткнетсѧ, John 11:10—"But if a man walketh in the night, he *stumbleth*"), aor. поткнѹхсѧ.

[со]_трети [to crush, grind up]; стерти (Octoechos, T. 7, Sunday at Matins, Ode 1—"having not the strength *to crush* Thy body with its teeth"); fut. сотрѹтъ, aor. сотрохъ, сотре (Exodus 32:20—"*ground* it very small"), active past part. стеръ, _ши, pass. past part. сотренъ (Canon of Theophany, Eirmos, Ode 3—"the jaws of devouring lions *have been broken*"); from the form сотрыти: сотрыетъ (Matth. 21:44—"it *shall grind* him to powder"), aor. сотры (Ps. 104:16—"he *brake in pieces* all the support of bread").

Ѵ (Оу)

ѹмрети [to die], fut. ѹмрѹтъ, aor. ѹмрохъ, 2nd-3rd p. ѹмре, active past part. ѹмеръ, _ши, _лъ-participle ѹмерлъ.

ѹснѹти [to fall asleep], fut. ѹснѹтъ, aor. ѹснѹхъ, or ѹспохъ, 2nd & 3rd p. ѹспе, past part. ѹснѹвъ.

[об]_ѹти [to shoe], fut. обѹютъ, aor. обѹхъ (обѹша, II Chronicles 28:15—"and arrayed them, and *shod* them"); active past part. ѡбꙋвъ, _ши; passive part. ѡбꙋвѣнъ (Mark 6:9—"But *be shod* with sandals").

Х

хотѣ́ти [to want, to be about to], pres. according to the 2nd conjugation: хощꙋ́, хотѧ́тъ (John 6:15—"When Jesus therefore perceived that they *would* come..."), the other forms are according to the 1st conjugation: хо́щеши, хо́щетъ (Matth. 20:32--"What *will ye* that I shall do unto you?"), не хо́щете (John 5:40—"And ye *will not* come to me"), хо́щꙋтъ (III Maccabees 3:13—"as men *unwilling* to submit to anything reasonable").

Ц

цвѣсти́ [to flower, bloom], pres. цвѣтꙋ́тъ.

Ч

[ис]_чезнꙋти [to vanish], fut. исчезнꙋтъ, aor. исчезо́хъ.

[по]_черпсти [to draw, ladle], (Pentecostarion, Sunday of the Samaritan Woman—[repeated mention]), with the с appearing only in the infinitive, fut. почерпꙋ́тъ, imperative почерпи́ (Kontakion of Mid-Pentecost—"come and *draw* the water of immortality"); aor. почерпо́хъ: active pass. part. поче́рпъ, _ши; from черпати: pres. че́рплютъ (Thursday in Bright Week at Vespers, Aposticha Doxasticon—"let kings and princes gather, and let them *draw* without envy from the source of Grace").

чести́ [to read; to honor], pres. чтꙋ́тъ, aor. что́хъ, impf. чтѧ́хъ, imperative чти́, чте́мъ, чти́те, active present part. чты́й, _ꙋщи, pass. pres. part. чго́мъ, act. past part. поче́тъ, _ши, long form почты́й, passive past part. почте́нъ.

Note: This word has the double meaning of *to read* [Russ. *читать*] aa well as *to honor, venerate* [Russ. *чтить*]. In a later period, to signify the latter meaning, the word чти́ти began to come into use (under the influence of the Russian language); hence in the acclamations (*Velichaniya*) for Saints, both forms are to be encountered—чте́мъ as well as чти́мъ.

[на_, за]-ча́ти [to begin], fut. начнꙋ́тъ, aor. нача́хъ, 2nd-3rd p. нача́тъ, active past part. наче́нъ, _шн (Mark 14:72—"and he *having begun* [to reflect], wept"); past pass. part. нача́тъ [зача́тъ].

Ꙗ

ꙗ́сти [to eat], pres. ꙗ́мъ, pres. act. part. ꙗдꙑ́й, _ꙋщꙂ, pres. pass. part. ꙗдо́мъ, past active part. ꙗ́дъ, _шн, past pass. part. снѣде́нъ.

ꙗ_ти [to take], builds its forms, for the most part with prefixes, from the stems є҆мл_ (present) and им_, and after the prefix по_ the и of the stem becomes й: pres. є҆млютъ (Luke 6:44—"nor of a bramble bush *gather they* grapes"), fut. по_им́ꙋтъ (по́ймеши, Ezek. 16:61—"when thou *shalt receive* thy sisters"; по́йметъ, Matth. 5:32--"whosoever *shall marry* her"); aor. ꙗ́хъ, поꙗ́хъ, 2nd-3rd p. ꙗ́тъ, поꙗ́тъ (John 19:27—"he *took* her unto his own home") ꙗ́ша (Luke 5:6--"they *caught* a great multitude of fishes"); impf. є҆мла́хъ, imperative понми́, (Matth. 2:13—"Arise, and *take* the young child..."), and пойми́ (Matth. 18:16—"*take* with thee one or two more"); active pres. part. є҆мла̀, pass. pres. part. є҆млемь, act. pass. part. є҆мъ, _шн, past pass. part. ꙗ́тъ, _а, _о;

From прїꙗ́ти: pres. прїе́млютъ (Matth. 7:8—"For every one that asketh, *receiveth*"), fut. прїи́мꙋтъ (Matth. 10:14—"And whosoever *shall not receive* you"); the other forms are like the preceding ones: imperative прїе́мли (прїе́млите, Rom. 14:1—"Him that is weak in the faith, *receive* ye") and прїими́; impf. прїима́хъ (from прїнма́ти, although прїе́млахъ seems also to occur); act. past part. прїе́мь and прїи́мь;

From вз_ꙗ́ти: pres. взе́млютъ, fut. во́змꙋтъ;

From вн_а́ти [to be attentive]: pres. внє́млю, imperative
вонмѝ and внємлѝ (Ps. 16:1—"*attend* to my supplication"; Gen.
24:6—"*Beware* that thou bring not my son hither again"); 1st person
plural во́нмємъ "*let us attend*", 2nd pl. внємлѝтє (Matth. 6:1—"*Take
heed* that ye do not your alms before men"), and in similar fashion
this verb а́ти builds forms with other prefixes as well.

Texts for Practice.

(1)Matth. 9:27-36:

Ѝ приходѧ́щꙋ ѿтꙋ́дꙋ і҆и҃сови, по нє́мъ и҆до́ста два̀ слѣпца̀,
зовꙋ́ща и҆ глагѡ́люща: помилꙋ́й ны̀, [і҆и҃сє] сн҃є дв҃довъ. Пришє́дшꙋ
жє є҆мꙋ̀ въ до́мъ, пристꙋпи́ста къ нємꙋ̀ слѣпца̀, и҆ гл҃а и҆́ма і҆и҃съ:
вѣ́рꙋєтє ли, ꙗ҆́кѡ могꙋ̀ сїѐ сотвори́ти; гл҃го́лаєта є҆мꙋ̀: є҆́й, гд҃и.
Тогда̀ прикоснꙋ́сѧ о҆́чїю и҆́хъ, глаго́лѧ: по вѣ́рѣ ва́ю бꙋ́ди ва́ма. и҆
ѿвєрзо́стасѧ о҆́чи и҆́ма. и҆ запрєти́ и҆́ма і҆и҃съ, глаго́лѧ: блюди́та, да
никто́жє о҆у҆вѣ́сть. о҆на̀ жє и҆зшє́дша просла́виста є҆го̀ по всє́й
зємлѝ то́й. Тѣ́ма жє и҆сходѧ́щєма, сѐ привєдо́ша къ нємꙋ̀ чл҃вѣ́ка
нѣ́ма бѣснꙋ́єма. и҆ и҆згна́нꙋ бѣ́сꙋ, проглаго́ла нѣмы́й: и҆ диви́шасѧ
наро́ди, глаго́лющє, ꙗ҆́кѡ николи́жє ꙗ҆ви́сѧ та́кѡ во і҆и҃ли[1]. Фарїсє́є
жє глаго́лахꙋ: ѡ̀ кнѧ́зѣ бѣсо́встѣмъ и҆зго́нитъ бѣ́сы. и҆
прохожда́шє і҆и҃съ гра́ды всѧ̀ и҆ вє́си, о҆у҆чѧ̀ на со́нмищахъ и҆́хъ, и҆
проповѣ́дꙋѧ є҆ѵлїє цр҃твїа, и҆ цѣлѧ̀ всѧ́къ нєдꙋ́гъ и҆ всѧ́кꙋ ꙗ҆́зю въ
лю́дєхъ. Ви́дѣвъ жє наро́ды, милосє́рдова ѡ̀ ни́хъ, ꙗ҆́кѡ бѧ́хꙋ
смѧтє́ни и҆ ѿвє́ржєни, ꙗ҆́кѡ о҆́вцы нє и҆мꙋ́щыѧ па́стырѧ.

(2). Luke 17:27-29:

Ѝ ꙗ҆́кожє бы́сть во днѝ нѡ́євы, та́кѡ бꙋ́дєтъ и҆ во днѝ сн҃а
чл҃вѣ́чєска: ꙗ҆да́хꙋ, пїа́хꙋ, жєнѧ́хꙋсѧ, посѧга́хꙋ, до нєгѡ́жє днѐ
вни́дє нѡ́є въ ковчє́гъ: и҆ прїи́дє пото́пъ, и҆ погꙋбѝ всѧ̀. Та́коджє и҆

---

[1])во і҆и҃ли = "во і҆сра́илн", "in Israel". See the list of other
common abbreviations in §3.c.--*Tr.*

ꙗ́коже бы́сть во дни̑ лѡ́товы:[1] ꙗда́хꙋ, пїа́хꙋ, кꙋпова́хꙋ, прода́ахꙋ, сажда́хꙋ, зда́хꙋ: во́ньже де́нь изы́де лѡ́тъ ѿ содо́млꙗнъ, ѡдожди̑ ка́мыкъ горѧ́щъ и ѻ́гнь съ небесѐ и погꙋби̑ всѧ̑.

(3) John 9:33:

а́ще не бы̀ бы́лъ се́й ѿ бг҃а, не мо́глъ бы̀ твори́ти ничесо́же.

(4) John 9:41:

речѐ и́мъ їис҃ъ: а́ще бы́сте слѣ́пи бы́ли, не бы́сте имѣ́ли грѣха̀: нынѣ́ же глаго́лете, ꙗ́кѡ ви́димъ: грѣ́хъ ѹ́бо ва́шъ пребыва́етъ.

(5) John 4:7-10:

Прїи́де жена̀ ѿ самарі́и почерпа́ти во́дꙋ. глаго́ла е̑́й їис҃ъ: да́ждь ми̑ пи́ти. Ѹ҆ченницы̀ бо е̑гѡ̀ ѿшли̑ бꙗ́хꙋ во гра́дъ, да бра́шно кꙋ́пꙗтъ. Глаго́ла е̑мꙋ̀ жена̀: ка́кѡ ты̀ жидови́нъ сы́й ѿ менѐ пи́ти про́сиши, жены̀ самарꙗны́ни сꙋ́щей; не прикаса́ютбосꙗ[2] жидове самарꙗ́нѡмъ. Ѿвѣща̀ е̑́й їис҃ъ и речѐ е̑́й: а́ще бы̀ вѣ́дала е̑си̑ да́ръ бж҃їй, и кто̀ е̑́сть глаго́лай ти̑: да́ждь ми̑ пи́ти: ты̀ бы проси́ла ѹ҆ негѡ̀, и да́лъ бы ти̑ во́дꙋ жи́вꙋ.

(6) Luke 5:17-18:

И҆ бы́сть во е̑ди́нъ ѿ дни́й, и то́й бѣ̀ ѹ́чꙗ: и бѣ́хꙋ сѣдꙗ́ще фарїсе́е и законоꙋчи́телїе, и́же бѣ́хꙋ пришли̑ ѿ всꙗ́кїꙗ ве́си галїле́йскїꙗ и і҆ꙋде́йскїꙗ и і҆ерꙋсали́мскїꙗ: и си́ла гд҃нꙗ бѣ̀ исцѣлꙗ́ющи и́хъ: и сѐ мꙋ́жїе носꙗ́ще на ѻдрѣ̀ человѣ́ка, и́же бѣ̀ разсла́бленъ, и и҆ска́хꙋ внести̑ е̑го̀ и положи́ти пред ни́мъ.

(7) Mark 1:33:

И҆ бѣ̀ ве́сь гра́дъ собра́лсꙗ къ две́ремъ.

---

[1])лѡ́товы= "of Lot"--son of Haran, cf. Gen. 11:27.--*Tr.*

[2])не прикаса́ют_бо_сꙗ=не прикаса́ютсꙗ бо, see the last 3 paragraphs of §71.--*Tr.*

THE ADVERB.

§105. Adverbs in General.

Adverbs are what we call the invariable words that, by category or circumstance, qualify verbs, adjectives and other adverbs. For example: Т Ꙋ́не* прїа́сте, т Ꙋ́не* дади́те (Matth. 10:8—"*Freely* have ye received, *freely* give"); дѣви́ца же бѧ́ше доброзра́чна ѕѣлꙋ̀* (Gen. 24:16--"And the damsel was *very* fair to look upon"); и̇ ѕѣлꙠ̀* заꙋ́тра* во є̇ди́нꙋ ѿ сꙋббѡ́тъ прїидо́ша на гро́бъ (Mark 16:2—"And *very early* in the morning, the first day of the week").

Adverbs include words formed from all classes of "names": nouns, adjectives and numerals, as well as pronouns and passive participles.

The adverbs were derived from various case forms, which in had often lost their connection with the cases in question, or else formed by means of suffixes. The first group consists mainly of adverbs from nouns, adjectives and numerals; the suffixes were used to form adverbs having the same stem as pronouns.

§106. Adverbs Formed from Various Declension Cases.

There is a very significant group of adverbs formed from qualitative adjectives, from the nominative singular neuter, in which the final o is written as ѡ: ра́нѡ [early], ско́рѡ [quickly, soon], по́зднѡ [late, too late], пра́мѡ [opposite to], кꙋ́пнѡ [together], пра́вѡ [rightly, correctly], хꙋ́дѡ [badly], мно́гѡ [much/ly, very], прилѣ́жнѡ [diligently], и̇звѣ́стнѡ [exactly], бога́тнѡ [richly]; the following adverbs end in _е: т Ꙋ́не [in vain], дале́че [far off, away], дре́вле [of old], є̇диначе (from є̇дина́ко [in accord, according],--until now, still, can it be that [expresses amazement, cf. Russ. неужели], Matth. 15:16—"Are ye *also yet* without undersanding?").

Adverbs from adjectives may end in _ѣ, from the prepositional case, though some of them can have either _ѡ or _ѣ: e.g. добрѣ [well], ѕлѣ [ill, badly], поздѣ [late], прїискреннѣ [likewise], горькѡ—горьцѣ [bitterly], достойнѡ—достойнѣ [rightfully], мꙋдрѡ—мꙋдрѣ [wisely], безбѣднѡ—безбѣднѣ [without mishap], тяжкѡ—тяжцѣ [gravely], бжественнѡ—бжественнѣ [divinely].

Like the forms from neuter singular adjectives, adverbs were also derived from present and past passive participles: невидимѡ [invisibly], неизреченнѡ [ineffably], несказаннѡ [ineffably, beyond expression].

Adverbs formed from qualitative adjectives may also have degrees of comparison: выше [higher], вᷱще [greater, better], лише [more], множайше [more], &c.

The comparative forms of the adjective and adverb are homonyms, and differ only in their use: the comparative adjective refers to its noun, while the comparative adverb refers to a verb-predicate: ꙷмꙋже предаша множайше*, множайше* просѧтъ ѿ негѡ (Luke 12:48—"To whom men have committed much, of him will they ask *the more*").

The adverbs тай, ѿтай [secretly], ницъ [down]—took their form from the nominative case of adjectives (падъ ницъ, Luke 5:12—"falling *on his face*"). The adverb ницъ can, with a subject in the plural, take the form ницъ or ницы, e.g. падоша ницы (Matth. 17:6—"they fell *on their face*"); in the service for Aug. 6: ницъ на земли покрывахꙋсѧ (at Vespers, "Lord I have cried"—"they fell to the ground upon their faces"); и на землю ницъ падахꙋ (Sessional Hymn after the Psalter—"they fell to the ground upon their faces"); и ницы на землю падше (Ode 8); ницы падше (at the Praises). It would appear that this adverb is on the border between parts of speech, and can also be viewed as an adjective found only in the nominative case: compare падѐ ницъ, падоша ницы with падѐ мє́ртвъ, падо́ша мє́ртви [he/they fell down; he/they fell down dead].

The following adverbs took their form from other declension cases of adjectives:

преи́злиха [exceedingly, beyond measure], и́злиха [excessively], испє́рва [from the first], изд'є́тска [from childhood], свы́ше [from above]—(from the genitive case); нє по мно́гу [presently, shortly], поистиннѣ [truly]—(from the dative case); всує [in vain], ѡдесну́ю [at the right hand], ѡшу́юю [at the left], воистинну [truly, in truth]—(from the accusative); грє́чєски [in Greek], єврє́йски [in Hebrew], му́жєски [manfully], жє́нски [in womanly fashion], ма́тєрски [maternally, as befits a mother]—(from the instrumental); вскорѣ [speedily, soon], вма́лѣ [in a little while, shortly], на мно́зѣ [for a long time; for a great price],—from numerals (in the prepositional case).

The following adverbs were formed from various cases of nouns:

зау́тра [early in the morning], вчєра́ [yesterday], искони́ [from the beginning], ѿча́сти [in part], изнача́ла [from the beginning], созади́ [in back], до вєрха́ [up to the top], бєзпристанни [without ceasing--Rom. 1:9]—(from the genitive); днє́сь [today--from дє́нь сє́й], у́тру [in the morning], вє́чєръ [in the evening], ѻ́крєстъ [round about], вну́трь [inside], вспа́ть [again], внєза́пу [suddenly, unexpectedly]--(from the accusative); посрєдѣ́ [in the midst], поря́ду [in order]--(from the dative); то́чїю [only], є́диною [once](from numerals), вто́рицєю [twice], трє́тицєю [thrice], чєтвєри́цєю [four times], сєдмєри́цєю [seven times], сто́рицєю [100 times], мно́жицєю [many times], полма́ [by halves; from dual of по́лъ]—(from the instrumental case); горѣ́ [up, on high], вєрху́ [above], до́лу [below, down], мєжду́ [between—dual number of мє́жда: [interval, limit, borderline], впрєди́ [in front], вну́три [inside], вку́пѣ [together], вмѣ́стѣ [together], кромѣ́ [without, except; from the noun кро́ма, "border", hence "far off", "absent"], послѣди́ [afterward], втайнѣ [in secret], ѻу҆́трѣ [tomorrow],—(from the prepositional case).

From the ordinal numbers come the adverbs пе́рвое [first of all; in the first place], второ́е [in the second place], пе́рвѣе: from the short numerals come двакра́ты [twice], трикра́ты [thrice], коликра́ты [how many times]. Some adverbs are formed from numerals with the aid of the suffix _жды: є҆ди́ножды [once], два́жды [twice], три́жды [thrice], and so on. From мно́гъ comes мно́гажды [many times].

Examples:

Бди́те ѹ҆́бо: не вѣ́сте бо, когда̀ госпо́дь до́мꙋ прїи́детъ, ве́черъ*, и҆лѝ полꙋ́нощи*, и҆лѝ въ пѣ́тлоглаше́нїе, и҆лѝ ѹ҆́трѡ* (Mark 13:35—"Watch ye therefore: for ye know not when the master of the house cometh, at even, or at midnight, or at cockcrow, or in the morning"). И҆ расте́шетъ є҆го̀ полма̀*, и҆ ча́сть є҆гѡ̀ съ невѣ́рными положи́тъ (Matth. 24:51—"And he shall cut him asunder, and appoint his portion with the unbelievers"). Є҆ди́ною* глаго́лахъ, втори́цею* же не приложꙋ̀ (Job 39:35—"I have spoken once, but will not add a second time"). И҆ ста́вши прѝ ногꙋ̀ є҆гѡ̀ созадѝ*, пла́чꙋщися, нача́тъ ѹ҆мыва́ти но́зѣ є҆гѡ̀ слеза́ми (Luke 7:38—"And stood at his feet behind, weeping, and began to wash his feet with tears"). Ше́дше рцы́те лисꙋ̀ томꙋ̀: сѐ и҆згоню̀ бѣ́сы и҆ и҆сцѣле́нїѧ творю̀ дне́сь* и҆ ѹ҆́трѣ*, и҆ въ тре́тїй сконча́юсѧ (Luke 13:32—"Go ye, and tell that fox, Behold I cast out devils, and I do cures to-day and to-morrow, and the third day I shall be consummated"). Дрꙋ́же, поса́ди вы́ше* (Luke 14:10—"Friend, take thy place higher").

§107. Adverbs from Pronoun Stems.

Pronoun adverbs were formed by means of the following suffixes, to which in some adverbs is further added the conjunction же:

1) -д‡, by means of which suffix adverbs are formed pertaining to place: гдѣ [where], здѣ [here], вездѣ [everywhere], идѣже [in the place where], ѻндѣ [in that manner; to that place; there yonder], инꙋдѣ [elsewhere].

2) -дꙁ: ѽнюдꙁ [not in the least, in no way];

3) -дꙋ: ѽкꙋдꙋ [whence], ѽсюдꙋ [hence], ѽтꙋдꙋ [thence], сюдꙋ и сюдꙋ [hither and thither], всюдꙋ [everywhere], ѽнюдꙋже or ѽнꙋдꙋже [whence, from the place where], ѽбоюдꙋ [from both sides].

4) -ꙋдꙋ: внѣꙋдꙋ [from without], внꙋтрьꙋдꙋ [from within];

5) -гда: всегда [always], иногда [once, at one time], когда [when], никогда [never], нѣкогда [at a certain time, once], тогда [then], ѻвогда [sometimes, once];

6) -лѣ: ѽселѣ [from now on], ѽтолѣ [since then, from that time], дотолѣ [until then], доколѣ [until when, how long], послѣ [afterward], послѣжде [afterwards], ҽлѣ [barely], ѽнелѣже [since the time that], донелѣже [until the time that], used as conjunctions.

7) -ли: николиже [never], -ль: коль [how much, to what extent];

8) -ми: кольми [how much more], ҽльми [in so far as, when], вельми [highly, very]; -ма: ҽльма [since, when], весьма [very much, greatly];

9) -мѡ: камѡ [whither, where], тамѡ [there], сѣмѡ [hither], ѻвамѡ [to another place, this way and that], мимѡ [past], токмѡ [only], аможе [whither, to the place where].

Some adverbs are formed from pronouns in the same way as from neuter adjectives: ҽликѡ [as much as—cf. ҽликꙁ, ҽлика, ҽлико], такѡ [thus], какѡ [how], всякѡ [in every, any way], селикѡ [as much as], толикѡ [that much, so much], инакѡ [otherwise], сицѣ [in this wise, manner].

A number of adverbs, connected with the stems of pronouns or prepositions, are formed without suffixes: тꙋ [here, there], вскꙋю

[why], ктомꙋ [henceforth, anymore], Ѻсобь [apart], пре́жде [beforehand], пото́мⷥ [afterward], ра́звѣ [except, but for], вы́нꙋ [ever, always—from вⷥ и̑нꙋ], во́нⷥ [yonder, behold afar off], внѣ̀ [outside], и̑звнѣ̀ [from outside], понѐ [even, at least], на то́лицѣ [for so much], на коли́цѣ [for how much], кольми́ [how much more], николи́же [never], да́же [even—from the conjunctions да and же], та́же [afterward, later, then][1].

The adverbs а̑бїе [at once, immediately], ны́нѣ [now], не оу̑ [not yet], па́ки [again], е̑два̀ [barely], е̑щѐ [still, furthermore, also], ни [neither, no (equivalent to Russian "ни" as well as "нѣтъ")], не [not]—are in the class of underived or primitive adverbs. The adverb оу̑жѐ [already] consists of the adverb оу̑ [already] plus the conjunction же.

§108. Adverbs Categorized by Meaning.

According to their meaning, adverbs fall into two main groups: determinative and circumstantial.

1) *Determinative* adverbs characterize action (in a verb) and distinguishing feature (in an adjective or another adverb) as to its quality, quantity or manner of implementation. On this basis, determinative adverbs are subdivided as follows:

a) Adverbs of quality (answering the question "How?"): хꙋ́дѡ [ill, badly], добрѣ̀ [well], ско́рѡ [quickly], досто́йнѡ [properly, worthily], та́жкѡ [gravely, heavily], неизречѣ́ннѡ [ineffably], and so on; e.g.: добрѣ̀*, оу̑чи́телю, вои̑стиннꙋ рекла̀ е̑сѝ (Mark 12:32—"Well, Master, thou hast truly spoken"); бѣ́ша всѝ а̑п҃толи е̑динодꙋ́шнѡ* вкꙋ́пѣ (Acts 2:1—"all the apostles were together in one accord").

---

[1]) Mark 4:17.

b) Adverbs of quantity and measure (answering the question: "How much, how many? For how much? In what measure?"): є҆ди́ножды [once], два́жды [twice], є҆ди́ною [once; all at once; for a short time], мно́гажды [many times], вельмѝ [highly], є҆два̀ [only just], толи́кѡ [to such an extent], на мно́зѣ [for long, for much], вма́лѣ [in a little while], and so on; e.g.: мно́жицею* бра́шася со мно́ю ѿ ю҆ности моеѧ̀ (Ps. 128:1—"Often have they fought against me from my youth"); коли́кѡ* нае́мникѡмъ ѻ҆ц҃а̀ моегѡ̀ и҆збыва́ютъ хлѣ́бы, а҆́зъ же гла́домъ ги́блю (Luke 15:17—"How many hired servants in my father's house abound with bread, and I here perish with hunger?"). Три́щи* па́лицами бїе́нъ бы́хъ, є҆ди́ною* ка́меньми наме́танъ бы́хъ, трикра́ты* кора́бль ѡ҆прове́ржеся со мно́ю (II Cor. 11:25—"Thrice was I beaten with rods, once I was stoned, thrice I suffered shipwreck").

c) Adverbs of manner (answering the question: "How? In what way?"): и҆злиха [exceedingly], вско́рѣ [soon], понѐ [at least], вма́лѣ [in a short time], внеза́пꙋ [suddenly], безпрестани [incessantly], полма̀ [in half, by halves], не́гли [perhaps, perchance], втайнѣ [in secret], ѡ҆тай [secretly, surreptitiously], та́й [secretly], гре́чески [in Greek], мꙋ́жески [manfully], ни́цъ [ни́цы] down, on one's face, всꙋ́е [in vain], пои́стиннѣ [truly], вои́стинꙋ [in truth] &c., for example: ѻ҆ни́ же и҆злиха* дивла́хꙋсѧ... (Mark 10:26—"But they wondered greatly"); и҆ та́кѡ* па́дъ ни́цъ*, поклони́тсѧ бг҃ови, возвѣща́ѧ, ꙗ҆́кѡ вои́стиннꙋ* бг҃ъ съ ва́ми є҆́сть (I Cor. 14:25—"And so, falling down on his face, he will adore God, affirming that God is among you indeed"); и҆ расте́шитъ є҆го̀ полма̀* (Matth. 24:51—"and shall cut him asunder"); наче́нъ же пе́тръ, сказоваше и҆̀мъ поря́дꙋ* (Acts 11:4—"But Peter began and told them the matter in order"). Ка́кѡ* воспое́мъ пѣ́снь гд҃ню (Ps. 136:4—"How shall we sing the song of the Lord?").

2) Adverbs of *circumstance* comprise those adverbs that signify circumstances of time or place in which the action occurs, as well as the reason for the action. Depending on this content, adverbs of circumstance are subdivided as follows:

a) Adverbs of time (answering the question: "When? Since when? Until when?"): а́нⷵℰⷵⷶ [today], за́ѹтра [early in the morning], вчера̀ [yesterday], и҆здѣ́тⷵка [from childhood], послѣди́ [afterward], ѹ҆́трⷼⷯ [in the morning], ѹ҆́трѣ [on the morrow, tomorrow, next day], всегда̀ [always], ны́нѣ [now], при́снⷿ [ever], and so on, for example: во є҆ди́нꙋ ѿ сꙋббⷬѿⷵ марі́а магдали́на прїи́де за́ѹтра*, є҆щѐ сꙋ́щей тмѣ̀, на гро́бⷹ (John 20:1—"And on the first day of the week, Mary Magdalene came early, when it was yet dark, unto the sepulchre"); пото́мⷹ* же ꙗ҆ви́са і҆а́кѡвꙋ... Послѣди́* же всѣ́хⷹ... ꙗ҆ви́са и҆ мнѣ̀ (I Cor. 15:7-8—"After that, he was seen by James... Last of all... he appeared also to me"); ѿсе́лѣ* бꙋ́детⷹ сн҃ⷹ чл҃вѣ́ческїй сѣда́й ѡ҆десн꙽ꙋю си́лы бж҃їа (Luke 22:69—"But hereafter the Son of Man shall be sitting on the right hand of the power of God").

b) Adverbs of place (answering the question: "Where? Whither? Whence? How far?"): здⷸ́ [here], та́мⷿ [there], ѻ҆ндⷸ́ [to that place], гдⷸ́ [where], и҆дⷸ́же [in that place, where--*used as a relative connecting word*], сю́дꙋ и҆ сю́дꙋ [this way and that], созади́ [in back, from behind], внⷸ́ꙋдꙋ [from outside], внꙋ́трьꙋдꙋ [from inside], впреди́ [in front], и҆нꙋдⷸ́ [elsewhere], а҆́може [in the place whither--*expresses relationship of place to which*] and so on, e.g.: пе́трⷹ же во слⷸ́дⷹ и҆да́ше и҆здалⷸ́ча* (Luke 22:54—"But Peter followed afar off"); и҆ и҆зше́дⷹ во́нⷹ* пла́каса го́рькⷿ (Luke 22:62—"And going out, he wept bitterly"); тогда̀* а҆́ще кто̀ рече́тⷹ ва́мⷹ: сѐ здⷸ́* хрⷵто́сⷹ, и҆лѝ ѻ҆ндⷸ́*: не и҆ми́те вⷸ́ры (Matth. 24:23—"Then if anyone shall say to you: Lo here is Christ, or there: do not believe him"); ѡ҆бозрⷸ́вса же сⷸ́мⷿ и҆ ѻ҆ва́мⷿ (Exodus 2:12—"And when he had looked about this way and that").

c) Adverbs of cause (answering the question: "Why? For what reason?") are represented in Church Slavonic by only a few words, for example: вскꙋ́ю мѧ̀ ѿри́нꙋлъ є҆сѝ (Eirmos at Sunday Matins, T. 8, Ode 5--"Wherefore hast Thou cast me off"); почто̀* червле́ны ри́зы твоѧ̑ (Isaiah 63:2—"Why then is thine apparel red?").

Adverbs of purpose are scarcely to be met with.

The negative particles не and ни stand by themselves, and are used with adverbs also.

The adverb когда̀ can have an interrogative or an indefinite sense, for example: рцы̀ на́мъ, когда̀ сїѧ̀ бꙋ́дꙋтъ; (Matth. 24:3—"Tell us when these things shall be?")—is interrogative; кто̀ ви́дѣ, кто̀ слы́ша, мертвеца̀ оу҆кра́дена когда̀ (=Russian "когда-нибудь"), [Octoechos, T. 5, at Vespers—"Who has ever seen, who has heard, of a dead form stolen at any time?")—is an example of indefinite use.

§109. The Orthography of Adverbs.

All adverbs that end in "o" are spelled with ѡ: та́йнѡ [secretly, mystically], ѻ҆па́снѡ [cautiously], неизглаго́ланнѡ [beyond words], оу҆́трѡ [in the morning], ка́кѡ [how], толи́кѡ [so, to such an extent], and so on.

The following adverbs are spelled with ѣ at the end of the word:

Adverbs that are formed from the dative or prepositional case: пои́стиннѣ [truly], оу҆́трѣ [on the morrow], вма́лѣ [shortly], вкꙋ́пѣ [together], вмѣ́стѣ [together], кромѣ̀ [except, without], до́брѣ [well], по́здѣ [late], ѕлѣ̀ [badly, wickedly], го́рцѣ [bitterly], прїискреннѣ [likewise], and so on, but всꙋ́е [in vain] (from the accusative case).

Adverbs with the suffixes дѣ and лѣ: гдѣ̀ [where], здѣ̀ [here], ѻ҆́ндѣ [in that place], и҆нꙋ́дѣ [elsewhere], ѿсе́лѣ [from henceforth], ѿне́лѣже [since the time that], and so on.

The following adverbs are written with є at the end:

Those that end in a "hushing" sibilant or a softened labial before є: дале́че [far away], є҆диначе [until now], дре́вле [of old], до́бле [bravely]; here, too, belong adverbs of the comparative degree: па́че [more than, beyond], наипа́че [the more], ва́ще [highly], as well as оу҆́не [better, more advantageous], тꙋ́не [for nothing], си́це [thus, as follows], but: бо́лѣ [more], пребо́лѣ [even more]: въ ра́нахъ пребо́лѣ (II Cor. 11:23—"in stripes above measure").

PREPOSITIONS

§110. *Prepositions* are what we call the auxiliary words which, together with nouns showing case endings, express various relationships between words, for example: гряди̑ по мнѣ̀, гряди̑ ко мнѣ̀, и҆дѝ со мно́ю, and so on.

Prepositions may be either primitive (underived), or derived.

1) To the prepositions with an *underived* stem, belong the following: бе́з [without], во́з [for], и҆́з [out of, from], ѡ҆́б [about], над [above], под [below], чре́з [through], пре́д[пре́до] [before], къ [ко] [to, towards], съ [со] [with], въ [во] [in], ѡ҆ [about], ѿ [from], по [along, according to], до [to, until], при [in the presence of, before], оу҆́ [by, at], за [for, by], на [on], ра́ди [for the sake of], дѣ́ла [for, on behalf of].

Note: The prepositions listed above with *yerok* [']are used also with ъ [бе́зъ, и҆́зъ, надъ &c.]. The Kievan editions followed an orthography in which prepositions were spelled with final -ъ.

The preposition [or postposition] ра́ди usually stands after the word that it governs, although it can also precede it: e.g. и҆ бꙋ́дете ненави́дими ѿ всѣ́хъ и҆́мене моегѡ̀ ра́ди (Luke 21:17—"And ye shall be hated of all men for my name's sake").

The preposition[postposition] дѣла [for, on behalf of] is met with quite rarely; it always stands after the word it governs, for example: на́съ бо дѣла ꙗви́лсѧ є҆си̍ чꙋдотво́рецъ и҆зѧ́щный (May 9, Kondak for St. Nicholas—"for on our behalf thou didst show thyself [as] a splendid worker of miracles"); пло́ть на́съ дѣла ѿ дѣвы прїѧ́тъ (Tetraode for the 4th Saturday after Pascha, 8th Ode[1]—"Having assumed flesh for our sake from the Virgin").

The preposition во́з is used mostly as a prefix (воз-, вз-), but sometimes occurs as a preposition also, for example: и ѿ и҆сполне́нїѧ є҆гѡ̀ мы̀ вси̍ прїѧ́хомъ блгода́ть воз блгода́ть (John 1:16—"And of his fulness have we all received, grace for grace"). Возда́ша мѝ дꙋка́вая воз блага́я (Ps. 34:12—"They repaid me evil for good").

2) To the *derivative* prepositions belong those derived from adverbs. Such adverb-prepositions are the following: бли́зъ [near], верхꙋ̀ [above, over], внꙋ́трь [inside], внѣ̀ [outside], вмѣ́стѡ [instead of], вскра́й [near, beside], вослѣ́дъ [following], кромѣ̀ [except, without], ни́зꙋ [down], послѣ̀ [after], посредѣ̀ [among, in the midst of], ра́звѣ [except], среди̍ [among], пра́мѡ [opposite, across from], проти́вꙋ [against] and certain others.

Examples: во́ини же ведо́ша є҆го̀ внꙋ́трь* двора̀ (Mark 15:16—"And the soldiers led him inside the court"). Не мо́жетъ гра́дъ оу҆кры́тисѧ верхꙋ̀* горы̍ стоѧ̀ (Matth. 5:14—"A city cannot be hid, standing atop a mountain"). И то́й прохожда́ше сквозѣ̀* гра́ды и вєси̍ (Luke 8:1—"And he passed through cities and villages"). И дрꙋго́е падѐ посредѣ̀* те́рнїѧ (Luke 8:7—"And other fell among thorns").

---

[1]) This text is not found in the current Greek editions of the Pentecostarion, and is relegated to an appendix in the Slavonic. --*Tr.*

The word governed by the adverb-preposition вмѣстѡ is often written between въ and мѣстѡ, e.g. є҆да̀ въ рыбы мѣстѡ ѕмїю̀ пода́стъ є҆мꙋ̀; (Luke 11:11—"Will he in place of a fish give him a viper?"); ра́дость же є҆ѵѣ въ печа́ли мѣстѡ подала̀ є҆сѝ (Sunday Matins, Evlogitaria—"Thou hast given joy to Eve in place of sorrow").

§111. Peculiarities in the Use of Prepositions.

In Church Slavonic, the prepositions take for the most part the same cases as they do in Russian. Among the uses of prepositions peculiar to Church Slavonic, the following may be noted:

1) къ in the sense of *"with"*: сло́во бѣ̀ къ бг҃ꙋ (John 1:1—"And the Word was with God");

2) до--used to express the direction or limit of motion: моля́ше є҆го̀ не ѡ҆блѣни́тисѧ прїитѝ до ни́хъ (Acts 9:38—"They entreated him not to be slack to come to them"); и҆ да́же до а҆́да низше́дшемꙋ (Octoechos, Sunday, T. 5 at *Lord I have cried*—"And having descended even unto Hades").

3) ѡ҆--used in the sense of *"in"*: ѡ҆ ма́лѣ былъ є҆сѝ вѣренъ (Matth. 25:23—"thou hast been faithful over a few things" [in Russian: "въ маломъ ты былъ вѣренъ"]); цѣлꙋ́йте ѹ҆рва́на споспѣ́шника на́шего ѡ҆ хрⷭ҇тѣ̀ (Romans 16:9—"Salute Urbanus, our helper in Christ"); in the sense of *"with, in the presence of"*: предвари́вшыѧ ѹ҆́тро ꙗ҆́же ѡ҆ мари́и (Hypakoe of Pascha—"Anticipating the dawn, the women with Mary"); и҆ по́ѧсъ ѹ҆сме́нъ ѡ҆ чре́слѣхъ свои́хъ (Matthew 3:4—"and a leather belt around his loins"); in the sense of *"for"*: ѡ҆ ѹ҆пова́нїи и҆ ѡ҆ воскрⷭ҇нїи ме́ртвыхъ а҆́зъ сꙋдъ прїе́млю (Acts 23:6—"of the hope and resurrection of the dead I am called in question"—in Russian: *за чаянїе воскресенїѧ мертвыхъ*); in the sense of an indicator of the person or instrument performing the action (see §139): ѡ҆ се́мъ се́й стои́тъ пред ва́ми здра́въ (Acts 4:10—"even by him doth this man stand before you whole"); signifying something joined or

combined (="*with*"): ѿ надѣ́ждѣ до́лженъ є҆́сть ѡ҆ра́й ѡ҆ра́ти (I Cor. 9:10—"he that ploweth, should plow in [i.e. *with*] hope").

4) над and пред can govern the accusative case: прїи́де над него̀ (Luke 10:33—"came near him"); also: Matth. 10:24[1]; пред воеводы и҆ цари̑ веде́ни бꙋ́дете менѐ ра́ди (Mark 13:9—"Ye shall be brought before governors and kings for My sake").

5) по can have the sense "*after, behind*": гряди́та по мнѣ̀ (Matth. 4:19—"follow Me"); it can also mean "*after*" (in expressing circumstances of time, both past and future): по дне́хъ шести́хъ поя́тъ... (Matth. 17:1—"After six days [Jesus] took..."); по трїе́хъ дне́хъ воста́нꙋ (Matth. 27:63—"After three days I will rise again").

6) за may signify *from, past*: и҆дѝ за мно́ю, сата́но̀ (Matth. 4:10—"Get thee hence, Satan").

§112. Prepositions as Prefixes.

Some prepositions are used as prefixes, in the formation of new words, so as to bring new shades of meaning to the basic word, for example: без-ꙋ́мїе [madness, mindlessness], без-зако́нїе [iniquity, lawlessness], воз-да́ти [to render], при-да́ти [to impart, attach], и҆з-да́ти [to issue, give out], со-и҆з-во́лити [to deign, be pleased], воз-со-зда́ти [to restore], and so on.

Besides prepositions, the following prefixes, both simple and compound, are used to form new words with various nuances of meaning: раз-[apart], про-[through], пре-[over], раз-про-, пре-про-, for example: раз-би́ти [break apart, shatter], про-сла́вленъ [glorified], пре-про-сла́вленъ [*most* glorified, cf. Lat. "super-exaltatus"], раз-про-страни́ти [to extend, spread], пре-вз-ыдо́ша [they went over, more-than-above] &c.

---

[1] Нѣ́сть ѹ҆чени́къ над ѹ҆чи́теля своего̀, ниже́ ра́бъ над господи́на своего̀: "The disciple is not above his master, nor the servant above his lord".

After the prepositions въ [in], къ [to, towards], съ [with, con-], which in the ancient period of the Slavonic language had н as part of their makeup (вън, кън, сън), the н is kept before words beginning with a vowel: въ нѐмъ, къ немꙋ̀, съ нн́мъ; these prepositions show the same peculiarity when they become prefixes: внꙋ́шн́тн (from вън_ꙋшн́тн, "to say/put [someting] into the ear", i.e. to instil, suggest], снѧ́тн (from сън_ѧ́тн, o take down), снн́дꙋ, внн́дꙋ, снн́скáтн [to obtain] and so on.

The pronoun of the 3rd person (о̏нъ, о̑нà, о̑нò), by analogy with the above, came to take an initial н after other prepositions as well: ѡ̀ нѐмъ, под нн́мъ, на негò, оӱ́ негѡ̀ and so forth.

Prefixes that end in a consonant (except for ѡ̈, въ_), when joined to words beginning with a vowel, are marked off with the *yerok:* н̑зѡбразн́тн [to depict], безоѻбрáзі̑е [outrage], ѡ̈бѧ́ті̑ѧ [embraces], подѐмлю [I raise], and so on; but ѡ̈ѐмлю [I take away], взѐмлю [I take].

In the verbs н́тн [to go], н́мꙋ [have, take], after the prefixes пре_, про_, по_, на_ the root-letter н usually becomes н̑: прейдꙋ̀ [I will cross], найдꙋ̀ [I will find], пойдꙋ̀ [I will go]; поймн̀ [take] and so on, for example: прей́демъ до вн̑дѹлеѐма (Luke 2:15—"Let us go unto Bethlehem"); поймн̀ съ собою е̑щѐ е̑дн́наго н̑лн̀ двà (Matth. 18:16—"take with thee one or two more"); ꙗ̑кw дꙋ̑хъ про́йде въ нѐмъ (Ps. 102:16—"For the spirit is passed in him"); but these words are also to be encountered written with н: востáвъ, поймн̀ о̑трочà н̑ мáтерь е̑гѡ̀ (Matth. 2:13—"Arise, take the young child and his mother").

In verbs that begin with н (aside from the forms of ꙗ́тн: н̑мáтн, н̑мꙋ̀), after the prefixes н̑з̀ [out of, ex-], въ̑з̀ [up], ѡ̈б [round, about] the н of the root becomes ы: н́зыѝде [went out], взыѝде [went up], ѡ̈быѝде [went around], взыскáтн [to exact, call to account], взыгрáтн [to leap], but: ѡ̈бн́мемъ [let us embrace]; for example: н̑з̀ тебѐ бо н̑зыѝдетъ во́ждь (Matth. 2:6—"For out of thee shall come a

Governor"); й и҆зы́щѹ́тъ до́мъ твой (III Kings 20:6—"and they shall search thine house"); взыгра́сѧ младе́нецъ (Luke 1:44—"the infant leaped").

The prefixes воз-, и҆з-, раз- before the voiceless consonants к, п, т, х, ц, and ч change their final з to с (see §12, d): рцы̀ сло́во, и҆ и҆сцѣлѣ́етъ о҆́трокъ мой (Luke 7:7—"say in a word, and my servant shall be healed"); о҆лтарѝ твоѧ̑ раскопа́ша (III Kings 19:10—"they have digged down Thine altars").

CONJUNCTIONS

§113. *Conjunctions* are the name for the auxiliary words that are used for a connection between the components of sentences, or between sentences themselves, e.g. варна́ва же и҆ са́влъ возврати́стасѧ и҆з і҆ерѹсали́ма во а҆нтїохі́ю (Acts 12:25—"And Barnabas and Saul returned from Jerusalem to Antioch"); є҆ди́на пое́млетсѧ, и҆ є҆ди́на ѡ҆ставлѧ́етсѧ (Matth. 24:41—"the one [woman] shall be taken, and the other left").

Conjunctions, according to their morphological makeup, can be *simple* or *compound*, for example: simple conjunctions—и҆ [and], а҆ [and, but], но [but], же [but], ли [or], &c; compound—поне́же [since], ниже́ [neither, nor], занѐ [for], и҆лѝ [or] and others.

The compound conjunctions took form out of various parts of speech, e.g. и҆-лѝ, и҆-бо [for], да́-же [even], ли-бо [or], and others (from simple conjunctions); за-[н]е́-же [because], по-[н]е́-же [because, since], тѣ́м-же [therefore] (from prepositions, pronouns and a conjunction); си́-рѣ́чь [that is to say], си́-єсть [that is, i.e.] (a preposition with a noun in the first case, and a verb in the second); ни-жѐ (from a negative adverb and a conjunction); до́ндеже [until] (from до-н-де-же = до-нь-де-же) and so on.

Conjunctions can also be *composite*: оу҆́бѡ—же [on the one hand—on the other], а҆́ще—о҆ба́че [if—moreover], не то́чїю—но [not only—but] and so on.

§114. Types of Conjunctions According to their Use.

Based on their use in speech, conjunctions are classed as either coördinating or subordinating.

1) *Coördinating* conjunctions serve to connect like members of a sentence, and also the segments of a compound sentence.

According to their meaning, coördinating conjunctions are divided into:

a) copulative: и̂, ни [nor], ни -- ни [neither -- nor], нижѐ, не то́кмѡ --- но и̂ [not only--but also], та́кождє [likewise; also];

b) adversative: а̂, но, да [but], ѻ҆ба́чє [however; but], же, не то́чїю—но, ѹ҆бо--же.

c) disjunctive: и̂ли̂, ли́бо, лю́бо [whether], а́щє [if].

d) causal: и̂бо, бо [for, because].

e) conclusive: тѣ́мже, тѣ́мъ [thereby], ѹ҆бо [therefore], тѣ́мже ѹ҆бо [for this reason, then], сегѡ̀ ра́ди [therefore; for this cause],

f) explanatory: си́єсть, сирѣ́чь [that is to say].

Many of the coördinating conjunctions can begin a sentence, connecting it with the sentence that went before, even though it ended with a period.

2) *Subordinating* conjunctions serve to join two clauses: a subordinate with a main clause.

Subordinating conjunctions can be of the following types:

a) causal: понéже, ꙗ́кѡ [for], занѐ, поели́кꙋ [since; inasmuch as], є҆да̀ ка́кѡ [lest; that...not...];

b) of purpose: да, дабы̀ [in order that]; ꙗ́кѡ да [so that], чесѡ̀ ра́ди [why, wherefore], да понѐ [so that at least];

c) of time: є҆гда̀ [when], ѿнéлѣже [since the time that], донéлѣже [until, till such a time as], прéжде да́же [before];

d) of place: и̂дѣ́же [where, in what place], а́може [whither, to what place];

e) conditional: а́щє, а́щє ли [if], а́щє ѹ҆бо [if indeed];

f) comparative: ꙗ́кѡ [like, as], ꙗ́коже [like], ꙗ́кн [like, as], ꙗ́кн бы [as if], не́же [than], не́желн [rather than];

g) concessive: а́ще н--но [and if--yet--], а́ще н--ѻба́че [for if--nevertheless--].

The conjunctions лн, є́да̀ [can it be?] often have the sense of interrogative particles: хо́щешн лн цѣ́лх бы́тн; (John 5:6—"Wilt thou be made whole?"); благодꙋ́шествꙋетх лн кто̀; да пое́тх (James 5:13—"Is anyone cheerful of mind? Let him sing"); є́да̀ н вы̀ хо́щете н́тн; (John 6:67—"Will ye also go away?").

The conjunctions лн, бо, же are placed after the first word in the sentence: оу̑до́бѣе бо є́сть (Luke 18:25—"For it is easier...").

§115. The functions of a conjunction are also carried out by certain adverbs and pronouns,—these are known as *conjunctive* or *relative* words. As conjunctions, the following adverbs and pronouns are used: нд̑ѣ́же, а́може, ка́кѡ [how], ѿкꙋ́дꙋ [whence, from where], кото́рый [which], какокы́й [of what sort], є́лнкх [as many as], что̀ [what], and others, e.g. н а́може а́зх нд̑ꙋ́, вѣ́сте (John 14:4—"And whither I go, ye know"); вы̀ же не вѣ́сте, ѿкꙋ́дꙋ прнхождꙋ̀, н ка́мѡ грѧдꙋ́ (John 8:14—"But ye know not whence I come, and whither I go"); вопроша́ше оу̑бо ѿ нн́хх ѡ часѣ́, вх кото́рый легча́е є́мꙋ бы́сть (John 4:52—"He asked them therefore the hour, wherein he grew better"); да оу̑вѣ́сть, какокꙋ́ кꙋ́плю сꙋ́ть сотворн́лн (Luke 19:15—"That he might know what purchase they had made"); н всѧ̑, є́лн́ка а́ще воспро́снте... прїн́мете (Matth. 21:22—"And all things whatsoever ye shall ask... ye shall receive"); н вы̀ не н́щн́те, что̀ ꙗ́сте, н́лн что̀ пїе́те (Luke 12:29—"And seek not what ye shall eat, or what ye shall drink"). One must also list the relative pronouns н́же, ꙗ́же, є́же among the conjunctive words, since their forms usually serve to express attributive connections, for example: прїн́детх господн́нх раба̀ тогѡ̀ вх де́нь, во́ньже* не ча́етх, н вх ча́сх, во́ньже* не вѣ́сть (Luke 12:46—"The lord of that servant will come in a day when he looketh not for him, and at an hour that he knoweth not").

§116. Peculiarities in the Meaning of Certain Conjunctions.

Certain conjunctions, as can be seen from the preceding categories, can have more than one meaning.

1) The conjunction ꙗ́кѡ can have the following meanings: *a)* "*that*", leading to a subordinate clause: слы́шано бы́сть, ꙗ́кѡ въ до́мѹ є҆́сть (Mark 2:1—"And it was heard, that he was in the house"); *b)* "*when*": и҆ бы́сть ꙗ́кѡ и҆спо́лнишасѧ дні́е слѹ́жбы є҆гѡ̀, и҆́де въ до́мъ сво́й (Luke 1:23—"And it came to pass, when the days of his ministration were accomplished, he departed to his own house"); *c)* as an indication of cause ("*since, due to the fact that...*"): дади́те на́мъ ѿ є҆ле́а ва́шегѡ, ꙗ́кѡ свѣти́льницы на́ши ѹ҆гаса́ютъ (Matth. 25:8—"Give us of your oil, for our lamps are going out"); *d)* as an indication of purpose, combined with the conjunction да: ѿкѹ́дѹ на́мъ въ пѹсты́ни хлѣ́би толи́цы, ꙗ́кѡ да насы́титсѧ толи́къ наро́дъ (Matth. 15:33—"Whence then should we have so many loaves in the desert, as to fill so great a multitude?"); *e)* in a sentence indicating result ("*so that*"): и҆ собра́сѧ па́ки наро́дъ, ꙗ́кѡ не мощѝ и҆̀мъ ни хлѣ́ба ꙗ́сти (Mark 3:20—"And the multitude came together again, so that they could not so much as eat bread"); *f)* with a comparative meaning (=*"as, than"*): и҆ бы́сть ꙗ́кѡ ме́ртвъ (Mark 9:26—"And he was as one dead"); *g)* with numerals to express approximation: пребы́сть же марі́амь съ не́ю ꙗ́кѡ трѝ мѣ́сѧцы (Luke 1:56—"And Mary abode with her about three months").

2) The conjunction а́ще can have the following senses: *a)* conditional (=*"if"*): и҆ а́ще цѣлѹ́ете дрѹ́ги ва́ша то́кмѡ, что̀ ли́шше творитѐ; (Matth. 5:47—"And if ye salute your friends only, what more do ye [than others]?"); *b)* concessive (=*"although"*): но а́ще и҆ внѣ́шній на́шъ человѣ́къ тлѣ́етъ, ѻ҆ба́че внѹ́тренній ѡ҆бновлѧ́етсѧ (II Cor. 4:16—"But though our outward man is corrupted, yet the

inward [man] is renewed"); *c)* disjunctive (=*"whether, be it"*): а́ще престо́ли, а́ще гд҃ствїѧ, а́ще нача́ла, а́ще вла́сти (Col. 1:16— "Whether thrones, or dominions, or principalities, or powers"); *d)* in conjunction with є҆ли́жды, а҆мо́же, и҆дѣ́же, є҆ли́ка, є҆́же it has the sense of *as often as, wherever (whithersoever)*, and so on: є҆ли́жды бо а́ще ꙗ҆́сте хлѣ́бъ се́й, и҆ ча́шꙋ сїю̀ пїе́те, сме́рть гд҃ню возвѣща́ете (I Cor. 11:26—"For as often as ye shall eat this bread, and drink of this chalice, ye do shew the Lord's death"); проси̂ ѹ҆ менѐ, є҆гѡ́же а́ще хо́щеши (Mark 6:22—"Ask of me what thou wilt").

3) The conjunction ѹ҆́бо---же (equivalent to the Greek μέν---δε) is used to express opposition or comparison, either of whole clauses or of like elements within a clause (sometimes with enumeration), for example: вси̂ ѹ҆́бо теку́тъ, є҆ди́нъ же прїе́млетъ по́честь (I Cor. 9:24—"All run, but one receiveth the prize"); нн҃ѣ же мно́зи ѹ҆́бо ѹ҆́дове, є҆ди́но же тѣ́ло (I Cor. 12:20—"But now there are many members, yet one body"); пе́рвѣе ѹ҆́бо чи́ста є҆́сть, пото́мъ же ми́рна... (James 3:17—"First it is chaste, then peaceable"); и҆ ѻ҆вомꙋ́ ѹ҆́бо дадѐ пѧ́ть тала̂нтъ, ѻ҆вомꙋ́ же два̀, ѻ҆вомꙋ́ же є҆ди́нъ (Matth. 25:15—"And to one he gave five talents, and to another two, and to another one"); та́кожде и҆ вы̀ помышлѧ́йте себѐ ме́ртвыхъ ѹ҆́бо бы́ти грѣхꙋ́, живы́хъ же бг҃ови (Romans 6:11—"Likewise reckon ye also yourselves dead unto sin, but alive unto God").

The conjunction ѹ҆́бо (without the correlative же) is also used as an affirmative particle (meaning *"indeed, of course, in particular"*): пе́рвое ѹ҆́бо сло́во (Acts 1:1—"The former treatise I have made"); подоба́ше ѹ҆́бо, ѽ мꙋ́жїе, послꙋ́шавше менѐ не ѿвезти́сѧ ѿ кри́та (Acts 27:21—"Ye should indeed, O ye men, have hearkened unto me, and not have loosed from Crete"); а́ще ѹ҆́бо совершє́нство леvі́тскимъ сщ҃е́нствомъ бы́ло... (Heb. 7:11—"If therefore perfection were by the Levitical priesthood...").

4) The conjunction оу҆́бо has the following meanings: *a)*
(equivalent to the Greek οὖν, μὲν οὖν) indicates a causative, and
sometimes a temporal, connection with the preceding clause, often
with a concluding sense (usually corresponds to such words as
therefore, accordingly, for this reason, although in many cases it is not
to be translated); for example: подоба́ше оу҆́бо теб'ѣ̀ вда́ти сребро̀ моѐ
тор́жникѡ́мъ (Matth. 25:27—"Thou oughtest therefore to have
committed my money to the exchangers"); возми́те оу҆́бо ѿ негѡ̀
тала́нтъ (Matth. 25:28—"Take ye away therefore the talent from
him"); и҆̀же оу҆́бо любе́знѡ прїа́ша сло́во є҆гѡ̀, крⷭ҇ти́шаса (Acts
2:41—"Then they that gladly received his word were baptized") (in
the Russian: *итакъ, "and so"*). *b)* In final clauses (equivalent to the
Greek ἄρα, ἄρα οὖν, ἄρα γε) with the meaning *thus, therefore,* usually
after the conjunction т'ѣ́мже, but it can also begin the sentence, for
example: Т'ѣ́мже оу҆́бо в'ѣ́ра ѿ слꙋ́ха (Rom. 10:17—"So then faith
[cometh] by hearing"); т'ѣ́мже оу҆́бо са́мъ а҆́зъ оу҆мо́мъ мои́мъ
рабо́таю зако́нꙋ бж҃їю (Rom. 7:25--"So, then, I myself with the mind
serve the law of God"); т'ѣ́мже оу҆́бо ѿ плѡ́дъ и҆́хъ позна́ете и҆́хъ
(Matth. 7:20--"Wherefore by their fruits ye shall know them"); оу҆́бо
свобо́дни сꙋ́ть сы́нове (Matth. 17:26--"Then are the children free").
c) In conditional sentences it begins the main clause (and corresponds
to the Greek ἄρα): а҆́ще ли же а҆́зъ ѡ҆ дс҃ѣ бж҃їи и҆згоню̀ б'ѣ́сы, оу҆́бо
пости́же на ва́съ црⷭ҇твїе бж҃їе (Matth. 12:28--"But if I cast out
demons by the Spirit of God, then is the kingdom of God come unto
you"); а҆́ще бо зако́номъ пра́вда, оу҆́бо хрⷭ҇то́съ тꙋ́не оу҆́мре (Gal. 2:21--
"For if justice be by the law, then Christ died in vain"). *d)* In
interrogative sentences (corresponds to the Greek οὖν, ἄρα): ѿкꙋ́дꙋ
оу҆́бо и҆́мать пле́велы; (Matth. 13:27--"From whence then hath it
tares?"); хо́щеши ли оу҆́бо, да ше́дше и҆спеле́мъ а҆̀; (Matth. 13:28--
"Wilt thou then that we go and pull them up?"); оу҆́бо разꙋм'ѣ́еши ли,
ꙗ҆̀же чте́ши; (Acts 8:30--"Understandest thou what thou readest?").

5) The conjunction жє is used in the following ways: *a)* with an adversative meaning, but weaker than но: въмалѣ нє сконча́ша менѐ на землѝ: а҆зъ же нє ѡ҆ста́вихъ за́повѣдєй твои́хъ (Ps. 118:87--"They had almost made an end of me upon earth: but I have not forsaken Thy commandments"); *b)* with a copulative sense: и҆ глаго́ла и҆́ма: грѧди́та по мнѣ̀, и҆ сотворю̀ вы̀ ло́вцѧ̑ чл҃вѣ́кѡмъ. Ѻ҆на́ же а҆́бїє ѡ҆ста́вльша мрє́жи, по нє́мъ и҆до́ста (Matth. 4:19-20--"And he said to them: Come ye after me, and I will make you fishers of men. And they immediately leaving their nets, followed him"). Cf. also: Matth. 8:10; 8:31; Luke 18:41. *c)* Introduces a new situation, or renews an interrupted course of narrative: во дни̑ же ѻ҆́ны прїи́дє і҆ѡа́ннъ крⷭти́тєль... (Matth. 3:1--"And in those days came John the Baptist..."); Ходѧ̀ же при мо́ри галїлє́йстѣмъ... (Matth. 4:18--"And walking by the Sea of Galilee..."); є҆гда̀ же прїи́дє въ галїлє́ю (John 4:45--"Then when he was come to Galilee"). *d)* Introduces an inserted, explanatory text: бѣ́же[1] и҆мє́нъ наро́да вкꙋ́пѣ ꙗ҆́кѡ стѡ̀ и҆ два́десѧть (Acts 1:16--"Now the number of persons together was about an hundred and twenty"); compare also Mark 7:26 and Acts 12:3. *e)* between clauses in apposition: слы́шастє, ꙗ҆́кѡ рєчє́но бы́сть дрє́внимъ: нє прєлюбы̀ сотвори́. а҆́зъ же глаго́лю ва́мъ... (Matth. 5:27-28--"Ye have heard that it was said to them of old time: Thou shalt not commit adultery. But I say unto you..."); see also: Matth. 5:31-32; 5:33-34; 6:16-17; 7:3. *f)* As a strengthening particle: во́льнаѧ ꙋ҆́стъ мои́хъ благоволѝ же, гдⷭи (Ps. 118:108--"The free offerings of my mouth make acceptable, O Lord"); бꙋ́ди же ми́ръ въ си́лѣ твоє́й (Ps. 121:7--"Let peace be in thy strength").

---

[1]) бѣ́же = бѣ̀ же

INTERJECTIONS.

§117. Invariable words that serve to express feelings and volitional impulses, are known as *interjections*.

In Church Slavonic, the following interjections are used, expressing wonder: ѽ, ѽле [o!]; sorrow: оу҆вы̀, ѽ лю́тѣ, о҆́хъ [alas! woe!]; assurance: є҆́й [yea]; reproach: оу҆а̀ [cf. Greek οὐά, "Ah"]; direction: сѐ [behold].

The interjection є҆́й is also equivalent to the affirmative particle *yes*: бꙋ́ди же сло́во ва́ше, є҆́й, є҆́й: нѝ, нѝ (Matth. 5:37--"But let your speech be Yea, Yea; Nay, Nay"); и҆лѝ і҆ꙋде́євъ бг҃ъ то́кмѡ, а҆ не ꙗ҆зы́кѡвъ; є҆́й, и҆ ꙗ҆зы́кѡвъ (Rom. 3:29--"Or is he the God of the Jews only, and not of the Gentiles? Yea, of the Gentiles also").

Сѐ is assigned to the interjections, though it usually has the value of a demonstrative particle, introducing some new element, especially together with the conjunction и҆: и҆ сѐ мꙋ́жъ нарицае́мый закхе́й (Luke 19:2--"And, behold, there was a man named Zacchæus").

Interjections do not interact with the parts of the sentence. Some interjections enter into combinations with other words, forming separate phrases, and constituting expressions of feelings; these words may be in the following cases: with ѽ, animate nouns are in the vocative case: ѽ же́но, ве́лїѧ вѣ́ра твоѧ̀! (Matth. 15:28--"O woman, great is thy faith!"); inanimate objects are in the genitive: ѽ преসла́внагѡ чꙋдесѐ! (Octoechos, Thursday at Vespers--"O most glorious miracle!"); ѽ мꙋ́жества твоегѡ̀! ѽ терпѣ́нїѧ твоегѡ̀! (March 15, 2nd Sticheron at *Lord I have cried*--"O thy courage! O thy patience!"); but not always: ѽ ди́вное чꙋ́до! (Dormition of the Theotokos, 1st Sticheron at *Lord I have cried*--"O wondrous miracle!"); with оу҆вы̀, ѽ лю́тѣ, nouns take the dative case: with ѽле, the genitive. Interjections, along with the words that relate to them, are set off by commas or an exclamation point.

Examples:

ѽ ро́де невѣ́рный и̑ развращѐнный, доко́лѣ бꙋ́дꙋ съ ва́ми; (Matth. 17:17--"O faithless and perverse generation, how long shall I be with you?"). Ѽле стра́шнагѡ та́инства« Ѽле бл҃гоꙋ̓тро́бїѧ бж҃їѧ« ка́кѡ бж҃е́ственнагѡ тѣ́ла и̑ кро́ве бре́нїе причаща́юсѧ (Canon for Holy Communion, Ode 8--"O dread Mystery! O Divine Compassion! How can I who am clay, partake of the divine Body and Blood!"). Сѣ́де а̓да́мъ пра́мѡ раѧ̑, и̑ свою̀ наготꙋ́ рыда́ѧ пла́каше: оу̓вы̀ мнѣ̀, пре́лестїю лꙋка́вою оу̓вѣща́ннꙋ бы́вшꙋ и̑ ѡ̓кра́денꙋ и̑ сла́вы оу̓дале́нꙋ« (Cheese-Fare Sunday: "Adam sat opposite Paradise, and bemoaning his nakedness wept: Woe is me, to have been persuaded by wicked deception, and led astray, and put far from glory!"). Ѽ лю́тѣ мно́жествꙋ ꙗ̓зы́кѡвъ мно́гихъ« а̓ки мо́ре волнꙋ́ющеесѧ, та́кѡ смѧте́тесѧ (Isaiah 17:12--"Woe to the multitude of many nations! As the swelling sea, so shall ye be confounded!). И̑ всѝ мѡаві́тане оу̓слы́шаша, ꙗ̓кѡ и̑зыдо́ша трѝ царѝ бра́тисѧ съ ни́ми, и̑ возопи́ша ѿвсю́дꙋ препоѧ́санніи Ѻ̓рꙋ́жїемъ, и̑ рѣ́ша: Ѻ̓хъ: и̑ ста́ша оу̓ предѣ́ла (IV Kings 3:21--"And all the Moabites heard that the three kings were come out to fight against them; and they cried out on every side, girt with armour, and they said: Oh! And they stood by the border"). Да взы́щетсѧ кро́вь всѣ́хъ прорѡ́къ, пролива́емаѧ ѿ сложе́нїѧ мі́ра, ѿ ро́да сегѡ̀, ... е҆́й, глаго́лю ва́мъ, взы́щетсѧ ѿ ро́да сегѡ̀ (Luke 11:50-51--"That the blood of all the prophets, which was shed from the foundation of the world, may be required of this generation; ... Verily I say unto you, it shall be required of this generation"). Оу̓а̀, разорѧ́ѧй цр҃ковь и̑ треми́ де́ньми созида́ѧй (Mark 15:29--"Ah, thou that destroyest the temple, and buildest in three days..."). И̑ сѐ, ѕвѣзда̀, ю̓́же видѣ́ша на восто́цѣ, и̑дѧ́ше пред ни́ми (Matth. 2:9--"And lo, the star, which they saw in the east, went before them").

SYNTAX.

§118. The segment of grammar that studies the composition of sentences and word combinations and their aspects, is called *syntax*.

§119. The Sentence.

A *sentence* is what we call a combination of words that expresses a complete thought.

As in other languages, in a Church Slavonic sentence we distinguish the main sentence elements: the *subject* and the *predicate;* secondary elements may also be part of the sentence structure: the *object*, the *attribute*, and *adverbial expressions*.

A sentence consisting only of the main sentence parts is known as *unextended*: Ѝ бы́сть свѣ́тъ (Gen. 1:3—"And there was light"). Unextended sentences are almost never met with in Church Slavonic texts.

A sentences that includes also secondary sentence parts in its makeup is known as *extended*: Авраа́мъ родѝ і̇саа́ка (Matth. 1:2—"Abraham begat Isaac").

A sentence whether unextended or extended, that includes both of the main parts (the subject and the predicate), is called *complete [bipartite]*. A sentence that has only one main part (for example, impersonal sentences), we call *incomplete [unipartite]*.

The secondary parts of the sentence relate either to the subject or the predicate; thus we distinguish two parts of the sentence: the *subject part*, and the *predicate part*.

Based on their structure, sentences may be categorized as *simple* and *compound/complex*. The *compound/complex* category consists of those which consist of two or more clauses, joined together by coördination or subordination.

§120. Forms of Combination in a Sentence.

In a sentence (simple or compound/complex), two basic types of syntactical joining are to be distinguished: *coördination* and *subordination.*

In coördination, equal and independent parts of the sentence (simple or compound) enter syntactically into a bond: мѝлость й истина [срѣтостеся] (Ps. 84:11—"Mercy and truth [have met each other]"). In subordination, unequal sentence elements, some depending on others, are united syntactically; for example: любити правдꙋ, домъ молитвы ["to love truth; a house of prayer"].

In *subordination*, three forms of syntactic ties are to be distinguished: agreement, government, and agglutination.

Agreement is a type of subordinate combination where the dependent word is likened in form to the main word, e.g. дивное чꙋдо ("wondrous miracle"—agreement in gender, case and number), оученицы̀ возвратишася ("the disciples returned"—agreement in person and number).

Government is a form of subordinate connection where the dependent word is put in the case demanded by the main word (with or without a preposition); in this case, when the governing word changes, the governed word remains in the same form; for example: чтꙋ книгꙋ, чтеши книгꙋ [I read a book, thou readest a book]; строенїе домꙋ, строенїѧ домꙋ [the building of the house; *of* the building of the house]; приставникъ домꙋ, приставника домꙋ [the custodian of the house; *of* the custodian of the house].

Agglutination is a type of subordinate binding in which the dependent word is joined to the main word only in sense (usually it is adverbs that enter into such a combination); for example, прїѧти тꙋне [to receive gratis], ѕѣлѡ красенъ [very splendid], ѕѣлѡ заꙋтра [very early].

§121. Combination of Words.

Words in a sentence that enter into a bond among themselves form *word combinations*.

In the basis of word combinations lie their lexcial functions; i.e. one word enlarges upon another to clarify its meaning; thus in every word combination there is a main word, and a word or words that explain it, for example: добрый рабъ [the good servant]; here рабъ is the main word, and добрый elucidates it.

Word combinations are formed by means of subordination, and therefore their members are joined together through agreement, government or agglutination, for example: рабъ бжїй (agreement [because бжїй is an adjective agreeing with рабъ: "the servant of God"]); рабъ живагw бга (government—"servant of the living God"), ити скорw (agglutination—"to go quickly").

Word combinations can be simple or complex. The complex are those that can be broken down into two or more word combinations, e.g.: небесныхъ воинствъ архистратизи consists of two word combinations: архистратизи воинствъ ["leaders of the hosts"] and воинствъ небесныхъ ["of the hosts of heaven"].

THE SIMPLE SENTENCE.

§122. The Subject.

The *subject* is what we call the main person, place or thing spoken of in the sentence; the subject answers the question: *Who? What?* For instance: Прїиде жена* ѿ самарїи почерпати водꙋ (John 4:5—"A woman of Samaria came to draw water").

Most often, the subject is expressed by a noun in the nominative case, but it may also be expressed by some other declinable part of speech in the nominative:

a) The subject expressed by a noun: Ѹченницы* же ѹжасахꙋсѧ ѡ словесехъ єгѡ (Mark 10:24—"And the disciples were astonished at his words"); сѐ грѧде́тъ ча́съ* (John 16:32—"Behold, the hour cometh").

b) The subject expressed by a pronoun: Ѻни́* же нача́ша скорбѣ́ти (Mark 14:19—"But they began to be sorrowful"); кто̀* прикосн̾у́сѧ мнѣ̀; (Mark 5:31—"Who touched me?"); Никто́же* у̾бо ꙗ̾вѣ глаго́лаше ѡ не́мъ (John 7:13—"Yet no one spake openly of him"); Не бѣ̀ то́й* свѣ́тъ (John 1:8—"He was not the Light"). A subject expressed by the personal pronoun of the 1st or 2nd person, is usually omitted. This occurs because the endings of the verbs themselves show the person; besides that, the 1st and 2nd persons are participants in the narrative, and therefore when the personal pronouns are left out, the utterance is clearer than it might be with the omission of 3rd person pronouns; e.g. ви́дѣхомъ бо ѕвѣздꙋ̀ є̾гѡ̀ на восто́цѣ (Matth. 2:2—"for [we] have seen his star in the East"); и̾дꙋ̀ ры̑бы лови́ти (John 21:3—"[I] go to fish"); сі́мѡне іѡ́ннинъ, лю́биши ли мѧ̀; (John 21:16—"Simon Bar-Jonas, lovest [thou] me?").

The 1st and 2nd-person pronouns are used as subjects only when a person needs to be set apart from several other possible persons, or when one performer of the action must be distinguished from another; for example: Слы́шесте, ꙗ̾кѡ рече́но бы́сть дре́внимъ: не у̾бїе́ши... А̾зъ* же глаго́лю ва́мъ... (Matth. 5:21-22—"Ye have heard that it was said to them of old: thou shalt not kill... But I say unto you..."); ты̀ вѣ́си, ꙗ̾кѡ люблю̀ тѧ̀ (John 21:17—"Thou knowest that I love thee").

c) The subject is often expressed by a substantivized adjective (i.e. an adjective used as if it were a noun), usually in the long form, although it may also be expressed by the short form, for example: Ю̾рѡ́дивыѧ* же мꙋ́дрымъ рѣ́ша... Ѿвѣща́ша же мꙋ́дрыѧ*, глаго́люще... (Matth. 25:8-9— "And the foolish said to the wise... But the wise answered, saying..."); Речѐ безꙋ́менъ* въ се́рдцѣ свое́мъ: нѣ́сть бг҃ъ (Ps. 13:1—"The fool hath said in his heart: There is no God").

d) The subject can be expressed by a substantivized participle, either active or passive, usually in its long form. A characteristic peculiarity of the Church Slavonic language lies in its rather frequent use of active participles as the subject, something much less common in Russian, for example: сѐ и҆зы́де сѣ́ѧй* (Matth. 13:3—"Behold, the sower went forth to sow"—in the Russian version "sower" is *"сѣятель"*); сѐ прнблн́жнсѧ предаѧ́й* мѧ̀ (Matth. 26:46—"Behold, he is at hand that will betray me"); Ше́дша же по́сланнаѧ*, ѡ҆брѣ́то́сѧ... (Luke 19:32—"And they that were sent, went their way, and found...").

e) The subject can be expressed by a numeral, either alone or in conjunction with a noun, and also by a substantivized ordinal number, for instance: Возвратн́шасѧ же се́дмьдесѧтх* сх ра́достїю (Luke 10:17—"The seventy returned with joy"); Се́дмь* бра́тїй* бѣ̀ (Mark 12:20—"There were seven brethren"); И҆ прнложн́шасѧ вх де́нь то́й дꙋ́шх ꙗ҆́кѡ* трѝ* ты́сѧщн* (Acts 2:41—"And in that day there were added some three thousand souls"); и҆ вторы́й* поѧ́тх ю̀ (Mark 12:21—"And the second took her [to wife]").

Since the cardinal numbers, from 5 and up, are etymologically viewed as singular nouns, yet at the same time logically interpreted as a quantity of items, the verb used with them may be either in the singular or plural, especially when it refers to the number of persons who perform an action; for example: Пѧ́ть же бѣ̀ ѿ ннхх мꙋ́дры (Matth. 25:2—"And five of them were wise"). In this example, the etymological approach is especially evident. The verb бѣ̀ (aorist, 3rd person singular) agrees with пѧ́ть in number, but does not agree with мꙋ́дры, with which it forms a composite nominal predicate. Other examples: Не пѧ́ть лн птн́цх цѣ́ннтсѧ пѣ́наꙃема двѣма̀ (Luke 12:6— "Are not five birds priced at two farthings?"). И҆ слы́шавше де́сѧть, нача́ша негодова́тн (Mark 10:41—"And the ten, hearing, began to be displeased").

f) The subject may be expressed by a word combination, consisting of such words as є҆ди́нъ, мно́зи, нѣ́цыи [one, many, some] and the like, combined with another word by means of the preposition ѿ (or without a preposition), for example: є҆ди́нъ* ѿ ва́съ преда́стъ мѧ̀ (Matth. 26:21—"One of you shall betray me"); сѐ нѣ́цыи* ѿ кꙋстѡді́и пришє́дше во гра́дъ, возвѣсти́ша а҆рхїерє́ѡмъ всѧ̑ бы́вшаѧ (Matth. 28:11—"Behold, some of the guards came into the city, and told the chief priests all the things that were done"); Нача́ша глаго́лати є҆мꙋ̀ є҆ди́нъ* кі́йждо* и҆́хъ* (Matth. 26:22—"They began, every one of them, to say to him...").

g) The infinitive, with the sense of a noun, can take the role of the subject, and therefore usually has the pronoun є҆́же placed before it as a sort of article, though this can also be absent (corresponding to the definite article τὸ in the Greek text): что̀ є҆́сть, є҆́же* и҆зъ мє́ртвыхъ воскре́снꙋти* (Mark 9:10—"What is the rising from the dead?"); є҆́же* не ѹ҆мовє́нныма рꙋка́ма ꙗ҆́сти*, не скверни́тъ человѣ́ка (Matth. 15:20—"to eat with unwashen hands defileth not a man"); Мнѣ̀ бо є҆́же* жи́ти* хрⷭ҇то́съ: и҆ є҆́же* ѹ҆мре́ти*, прїѡбрѣ́тенїе є҆́сть (Philippians 1:21—"For me, to live is Christ, and to die is gain"); лꙋ́чше бо є҆́сть жени́тисѧ*, не́жели разжиза́тисѧ* (I Cor. 7:9— "It is better to marry than to burn"); Мнѣ̀ же прилѣпля́тисѧ* бѣгови бла́го є҆́сть (Ps. 72:28—"But it is good for me to adhere to God").

h) The subject may be expressed by an indeclinable part of speech with the sense of a noun, before which is put the pronoun є҆́же, used as an article (for the Greek τὸ); or else by an oblique case with a preposition, likewise in combination with є҆́же: бꙋ́ди же ва́мъ, є҆́же* є҆́й, є҆́й*, и҆ є҆́же* нѝ, нѝ* (James 5:12—"But let your Yea be Yea, and your Nay be Nay"); и҆́бо є҆́же* ѡ҆ мнѣ̀*, кончи́нꙋ и҆́мать (Luke 22:37—"For the things concerning me have an end").

Note. Examples such as the preceding can hardly be viewed as subordinate clause subjects with an omitted predicate, since they merely copy the construction of the Greek: Καὶ γὰρ τὸ περὶ ἐμοῦ τέλος ἔχει.

*i)*Pronouns, substantivized adjectives and participles, if used as the subject with a collective sense, in Church Slavonic (on the Greek model) are in the neuter nominative plural, for example: Сїѧ* бо сꙋщаѧ* въ васъ и мнѡжащаѧсѧ*, не пра́здныхъ нижѐ безпло́дныхъ сотворѧ́тъ вы̀... (II Peter 1:8—"For if these things be in you and abound, they will make you neither empty nor unfruitful..."); Неви́димаѧ* бо є҆гѡ̀, ѿ созда́нїѧ мі́ра творе́ньми помышлѧ́єма ви́дима сꙋ́ть (Rom. 1:20—"For the visible things of him, from the creation of the world, being understood by the things that are made, are clearly seen").

§123. The Predicate.

The *predicate* is what is said about the subject of a sentence: the predicate answers the question *"What is done/what does he do? What/who is it?"* For example: Сѐ грѧде́тъ* ча́съ (John 16:32—"Behold, the hour cometh"); а҆́зъ бо є҆́смь* ста́ръ* (Luke 1:18—"For I am old"); не бѣ̀* то́й свѣ́тъ* (John 1:8—"He was not the Light"); пло́дъ же дꙋхо́вный є҆́сть* любы̀*... (Gal. 5:22—"The fruit of the Spirit is love").

The predicate is of the following forms: *simple, composite nominal, composite verbal,* and *complex.* A simple predicate can be expressed by simple conjugation forms of verbs, or by compound forms, of which there are the following:

The Perfect (є҆́смь сотвори́лъ, §88),
The Pluperfect (бѣ́хъ сотвори́лъ, §89),
The Future Composite (и҆́мамъ твори́ти, §85),
The Subjunctive Mood (сотвори́лъ бы́хъ, §91).

With the demonstrative-introductory particle сѐ (behold) or и҆ сѐ (and behold) the predicate from the verb бы́ти (in the present, past or future) is often omitted, for example: Сѐ мы̀ днесь *(есмы)* въ пресєлє́нїи на́шемъ (Baruch 3:8—"Behold, we are yet this day in our captivity"); Й сѐ ва́мъ *(есть* or *будетъ)* зна́мєнїє (Luke 2:12—"And this shall be a sign unto you"). The predicate (of the verb бы́ти, *to be*) is omitted in the past tense, no doubt, to represent some event as occurring before the eyes, for the sake of greater vividness: Й сѐ *(бысть)* гла́съ съ нєбєсѐ, глаго́ла (Matth. 3:17—"And behold *(there was)* a voice from heaven, saying"); Й сѐ *(бяше)* мѹ́жъ, нарицаємый закхє́й (Luke 19:2 —"And behold, *(there was)* a man named Zacchæus"); Й ви́дѣхъ, и сѐ *(бяше)* ко́нь бѣ́лъ (Rev. 6:2— "And I saw, and behold *(there was)* a white horse"); sometimes this occurs in sentences without сѐ: А́ггльскїѧ си́лы *(бяху)* на гро́бѣ твоє́мъ, и стрегѹ́щїи ѡ̀мертвѣ́ша (Sunday Troparion of the 6th Tone:—"The Angelic Hosts *(were)* at Thy tomb, and the guards were as dead men"). With сѐ, sometimes other verbs can be "understood", for example: Сѐ *(слы́шу)* гла́съ во́пля дщє́рє людє́й мои́хъ ѝзъдалє́ча (Jer. 8:19—"Behold *(I hear)* the voice of the cry of the daughter of my people from afar"); Сѐ а́зъ *(есмь, гряду)* на проро́ки (Jer. 23:31—"Behold, I *(am,* or *come)* against the prophets").

The predicate from бы́ти is also omitted:

a) in questions: что̀ къ тебѣ̀; (John 21:22—"What is that to thee?"); ка́ѧ мѝ по́льза; (I Cor. 15:32—"What doth it profit me?"); что̀ сло́во сїѐ; (Luke 4:36—"What word is this?");

b) in expressions of desire (to be understood, evidently, are the forms of бы́ти in the imperative or optative moods): ми́ръ ва́мъ (John 20:19—"Peace *(be)* unto you"); гд҇ь съ тобо́ю (Luke 1:28—"The Lord *(is* or *be)* with thee"); благословє́нїє гд҇не на ва́съ (Liturgy—"The blessing of the Lord *(be)* upon you"); ѐмѹ́же сла́ва во вѣ́ки вѣкѡ́въ (I Peter 1:5—"To whom *(be)* glory for ages of ages"); бг҇ѹ же благодарє́нїє (I Cor. 15:57; II Cor 8:16; 9:15—"But thanks *(be)* to God").

c) In conjunction with the word и́ма (name): и́ма є҆м҄ꙋ іѡа́ннъ (John 1:6—"Whose name was John"); є҆й́ же и́ма ге҆ѳсима́нїа (Mark 14:32—"Which was named Gethsemane").

§124. The Composite Nominal Predicate.

The *composite nominal predicate* consists of a *verb-copula* and the *nominal part* of the predicate. The copula is usually a form of the verb бы́ти. This copula has a purely grammatical role, that is, it merely connects the nominal (noun, adjective) part of the predicate with the subject, and indicates the mood and the personal tense forms. The nominal part of the predicate shows what is said about the subject. For example: прⷪ҇ро́къ* є҆сѝ* ты̀: (John 4:19—"[I see that] Thou art a prophet"); ты̀ є҆сѝ* цр҃ь* і҆и҃левъ (John 1:49—"Thou art the King of Israel"); бѣ̀* же вара́вва разбо́йникъ* (John 18:40—"Now Barabbas was a robber"); вы̀ є҆стѐ* со́ль* землѝ (Matth. 5:13—"Ye are the salt of the earth").

The verb-copula in the present tense in a composite predicate usually is not omitted, although constructions without a copula are also to be encountered, for instance: бл҃же́ни рабѝ ті́и (Luke 12:37 —"Blessed are those servants"); cf. бл҃же́ни сꙋ́ть рабѝ ті́и (Luke 12:38); ю҆нцы̀ моѝ и҆ ѹ҆пита́нная и҆сколе́на, и҆ всѧ̑ гото́ва (Matth. 22:4—"My oxen and my fatlings [*are*] killed, and all is ready").

With the demonstrative-introductory particle сѐ, the copula (not only in the present, but also in the past) is for the most part omitted, for example: и҆ со́нъ ви́дѣ: тꙋ̀ и҆ сѐ лѣ́ствица ѹ҆твержде́на на землѝ (Gen. 28:12—"And he dreamed, and behold a ladder set up on the earth")(=ба́ше ѹ҆твержде́на); и҆ сѐ мꙋ́жїе носѧ́ще на ѻ҆дрѣ̀ челов́ѣ́ка, и́же бѣ̀ разсла́бленъ (Luke 5:18—"And behold, men brought in a bed a man which was taken with the palsy")(=ба́хꙋ носѧ́ще); и҆ сѐ по́лнъ сла́вы до́мъ гдⷭ҇нь (Ezek. 43:5—"And behold, the glory of the Lord filled the house")(=ба́ше по́лнъ). The copula in the past tense is omitted, it would appear, for greater vividness of the events described (§123).

Sometimes one meets with cases of an omitted copula in the imperative: Премꙋдрость. Прости (Liturgy—"Wisdom. [Let us] attend") (=бꙋдите прости [be attentive]); Братолюбїемъ дрꙋгъ ко дрꙋгꙋ любезни (Rom. 12:10—"[Be] kindly disposed to one another with brotherly love")— (=бꙋдите любезни); Проклѧтъ всѧкъ... (Gal. 3:10—"Cursed is everyone [that continueth...]"); Благословено цртво (Liturgy—"Blessed [is] the Kingdom...").

The copula is omitted with the words горе, времѧ, потреба [woe, time, need] when they are used impersonally, for example: Горе вамъ (Matth. 23:13—"Woe to you"); Времѧ плакати, и времѧ смѣѧтисѧ (Eccl. 3:4—"[There is] a time to weep, and a time to laugh"); see §175, 3) d).

In the following examples, it would appear that the copula also has been omitted: рахиль плачꙋщисѧ чадъ своихъ и не хотѧше оутѣшитисѧ, ꙗкw не сꙋть (Matth. 2:18—"Rachel weeping for her children, and would not be comforted, because they are not")—(=бѧше плачꙋщисѧ); взе́млеши ꙲гẃже не положи́, и жне́ши ꙲гẃже не сѣѧвъ (Luke 19:21-22—"Thou takest up that thou layedst not down, and reapest that thou didst not sow")—(=не сѣѧвъ ꙲си), cf. Luke 7:18. In revised editions of the Gospel, this reading has been changed to не сѣѧлъ ꙲си.

In the function of a copula, the following verbs, expressing the manifestation or display of some characteristic, are also used: —бывати [to be, over a period of time]; ꙗвлѧтисѧ [appear]; показатисѧ [show oneself]; познатисѧ [be known, make oneself known]; видѣтисѧ [be seen, seem]; a transition from one state to another, or the retention of a previous condition: —содѣлатисѧ [become], wстатисѧ [stay], wставатисѧ, пребывати [remain], wбрѣстисѧ [be found] and certain others (some of the verbs indicated may be in a composite passive form: видимъ бѣ [he was seen], ꙗвленъ бѣ [he was shown, manifest] &c.). These verbs, fulfilling the functions of a copula, retain to some extent their lexical meaning, and therefore are called *semi-significant* copulas[1]). Examples:

Ма́ти* ѹ҆́бо позна́ласѧ* є҆сѝ*, па́че є҆стества̀, бцⷣе, пребыла̀* же є҆сѝ дв҃а*, па́че сло́ва и҆ ра́зꙋма (Dogmatik, T. 7—"Thou hast been acknowledged to be a Mother above and beyond nature, O Theotokos, for thou didst remain a Virgin, beyond word and reason"); Бл҃же́ни миротво́рцы: ꙗ҆́кѡ ті́и сн҃ове* бж҃їи нарекꙋ́тсѧ* (Matth. 5:9—"Blessed [are] the peacemakers: for they shall be called the children of God"); ви́дѣнъ* бы́сть* невѣще́ственъ* (Matins for Aug. 6, Ode 4—"Thou wast revealed [to be] an immaterial [fire]").

Note. The forms of the verb бы́ти, along with several other of those given above that can be used as copulas, are also used with their full lexical meaning as independant predicates: Бѣ̑ же фі́лїппъ ѿ виѳсаі́ды (John 1:44—"Now Philip was of Bethsaida"); Бг҃ъ ꙗ҆ви́сѧ во пло́ти (I Tim. 3:16—"God was manifest in the flesh").

In the role of a copula, certain verbs with full lexical meaning can also be used — these are known as a *significant* copula. To their number belong verbs of motion or condition: и҆тѝ [to go], ходи́ти [go, walk], посыла́тисѧ [be sent], возврати́тисѧ [return], стоѧ́ти [stand], лежа́ти [lie], сѣдѣ́ти [sit], вста́ти [rise], роди́тисѧ [be born], жи́ти [live], ѹ҆мре́ти [die] and others, for example: слѣ́пъ* роди́сѧ* (John 9:2—"he was born blind"); на́гъ* и҆зыдо́хъ* ѿ чре́ва ма́тере моеѧ̀, на́гъ* и҆ ѿи҆дꙋ̀ та́мѡ (Job 1:21—"Naked came I out of my mother's womb, and naked shall I return thither"); вста́ни* на нѡ́гꙋ твою̀ пра́въ* (Acts 14:10—"Stand upright on thy feet"); но ѻ҆ба́че проповѣ́дница* посыла́етсѧ* твои҆́мъ ѹ҆чени́кѡмъ (Gospel Sticheron 8—"But she was also sent to preach ("*въ качествѣ проповѣдницы*"—Russ.) the good tidings unto Thy Disciples"); та́кѡ дв҃а* родила* є҆сѝ* и҆ дв҃а пребыла̀ є҆сѝ (Dogmatik, T. 2—"so hast thou given birth as a Virgin ("*дѣвою*"— Russ.), and remained a

[1])For the meaning of the term "significant", see §18.

Virgin"); бг҃ъ* бо пріidо́хъ* за бл҃гоу́тробїе а҆да́ма ѡ҆чи́стити ѿ паде́нїѧ (Matins for Jan. 5, 1st Sticheron at the Praises—"[As] God I have come, out of mercy, to cleanse Adam from his fall").

§125. The Nominal Part of the Composite Predicate.

The nominal part of a composite predicate may be expressed by any of the declinable parts of speech, which in Church Slavonic are always put in the nominative case; for example:

a) A noun: вы̀ є҆стѐ* свѣ́тъ* мі́ра (Matth. 5:14—"Ye are the light of the world"); дв҃а* пребыла̀* є҆сѝ (Dogmatik, T. 2—"thou hast remained a Virgin"); и҆ ты̀, ѻ҆троча̀, пр҃ро́къ* вы́шнѧгѡ нарече́шисѧ* (Luke 1:76—"And thou, child, shalt be called the prophet of the Highest").

Note: Sometimes, as an exception, the nominal part of the predicate is encountered in the instrumental case: И҆ ма́ти по рождествѣ̀ па́ки пребы́сть* дв҃ою* (Octoechos, Sunday Vespers T. 5, Theotokion at the Aposticha—"And the Mother, after childing, again remaineth a Virgin").

b) A pronoun: И҆ моѧ̑ всѧ̑ твоѧ̑* су́ть, и҆ твоѧ̑ моѧ̑* (John 17:10—"And all mine are thine, and thine are mine"); а҆́зъ є҆́смь*, не бо́йтесѧ (John 6:20—"It is I, be not afraid").

c) An adjective: Бу́дите* оу҆́бо соверше́ни*, ꙗ҆́коже ѻ҆ц҃ъ ва́шъ соверше́нъ є҆́сть (Matth. 5:48—"Be ye therefore perfect, even as your Father is perfect"); Се́й ве́лїй нарече́тсѧ* въ цр҃твїи нб҃е́снѣмъ (Matth. 5:19—"the same shall be called great in the kingdom of heaven").

d) A participle: here belong the compound passive forms (§102): и҆ ни ко є҆ди́ной и҆́хъ по́сланъ* бы́сть* и҆лїа̀ (Luke 4:26—"But unto none of them was Elias sent"); and the descriptive tense forms (§90): и҆ бѣ̀ проповѣ́даѧ* на со́нмищахъ галїле́йскихъ (Luke 4:44—"And he preached in the synagogues of Galilee"). As the nominal part of the predicate, the long form of the participle (substantivized) may also be used: Вѣ́дѧше бо и҆сконѝ і҆и҃съ, кі́и су́ть* не вѣрующїи*, и кто̀ є҆́сть* преда́ѧй* є҆го̀ (John 6:64—"For Jesus knew from the beginning who they were that believed not, and who should betray him").

e) A numeral: и҆ да бꙋ́дꙋтъ* о҆́смь* столпы̀, и҆ стоѧ́ла и҆́хъ сре́бранаѧ шестьна́десѧть* (Exodus 26:25—"And there shall be eight posts, and their bases of silver, sixteen").

Numerals expressing *age* or *measure* may be in the genitive case: и҆ є҆гда̀ бы́сть* двоюна́десѧти* лѣ́тъ* (Luke 2:42—"And when he [the child Jesus] was twelve years old"); долгота̀ о҆по́ны є҆ди́ныѧ да бꙋ́детъ* тридесѧти* лакте́й* (Ex. 26:8—"The length of one curtain shall be thirty cubits").

f) An infinitive, with a substantivized meaning, and therefore the pronoun є҆́же is placed before it with the sense of an article (in the Greek text τὸ): Твое́ бо є҆́сть, є҆́же* ми́ловати* и҆ спаса́ти ны̀, бж҃е на́шъ (Exclamation at Matins—"For Thine it is to have mercy on us and save us, O our God...").

§126. The Composite Verbal Predicate.

A *composite verbal predicate* consists of a conjugational personal form of a verb together with an infinitive. The conjugated personal form in this combination has a weakened lexical meaning and is an auxiliary verb. The following may be used as auxiliary verbs in a composite verbal predicate:

1) Verbs signifying the beginning or end of an action: нача́ти [to begin], сконча́ти [to finish], преста́ти [to cease, stop]: и҆ нача́ша* моли́ти* є҆го̀ ѿити ѿ предѣ̑лъ и҆́хъ (Mark 5:17—"And they began to pray him to depart out of their coasts"); нн҃ѣ же сїѐ твори́ти* сконча́йте* (II Cor. 8:11—"Now therefore perform [i.e. complete] the doing of this"); преста́ша* би́ти* па́vла (Acts 21:32—"they left off beating Paul").

Note. Composite verbal predicates that consist of an auxiliary verb, signifying continuous action, in combination with an infinitive, are not normally used in Church Slavonic, but instead of this type of verb combination the descriptive tense forms are used (see §90, §161), for example: (Апостолы) не престаа́хꙋ* оучаще и благовѣ́ствꙋюще* і҆и҃са х҃рта̀, Acts 5:42 (cf. in the Russian version не переставали учить и благовѣствовать—"they ceased not to teach and to preach Jesus Christ"); yet sometimes: пребꙋ́демъ х҃рта̀ ви́дѣти (rather than ви́дѧще), Sunday Matins Exaposteilarion 4—"let us stay to behold Christ".

2) Verbs with a modal meaning: *a)* expressing ability, possibility or obligation: мощи́, имѣ́ти, оумѣ́ти. *b)* expressing intention: хотѣ́ти [to want, be about to], желати [to wish, desire], и҆скати [to seek—in the sense of 'desire, try'], тщатисѧ [to strive, take pains], дерзнꙋ́ти [to dare, be bold], покꙋшатисѧ [to attempt], смѣ́ти [to be bold], ѿрекатисѧ [to refuse, renounce]; *c)* expressing inner experience: надѣ́ѧтисѧ [to hope], боятисѧ [to fear] and certain others, for example: вы̀ спастисѧ* не мо́жете* (Acts 27:31—"ye cannot be saved"); кля́твы же ра́ди и҆ за возлежащихъ не восхотѣ̀* ѿрещи́* е҆ѝ (Mark 6:26—"for [his] oath's sake and for their sakes which sat with him, he would not refuse her"); е҆гда̀ же хотѧ́ше* де́нь бы́ти* (Acts 27:33—"and while the day was coming on"); Рахи́ль плачꙋ́щисѧ ча́дъ свои́хъ, и҆ не хотѧ́ше* оутѣ́шитисѧ, я́кω не сꙋ́ть (Matth. 2:18—"Rachel weeping for her children, and would not be comforted, because they are not"); си́це же тщахсѧ* благовѣ́стити* (Rom. 15:20—"so have I strived to preach the gospel"); а҆бїе взыскахомъ* изытѝ* въ македо́нїю (Acts 16:10—"immediately we endeavoured to go into Macedona"); покꙋшахꙋсѧ* въ вⷣивⷤнїю понтѝ* (Acts 16:7—"they assayed to go into Bithynia"); Никто́же смѣ́аше* прилѣплѧ́тисѧ* и҆мъ (Acts 5:13—"No man durst join himself unto them"); оубоѧ́сѧ* та́мω итѝ* (Matth. 2:22—"he was afraid to go thither").

§127. The Compound Predicate.

A *compound predicate* is a predicate that consists of three (or four) members. In most cases it is a combination of a composite nominal and a composite verbal predicate, for example: є̂да̀ и̂ вы̀ оу҆ченицы̀* є҆гѡ̀ хо́щете* бы́ти*; (John 9:27—"Will ye also be his disciples?"); вѣ́рою, мѡѷсе́й вели́къ бы́въ, ѿве́ржеса* нарица́тиса* сы́нъ дще́ре фараѡ́новы (Heb. 11:24—"By faith Moses, when he was come to years, refused to be called the son of Pharaoh's daughter"); можа́ше* бо сїѐ мѵ́ро про́дано* бы́ти* на мно́зѣ (Matth. 26:9—"For this ointment might have been sold for much"); по зако́нꙋ на́шемꙋ до́лженъ* є҆́сть* оу҆мре́ти* (John 19:7—"by our law he ought to die"); нѣ́смь* досто́инъ* нареши́са* сы́нъ* тво́й (Luke 15:19—"I am not worthy to be called thy son").

§128. Agreement of the Predicate with the Subject.

a) With a subject signifying two persons or things, the predicate is usually put in the dual number; although, under the influence of Russian, deviations from this rule are also encountered. For example: ꙗ҆́кѡ ви́дѣстѣ ѻ҆́чи мои̑ спасе́нїе твоѐ (Luke 2:30—"for mine eyes have seen thy salvation"); человѣ́ка два̀ внидо́ста въ це́рковь помоли́тиса (Luke 18:10—"Two men went up into the temple to pray"); also: не двѣ́ ли пти̑цы цѣ́нꙗтса є҆ди́нымъ а҆сса́рїемъ; (Matth. 10:29—"Are not two sparrows sold for a farthing?").

b) A predicate that accompanies a subject in the form of a collective noun, has a tendency to agree according to the sense, i.e. it may be in the plural. In the Holy Scriptures the following collective nouns are used: бра́тїа [brethren, group of brothers], наро́дъ [people, folk], гра́дъ [city], до́мъ [household], мно́жество [multitude], собра́нїе [gathering, assembly].

The predicate with бра́тїа is always put in the plural, for example: цѣлꙋ́ютъ вы̀ бра́тїа вса̀ (I Cor. 16:20—"All the brethren greet you"); пріндо́ша бра́тїѧ їѡ́сифова (Gen. 45:16—"Joseph's brethren are come") cf. §37, 12.

With the other words indicated, the predicate if immediately next to them, is comparatively rare in the plural; generally adjacent predicates are in the singular, while remote predicates, usually in subordinate clauses, are in the plural. Adverbial participles (equivalent to gerunds) used with these words are also in the plural.

Examples: Adjacent predicates in the plural; collective nouns, usually combined with other nouns signifying persons: Мно́гъ наро́дъ сще́нникѡвъ послꙋшахꙋ вѣ́ры (Acts 6:7—"A great company of the priests were obedient to the faith"); ѡ не́мже всѐ мно́жество їꙋде́й стꙋжахꙋ мнѝ (Acts 25:24 —"about whom all the multitude of the Jews have dealt with me"); И воста́вше всѐ мно́жество и́хъ, ведо́ша є҆го̀ къ пїла́тꙋ (Luke 23:1—"And the whole multitude of them arose, and led him unto Pilate"); Собра́нїе їꙋде́йское оу҆ пїла́та и҆спроси́ша распѧ́ти тѧ̀, гд҃и (Good Friday Matins, 13th Antiphon—"The assembly of the Jews besought Pilate to crucify Thee, O Lord"). Proximate predicates— in the singular; remote predicates as well as adverbial participles—in the plural: и се весь гра́дъ и҆зы́де въ срѣ́тенїе і҃совн: и҆ ви́дѣвше є҆го̀, моли́ша... (Matth. 8:34—"And behold, the whole city came out to meet Jesus, and when they saw him, they besought him..."); И моли́ є҆го̀ весь наро́дъ страны̀ гадари́нскїѧ ѿити ѿ ни́хъ, ꙗ҆́кѡ стра́хомъ ве́лїимъ ѡ҆держи́ми бѣ́хꙋ (Luke 8:37—"Then the whole multitude of the country of the Gadarenes besought him to depart from them, for they were taken with great fear"); Но наро́дъ се́й, и́же не вѣ́сть зако́на, про́клѧти сꙋ́ть (John 7:49— "But this people who know not the law, are cursed"); вѣ́сте до́мъ стефани́новъ, ꙗ҆́кѡ є҆́сть нача́токъ а҆ха́їи, и҆ въ слꙋже́нїе оу҆чини́ша себѐ (I Cor. 16:15—"ye know the house of Stephanas, that is is the firstfruits of Achaia, and that they have dedicated themselves to the ministry..."); see also John 6:2; Acts 5:16; Mark 3:9; Acts 15:12.

c) If the subject is expressed by a cardinal numeral, with or without a noun, then the predicate is in the plural, for example: срѣто́ша є҆го̀ де́сать прокаже́ныхъ мꙋже́й (Luke 17:12—"there met him ten men that were lepers"); и҆ слы́шавше де́сать, негодова́ша ѡ҆ ѻ҆бою̀ бра́тꙋ (Matth. 20:24—"And when the ten heard it, they were moved to indignation against the two brethren").

d) The nominal part of a composite predicate agrees (as far as possible) with its subject in gender, number and case, for example: бѣста ѻ҆ба на́га (Gen. 2:25—"They were both naked").

The numeral є҆ди́нъ, as the nominal part of a composite predicate, in expressing singleness, is put in the neuter singular: и҆ сі́и трѝ є҆ди́но сꙋть (I John 5:8—"and these three are one"); а҆́зъ и҆ ѻ҆ц҃ъ є҆ди́но є҆сма̀ (John 10:30—"I and [my] Father are one").

§129. Agreement of the Predicate with Several Subjects.

The agreement of a predicate with several subjects of the same gender (with or without conjunctions), being either in the singular number, or singular and plural:

a) A predicate preceding the subjects (singular + singular or sing. + plural), agrees with the first, except for the cases listed below under point *d)*, for example: до́ндеже пре́йдетъ нб҃о и҆ землѧ̀ (Matth. 5:18—"till heaven and earth pass away"); ꙗ҆́кw преста̀ до́ждь и҆ гра́дъ и҆ гро́мн (Ex. 9:34 — "And the rain and hail and thunders ceased"); зва́нъ же бы́сть і҆и҃съ и҆ ᲂу҆чєнницы̀ є҆гẁ на бра́къ (John 2:2—"And both Jesus was called, and his disciples, to the marriage"); likewise John 18:15; John 20:3; Acts 11:14; Acts 16:31; Rom. 16:21; II Tim. 1:15.

b) A predicate standing between the first subject and the others (sing. + sing. or sing. + plu.), agrees with the first, e.g.: то́й влѣ́зе въ кора́бль и҆ ᲂу҆чєнницы̀ є҆гẁ (Luke 8:22—"he went into a ship with his disciples"); да и҆ сѣ́ай вкꙋ́пѣ ра́дꙋетсѧ и҆ жнѧ́й (John 4:36—"that both he that soweth and he that reapeth, may rejoice together").

c) A predicate standing after its subjects (sing. + sing.), may be in either the singular or the plural:

When the subjects are inanimate objects, of the same grammatical gender and close in substance, the predicate is usually in the singular; when the subjects are of various genders, it is in the plural, for example: и гра́дъ и до́ждь не бꙋ́детъ ктомꙋ̀ (Ex. 9:31—"and there shall be no more rain and hail"); also Ex. 9:33; ле́нъ и ꙗчме́нь побꙋ́тъ е҆́сть (Ex. 9:31—"And the flax and the barley was smitten"); зла́то ва́ше и сребро̀ проржа́вѣ (James 5:3—"Your gold and silver is cankered"); but also: ми́лость и и҆́стина пред҆и́детъ пред҆ лице́мъ твои́мъ (Ps. 88:15—"Mercy and truth shall go before thy face"); with different grammatical genders: пшени́ца и жи́то не побꙋ́ты (Ex. 9:32—"the wheat and rye were not smitten"); и вѣ́тръ и мо́ре послꙋ́шаютъ е҆гѡ̀ (Mark 4:41—"the wind and sea obey him"), but also: нбо и землѧ̀ мимои́детъ (Matth. 24:35—"Heaven and earth shall pass away"); нбо и землѧ̀ пре́йдетъ (Mark 13:31—"Heaven and earth shall pass away").

The predicate is in the singular with subjects (sing. + sing.) expressing varied activity, i.e. when the subject does not represent a joint action and the predicate relates as it were to each subject individually, for example: всѧ́ка го́ресть и гнѣ́въ, и ꙗ́рость, и кли́чь, и хꙋ́ла, да во́зметсѧ ѿ ва́съ (Eph. 4:31—"Let all bitterness, and wrath, and anger, and clamour, and evil speaking, be put away from you"); блꙋ́дъ же и всѧ́ка нечистота̀ и лихои́мство нижѐ да и҆менꙋ́етсѧ въ ва́съ (Eph. 5:3— "But fornication, and all uncleanness, or covetousness, let it not once be named among you"); нечести́вый и грѣ́шный гдѣ̀ ꙗви́тсѧ (I Peter 4:18—"where shall the ungodly and sinner appear?"); благода́ть ва́мъ и ми́ръ да ѹ҆мно́житсѧ въ позна́нїи бга (II Peter 1:2—"Grace and peace be multiplied unto you through the knowledge of God").

d) If the action of the subjects is combined (sing. + sing. or sing. + plu.), which usually occurs when the subjects signify persons, the predicate agrees with the subjects in the plural or in the dual number, regardless of its position in the sentence: whether it stands before or after the subjects, for example: й пред него прїидоста* іакѡвъ й іѡаннъ (Mark 10:35—"And there came before him James and John"); Прїидоша* же къ немꙋ̀ мати й братїа єгѡ̀ (Luke 8:19—"Then came to him his mother and his brethren"); Вкꙋпѣ же петръ й іѡаннъ восхождаста* во свѧтилище (Acts 3:1—"Now Peter and John went up together into the temple"), as well as Luke 23:12; Acts 5:24; Acts 17:14.

e) If the subjects (sing. + sing or sing. + plu.) are located between an adverbial participle (equivalent to a gerund) and a conjugated verb form (predicate), then, based on the Greek text, the participle agrees in the singular, but the conjugated verb does so in the plural, for example: Воставъ* же архїерей й вси, йже съ нимъ сꙋщаѧ єресь саддꙋкейскаѧ, исполнишаса* зависти (Acts 5:17— "Then the high priest rose up, and all they that were with him, which is the sect of the Sadducees, and were filled with indignation"); пришедъ* же архїерей й йже съ нимъ, созваша* соборъ (Acts 5:21— "But the high priest came, and they that were with him, and called the council together"); Ѿвѣщавъ* же петръ й апли рѣша* (Acts 5:29—"Then Peter and the apostles answered and said"). A similar agreement is possible in the inverse order, i.e. the conjugated verb agrees in the singular, but the participle in the plural (or the dual), for example: й бѣ* іѡсифъ й мати єгѡ̀ чꙋдѧщаса* (Luke 2:33 —"And Joseph and his mother marvelled").

f) With a subject (sing. + sing.) connected by the disjunctive conjunction или, the predicate is in the singular, for example: іѡта єдина, или єдина черта не прейдетъ* ѿ закона (Matth. 5:18 —"one jot or one tittle shall in no wise pass from the law"); всѧкъ градъ или домъ раздѣливыйса на сѧ не станетъ (Matth. 12:25—"every city or house divided against itself shall not stand"); аще ли рꙋка твоа, или нога твоа соблажнаетъ тѧ (Matth. 18:8—"if thy hand or thy foot

offend thee"); also I Cor. 14:24; Gal. 1:8; Eph. 5:5; an exception: а́ще
же бра́тъ и́ли сестра́ на́ги бу́дутъ (James 2:15 —"If a brother or sister
be naked").

g) With the reflexive mood, the predicate is put in the plural
(or the dual), for example: Ми́лость и и́стина срѣто́стѣсѧ, пра́вда и
ми́ръ ѡблобыза́стасѧ (Ps. 84:11—"Mercy and truth have met each
other: justice and peace have kissed").

h) If the forms of the predicate show gender (for instance, in
the dual number or in certain forms of the composite predicate), then
the agreement of the predicate in the dual and plural with subjects of
various gender follows the predominant gender, e.g.: пра́вда и ми́ръ
ѡблобыза́стасѧ (Ps. 84:11, above).

§130. Attributes.

Attribute is the term for a secondary part of the sentence,
showing a quality of some entity and answering the question: What
sort of? Whose? Which? For example: Благі́й* человѣ́къ ѿ
блага́гѡ* сокро́вища се́рдца своегѡ̀ изно́ситъ благо́е (Luke 6:45—"A
good man out of the good treasure of his heart bringeth forth that
which is good"); Бѣ̀ же фїли́ппъ ѿ виѳсаі́ды, ѿ гра́да андре́ова* и
петро́ва* (John 1:44—"Now Philip was of Bethsaida, the city of
Andrew and Peter"); Па́ки же изше́дъ въ шесты́й*, и деѧ́тый*
ча́съ, сотворѝ та́кожде (Matth. 20:5—"Again he went out about the
sixth and ninth hour, and did likewise").

The word to which the attribute relates is called the
determinate [Russ. опредѣляемое, "entity which is defined"].

Depending on the grammatical bond between the attribute
and the determinate, attributes may be, as in Russian, either
coördinated or *uncoördinated*.

1) Coördinated [concordant] attributes usually are expressed
by adjectives, but also by equivalent participles, pronouns and
numerals, for example: И бли́зъ бѣ̀ па́сха їуде́йска* (John 2:13—

"And the Jews' Passover was at hand"); є҆ди́нъ же ѿ ѡ҆б҆ѣшеною* ѕлодѣ́ю хꙋлаше є҆го̀ (Luke 23:39—"And one of the malefactors which were hanged railed against him"); вѣ́ра твоѧ̀* спасе́ тѧ̀ (Luke 18:42—"thy faith hath saved thee"); и҆ въ тре́тїй* де́нь воскре́снетъ (Luke 18:33—"and the third day he shall rise again").

An attribute may be expressed by either the long or the short form of adjectives (see §171).

2) When there are several determinates [modified entities], the concordant attribute usually agrees with that nearest to it, for example: во всѧ́къ* гра́дъ и҆ мѣ́сто (Luke 10:1—"into every city and place"); и҆ соверше́нъ* ва́шъ дꙋ́хъ и҆ дꙋша̀ и҆ тѣ́ло непоро́чно въ прише́ствїе гд҃а на́шегѡ і҆и҃са хр҃та̀ да сохрани́тсѧ (I Thess. 5:23—"and [may] your whole spirit and soul and body be preserved blameless unto the coming of our Lord Jesus Christ"); въ не́же да́рове и҆ же́ртвы прино́сѧтсѧ не могꙋ́щыѧ* по со́вѣсти соверши́ти слꙋжа́щаго (Heb. 9:9—"in which were offered gifts and sacrifices, that could not make him that did the service perfect, as pertaining to the conscience"); слы́шавъ любо́вь твою̀* и҆ вѣ́рꙋ (Philemon 5—"Hearing of thy love and faith").

3) Uncoördinated [non-concordant] attributes are expressed by the oblique cases of nouns and other declinable parts of speech (having the value of nouns). To express an attribute, the most common case used is the genitive without a preposition, for example: и҆зы́ди ско́рѡ на распꙋ́тїѧ и҆ сто́гны гра́да* (Luke 14:21—"Go out quickly into the streets and lanes of the city"); и҆ посла̀ раба̀ своегѡ̀ въ го́дъ ве́чери* (Luke 14:17—"And sent his servant at supper time"); го́дъ ѳѷмїа́ма* (Luke 1:10—"at the time of incense"); ро́гъ спасе́нїѧ* (Luke 1:69—"an horn of salvation").

Such expressions are especially often encountered in liturgical texts, for example: ра́дꙋйсѧ свѧти́телей* тро́ица, цр҃кве* вели́каѧ забра́ла, столпѝ бл҃гоче́стїѧ*, вѣ́рныхъ* оу҆твержде́нїе, є҆ретїчествꙋ́ющихъ* низпаде́нїе (Matins of Jan. 30, at the Praises

[Pss. 148-150]—"Rejoice, O threesome of hierarchs, great towers of the Church, pillars of piety, confirmation of the faithful, downfall of heretics!").

4) In many cases, an attribute expressed by the genitive case can be replaced by an adjective, for example: бѧ́ше же дале́че ѿ негѡ̀ ста́до свинíй* мно́го пасо́мо... ста́до свино́е* (Matth. 8:30-31 —"And there was a good way off from them an herd of many swine feeding... [suffer us to go away into] the herd of swine"); ѿ маммѡ́ны непра́вды (Luke 16:9—"[friends] of the mammon of unrighteousness") and въ непра́ведн҄ѣмъ и҆мѣ́нïи (Luke 16:11—"in the unjust mammon [*lit.* in unjust possession]").

5) Sometimes, instead of a genitive with attributive meaning, the dative case is to be met with: лицемѣ́ри, лицѐ небꙋ̀* и҆ землѝ* вѣ́сте и҆скꙋша́ти (Luke 12:56—"Ye hypocrites, ye can discern the face of the sky and of the earth"); моли́тесѧ ᲂу҆́бо гдⷭ҇нꙋ жа́твѣ̀* (Luke 10:2—"pray ye therefore the Lord of the harvest"); приста́вникъ домꙋ̀ (Luke 16:3—"the steward [of the house]"), although домꙋ̀ can also be construed as the genitive case.

6) An attribute of belonging can also be expressed by the genitive case, or on occasion by the dative, for example: прïи́де господи́нъ ра́бъ* тѣ́хъ (Matth. 25:19—"the lord of those servants cometh [*lit.* shall come]"); послѝ въ до́мъ ѻ҆ц҃а̀* моегѡ̀ (Luke 16:27—"send [him] to my father's house]"); предае́тсѧ въ рꙋ́ки грѣ́шникѡвъ* (Matth. 26:45—"is betrayed into the hands of sinners"); dative case: вы̀ же сотвори́сте и҆ вертѣ́пъ разбо́йникѡмъ* (Matth. 21:13—"But ye have made it a den of thieves"), also Luke 19:46; и҆ старѣ́йшины лю́демъ* (Luke 19:47—"and the rulers of the people"); занѐ дрꙋ́гъ е҆мꙋ̀ е҆́сть (Luke 11:8—"because he is his friend"); въ рꙋ́цѣ человѣ́кѡмъ (Matth. 17:22— "into the hands of men"), cf. въ рꙋ́цѣ человѣ́къ грѣ́шникъ (Luke 24:7—"into the hands of sinful men").

Since in Church Slavonic the concept of individual possession is indicated wherever possible by possessive adjectives, the following cases must be noted in which the genitive case (sometimes the dative) is used:

a) when the attribute is expressed by substantivized adjectives or participles, or by personal pronouns (in which case the formation of possessive adjectives is impossible): мно́гѡ бо мо́жетъ моли́тва пра́веднагѡ* (James 5:16—"for the prayer of a righteous [man] availeth much"); ѿ гла́са поноша́ющагѡ* и ѡ҆клевета́ющагѡ* (Ps. 43:17—"at the voice of him that reproacheth and detracteth"); и ст҃о и҆́мѧ є҆гѡ́* (Luke 1:49—"and holy is his name"); as an exception: се́й нѣ́сть є҆гѡ́въ* (Rom. 8:9—"he is none of his"); *b)* when the word expressing possession is accompanied by explanatory words, i.e. when it becomes at the same time a determinate [modified word], for example: ѿ ве́си мари́нны* и мар҆ѳ҆ы* сестры̀ є҆ѧ̀ (John 11:1—"of the town of Mary and her sister Martha"), where the second possessive attribute is expressed by the genitive case, since a possessive adjective would have made the text ambiguous. Compare also: ѿ до́ма и҆ ѻ҆те́чества дави́дова* (Luke 2:4—"of the house and lineage of David"), but: въ до́мꙋ дави́да* ѻ҆́трока своегѡ̀ (Luke 1:69 —"in the house of his servant David"). However, by way of exception, possessive adjective attributes can be encountered with modifying words, for example: Тогда̀ собра́шасѧ а҆рхїере́є и҆ кни́жницы и҆ ста́рцы людсті́и во дво́ръ а҆рхїере́овъ*, глаго́лемагѡ каїа́фы (Matth. 26:3—"Then assembled together the chief priests, and the scribes, and the elders of the people, unto the palace of the high priest, who was called Caiaphas"); съ жена́ми и҆ мари́ею мт҃рїю і҆и҃совою* и҆ съ бра́тїею є҆гѡ̀ (Acts 1:14 —"with the women, and Mary the mother of Jesus, and with his brethren"); и҆ ѿверго́стеся є҆гѡ̀ пред лице́мъ пїла́товымъ*, сꙋ́ждшꙋ ѻ҆́номꙋ пꙋсти́ти (Acts 3:13—"and [ye] denied him in the presence of Pilate, when he was determined to let him go").

7) Uncoördinate [non-agreeing] attributes can also be expressed by the oblique cases with a preposition, and in such cases the pronouns и́же, я́же, є́же usually are added, although, far less often, this type of attribute may alse be found without the pronoun. Examples: и҆ воскресе́нїе, є́же ѿ ме́ртвыхъ* (Luke 20:35—"and the resurrection from the dead"); И҆стреби́въ є́же на на́съ* рꙋкописа́нїе оу҆че́ньми (Col. 2:14—"Blotting out the handwriting [of ordinances] that was against us"); не и҆мы́й моеѧ̀ пра́вды, я́же ѿ зако́на* (Philipp. 3:9—"not having mine own righteousness, which is of the law"), as well as Acts 3:16; 26:18; 26:22; Gal. 1:22. Without the pronouns: бѣ̀ въ со́нмищахъ человѣ́къ въ дꙋсѣ* нечи́стѣ* (Mark 1:23—"And there was in [their] assemblies a man with an unclean spirit"); бра́тїѧ ѡ҆ гдѣ* (Philipp. 1:14—"brethren in the Lord"); И҆мамъ оу҆бо похвалꙋ̀ ѡ҆ хртѣ̀* і҆исѣ* (Rom. 15:17—"I have therefore whereof I may glory in Christ Jesus").

These word groups with pronouns aim at conveying Greek phrases with a definite article: compare the 1st example above: καὶ τῆς ἀναστάσεως τῆς ἐκ νεκρῶν (Luke 20:35), but, strictly speaking, only the pronoun я́же (fem.), when it refers to nouns in the accusative, clearly expresses the sense of the article, for example: Мѡѵсе́й бо пи́шетъ пра́вдꙋ, ю́же (and not "я́же") ѿ зако́на (Rom. 10:5—"For Moses describeth the righteousness which is of the law").

8) Non-agreeing attributes can be expressed by the infinitive of verbs, e.g. и҆зы́де повелѣ́нїе ѿ ке́сара а́ѵгꙋста написа́ти* всю̀ вселе́ннꙋю (Luke 2:1—"there went out a decree from Cæsar Augustus, that all the world should be enrolled"); и҆спо́лнишасѧ дні́е роди́ти* є́й (Luke 2:6— "the days were completed for her to give birth"), (see §142, 12).

9) Possessive adjectives in Church Slavonic may, in some cases, go beyond the limits of their normal use, and rather than showing possession, have the sense of an oblique object, e.g.: оу҆слы́шавъ и́рѡдъ четвертовла́стникъ слꙋхъ і҆исовъ (Matth.

14:1—"Herod the tetrarch, having heard of the fame of Jesus"), i.e. *the fame concerning Jesus;* По преда́нїи же і҆оа́нновѣ (Mark 1:14—"And after that John was delivered up"); ре́вность бж҃їю и҆мꙋ́тъ (Rom. 10:2—"they have a zeal of God")—i.e. *they have a zeal about [regarding] God.*

§131. Apposition.

Apposition is the setting of one noun beside another as an attributive [a modifier, or an explaining or limiting adjunct], agreeing with the modified word in number and case.

The use of appositives in Church Slavonic generally does not differ from their use in Russian [or English], save for the peculiarity that in Slavonic, nouns in apposition are only rarely set off by commas. Examples: Слы́шавъ же и҆рѡ́дъ ца́рь* смꙋти́ся (Matth. 2:3—"When Herod the king had heard [these tings], he was troubled"); ви́дѣша ѻ҆троча̀ съ марі́ею ма́терїю* є҆гѡ̀ (Matth. 2:11—"they saw the young child with Mary his mother"); и҆ сѐ мꙋ́жъ мꙋ́ринъ є҆ѵнꙋ́хъ* си́ленъ* кандакі́и цари́цы* мꙋ́ринскїѧ (Acts 8:27—"and behold, an man of Ethiopia, an eunuch of great authority under Candace queen of the Ethiopians"), cf. in the Russian version: "и вотъ, мужъ еѳіоплянинъ, евнухъ, вельможа Кандакіи, царицы Еѳіопской..."

Apposition with the words и҆́менемъ, ро́домъ, мꙋ́жъ: і҆ꙋде́анинъ же нѣ́кто а҆поллѡ́съ* и҆́менемъ, а҆леѯа́ндранинъ* ро́домъ, мꙋ́жъ* слове́сенъ, прїи́де во є҆фе́съ (Acts 18:24—"And a certain Jew named Apollos, born at Alexandria, an eloquent man, ...came to Ephesus"); є҆ди́нъ ѿ а҆рхїсѷнагѡ́гъ, и҆́менемъ і҆аі́ръ* (Mark 5:22—"one of the rulers of the synagogue, Jairus by name").

§132. The Object.

The *object* is the term for a secondary part of the sentence, signifying the recipient of the action or quality. The object answers the questions of the oblique cases, for example: и҆ посла̀ вѣ́стника* пред̾ лице́мъ* свои́мъ (Luke 9:52—"and sent a messenger before his face").

The object in most cases relates to a verb, but it can also relate to nouns and adjectives.

a) The object is usually expressed by a noun in one of the oblique cases, for example: Не носи́те влага́лища*, ни пи́ры*, ни сапогѡ́въ* (Luke 10:4—"Carry neither purse, nor scrip, nor shoes"); but it can also be expressed by other parts of speech, used as if they were nouns, for example: *pronoun:* Слꙋшаѧй ва́съ*, менѐ* слꙋшаетъ (Luke 10:16—"He that heareth you, heareth me"); *adjective:* Юрѡ́дивыѧ же мꙋ́дрымъ* рѣ́ша (Matth. 25:8—"And the foolish said unto the wise"); *participle:* иди́те же па́че къ продаю́щымъ*, и҆ кꙋпи́те себѣ̀ (Matth. 25:9—"but go ye rather to them that sell, and buy for yourselves"); *numeral:* трі́е на два̀*, и҆ два̀ на трѝ* (Luke 12:52—"three against two, and two against three").

b) The object may be expressed by an infinitive: повелѣ̀ принестѝ* главꙋ̀ є҆гѡ̀ (Mark 6:27— "[he] commanded his head to be brought").

c) The object can be expressed by a phrase with a sense of quantity: и҆ призва́въ є҆ди́наго* ѿ ѻ҆трѡ́къ*, вопроша́ше (Luke 15:26—"And he called one of the servants, and asked"); человѣ́къ нѣ́кїй и҆мѧ́ше два̀* сы́на* (Matth. 21:28—"A certain man had two sons").

d) The object may also be expressed by a special combination of words with the sense of an entity; before it, in such cases, stands the pronoun є҆́же used as an article: на є҆́же* по подо́бїю* возведѝ дре́внею добро́тою возѡбрази́тисѧ (Pannikhida—"raise [me] up to be transformed, to [my] ancient beauty [which is] according to [Thy] likeness"); here є҆́же по подо́бїю is a special concept or term.

e) The object can be expressed by a demonstrative pronoun with a phrase attached to it, consisting of the relative pronouns и҆́же, ꙗ́же, є҆́же and an oblique case with a preposition, for example: Й҆ма́мъ ѹ҆́бо похвалѹ̀ ѡ҆ хрⷭ҇тѣ̀ і҆и҃сѣ въ тѣ́хъ*, ꙗ҆́же* къ бг҃ѹ (Rom. 15:17—"I have therefore whereof I may glory through Jesus Christ in those things which pertain to God").

§133. Verb Objects.

Objects that occur with verbs are of two kinds: direct and indirect.

A *direct object* receives the action of a transitive verb, and is in the accusative case without a preposition (see §72), e.g.: ли́си ꙗ҆́звинны* и҆мѹ́тъ, и҆ пти́цы нбⷭ҇ныꙗ гнѣ́зда* (Matth. 8:20 — "The foxes have holes, and the birds of the air have nests").

With transitive verbs and negation, the object is usually put in the genitive case: Тро́сти* сокрѹше́нны не прело́митъ, и҆ лена* внемшаса не ѹ҆гаси́тъ (Matth. 12:20—"A bruised reed shall he not break, and smoking flax shall he not quench"); Нижѐ влива́ютъ вїна̀* но́ва въ мѣ́хи ве́тхи (Matth. 9:17—"Neither do [men] put new wine into old bottles").

Note. In certain cases, however, a direct object may also be found in the accusative case after a negated verb: не дади́те ст҃а́а псѡ́мъ (Matth. 7:6—"Give not that which is holy unto the dogs").

With the passive mood, the direct object becomes the subject, while the performer of the action (the subject of a verb in the active mood) becomes an object in the genitive case with the preposition ѿ or in the instrumental case (see §§ 73, 102), e.g.: и҆ ви́дѣнъ бы́сть ѿ неꙗ* (Mark 16:11 —"and had been seen of her"); Прїидо́ша же и҆ мыта́рѝ крⷭ҇ти́тиса ѿ негѡ̀* (Luke 3:12—"Then came also publicans to be baptized by him"); и҆́мже* держи́ми бѣ́хомъ (Rom. 7:6—"wherein we were held").

Objects in the other oblique cases, as well as in the accusative case with a preposition, are called *indirect objects*, for example: Пре́дани же бѹ́дете и҆ роди́тели* и҆ бра́тїею* и҆ ро́домъ* и҆ дрѹ́ги* (Luke

21:16—"And ye shall be betrayed both by parents, and brethren, and kinsfolks, and friends").

Concerning objects expressed by an infinitive, see §143, 2.

§134. Objects of Nouns and Adjectives.

Nouns can have objects, for the most part in those cases where they are formed from verbs or are related to them in meaning. Most often, objects of nouns are in the genitive case (genitive of object), for example: жа́лость до́мꙋ* твоегѡ̀ снѣдѐ мѧ̀, (John 2:17—"The zeal of thine house hath eaten me up"—i.e. concern for Thy house); и̑ проповѣ́даѧ є҆ѵⷢ҇лїе црⷭ҇твїѧ* (Matth. 4:23—"and preaching the gospel of the kingdom"[= *concerning* the kingdom]); и̑ за оу҆множе́нїе беззако́нїа*, и҆зсѧ́кнетъ любы̀ мно́гихъ (Matth. 24:12—"And because iniquity shall abound, the love of many shall wax cold"); И̑стинный по́стъ є҆́сть, ѕлы́хъ* ѿчꙋжде́нїе, воздержа́нїе ѧ҆зы́ка*, ꙗ҆́рости* ѿложе́нїе, похоте́й* ѿлꙋче́нїе (1st week of Great Lent, Monday at Vespers [Aposticha]— "A true fast is the rejection of evils, control of the tongue, forbearance from anger, abstaining from lusts").

In some cases the genitive case is replaced by the dative: Оу҆слы́шати и́мате бра́ни и̑ слы́шанїѧ бра́немъ* (Matth. 24:6—"And ye shall hear of wars and rumours of wars"); творца̀ нбꙋ* и̑ землѝ*, ви́димымъ же всѣмъ* и̑ неви́димымъ* (Creed—"Maker of heaven and earth, and of all things visible and invisible"); и̑ вся́комꙋ бла́гꙋ* промы́сленникъ и̑ пода́тель (Morning Prayer 3— "and [Thou art] the Provider and Giver of everything good").

There can be an object of predicate adjectives as well as of appositives (in subordinate clauses), and sometimes also of substantivized adjectives, for example: на́гъ є҆́смь черто́га* (Great Canon, Ode[Canticle] 4—"I am deprived of the Bridal Chamber"); Красе́нъ добро́тою* па́че сынѡ́въ человѣ́ческихъ (Ps. 44:3—"Splendid in beauty beyond the sons of men"); и̑ свѣти́ло є҆гѡ̀ подо́бно ка́мени* драго́мꙋ (Rev. 21:11—"and the light thereof was like to a precious stone"); Сотворите оу́бо плоды досто́йны покаѧ́нїѧ* (Luke 3:8—"Bring forth therefore fruits worthy of repentance"); испо́лнь благода́ти* и и́стины* (John 1:14—"full of grace and truth"); ѽ несмы́сленнаѧ и ко́снаѧ се́рдцемъ* (Luke 24:25—"O [ye] foolish and slow of heart"); ѽ исполне́нне всѧ́кїѧ льсти́* и всѧ́кїѧ ѕло́бы (Acts 13:10—"O [thou] full of all guile and all wickedness").

Peculiarities in the Use of the Cases to Express an Object.

§135. *The Accusative.* Pronouns, adjectives and participles with a *collective* sense are used in the accusative, and also in the other oblique cases, as in the nominative (§120) in the neuter plural, for example: є҆гда̀ оу҆́зрите сїѧ̀* быва́юща* (Luke 21:31—"when ye see these things come to pass"); и всѝ лю́дїе ра́довахꙋсѧ ѡ всѣ́хъ* сла́вныхъ* быва́ющихъ* ѿ негѡ̀ (Luke 13:17—"and all the people rejoiced for all the glorious things that were done by him"). With an *abstract sense*, they are put in the neuter singular: Ма́рѳѣ показꙋ́а самовла́стное* (Lazarus Saturday, 3rd Song—"showing Martha Thy power"). Ст҃ы́ѧ бо тр҃цы є҆диносꙋ́щное* правосла́внѡ наꙋчи́вше (7th Sunday after Pascha at Vespers, Doxasticon at the Aposticha—"Having taught in Orthodox manner the unity of the Holy Trinity"). Го́ре глаго́лющымъ лꙋка́вое* до́брое*, и до́брое* лꙋка́вое*, полага́ющымъ тьмꙋ̀ свѣ́тъ, и свѣ́тъ тьмꙋ̀, полага́ющымъ го́рькое* сла́дкое*, и сла́дкое* го́рькое* (Isaiah 5:20—"Woe to them that call evil good, and good evil; who make darkness light, and light darkness; who make bitter sweet, and sweet bitter").

Nouns (or other declinable parts of speech used as nouns), signifying animate beings, have in the singular an accusative case that coincides with the genitive, but in the plural their accusative case is usually the same as the nominative, though it can also coincide with the genitive (§22, §35, 1), §40, 4), for example: раздѣли́тсѧ ѻ҆те́цъ на сы́на*, и҆ сы́нъ на ѻ҆тца̀* (Luke 12:53—"The father shall be divided against the son, and the son against the father"; взыска́ти и҆ спасти́ погибшаго* (Luke 19:10—"to seek and to save that which was lost"); нача́тъ и҆згони́ти продаю́щыѧ* въ не́й и҆ ку̑пꙋ́ющыѧ* (Luke 19:45—"began to cast out them that sold therein, and them that bought").

The verbs подража́ти [to imitate], гони́ти [to pursue], слы́шати [to hear], внꙋши́ти [to inspire, suggest—from въи-ꙋш-ити], воспомина́ти [to recall], also помина́ти [mention, commemorate], помышля́ти [to think of] usually call for the accusative case, for example: прⷪ҇ро́ка* і҆ѡ́нꙋ* подража́ѧ вопїю̀ (Eirmos: Tone 1, Monday at Compline, Ode 6—"Imitating the Prophet Jonah I cry out"); но ты̀ подража́ла є҆сѝ тогѡ̀ стра̑стнаѧ и҆ любостра̑стнаѧ стремлє́нїѧ* (Great Canon, Ode 7—"But thou hast imitated his [Absalom's] passionate and pleasure-loving cravings"); but also the dative case: подража́йте вѣ́рѣ* и҆́хъ (Heb. 13:7—"follow their faith"); є҆гѡ̀ произволе́нїю* подража́й (Great Canon, Ode 3—"imitate his [Abraham's] resolution"); гонѝ же пра́вдꙋ*, бл҃гоче́стїе*, вѣ́рꙋ*... (I Tim. 6:11—"follow after righteousness, godliness, faith..."); і҆ѡа́ннъ слы́шавъ во ᲂу҆зи́лищи дѣла̀* хрⷭ҇то́ва (Matth. 11:2—"Now when John had heard in prison the works of Christ"); моле́нїе* моѐ внꙋши́ (Ps. 38:13—"give ear to my supplication"); помина́йте женꙋ̀* лѡ́товꙋ (Luke 17:32—"Remember Lot's wife"); помина́ѧ слє́зы* твоѧ̑ (II Tim. 1:4— "being mindful of thy tears"); дѣѧ̑нїѧ* твоѧ̑, ꙗ҆̀же содѣ́лала є҆сѝ, помышля́й (Great Canon, Ode 4— "Consider the deeds thou hast done").

§136. A characteristic peculiarity of the Church Slavonic language is the use of the so-called *double accusative case*. The first accusative is the direct object, and the second takes on the role of a predicate complement; it is called a *second predicate accusative* (cf. §124; many verbs, acting as semi- significant copulas in a composite nominal predicate, in the active voice are followed by two accusatives). In Russian, the instrumental case corresponds to such a second accusative.

This second accusative, by its derivation, is nothing other than a predicate adjunct of the verb бы́ти, in a construction of the accusative with an infinitive (see §143, 3), for example: ѡсꙋди́ша є҆го̀* бы́ти пови́нна* сме́рти, (Mark 14:64—"they condemned him to be guilty of death"); however, with the following verbs, since they are semi-significant, бы́ти becomes superfluous and therefore disappears, for example: Что̀ мѧ̀ глаго́леши [бы́ти] бла́га (Mark 10:18—"Why callest thou me good?"); but sometimes бы́ти is present: Кого̀ мѧ̀ глаго́лютъ человѣ́цы бы́ти; (Mark 8:27—"Whom do men say that I am?").

Verbs taking a second accusative, according to their use, can be divided into two groups:

I. Those meaning *"to make, call or consider someone something"*: 1) сотвори́ти [to make], прїѧ́ти [to receive], положи́ти [to place], поста́вити [to set], ꙗви́ти [to reveal], ѹ҆гото́вати [to prepare], да́ти [to give], дарова́ти [to bestow], показа́ти [to show], возвы́сити [to raise up]; 2)рещѝ [to say], нарица́ти [to name], и҆сповѣ́дати [to confess], глаго́лати [to speak], глаша́ти [to call]; 3) и҆мѣ́ти [to have], вмѣнѧ́ти [to consider], помышлѧ́ти [to think], непщева́ти [to estimate], представлѧ́ти [to represent] and others.

With these verbs the main object is for the most part a *person* and is usually expressed by a pronoun, but also by a noun (or a substantivized adjective or participle), while the second accusative indicates a *duty, calling, thing* or *quality* and is expressed by a noun or adjective (or participle), as a general rule in the short form, though in the plural this may not be the case, for example:

1) вы̀ же сотвори́сте є҆го̀* пеще́рꙋ* разбо́йникѡмъ (Luke 19:46—"but ye have made it a den of thieves"); и҆ сотворѧ́тъ є҆го̀* царѧ̀* (John 6:15—"and [they would] make him a king"); и҆

запꙋстѣвшꙋ* сотворѧ́тъ ю̀* и нагꙋ̀* (Rev. 17:16—"and shall make her desolate and naked"); Ѻ҆́бразъ* прїими́те, бра́тїѧ моѧ̀, ѕлострада́нїѧ и долготерпѣ́нїѧ, проро́ки* (James 5:10—"Take, my brethren, the prophets...for an example of suffering affliction, and of patience"); є҆го́же* положѝ наслѣ́дника* всѣ́мъ (Heb. 1:2—"whom he hath appointed heir of all things"); кто̀ мѧ̀* поста́ви сꙋдїю̀* и дѣли́телѧ* над ва́ми (Luke 12:14—"who made me a judge or a divider over you?"); поста́ви ю̀* жи́вꙋ* (Acts 9:41—"presented her alive"); бг҃ъ ны̀* посла́нники* ꙗ҆вѝ (I Cor. 4:9— "God hath set forth us the apostles last"); оу҆гото́вати гд҃еви лю́ди* соверше́ны* (Luke 1:17—"to prepare unto the Lord a perfect people"); всѧ́ческихъ творца̀ на рꙋкꙋ̀ твоє́ю понє́сши, сего̀* на́мъ твои́ми моли́твами бл҃гопремѣ́нна* дава́й (Jan. 30, Matins, Ode 5—"having borne in thine arms the Creator of all, render Him propitious to us by thy prayers"); и҆хже* да́рꙋй ст҃ы́мъ твои́мъ цр҃квамъ, въ ми́рѣ, цѣ́лыхъ*, чє́стныхъ*, здра́выхъ*... (Liturgy: commemoration of the hierarchy after the Consecration—"whom [do Thou] grant unto Thy holy Churches in peace: safe, honourable, healthy..."); стра́нна* мꙋ́ки всѧ́кїѧ покажѝ мѧ* (Morning Prayers, Prayer 7: [Midnight Song to the Most Holy Theotokos]—"Present me untouched by [lit. 'estranged from', 'alien to'] all torments"); сего̀* бг҃ъ нача́льника* и сп҃са* возвы́си десни́цею своє́ю (Acts 5:31—"Him hath God exalted with his right hand to be a Prince and a Saviour");

2) а҆́ще ѻ҆́ныхъ* речѐ бого́въ*(John 10:35—"If he called them gods"); и нарица́хꙋ є҆* и҆́менемъ Ѻ҆тца̀ є҆гѡ̀, заха́рїю* (Luke 1:59—"and they called him Zacharias, after the name of his father"); а҆́ще кто̀ є҆го̀* и҆сповѣ́сть хр҃та̀* (John 9:22—"if any [man] did confess that he was the Christ"); не ктомꙋ̀ ва́съ* глаго́лю рабы́*... ва́съ же рекохъ дрꙋ́ги* (John 15:15—"Henceforth I call you not servants... but I have called you friends"); Что̀ мѧ̀* глаго́леши бла́га* (Mark 10:18—"Why callest thou me good?"); Вы̀ глаша́ете мѧ̀* оу҆чи́телѧ* и гд҃а* (John 13:13—"Ye call me Master and Lord").

3) нижѐ и́мамъ дꙋшꙋ* мою̀ честнꙋ* себѣ̀ (Acts
20:24—"neither count I my life dear unto myself"); сїѧ̀* вмѣни́хъ
хрⷭ҇та̀ ра́ди тщетꙋ* (Philipp. 3:7—"those [things] I counted loss for
Christ"); поне́же вѣ́рна* непщева̀ ѡ̑бѣтова́вшаго* (Heb.
11:11—"because [she] judged him faithful who had promised"). The
second accusative in some cases may be joined with the conjunctions
ꙗ́кѡ, ꙗ́коже, а́ки [like, as]: Та́кѡ на́съ* да непщꙋ́етъ человѣ́къ,
ꙗ́кѡ слꙋгъ* хрⷭ҇то́выхъ и̑ строи́телей* та́инъ бж҃їихъ (I Cor.
4:1—"Let a man so account of us, as of the ministers of Christ, and
stewards of the mysteries of God"); Но во все́мъ представлѧ́ющихъ
себѐ* ꙗ́коже бж҃їѧ слꙋги̑* (II Cor. 6:4—"But in all things approving
ourselves as the ministers of God"); и̑ не а́ки врага̀* и̑мѣ́йте є̑гѐ* (II
Thess. 3:15—"Yet count him not as an enemy").

4) With verbs signifying dependent motion or condition:
ѿпꙋсти́ти [let go, send away, dismiss], посла́ти [send],
препроводи́ти [accompany], возврати́ти [bring back, return],
привестѝ [bring], возста́вити [raise up], спаса́ти [save], соблюстѝ
[keep], &c., *someone as such*, —with these there can also be a double
accusative: и̑ богатѧ́щыѧсѧ* ѿпꙋстѝ тщы̀* (Luke 1:53—"and the
rich he hath sent away empty"); и̑ послѝ ми а́гг҃ла* ми́рна,
храни́телѧ* и̑ наста́вника* дꙋши̑ и̑ тѣ́лꙋ моемꙋ̀ (Prayers Before
Sleep, Prayer 4, of St. Macarius the Great—"And send me an Angel
of peace, a guardian and guide of my soul and body"); ѡ̑ є̑́же
покры́ти и̑хъ* и̑ невреди́мыхъ* соблюстѝ ѿ все́хъ вра́жїихъ
навѣ́товъ и̑ ѡ̑бстоѧ́нїй, и̑ безпа́косныхъ* препроводи́ти и̑
возврати́ти (Prayer Service for Travellers—"That He will protect
them and preserve [them] unscathed from all adverse incursions and
circumstances, and accompany and bring them back unharmed");
мꙋ̑жи* же и̑ жены̀* свѧ́заны* приведе́тъ во і̑ерꙋсали́мъ (Acts
9:2—"[that he might] bring men and women bound to Jerusalem");
возста́ви же на́съ* во вре́мѧ моли́твы, оу҆твержде́ны* въ
за́повѣдехъ твои́хъ, и̑ па́мѧть* сꙋде́бъ твои́хъ въ себѣ̀ тве́рдꙋ*

и҆мꙋ́ща* (Compline, Another Prayer to our Lord Jesus Christ, by Antiochus the Monk—"And raise us up at the time of prayer, confirmed in Thy precepts, and keeping the memory of Thy judgments firm within us"); ѿ мі́рскихъ напа́стей спаса́й ны̀* невреди́мы* (Octoechos, T. 3, Thursday at Matins, Ode 6—"From worldly assaults, save us unharmed"); и҆ на́съ* неѡсꙋжде́ны* сохранѝ во сщ҃еннодѣ́йствїи бж҃е́ственныхъ твои́хъ та́инъ (Liturgy, Prayer of the Proskomedia—"and keep us without condemnation in the sacred service of Thy Divine Mysteries").

If the above verbs occur with negation, then they call for two genitives: не твори́те до́мꙋ* ѻ҆ц҃а̀ моегѡ̀ до́мꙋ* кꙋ́пленагѡ (John 2:16—"make not my Father's house an house of merchandise").

With the verb проси́ти there can be a second predicate *genitive,* for example: днѐ всегѡ̀ (бы́ти) соверше́нна*, ст҃а*, ми́рна* и҆ безгрѣ́шна*, ѹ҆ гд҃а про́симъ (Liturgy); in this case what is asked for is not "a perfect, holy... day", but rather that the day *be* perfect, holy and so on; cf. the English text—"For this whole day, that it may be perfect, holy, peaceful and sinless, let us entreat the LORD".

With verbs meaning "to elevate someone [to some calling or position]" there are also two accusatives used, with the second preceded by the preposition въ: воздви́же и҆мъ даві́да* въ цара̀* (Acts 13:22—"he raised up unto them David to be their king"); Пома́захъ тѧ̀* въ цара̀* над ї҆и҃лемъ (IV Kings 9:3—"I have anointed thee king over Israel"); и҆ воспита̀ и҆* себѣ̀ въ сы́на* (Acts 7:21 — "and [the Pharaoh's daughter] nourished him for her own son").

II. The *second* group consists of verbs signifying perception and knowledge: 1) *perception:* ви́дѣти, зрѣ́ти [to see], слы́шати [to hear]; 2) *knowledge:* вѣ́дати, свѣ́дѣти [to know, be aware], ѡ҆брѣсти́ [to find], и҆скꙋси́ти [to try, test], разꙋмѣ́ти [understand]; 3) *opinion:* мнѣ́ти [to opine], и҆мѣ́ти [to have], и҆сповѣ́дати [to confess] (the same as in the first group) &c.

With these verbs, the direct object is expressed, as in the verbs of the first group, by a pronoun or a noun, and the second accusative is usually a short participle. This 2nd-accusative construction is of a somewhat different character than with the verbs of the first group, and in some cases it can be regarded as a simplified replacement of a subordinate clause as object, for example: ви́диши наро́дъ оу҆гнета́ющъ тѧ̀ (Mark 5:31—"Thou seest the multitude thronging thee"); cf. the Russian version: *Ты видишь, что народъ тѣснитъ Тебя*—"*Thou seest that the people throng Thee*"; мнѧ̀ и҆збѣ́гша ю҆зники (Acts 16:27—"supposing the prisoners to have fled"), in the Russian: *думая, что узники убѣжали*—"supposing *that* the prisoners had fled". If the second accusative is related to a composite noun predicate of a subordinate clause, then it is expressed by a noun or an adjective (or a passive participle) in combination with the participles сы́й, бы́въ [being, having been], for example:

ѿ мно́гихъ лѣ́тъ су́ща* тѧ̀* су́дїю̀* пра́ведна ꙗ҆зы́ка семꙋ̀ свѣ́дый (Acts 24:10—"Forasmuch as I know thee to have been of many years a righteous judge unto this nation"—Russian: *зная, что ты много лѣтъ былъ праведнымъ судьей:* "Knowing *that* for many years thou hast been a righteous judge"); ꙗ҆́кѡ вѣ́дахꙋ є҆го̀* хрⷭ҇та̀* су́ща* (Mark 1:34—"because they knew him to be the Christ"—Russian: *что они знаютъ, что Онъ Христосъ:* "because they knew *that* He was the Christ").

There is, however, no strict demarcation between the verbs of the first and second group, and therefore, just as with the verbs of the 1st group the second accusative can be expressed by a participle, so, on the contrary, the second accusative with verbs of the 2nd group may be expressed by an adjective (without the participles сы́й, бы́въ). Examples: ви́дѣвше є҆го̀* ходѧ́ща* по мо́рю (Mark 6:49—"Having seen him walking on the sea"); ви́дѧщымъ нѣмы́ѧ* глаго́лющѧ*, вѣ́дныѧ* здра́вы*, хрѡмы́ѧ* ходѧ́щѧ*, и҆ слѣпы́ѧ* ви́дѧщѧ*

(Matth. 15:31—"when they saw the dumb to speak, the maimed[2] to be whole, the lame to walk, and the blind to see"); мы̀ слы́шахомъ є҆гѡ̀* глаго́люща* (Mark 14:58—"We heard him say"); вѣ́дый є҆гѡ̀* мѫ́жа* пра́ведна и҆ ст҃а (Mark 6:20— "knowing that he was a just man and an holy"); и҆ прише́дъ ѡ҆брѧ́щетъ (домъ) пра́зденъ*, помете́нъ*, и҆ оу҆кра́шенъ* (Matth. 12:44—"and when he is come, he findeth [the house] empty, swept, and garnished"); є҆го́же* и҆скꙋси́хомъ во мно́гихъ мно́гащи вста́нлива* сꙋща* (II Cor. 8:22 —"whom we have oftentimes proved diligent in many thngs"); разꙋмѣ́йте посла́нника* и҆ ст҃и́телѧ* и҆сповѣ́данїѧ на́шегѡ і҆и҃са* хр҃та̀*: вѣ́рна* сꙋща* сотко́ршемꙋ є҆го̀ (Heb. 3:1-2—"consider the Apostle and High Priest of our confession, Jesus Christ: Who is faithful to him that made him"); и҆мѣ́й мѧ̀* ѡ҆рече́на* (Luke 14:18—"have me excused"); всѧ́къ дꙋ́хъ, и҆́же и҆сповѣ́дꙋетъ і҆и҃са* хр҃та̀* во пло́ти прише́дша*, ѿ бг҃а є҆́сть (I John 4:2—"Every spirit that confesseth that Jesus Christ is come in the flesh, is of God").

§137. The *genitive case*. Among the special uses of the genitive there should be listed the *distributive* or *partitive* genitive. The distributive genitive may occur in a verbal or nominal combination.

The distributive genitive is used in those cases where the action affects an entity not in its entirety, but only in part. This genitive is usually employed after the verbs напита́ти [to feed], насы́тити [to satiate], напоѧ́ти [to give drink], вкꙋси́ти [to taste], причасти́тисѧ [to communicate, take part], напо́лнити [to fill], and others without a preposition (which does not always correspond to usage in Russian), or else with the preposition ѿ, for example: насы́ти мѧ̀ го́рести, напои́ мѧ же́лчи (Lam. 3:15—"He hath filled me with bitterness, he hath given me gall to drink"); compare the Russian text: *Онъ пресытилъ меня горечью, напоилъ меня*

---

[2] The Slavonic вѣ́дный here means "lacking some limb".—*Tr.*

полынью—"He has filled me with bitterness, he has given me wormwood to drink" [instrumental instead of genitive]; и хлѣба небеснагѡ насыти ѧ (Ps. 104:40—"and he filled them with the bread of heaven"); наполни рогъ твой елеа (I Kings 16:1—"fill thy horn with oil"); Пїѧй ѿ воды сеѧ, вжаждетсѧ паки (John 4:13—"Whosoever drinketh of this water, shall thirst again"); желаше насытитисѧ ѿ крꙋпицъ (Luke 16:21—"he desired to be fed with the crumbs"). Thus also after certain other verbs: Ко'тѡраго же васъ Ѿца̀ вопроситъ сн҃ъ хлѣба* (Luke 11:11—"And which of you, if he [as son] ask his father bread"); оу҆слышимъ ст҃агѡ е҆ѵа́лїа* (Sluzhebnik—"Let us hear the Holy Gospel [reading]").

The *distributive genitive with nouns* signifies the totality of objects or persons (or other living beings) from which a part is taken; it is used with the preposition ѿ or the pronoun кі́йждо, or without them, for example: е҆ди́нъ ѿ васъ* преда́стъ мѧ̀...нача́ша глаго́лати е҆мꙋ̀ е҆ди́нъ кі́йждо, и҆хъ* (Matth. 26:21-22—"one of you shall betray me... they began to say to him, every one of them..."); и҆ сѐ е҆ди́нъ ѿ сꙋ́щихъ* со і҆и҃сомъ (Matth. 26:51—"And behold, one of them that were with Jesus"); сѐ нѣцыи ѿ кꙋстѡді́и* (Matth. 28:11—"behold, some of the watch"); посла̀ два̀ оу҆чени́къ* свои́хъ (Luke 19:29—"he sent two of his disciples"); и҆ бы́сть во е҆ди́нъ ѿ дней ѻ҆нѣхъ* (Luke 20:1—"And it came to pass, that on one of those days"); а҆зъ бо е҆смь мні́й а҆п҃лѡкъ* (I Cor. 15:9—"For I am the least of the Apostles"); ко'то́рый оу҆бо е҆ю̀* (Luke 7:42—"which of them"); ко'то́рагѡ ѿ васъ* ѻ҆сѣлъ и҆лѝ волъ (Luke 14:5—"Which of you shall have an ass or an ox"). In some cases there is not even a word indicating a part taken from the whole of the entities; but such may be inferred at times from the person-ending of the verb, for example: Рѣша же ѿ оу҆чени́къ* е҆гѡ̀ къ себѣ̀ (John 16:17 —"Then said [some] of his disciples among themselves"); и҆ оу҆мертвѧ́тъ ѿ васъ* (Luke 21:16—"and [some] of you shall they cause to be put to death"); внемли́те же ѿ человѣ́къ* (Matth. 10:17— "But beware of men"—i.e. of *certain* men). Such constructions are also to be encountered without ѿ: и не бꙋдетъ тамѡ лвва, ниже ꙸꙁвѣрей* лютыхъ взыдетъ нань (Isaiah 35:9, as printed in the Prophecy at the Blessing of Waters—"No lion shall be there, nor [any] ravenous beast shall go up thereon"— compare with the Greek text: οὐδὲ τῶν θηρίων τῶν πονηρῶν), i.e. *any of the ravenous beasts;* but the usual edition of the [Slavonic] Bible gives the reading ни ѿ ꙁвѣрей ѕлыхъ, "neither of the evil beasts". Насытишасѧ сынѡвъ* и ѡставиша ѡстанки младенцемъ своимъ (Ps. 16:14 —"[Certain of] The sons have been filled, and left the remnants to their babes"—compare with the Greek: Ἐχορτάσθησαν υἱῶν: i.e."*some or many of the sons*").

In some cases the sense of a part is expressed by the prepositional case with the preposition въ: болитъ ли кто въ васъ (James 5:14—"Is any sick among you?").

With the verbs смотрѣти [to regard, consider], слꙋшати [to listen], the object is often put in the genitive case: смотрите крінъ сельныхъ (Matth. 6:28—"Consider the lilies of the field"); Смотрите вранъ (Luke 12:24—"Consider the ravens"); послꙋшайте словесъ моихъ (Numbers 12:6 —"Hear now my words"); послꙋшай ѡправданій и сꙋдѡвъ (Deut. 4:1—"Hearken unto the statutes and unto the judgments").

With verbs signifying *removal, deprivation:* бѣгати [to flee], лишатисѧ [to be deprived of], рѣшити [to free], свободити [to liberate], ѡпꙋстити [to let go], боѧтисѧ [to fear], трепетати [to tremble], ꙋжасатисѧ [to be amazed], плакати [to weep], рыдати [to sob] and the like, the object is put in the genitive case *(the genitive of detachment)* without a preposition or with the preposition ѿ. The combination without a preposition does not always correspond to the use of such combinations in Russian, for example: бѣгай дꙋше моа грѣха*: бѣгай содомы* и гоморры*, бѣгай пламене* всѧкагѡ безсловеснагѡ желанїа (Great Canon, Ode 3—"Flee, O my soul, from sin: flee from Sodom and Gomorrah; flee from the flame of every irrational desire"); трепе́щꙋ стра́шнагѡ днѐ* сꙋ́днагѡ (Sunday of the Publican and Pharisee, Matins—"I tremble before the dread day of judgment"); ѿчꙋжде́ни житїѧ̀* і҆и҃лева (Eph. 2:12—"being estranged from the life of Israel"); пла́кахꙋ всѝ, и҆ рыда́хꙋ є҆ѧ̀* (Luke 8:52—"all wept, and bewailed her"); не пла́читеса ѡ҆ мнѣ̀, ѻ҆ба́че себє̀* пла́чите и҆ ча́дъ* ва́шихъ (Luke 23:28—"weep not for me, but weep for yourselves, and for your children").

§138. The *dative case.* The verbs сꙋди́ти [to judge], брани́ти [to reproach], рꙋга́тисѧ [to make sport of], поноси́ти [to revile], наси́ловати [to force], смѣ́ѧтисѧ [to laugh], терпѣ́ти [to bear patiently], ѡ҆долѣ́ти [to overcome], оу҆вѣ́ровати [to believe], стꙋжа́ти [to annoy, trouble], хотѣ́ти [want, be about to](the last in some circumstances), and certain others usually have their object in the dative case (though in Russian they may take various other cases); for example: сꙋдѝ и҆мъ*, бж҃е (Ps. 5:11—"Judge them, O God"); хо́щетъ сꙋди́ти вселе́ннꙋй* (Acts 17:31—"he will judge the world"); не брани́те и҆мъ* (Mark 10:14—"forbid them not"); рꙋга́хꙋсѧ є҆мꙋ* (Matth. 9:24—"they laughed him to scorn"); разбѡ́йника распѧ̑таѧ съ ни́мъ поноша́ста є҆мꙋ (Matth. 27:44—"The [two] thieves also, that were crucified with him, mocked him"); да не когда̀ посмѣю́тсѧ на́мъ* (Gen. 38:23 —"lest we be shamed"); доко́лѣ терплю̀ ва́мъ* (Matth. 17:17—"how long shall I suffer you?"); и҆ врата̀ а҆́дѡва не ѡ҆долѣ́ютъ є҆́й* (Matth. 16:18—"and the gates of hell shall not prevail against it"); и҆ ѡ҆долѣ́въ и҆мъ* (Acts 19:16—"and prevailed against them"); да оу҆вѣ́рꙋютъ тѝ* (Ex. 4:5, 8, 9— "that they might believe thee"); а҆́зъ ви́дѣхъ тꙋгꙋ́, є҆́юже є҆гѵ́птѧне стꙋжа́ютъ и҆мъ* (Ex. 3:9—"I have seen the oppression, wherewith the Egyptians oppress them"); а҆́ще хо́щетъ є҆мꙋ̀* (Matth. 27:43 —"if he will have him"); расточѝ ꙗ҆зы́ки хотѧ́щыѧ бра́немъ* (Ps. 67:31—"Scatter thou the nations that delight in wars").

To express the idea *"in the possession of someone"* the dative case is generally used: а҆хаа́вꙋ* бѣ́ша се́дмьдесѧтъ сн҃ы въ самарі́н (IV

Kings 10:1—"Ahab had seventy sons in Samaria"); челове́кꙋ* не́коемꙋ бога́тꙋ ѹ҆гобзи́са ни́ва (Luke 12:16—"The ground of a certain rich man brought forth plentifully"); восⷮрепета̀ даві́дꙋ* се́рдце є҆гѡ̀ (I Kings [Samuel] 24:6—"David's heart smote him"); вскꙋю бо́ше и҆ме́нїе безꙋ́мномꙋ* (Prov. 17:16—"Wherefore did the fool have property?").

With verbs signifying *speaking,* the object is in the dative, usually without a preposition, but there can also be the preposition кꙋ: Рече́ же кꙋ вінаре́ви (Luke 13:7—"Then he said to the dresser of the vineyard"); Глаго́лаше же и҆ ко зва́вшемꙋ є҆гѡ̀ (Luke 14:12—"Then said he also to him that bade him"); so also Luke 14:23, 25; 15:3, 22.

In the books of the Holy Scriptures, idiomatic expressions are not infrequently to be met with that consist of two datives with the pronoun что̀ (ничто́же), with a meaning along the lines of *"What business hast thou with me?"* For example: что̀ мне́ и҆ тебе́; и҆ди́ кꙋ проро́кѡмꙋ ѻ҆ц҃а̀ твоегѡ̀ (IV Kings 3:13—"What have I to do with thee? get thee to the prophets of thy father"); ничто́же тебе́ и҆ пра́веднникꙋ то́мꙋ (Matth. 27:19—"Have thou nothing to do with that just man").

§139. The *instrumental case.* An object in the instrumental, in its main meanings, that of the means used and that of jointness (the sociative instrumental), for the most part does not differ from its corresponding use in Russian: і҆и҃съ пома́за ѻ҆́чи бре́нїемꙋ* сле́помꙋ (John 9::6—"Jesus anointed the eyes of the blind man with the clay"); прїидо́ша сваще́нницы и҆ кни́жницы со ста́рцы* (Luke 20:1—"the chief priests and the scribes came [upon him] with the elders").

When *buying, selling* and *paying* are signified, the price is given in the instrumental case: и҆́же бѐ до́лженꙋ є҆мꙋ сто́мꙋ* пе́нязь (Matth. 18:28—"which owed him an hundred pence").

§140. The *prepositional case.* The prepositional is used much as in Russian. As peculiar to its use in Slavonic, the following cases can be listed:

The price named for a sale can be in the prepositional case: Чесѡ̀ ра́ди мѵ́ро сїѐ не про́дано бы́сть на тре́хъ сте́хъ* пѣ́нязь (John 12:5—"Why was not this ointment sold for three hundred pence?").

With the preposition ѡ̀ it can have a meaning close to that of the instrumental of means: Ѡ не́мъ* бо живе́мъ, и дви́жемся и є҆смы̀ (Acts 17:28—"For in him we live, and move, and have our being"); не ѡ хлѣ́бѣ є҆ди́номъ жи́въ бꙋ́детъ человѣ́къ (Matth. 4:4—"Not by bread alone shall man live").

Some meanings are conveyed in Church Slavonic by the prepositional, even though other cases are used in Russian: потерпѝ на мнѣ̀*, и҆ вся̂ тѝ возда́мъ (Matth. 18:26—"Be patient with me, and I will return all to thee"); дадѐ и҆̀мъ вла́сть на дꙋ́сѣхъ* нечи́стыхъ (Matth. 10:1—"He gave them power against unclean spirits").

Adjuncts [Circumstance]: Adverbial Modifiers.

§141. *Adverbial modifiers* are a secondary part of the sentence, signifying the circumstance under which an action or condition occurs, for example: И҆ нача́ша вкꙋ́пѣ* ѿрица́тися вси́ (Luke 14:18—"And they began all at once to make excuse"); а҆зъ же гла́домъ* ги́блю (Luke 15:17—"and I perish with hunger").

The usual form by which circumstances are expressed is the adverb. Circumstances can also be expressed by the oblique cases of nouns and by the infinitives of verbs. Adjectives and participles signifying circumstance occupy a special place.

Adverbial modifiers usually refer to the predicate: доко́лѣ* терплю̀ вы̀ (Mark 9:19—"how long shall I suffer you?"); бѣ̀ бо ве́лїй ѕѣлѡ̀* (Mark 16:4—"for it was very great"); but they can also refer to other parts of the sentence, albeit very rarely: и҆ ѕѣлѡ̀* заꙋ́тра во є҆ди́нꙋ ѿ сꙋббѡ́тъ (Mark 16:2—"And very early in the morning, the first day of the week").

According to their meaning, adverbial modifiers can be divided into the following categories: 1) circumstances of time, 2) of place, 3) of purpose, 4) of cause, 5) manner of action, 6) of measure.

The methods of expressing circumstances, both by adverbs and by the oblique cases of nouns, are in many respects close to the methods of expressing circumstances in Russian. Out of all the classes of expression above, there is a significant difference in usage only in those of time, place, and of circumstance as expressed by the infinitives of verbs.

§142. 1) *Circumstances of Time.* Adverbial modifiers of time answer the questions: *When? How long? At what time?*

Circumstances of time can be expressed by adverbs: Бди́те оу҆́бо: не ве́сте бо, когда̀ гд҇ь до́мꙋ прїи́детъ, ве́черъ*, и҆лѝ полꙋ́нощи*, и҆лѝ въ пѣтлоглаше́нїе, и҆лѝ оу҆́трѡ* (Mark 13:35—"Watch ye therefore: for ye know not when the master of the house cometh, at even, or at midnight, or at the cockcrowing, or in the morning").

Circumstances of time can be expressed by all the oblique cases of nouns:

a) genitive: и҆ пройдꙋ̀ зе́млю е҆гѷпетскꙋ́ю сея̀ но́щи* (Ex. 12:12—"For I will pass through the land of Egypt this night");

b) dative: а҆рхїере́й сы́й ле́тꙋ* то́мꙋ (John 11:49—"being the high priest that year");

c) accusative: with the preposition въ to signify a *definite* time, and without a preposition to signify a *measure* of time: И҆ въ тре́тїй* де́нь* бра́къ бы́сть въ ка́не галїле́йстей (John 2:1—"And the third day there was a marriage in Cana of Galilee"); Ꙗ҆́коже бо бе і҆ѡ́на во чре́ве ки́товѣ трѝ дни̑* и҆ трѝ но́щи* (Matth. 12:40—"For as Jonas was three days and three nights in the whale's belly"); и҆ ми́лость твоѧ̀ пожене́тъ мѧ̀ всѧ̑* дни̑* живота̀ моегѡ̀ (Ps. 22:6—"And thy mercy will follow me all the days of my life").

d) instrumental, signifying a *specific* time: и҆ воста́етъ но́щїю* и҆ дні́ю* (Mark 4:27—"[as if a man should] rise night and day"); signifying a *measure* of time: четы́редесѧть* и҆ шестїю* ле́тъ* созда́на бы́сть це́рковь сїѧ̀, и҆ ты́ ли треми́* де́ньми* воздви́гнеши ю̇; (John 2:20—"Forty and six years was this temple in building, and wilt thou rear it up in three days?");

e) prepositional with the preposition въ *and* по: Бж҃е мо́й, воззову̀ во дни̑* и̇ не оу̇слы́шиши, и̇ въ нощи̑*, и̇ не въ безу́мїе мнѣ̀ (Ps. 21:3—"O my God, I shall cry by day, and thou wilt not hear: and by night, and it shall not be reputed as folly in me"); По дне́хъ* шести́хъ* поѧ́тъ і̇и҃съ петра̀, и̇ і̇а́кѡва, и̇ і̇ѡа́нна (Matth. 17:1—"After six days Jesus took Peter, and James, and John"); по двою̇ дню̇* па́сха бу́детъ (Matth. 26:2—"after two days shall be the Pasch").

Circumstances of time can also be expressed by combinations of words: ѿ дне́й* до дне́й* и̇схожда́ху дще́ри і̇сра̑илевы пла́кати ѡ̇ дще́ри і̇еф,ѳ,а́ѧ галаади́тина (Judges 11:40—"From year to year the daughters of Israel went forth to lament the daughter of Jephtha the Galaadite[=Gileadite]").

2) *Circumstances of Place.* Adverbial modifiers of place answer the questions: *Where? Whither? Whence?*

Circumstances of place can be expressed by adverbs: Ту̀* оу̇бо па́тка ра́ди і̇у̇де́йска, ꙗ́кѡ бли́зъ* бѧ́ше гро́бъ, положи́ша і̇и҃са (John 19:42—"There, therefore, because of the parasceve [=preparation day] of the Jews, they laid Jesus, because the sepulchre was nigh at hand").

Circumstances of place can be expressed by the oblique cases of nouns:

a) Answering the question Where? — the prepositional case with the prepositions въ, при, на: е́сть во і̇ер́у̇салими́хъ* Ѻ̇вча́ѧ ку́пѣль (John 5:2—"There is at Jerusalem by the sheep [market] a pool"); сѣдѧ́ше при мо́ри* (Matth. 13:1—"sat by the sea"); и̇ ве́сь наро́дъ на бре́зѣ* стоѧ́ше (Matth. 13:2—"and the whole multitude stood on the shore"); — the dative case with the preposition по: бы́сть же и̇ду́щымъ и̇̀мъ по пути̑* (Luke 9:57—"And it came to pass, that, as they went in the way").

b) Answering the question *Whither?* — the accusative case with the preposition въ: і҃нсъ ѿи́де во страны̀* тѵ́рскїѧ и сїдѡ́нскїѧ (Matth. 15:21—"Jesus went into the coasts of Tyre and Sidon"); the genitive case with the preposition до, although, if the verb has the prefix до_, then the genitive case is normally used without the preposition: Пре́йдемъ до вн҃ѳлее́ма (Luke 2:15—"Let us now go even unto Bethlehem"); вн҃ѳлее́ма же доше́дше (Canon of Christmas, Ode 7—"Having reached Bethlehem").

c) Answering the question *Whence?* — the genitive case with the preposition ѿ: Б҃ѣ же фїлі́ппъ ѿ вн҃ѳсаі́ды*, ѿ гра́да* андре́ова и петро́ва (John 1:44—"Now Philip was of Bethsaida, the city of Andrew and Peter").

3) *Circumstances of Purpose:* these answer the questions, *To what goal? With what aim?* They are usually expressed by the infinitive mood of verbs (see §143, 8), or by the oblique cases of nouns with a preposition, for example: и ведо́ша є҆го̀ на пропѧ́тїе* (Matth. 27:31—"and they led him [away] to crucify him").

4) *Circumstances of Cause:* they answer the questions *Why? Because of what?* They can be expressed by an adverb, the oblique cases of nouns or by the infinitive of a verb (see §143, 10), for example: почто̀* мѧ забы́лъ є҆сѝ; и вск҃ю* сѣ́тѹѧ хожда̀; (Ps. 41:10—"Why hast thou forgotten me? and why go I mourning?"); О́чи моѝ и҆знемого́стѣ ѿ нищеты̀* (Ps. 87:10—"My eyes languished through poverty).

5) *Circumstances of Manner:* they answer the questions, *How? In what way?* They can be expressed by qualitative adverbs and adverbs of manner: ѕлы́хъ ѕлѣ* погѹби́тъ (Matth. 21:41— "He will miserably destroy those wicked men"); и расте́шитъ є҆го̀ полма̀* (Matth. 24:51—"And shall cut him asunder"); by an oblique case with a preposition: И҆ и҆зше́дше ско́рѡ ѿ гро́ба со стра́хомъ* и ра́достїю* ве́лїею, теко́стѣ возвѣсти́ти оу҆ченикѡ́мъ є҆гѡ̀ (Matth. 28:8—"And they departed quickly from the sepulchre with fear and great joy; and

did run to bring his disciples word"); рече́ въ себѣ́*, глаго́ла... (Luke 7:39—"he spake within himself, saying..."); by comparative turns of speech with the conjunctions ꙗ́кѡ, ꙗ́ки: Бѣ̀ же зра́къ є҆гѡ̀ ꙗ́кѡ мо́лнїа*, и҆ ѡ҆дѣ́анїе є҆гѡ̀ бѣ́ло ꙗ́кѡ снѣ́гъ* (Matth. 28:3—"His countenance was like lightning, and his raiment white as snow").

6) *Circumstances of Measure:* these answer the questions, *How much? In what measure?* They can be expressed by adverbs or numeral combinations, or by a definite pronoun with a noun, for example: а҆ми́нь, а҆ми́нь глаго́лю тебѣ̀, не возгласи́тъ а҆ле́ктѡръ, до́ндеже ѿве́ржешисѧ менѐ три́щи* (John 13:38—"Verily, verily I say unto thee, the cock shall not crow, till thou hast denied me thrice"); ѿ дне́й до дне́й и҆схожда́хꙋ дще́ри і҆сра́илевы пла́кати ѡ҆ дще́ри і҆еф́ѳа́ѧ галаади́тина четы́ре* дни̑* въ лѣ́тѣ (Judges 11:40—"The daughters of Israel went yearly to lament the daughter of Jephthah the Gileadite four days in a year"); ве́сь* де́нь* сѣ́тꙋѧ хожда́хъ (Ps. 37:7—"I walked sorrowfully all the day long").

§143. The Use of the Infinitive.

1) The infinitive is for the most part combined with the conjugated forms of verbs (and also with participles), and has the role of an object or a modifier. In combinations of infinitives with conjugation forms of verbs, the following peculiarities are to be noted: if the subject of the action indicated by the infinitive coincides with the subject of the conjugated verb, then such an infinitive is known as *simple*, for example: хотѧ́ше минꙋ́ти и҆́хъ (Mark 6:48—"he would have passed by them", *lit.* "he was about to pass them by"); here the subject of the action shown by минꙋ́ти is the same as the subject of the action shown by хотѧ́ше, i.e. *He (Jesus).* If the subject of the infinitive and the subject of the conjugated verb are different, then such an infinitive is equivalent to a subordinate clause, for example: и҆ повелѣ̀ наро́дѡмъ возлещѝ на землѝ (Matth. 15:35—"and he commanded the multitude to sit down on the

ground"—cf. Russ. *(Господь) повелѣлъ, чтобы народъ возлегъ:* "[the Lord] commanded that the people should recline"). In such a construction with the infinitive, the subject of the infinitive is the object of the governing verb, and in that case the subject of the infinitive is either in the accusative case: и молѧше є҆го̀* ѿвратѝти* ѕло́бꙋ а҆ма́новꙋ (Esther 8:3 — "and besought him to turn away the malice of Aman [Haman]"), or else in the dative: [бг҃ъ] повелѣва́етъ человѣ́кѡмъ всѣмъ всю́дꙋ ка́ѧтисѧ* (Acts 17:30—"[God] commandeth all men everywhere to repent"). Such a construction is called, in the first case, *accusative with infinitive,* in the second — *dative with infinitive.* The examples brought forth coincide with the usage of Russian, although in Church Slavonic the use of both the accusative with an infinitive, and of the dative with an infinitive, is much broader than in Russian.

2) *The Infinitive as Object.* The simple infinitive is generally used with "semi-significant" verbs (such as нача́ти, мощѝ, хотѣ́ти, и҆ска́ти, смѣ́ѧтисѧ, боѧ́тисѧ and the like) as auxiliaries, forming together with them composite predicate verb forms (§126).

In conjunction with some verbs, if they have an independant meaning (as opposed to being auxiliaries), the simple infinitive can be viewed as an object (in such cases the infinitive could be replaced by a noun), for example: ѕвѣздо́ю оу҆ча́хꙋсѧ* тебѣ̀ кла́нѧтисѧ* со́лнцꙋ пра́вды (Troparion of the Nativity of Christ —"they learned to worship Thee, the Sun of righteousness"—i.e. "they learned Thy worship"); совѣща́ша* оу҆би́ти* и҆̀хъ (Acts 5:33—"[they] took counsel to slay them"); да сподо́битесѧ* оу҆бѣжа́ти* всѣ́хъ си́хъ хотѧ́щихъ бы́ти (Luke 21:36—"that ye may be accounted worthy to escape all these things that shall come to pass"); Забы́ша* хлѣ́бы взѧ́ти* (Matth. 16:5 —"They had forgotten to take bread"); что̀ ꙗ҆́кѡ согласи́стасѧ* и҆скꙋси́ти* дх҃а гд҇нѧ; (Acts 5:9— "How is it ye have agreed together to tempt the Spirit of the Lord?").

3) *The Accusative with the Infinitive* is, in Russian, normally used after the verbs упросить, заставить and the like ("прошу васъ остаться дома"—"I request you to remain at home"), whereas, in Church Slavonic, such a construction can follow many other verbs in the active voice: ѡстáвнти [to leave], твори́ти [to make], хотѣ́ти [want, be about to], нарицáти [to name], глагóлати [to say] and others, for example: Й не ѡстáви по себѣ ни є҆ди́наго* и҆ти́* (Mark 5:37—"And he suffered no man to follow him"); Й глухі́а* твори́тъ слы́шати*, и҆ нѣмы́а* глагóлати* (Mark 7:37—"he maketh both the deaf to hear, and the dumb to speak"); и҆ сотвори́ є҆гó* прозрѣ́ти* (Mark 8:25— "and he made him to see"); Не хощу́ же вáсъ*, брáтїе, не вѣ́дѣти* ѡ оу҆мéршихъ (I Thess. 4:13— "I would not have you to be ignorant, brethren, concerning them that have died").

The infinitive of the verb бы́ти usually has with it a predicate part in the accusative case (*second predicate accusative*): ѡсуди́ша є҆гó* бы́ти* пови́нна* смéрти (Mark 14:64—"they condemned him to be guilty of death"); когó* мѧ̀* глагóлютъ человѣ́цы бы́ти*; (Mark 8:27—"Whom do men say that I am?").

The second predicate accustive can occur with the infinitives of several other verbs also (signifying *"to make or call someone something"*, cf. §136): и҆ мнѣ́ бг҃ъ показá ни є҆ди́наго* сквéрна* и҆ли нечи́ста* глагóлати* человѣ́ка (Acts 10:28—"but God hath shewed me that I should not call any man common or unclean").

The second predicate accusative with the infinitive (not бы́ти, but another), may occur also in those cases where a second accusative-participle + infinitive relates to a composite verbal predicate (§126), or the second accusative + infinitive relates to a noun predicate with a semi-significant or fully significant copula (§124), in the construction of a subordinate clause, for example: Они́ же чáаху є҆гó* и҆му́ща* возгордѣ́тисѧ*, и҆ли пáсти* внезáпу мéртва* (Acts 28:6—"But they supposed that he would begin to swell up, or suddenly fall dead");—(this verse could also be expressed as "Они́ же чáаху, я҆́кω Óнъ и҆́мать* возгордѣ́тисѧ* и҆ли падéтъ* внезáпу мéртвъ*").

4) An infinitive (equivalent to a subordinate clause) can also have the sense of an accusative with infinitive, when the subject of the infinitive is the same as that of its governing verb, and in such cases the subject of the infinitive is usually not restated, though it may be found in the reflexive _ся of the governing verb or the infinitive (in Russian [and English] a subordinate clause is used in place of such a construction), for example: вся́къ, и́же оубїе́тъ вы̀, возмни́тся слу́жбу приноси́ти* бг҃у (John 16:2—"whosoever killeth you will think that he doeth God service"), cf. the Russian text: *"всякій, убивающій васъ, будетъ думать, что онъ тѣмъ служитъ Богу"*). Но благода́тїю гд҃а і҆и҃са хр҃та̀ вѣ́руемъ спасти́ся* (Acts 15:11—"But we believe that through the grace of our Lord Jesus Christ we shall be saved"); бг҃а и҆сповѣ́дуютъ вѣ́дѣти* (Tit. 1:16—"They profess that they know God" [*or:* "They profess to know God"]); Въ хра́мѣ стоя́ще сла́вы твоея̀ на небесѝ стоя́ти* мни́мъ (Lenten Matins—"Standing in the temple of thy glory, we seem to stand in heaven").

Note. In the following example instead of the infinitive the short active participle is used (a remnant, no doubt, of the ancient possible use of the participle): Оу҆боя́вшеся же и҆ пристра́шни бы́вше, мня́ху ду́хъ ви́дяще* (Luke 24:37—"But they were terrified and affrighted, and supposed had seen that they a spirit"); but in newer revised editions of the Gospel, ви́дѣти has been substituted for ви́дяще.

The subject of the action of the infinitive, in the construction indicated above, can however be expressed by a reflexive pronoun in the accusative case, which can occur with the infinitve бы́ти, and бы́ти usually has a predicate part, the *second predicate accusative*, for example: Оу҆пова́я же себѐ* вожда̀* бы́ти* слѣпы́мъ, свѣ́тъ* су́щымъ во тьмѣ̀, наказа́теля* безу́мнымъ, оу҆чи́теля* младе́нцемъ (Rom. 2:19-20—"And art thou confident that thou thyself art a guide of the blind, a light of them which are in darkness, An instructor of the foolish..."); глаго́ля нѣ́коего бы́ти* себѐ* кєли́ка* (Acts 8:9—"giving out that himself was some great one"); притꙿкора́щихъ ꙁєбѐ* пра́ведники* бы́ти* (Luke 20:20—"[spies] which should feign themselves just men"). The predicate part can also be in an oblique case with a preposition: Глаго́лай ꙁєбѐ* во ꙁвѣ́тѣ* бы́ти* (I John 2:9—"He that saith he is in the light"), cf. Russ. *Кто говоритъ, что онъ во свѣтѣ.*

5) With a governing verb in the passive voice, the subject of the action of the infinitive is in the nominative case (if present), resulting in a *nominative with the infinitive,* while the predicate part with бы́ти is a *second predicate nominative,* for example: є҆́ю же ꙁвидѣ́тєльꙁтвованъ бы́ꙁть бы́ти* пра́ведникъ* (Heb. 11:4—"by which he [Abel] obtained witness that he was righteous"); Но ꙗ҆́коже и҆ꙁкꙋꙁи́хомꙁѧ ѿ бга вѣ́рни* бы́ти* прїѧ́ти бл҃говѣ́ꙁтвова́нїе (I Thess. 2:4—"But as we were approved of God to be put in trust with the Gospel").

6) The *Dative with the infinitive* in Church Slavonic is quite often employed in impersonal constructions with the sense of a logical subject: нє добро̀ бы́ти* чєловѣ́кꙋ* є҆ди́номꙋ (Gen. 2:18 —"[It is] not good for man to be alone"). The use of the dative with the infinitive is especially frequent with the verbs бы́ꙁть (="it came to pass", "it happened", see §160) and подоба́етъ (impersonal sense: "it is proper, fitting; it behooveth, becometh"): бы́ꙁть же оу҆мрє́ти* ни́щемꙋ*, и҆ нєꙁє́нꙋ* бы́ти* а҆́гг҃лы на ло́но а҆враа́млє (Luke 16:22—"And it came to pass, that the beggar died, and was carried by the angels into Abraham's bosom"); бы́ꙁть же внегда̀ бы́ти* а҆поллѡ́ꙁꙋ въ корі́нѳѣ (Acts 19:1—"And it came to pass, that, while Apollos was at Corinth"); ꙗ҆́кѡ подоба́етъ ꙁн҃ꙋ* чєловѣ́чєꙁкомꙋ мно́гѡ поꙁтрада́ти (Mark 8:31—"that the Son of Man must suffer many things").

The dative with the infinitive can be used also with personal verbs, for example: И҆ прїидо́ша ꙁаддꙋкє́є къ немꙋ̀, и҆̀же глаго́лютъ воꙁкреꙁє́нїю* нє бы́ти* (Mark 12:18—"Then came unto him the

Sadducees, who say there is no resurrection"); но хота́тъ ва́мъ* ѡбрѣ́зоватиса (Gal. 6:13—"But [they] desire to have you circumcised"); Не хощꙋ̀ же не вѣ́дѣти* ва́мъ*, бра́тїе, ꙗ́кѡ мно́жицею восхотѣ́хъ прїитѝ къ ва́мъ (Rom. 1:13—"Now I would not have you ignorant, brethren, that oftentimes I purposed to come to you"). The two last examples could also have been expressed by the accusative with the infinitive, cf. the preceding point 3).

With the verbs подоба́етъ, повелѣ́ти [to command], бл҃говоли́ти [to deign, see fit], моли́ти [to entreat] (*"someone to be such-and-such to someone"*), да́ти and the like there can be two datives with an infinitive, a second *predicate dative* with бы́ти (in Russian, such constructions would use a predicate instrumental): Подоба́етъ ѹ́бо є҆пи́скопꙋ* бы́ти* непоро́чнꙋ*, є҆ди́ныа жены̀ мꙋ́жꙋ, тре́звенꙋ*, цѣломꙋ́дрꙋ*... (I Tim. 3:2—"A bishop then must be blameless, the husband of one wife, vigilant, sober,..."); и повели́тъ є҆мꙋ* гдⷭ҇ь властели́нꙋ* бы́ти* над людьмѝ свои́ми (I Kings [Samuel] 13:14—"and the Lord shall appoint him to be a ruler over his people"); Ты́ же глаго́ли ... ста́рцемъ* тре́звеннымъ* бы́ти* (Titus 2:1-2—"But speak thou... that the aged men be sober"); бл҃говолѝ ѹ́бо, гдⷭ҇и, бы́ти на́мъ* слꙋжи́телємъ* но́вагѡ твоегѡ̀ завѣ́та (Liturgy of St. Basil the Great—"look favorably upon us, O Lord, to be ministers of Thy New Testament"); ю҆́ношы та́кожде молѝ цѣломꙋ́дрствовати... Рабы̀, свои́мъ господє́мъ* повиноватиса, во все́мъ бл҃гоꙋгѡ́днымъ* бы́ти*, непрекослѡ́внымъ* (Titus 2:6,9—"Young men likewise exhort to be sober minded... Servants, to be obedient unto their own masters, to please them well in all things; not answering again"); Ты̀ сподо́билъ є҆сѝ на́съ бы́ти слꙋжи́телємъ ст҃а́гѡ твоегѡ̀ же́ртвенника (Lit. of St. Basil—"Thou hast granted us to be ministers of Thy holy table of oblations"); гдⷭ҇ь даде́ тѧ жерца̀ вмѣ́стѡ і҆ѡда́а жерца̀, бы́ти* приста́вникꙋ* въ домꙋ̀ гдⷭ҇ни, вса́комꙋ человѣ́кꙋ* проринца́ющꙋ... (Jer. 29:26—"The Lord hath made thee a priest in the stead of Jehoiada the priest, that thou shouldst be an officer in the house of the Lord, for every man that is mad...").

The subject of the action of an infinitive can in some cases be lacking: Ѻнá же крѣплѧ́шесѧ та́кѡ бы́ти* (Acts 12:15—"But she constantly affirmed that it was even so"); cf. глаго́люще си́мъ* та́кѡ бы́ти* (Acts 24:9—"saying that these things were so"); сїѧ̂ же подоба́ше твори́ти* и̂ ѻ̂нѣ́хъ не ѡ̂ставлѧ́ти* (Matth. 23:23—"these ought ye to have done, and not to leave the other undone"); Тѣ́мже потре́ба повинова́тисѧ* (Rom. 13:5—"Wherefore ye must needs be subject"); внемли́те (себѣ̀) ми́лостыни ва́шеѧ не твори́ти* (вамъ) пред̾ человѣ́ки (Matth. 6:1—" Take heed that ye do not your alms before men").

The syntactic constructions in Church Slavonic known as the accusative and dative with the infinitive correspond in the Greek text to the accusative with the infinitive.

7) *The Infinitive in the role of Adverbial Modifier.* The infinitive as an adverbial modifier is used to express the circumstances of *purpose, result, cause* or *time*. These circumstances can be expressed either by the *simple* infinitive (§143, 1): и̂дꙋ̀ ры̑бы лови́ти* (John 21:3 —"I go a fishing"[1]), or by the *accusative* or *dative* with the infinitive (§143, 1): да посыла́етъ и̂хъ* проповѣ́дати* (Mark 3:14—"that he might send them forth to preach"); преда́ѧше и̂мъ* храни́ти* оу̂ста́вы (Acts 16:4—"they delivered them the decrees for to keep").

8) The infinitive is generally used after verbs of motion [и̂ти, приходи́ти and the like] to express *purpose* [see footnote on this page], as well as dependent motion or condition (посла́ти, to send; призва́ти, to call; поста́вити, to set up, ordain; преда́ти, to give

---

[1]) In Old Church Slavonic, after verbs of motion, the supine was used to express circumstances of purpose, for example: идоу ръібъ ловитъ (John 21:3). [Cf. Latin *eo piscatum*.].

over; и҆збра́ти, to choose, and the like) as well as certain others, for example: ви́дѣхомъ бо ѕвѣздꙋ̀ є҆гѡ̀ на восто́цѣ, и҆ прїидо́хомъ поклони́тисѧ* є҆мꙋ̀ (Matth. 2:2—"for we have seen his star in the east, and are come to worship him"); и҆ посла́ша во ѹ҆зи́лище привести́* и҆хъ (Acts 5:21—"and [they] sent to the prison to have them brought"); и҆ли̑ ѡ҆ꙋбо́жити* призва́сте ны̀; (Judges 14:15—"or have ye called us [to the wedding] to despoil us?"); въ не́мже ва́съ дх҃ъ ст҃ы́й поста́ви є҆пі́скопы, пасти́* цр҃ковь гд҃а и҆ бг҃а (Acts 20:28—"[the flock] over which the Holy Ghost hath placed you [as] bishops, to feed the Church of the Lord and God"); преда́въ четы́ремъ четвери́цамъ во́инѡвъ стрещи́* є҆го̀ (Acts 12:4—"[having] delivered him to four quaternions of soldiers to keep him"); покажѝ, є҆го́же и҆збра́лъ є҆сѝ ѿ сею̀ двою̀ є҆ди́наго, прїѧ́ти* жре́бїй слꙋже́нїѧ сегѡ̀ и҆ а҆п҇то́льства (Acts 1:24-25—"shew whether of these two thou hast chosen, to take the place of this ministry and apostleship"); бꙋ́ди мѝ въ бг҃а защи́тителѧ, и҆ въ мѣ́сто крѣ́пко спасти́* мѧ (Ps. 70:3—"Be thou unto me a God, a protector, and a place of strength, that thou mayest save me"); но́щь и҆ де́нь преизли́ха молѧ́щесѧ ви́дѣти* лицѐ ва́ше (I Thess. 3:10—"Night and day praying exceedingly that we might see your face").

The infinitive signifying circumstances of *purpose* of verbs used as a semi-significant copula in a composite noun predicate, can have with it a predicate part (in the nominative), for example: происхо́дитъ пло́тїю въ виѳлее́мскомъ верте́пѣ роди́тисѧ... ви́дѣтисѧ* же младе́нецъ* (Sedalen [sessional hymn] for Matins of Dec. 20—"[He] cometh forth in the flesh to be born in the cave of Bethlehem... to be seen as a babe"); while the infinitive of verbs meaning *to make or call someone something* may have a second predicate accusative, for example: прїи́де бо влⷣка, тѧ̀ многоча́днꙋ* содѣ́лати* (Dec. 24, 1st Ode—"the Master is come, to make thee the mother of many children").

An infinitive expressing adjuncts of *purpose* can be replaced
by the optative mood, which is permissible in cases where the subjects
of the main verb and the infinitive are different; although
replacement of the simple infinitive is also encountered, i.e. with the
subject of the governing verb, for example: і҆и҃са же би́въ предадѐ и҆̀мъ,
да* е҆гò про́пн8тъ* (Matth. 27:26—"when he had scourged Jesus, he
delivered him to be crucified"); и҆ посла́ша фарїсе́є и҆ а҆рхїере́є сл8гѝ,
да* и҆м8тъ е҆гò (John 7:32—"the Pharisees and the chief priests sent
officers to take him"); я҆́кю и҆́детъ на гро́бъ, да* пла́четъ* та́мю
(John 11:31—"[saying] that she goeth unto the grave, to weep there").

The infinitive showing adjuncts of *purpose* can be used in
combinations with е҆́же or во е҆́же (="so as to", "in order to"), which
in this case have the role of conjoining words, while the infinitive
along with its dependent words forms a subordinate clause. With the
aid of е҆́же, and especially во е҆́же, the infinitive of purpose can be
joined with verbs of various meaning. Examples: да помрача́тсѧ
о҆́чи и҆́хъ, е҆́же не ви́дѣти* (Ps. 68:24—"Let their eyes be darkened
that they see not"); я҆́кю предста̀ ю҆деснꙋ́ю ꙋ҆бо́гагю, е҆́же спастѝ* ю҆
гонѧ́щихъ дꙋ́шꙋ мою̀ (Ps. 108:31 — "Because he hath stood at the
right hand of the poor, to save my soul from persecutors"); и҆ ю҆ се́мъ
молю́сѧ, да любо́вь ва́ша е҆щѐ па́че и҆ па́че и҆збы́точествꙋетъ въ
ра́зꙋмѣ и҆ во всѧ́комъ чꙋ́вствїи, во е҆́же и҆скꙋша́ти* ва́мъ лꙋ́чшаѧ
(Philippians 1:9-10—"And this I pray, that your charity may more
and more abound in knowledge, and in all understanding: that ye
may approve the better things"); ва́мъ пе́рвѣе бг҃ъ воздви́гїй о҆́трока
своегò і҆и҃са, посла̀ е҆гò блгⷭ҇ловѧ́ща ва́съ, во е҆́же ю҆брати́тисѧ* ва́мъ
комꙋ́ждо ю҆ ѕлẃбъ ва́шихъ (Acts 3:26—"Unto you first, God raising
up His Son Jesus, sent him to bless you, that ye may every one of you
turn from your iniquities").

The infinitive signifying adjuncts of *purpose*, while remaining
a subordinate clause, may also be used without the above-mentioned
linking words, in which case the infinitive with its dependent words

is set off by a comma, for example: и вше́дъ вну́трь, сѣдѧ́ше со слу́гами, ви́дѣти кончи́ну (Matth. 26:58—"and having gone in, [Peter] sat with the servants, to see the end"), compare the Russian version: чтобы видѣть конецъ—"*so as* to see the outcome"; и воздви́же ру́ку свою̀ на нѧ̀, низложи́ти ѧ̀ въ пусты́ни (Ps. 105:26—"and he lifted up his hand over them: to overthrow them in the desert"); ѡѕло́би Ѻ҆тцы̀ на́ши, у҆мори́ти младе́нцы и҆́хъ (Acts 7:19—"[another king] afflicted our fathers, to mortify their babes").

Adjuncts of *purpose* can be expressed by the infinitive with the conjunction ꙗ́кѡ: свѧжи́те и҆́хъ въ снопы̀ ꙗ́кѡ сожещѝ* ѧ̀ (Matth. 13:30—"bind them in bundles [as] to burn them"); а҆́зъ [є҆́смь] бг҃ъ и҆зведы́й тѧ̀ ѿ страны̀ халде́йскїѧ ꙗ́кѡ да́ти* тебѣ̀ зе́млю сїю̀ наслѣ́довати (Gen. 15:7—"I am God that brought thee out of the land of the Chaldeans, so as to give thee this land to inherit").

9) Adjuncts of *result* most often are expressed by the dative with the infinitive, with the conjunction ꙗ́кѡ [же] and constitute a subordinate clause, for example: во́лны влива́хусѧ въ кора́бль, ꙗ́кѡ у҆жѐ погружа́тисѧ* є҆му̀* (Mark 4:37—"The waves poured into the ship, so that it was filled"); и҆ и҆сцѣлѝ є҆го̀, ꙗ́кѡ слѣпо́му* и҆ нѣмо́му* глаго́лати*, и҆ глѧ́дати* (Matth. 12:22—"and he healed him, so much that the blind and dumb both spake and saw"); и҆ бы́сть ꙗ́кѡ ме́ртвъ, ꙗ́коже мнѡ́зѣмъ* глаго́лати*, ꙗ́кѡ у҆мре (Mark 9:26—"and he was as one dead; insomuch that many said, He is dead").

However, *result* can also be expressed by the infinitive with the subject of the governing verb, i.e. by the *simple* infinitive, e.g.: а҆́ще и҆ма́мъ всю̀ вѣ́ру, ꙗ́кѡ и҆ го́ры преставлѧ́ти* (I Cor. 13:2—"and though I have all faith, so that I could remove mountains"); и҆́же мі́ръ тво́й та́кѡ возлюби́лъ є҆сѝ, ꙗ́коже сн҃а твоегѡ̀ є҆диноро́днаго да́ти* (Liturgy of St. John Chrysostom—"Who didst so love the world as to give Thine Only-begotten Son"); и҆ а҆́бїе собра́шасѧ мно́зи, ꙗ́коже ктому̀ не вмѣща́тисѧ* ни при две́рехъ (Mark 2:2—"And straightway many were gathered together, insomuch that there was no room to receive them, no, not so much as about the door").

The infinitive showing adjuncts of *result* can also be used without the conjunction ꙗ́кѡ, while remaining a subordinate clause, for example: Нє ѹ҆клонѝ сє́рдцє моѐ въ словєса̀ лꙋка́вствїѧ, нєщєва́ти* вины̀ ѡ҆ грѣсѣ́хъ (Ps. 140:4—"Incline not my heart to evil words, to make excuses for sins"); почто̀ и҆спо́лни сатана̀ сє́рдцє твоѐ, солга́ти* дх҃ꙋ ст҃о́мꙋ (Acts 5:3—"why hath Satan filled thy heart to lie to the Holy Ghost"); Нє ѡ҆би́дливъ бо бг҃ъ, забы́ти* дѣ́ла ва́шєгѡ и҆ трꙋда̀ любвѐ (Heb. 6:10—"For God is not unrighteous to forget your work and labour of love"); see also Rev. 5:5; Luke 1:54; Rev. 16:9.

Adjuncts of *result* may be expressed by the infinitive with the conjunction во є҆́жє (forming a subordinate clause): Нєви́димаѧ бо є҆гѡ̀, ѿ созда́нїѧ мі́ра творє́ньми помышлѧ́ємма ви́дима сꙋ́ть, и҆ присносꙋ́щнаѧ си́ла є҆гѡ̀ и҆ бж҃єство̀: во є҆́жє бы́ти и҆̃мъ бєзѿвѣ́тнымъ (Rom. 1:20—"For the invisible things of him, from the creation of the world, are clearly seen, being understood by the things that are made; his eternal power also, and divinity: so that they are without excuse"), compare with the Russian: *такъ что они безотвѣтны.* Likewise: вѣ́рою, разꙋмѣва́ємъ совєршѝтисѧ вѣ́кѡмъ глаго́ломъ бж҃їнмъ, во є҆́жє (и҆зъ) нєѧвлѧ́ємыхъ ви́димымъ бы́ти (Heb. 11:3—"Through faith, we understand that the worlds were framed by the word of God; that from things invisible, visible things might be made"); see also Rom. 1:24.

10) Adjuncts of *result* are expressed by the dative with the infinitive and the conjunction занѐ and constitute a subordinate clause, for example: Взы́дє жє и҆ і҆ѡ́сифъ ѿ галїлє́и, и҆з гра́да назарє́та, во і҆ꙋдє́ю, во гра́дъ дв҃довъ, и҆̃жє нарица́єтсѧ вихлєє́мъ, занѐ бы́ти* є҆мꙋ́* ѿ до́мꙋ и҆ ѻ҆́чєства² дв҃дова (Luke 2:4—"And

---

²) Ѻ҆́чєства = Ѻ҆тє́чєства

Joseph also went up from Galiliee, out of the city of Nazareth, into Judæa, unto the city of David, which is called Bethlehem; because he was of the house and lineage of David"); Слы́шацымх же и́мх сїѧ̀, приложь ре́че при́тчꙋ, занѐ бли́зх є҆мꙋ* бы́ти* і҆ерꙋсали́ма... (Luke 19:11—"And as they heard these things, he added and spake a parable, because he was nigh to Jerusalem...").

11) Adjuncts of *time* are expressed by the dative with the infinitive, with the conjunctions внегда̀ (when), пре́жде да́же (before), дондеже (until) and form a subordinate clause, for example: Ко гꙋꙋ, внегда̀ скорбѣ́ти* мѝ*, воззва́хх (Ps. 119:1—"To the Lord, when I was troubled, I cried"); ꙗ҆́кѡ внегда̀ оу҆мре́ти* є҆мꙋ*, не во́зметх всѧ̑ (Ps. 48:18—"For when he shall die, he shall not take anything"); пре́жде да́же гора́мх не бы́ти* и҆ созда́тисѧ* земли̂* и҆ вселе́ннѣй*, и҆ ѿ вѣ́ка и҆ до вѣ́ка ты̀ є҆сѝ (Ps. 89:2—"Before the mountains came into being, and the earth and universe were made, from age to age thou art"); Со́лнце приложи́тсѧ во тьмꙋ̀, и҆ лꙋна̀ вх кро́вь, пре́жде да́же не прїити́* дню̀* гꙋꙋню вели́комꙋ и҆ просвѣще́нномꙋ (Acts 2:20—"The sun shall be turned into darkness, and the moon into blood, before that great and notable day of the Lord come"); и҆ и҆да́ше и҆дый и҆ проррица́ѧ, дондеже прїити́* є҆мꙋ* вх нава́,д,х и҆́же вх ра́мѣ (I Kings [Samuel] 19:23 —"and going he went and prophesied, until he came to Nabath in Ramah"); и҆ проходѧ̀ блговѣ́ствова́ше градѡ́мх всѣ̑мх, дондеже прїити́* є҆мꙋ* вх кеса́рїю (Acts 8:40—"and passing through he preached in all the cities, till he came to Cæsaria").

12) The infinitive, which by origin is a frozen case form of a verbal noun, may be used as if tify a thing, and acts as various parts of the sentence in the manner of a noun, for which reason the pronoun є҆́же is put before it as an article in such cases, although it can also be absent.

The infinitive may have the following roles:

As a *subject* (see §122, g), which occurs most often with an impersonal construction of the predicate. The impersonal form of the predicate in such cases is for the most part expressed by a neuter adjective of the positive or comparative degree with a copula (or sometimes without a copula), for example: Бла́го є҆́сть ѹ҆пова́ти* на гд҃а, не́жели ѹ҆пова́ти* на кнѧ́зи (Ps. 117:9—"It is good to trust in the Lord, rather than to trust in princes"); добрѣ́йше тѝ є҆́сть вни́ти* къ живо́тꙋ хро́мꙋ и҆лѝ бѣ́днꙋ (Matth. 18:8—"it is better for thee to enter into life halt or maimed[3], [rather than...]"); also: Мнѣ̀ бо є҆́же жи́ти*, хрⷭ҇то́съ: и҆ є҆́же ѹ҆мре́ти*, прїѡбрѣ́тенїе є҆́сть (Philipp. 1:21—"For me to live is Christ, and to die is gain").

As a *direct object:* Ꙗ҆́кѡ ва́мъ дарова́сѧ... не то́кмѡ є҆́же въ него̀ вѣ́ровати*, но и҆ є҆́же по не́мъ страда́ти* (Philipp. 1:29—"For unto you is given ... not only to believe on him, but also to suffer for his sake");

In combination with a preposition and є҆́же it can express case-relationships like those of nouns (є҆́же may be absent when the sense of the prepositional case is expressed): as an *object:* и҆́же ѿ небытїѧ̀ во є҆́же бы́ти приве́дый всѧ́ческаѧ (=въ бытїѐ), Liturgy of St. John Chrysostom—"Who hast brought all things out of nonexistence into being"; за є҆́же люби́ти мѧ̀ (=за любо́вь ко мнѣ̀), Good Friday at the 6th Hour—"instead of loving me"; вмѣ́стѡ є҆́же люби́ти мѧ̀ (= вмѣ́стѡ любвѐ ко мнѣ̀), Ps. 108:4—"Instead of making me a return of love"; ѡ҆ є҆́же поми́ловати рабѡ́въ свои́хъ (=ѡ҆ поми́лованїи рабѡ́въ свои́хъ), Moleben for Travellers—"That He will have mercy upon His servants..."; ѡ҆ є҆́же посла́ти и҆̀мъ а҆́гг҃ла ми́рна... (ibid.—"That He will send them an Angel of peace..."); but also: ѡ҆ прости́ти и҆̀мъ... (Pannikhida—"For their forgiveness...", or "That He will forgive them..."); ѡ҆ неѡсꙋжде́ннымъ предста́ти (ibid.—"That they may appear uncondemned"); with the sense of *circumstance of cause:* Ꙗ҆́коже є҆́сть пра́ведно мнѣ̀ сїѐ мꙋ́дрствовати

---

[3])for the meaning of бѣ́днꙋ in this verse, see Note 4 on p. 172.—*Tr.*

ѿ всѣхъ васъ, за є҆́же и҆мѣ́ти* мѝ въ се́рдцѣ ва́съ (Philipp.
1:7—"Even as it is meet for me to think this of you all, because I have
you in my heart"); И҆счезо́стѣ о́чи моѝ, ѿ є҆́же ѹ҆пова́ти* мѝ на бг҃а
моего̀ (Ps. 68:4—"My eyes have failed, whilst I hope on my
God"—[=ѿ ѹ҆пова́нїѧ, cf. in the Russian version: истомились глаза
мои отъ ожиданія Бога [моего]); signifying *circumstance of purpose*:
ко є҆́же вожделѣ́ти* є҆ѧ̀ (Matth. 5:28—"to lust after her").

However, if one adds to є҆́же the subjunctive particle бы, the
verbal significance outweighs the sense of a noun, and such a
combination can be viewed as a *short* subordinate clause (§196, III),
for example: Вмѣ́стѡ є҆́же бы̀ глаго́лати: а҆́ще гд҃ь восхо́щетъ (James
4:15—"For that ye ought to say, If the Lord will": cf. Russ. *Вмѣсто
того, чтобы вамъ говорить…—"Instead of you saying…"*)

As a direct object with a noun-like coloring, also used are the
verbs ꙗ҆́сти, пи́ти: дади́те и҆̀мъ вы̀ ꙗ҆́сти (Matth. 14:16—"Give ye
them to eat"); да́ждь мѝ пи́ти (John 4:7—"Give me to drink").

With certain adjectives (such as досто́инъ, worthy; дово́ленъ,
enough; си́ленъ, able; гото́въ, ready, &c.) the infinitive can be
viewed as an *indirect object*, for example: да бу́детъ всѧ́къ человѣ́къ
ско́ръ* ѹ҆слы́шати*, и҆ ко́сенъ* глаго́лати* (James 1:19—"let every
man be swift to hear, and slow to speak": cf. Russ. всякій человѣкъ
да будетъ скоръ на слышаніе, медленъ на слова— "*Let every man be
swift at hearing, slow at words*"); досто́инъ* є҆сѝ гд҃и прїѧ́ти* сла́ву и҆
че́сть и҆ си́лу (Rev. 4:11—"Thou art worthy, O Lord, to receive [="to
the reception of"] glory and honour and power"); и҆̀же дово́льни*
бу́дутъ и҆ и҆ны́хъ научи́ти* (II Tim. 2:2—"who shall be able to teach
['to the teaching of'] others also"); а҆́ще си́ленъ* є҆́сть срѣ́сти* съ
десѧ́тїю ты́сѧщъ (Luke 14:31—"whether he be able with ten thousand
to meet [to the meeting with] him…"); Сѐ тре́тїе гото́въ* є҆смь
прїити́* къ ва́мъ (II Cor. 12:14—"Behold, the third time I am ready
to come ['to coming'] to you").

If the adjectives indicated above (usually with a copula) occur with the infinitive of one of the semi-significant verbs or бы́ти accompanied by a predicate part, such a combination can be construed as a special type of composite predicate (see §127), for example: ѹ҆жѐ нѣ́смь* досто́инъ* нарещи́сѧ* сы́нъ* тво́й (Luke 15:21—"[I] am no more worthy to be called thy son"); however, the infinitive could also be construed as an object, i.e. *worthy of the name of a son.*

14) Used with nouns, the infinitive has a *determinant* role (§130, 8), for example: бж҃е на́шъ, бж҃е спаса́ти* (=спасе́нїѧ), Liturgy of St. Basil—"Our God, the God of salvation"; сѐ даю̀ ва́мъ вла́сть наступа́ти* на ѕмїю̀… (Luke 10:19—"Behold, I give you power to tread on serpents"). With бы́ти or the infinitive of the semi-significant verbs, there is always a predicate part — in the nominative case: ꙗ҆́кѡ вѣ́рꙋ и҆́мать здра́въ* бы́ти* (Acts 14:9—"[perceiving] that he had faith to be healed"); or else a *second predicate dative*, for example: дадѐ и҆̀мъ ѻ҆́бласть ча́дѡмъ* бж҃їимъ [и҆̀мъ] бы́ти* (John 1:12—"to them he gave power to become the sons of God"). The subject (и҆мъ) of the action of the verb бы́ти is left out, because it coincides with the object (и҆̀мъ) of the action of дадѐ.

With a *determinant* meaning, the infinitive may be combined with the conjunctive words є҆́же, во є҆́же, ѡ҆ є҆́же, ка́кѡ (which can be viewed as forming a subordinate clause), for example: мл҃тва, є҆́же бл҃гослови́ти нѡ́выѧ покро́вцы (Heading in the Slavonic Trebnik [*Book of Needs*]— "A Prayer for the Blessing of New Covers [for the Eucharistic Vessels]"); мл҃тва, во є҆́же бл҃гослови́ти ста́до (ibid., —"Prayer for Blessing a Flock"); мл҃тва, ѡ҆ є҆́же бл҃гослови́ти мре́жи (ibid., — "Prayer for the Blessing of Nets"); чи́нъ, ка́кѡ прїима́ти приходѧ́щихъ ко правосла́внѣй цр҃кви ѿ ри́мско-лати́нскагѡ вѣроисповѣ́данїѧ (ibid., —"An Order for the Reception of Converts [*lit., "those who come"*] to the Orthodox Church from the Roman-Latin Confession"). The dative with the infinitive may also be used with a determinant meaning (and the sense of a subordinate clause), for example: Моли́твы въ пе́рвый де́нь, по внегда̀ роди́ти жен녀 Отроча̀ (Trebnik heading — "Prayers [to be said] on the First Day After Childbirth [*lit.*, "*after a woman has given birth to a child*"]).

15) The infinitive is not used in Church Slavonic with the independent function of a verb. Nevertheless there are some cases (based on the Greek text) when, as an expression of command or desire, the infinitive stands alone, for example: ничесо́же возми́те на пꙋ́ть... ни по двѣ̀ ри̑зѣ имѣ́ти* (Luke 9:3—"Take nothing for your journey... neither have two coats apiece"); кла́ꙋдїй лꙋ́сіа держа́вномꙋ игемонꙋ фили̑зꙋ ра́доватиса* (Acts 23:26—"Claudius Lysias unto the most excellent governor Felix [sendeth] greeting"), in this example жела́етъ should be understood; Ра́доватиса* съ ра́дꙋющимиса, и пла́кати* съ пла́чꙋщими (Rom. 12:15—"Rejoice with them that do rejoice, and weep with them that weep"), where one can also assume an omitted verb; one might see here a connection to the word Глаго́лю which appears in the 3rd verse. Likewise: Acts 15:23 and Jas. 1:1.

§144. Isolated Parts of the Sentence.

Isolated Objects. Declension forms of nouns when combined with the conjunctions то́кмѡ, ра́звѣ, кромѣ̀ ["except for, other than, but for"] indicating *limitation*, can be viewed as isolated *objects*, which are therefore set apart by a comma, for example: Ктомꙋ никого́же ви́дѣша, то́кмѡ і҆и҃са е҆ди́нагѡ съ собо́ю (Mark 9:8—"they saw no man anymore, save Jesus only with themselves"); Ꙗдꙋщихъ же бѣ̀ мꙋже́й ꙗ҆кѡ па́ть ты́сацъ, ра́звѣ же́нъ и дѣ́тей (Matth. 14:21—"And they that had eaten were about five thousand men, beside women and children"); Пꙋсты́ннымъ непреста́нное бж҃е́ственное жела́нїе быва́етъ, мі́ра сꙋ́щымъ сꙋ́егнагѡ кромѣ̀ (Octoechos, "Hymn of Ascent" [Stepenna], T. 1—"They that live in the wilderness have an unquenchable longing for God, as they are far from the tumult of life"—or thus: "For the wilderness dwellers there is an incessant Divine striving, to them that are apart from the vain world"). Sometimes a word combination with вмѣстw can be taken as an isolated object and set apart by a comma: вмѣстw є҆же люби́ти мѧ̀, ѡ҆болга́хꙋ мѧ̀ (Ps. 108:4—"Instead of making me a return of love, they detracted me").

Isolated Circumstances. Adverbial modifiers of place and time can be accompanied by circumstances that define them more precisely, and which may be viewed as *isolated*. Such circumstances are set apart by commas, for example: и҆до́ша въ галїле́ю, въ го́рꙋ, а́може повелѣ̀ и҆мъ і҆и҃съ (Matth. 28:16—"[the eleven disciples] went away into Galilee, unto a mountain where Jesus had appointed them"); и҆ прише́дшꙋ є҆мꙋ̀ на ѻ҆́нъ по́лъ, въ странꙋ̀ гергесі́нскꙋю, срѣ́то́ста є҆го̀ два̀ бѣ́сна (Matth. 8:28—"And when he was come to the other side, into the country of the Gergesenes, there met him two possessed with devils"); И҆ бы́сть по возвраще́нїи лѣ́та, во вре́мѧ и҆схожде́нїѧ царе́й [на бра́нь], и҆ посла̀ даві́дъ і҆ѡа́ва (II Kings [Samuel] 11:1—"And it came to pass, after the year was expired, at the time when kings go forth [to battle], that David sent Joab"); Но въ ты̀ѧ дни̑, по ско́рби то́й, со́лнце поме́ркнетъ (Mark 13:24—"But in those days, after that tribulation, the sun shall be darkened").

§145. Circumstantial Attributes.

Certain adjectives, always in the short form, relate not only to the subject but to the predicate as well, and have the role of *adverbial modifiers (adjuncts)*, for example: Тридне́венъ* воскре́слъ є҆сѝ, хр҃тѐ ѿ гро́ба (Octoechos, Sunday Tone 6, at the Praises—"On the third day, O Christ, Thou art risen from the tomb"). Such attributes are related to the use of participles as subordinate clauses, cf. сы́й тридне́венъ, воскре́слъ є҆сѝ (*"being* of-three-days [i.e. three days in the tomb], Thou art risen...") Similarly: Въ пе́рсть сме́ртнꙋю соше́дъ, влⷣко, сме́ртнꙋю держа́вꙋ разрꙋши́лъ є҆сѝ, и҆ ме́ртвъ* тридне́венъ* воскре́съ, въ нетлѣ́нїе мѧ̀ ѡ҆бле́клъ є҆сѝ (Sunday T. 1,

Ode 3—"Having descended into mortal dust, O Master, Thou didst destroy the power of death, and being one dead three days, rising didst clothe me in incorruption"), as if "[сый] мертвъ триднебенъ, воскресъ, въ нетлѣнїе..." (Compare with constructions in the Russian language: *Терекъ воетъ, дикъ* и злобенъ*, межъ утесистыхъ громадъ*—"*Terek roars, wild and enraged, amid the massive crags [craggy masses]*", Lermontov: The Gifts of Terek; *Но равнодушно ей, задумчивъ*, онъ внимаетъ*—"*But he, indifferent [=with indifference] listens to her*"—*Pushkin*).

In some cases, similar circumstantial attributes can be translated by adverbs, for example: видѧ же силы и знаменїѧ велїѧ бывбаема, оужасенъ* дивлѧшеса (Acts 8:13—"seeing the miracles and great signs that were done, he wondered, being astonished"), i.e. оужасенъ = въ оужасѣ: "in amazement, astonishment"; ѿонудуже небесныѧ силы, зрѧще, апломъ страшливн* (i.e. "со страхомъ") глаголаху (Pentecostarion, 6th week, Saturday [after the Ascension] Matins, at the Aposticha/Stichovna—"For which cause [*lit.*, "whence"] the Powers of Heaven, having seen, spake affrighted [=in fright] to the Apostles".

§146. Circumstantial Participles.

The short forms of the participles, either alone or with dependent words, may relate to the predicate and limit it in terms of circumstance — they can be called *circumstantial participles* [*i.e* participles that act as adverbs]. Such participles, if they have dependent words, generally have a meaning equivalent to subordinate clauses of circumstance [adverbial phrases]. Since these participles refer to the predicate, and have a connection to the subject as well, they are used only in the nominative case (in all numbers and genders). Circumstantial participles, by meaning and use (with the exception of certain peculiarities), are equivalent to gerunds in Russian [and other languages], for example: во дни ѻны прїиде їѡа́ннх кр҃ти́тель, проповѣ́даѧ* вх пꙋстьı́нн і꙳ꙋде́йстѣ́н (Matth. 3:1—"In those days came John the Baptist, preaching in the wilderness of Judæa"); Ѻ҆на́ же а҆́бїе ѡ꙳ста́вльша* (*dual number*) мрѐ́жн, по не́мх и꙳до́ста (Matth. 4:20—"And they straightway left their nets, and followed him").

One might list the following types of circumstantial [adjunct] participles:

1) Active adverbial present participles: Ѻ҆ни́ же помышлѧ́хꙋ кх себѣ̀, глаго́люще*: ꙗ́кw хлѣ́бьı не взѧ́хомх (Matth. 16:7—"And they reasoned among themselves, saying, It is because we have taken no bread"); вх четве́ртꙋю же стра́жꙋ но́щн и꙳де кх ни́мх і҆н҃сх, ходѧ̀* по мо́рю (Matth. 14:25—"And in the fourth watch of the night Jesus went unto them, walking on the sea").

Note: In the text и҆ хотѧ́щх (in place of хотѧ̀) е҆го̀ ꙋби́тн, ꙋбоѧ́сѧ наро́да (Matth. 14:5 — "And when he would have put him to death, he feared the multitude"), the form хотѧ́щх as an adverbial participle must be considered irregular, since it is used in a determinant sense, cf. и҆ не хотѧ̀* е҆ѧ̀ ѡ꙳бличи́тн, восхотѣ́ та́й пꙋсти́тн ю҆ (Matth. 1:19—"and not willing to make her a publick example, [Joseph] was minded to put her away privily").

2) Adverbial past participles: а҆́зх пришѐ́дх* и҆сцѣлю̀ е҆го̀ (Matth. 8:7—"I will come and heal him"); и҆ прнстꙋ́пль* е҆ди́нх кни́жникх, речѐ е҆мꙋ̀... (Matth. 8:19—"And a certain scribe came, and said unto him..."); и҆ прнше́дше* ꙋ҆ченнцьı̀ е҆гѡ̀, возбꙋди́ша е҆го̀ (Matth. 8:25—"And his disciples came to him, and awoke him..."); кто́ же ѿ ва́сх пекі́йсѧ* (instead of the short form, see §95), мо́жетх прнложи́тн во́зрастꙋ своемꙋ̀ ла́коть е҆ди́нх; (Matth. 6:27—"Which of you by taking thought can add one cubit unto his stature?").

3) Adverbial present passive participles: Ѻ҆укорѧ́емн, блгослоВлѧ́емх: гони́мн, терпи́мх: хꙋли́мн, ꙋ҆тѣшѧ́емсѧ (I Cor. 4:12-13—"Being reviled, we bless; being persecuted, we we suffer it; being defamed, we intreat"); but the Church Slavonic adverbial

passive participles (present as well as past) are not accompanied by a copula, the present active participle of the verb бы́ти [сы́й, сꙋ́щꙇи].

4) Adverbial past passive participles: да не па́дше и ѡблѣни́вшесѧ, но бо́дрствꙋюще и воздви́жени* въ дѣла́нꙇе, ѡбраща́емсѧ гото́ви (Morning Prayer 5—"May we not be found fallen and idle, but watching, and upright in activity, ready..."); посредѣ́ же ѻгнѧ̀ вве́ржени*, ѡроша́еми поѧ́хꙋ (Eirmos, T. 2, Ode 7—"cast into the midst of the fire, [but] moistened by dew, they sang...").

An adverbial past participle may also be composite, with the active past participle of бы́ти [бы́въ, бы́вши] as a copula [connecting verb]: Слы́шавше же и бы́вше* испо́лнени* ꙗ́рости, вопꙇа́хꙋ... (Acts 19:28—"And when they heard these sayings, they were full of wrath, and cried out"); Мно́гѡ ѹ̑бо па́че, ѡправда́ни* бы́вше* ны́нѣ кро́вꙇю є̑гѡ̀, спасе́мсѧ и̑мъ ѿ гнѣ́ва (Rom. 5:9—"Much more then, being now justified by his blood, we shall be saved from wrath...").

5) Since adverbial participles have the value of a collateral predicate, therefore, by analogy with compound predicates, they too can have compound forms, consisting of forms of the participle of the verb бы́ти [сы́й, сꙋ́щꙇи] and a noun part, for example: Сꙇѝ человѣ́цы возмꙋща́ютъ гра́дъ на́шъ, і̑ꙋде́є* сꙋ́ще* (Acts 16:20—"These men being Jews, do exceedingly trouble our city"); а́ще ѹ̑бо вы̀ лꙋка́ви* сꙋ́ще*, ѹ̑мѣ́ете даѧ̑нꙇѧ бл҃га даѧ́ти ча́дѡмъ ва́шымъ (Matth. 7:11—"If ye then, being evil, know how to give good gifts unto your children..."); Бг҃а и̑сповѣ́дꙋютъ вѣ́дѣти, а̑ дѣ́лы ѿмеща́ютсѧ є̑гѡ̀, ме́рзцы* сꙋ́ще* и̑ непокорли́ви*, и̑ на всѧ́ко дѣ́ло бл҃го́е неискꙋ́сни* (Titus 1:16 —"They profess that they know God, but in works they deny him, being abominable, and disobedient, and unto every good work reprobate"); и̑ тре́петенъ* бы́въ*, припадѐ къ па́влꙋ и̑ сꙇлѣ̀ (Acts 16:29—"and trembling, [he] fell down before Paul and Silas"); И̑бо до́лжни* сꙋ́ще* бы́ти* ѹ̑чи́телꙇ* лѣ́тъ ра́ди, па́ки тре́бꙋете ѹ̑чи́тисѧ (Heb. 5:12—"For when for the time ye ought to be

teachers, ye have need that one teach you again"). Such compound forms can be called *compound circumstantial participles*.

In the role of a connecting-verb participle [copula-participle], one may also encounter passive participles formed from those verbs that can be used as semi-significant copulas (§123), for example: а҆́гг҃льскаѧ спсе ра́дость бы́въ, ны́нѣ и҆ печа́ли сѧ́мъ бы́лъ є҆сѝ кѷнонешъ, ви́димь* пло́тїю безды́ханенъ* ме́ртвъ* (Holy Saturday, Stasis 1, v. 36—"Thou art the joy of the Angels, O Saviour, but now art become the cause of their grief, as they see Thee in the flesh a lifeless corpse"), i.e *being seen without breath, dead in the flesh.*

6) The sphere of circumstantial [adjunct] participles is somewhat broader than that of the gerund in Russian. Thus, for example, where Russian has the combinations пойду посмотрю, встану и пойду, возьму и сдѣлаю — Church Slavonic has corresponding expressions using adjunct participles: ше́дъ посмотрю̀ (Exodus 3:3—"I will go [near] and see"); воста́въ и҆дꙋ̀ (Luke 15:18—"I will arise and go"); взе́мъ сотворю̀ (Matth. 13:33—"having taken... I will make...", cf. §147, 2).

7) Individual adjunct participles in Church Slavonic are viewed as simple adverbial modifiers and not set off by commas, for example: ше́дше* и҆спыта́йте и҆звѣ́стнѡ ѡ҆ ѻ҆троча́ти (Matth. 2:8—"Go and search diligently for the young child"); посредѣ́ же ѻ҆гнѧ̀ вве́ржени, ѡ҆роша́еми* поѧ́хꙋ (Eirmos—"But cast in the midst of fire, moistened by dew, they sang").

Note. Adjunct participles such as глаго́лѧ, зовы́й—are always set off by a comma, in view of the fact that the quotation following them has the role of an object [the thing said]: а҆́бїе же речѐ и҆̀мъ і҆и҃съ, глаго́лѧ: дерза́йте (Matth. 14:27—"But straightway Jesus spake unto them, saying: Be of good cheer").

§147. Pleonastic Expressions.

1) In the books of Holy Scripture, special *pleonastic expressions* are not infrequently to be encountered (from πλεονασμός —

"excess"), consisting of a verb with a personal ending (the predicate) in combination with a circumstantial present participle (§146, 1) or a noun in the instrumental case (in Greek in the *dative*), derived from the same word-root as the personal verb. This kind of figurative turn of speech is used to emphasize and intensify the content expressed by the verb, for example: Ревнꙋ́ѧ* поревнова́хꙋ* по гдⷭ҇ѣ бѕ҃ѣ вседержи́тели (III Kings 19:14—"I have been very zealous for the Lord God Almighty"); Разоре́нїемꙋ* разори́ши* и̑ сокрꙋше́нїемꙋ* сокрꙋши́ши* ка̑пища ихꙋ (Ex. 23:24—"Thou shalt utterly overthrow them, and quite break down their images").

These expressions are copies of similar expressions in the Greek text of the Holy Scriptures. And in the Greek text they are a transmission of the Hebrew INFINITIVE ABSOLUTE[4]), for which reason these pleonastic expressions are mostly to be found in the books of the Old Testament, while in the New Testament they are for the most part found where the Old Testament is quoted, although examples [of such hebraicisms] do occur even without reference to the Old Testament text, for example: слꙋ́хомꙋ* оу̑слы́шите*, и̑ не и̑мате разꙋмѣ́ти: и̑ зрѧ́ще* оу̑́зрите*, и̑ не и̑мате ви́дѣти (Matth. 13:14, from Isaiah 6:9—"By hearing ye shall hear, and shall not understand; and seeing ye shall see, and shall not perceive"); Не запреще́нїемꙋ* ли запрети́хомꙋ* ва́мꙋ не оу̑чи́ти ѿ и̑мени сегꙋ (Acts 5:28—"Did we not straitly command you that ye should not teach in this name?"); see also Acts 7:34 and Heb. 6:14.

2) In the text of the Holy Scriptures there are also frequently pleonastic expressions that consist of a circumstantial participle (present or past) and a personal verb form (predicate), close to each other in meaning. These combinations are either from Hebrew or Greek idioms. The following combinations are the most common:

---

[4]) A Greek Grammar of the New Testament, by Robert W. Funk, §422.

ѿвѣщавъ глаго́ла, ѿвѣщà глаго́ла, речѐ глаго́ла, написа̀ глаго́ла, воста́въ ида̀, изы́де проходà and others like them: Піла́тъ же ѿвѣща* и́мъ, глаго́ла* (Mark 15:9—"But Pilate answered them, saying"); Она̀ же ѿвѣща́вши* глаго́ла* е҆мꙋ̀ (Mark 7:28—"And she answered and said unto him"); ѿвѣща́въ* и́мъ речѐ* (Luke 17:20—"he answered them and said"); воста́въ* ида̀ ко О҆ц҃ꙋ̀ моемꙋ̀ (Luke 15:18—"I will arise and go to my father"); изы́де* проходà* по ря́дꙋ галати́йскꙋю страну̀ и҆ фрꙋ́гію (Acts 18:23—"he departed, and went over all the country of Galatia and Phrygia"); е҆го́же взе́мши* жена̀ скры̀* въ са́тѣхъ тре́хъ мꙋкѝ (Matth. 13:33—"which a woman took, and hid in three measures of meal").

Similar pleonastic expressions may also consist of two conjugated verb forms, for example: ѿвѣща́ша и҆ рѣ́ша е҆мꙋ̀ (John 18:30—"They answered and said unto him"); и҆ свидѣ́тельствова и҆ речѐ (John 13:21—"and [he] testified, and said"); И҆са́їа же дерза́етъ и҆ глаго́летъ (Rom. 10:20—"But Esaias is very bold, and saith"); О҆нъ же ѿве́ржеса и҆ речѐ (John 18:25—"He denied [it], and said").

§148. Word Order in the Sentence.

The position of the subject, predicate, object and circumstance [adverbial modifiers] in the sentence. The sequence followed for the subject, predicate, object and circumstance in a sentence is, in general, much the same as in Russian. However, there can also be an order of words proper to the Greek language rather than to the Slavonic:

In sentences of the determinant type, the noun part of the predicate sometimes is put before the subject, for example: и҆ бг҃ъ бѣ̀ сло́во (John 1:1—"and the word was God"); from the viewpoint of Russian speech, the word бг҃ъ is taken for the subject, but in reality the subject is сло́во, while бг҃ъ is the noun part of a composite predicate. In the Greek text this kind of ambiguity is avoided because the subject is accompanied by the definite article, whereas the noun part of the predicate is not: καὶ Θεὸς ἦν ὁ λόγος. Likewise: Дх҃ъ [є́сть] бг҃ъ (John 4:24—"God is a Spirit"); бг҃ъ бо въ человѣ́цѣхъ, человѣ́къ бг҃ъ возда́анїемъ (Dec. 21, service for Metropolitan Peter of Kiev, Theotokion at Little Vespers—"For God is among men, God is a man by retribution").

Similarly, a second predicate accusative also sometimes precedes the accusative direct object, for example: и̂ Ѻ̂ц҃а̀ своего̀ глаго́лаше бг҃а, καὶ Πατέρα ἴδιον ἔλεγεν τὸν Θεόν (John 5:18—"[but] said also that God was his Father"); человѣ́къ быва́етъ бг҃ъ, да бг҃а а́да́ма содѣ́лаетъ (Vespers for March 24, Theotokion—"God becomes man, so as to make Adam divine"). When two accusatives are expressed by adjectives (or by participles), the predicate accusative is in the short form, which can be an indicator to eliminate ambiguity, for example: нареку̀ не лю́ди моа̂, лю́ди моа̂: и̂ невозлю́бленну́ю, возлю́бленъ* (Rom. 9:25—"I will call them my people, which were not my people; and her beloved, which was not beloved"). The following text from the Akathist to the Theotokos: Ра́ду́йса, любому́дрыа нему́дрыа ꙗ̂вла́ющаа: ра́ду́йса, хитрослове́сныа безслове́сныа ѡ̂блича́ющаа (9th Oikos—"Rejoice, thou that shewest philosophers to be fools: Rejoice, thou that constrainest the learned to silence") might be written more correctly thus: Ра́ду́йса, любому́дрыа нему́дры* ꙗ̂вла́ющаа: ра́ду́йса, хитрослове́сныа безслове́сны* ѡ̂блича́ющаа.

§149. The Position of the Attribute in a Sentence.

Attributive short adjectives usually stand before the modified noun in a sentence, but they can also stand after it, for example: Не мо́жетъ дре́во добро̀ плоды̀ ѕлы̀ твори́ти, ни дре́во ѕло̀ плоды̀ добры̀ твори́ти (Matth. 7:18—"A good tree cannot bring forth evil fruit, neither can a corrupt tree bring forth good fruit"); а́ще бо вни́детъ въ со́нмище ва́ше му́жъ, зла́тъ пе́рстень носа̀, въ ри́зѣ свѣ́тлѣ, вни́детъ же и̂ ни́щъ въ ху́дѣ ѡ̂де́ждѣ (James 2:2—"For if there come unto your assembly a man with a gold ring, in goodly apparel, and there come in also a poor man in vile raiment").

Attributive adjectives in the long form (as also participles) can stand either before or after their modified noun, for example: Вни́дите ѹ҆́зкими враты̀: ꙗ҆́кѡ простра́ннаѧ врата̀ и҆ широ́кїй пꙋ́ть вводѧ́й въ пагꙋбꙋ (Matth. 7:13—"Enter ye in at the strait gate: for wide is the gate, and broad is the way, that leadeth to destruction"); согрѣши́хъ преда́въ кро́вь непови́ннꙋю (Matth. 27:4—"I have sinned, [in that I have] betrayed innocent blood"); ка́мень жерно́вный (Mark 9:42—"a millstone"); мѡѷсе́й повелѣ́ кни́гꙋ распꙋ́стнꙋю написа́ти (Mark 10:4—"Moses suffered to write a bill of divorcement").

Possessive adjectives and pronouns (here belong possessive adjectives with the suffix -ск- as well), as a rule, follow the modified noun (perhaps this shows the influence of Greek, where possession is shown by a genitive following the modified noun), for example: Те́ща же сі́мѡнова* лежа́ше ѻ҆гне́мъ жего́ма (Mark 1:30—"But Simon's wife's mother lay sick of a fever"); во дни̑ нѡ́евы* (Matth. 24:37—"But as the days of Noe were"); сы́на подꙗре́мнича* (Matth. 21:5—"[upon] the colt of-her-that-is-under-the-yoke [a colt the foal of an ass]"); къ горѣ̀ є҆леѡ́нстѣй* (Matth. 21:1—"unto the mount of Olives"); ѻ҆́чи на́ши* (Matth. 20:33—"[that] our eyes [may be opened]); ѹ҆срамѧ́тсѧ сн҃а моегѡ̀ (Matth. 21:37—"They will reverence my son").

The possessive pronoun, however, is also met with before the modified noun: сїѐ твори́те въ моѐ* воспомина́нїе (Luke 22:19—"Do this in remembrance of me"); Бра́тїе, бл҃говоле́нїе ѹ҆́бѡ моегѡ̀* се́рдца (Rom. 10:1—"Brethren, my heart's desire..."); слы́шасте бо моѐ* житїѐ (Gal. 1:13 —"For ye have heard of my way of life").

When there are two attributive long adjectives (or participles), the modified word is often placed between them: Кто̀ ѹ҆́бо є҆́сть вѣ́рный ра́бъ и҆ мꙋ́дрый (Luke 12:42—"Who then is that faithful and wise steward"); лꙋка́вый ра́бе и҆ лѣни́вый (Matth. 25:26—"Thou wicked and slothful servant").

Two or more attributive adjectives or participles, standing after the modified noun, frequently carry the main force of the logical accent, i.e. their meaning is somewhat emphatic: до́брѣ, ра́бе бла́гíй и вѣ́рный (Matth. 25:21—"Well done, thou good and faithful servant"); ра́дꙋется ра́достію неизглаго́ланною и препросла́вленною (I Peter 1:8—"ye rejoice with joy unspeakable and full of glory"); пре́жде да́же не прíйти дню́ гд҃ню велíкомꙋ и просвѣще́нномꙋ (Acts 2:20—"before that great and notable day of the Lord come"); въ наслѣ́дïе нетлѣ́нно и нескве́рно и неꙋвада́емо (I Peter 1:4—"To an inheritance incorruptible, and undefiled, and that fadeth not away").

In some cases individual attributes in agreement with their modified noun and standing after it, may bear the logical accent, for example: і҆и҃се, си́ло непобѣдíмаѧ: і҆и҃се, ми́лости безконе́чнаѧ. і҆и҃се, красото̀ пресвѣ́тлаѧ: і҆и҃се, любы̀ неизрече́ннаѧ (Akathist [to the Sweetest Jesus], Oikos 3— "Jesus, Invincible Power! Jesus, Infinite Mercy! Jesus, Radiant Beauty! Jesus, Unspeakable Love!").

Two or more adjectives or participles in the long form, following the modified noun, may show an added characteristic; in such cases they are usually set off by a comma: та́кѡ изво́ли внíти и въ до́мъ смире́нныѧ моеѧ̀ дꙋшѝ, прокаже́нныѧ* и грѣ́шныѧ* (2nd Prayer Before Communion —"so consent also to enter the house of my humble soul which is leprous and sinful"); си́це ꙋмилосе́рдисѧ и ѡ мнѣ̀ грѣ́шнемъ, приходѧ́щемъ и прикаса́ющемтисѧ (ibid., —"so also be compassionate with me, a sinner, as I approach and touch Thee"); бл҃гознамени́тыѧ трꙋбы̀ проповѣ́данïа, стра́шныѧ* и достослы́шанныѧ* (Vespers for Jan. 30, at 'Lord I have cried'— "those well-sounding trumpets of preaching, fearsome and meet to be heard").

§150. *Uncoördinated* attributes, expressed by the genitive case, usually follow the modified noun: вре́мѧ плодѡ́въ (Matthew 21:34—"the time of the fruit"); во дн҃и написа́нïа (Acts 5:37—"in the days of the taxing").

An uncoördinated attribute (in the genitive case), accompanied by a coördinate attribute [one agreeing in gender, number and case], usually precedes the modified noun: небе́сныхъ ко́ннствъ архїстрати́зи (Tropar for Monday—"Ye Rulers of the Heavenly Host").

However, various combinations are possible of uncoördinated attributes (in the genitive) and modified nouns, especially in Sticheras, for example: це́рквє* вели́кая забра́ла: заключе́ннꙋю сло́ва* две́рь: доброт́ѡ́чныя присножи́вꙋ́тныя дꙋ́ха* па́стырїе и оу́чи́телїе (Jan. 30, at the Praises— "those great towers of the Church: the sealed Door of the Word: free-flowing pastors and teachers, forever reviving the spirit"); земнꙋю тро́ицꙋ ст́ыхъ їера́рхѡвъ* да восхва́лимъ (Jan. 30, at the Litiya—"Let us praise the earthly trinity of holy hierarchs").

Uncoördinated attributes, expressed by oblique cases with a preposition and и́же, ꙗ́же, є́же, may be either before or after the modified noun, for example: Ста́рцы и́же въ ва́съ* молю́ (I Peter 5:1—"The elders which are among you I exhort"); паси́те є́же въ ва́съ* ста́до б́жїе (I Peter 5:2— "Feed the flock of God which is among you").

Uncoördinated attributes with и́же, ꙗ́же, є́же, placed after the modified noun, are usually set apart by a comma (although not always), but those that precede the noun are not set apart, for example: но и во вся́ко ме́сто ве́ра ва́ша, ꙗ́же къ бѓꙋ*, и́зыде (I Thess. 1:8—"but also in every place your faith to God-ward is spread abroad"); but also: ꙗ́кѡ сло́во на́ше є́же къ ва́мъ* не бы́сть є́й и ни (II Cor. 1:18—"[that] our word toward you was not yea and nay"); По є́же во а́дъ* соше́ствїи*, и є́же и́з ме́ртвыхъ* воскресе́нїи (Octoechos, 10th Matins Stichera—"After the descent into hell and the resurrection from the dead…")

Use of the Negations «не» and «ни».
§151. *The particle* не.

1) The negative particle не, as in Russian, can be placed with any part of the sentence, although for the most part it is used with the predicate, for example: и и́же не собира́етъ со мно́ю, расточа́етъ (Matth. 12:30—"and he that gathereth not with me scattereth abroad"); Не се́й ли є́сть текто́новъ сы́нъ; не ма́ти ли є̓гѡ̀ нарица́етса марі́амь; (Matth. 13:55—"Is not this the carpenter's son? is not his mother called Mary [Mariam]?").

2) The particle не may be used in sentences with a limiting sense, for example: Се́й не и̓зго́нитъ бѣ́сы, то́кмѡ ѡ̓ вельзеву́лѣ кна́зѣ бѣсо́встѣмъ (Matth. 12:24—"This [fellow] doth not cast out devils, but by Beelzebub the prince of devils"); Та́ть не прихо́дитъ, ра́звѣ да оу̓кра́детъ и̓ оу̓бі́етъ и̓ погу́битъ (John 10:10—"The thief cometh not, but for to steal, and to kill, and to destroy").

3) The particle не may be part of the conjunctive combination да не [когда̀] in subordinate clauses of cause or purpose with negation, e.g. да не когда̀ восторга́юще пле́велы, восто́ргнете ку́пнѡ съ ни́ми [и̓] пшени́цу (Matth. 13:29—"lest while ye gather up the tares, ye root up also the wheat with them"); да не когда̀ оу̓сну̀ въ сме́рть, да не когда̀ рече́тъ вра́гъ мо́й... (Evening Prayers —"lest I ever fall asleep unto death, lest mine enemy ever say..."); да не кто̀ поплы́въ, и̓збѣ́гнетъ (Acts 27:42—"lest any of them should swim out, and escape").

4) In the case of some verbs with a negative meaning (запрети́ти, to forbid; возбрани́ти, to prohibit, forbid) an infinitive dependant upon them (as in the Greek text) is encountered with the negation не, and in this case the не does not change the negative sense, for example: Не запреще́нїемъ ли запрети́хомъ ва́мъ не оу̓чи́ти ѡ̓ и́мени се́мъ (Acts 5:28—"Did we not straitly command you that ye should not teach in this name?" [*i.e.* 'Did we not forbid you to teach...']); likewise cf. Acts 5:40; Кто̀ ва́мъ возбранѝ не покора́тиса

и́стиннⷦ (Gal. 5:7—"who did hinder you that ye should not obey the truth?"—*i.e.* 'who prevented you from obeying the truth"); є҆два̀ оу҆ста́кнста наро́ды не жре́ти и҆́ма (Acts 14:18—"scarce restrained they the people, that they had not done sacrifice unto them"— *i.e.* 'lest they do sacrifice', 'from doing sacrifice').

5) To indicate a limit of action, the combination не ктомꙋ̀ (=no more, no longer) is used: не вза́лчꙋтъ ктомꙋ̀, нижѐ вжа́ждꙋтъ (Rev. 7:16—"They shall hunger no more, neither thirst any more"); и҆ не ктомꙋ̀ ѡ҆ставля́ете є҆го̀ что̀ твори́ти (Mark 7:12—"And ye suffer him no more to do ought"); see also the Sunday Kondak of the 7th Tone.

6) With two verbs (or a circumstantial participle + a verb with a person-ending), having a mutual relationship of cause or result, there may be only one negation: да не вѣ́ровавше* спасꙋ́тса* (Luke 8:12—"lest they should believe and be saved"); нѣ́сть бо та́йно, є҆́же не ꙗ҆вле́но бꙋ́детъ: нижѐ оу҆та́ено, є҆́же не позна́етса*, и҆ въ ꙗ҆вле́нїе прїи́детъ* (Luke 8:17—"For nothing is secret, that shall not be made manifest; neither any thing hid, that shall not be known and come abroad"); а҆́ще не ѡ҆брати́теса*, и҆ бꙋ́дете* ꙗ҆́кѡ дѣ́ти, не вни́дете въ ца́рство нбⷭ҇ное (Matth. 18:3—"Except ye be converted, and become as little children, ye shall not enter into the kingdom of heaven").

7) A double negation gives an affirmative meaning, for example: не возмо́жно є҆́сть не прїитѝ соблазнѡ́мъ (Luke 17:1—"It is impossible but that offences will come", *i.e.* *they will come)*; и҆ ꙗ҆́коже не не оу҆досто́йла є҆сѝ вни́ти (Prayer before Communion—"and as Thou didst not find unworthy to enter"), *i .e.* *Thou didst find worthy;* никто́же да не вѣ́рꙋетъ (Octoechos, Suday Exaposteilarion 3—"Let no man not believe"), that is, *let every man believe.* (Cf. §152, 3).

8) The particle не sometimes is not put next to the word to which it relates, for example: и҆ не ꙗ҆́сти и҆́мъ бѣ̀ когда̀ (Mark 6:31—"and the had no leisure so much as to eat"), in place of the

expected й ꙗ́сти й́мъ не бѣ̀ когда̀. а҆́ще не сі́и пребꙋ́дꙋтъ (Acts 27:31—"Except these abide [in the ship]") instead of а҆́ще сі́и не пребꙋ́дꙋтъ.

§152. *The particle* ни.

The basic meaning of the particle ни is that of a negatively-joining conjunction, and, depending on the order of sequence, it can mean *"neither"* or *"nor"*:

1) If the predicate with the negation не precedes, the particle ни has the meaning of *"neither"*, *"neither/nor"*, for example: Не вреди́те ни зе́млѝ, ни мо́ра, ни дре́весъ (Rev. 7:3—"Hurt not the earth, neither the sea, nor the trees"); before the first enumerated item, the particle ни may be omitted: Не стѧжи́те зла́та, ни сребра̀, ни мѣ́ди при поѧсѣ́хъ ва́шихъ, ни пи́ры въ пꙋ́ть, ни двою̀ ри́зꙋ, ни сапѡ́гъ, ни же́злъ (Matth. 10:9-10—"Provide neither gold, nor silver, nor nor brass in your purses, nor script for your journey, neither two coats, neither shoes, nor yet staves").

2) If, however, the predicate (or the conjugated part of a composite predicate) follows the word (or words) with the particle ни, then the negation не in such cases is *absent*, for example: и҆́же ни ви́дѣти мо́гꙋтъ, ни слы́шати, ни ходи́ти, cf. in the Russian: *которые не могутъ ни видѣть, ни слышать, ни ходить* (Rev. 9:20—"which can neither see, nor hear, nor walk"); ꙗ́кѡни на зако́нъ і҆ꙋде́йскїй, ни на це́рковь, ни на ке́сарѧ что̀ согрѣши́хъ (Acts 25:8—"[that] neither against the law of the Jews, neither against the temple, nor yet against Cæsar, have I offended any thing at all"), but if the predicate were moved forward, then the particle не would have to be inserted: «ꙗ́кѡ не согрѣши́хъ что̀ (*anything*) ни на зако́нъ і҆ꙋде́йскїй, ни на це́рковь, ни на ке́сарѧ». Ꙗ́кѡ ни сме́рть, ни живо́тъ, ни а҆́гг҃ли, ни нача́ла, нижѐ си́лы, ни настоѧ́щаѧ, ни грѧдꙋ́щаѧ, ни высота̀, ни глꙋбина̀, ни и҆́на тва́рь ка́ѧ возмо́жетъ на́съ разлꙋчи́ти ѿ любвѐ бж҃їѧ (Rom. 8:38-39—"For [I am persuaded that] neither death, nor life, nor angels, nor principalities, nor

powers, nor things present, nor things to come; nor height, nor depth, nor any other creature, shall be able to separate us from the love of God"), but — if the conjugated part of the composite predicate is before the enumeration: ꙗ́кѡ не возмо́жетъ ни сме́рть, ни живо́тъ, ни а́гг҃ли... ни и́на ка́ѧ тва́рь на́съ разлꙋчи́ти... Such a construction, when the predicate comes *after* the word with the particle ни, has the sense *"and not"*. One might note also the following case of such usage:

A single ни may be used with nouns, pronouns or adverbs, for example: ни во і҆и҃ли толи́ки вѣ́ры ѡ҆брѣто́хъ, compare with the Russian: и* въ Израилѣ не* нашелъ я такой вѣры (Matth. 8:10 —"I have not found so great faith, no, not in Israel"); и҆ ни тѣ́ма вѣ́ры ꙗ́ша, Russ.: но и* имъ не* повѣрили (Mark 16:13—"neither believed they them"); и҆ ни та́кѡ ра́вно бѣ̀ свидѣ́тельство и́хъ, Russ.: Но и* такое свидѣтельство ихъ не* было достаточно (Mark 14:59—"But neither so did their witness agree together").

But if a single ни is preceded by the predicate, then the negation by не is used (as indicated in point 1), and in that case ни has a somewhat emphatic meaning — *"even"*, *"even so much as"*, for example: не хотѧ́ше ни о҆́чїю возвестѝ (Luke 18:13—"would not lift up so much as his eyes"); ꙗ́кѡ не мощѝ и́мъ ни хлѣ́ба ꙗ́сти (Mark 3:20—"so that they could not so much as eat bread"); ꙗ́кѡ ктомꙋ̀ не вмѣща́тисѧ ни при две́рехъ (Mark 2:2—"insomuch that there was no room to receive them, no, not so much as about the door").

The double ни ("neither... nor...") is used with the same parts of speech as the single: Ни со́лнцꙋ же, ни ѕвѣзда́мъ ꙗ́вльшымсѧ на мно́ги дни̑ (Acts 27:20—"And when neither sun nor stars in many days appeared"); ни се́й согрѣшѝ, ни роди́тела е҆гѡ̀ (John 9:2—"Neither hath this man sinned, nor his parents"); О҆ба́че ни мꙋ́жъ без женьі̀, ни жена̀ без мꙋ́жа (I Cor. 11:11— "Nevertheless neither is the man without the woman, neither the woman without the man [in the Lord]"); it can also be used with verb forms: е҆гда̀ бо и҆з̀ ме́ртвыхъ воскре́снꙋтъ, ни же́нѧтсѧ, ни посага́ютъ (Mark 12:25—"For when they shall rise from the dead, they neither marry, nor are given in marriage"); Прїи́де бо і҆ѡа́ннъ не ꙗ҆ды́й, ни пїѧ́й (Matth. 11:18—"For John came neither eating nor drinking"), cf. ни хлѣ́ба ꙗ҆ды́й, ни ни вїна̀ пїѧ̀ (Luke 7:34—"neither eating bread nor drinking wine"); cf. such Russian expressions as "*ни тотъ, ни этотъ*", "*ни дать, ни взять*".

3) Negative pronouns and adverbs: никто́же [no one], ничто́же [nothing], нікі́й же, ни кото́рый [none], николи́же, никогда́же [never], нигдѣ́же [nowhere, in no place], ника́може [nowhere, *to* no place], and the numeral ни є҆ди́нъ [же] (not one, not a single...) have a similar use, i.e. if the predicate follows *after* them, then the negation не is eliminated, for example: и҆ никомꙋ́же ничто́же рѣ́ша: боѧ́хꙋбосѧ (Mark 16:8—"and they said nothing to anyone, for they were afraid"); нікі́й же ра́бъ мо́жетъ двѣма̀ господи́нома рабо́тати (Luke 16:13—"no servant can serve two masters"); ни кото́рый прⷪ҇ро́къ прїѧ́тенъ є҆́сть во Ѻ҆те́чествѣ свое́мъ (Luke 4:24—"No prophet is accepted in his own country"); и҆ мнѣ̀ николи́же да́лъ є҆сѝ козлѧ́те (Luke 15:29—"and yet thou never gavest me a kid"); ни гла́са є҆гѡ̀ нигдѣ́же слы́шасте, ни видѣ́нїѧ є҆гѡ̀ ви́дѣсте (John 5:37—"Ye have neither heard his voice at any time, nor seen his shape"); се́й же ни є҆ди́нагѡ ѕла̀ сотворѝ (Luke 23:41—"but this man hath done nothing amiss"); but if the predicate precedes, then the negative particle не is used, for example: Не могꙋ̀ а҆́зъ ѿ себѐ твори́ти ничесо́же (John 5:30—"I can of mine own self do nothing"); Ѹ҆таи́тисѧ бо є҆мꙋ̀ ѿ си́хъ не вѣ́рꙋю ничесомꙋ́же (Acts 26:26—"For I am persuaded that none of these things are hid from him"); въ не́мже не бѣ̀ никто́же никогда́же положе́нъ (Luke 23:53—"wherein never before man was laid"); и҆ не восхи́титъ и҆̀хъ никто́же ѿ рꙋкѝ моеѧ̀ (John 10:28—"neither shall any man pluck them out of my hand"); but: и҆ никто́же мо́жетъ восхи́тити и҆̀хъ ѿ

рꙋ́ки ѻ҆ц҃а̀ моегѡ̀ (John 10:29—"and no man is able to pluck them out of my Father's hand"); не и҆сходѧ́лъ ра́бъ тво́й никáможе (IV Kings 5:25—"Thy servant went no whither"); зна́менїѧ не сотворѝ ни є҆ди́нагѡ (John 10:41—"[John] did no miracle"); nevertheless sometimes, as an exception, the negative particle не may be encountered even with a predicate that comes after the above mentioned words, for example: и҆ ничесѡ́же є҆мꙋ̀ не глаго́лютъ (John 7:26—"and they say nothing unto him"); see also John 16:29.

4) With negation by не, the combination нижѐ has the sense of "not even"; the repeated ни often concludes with it, for example: Не коснѝсѧ, нижѐ вкꙋсѝ, нижѐ ѡ҆сѧжѝ (Col. 2:21—"Touch not; taste not; handle not"); Не пререче́тъ, ни возопїе́тъ, нижѐ оу҆слы́шитъ кто̀ на распꙋ́тїахъ гла́са є҆гѡ̀ (Matth. 12:19—"He shall not strive, nor cry; neither shall any man hear his voice in the streets").

5) The particle ни is used also as the negative reply, "No", for example: ни: да не когда̀ восторга́юще пле́велы... (Matth. 13:29—"Nay; lest while ye gather up the tares [ye root up also...].

§153. Address.

Address is what we call a word or a combination of words indicating a person (or a thing) to whom speech is addressed.

Most often, address is expressed by a noun in the vocative case, for example: оу҆чи́телю, гдѣ̀ живе́ши; (John 1:38—"Master, where dwellest thou?").

Address can also be expressed by substantivized adjectives and participles. The short forms of adjectives and passive participles show address in the vocative case with a special form (see §171, 6). The long forms of adjectives and participles (both passive and active) show address by means of a form identical with the nominative, for example: безꙋ́мне, въ сїю̀ но́щь дꙋ́шꙋ твою̀ и҆стѧ́жꙋтъ ѿ тебѐ (Luke 12:20—"Thou fool, this night thy soul shall be required of thee"); Возлю́бленнїи, молю̀ я̑́кѡ пришéльцєвъ и̑ стрáнникѡвъ (I Peter 2:11—"Dearly beloved, I beseech you as strangers and pilgrims").

Address may be *unextended*, if it is expressed by a single word, or *extended*, if expressed by a combination of words. The makeup of an extended address can be quite varied, for example: Ѽ ро́де невѣ́рный и̑ развращéнный, доко́лѣ бꙋ́дꙋ съ вáми; (Matth. 17:17—"O faithless and perverse generation, how long shall I be with you?"); Ѽ и̑спо́лненне вса́кїѧ льсти и̑ вса́кїѧ ѕло́бы, сы́не дїáволь, врáже вса́кїѧ прáвды, не престáнеши ли развращáѧ пꙋ́ти гⷣни прáвыѧ; (Acts 13:10—"O full of all subtilty and all mischief, thou child of the devil, thou enemy of all righteousness, wilt thou not cease to pervert the right ways of the Lord?").

An address is often extended by a subordinate clause, for example: Иже ѡ̑ всѣ́хъ благі́й гⷣн, слáва тебѣ̀ (Tropar of Holy Thursday—"O Lord, Who art good towards all, glory to Thee"); Стрáстїю твоéю, хрⷵтѐ, ѡ̑мрачи́вый со́лнце, и̑ свѣ́томъ твоегѡ̀ воскрⷵнїѧ, просвѣти́вый всѧ́чєскаѧ, прїими́ нáшꙋ вечéрнюю пѣ́снь, чл҃вѣколю́бче (Octoechos, Tone , Saturday Great Vespers at the Aposticha [Stichovna]—"By Thy passion, O Christ, Thou hast darkened the sun, and by the light of Thy Resurrection, Thou hast given all things light; accept our evening hymn, O Thou Who lovest mankind"). In most cases a subordinate clause is itself the address, since the 2nd-person pronoun, to which the subordinate clause refers, is in such cases omitted, e.g.: [Ты̀] Я̑́же свѣ́тъ невечéрнїй рождшáѧ, дꙋ́шꙋ мою̀ ѡ̑слѣ́пшꙋю просвѣти́ (7th Morning Prayer—"O thou who barest the Unwaning Light, enlighten my blinded soul"); Иже богáтый въ ми́лости, во́лею погрéблсѧ є̑сѝ (Octoechos, T. 2, Sunday at the 8th Ode—"Thou Who art rich in mercy, wast of Thine own will buried"); [Ты̀] На дрéвѣ распны́йсѧ, и̑ и̑з мéртвыхъ воскрéсый, и̑ сы́й въ нѣ́дрѣхъ Ѻ̑́чихъ, ѡ̑чи́сти грѣхѝ нáша (Saturday at Vespers,

T. 2, at "Lord I have cried"—"O Thou Who wast crucified on the tree, and didst rise from the dead, and art [forever] in the bosom of the Father, cleanse our sins").

The interjection ѽ is often used in direct address to reinforce the strength of a vocative, for example: ѽ всепѣ́таѧ ма́ти (Akathist—"O All-Praised Mother").

———

The Use of Tenses.
§154. The Present Tense.

In Church Slavonic, the present tense forms have for the main part a use similar to that in Russian. One might note the following meanings of present tense forms:

1) The forms of the present tense indicate an action that coincides with the time of speaking, for example: а́зъ требу́ю* тобо́ю крести́тисѧ, и҆ ты̀ ли грѧде́ши* ко мнѣ̀ (Matth. 3:14—"I have need to be baptized of thee, and comest thou to me?").

2) The present tense may be used for a pictorial description of past time. Such a present tense is known as the *historical* (or *descriptive*) present, for example: Тогда̀ прихо́дитъ* і҆и́съ ѿ галїле́и на і҆ѻрда́нъ ко і҆ѡа́нну кр̑ти́тисѧ ѿ негѡ̀ (Matth. 3:13—"Then cometh Jesus from Galilee to Jordan unto John, to be baptized of him").

3) The present tense may be used to express actions that are a constant characteristic of the given item or person, for example: И҆спыта́й и҆ ви́ждь, ꙗ҆́кѡ прро́къ ѿ галїле́и не прихо́дитъ* (John 7:52—"Search, and see, that out of Galilee ariseth no prophet"); Всѧ̑ ѹ҆́бо, е҆ли̑ка а҆́ще реку́тъ ва́мъ (фарисеи) блюстѝ, соблюда́йте и҆ твори́те: по дѣлѡ́мъ же и҆́хъ не твори́те: глаго́лютъ* бо, и҆ не творѧ́тъ*. Свѧзу́ютъ* бо бремена̀ тѧ̑жка и҆ бѣ́днѣ носи̑ма, и҆ возлага́ютъ* на плеща̀ человѣ́ческа: пе́рстомъ же свои́мъ не хотѧ́тъ* дви́гнути и҆́хъ (Matth. 23:3-4—"All therefore whatsoever they [*the Pharisees*] bid

you observe, that observe and do; but do not ye after their works: for they say, and do not. For they bind heavy burdens and grievous to be borne, and lay them on men's shoulders; but they themselves will not move them with one of their fingers").

4) Action in the immediate future may be expressed by means of the present tense forms of verbs of motion (и́дꙋ, гра́дꙋ), for example: воста́въ и́дꙋ* ко Ѻ҆цꙋ̀ моемꙋ̀ (Luke 15:18—"I will arise and go to my father"); и҆ди́ же ко бра́тїи мое́й, и҆ рцы̀ и҆̀мъ: восхождꙋ̀* ко Ѻ҆цꙋ̀ моемꙋ̀ и҆ Ѻ҆цꙋ̀ ва́шемꙋ (John 20:17—"but go to my brethren, and say unto them, I ascend unto my Father, and your Father"); є҆́й, гра́дꙋ* ско́рѡ (Rev. 22:20—"Yea, I come quickly").

5) In Church Slavonic, present forms of certain verbs (not only verbs of motion) are encountered with a future meaning, determined by the context (see §84), for example: и҆̀мже ѿпꙋститѐ грѣхѝ, ѿпꙋ́стѧтсѧ и҆̀мъ: и҆ и҆̀мже держитѐ*, держа́тсѧ* (John 20:23—"Whose soever sins ye remit, they are remitted unto them; and whose soever sins ye retain, they are retained").

§155. The Future Tense.

The forms of the simple future tense are used to indicate future time in the perfective aspect, for example: и҆̀же сотвори́тъ и҆ наꙋчи́тъ, се́й ве́лїй нарече́тсѧ въ ца́рствїи небе́снѣмъ (Matthew 5:19 —"whosoever shall do and teach them, the same shall be called great in the kingdom of heaven").

The forms of the compound future tense are used to signify future time in the imperfective aspect, and here the copula [connecting verb] does not entirely lose its lexical significance, so that besides showing action in the future it also adds its own additional meaning: и҆ма́мъ — can add a sense of obligation or need: и҆́мать* пострада́ти* ѿ ни́хъ (Matth. 17:12—"[the Son of Man] shall also suffer of them"); и҆́же а҆́ще не прїи́метъ цр҃твїѧ бж҃їѧ, ꙗ҆́кѡ Ѻ҆троча̀, не и҆́мать* вни́ти* въ нѐ (Luke 18:17—"Whosoever shall not receive

the kingdom of God as a little child shall in no wise enter therein");
є҆гда̀ и҆мᲂу҆тъ* всѧ̑ сїѧ̑ сконча́тисѧ* (Mark 13:4—"[Tell us] when all
these things shall be fulfilled"); but note the following example: и҆
и҆мѣ́ти* и҆маши* сокро́вище на нб҃есѝ (Matth. 19:21—"and thou
shalt have treasure in heaven"), where и҆маши approximates a "pure"
copula [i.e. a mere tense indicator]. The connecting verb хощᲂу҆
brings with it nuances of desire, especially the manifestation of will,
fate, providence or the elements: мᲂу҆жїе, ви́ждᲂу҆, га́кѡ съ
досажде́нїемъ и҆ мно́гою тщето́ю, не то́кмѡ бре́мене и҆ кораблѧ̀, но
и҆ дᲂу҆шъ на́шихъ хо́щетъ* бы́ти* пла́ванїе (Acts 27:10—"Men, I
perceive that this sailing will be with hurt and much damage, not
only of the cargo and ship, but also of our lives"); что̀ оу҆̀бо сїѐ
хо́щетъ бы́ти (Acts 2:12—"What meaneth this?"). The copula
на́чнетъ, besides indicating the start of a future action, can also show
the inescapability or obligatory quality of an action: и҆ тогда̀
на́чнеши* со стыдо́мъ послѣ́днее мѣ́сто держа́ти* (Luke 14:9—"and
[lest] thou begin with shame to take the lowest room"), i.e. one "will
have" to be in the lowest place.

Sometimes the verb бᲂу҆ди is also to be met with as a copula,
used with infinitives, for example: и҆ а҆́ще бᲂу҆детъ* ѡ҆брѣстѝ* ю҆̀
(Matthew 18:12—"and if so be that he find it"), in the Russian
version: и если случится найти ее; госпо́дствовати бᲂу҆детъ рᲂу҆ка̀
моѧ̀ (Psalter, 1st Old Testament Canticle, Song of Moses [Exodus
15:9]—"my hand shall have dominion").

§156. The Aorist.

The aorist expresses a simple action which preceded the
moment of narration, without any characterization of the action in
terms of duration or lack of duration, or distance in time.

The aorist may be formed from verbs of either the perfective
or imperfective aspect, and for this reason the aorist of the perfective
aspect indicates the limits of duration: that is, the completed state of

the action; however, this is a quality not of the aorist, but of the aspect of the verb (и҆ти́ — и҆до́хъ, прїити́ — прїидо́хъ ["I was going" *vs.* "I arrived/I have come"]).

The function of the aorist is to tell a story. The narrator uses the aorist to express the main actions of the case or event. Inherent is the aorist is the vivid sense of what has happened, reflecting the direct interest of the narrator.

Входѧ́щꙋ же є҆мꙋ̀ въ нѣ́кꙋю ве́сь, срѣто́ша (1) є҆го̀ де́сѧть прокаже́нныхъ мꙋже́й и҆̀же ста́ша (2) и҆здале́ча: И҆ ті́и вознесо́ша (3) гла́съ, глаго́люще: і҆и҃се наста́вниче, поми́лꙋй ны̀. И҆ ви́дѣвъ речѐ (4) и҆̀мъ: ше́дше покажи́тесѧ свѧще́нникѡмъ: и҆ бы́сть (5) и҆дꙋ́щымъ и҆̀мъ ѡ҆чи́стишасѧ (6). (Luke 17:12-14—"And as he entered into a certan village, there met him ten men that were lepers, which stood afar off: And they lifted up their voices, and said: Jesus, Master, have mercy on us. And when he saw them, he said unto them, Go shew yourselves unto the priests. And it came to pass, that, as they went, they were cleansed").

The chain of the main events of this incident are expressed in the aorists numbered 1, 2, 3, 4, 5, 6.

§157. The Imperfect (Past Continuous).

The imperfect expresses an action that is correlative to another main action (or fact), usually expressed by an aorist, or sometimes by a predicate participle.

The aorist tells a story, while the imperfect, wedged in as it were, adds to the main action another, additional action, one that clarifies or accompanies the main action.

The imperfect may not always be relative to a specific action in the incident described; it may express an action related to the general circumstances of the incident or event, and its relationship is then viewed only in context; in such a case, for convenience, one might add "at that time".

An example of the combined use of the aorist and the imperfect:

Ѿ оу҆слы́ша (1) ца́рь и҆рѡдъ: [ꙗ҆вѣ̀ бо бы́сть и҆́ма е҆гѡ̀] и҆ глаго́лаше, (2) ꙗ҆кѡ і҆ѡа́ннъ кр҃ти́тель ѿ ме́ртвыхъ воста̀, и҆ сегѡ̀ ра́ди си́лы дѣ́ютсѧ ѡ҆ не́мъ. И҆ни́и глаго́лахꙋ, (3) ꙗ҆кѡ и҆лїа̀ е҆́сть: и҆ни́и же глаго́лахꙋ, (4) ꙗ҆кѡ прⷬ҇о́къ, и҆ли́ ꙗ҆кѡ е҆ди́нъ ѿ прⷬ҇о́къ. Слы́шавъ же и҆рѡдъ речѐ (5), ꙗ҆кѡ, е҆го́же а҆́зъ оу҆сѣкнꙋ́хъ і҆ѡа́нна, то́й е҆́сть: то́й бо воста̀ ѿ ме́ртвыхъ. То́й бо и҆рѡдъ посла́въ, ꙗ҆́тъ (6) і҆ѡа́нна, и҆ свѧза̀ (7) е҆го̀ въ темни́цѣ, и҆рѡдїа́ды ра́ди жены̀ фїли́ппа бра́та своегѡ̀, ꙗ҆кѡ ѡ҆жени́сѧ (8) е҆́ю. Глаго́лаше (9) бо і҆ѡа́ннъ и҆рѡдови: не досто́итъ тебѣ̀ и҆мѣ́ти женꙋ̀ [фїли́ппа] бра́та твоегѡ̀. И҆рѡді́а же гнѣ́вашесѧ (10) на него̀, и҆ хотѧ́ше (11) е҆го̀ оу҆би́ти: и҆ не можа́ше (12). И҆рѡдъ бо боѧ́шесѧ (13) і҆ѡа́нна, вѣ́дый е҆го̀ мꙋ́жа пра́ведна и҆ ст҃а, и҆ соблюда́ше (14) е҆го̀: и҆ послꙋ́шавъ е҆го̀, мнѡ́га творѧ́ше (15), и҆ въ сла́дость е҆гѡ̀ послꙋ́шаше (16). (Mark 6:14-20 —"And king Herod heard of him (for his name was spread abroad), and he said, That John the Baptist was risen from the dead, and therefore mighty works do shew forth themselves in him. Others said, That it is Elias, and others said, That it is a prophet, or as one of the prophets. But when Herod heard thereof, he said, It is John whom I beheaded: he is risen from the dead. For Herod himself had sent forth and laid hold upon John, and bound him in prison for Herodias' sake, his brother Philip's wife: for he had married her. For John had said unto Herod, It is not lawful for thee to have thy brother's wife. Therefore Herodias had a quarrel against him, and would have killed him, but she could not: For Herod feared John, knowing that he was a just man and an holy, and observed him; and when he heard him, he did many things, and heard him gladly").

The aorists 1, 5, 6, 7, 8 present an outline of the incident's main actions. Глаго́лаше (2) corresponds to оу҆слы́ша (2): the aorist 1 in the perfective aspect shows a completed action; the imperfect 2 reveals the result of the aorist's action. The imperfects 3 and 4 add secondary information and are correlative to the general circumstances of this incident, that is, the report of the works of the Saviour. Imperfects 10, 11, 12, 13, 14, 15 and 16 relate to the aorists ѧ҃тъ (6) and сказа̀ (7) and explain the reasons why St. John the Baptist was confined to prison.

Correlation almost always coincides with simultaneity [events happening at the same time]. One might note the following cases of the use of the imperfect:

1) An accompanying action:

По си́хъ и́де і҃нсъ на о҃нъ по́лъ мо́рѧ галїле́н тїверіа́дска: А по не́мъ и́дѧше наро́дъ мно́гъ (John 6:1-2—"After these things Jesus went over the sea of Galilee, which is the sea of Tiberias. And a great multitude followed him").

The imperfect и́дѧше is correlative to и́де.

2) Independant action of the imperfect:

И҆до́ста же па́ки къ себѣ̀ оу҆чеnnка̀. Марі́а же стоѧ́ше оу҆ гро́ба внѣ̀ пла́чꙋщи (John 20: 10-11 —"Then the disciples went away again unto their own home. But Mary stood without at the sepulchre weeping").

The imperfect стоѧ́ше is correlative to и҆до́ста, i.e. at the time that the Apostles went away, Mary stood (was remaining) at the sepulchre.

Ма́рѳа оу҆́бо е҆гда̀ оу҆слы́ша, ꙗ҆кw і҃нсъ грѧде́тъ, срѣ́те е҆го̀: марі́а же до́ма сѣдѧ́ше (John 11:20 —"Then Martha, as soon as she heard that Jesus was coming, went and met him: but Mary sat still in the house").

The imperfect сѣдѧ́ше is correlative to the main action, expressed by the aorist срѣ́те.

3) The action of the imperfect as a result. It follows an aorist of the perfective aspect and reveals the result of the aorist's action:

И҆ а҆бїе прозрѣ̀ и҆ вслѣ́дъ е҆гẁ и҆дѧ́ше, сла́вѧ бг҃а (Luke 18:43—"And immediately he received his sight, and followed him, glorifying God"); По си́хъ же прїи́де і҃нсъ и҆ оу҆ченицы̀ е҆гẁ въ жидо́вскꙋ́ю зе́млю: и̑ тꙋ̑ жива́ше съ ни́ми и̑ креста́ше (John 3:22—"After these things came Jesus and his disciples into the land of Judæa; and there he tarried with them, and baptized").

The actions of the imperfects are correlative to the actions of the aorists.

4) The action of the imperfect serves as a background for that of the aorist:

Ꙗ́коже пла́кашеса, приниче во гро́бъ (John 20:11—"as she wept, she stooped down, [and looked] into the sepulchre"). Ꙗ́коже и̑да́хꙋ пꙋте́мъ, прїидо́ша на нѣ́кꙋю во́дꙋ (Acts 8:36—"And as they went on the way, they came unto a certain water"). И̑ бы́сть, є̑гда̀ мола́шеса, видѣ́нїе лица̀ є̑гѡ̀ и̑но, и̑ ѡ̑дѣ́ѧнїе є̑гѡ̀ бѣ́ло блиста́ѧса (Luke 9:29—"And as he prayed, the fashion of his countenance was altered, and his raiment was white and glistening").

The action of the imperfect as a background can be presented in a more extended manner:

Жи́знь во гро́бѣ возлежа́ше (1), и̑ печа́ть на ка́мени надлежа́ше (2), ꙗ́кѡ царѧ̀ спѧ́ща во́ини стрежа́хꙋ (3) хрⷭта̀: и̑ а̑́гг҃и сла́вахꙋ (4), ꙗ́кѡ бг҃а безсме́ртна, жены̀ же взыва́хꙋ (5): воскрⷭе гдⷭь, подаѧ̀ мі́рови ве́лїю мⷧлость (Octoechos, T. 7, Sedalen at Sunday Matins—"After Life had been laid in the tomb, and the seal had been set upon the stone, the soldiers watched Christ as it were a sleeping King; and the Angels glorified Him as God immortal, while the women cried out: The Lord is risen, granting the world great mercy").

The imperfects 1, 2, 3, 4, and 5 of this example are correlative to the circumstances of the death and resurrection of Christ. They are a contrasting background for the aorist воскрⷭе.

5) Imperfect with an explanatory meaning:

По си́хъ и̑́де і҆и҃съ на ѻ̑нъ по́лъ мо́ра галїле́и тїверїа́дска: И̑ по не́мъ и̑да́ше наро́дъ мно́гъ, ꙗ́кѡ ви́дахꙋ зна́менїа є̑гѡ̀, ꙗ́же твора́ше над недꙋ́жными (John 6:1-2—"After these things Jesus went over the sea of Galilee, which is [the sea] of Tiberias. And a great multitude followed him, because they saw his miracles which he did on them that were diseased").

Ви́дах8 and твора́ше are correlative to the activity of the Saviour and to the imperfect ида́ше and are explanatory.

Тогда̀ оу́бо вни́де и дру́гі́й оу̓ченни́къ, прише́дый пре́жде ко гро́бу, и ви́д'ѣ и в'ѣ́рова. Но оу̓ бо в'ѣ́дах8 писа́ні́а, ꙗ́кw подоба́етъ є̓му̀ и́з ме́ртвыхъ воскре́сну́ти (John 20:8-9—"Then went in also that other disciple, which came first to the sepulchre, and he saw, and believed. For as yet they knew not the scripture, that he must rise again from the dead").

Не в'ѣ́дах8 is correlative to ви́д'ѣ и в'ѣ́рова and is explanatory.

Ѡ̓бра́щьса же пе́тръ ви́д'ѣ оу̓ченика̀, є̓го́же любла́ше і̓н҃съ, во сл'ѣ́дъ иду́ца (John 21:20—"Then Peter, turning about, saw the disciple whom Jesus loved following").

The imperfect любла́ше is explanatory.

6) Imperfects in a description of the details of an incident or event:

И̓ по́аша ю̓нца̀ и̓ сотвори́ша [та́кw], и̓ призыва́х8 (1) и́ма ваа́лово ѿ оу́тра до полу́дне, и̓ р'ѣ́ша: послу́шай на́съ, ваа́ле, послу́шай на́съ, и̓ не б'ѣ́ гла́са ни послу́ша́ні́а. и̓ ристах8 (2) о́коло же́ртвенника, є̓го́же сотвори́ша... и̓ зова́х8 (3) гла́сомъ вели́кимъ, и̓ кроа́х8са (4) по о̓бы́чаю свое́му̀ ножа́ми, и̓ мно́зи би́шаса би́чми, до проли́ті́а кро́ве свое́а. И̓ прорица́х8 (5), до́ндеже пре́йде ве́черъ (III Kings 18:26-29—"And they took a bullock, and dressed it, and called on the name of Baal from the morning till noon, and said, Hear us, O Baal, hear us. And there was no voice nor any that answered. And they leaped about the altar which they had made... And they cried out in a great voice, and cut themselves according to their custom with knives, and many flogged themselves with whips until their blood flowed. And they prophesied until the evening came").

The imperfects 1, 2, 3, 4, and 5 express details of this incident, and are correlative to the facts of bringing sacrifice to Baal — по́аша and сотвори́ша.

7) Descriptive imperfects with a sense of characterization:

Бы́сть же на вса́кой дꙋши стра́хъ, мно́га бо чꙋдеса̀ и зна́менїа а҆пⷵтолы бы́ша во і҆ерꙋсали́мѣ. стра́хъ же вели́й ба́ше (1) на все́хъ и́хъ. всѝ же вѣ́ровавшїи ба́хꙋ (2) вкꙋ́пѣ, и҆ и҆ма́хꙋ (3) всꙗ̂ Ѻ҆́бща. И҆ стажа̂нїа и҆ и҆мѣ́нїа прода́ахꙋ (4), и҆ розда́ахꙋ (5) всѣ́мъ, е҆го́же а҆́ще кто̀ тре́боваше (6): По всꙗ̂ же дни̑ терпꙗ́ще е҆диноⷣꙋшнѡ въ цр҃кви, и҆ лома́ще по домѡ́мъ хлѣ́бъ, прїима́хꙋ (7) пищꙋ̀ въ ра́дости и҆ въ простотѣ̑ се́рдца, Хва́лꙗще бг҃а и҆ и҆мꙋ́ще бл҃года́ть оу҆̀ все́хъ люде́й. Гдⷵь же прилага́ше (8) по всꙗ̂ дни̑ цр҃кви спаса́ющїесꙗ (Acts 2: 43-47—"And fear came upon every soul: and many wonders and signs were done by the apostles. And all that believed were together, and had all things common; And sold their possessions and goods, and parted them to all, as every man had need. And they, continuing daily with one accord in the temple, and breaking bread from house to house, did eat their meat with gladness and singleness of heart, Praising God, and having favour with all the people. And the Lord added to the church daily such as should be saved").

The aorists бы́сть and бы́ша give the facts, while the imperfects 1, 2, 3, 4, 5, 6, 7 and 8 give the details, characterizing the first community of Christians. The imperfects are correlative to бы́сть and бы́ша.

8) Imperfects showing repetition:

Е҆́сть же во і҆ерꙋсали́мѣхъ Ѻ҆́вчаа кꙋ́пѣль, ꙗ҆́же глаго́летсꙗ е҆вре́йскⷯи ви.ѳесда̀, па́ть притвѡ́рх и҆мꙋ́щи. Въ тѣ́хъ слежа́ше (1) мно́жество болꙗ́щихъ, слѣ́пыхъ, хромы́хъ, сꙋхи́хъ, ча́ющихъ движе́нїа воды̀. А҆́ггл҃ъ бо гдⷵень на всꙗ́ко лѣ́то схожда́ше (2) въ кꙋ́пѣль, и҆ возмꙋща́ше (3) во́дꙋ: и҆ и҆́же пе́рвѣе влаза́ше (4) по возмꙋще́нїи воды̀, здра́въ быва́ше (5), ꙗ҆цѣ́мъ же недꙋ́гомъ ѡ҆держи́мъ быва́ше (6) (John 5:2-4—"Now there is at Jerusalem by the sheep market a pool, which is called in the Hebrew tongue Bethesda, having five porches. In these lay a great multitude of impotent folk, of blind, halt, withered, waiting for the moving of the water. For an angel went down at a certain season into the pool, and troubled the water: whosoever then first after the troubling of the water stepped in, was made whole of whatsoever disease he had").

The imperfect слежаше (1) shows the duration of the action; the other imperfects, 2, 3, 4, 5 and 6 show repeated action. All the imperfects are correlative to the fact of healing at the pool, taken in context, so that one could add "at that time".

9) Fairly often, the imperfect is employed as an introductory word for someone else's speech (usually the words глаго́лаше, вопїаше, взыва́ше [said, exclaimed, cried out] and others): и глаго́лаше и́мъ: и́дѣ́же а́ще вни́дите въ до́мъ, тꙋ пребыва́йте (Mark 6:10—"And he said unto them, In what place soever ye enter into an house, there abide").

The Perfect (Past Complete)

§158. The perfect expresses a retrospective viewpoint of the speaker, i.e a looking back. For this reason the perfect does not develop the action, but puts the process that it signifies *outside the main context* that makes up the action of the narrative, and reflects the vivid involvement of the speaker; in other words, the perfect *objectivizes* [1] the process it signifies. Thus, the speaker makes use of the perfect to express those actions or facts, which in his consciousness have an objective meaning. To make this easier to understand, one could periphrase the meaning of the perfect by such words as "this is an indisputable fact", or "as everyone knows perfectly well..." [2].

---

[1] C. H. Van Schooneveld, "A Semantic Analysis of the Old Russian Finite Preterite System". 1959. p. 92.

[2] Ibid., p. 95.

The point of departure for "looking back" is the present, as shown by the copula (е҆́смь, е҆си̑, е҆́сть...). Hence the perfect is for the most part to be met with in conjunction with the present or future tenses.

Since the perfect signifies a process outside of its development in time, outside of showing objectiveness, the action of the perfect can also have the sense of result as seen from the moment of narration, sometimes having a characterizing relationship to the subject.

The forms of the perfect can be either in the perfective or imperfective aspect, depending on the present stems they are derived from.

Examples:

1) Предста́ша (1) ца́рїе зе́мстїн, и҆ кнѧ́зн собра́шасѧ (2) вкꙋ́пѣ: на гⷣа, и҆ на хрⷭта̀ е҆гѡ̀. Собра́шасѧ (3) бо вои́стиннꙋ во гра́дѣ се́мъ на стⷮа́го ѻ҆́трока твоегѡ̀ і҆и҃са, е҆гѡ́же пома́залъ е҆си̑, и҆́рѡдъ же и҆ понті́нскїй пїла́тъ, съ ꙗ҆зы́ки и҆ людьми̑ і҆и҃левыми (Acts 4:26-27—"The kings of the earth rose up, and the rulers were gathered together against the Lord, and against his Christ. For of a truth against thy holy child Jesus, whom thou hast anointed, both Herod, and Pontius Pilate, with the Gentiles, and the people of Israel, were gathered together").

Here the aorists 1, 2 and 3, developing the action, comprise the main context of the narrative; the action of the perfect is outside of this context and constitutes an objective fact — е҆гѡ́же пома́залъ е҆си̑. The perfect expresses an action earlier than that of the aorists, yet it had an equally important significance at the moment of telling.

2) Занѐ, разꙋ́мное бж҃їе, ꙗ҆вѣ̀ е҆́сть въ ни́хъ: бг҃ъ бо ꙗ҆ви́лъ е҆́сть и҆̀мъ (Rom. 1:19—"Because that which may be known of God is manifest in them; for God hath shewed it unto them").

The action of the perfect is an objective fact; its result is at hand at the moment of telling — ꙗ҆вѣ̀ е҆́сть...

3) Оучи́тель пришéлъ є҆́сть и҆ глашáетъ тѧ (John 11:28—"The Master is come, and calleth for thee").

4) Во грѣсѣ́хъ ты̀ роди́лсѧ є҆́си вéсь, и҆ ты̀ ли ны̀ оучи́ши; (John 9:34—"Thou wast altogether born in sins, and dost thou teach us?").

5) Й҆́кш бри́твꙋ и҆зшщрéнꙋ сотвори́лъ є҆́си лéсть. Возлюби́лъ є҆́си ѕло́бꙋ пáче благостьнни... Возлюби́лъ є҆́си всѧ̀ глаго́лы потшпныѧ, ꙗ҆зы́къ льсти́въ. Сегш рáди бг҃ъ разрꙋши́тъ тѧ до концà... (Ps. 51:4-7—"As a sharp razor thou hast wrought deceit. Thou hast loved malice more than goodness... Thou hast loved all the words of ruin, O deceitful tongue. Therefore God will destroy thee forever...").

In these examples, besides the sense of objectivity from the viewpoint of the speaker, example 3) shows the result at the moment of speaking; in examples 4) and 5) the action of the perfect is one of characterization, and one might paraphrase them by the question "what is the nature of... ?".

Note. In dialectal forms of Russian there exist special participial expressions: «онъ пришодце (есть пришедши)», cf. example 3) above, «онъ поѣмши (есть поѣвши)». These expressions would appear to be nothing else than forms of the perfect with a resultative sense, only composed with the active participle in -ш. On the other hand, forms with a past tense copula such as «когда мы пришли, онъ былъ уставши» — can be viewed as a pluperfect. Forms with the copula in the future tense may be seen as a future resultative, for example: «Нешто я неѣмши буду».

§159. Based on the perfect tense's sense of objectiveness, as speaking of a known fact, its uses may be grouped as follows:[3]

---

[3] Op. cit., p. 95.

I. The case is known to all, besides those addressed. Encountered with a sense of conviction:

7) Тве́рдѡ ѹ́бо да разꙋмѣ́етъ ве́сь до́мъ і҆и҃левъ, ꙗ́кѡ и҆ г҃да и҆ хрⷭта̀ є҆гѡ̀ бг҃ъ сотвори́лъ є҆́сть (1), сего̀ і҆и҃са, є҆го́же вы̀ распа́сте (Acts 2:36—"Therefore let all the house of Israel know assuredly, that God hath made that same Jesus, whom ye have crucified, both Lord and Christ").

The speaker urges the hearer to accept an objective fact (1), which is obvious to the speaker. The action of the perfect (1) took place prior to that of the aorist (2) (that of the main context), but its meaning still had effect at the moment of utterance.

8) І҆ѡа́ннъ ѹ́бо крести́лъ є҆́сть водо́ю, вы̀ же и҆́мате крести́тисѧ дх҃омъ ст҃ы́мъ (Acts 11:16 —"John indeed baptized with water, but ye shall be baptized with the Holy Ghost").

9) И҆ ви́дѣлъ є҆сѝ є҆го̀, и҆ глаго́лай съ тобо́ю, то́й є҆́сть (John 9:37—"Thou hast both seen him, and it is he that talketh with thee").

Here one could also add examples 2) and 3) from above.

II. The case is generally known to all, except the speaker. This is encountered as the conclusion of a thought:

10) Ѹ́чи́телю, до́брѣ ре́клъ є҆сѝ (Luke 20:39—"Master, thou hast well said").

11) Слы́шавъ же сїѧ̀ і҆и҃съ, речѐ є҆мꙋ̀: є҆щѐ є҆ди́нагѡ не доконча́лъ є҆сѝ (Luke 18:22—"Now when Jesus heard these things, he said unto him, Yet lackest thou one thing").

III. The case is generally known to all, except the speaker and the person addressed. This is encountered as an expression of doubt, in a direct or indirect question, or in conditional sentences.

12) Ке́сарѧ ли нарекла́ є҆сѝ, къ ке́сарю по́йдеши (Acts 25:12—"Hast thou appealed unto Cæsar? Unto Cæsar shalt thou go").

13) Кто́ о҆у́бо є҆́сть, и҆ что́ є҆́сть сотвори́лъ; (Acts 21:33—"[and the chief captain demanded] who he was, and what he had done").

14) И҆ бы́сть, є҆гда̀ возврати́ся, прїи́мъ ца́рство, речѐ пригласи́ти рабы̀ тїи, и҆́мже дадѐ сребро̀, да о҆у҆вѣ́сть, каково́у ку́плю су́ть сотвори́ли (Luke 19:15—"And it came to pass, that when he was returned, having received the kingdom, then he commanded these servants to be called unto him, to whom he had given the money, that he might know how much every man had gained by trading").

IV. The case is generally known to all, including the speaker and the person addressed. This is encountered in corroborations:

15) Поклоню́ся ко хра́му свято́му твоему́, и҆ и҆сповѣ́мся и҆́мени твоему̀ ѡ҆ ми́лости твое́й и҆ и҆́стиннѣ твое́й: ꙗ҆́кѡ возвели́чилъ є҆сѝ над всѣ́ми и҆́мя твоѐ свято́е (Ps. 137:2—"I will worship towards thy holy temple, and I will give glory to thy name, for thy mercy, and for thy truth: for thou hast magnified thy holy name above all").

16) И҆скуси́лъ є҆сѝ се́рдце моѐ, посѣти́лъ є҆сѝ но́щїю: и҆скуси́лъ мѧ̀ є҆сѝ, и҆ не ѡ҆брѣ́теся во мнѣ̀ непра́вда (Ps. 16:3—"Thou hast proved my heart, and visited it by night: thou hast tried me by fire, and iniquity hath not been found in me").

This last type of perfect is especially frequent in liturgical texts, where the good works of a Saint or the mercies of God towards mankind are usually enumerated, as having an objective significance in the consciousness of the speaker, and usually expressed in the 2nd person. Hence, as it would appear, out of frequent usage, the 2nd person singular of the perfect almost completely displaced the 2nd person singular of the aorist; the latter occurs only as an exception, although in the texts prior to Patriarch Nikon's reforms, the 2nd person singular of the aorist was as common as that of the perfect.

An example of the modern text:

Роди́лся є҆сѝ ꙗ҆́кѡ са́мъ восхотѣ́лъ є҆сѝ, ꙗ҆ви́лся є҆сѝ ꙗ҆́кѡ са́мъ и҆зво́лилъ є҆сѝ: пострада́лъ є҆сѝ пло́тїю бж҃е на́шъ, и҆з̾ ме́ртвыхъ воскрл҃ъ є҆сѝ попра́въ сме́рть. вознесл҃ся є҆сѝ во сла́вѣ, всѧ́ческаѧ и҆сполнѧ́ай, и҆ посла́лъ є҆сѝ на́мъ дх҃а бж҃е́ственнаго, є҆́же воспѣва́ти и҆ сла́вити твоѐ бж҃ество̀ (From the service for Ascension Day, the Aposticha [Stichovna] at Vespers—"Thou wast born as Thou didst will, Thou didst appear of Thine own choice: Thou didst suffer in the flesh, O our God: Thou didst rise from the dead, trampling down death. Thou didst ascend in glory, fulfilling all, and dist send us the Divine Spirit, that we may praise and glorify Thy Godhead").

Here is the same text as it was printed under Patriarch Joseph:
Роди́сѧ ꙗ҆́кѡ са́мъ восхотѣ̀, ꙗ҆ви́лсѧ є҆сѝ ꙗ҆́кѡ са́мъ и҆зво́ли, пострада̀ пло́тїю бж҃е на́шъ. и҆змр҃твыхъ воскр́се, попра́въ сме́рть. вознесе́сѧ во сла́вѣ, и҆́же всѧ́ческаѧ и҆сполнѧ́ай. и҆ посла́лъ є҆сѝ на́мъ дх҃ъ бж҃е́ственный, воє́же воспѣва́ти и҆ сла́вити твоѐ бж҃ество̀.

The 2nd person singular of the aorist and imperfect have been preserved intact only in the Gospel text used in Divine services (and even then not in all editions), while in editions of the Gospel in Church Slavonic for private reading, the 2nd person of the aorist and imperfect have been replaced by the 2nd person of the perfect tense.

For example, in the liturgical text:
Є҆гда̀ бѣ̀ (1) ю҆́нъ, поѧса́шесѧ (2) са́мъ, и҆ хожда́ше (3), а҆́може хотѧ́ше (4): є҆гда̀ же состарѣ́ешисѧ, и҆ воздѣ́жеши рꙋцѣ̀ твоѝ, и҆ и҆́нъ тѧ̀ поѧ́шетъ, и҆ веде́тъ, а҆́може не хо́щеши (John 21:18—"When thou wast young, thou girdedst thyself, and walkedst whither thou wouldest: but when thou shalt be old, thou shalt stretch forth thy hands, and another shall gird thee, and carry thee whither thou wouldest not").

The aorist бѣ̀ introduces a new action into the narrative: the imperfects 2, 3 and 4 are correlative to бѣ̀ and add details.

In non-liturgical editions, the 2nd person aorist 1 and the imperfects 2, 3 and 4 have been replaced by perfects, which upsets the system of past tenses: є҆гда̀ бы́лъ є҆сѝ ю҆́нъ, по́ѧсалсѧ є҆сѝ са́мъ, и҆ ходи́лъ є҆сѝ, а҆́може хотѣ́лъ є҆сѝ...

§160. Concerning the Forms бы́хъ, бѣ́хъ, ба́хъ.

The forms of бы́хъ and бѣ́хъ are both aorists, in both form and meaning, only the forms of бы́хъ are in the perfective aspect, while those of бѣ́хъ are imperfective:

И҆́же по мнѣ̀ грѧды́й, предо мно́ю бы́сть: ꙗ҆́кѡ пе́рвѣе менѐ бѣ̀ (John 1:15—"He that cometh after me, is preferred before me: for he was before me").

Бы́сть expresses a state, with an indication of the limits of duration, whereas бѣ̀ expresses a state in general, without indicating limits of duration.

Всѧ̑ тѣ́мъ бы́ша (1), и҆ без̾ негѡ̀ ничто́же бы́сть (2), є҆́же бы́сть (3) (John 1:3—"All things were made by him; and without him was not any thing made that was made").

The aorists 1, 2 and 3 signify a completed action (compare the Russian version: *Все черезъ Него начало быть, и безъ Него ни что не начало быть, что начало быть*).

Въ нача́лѣ бѣ̀ (1) сло́во, и҆ сло́во бѣ̀ (2) къ бг҃ꙋ, и҆ бг҃ъ бѣ̀ (3) сло́во (John 1:1—"In the beginning was the Word, and the Word was with God, and the Word was God").

The aorists 1, 2 and 3 express a state in general, as in the first example.

The 3rd person aorist of the perfective aspect — бы́сть — is fairly frequently used as an impersonal clause, expressed by a single word (equivalent to the English "and it came to pass"); the comparable Russian expression would be "случилось": И҆ бы́сть є҆гда̀ благословлѧ́ше и҆́хъ, ѿстꙋпѝ ѿ ни́хъ, и҆ вознош́ашесѧ на нб҃о (Luke 24:51—"And it came to pass, while he blessed them, he was parted from them, and carried up to heaven").

The forms of ба́ху are used with all the peculiarities characteristic of the imperfect, i.e. they express actions that are relative to the main action: Бѣ̀ (1) же і҆ѡа́ннъ крестѧ̀ во є҆нѡ́нѣ бли́зъ салі́ма, ꙗ҆́кѡ во́ды мно́ги ба́хꙋ (2) тꙋ̀ (John 3:23—"And John also was baptizing in Ænon near to Salim, because there was much water there").

Ба́хꙋ (2) expresses an action relative to the main action, the latter being expressed by the aorist (1), and so ба́хꙋ is explanatory.

§161. The Pluperfect (Distant Past).

The pluperfect expresses action previous to another past action. The copula of the pluperfect (бѣ́хъ or ба́хъ) indicates a certain moment in the past, while the participle ending in -лъ signifies some action that took place at a still more distant time, but which is represented as being resultant in the time indicated by the copula. The copula of the pluperfect, бѣ́хъ (aorist) and ба́хъ (imperfect) retains its time significance, and therefore the pluperfect has two forms of use.

a) The copula бѣ́хъ always stands in a chain of aorists that convey the action of the narrative, presenting new actions or facts: consequently, the partiple in -лъ with the copula бѣ́хъ indicates a preceding action within the chain of aorists. For example:

1) Мно́гꙋ же вре́мени минꙋ́вшꙋ, и҆ сꙋ́щꙋ ᲂу҆жѐ не безбѣ́днꙋ пла́ванїю, зане́же и҆ по́стъ ᲂу҆жѐ бѣ̀ прѣше́лъ, совѣ́товаше па́велъ... (Acts 27:9—"Now when much time was spent, and when sailing was now dangerous, because the fast was now already past, Paul admonished them...").

The pluperfect бѣ̀ прѣше́лъ introduces a new report. Бѣ̀ is linked to the actions indicated by the predicate participles минꙋ́вшꙋ, сꙋ́щꙋ (dative absolute [see §197]); прѣше́лъ indicates that by this time (бѣ̀) the fast had already ended; совѣ́товаше (imperf.) indicates an action contemporaneous and correlative to the main action (which is understood — минꙋ́вшꙋ).

Other examples:

2) Иже въ мимошедшыѧ роды ѡстáвилъ* бѣ* всѧ ꙗзыки ходити въ пꙋтехъ ихъ (Acts 14:16—"Who in times past had suffered all nations to walk in their own ways").

3) И нѣкто мꙋжъ въ лꙋстрѣхъ немощенъ ногáма сѣдáше, хрóмъ ѿ чрéва мáтере своеѧ сый, иже николиже бѣ* ходилъ* (Acts 14:8—"And there sat a certain man at Lystra, impotent in his feet, being a cripple from his mother's womb, who never had walked").

4) Сей не бѣ* пристáлъ* совѣтꙋ и дѣлꙋ ихъ, ѿ аримаѳéа грáда іꙋдéйска, иже чáаше и сáмъ цáрствіѧ бжíѧ (Luke 23:51—"The same had not consented to the counsel and deed of them; he was of Arimathæa, a city of the Jews, who also himself waited for the kingdom of God").

5) Мы же пришéдше въ корáбль, ѿвезóхомсѧ въ áссонъ, ѿкꙋдꙋ хотѧ́ше поѧ́ти пáвла: тáкѡ бо нáмъ бѣ* повелѣ́лъ*, хотѧ́ сáмъ пѣшъ ити (Acts 20:13—"And we went before to ship, and sailed unto Assos, there intending to take in Paul: for so had he appointed, minding himself to go afoot").

6) Тысѧщникъ же оубоѧ́сѧ, разꙋмѣ́въ, ꙗ́кѡ рꙋмлѧнинъ є́сть, и ꙗ́кѡ бѣ* є́го свѧзáлъ* (Acts 22:29—"And the chief captain was afraid, after he knew that he was a Roman, and because he had bound him").

Often the pluperfect combined with не оу̑ indicates a preceding unrealized action.

7) Искáхꙋ оубо да имꙋтъ є́го: и никтóже возложи нáнь рꙋ́ки, ꙗ́кѡ не оу̑ бѣ* пришéлъ* чáсъ є́гѡ (John 7:30—"Then they sought to take him: but no man laid hands on him, because his hour was not yet come").

8) Не оу́же бо бѣ* пришéлъ* інсъ въ вéсь, но бѣ на мѣ́стѣ, идѣ́же срѣ́те є́гѡ мáрѳа (John 11:30—"Now Jesus was not yet come into the town, but was in that place where Martha met him").

9) Й никто́же ꙗ́тъ є҆го̀, ꙗ́кѡ не оу҆ бѣ̀* пришélъ* ча́съ є҆гѡ̀ (John 8:20—"and no man laid hands on him, for his hour was not yet come").

b) The copula ба́хъ expresses an action that is correlative to the main action (usually expressed by an aorist), and therefore a pluperfect of this type shows all the characteristics of the imperfect. For example:

10) Сїѧ̀ реко́ша роди́телѧ є҆гѡ̀, ꙗ́кѡ боѧ́хꙋсѧ жидѡ́въ: оу҆же́ бо ба́хꙋ сложи́лисѧ жи́дове, да а҆́ще кто̀ є҆го̀ и҆сповѣ́сть хрⷭ҇та̀, ѿлꙋчéнъ ѿ со́нмища бꙋ́детъ (John 9:22—"These words spake his parents, because they feared the Jews: for the Jews had agreed already, that if any man did confess that he was Christ, he should be put out of the synagogue").

The copula ба́хꙋ is correlative to the main action (реко́ша, боѧ́хꙋсѧ): сложи́лисѧ indicates a prior action, the result of which was felt at that time (ба́хꙋ). The pluperfect has an explanatory sense.

11) Й ꙗ́коже хотѧ́хꙋ (1) сéдмь дні́й сконча́тисѧ, и҆́же ѿ а҆сі́и і҆ꙋдéи ви́дѣвше є҆го̀ во ст҃и́лищи, наба́дниша (2) вéсь наро́дъ, и҆ возложи́ша (3) на́нь рꙋ́цѣ... ба́хꙋ бо ви́дѣли (4) трофі́ма є҆фéсѧннина во гра́дѣ съ ни́мъ, є҆го́же мнѧ́хꙋ (5) ꙗ́кѡ въ цéрковь ввéлъ є҆́сть (6) па́велъ (Acts 21:27-29—"And when the seven days were almost ended, the Jews which were of Asia, when they saw him in the temple, stirred up all the people, and laid hands on him... For they had seen before with him in the city Trophimus an Ephesian, whom they supposed that Paul had brought into the temple").

The main action of this incident is expressed by the aorists 2 and 3; the imperfect хотѧ́хꙋ (1) forms a background (see §157, 4), against which the action of aorists 2 and 3 took place; the copula ба́хꙋ and мнѧ́хꙋ (5) are correlative to the action of aorists 2 and 3, expressing action that takes place contemporaneously with them, and are explanatory; consequently, the pluperfect бѧхꙋ вид҃ѣли (4) is explanatory, pointing to a prior resultative action; ввелъ є҆́сть (6) is expressed by the perfect because in the consciousness of the Jews, this incident had an objective nature, as an undoubted fact ("this is well known to all").

12) Глаго́ла є҆́й і҆и҃съ: да́ждь мѝ пи́ти. оу҆ченицы́ бо є҆гѡ̀ ѿшлѝ бѧхꙋ во гра́дъ, да бра́шно кꙋ́пѧтъ (John 4:7-8—"Jesus said unto her, Give me to drink. For his disciples were gone away into the city to buy meat").

The pluperfect ѿшлѝ бѧхꙋ is, by its copula, correlative and simultaneous with the main action — the conversation with the Samaritan woman (глаго́ла).

13) Сосѣ́ди же, и҆ и҆́же бѧхꙋ вид҃ѣли є҆го̀ пре́жде, ꙗ҆́кѡ слѣ́пъ бѣ̀, глаго́лахꙋ: не се́й ли є҆́сть сѣдѧ́й и҆ просѧ́й; (John 9:8—"The neighbors therefore, and they which before had seen him that he was blind, said, Is not this he that sat and begged?").

14) Во слѣ́дъ же ше́дшыѧ жены̀, ꙗ҆́же бѧхꙋ пришлѝ съ ни́мъ ѿ галїле́и, вид҃ѣша гро́бъ, и҆ ꙗ҆́кѡ положе́но бы́сть тѣ́ло є҆гѡ̀ (Luke 23:55—"And the women also, which came with him from Galilee, followed after, and beheld the sepulchre, and how his body was laid").

Бѧхꙋ вид҃ѣли is correlated by its copula to the aorist бѣ̀: бѧхꙋ пришлѝ is correlative to the aorist вид҃ѣша: these pluperfects are used in an explanatory fashion.

15) Ꙗ҆́кѡ причте́нъ бѣ̀ съ на́ми, и҆ прїѧ́лъ бѧ́ше жре́бїй слꙋ́жбы сеѧ̀ (Acts 1:17—"For he was numbered with us, and had obtained part of this ministry").

Причте́нъ бѣ̀ is a pluperfect passive, and due to the aorist connecting verb [copula], it leads us into the main context of a new incident; прїѧ́лъ бѧ́ше is correlated by its copula with the copula бѣ̀, and expresses an explanatory detail.

§162. The Future Perfect (Preceding Future).

The future perfect tense went out of use in Church Slavonic and is encountered by way of exception. The forms of the future perfect consist of the participle ending in -лъ and the copula бꙋдꙋ, бꙋдєши, &c. It signifies a future action that precedes another future action, and is used with the conjunction а́ще, for example: и а́ще грѣхѝ бꙋдетъ* сотворилъ*, ѿпꙋстѧтсѧ є҆мꙋ (James 5:15 in the liturgical Epistolary—"and if he [shall] have committed sins, they shall be forgiven him").

§163. The Descriptive (Periphrastic) Form of the Tenses.

The descriptive tense forms, consisting of forms of the verb бы́ти (as a copula) and the present active participle, are used to emphasize some particular duration or continuity of action, or in some cases more to express a state or condition than an action.

И бѣ* проповѣ́даѧ* на со́нмищахъ и҆хъ, по всєй галїлє́и, и бѣсы и҆згонѧ̀* (Mark 1:39—"And he preached [lit. 'was preaching'] in their synagogues thoughout all Galilee, and cast out devils"). И бѧхꙋ* о҆ученицы̀ і҆ѡа́нновы и фарїсє́йстїи постѧщєсѧ* (Mark 2:18—"And the disciples of John and of the Pharisees used to fast"). И а́ще на нєго̀ надѣ́ѧсѧ* бꙋдꙋ*, бꙋдетъ мнѣ̀ во ѡ҆свѧщє́нїе. И о҆уповаѧ* бꙋдꙋ* на нєго̀, и спасꙋсѧ и҆́мъ (Great Compline, "God is with us"—"And if I be trusting unto Him, He shall be unto sanctification for me. And hoping upon Him, I shall be saved by Him").

A similar form is rather often to be met with, when two simultaneous actions are presented: the main action, expressed by the aorist, and another, correlative to it, expressed by the imperfect; and here, the descriptive form may be taken by either the aorist or the imperfect.

The descriptive form of the aorist:

И є҆гда̀ и҆зливашесѧ кро́вь стєфа́на свидѣ́тєла твоєгѡ̀, и са́мъ бѣ́хъ* стоѧ̀* и соизволѧ́ѧ* о҆убїє́нїю є҆гѡ̀, и стрєгїй* ри́зъ оу҆бнка́ющнхъ є҆гѡ̀ (Acts 22:20—"And when the blood of thy martyr Stephen was shed, I also was standing by, and consenting unto his death, and kept the raiment of them that slew him"). Не се́рдце лн на́ю горѧ̀* бѣ̀* въ на́ю, є҆гда̀ глаго́лаша на́ма на пꙋтѝ, и҆ є҆гда̀ сказоваше на́ма писа́нїѧ (Luke 24:32—"Did not our heart burn within us, while he talked with us by the way, and while he opened to us the scriptures?").

The descriptive form of the imperfect:

И҆ є҆гда̀ взира́юще(1) бѧ́хꙋ (1) на не́бо, и҆дꙋщꙋ є҆мꙋ̀, и҆ сѐ мꙋжа два̀ ста́ста (2) пред нѝмн во ѻ҆де́жди бѣ́лѣ (Acts 1:10—"And while they looked stedfastly toward heaven as he went up, behold, two men stood by them in white apparel").

In the example given above, the descriptive form of the imperfect (1) underlines the contrast of the background against which the action of the aorist (2) took place.

The semi-significant copulas не преста́ти (or не преста̀ѧ́ти), пребыва́ти, прилѣжа́ти, не ѻ҆скꙋдѣва́ти [not to cease, to continue], indicate a continued action, while преста́ти, соверши́ти [to cease, complete] signify the end of an action. In Russian, these descriptive forms with the copulas indicated often correspond to word combinations consisting of personal verb forms (of не переставать, продолжать, перестать, окончить) and the infinitive, for example: не преста́ахꙋ* оу҆ча́ще* и҆ благовѣ́ствꙋ́юще* (Acts 5:42—"they ceased not to teach and to preach"), which in the Russian text is: не переставали учить и благовѣствовать; человѣ́къ се́й не преста́етъ* глаго́лы хꙋ́льныѧ глаго́лѧ* (Acts 6:13—"This man ceaseth not to speak blasphemous words"), in the Russian: не перестаетъ говорить хульныя слова; Пе́трꙋ же пребыва́ше* толкі́й (instead of толкы̀, see §95), Acts 12:16—"But Peter continued knocking"), in the Russian: продолжалъ стучать; ꙗ҆́коже преста̀* глаго́лѧ*, речѐ къ сі́мшнꙋ (Luke 5:4—"Now when he had left off speaking, he said unto Simon"), in the Russian: когда пересталъ учить... И҆ бы́сть, є҆гда̀ совершѝ* і҆н҃съ заповѣ́даѧ* ѻ҆бѣманадесѧте оу҆ченнко́ма свои́ма, пре́йде ѿт҂́дꙋ оу҆чи́ти (Matth. 11:1—"And it came to pass, when Jesus had made an end of commanding his twelve disciples, he departed thence to teach"), in the Russian: *И когда окончилъ Іисусъ наставленіе (наставлять).*

Note: With certain of the copulas mentioned above, combinations using the infinitive are also to be met with, for example: и҆ не преста́нетъ твори́ти плода̀ (Jeremiah 17:8—"neither shall cease from yielding fruit"); преста́ша би́ти па́vла (Acts 21:32—"they left off beating of Paul").

The descriptive tense forms almost always correspond to similar forms in the Greek text. Cf. the 2nd example above: Καὶ ἦσαν οἱ μαθηταὶ Ἰωάννου καὶ οἱ φαρισαῖοι νηστεύοντες (Mark 2:18—"And the disciples of John and the Pharisees used to fast").

Note: These descriptive tenses are close, in both form and meaning, to the English "continuous forms", for example: и҆ са́мъ бѣ́хъ* стоѧ̀* и҆ соизволѧ́ѧ* оу҆бїе́нїю є҆гѡ̀ — "I also was* standing* by, and consenting* unto his death" (Acts 22:20).

§164. Passive Forms.

The passive forms consist of passive participles and a copula. The present passive participle expresses a characteristic, found in the action (e.g. несо́мъ); the past passive participle expresses a characteristic, seen as the result of a past action (принесе́нъ); therefore to express an unfinishd process, the present participle is used (несо́мъ бꙋ́дꙋ, є҆́смь or бѣ́хъ—"I shall be [in the process of being] carried, am being carried, was..."), whereas to express a completed process (or its result) the past participle is used (принесе́нъ бꙋ́дꙋ—"I shall be [in the state of having already been] brought"). The past passive participle of the imperfective aspect expresses a process that was begun, but continues in effect (несе́нъ). In the passive tense forms of a verb, the participle indicates a process that has been completed (принесе́нъ) or is incomplete (несо́мъ), while the copula indicates its relationship to the action in time (the present time, future, or past).

§165. The Present Tense and the Imperfect.

Since the present tense and the imperfect by their meaning cannot express a completed action, their passive forms are derived only from the present participle, with the copula є҆́смь for the present tense, and бѧ́хꙋ for the imperfect.

Examples.

Present tense: На̀ сїѐ бо и҆ трꙋжда́емсѧ и҆ поношла́еми є҆смы̀, ꙗ҆́кѡ оу҆пова́хомъ на бга жи́ва (I Tim. 4:10—"For therefore we both labour and suffer reproach, because we have put our trust in the living God").

Imperfect: Бы́сть ропта́нїе є҆́ллинѡвъ ко є҆вре́ѡмъ, ꙗ҆́кѡ презира́еми быва́хꙋ во вседне́вныⸯ слꙋже́нїи вдовицы и҆хъ (Acts 6:1—"There arose a murmuring of the Grecians against the Hebrews, because their widows were neglected in the daily ministration").

§166. The Aorist.

The passive participles of the present and past tenses, in combination with бы́хъ (perfective aspect) must be viewed as passive forms of the aorist. The combination of a present passive participle with бѣ́хъ (imperfective aspect) is also a passive form of the aorist.

Examples.

Ꙗ҆́кѡ кнѧ́зь мі́ра сегѡ̀ ѡ҆сꙋжде́нъ бы́сть (John 16:11—"For the prince of this world is judged"). Е҆ли́ка бо преднапи́сана бы́ша, въ на́ше наказа́нїе преднаписа́шесѧ (Rom. 15:4—"For whatsoever things were written aforetime were written for our learning"). Слы́шасте, ꙗ҆́кѡ рече́но бы́сть дре́внимъ: не оу҆бі́еши (Matth. 5:21—"Ye have heard that it was said to them of old time, Thou shalt not kill"). Бѣ́хъ же не зна́емь лице́мъ цр҃квамъ і҆ꙋде́йскимъ, ꙗ҆́же ѡ҆ хр҃тѣ̀ (Gal. 1:22 — "And I was unknown by face unto the churches of Judæa which were in Christ"). Вда́вшесѧ волна́мъ, носи́ми бѣ́хомъ (Acts 27:15—"Having given up the ship to the winds, we were driven").

§167. The Perfect.

The perfect passive is formed by combining the past passive participle with the copula є҆́сть. In the forms of the perfect, the active participle ending in -лъ is counterposed to the passive participle ending in -нъ, -тъ, since they have common characteristics signifying 1) the process of an objective fact, and 2) the beginning of the process up to the moment of utterance[4]. However, there is a significant difference of meaning between them besides that of voice. In the -лъ participles, the sense of result is only partially present, while the main meaning os that of objectivized action in the past; this circumstance led to their taking on, in Russian, the role of past indicative participles. In the past passive participle the sense of result is far stronger than in the -лъ participle, for which reason the passive participles easily take on a qualitative sense and are close to adjectives.

Examples.

Всѝ бо согрѣши́ша и҆ лишенѝ* сꙋ́ть сла́вы бж҃їѧ (Rom. 3:23—"For all have sinned, and come short of the glory of God"). Ничто́же бо є҆́сть* покрове́но*, є҆́же не ѿкры́етсѧ (Matth. 10:26 —"There is nothing covered, that shall not be revealed"). Ва́мъ же и҆ вла́си главні́и всѝ и҆зочте́нѝ* сꙋ́ть* (Matth. 10:30—"But the very hairs of your head are all numbered").

In the forms of the perfect, the passive participle indicates an objective fact, the result of which is evident at the moment of utterance.

In Russian, the predicate past passive participles (without a copula) have the same meaning.

Cf. in the first example: "потому что всѣ согрѣшили и лишены славы Божіей" (Rom. 3:23).

---

[4] Op. cit., p. 152.

§168. The Pluperfect.

The pluperfect derives its forms from the past passive participle and the copula в҃ѣхъ or бѧ́хъ. In the forms of the pluperfect, the difference between the active and passive voices is the same as in the perfect, i.e. it lies in the meaning of the participle. Like the pluperfect active, the passive forms, depending on the copula, may be used as an aorist or as an imperfect.

Examples.

Ѡбрѣ́те же та́мѡ человѣ́ка нѣ́коего и҆́менемъ є҆нє́а, ѿ о҆смѝ лѣ́тъ лежа́ща на о҆дрѣ̀, и҆́же бѣ̀* разсла́бленъ* (Acts 9:33—"And there he found a certain man named Æneas, which had kept his bed eight years, and was sick of the palsy").

The copula бѣ̀ is in line with another aorist (ѡбрѣ́те); the passive participle indicates the result at the time shown by the copula (бѣ̀).

Бѧ́хꙋ же свѣщы̀ мнѡ́ги въ го́рницѣ, и҆дѣ́же бѣ́хомъ* со́брани* (Acts 20:8—"And there were many lights in the upper chamber, where we were gathered together").

The imperfect бѧ́хꙋ is explanatory and adds detail, and is correlative to the aorist-copula (бѣ́хомъ); the passive participle shows the result as of the time indicated by the copula.

Во і҆оппі́н же бѣ̀ нѣ́кая ᲂу҆чени́ца и҆́менемъ таві́ѳа, ꙗ҆́же сказа́ема глаго́летсѧ се́рна: сїѧ̀ бѧ́ше* и҆спо́лнена* бла҃ги́хъ дѣ́лъ и҆ ми́лостынь, ꙗ҆̀же творѧ́ше (Acts 9:36—"Now there was at Joppa a certain disciple named Tabitha, which by interpretation is called Dorcas: this woman was full of good works and almsdeeds which she did").

The copula бѧ́ше is correlative to the aorist бѣ̀: the passive participle indicates the result of an objective fact (good works) at the moment shown by the copula (бѧ́ше); the pluperfect has an explanatory, characterizing sense.

є҆щѐ бо ни на є҆ди́ннаго и҆хъ бѣ̀ пришелъ, то́чїю креще́нн* бА́хꙋ* во и҆́мѧ гда і҆и҃са (Acts 8:16— "For as yet he [i.e. the Holy Ghost] was fallen upon none of them: only they were baptized in the name of the Lord Jesus").

The puperfect with бѣ̀ introduces a new report—it shows an unrealized fact; the pluperfect with бА́хꙋ has an explanatory sense.

The pluperfect can also be formed by means of the copula бы́лъ є҆смь (active perfect), in which case the copula retains its meaning — that of an objective fact in the past, for example: є҆мли́сѧ за вѣ́чнꙋю жи́знь, въ ню́же зва́нъ бы́лъ є҆сѝ (I Tim. 6:12—"Lay hold on eternal life, whereunto thou art also called").

Since the copula (regardless whether бѣ́хъ, бА́хъ or бы́лъ є҆смь) expresses a falling back in past time by one temporal step, one could say that the past passive participle in Russian with the copula былъ might altogether correspond to the Slavonic pluperfect, albeit without those specific distinctions of use that there is between the copulas (бѣ́хъ, бА́хъ or бы́лъ є҆смь). Compare the 3rd example: "она была исполнена добрыхъ дѣлъ" (Acts 9:36). The 4th example: "только были они крещены во имя Господа Іисуса" (Acts 8:16).

§169. The Future Tense, Subjunctive Mood, and the Imperative.

The use of the passive forms of the *future* tense, *subjunctive* and *imperative* moods is the same as their use in Russian.

§170. The Church Slavonic Article and Its Use.

The relative pronouns и҆́же, ꙗ҆́же, є҆́же can be used as articles in Church Slavonic. These pronouns used as articles can have the following forms: in the singular and plural, in the nominative and accusative cases. Constructions using articles in Church Slavonic must be considered Grecisms [imitations of Greek syntax].

The pronoun-articles are used in the following cases:

1) With the infinitive, to express substantivization (see §143, 12), for example: Мнѣ́ бо є҆́же жи́ти, хрⷭ҇то́съ: и҆ є҆́же оу҆мре́ти, приwкрѣ́тенїе є҆́сть (Philipp. 1:21—"For me to live is Christ, and to die is gain"), compare with the Russian: "Ибо для меня жизнь—Христосъ, и смерть—пріобрѣтеніе". Гдⷭ҇и, во є҆́же помощи́ ми вонми́ (Ps. 39:14—"O Lord, make haste to help me"); cf. in Russian: "Господи! поспѣши на помощь мнѣ".

2) Before invariable words, which in such cases take on a substantive meaning, for example: да бꙋ́детъ оу҆ менѐ є҆́же є҆́й є҆́й, и҆ є҆́же нѝ нѝ (II Cor. 1:17—"with me there should be Yea, Yea, and Nay, Nay").

3) є҆́же is often put before quotations or an indirect question: а҆́гг҃лъ оу҆́бо принесѐ дв҃ѣ, є҆́же ра́дꙋйсѧ, пре́жде твоегẁ зача́тїѧ, хрⷭ҇тѐ (Octoechos, 2nd Sunday Exaposteilarion, Theotokion: "The Angel brought the Virgin the salutation [lit., the 'Rejoice'], before Thy conception, O Christ"); И҆́бо ве́сь зако́нъ во є҆ди́номъ словесѝ и҆сполнѧ́етсѧ, во є҆́же: возлю́биши бли́жнѧго твоего̀ ꙗ҆́коже себѐ (Gal. 5:14—"For all the law is fulfilled in one word, even in this: Thou shalt love thy neighbor as thyself"); і҆и҃съ же речѐ є҆мꙋ̀: є҆́же а҆́ще что̀ мо́жеши вѣ́ровати, всѧ̑ возмо́жна вѣ́рꙋющемꙋ (Mark 9:23—"[And] Jesus said unto him, If thou canst believe, all things are possible to him that believeth"). Other examples may be seen in Rom. 13:9; Heb. 12:27; Luke 1:62.

4) Before expressions that consist of oblique cases of nouns with a preposition, and are then taken as a single unit, with the value of an attribute (§130, 7), a subject (§122, h), or an object (§132, d), for example: Мѡѷсе́й бо пи́шетъ пра́вдꙋ, ю҆́же* ѿ зако́на* (Rom. 10:5—"For Moses describeth the righteousness which is of the law"); крⷭ҇то́мъ твои́мъ оу҆праздни́лъ є҆сѝ, ю҆́же* ѿ дре́ва* клѧ́твꙋ (Octoechos, T. 2, Saturday at Great Vespers of Sunday—"By Thy

Cross Thou hast abolished the curse of the tree"); є҆́же* по ѻ҆́бразꙋ* соблю́дъ некреди́мо, ᲂу҆́мъ ка́кꙋ на стра́сти пагꙋбныѧ по́стнически поста́вивъ, во є҆́же* по подо́бїю* ꙗ҆́кѡ мо́щно возше́лъ є҆сѝ (General service for monastic Saints, Vespers—"Having kept that which is after the image unharmed, and, by fasting, setting [thy] mind as master over the ruinous passions, thou didst ascend to that which is according to the likeness").

5) Determinant participles with dependant words often are accompanied by a pronoun-article. In this case the article points to one or another person, well known to all in connection with the incident or event indicated by the participle, for example: Ѻ҆́крестъ ста́ша, и҆́же ѿ і҆ерꙋсали́ма сше́дшїи і҆ꙋде́и (Acts 25:7—"Round about stood the Jews which had come from Jerusalem"), i.e the same ones who had arrived from Jerusalem and who are spoken of in verses 2 and 5 of the same Chapter. In this regard, the festival Dismissals are especially characteristic, for example: И҆́же въ верте́пѣ роди́выйсѧ и҆ въ ꙗ҆́слехъ возлеги́й, на́шегѡ ра́ди спасе́нїѧ... ("[May] He that was born in a cave and lay in a manger, for our salvation..."); И҆́же во і҆ѻрда́нѣ крести́тисѧ и҆зво́ливый ѿ і҆ѡа́нна... ("[May] He that saw fit to be baptized in the Jordan by John..."); И҆́же на горѣ̀ ѳаво́рстѣй преѡбрази́выйсѧ во сла́вѣ... ("[May] He that was transfigured on Mt. Tabor in glory...") and so on (texts from the Sluzhebnik); other examples: А҆́зъ є҆́смь хлѣ́бъ живо́тный, и҆́же сше́дый съ небесѐ (John 6:51—"I am the Living Bread which came down from heaven"); и҆́же ѿ ѻ҆ц҃а̀ и҆сходѧ́щагѡ, и҆́же со ѻ҆ц҃е́мъ и҆ сн҃омъ спокланѧ́ема и҆ сла́вима (Nicene Creed—"Who proceedeth from the Father, Who with the Father and the Son together is worshipped and glorified").

Such a participial word combination with an article may be governed by a preposition, for example: тогѡ̀ ᲂу҆́бо молѝ при́снѡ, ѡ҆ и҆́же вѣ́рою покланѧ́ющихсѧ, ѡ҆ всѧ́кагѡ навѣ́та вра́жїѧ и҆зба́витисѧ (Octoechos, 8th Sunday Exaposteilarion, Theotokion—"entreat Him then for us who venerate thee in faith, that we may be delivered from every assault of the enemy").

Similarly, there may be an article before adjectives that have dependant words, for example: и́же ѡ всѣхъ благі́й гдⷭ҇и, сла́ва тебѣ̀ (Holy Thursday, Tropar—"O Lord, Who art good towards all, glory to Thee"); и́же въ мéртвыхъ свобо́дь (Octoechos, T. 6, Saturday at Great Vespers of Sunday—"Who art free among the dead").

Note: Strictly speaking, the equivalent in Church Slavonic to the Greek participles with an article, is the long form of the participles (see §170); however, in many cases the long participles, as said above, also take a pronoun-article. But as an exception, short forms of the participles, with dependant words, are encountered with the pronoun-articles, thus presenting a literal equivalent of the Greek text, for example: ты̀ є҆сѝ, и́же всѣ́мъ подаѧ̀, хрⷭ҇тѐ, воскресéнїе (cf. Greek: Σὺ εἶ ὁ πᾶσιν παρέχων, Χριστέ, τὴν ἀνάστασιν), Sunday Kondak T. 1—"Thou, O Christ, art He that granteth resurrection to all"; и́же херꙋві́мы та́йнѡ ѡ҆браꙁꙋ́юще... (Liturgy—"We who mystically represent the Churubim..."); и́же ꙁемны́ѧ сла́дѡсти не возлюби́вше стрⷭ҇тотéрпцы, небéсными благи́мъ сподо́бльшесѧ (Octoechos, T. 2, Sunday Vespers at the Aposticha [Stichovna]—"Ye who did not love earthly pleasures, O passion-bearers, have attained unto the good things of heaven").

The Use of the Short and Long Forms of Adjectives and Participles.

§171. Adjectives and partiiples, accoding to their use, may be of three types: substantivized — used in place of nouns; attributive — used to define nouns; and predicative — those which relate to the predicate part of a sentence.

Attributive adjectives and participles may be in the short or long form.

As said above in §49, the long forms of adjective (and participles) were arrived at by means of the demonstrative pronouns ӥ, ꙗ and є̈, which in the beginning were attached to adjectives and had approximately the same meaning as the definite article does in other languages. In this manner, the use of these long forms of adjectives and participles was connected with the category of definite-ness, while the use of the short form showed the category of indefinite-ness. However, in Church Slavonic this distinction between definite and indefinite categories is not clearly expressed. However, if one compares the Slavonic texts with the Greek, the Greek adjectives and participles with a definite article correspond, in most cases, to the long forms in Slavonic.

One might note the following cases in the use of short and long forms of Slavonic adjectives and participles.

1) The short forms of substantivized adjectives and determinative adjectives, standing usually after the modified noun, indicate some new item, mentioned for the first time, or else indefinite, whereas the long forms indicate an item already mentioned or generally known, for example: сѐ привед́оша кꙋ немꙋ̀ чл҃вѣ́ка нѣма̀*, бѣсн́ꙋема*. Й ꙗзгна́нꙋ бѣсꙋ̀, проглаго́ла нѣмы́й* (compare the Greek text: ἰδοῦ, προσήνεγκαν Αὐτῷ ἄνθρωπον κωφὸν δαιμονιζόμενον. Καὶ ἐκβληθέντος τοῦ δαιμονίου, ἐλάλησεν ὁ κωφός, Matth. 9:32-33—"And behold, they brought to him a dumb man possessed with a devil. And when the devil was cast out, the domb spake"); Й приведо́ша кꙋ немꙋ̀ слѣпа... й є̈мꙋ за рꙋ́кꙋ слѣпа́го (Mark 8:22-23—"And they brought a blind man unto him... and he took the blind man by the hand"); Ймꙋ́ща дꙋ́ха нѣма... запрети̍ дꙋ́хꙋ нечи́стомꙋ (Mark 9:17, 25 —"which hath a dumb spirit... he rebuked the foul spirit"); in James 2:2-3: ни́щꙋ... ни́щемꙋ ["a poor man... to the poor man"]; cf. also: ѿ вѣ́ка нѣсть слы́шано, ꙗ́ки кто̀ ѿве́рзе о̀чи слѣпꙋ̀ рожде́нꙋ* [John 9:32—"Since the world began was it not heard that any man opened the eyes of one that was born blind"]; (here the sense is indefinite — although слѣпꙋ̀ is of predicate origin, compare: роди́са слѣпꙋ, рожде́нꙋ слѣпꙋ, слѣпꙋ

ро́жден8) and не мо́жаше ли се́й ѿве́рзый о́чи слѣпом8*, сотвори́ти, да и се́й не оу́мретъ; (John 11:37—"Could not this man, which opened the eyes of the blind, have caused that even this man should not have died?"); (here an incident is had in view that is known to all, the healing of the man born blind).

Comparative adjectives are used in a similar manner — with a definite sense: Честнѣйш8ю* хер8ви́мъ и славнѣйш8ю без сравне́нїѧ серафи́мъ (from "It is truly meet"—"More honourable than the Cherubim, and more glorious beyond compare than the Seraphim"); Превы́шшаѧ* а́гглъ, мі́рскагѡ мѧ превы́шша слитїѧ сотвори́ ([Private] Morning Prayer No. 8—"Thou that art higher than the Angels, make me to be above worldly turmoil"); with an indefinite sense: Бре́мене па́че себѐ не воздви́жи, и крѣпльш8* и богатѣйш8* себѐ не прїѡбща́йсѧ (Ecclesiasticus [Wisom of Sirach], 13:2—"Lift not a burden that is beyond thee, and have no fellowship with one that is mightier and richer than thyself"—see §58).

2) Substantivized adjectives with a generic sense (i.e. ни́щїй, бога́тый as representing a whole class) or signifying isolated cases are used with the long endings, for example:

With a generic sense: нечести́вый и грѣ́шный гдѣ̀ ꙗви́тсѧ (I Peter 4:18—"where shall the ungodly and the sinner appear?"); слѣпі́и прозира́ютъ, хромі́и хо́дѧтъ, прокаже́нїи ѡчища́ютсѧ, глу8сі́и слы́шатъ, ме́ртвїи востаю́тъ, ни́щїи благовѣств8ю́тъ (Luke 7:22—"the blind see, the lame walk, the lepers are cleansed, the deaf hear, the dead are raised, the poor preach the Gospel"); Вы́ же оу́кори́сте ни́щаго. не бога́тїи ли наси́л8ютъ ва́мъ (James 2:6—"But ye have despised the poor. Do not rich men oppress you?").

As as isolated case: вѣ́мъ тѧ̀, кто̀ є҆сѝ, ст҃ы́й бж҃їй (Luke 4:34—"I know thee who thou art: the Holy One [Jesus Christ] of God"); и҆ оу́би́ша предвозвѣсти́вшыѧ ѡ҆ прише́ствїи првнагѡ (Acts 7:52—"and they have slain them which shewed before of the coming of the Just One [Jesus Christ]); но и҆зба́ви на́съ ѿ л8ка́вагѡ (Matth.

6:13—"but deliver us from evil [the devil]); ѧ́кѡ сотворѝ мнѣ̀ вели́чїе си́льный (Luke 1:49—"For he that is mighty [God] hath done great things for me").

But in the following examples it has an indefinite sense: избавлѧ́ѧй ни́ща и҆з рꙋкѝ крѣпльшихъ е҆гѡ̀, и҆ ни́ща, и҆ оу҆бо́га ѿ расхищѧ́ющихъ е҆го̀ (Ps. 34:10—"Who deliverest the poor from the hand of them that are stronger than he; the needy and the poor from them that strip him"); и҆лѝ ни́щъ прїи́де ко мнѣ̀, и҆ презрѣ́хъ е҆го̀ (Evening Prayers—"or else a beggar came to me, and I despised him").

In like manner, when determinative adjectives are used with generic nouns, they take the long form, for example: Бл҃гі́й* человѣ́къ ѿ бл҃га́гѡ сокро́вища и҆зно́ситъ бл҃га̑я: и҆ лꙋка́вый* человѣ́къ ѿ лꙋка́вагѡ сокро́вища и҆зно́ситъ лꙋка̑вая (Matth. 12:35—"A good man out of the good treasure of the heart bringeth forth good things: and an evil man out of the evil treasure bringeth forth evil things").

3)Determinative adjectives that are used with nouns showing some generally-known institution or concept in the realm of faith, have the long form, for example: бж҃е́ственная лїтꙋргі́а, недѣ́лѧ цвѣ́тоно́сная, свѣ́тлая седми́ца, жи́знь вѣ́чная, цр҃тво нб҃е́сное (Divine Liturgy, Palm Sunday, Bright Week, eternal life, the Kingdom of Heaven) and so on.

4) The short form of determinative adjectives may appear even in those cases where there is no need to indicate a definite quality, because this is inherent in the lexical meaning of the word itself. First and foremost in this class are possessive adjectives:

Possessive adjectives (showing that which belongs or is proper to one person, answering the question *whose?*) are used only in the short form, for example: ѿса́нна сн҃ꙋ дави́довꙋ*: бл҃гослове́нъ грѧды́й во и҆́мѧ гд҃не* (Matth. 21:9—"Hosanna to the Son of David: Blessed is he that cometh in the name of the Lord"); мꙋ́жа марі́ина* (Matth.

1:16—"the husband of Mary"); а́гг҃лъ гд҃нь* (Matth. 1:20—"the Angel of the Lord").

Possessive adjectives ending in _ск_ (showing that which belongs to a group of persons or to a particular place) are customarily used in the long form (a quality of being definite is expressed morphologically), but they can also have short forms, for example: гдѣ̀ є́стъ рожде́йся ца́рь і҆уде́йскїй (Matth. 2:2—"Where is he that is born King of the Jews?"); страна̀ і҆ѻрда́нскаѧ (Matth. 3:5—"the region round about Jordan"); but also: ѿ назаре́та галїле́йска (Matth. 21:11—"of Nazareth of Galilee"); при є҆зе́рѣ геннисаре́тстѣ (Luke 5:1—"by the lake of Gennesaret"); во страну̀ гадари́нску (Luke 8:26—"at the country of the Gadarenes").

5) With the word бг҃ъ (which has an inherent 'definite' meaning), adjectives are usually in the long form, but they may also take the short, for example: Ко гра́ду бг҃а жива́гѡ (Heb. 12:22—"unto the city of the Living God"); but also: ꙗ҆́кѡ оу҆пова́хомъ на бг҃а жи́ва (I Tim. 4:10—"because we trust in the Living God"); see also II Cor. 6:16.

6) In the vocative case, only *masculine* singular adjectives can have the short form: *a)* substantivized adjectives (or passive participles) have only the short form: тѣ́мже, неизслѣ́дованне, со стра́хомъ зову́ ти (Akathist to the Sweetest Jesus, Oikos 2—"therefore, Thou inscrutable One, I call out to Thee in fear"); и҆ спаси́, бла́же, ду́шы на́шѧ (Invocation of the Holy Spirit—"and save our souls, O Good One"); *b)* determinants have the short and long form: Многоми́лостиве и҆ всеми́лостиве бж҃е мо́й (Morning Prayer 8-9—"O my God, Who art of many mercies, and all-merciful"); ѽро́де невѣ́рный и҆ развраще́нный (Matth. 17:17—"O faithless and perverse generation"); фарїсе́е слѣпы́й (Matth. 23:26—"Thou blind Pharisee"); here it should be noted that the short forms usually precede the modified word, whereas the long forms come after; but the reverse usage is also possible (§54): ѽ человѣ́че су́етне (Jas. 2:20—"O vain man").

In the feminine (and neuter) singular, and in the plural in all genders, adjectives and participles (both substantivized and determinant) have the vocative case only in the long form.

7) Substantivized adjectives and participles with a collective meaning are usually in the long form of the neuter plural, for example: невозмѡ́жнаѧ* оу̓ человѣ́кѣхъ возмѡ́жна сꙋ́ть оу̓ бг҃а (Luke 18:27—"The things which are impossible with men are possible with God"); и̓ вси лю́дїе ра́довахꙋсѧ ѡ всѣ́хъ сла́вныхъ* быва́ющихъ* ѿ негѡ̀ (Luke 13:17—"And all the people rejoiced for all the glorious things that were done by him"); but (with an indefinite sense): стра̑нна* бо нѣ̑каѧ влага́еши во оу̓шеса̀ на́шѧ (Acts 17:20—"For thou bringest certain new things to our ears").

Substantivized adjectives, relating to some definite concept, with a general or abstract sense, are used in the long form in the neuter singular, for example: и̓́же мно́гое*, не оу̓мно́жилъ е҆́сть, и̓ ма́лое* не оу̓ма́лилъ (II Cor. 8:15—"He that [had gathered] much, had nothing over; and he that [had gathered] little had no lack"); не по повелѣ́нїю глаго́лю, но за ины́хъ тща́нїе и̓ ва́шеѧ любвѐ и̓́стинное* и̓скꙋша́ѧ (II Cor. 8:8—"I speak not by commandment, but by occasion of the forwardness of others, and to prove the sincerity of your love"); до́брое* же творѧ́ще да не стꙋжа́емъ сѝ... да дѣ́лаимъ бл҃го́е* ко всѣ́мъ (Gal. 6:9-10—"Let us not be weary in well doing... let us do good to all men").

9) Substantivized participles are employed, usually, only in the long form, for example: сѐ прибли́жисѧ предаѧ́й* мѧ̀ (Matth. 26:46—"he is at hand that doth betray me"); всѧ́къ бо просѧ́й* прїе́млетъ, и̓ и̓щѧ́й* ѡ҆брѣта́етъ, и̓ толкꙋ́щемꙋ* ѿве́рзетсѧ (Matth. 7:8—"For every one that asketh receiveth; and he that seeketh findeth; and to him that knocketh it shall be opened"); благослови́те кленꙋ́щыѧ* вы̀ (Luke 6:28—"Bless them that curse you"); и̓змове́нный* не тре́бꙋетъ, то́кмѡ но́зѣ оу̓мы́ти (John 13:10—"He that is washed needeth not save to wash his feet").

Substantivized passive participles, since they are close to adjectives, can have a short form, for example, when they designate an entity mentioned for the first time: Й прїиде къ немꙋ прокаженъ* (Mark 1:40—"And there came a leper to him"); see also Matth. 8:2; Matth. 9:2; Mark 2:3.

When two substantivized participles are connected by a conjunction, if they both express one and the same individual, then the first is in the long form, the second in the short (this may reflect the influence of the Greek language, where, in such cases, one definite article, common to both, is placed before the first participle), for example: Блажени не видѣвшїи* й вѣровавше* (John 20:29— "Blessed are they that have not seen, and yet have believed"); Тꙗкѡ собнрааи* себѣ, а не въ бга богатѣꙗ* (Luke 12:21—"So is he that layeth up treasure for himself, and is not rich toward God"); see also: Luke 11:28; Matth. 13:19; Matth. 7:26; Matth. 23:24.

10) Determinant participles usually are used in the long form, although short forms also occur (for the most part passive participles); for example, *long forms:* Тѣмже ꙋбо ни хотꙗщагѡ*, ни текꙋщагѡ*, но милꙋющагѡ* бга (Rom. 9:16—"So then it is not of him that willeth, nor of him that runneth, but of God that sheweth mercy"); Ꙗкѡ скорбь ми есть велїа, й не престающаа* болѣзнь сердцꙋ моемꙋ (Rom. 9:2—"That I have great heaviness and continual sorrow in my heart"); Тѣмже ѡслабленнаа* колѣна исправите (Heb. 12:12—"Wherefore lift up [the hands which hang down, and] the feeble knees"); радꙋйтеса радостїю неизглаголанною* й прославленною* (I Peter 1:8—"rejoice with joy unspeakable and full of glory"); *short forms:* да искꙋшенїе вашеа вѣры многочестнѣйше злата гибнꙋща*, Огнемъ же искꙋшена, ѡбращаетса въ похвалꙋ (I Peter 1:7 —"That the trial of your faith, being much more precious than of gold that perisheth, thoughit be tried with fire, might be found unto praise"); созданїе ѿ бга имамы, храминꙋ нерꙋкотворенꙋ* (II Cor. 5:1—"we have a building of God, an house

not made with hands"); Тѣ́мже ца́рство непоколеби́мо* прїе́млюще, да и́мамы благода́ть (Heb. 12:28—"Wherefore we receiving a kingdom which cannot be moved, let us have grace").

11) Determinant participles, when used with personal pronouns, are usually in the short form (though passive participles are to be met with in the long form as well), for example: я́кw лѣна́щаса менѐ на твоѐ оу̓гожде́нїе (4th Evening Prayer—"for when I was slothful in seeking to please Thee"); да́рꙋй мн воста́вшꙋ словесѐмх твои́мх поꙋчи́тнса (ibid.—"grant me, upon rising, to be instructed by Thy sayings"); оу̓мерщвле́на ма̀ страстьмѝ ѡ̓живѝ (7th Morning Prayer [Midnight Hymn to the Most Holy theotokos]—"enliven me who am deadened by passions"). However, if the participle refers more to a person than to an action, then the long form is used, for example: и̓ призовѝ ма̀ оу̓нываю́щаго (Akathist to the Sweetest Jesus, Kondak 12—"and call me who am downcast").

12) Concerning the determinant participles and adjectives, when they stand in place of a predicate in subordinate clauses, see §196, 1).

13) Of the two short forms of participles in the nominative masculine singular, (§§95 — 96), the forms with the suffixes -щ, _ш are generally used in a determinant sense, while the forms without a suffix are used in a predicative sense (§172, 4). The short forms of participles in the neuter nominative/accusative case ending in _що, _шо have a like determinant use, for exmple: Предпра́зднственный днесь мꙋ́ченнкwвх наста̀ пра́здникх: ржде́ственный на́мх предподпнсꙋ́ющх* де́нь, ѿ сл́нца со́лнце, ѿ дѣ́вы бга я̓́вльшаса пло́тїю проповѣ́дающх* (Dec. 23 at 'Lord I have cried'—"Today the martyrs' pre-festive feast is come, anticipating the day of the Nativity, proclaiming Him Who is the Sun from the Sun, God Who came forth from the Virgin"); Торжествꙋ́ющїй свѣ́тлw жела́ющх* та̀ гра́дх (Feb. 24, Ode 3—"The city that, celebrating brightly,

seeketh thee"); нεвέщεⷭтвεнⷤ сьıй пρέждε, но послѣ́ждε сло́во ѡ̀дεкεлѣ́кшю* пло́тїю (Nativity of Christ, Ode 3—"He that was before without material body, but was in after times vested in flesh"); the neuter participle is sometimes to be met with in a substantivized sense as well: Смотрѧ́ющε пρεбывáющихⷶ, мꙋ́дρїи, пρисносꙋ́щноε, нεпостоáнныхⷶ и тлѣ́нныхⷶ до́лꙋ влεкꙋ́що* ѿрини́стε (Jan. 13, 3rd Canon, Ode 3—"Looking at those things that remain [eternally], ye wise ones, ye cast aside those things the downward pull of those things that pass away and are subject to corruption").

§172. *Predicate adjectives and participles.* Adjectives and participles, when they become predicative, are as a general rule used in the short form. One might note the following positions in which adjectives and participles are predicative:

1) In the strict sense, those adjectives and participles are classed as predicative, that make up the nominal part of a composite predicate (§125, *c), d)*, for example: *adjectives:* вѣ́ρεнⷤ є҆́сть и̑ пρáвεдεнⷤ (I John 1:9—"he is faithful and just"); по́лни сꙋ́ть косте́й (Matth. 23:27—"[but] are [within] full of [dead men's] bones"); *passive participles:* ѿ бг҃а ρождέнⷤ є҆́сть (I John 5:1—"is born of God"); вεдέни бꙋ́дεтε мεнέ ρáди (Matth. 10:18—"ye shall be brought [before governors and kings] for my sake"); *active participles, descriptive forms* (§§90, 163): бѣ̀ бо оу̑чѧ̀ и̑хⷶ, ꙗ҆́кѡ влáсть и̑мы́й (Mark 1:22—"for he taught them as one that had authority"); нε пρεстà ѡ̀блобы́заю́щε ми́ но́зѣ (Luke 7:45—"hath not ceased to kiss my feet"); ѡ̀бρѣ́тεсѧ и̑мꙋ́щи во чρέвѣ (Matth. 1:18—"she was found with child").

Adjectives and participles that make up the nominal part of a predicate, however, may be in the long form, if they are used like nouns (i.e. if they are substantivized), for example: кто̀ є҆́сть ближнїй мо́й (Luke 10:29—"who is my neighbor?"); вѣ́даше .о̀ и̑сконѝ і҆и҃съ, кі́и сꙋ́ть нε вѣ́ρꙋющїи, и̑ кто̀ є҆́сть пρεдаáй є҆го̀ (John

6:64—"For Jesus knew from the beginning who they were that believed not, and who should betray him").

2) When there is a double accusative, the second predicate accusative (see §136, §143, 3 and 8), for example: и҆ запꙋстѣвшꙋ* со'тко́рѧтъ ю҆ и҆ на́гꙋ* (Rev. 17:16—"and shall make her desolate and naked"); ѡ҆сꙋди́ша є҆го̀ бы́ти пови́нна* сме́рти (Mark 14:64—"they [all] condemned him to be guilty of death"). When there is a double genitive, the second predicate genitive (§136): Хрⷭ҇тїа́нскїѧ кончи́ны живота̀ на́шегѡ, безболѣ́зненны*, непосты́дны*, ми́рны*... про́симъ (Litany of fervent supplication—"A Christian ending to our life, without pain, without shame, peaceful... let us ask"). When there is a double dative, the second predicate dative (§143, 6): Подоба́етъ ѹ҆́бо є҆пⷭ҇копꙋ бы́ти непоро́чнꙋ*... тре́звенꙋ, цѣломꙋ́дрꙋ*... (I Tim. 3:2—"A bishop then must be blameless... vigilant, sober...");

3) Adjunct [adverbial] adjectives (§145), for example: Трїдне́венъ* воскре́слъ є҆сѝ, Хрⷭ҇тѐ ѿ гро́ба (Octoechos, T. 6, Sunday at the Praises—"Thou art risen on the third day [as one who is of three days], O Christ, from the tomb").

4) Adjunct participles (see §146), for example: и҆ возопи́въ*, и҆ мно́гѡ прꙋжа́вса*, и҆зы́де (Mark 9:26—"And [the spirit] cried, and rent him sore, and came out [of him]").

5) A participle in the dative absolute (see §197), for example: и҆ вше́дшꙋ* є҆мꙋ̀ въ до́мъ, ѹ҆ченицы̀ є҆гѡ̀ вопроша́хꙋ є҆го̀ є҆ди́наго (Mark 9:28—"And when he was come into the house, his disciples asked him privately").

6) An adjective and a passive participle with an active copula participle — determinatives: сы́й, сꙋ́щаѧ, бы́вый, бы́вшаѧ: circumstantial: сы́й, сꙋ́щи, бы́въ, бы́вши (see §146, 4 and 5; §196, b), for example: херꙋві́мѡвъ свѣтлѣ́йши*, и҆ серафі́мѡвъ честнѣ́йши* сꙋ́щаѧ (Prayer after the Akathist [to the Theotokos]—"Being brighter than the Cherubim, and more honourable than the Seraphim"); и҆ вїю́ще и҆́хъ со́вѣсть не́моцинꙋ* сꙋ́щꙋ (I Cor.

8:12—"and [when ye] wound their weak conscience"); и҆ трепе́тенъ* бы́въ, припадѐ къ па́ѵлꙋ и҆ сі́лѣ (Acts 16:29—"and trembling, he fell down before Paul and Silas").

With copula-participles (determinant or adverbial) from the semi-significant verbs (see §124): ꙗ҆вле́йсѧ, ꙗ҆́вльсѧ, показа́выйсѧ, показа́всѧ, пребыва́ѧй, пребыва́ѧ and the like, for example: ѡ҆́бразы несвѣ́тлы, и҆ сѣ́ни приведе́ны... ви́дѣвше сло́ва, но́ва* ꙗ҆́вльшагѡсѧ ѿ вра́тъ заключе́нныхъ (Nativity of the Lord, Ode 9—"Having seen dark images and diverted shadows [O pure Mother] of the new Word that hath shone forth [from a closed portal, and believing Him to be the True Light, we rightfully bless thy womb]").

With the participles (determinant or adverbial) of verbs that have a second predicate accusative: сотвори́вый, сотво́рь, показа́вый, показа́въ, зрѧ́й, зрѧ̀ [making, showing, seeing], and the like, for example: печа́ть бо дѣ́вства моегѡ̀ зрѧ́щи неразрꙋ́шимꙋ* (Dec. 26, Oikos—"seeing the seal of my virginity [to be] unbroken").

7) With the conjunction ꙗ҆́кѡ [since, because], for example: Ꙗ҆́кѡ бл҃гъ* и҆ чл҃вѣколю́бецъ (Sluzhebnik, exclamation—"For [Thou art] a good [God] and lovest mankind").

The use of the shorts forms of adjectives or passive participles, when they are predicate parts with a copula-participle, however, is not always strictly adhered to: the full forms are also encountered in this position, for example: Ѻ҆ба́че блага́ѧ* сꙋ́щи, вѣ́рꙋ прїимѝ (Theophany, 9th Eirmos—"But inasmuch as thou art gracious, accept thou our faith"); но пребыва́ѧ неѿстꙋ́пный* (Kondak of the Ascension—"but abiding uninterruptedly [with us]"); всѣ́хъ тва́рей нб҃сныхъ и҆ зе́мныхъ вы́шшаѧ* ꙗ҆́вльшаѧсѧ (Prayer after the Akathist Hymn—"thou who art [*lit.* hast shown thyself] higher than all the creatures of heaven and earth").

The Main Sentence Types.

§173.   *Types of sentences according to the nature of the utterance.* Based on the nature of their content, sentences may be divided, as in Russian and other languages, into these categories: narrative, interrogative, exhortative [expressing a command or incitement], and exclamatory.

1) *Narrative* sentences are those that inform us of some fact or event, for example: и҆ и҆зы́де сло́во сїѐ по все́й і҆ꙋде́и ѡ҆ не́мъ, и҆ по все́й стране́ (Luke 7:17—"And this rumour of him went forth throughout all Judæa, and throughout all the region round about").

2) *Interrogative* sentences are those that ask a question. Interrogative sentences are usually formed by means of interrogatory pronouns, adverbs or particles (кто̀, что̀, что̀ ꙗ҆́кѡ, кі́й, чі́й, гдѣ̀,вскꙋ́ю, ли, а҆́ще, є҆да̀ [who? what? what for? what kind of? whose? where? why? {untranslated interrogative particle}, if? can it be?] and the like). After interrogative sentences, a question mark (;) is normally used. Examples: Ты̀ ли є҆сѝ гряды́й, и҆лѝ и҆но́гѡ ча́емъ; (Luke 7:20—"Art thou he that should come? or look we for another?"); Но чесѡ̀ и҆зыдо́сте ви́дѣти; прⷬо́ка ли; (Luke 7:26—"But what went ye out for to see? A prophet?"); ѽ ро́де невѣ́рный и҆ развраще́нный, доко́лѣ терплю̀ ва́мъ; (Matth. 17:17—"O faithless and perverse generation, how long shall I suffer you?").

3) *Hortatory*   sentences are those that express the will [command] of the speaker. Hortatory sentences are usually expressed by means of the imperative or optative mood, for example: ѡ҆бла́зи съ на́ма, ꙗ҆́кѡ къ ве́черꙋ є҆́сть (Luke 24:29—"Abide with us, for it is toward evening"); гдⷭ҇и, да прозрю̀ (Luke 18:41—"Lord, that I may receive my sight").

4) *Exclamatory* sentences are those that express an emotional attitude of the speaker to that which is said. In Church Slavonic, exclamatory sentences are usually set apart by a comma or period;

however, after an exclamatory sentence expressing amazement, there may be an exclamation mark (called ѹ҆диви́тельнаѧ), for example: Полꙋ́нощи же во́пль бы́сть: сѐ жени́хъ гряде́тъ, и҆сходи́те въ срѣ́теніе є҆гѡ̀ (Matth. 25:6—"And at midnight there was a cry made, Behold, the bridegroom cometh; go ye out to meet him"). Сн҃е даві́довъ, поми́лꙋй мѧ̀ (Mark 10:48—"[Thou] Son of David, have mercy on me"). Ѽ ка́кѡ, въ вы́шнихъ непости́жимь сы́й, ѿ дв҃ы ражда́етсѧ! (Annunciation, at "Lord I have cried"—"O, how can He Who on high is beyond comprehension be born of a Virgin!").

§174. *Incomplete sentences.* These are sentences lacking one or more parts, but which are easily grasped from the context. Incomplete sentences are usually found in a dialogue, but they may occur also in the narrative form of a story, for example: є҆гда̀ пѧ́ть хлѣ́бы преломи́хъ въ пѧ́ть ты́сѧщъ, коли́кѡ кѡ́шъ и҆спо́лнь ѹ҆крꙋ́хъ прїѧ́сте; глаго́лаша є҆мꙋ̀: двана́десѧть* (Mark 8:19—"When I brake the five loaves among five thousand, how many baskets full of fragments took ye up? They said unto him, Twelve"); чі́й ѻ҆́бразъ сі́й и҆ написа́ніе; ѻ҆ни́ же рѣ́ша є҆мꙋ̀: ке́саревъ* (Mark 12:16—"Whose is this image and superscrition? And they said unto him, Caesar's"); и҆ вторы́й поѧ́тъ ю̀, и҆ ѹ҆́мре, и҆ ни то́й ѡ҆ста́ви сѣ́мене: и҆ тре́тїй* та́кожде* (Mark 12:21—"And the second took her, and died, neither left he any seed: and the third likewise").

§175. *One-part sentences.* One-part sentences may be of the following types: indefinite-personal, generalized-personal, and impersonal.

Nominative sentences are those that consist of only a subject as the main part. This type of sentence is met with only rarely in Church Slavonic, for the most part in liturgical chants, for example: Безсѣ́меннагѡ зача́тїѧ рождество̀ несказа́нное, мт҃ре безмꙋ́жныѧ нетлѣ́нный пло́дъ*, бж҃їе бо рожде́ніе ѡ҆бновлѧ́етъ є҆стества̀ (Great Canon—"From a conception without seed, a nativity beyond understanding; from a Mother who knew not man, a fruit without corruption*; for the birth of God makes [both] natures new"). Here the first is a nominative sentence, while the second is of a connective character, clarifying the first. Є҆́же ѿ вѣ́ка ѹ҆таѐнноє, и҆ а҆́гг҃лѡмъ несвѣ́домоє та́инство*: тобо́ю, бц҃е, сꙋ́щымъ на землѝ ꙗ҆ви́сѧ бг҃ъ. (Sunday Tropar-Theotokion, T. 4: "The mystery hidden from all ages and unknown to the Angels*: through thee, God was manifest to those on earth"). Here the construction is similar to that in the preceding example.

1) *Indefinite-personal.* To the indefinite personal sentences belong those in which the predicate, expressed by a 3rd person plural verb form, signifies an action carried out by persons unspecified, for example: глаго́ла и҆́ма, ꙗ҆́кѡ взѧ́ша* гд҃а моего̀, и҆ не вѣ́мъ, гдѣ̀ положи́ша* є҆го̀ (John 20:13—"She said unto them, Because they have taken away my Lord, and I know not where they have laid him"); безꙋ́мне, въ сїю̀ но́щь дꙋ́шꙋ твою̀ и҆стѧ́жꙋтъ ѿ тебѐ (Luke 12:20—"[Thou] fool, this night thy soul shall be required of thee").

In Church Slavonic, such sentences are comparatively rare.

2) *Generalized personal sentences.* In these, the action indicated by the predicate refers to any individual. The predicate verb is usually expressed by the second person singular or plural, or sometimes by a 3rd person plural form, for example: лицемѣ́ре (in a generalized sense), и҆змѝ* пе́рвѣе бервно̀ и҆з̾ ѻ҆чесѐ твоегѡ̀ и҆ тогда̀ ѹ҆́зриши* и҆з̾ѧ́ти сꙋче́цъ и҆з̾ ѻ҆чесѐ бра́та твоегѡ̀ (Matth. 7:5—"Thou hypocrite, first cast out the beam out of thine own eye; and then shalt thou see clearly to cast out the mote out of thy brother's eye"); и҆́мже сꙋдо́мъ сꙋ́диши* дрꙋ́га, себѐ ѡ҆сꙋжда́еши* (Rom. 2:1—"For wherein thou judgest another, thou condemnest thyself"); и҆щи́те* и҆ ѡ҆брѧ́щете* (Matth. 7:7—"seek, and ye shall find"); не сꙋди́те* и҆ не сꙋ́дѧтъ* ва́мъ (Luke 6:37—"Judge not, and ye shall not be judged").

A verb in the 3rd person plural more often indicates a generalized action, for example: не ѿ те́рнїѧ бо че́шꙋтъ смо́квы, ни ѿ кꙋпины̀ є҆́млютъ гро́здїѧ (Luke 6:44—"For of thorns men do not gather figs, nor of a bramble bush gather they grapes"); Всѧ́ко ᲂу҆́бѡ др+́во, є҆́же не тво́ритъ плода̀ добра̀, посѣка́ютъ є҆̀, и҆ во ѻ҆́гнь вмета́ютъ (Matth. 7:19—"Every tree that bringeth not forth good fruit is hewn down, and cast into the fire").

3) *Impersonal sentences.* To these belong one-part sentences in which the predicate expresses an action or condition without any relation to the one who performs it. The predicate in impersonal sentences may be expressed in the following ways:

a) By a conjugated form of the verb in the 3rd person singular, with the reflexive pronoun -сѧ. The verb довлѣ́етъ [it is enough, suffices] is used impersonally without -сѧ. For example: да́йте, и҆ да́стсѧ* ва́мъ (Luke 6:38—"Give, and it shall be given unto you"); въ ню́же мѣ́рᲂу мѣ́рите, возмѣ́ритсѧ* ва́мъ (Matth. 7:2—"with what measure ye mete, it shall be measured to you again"); покажѝ на́мъ ѻ҆ц҃а̀, и҆ довлѣ́етъ на́мъ (John 14:8—"shew us the Father, and it sufficeth us").

b) By the semi-significant verbs подоба́етъ, досто́итъ [it is proper, right] in combination with the infinitive, for example: и҆ ты̑ѧ мѝ подоба́етъ привестѝ (John 10:16—"them also must I bring [it behooveth me to bring]"); не подоба́ше ли и҆ тебѣ̀ поми́ловати клевре́та твоегѡ̀ (Matth. 18:33—"Shouldest not thou also have had compassion on thy fellow servant?"); досто́итъ ли въ сᲂу́ббѡ̑ты добро̀ твори́ти (Mark 3:4—"Is it lawful to do good on the sabbath days?"); досто́итъ ли кинсо́нъ ке́саревн да́ти, и҆лѝ нѝ; (Mark 12:14—"Is it lawful to give tribute to Cæsar, or not?").

c) By neuter passive participles or adjectives (to which might be added the invariable word лѣ́ть ["it is permissible"]) with a 3rd person copula from the verb бы́ти, for example: па́ки пи́сано* є҆́сть*: не и҆скᲂуси́ши гд҃а бг҃а твоегѡ̀ (Matth. 4:7—"It is written again: Thou shalt not tempt the Lord thy God"); слы́шасте, ꙗ҆́кѡ рече́но* бы́сть* дре́внимъ (Matth. 5:21—"Ye have heard that it was said to them of old time"); досто́йно* ли є҆́сть* да́ти кинсо́нъ ке́саревн, и҆лѝ нѝ;

(Matth. 22:17—"Is it lawful to give tribute unto Cæsar, or not?");
человѣка ри́млѧни́на и̂ неѡсꙋжде́на лѣ́ть* ли е҆сть* ва́мъ би́ти;
(Acts 22:25—"Is it lawful for you to scourge a man that is a Roman,
and uncondemned?").

d) By nouns, to which го́ре, нꙋжда, вре́мѧ, потре́ба and the
like refer. Such nouns form the nominal [noun-] part of a composite
predicate with omitted copula. For example: Го́ре* ва́мъ кни́жницы
и̂ фарїсе́є лицемѣ́ри (Matth. 23:13—"Woe unto you, scribes and
Pharisees, hypocrites!"); нꙋжда* бо е҆сть прїити́ собла́зншмъ
(Matth. 18:7—"for it must needs be that offences come"); ꙗ̂кѡ
вре́мѧ* нача́ти сꙋдъ ѿ до́мꙋ бж҃їѧ (I Peter 4:17—"For the time is
come that judgment must begin at the house of God"); Тѣ́мже
потре́ба* повинова́тисѧ не то́кмѡ за гнѣ́въ, но и̂ за со́вѣсть
(Rom. 13:5—"Wherefore ye must needs be subject, not only for
wrath, but also for conscience sake").

e) By forms of the verb бы́ти with negation, in combination
with nouns in the genitive case, for example: и̂дѣ́же бо нѣ́сть*
зако́на*, [тꙋ] ни* престꙋпле́нїѧ* (Rom. 4:15—"for where no law
is, there is no transgression"); и̂ но́щи* не бꙋ́детъ* та́мѡ (Rev.
22:5—"And there shall be no night there").

f) By forms of the verb бы́ти with words indicating time, for
example: ѡ̂бла́зи съ на́ма, ꙗ̂кѡ къ ве́черꙋ* е҆сть* (Luke
24:29—"Abide with us, for it is toward evening"); и̂ ꙗ̂кѡ по́здѣ*
бы́сть*, и̂схожда́ше во́нъ и̂зъ гра́да (Mark 11:19—"And when even
was come, he went out of the city").

g) By the verb бы́сть in the sense of "it came to pass" (§160),
for example: и̂ бы́сть* во е̂ди́нъ ѿ дне́й (Luke 8:22—"Now it came
to pass on a certain day").

§176. Sentence Members of the Same Kind.

Several syntactically alike members, having the same relationship to one and the same part of the sentence, are known as sentence members *of the same kind*, for example: Привед0́ста Осла̀* и̂ жреба̀* (Matth. 21:7—"They brought the ass, and the colt").

Both the main and the secondary sentence parts may be 'of the same kind', for instance, subjects of the same kind: На мѡѷсе́овѣ сѣдалищи сѣд0́ша кни́жницы* и̂ фарїсе҄є (Matth. 23:2—"The scribes and the Pharisees sit in Moses' seat"); predicates of the same kind: и̂дѣ́же та́тїе подкопыва́ютъ* и̂ кра́дꙋтъ* (Matth. 6:20—"where thieves break through and steal"); вїноградъ насади́* чл҃вѣ́къ, и̂ ѡ̂гради́* ѡ̂пло́томъ, и̂ и̂скопа̀* точи́ло, и̂ созда̀* сто́лпъ, и̂ преда́дѐ* є҄го̀ та́жателємъ, и̂ ѿи́де* (Mark 12:1—"A certain man planted a vineyard, and set an hedge about it, and dug a place for the wine press, and built a tower, and let it out to husbandmen, and went away"); complements of the same kind: Но е҄гда̀ твори́ши пи́ръ, зовѝ ни́щыѧ*, маломѡ́щныѧ*, хрѡмы́ѧ*, слѣпы́ѧ*, (Luke 14:13—"But when thou makest a feast, call the poor, the maimed, the lame, the blind"); attributes of the same kind: въ наслѣ́дїе нетлѣ́нно* и̂ нескве́рно* и̂ неꙋвада́емо* (I Peter 1:4—"To an inheritance incorruptible, and undefiled, and that fadeth not away"); adjuncts of the same kind: и̂ прїи́дꙋтъ ѿ восто́къ* и̂ за́падъ* и̂ сѣ́вера* и̂ ю́га* (Luke 13:29—"And they shall come from the east, and from the west, and from the north, and from the south").

Sentence members of the same kind are usually connected by conjunctions, be they connective,adversative, or disjunctive conjunctions (see §114). In a construction joining like members of the sentence, the following characteristics occur: the connective conjunction и̂ may be repeated before each of the like members, or else it may stand only before the last one; the enumeration of members of the same kind is also possible without a conjunction. Examples: With connective conjunctions: и̂ бꙋ́дꙋтъ гла́ди и̂ па́гꙋбы и́ гр҃си по мѣстѡ́мъ (Matth. 24:7—"and there shall be famines, and pestilences, and earthquakes, in diverse places"); и҆збра́ннымъ прише́льцємъ разсѣ́аніѧ по́нта*, галаті́и*, каппадокі́и*, а҆сі́и* и҆ ві҃,о,ѵні́и* (I Peter 1:1—"To the chosen wanderers in the diaspora, of Pontos, Galatia, Cappadocia, Asia and Bithynia"); не стѧжи́те зла́та*, ни сребра̀*, ни мѣ́ди* при поѧсѣ́хъ ва́шихъ (Matth. 10:9—"Provide neither gold, nor silver, nor brass in your purses"); въ тѣ́хъ слежа́ше мно́жество болѧ́щихъ*, слѣпы́хъ*, хромы́хъ*, сꙋхи́хъ*, ча́ющихъ движе́ніѧ воды̀ (John 5:3—"In these lay a great multitude of impotent folk, of blind, halt, withered, waiting for the moving of the water"). With adversative conjunctions: не ѹ҆́мре* дѣ́вица, но спи́тъ* (Matth. 9:24—"the maid is not dead, but sleepeth"); благослови́те*, а҆ не клени́те* (Rom. 12:14—"bless, and curse not"); и҆ прини́къ ви́дѣ* ри́зы лежа́щѧ: Ѻ҆ба́че не вни́де* (John 20:5—"And stooping down, he saw the linen clothes lying; yet went he not in"); не то́кмѡ бре́мене* и҆ корабла̀*, но и҆ дꙋ́шъ* на́шихъ хо́щетъ бы́ти пла́ваніе (Acts 27:10—"this voyage will be [with hurt and much damage] not only of the lading and ship, but also of our lives"); With disjunctive conjunctions: и҆ всѧ́къ и҆́же ѡ҆ста́витъ до́мъ*, и҆лѝ бра́тїю*, и҆лѝ сестры̀*, и҆лѝ ѻ҆ц҃а̀*, и҆лѝ ма́терь*, и҆лѝ женꙋ̀*, и҆лѝ ча́да*, и҆лѝ села̀*, и҆́мене моегѡ̀ ра́ди, сторице́ю прїи́метъ... (Matth. 19:29—"And everyone that hath forsaken houses, or brethren, or sisters, or father, or mother, or wife, or children, or lands, for my name's sake, shall receive an hundredfold..."); Никто́же мо́жетъ двѣма̀ господи́нома рабо́тати: лю́бо є҆ди́наго возлю́битъ*, а҆ дрꙋга́го возненави́дитъ*: и҆лѝ є҆ди́нагѡ держи́тсѧ*, ѡ҆ дрꙋзѣ́мъ же неради́ти* на́чнетъ* (Matth. 6:24—"No man can serve two masters: for either he will hate the one, and love the other, or else he will hold to the one, and become careless of the other").

Note: In older grammars, sentences having members of the same kind were viewed as **joint sentences**, based on the idea that they could be logically divided into several sentences, for example: Приведо́ста ѻ҆сла̀ и҆ жреба̀ (Matth. 21:7) = прикедо́ста Ѻ҆сла̀ и҆ прикедо́ста жреба̀ — "they brought an ass and they brought a colt".

Sentence members of the same kind, in general, are set apart by a comma in the same manner as in other languages, except for the following peculiarity: two like predicates, joined by the conjunction и҆, if they have dependant words with them, are separated by a comma, for example: се́ мы̀ ѡ҆ста́вихомъ* всѧ̑, и҆ въ слѣ́дъ тебѐ и҆до́хомъ* (Matth. 19:27—"Behold, we have forsaken all, and followed thee"); прїиди́те, ѹ҆бїе́мъ* є҆го̀, и҆ ѹ҆держи́мъ* достоѧ́нїе є҆гẁ (Matth. 21:38—"come, let us kill him, and [let us] seize on his inheritance").

The Compound Sentence.

§177. General Observations on Compound Sentences.
Compound sentences in Church Slavonic may be put together either as coördinate or as subordinate sentences. The construction of compound sentences is in many ways quite close to such sentences in Russian, making it possible to use the same classification as in Russian grammars. However, despite a certain similarity there is also a noteworthy difference — Church Slavonic has considerably fewer conjunctions (though some conjunctions do have more than one meaning, for example ꙗ҆́кw, а҆́ще), and consequently, sentences have less variety as to how they can express one thought or another. Besides that, Church Slavonic also has constructions not found in Russian — such as sentences with the infinitive and sentences with a peculiar use of the participle, known as the "dative absolute".

Compound sentences, according to their structure, are subdivided into compound coördinate and compound subordinate.

The subordinate clause forms a special section under the compound subordinate sentences.

§178. Compound [Coördinate] Sentences.

Two or more simple sentences, joined by a copulative conjunction, constitute a *compound [coördinate] sentence.*

The phrases that make up a compound sentence are considered independent, although their independence is conditional, and in a number of situations the components of a compound coördinate sentence set conditions for each other, for example: и̑ желаше насытити чрево ѿ рожецъ...: и̑ никто̀ же даꙗше є̑мꙋ (Luke 15:16—"And he would fain have filled his belly with the husks...: and no man gave unto him"). In the second clause the word рожецъ is omitted, since it is common to both clauses.

Depending on the conjunctions joining them, compound coördinate sentences are divided into copulative, adversative, disjunctive and causative categories.

§179. Copulative Coördination.

Copulative compound [coördinate] sentences are joined together by means of the conjunctions и̑, и̑ — и̑, ни[жѐ], ни — ни[жѐ], та́кожде. In Scriptural texts, the link effected in sentences by the conjunction и̑ is not too strong — this conjunction is often more *connective* than copulative, and it serves merely to show the continuation of a narrative, for which reason it occurs with a high frequency: for instance, in the 3rd chapter of the Gospel of St. Mark, out of 35 verses, 28 begin with the conjunction и̑ (which corresponds literally to the Greek text).

In compound coördinate sentences with the conjunction и̑, temporal relationships are usually expressed: coördinate sentences may express *simultaneous* actions, *sequence* of actions, or else relationships of *cause* and *result* between actions.

For example:

1) Sentences expressing simultaneous actions: и̑ поме́рче со́лнце, и̑ завѣ́са црко́внаꙗ раздра́са посредѣ̀ (Luke 23:45—"And the

sun was darkened, and the veil of the temple was rent in the midst");
Не вѣсте ли ꙗкѡ храмъ Бжїй є҆сте, и҆ дх҃ъ Бж҃їй живе́тъ въ ва́съ (I
Cor. 3:16—"Know ye not that ye are the temple of God, and that the
Spirit of God dwelleth in you?"); А҆бїе по ско́рби дні́й тѣ́хъ, со́лнце
поме́ркнетъ, и҆ луна̀ не да́стъ свѣ́та своегѡ̀, и҆ звѣ́зды спаду́тъ съ
нб҃сѐ, и҆ си́лы нб҃сны҆ꙗ подви́гнутсѧ (Matth. 24:29—"Immediately
after the tribulation of those days shall the sun be darkened, and the
moon shall not give her light, and the stars shall fall from heaven, the
powers of the heavens shall be shaken").

2) Sentences expressing a sequence of actions: ѻ҆́ва падо́ша на
путѝ: и҆ прїидо́ша пти́цы и҆ позоба́ша ꙗ҆̀ (Matth. 13:4—"some
[seeds] fell by the wayside, and the fowls came and devoured them
up"); прїи́де въ до́мъ і҆и҃съ, и҆ приступи́ша къ нему̀ о҆у҆ченицы̀ є҆гѡ̀
(Matth. 13:36—"Jesus... went into the house, and his disciples came
unto him"); и҆ и҆зы́де во́нъ на придво́рїе: и҆ а҆ле́кторъ возгласи́ (Mark
14:68—"And he went out into the porch: and the cock crew"); и҆ сни́де
до́ждь, и҆ прїидо́ша рѣ́ки, и҆ возвѣ́ꙗша вѣ́три (Matth. 7:25—"And
the rain descended, and the floods came, and the winds blew").

3) Sentences expressing a cause-and-effect relationship: тогда̀
воста́въ запретѝ вѣ́трѡмъ и҆ мо́рю, и҆ бы́сть тишина̀ ве́лїꙗ (Matth.
8:26—"Then he arose, and rebuked the winds and the sea; and there
was a great calm"); Ѻ҆ни́ же и҆зше́дше и҆до́ша въ ста́до свино́е: и҆ сѐ,
[а҆бїе] о҆у҆стреми́сѧ ста́до всѐ по брегу̀ въ мо́ре, и҆ о҆у҆топо́ша въ вода́хъ
(Matth. 8:32—"And when they were come out, they went into the
herd of swine: and, behold, the whole herd of swine ran violently
down a steep place into the sea, and perished in the waters");
Прибли́житесѧ бг҃у, и҆ прибли́житсѧ ва́мъ (James 4:8—"Draw nigh
to God, and he will draw nigh to you").

Relations of cause and result between clauses are especially
evident when the conjunction и҆ is followed by the conjoining
expression сегѡ̀ ра́ди: то́й воскре́се ѿ ме́ртвыхъ, и҆ сегѡ̀ ра́ди си́лы
дѣ́ютсѧ ѡ҆ не́мъ (Matth. 14:2—"he is risen from the dead; and
therefore mighty works do shew themselves in him").

To this form of compound sentence belong those sentences, also, that are composed using conjunctions of result or conclusion: тѣмже, тѣмъ, сегѡ ради, оубо, ѿсюдꙋ, ѿнюдꙋже, [="therefore, hence"], for example: кольми оубо лꙋчши человѣкъ ѻвча́те; тѣмже* достоитъ въ сꙋббѡ́ты добро̀ твори́ти (Matth. 12:12—"How much better then is a man than a sheep? Wherefore it is lawful to do good on the sabbath days"); Ибо не со́зданъ бы́сть мꙋжъ жены̀ ради, но жена̀ мꙋжа ради: сегѡ̀ ради* должна̀ є҆сть жена̀ власть имѣ́ти на главѣ̀ а҆́гглъ ради (I Cor. 11:9-10—"Neither was the man created for the woman; but the woman for the man. For this cause ought the woman to have power on her head because of the angels"); а҆́ще же хрⷭ҇то́съ не воста̀, сꙋе́тна вѣ́ра ва́ша, є҆щѐ є҆стѐ во грѣсѣ́хъ ва́шихъ: оубо* и҆ оу҆ме́ршїи ѡ хрⷭ҇тѣ́, погибо́ша (I Cor. 15:17-18—"And if Christ be not risen, your faith is in vain; ye are yet in your sins. Then also they which are fallen asleep in Christ, are perished"); и҆ на тѣ́хъ взꙗ́лъ є҆сѝ побѣ́ды, бжⷤїею си́лою, достосла́вне. Ѿсюдꙋ* по́честн тебѣ̀ о҆́че чꙋде́съ бл҃гі́й дарова̀ (Nov. 4, at "Lord I have cried"—"against them also [i.e. the demons] thou wast victorious, by the power of God, O thou who art worthy of glory. Therefore He that is good hath honoured thee by miracles"); и҆ бѡлѣ́зни на́ша подꙗ́лъ є҆сѝ. Ѿнюдꙋже* ра́нами твои́ми мы̀ и҆сцѣлѣ́вше, пѣ́ти навыко́хомъ: а҆ллилꙋ́їа (Akathist to the Sweetest Jesus—"and Thou hast borne our illnesses. Therefore, being healed through Thy wounds, we have learned to sing: Alleluia!").

Compound sentences with the conjunction и҆ may also express adversative relationships, for example: Бл҃гі́й человѣ́къ, ѿ бл҃га́гѡ сокро́вища, и҆зно́ситъ бл҃га́ꙗ: и҆ лꙋка́вый человѣ́къ, ѿ лꙋка́вагѡ сокро́вища, и҆зно́ситъ лꙋка́вꙗ (Matth. 12:35—"A good man out of the good treasure [of the heart] bringeth forth good things: and an evil man out of the evil treasure bringeth forth evil things").

The conjunctions ни[же], ни — ни[же] "neither — nor" are used in combining clauses of the same kind, with negation, for example: Нѣсть бо дрéво добрò, творѧ̀ плодà ѕлà: нижè дрéво ѕлò, творѧ̀ плодà добрà (Luke 6:43—"For a good tree bringeth not forth corrupt fruit; neither doth a corrupt tree bring forth good fruit"); не ѿ тéрнїѧ бо чéшꙋтъ смѡ́квы, ни ѿ кꙋпины̀ ꙟмлютъ грѡ́здїѧ (Luke 6:44—"For of thorns men do not gather figs, nor of a bramble bush gather they grapes").

The conjunction тáкожде ["likewise, also, as well"] is used with a suggestion of adding or incorporating some element, for example: Прїѧ́тъ же хлѣ́бы і҆и҃съ, и҆ хвалꙋ̀ воздáвъ, подадѐ о҆у҆ченникѡ́мъ, о҆у҆ченницы̀ же возлежáщымъ: тáкожде и҆ ѿ ры́бъ, ꙟлико хотѧ́хꙋ (John 6:11—"And Jesus took the loaves; and when he had given thanks, he distributed to the disciples, and the disciples to them that were set down; and likewise of the fishes, as much as they would"); и҆ трéтїй поѧ́тъ ю҆̀: тáкожде же и҆ всѝ сéдмь (Luke 20:31—"And the third took her; and in like manner the seven also").

Compound [coördinate] sentences may also be without a conjunction, for example: Тáмѡ пти̑цы вогнѣздѧ́тсѧ, е҆рѡдíево жили́ще предводи́тельствꙋетъ и҆ми (Ps. 103:17—"There the birds shall make their nests; the house of the heron is the foremost among them"); ѡ҆бы́доша мѧ̀ тельцы̀ мнóзи, ю҆нцы̀ тꙋ́чнїи ѡ҆держáша мѧ̀: ѿверзóша на мѧ̀ о҆у҆стà своѧ̀, ꙗкѡ лéвъ восхищáѧй и҆ рыкáѧй (Ps. 21:13-14—"Many calves have surrounded me, fat bulls have besieged me; they have opened their mouths against me, as a lion ravening and roaring"); и҆ ввéргꙋтъ и҆хъ въ пéщь óгненнꙋю: тꙋ̀ бꙋ́детъ плáчь и҆ скрéжетъ зꙋбѡ́мъ (Matth. 13:50—"And [they] shall cast them into the furnace of fire: there shall be wailing and gnashing of teeth"); тꙋне прїѧ́сте, тꙋне дади́те (Matth. 10:8—"freely ye have received, freely give"); Хр҃тóсъ раждáетсѧ, слáвите: хр҃тóсъ съ небéсъ, срѧ́щите: хр҃тóсъ на землѝ, возноси́тесѧ (Eirmos from the Canon of the Nativity, Ode 1—"Christ is born: glorify Him! Christ is from heaven: go to meet him! Christ is on earth: be ye exalted!").

§180. Adversative Coördination.

In adversative compound sentences, a relationship of *contrast* or *opposition* is expressed, sometimes with additional overtones (of disparity, restriction, concession and the like). Sentences of this type are composed with the aid of the conjunctions но, а, оу҆бо — же, ѻ҆ба́че, да. Of these, а and же are the most frequent. Examples: Не входѧ́щее во оу҆ста̀ скверни́тъ челов҄ѣка: но* и҆сходѧ́щее и҆зоу́стъ, то̀ скверни́тъ челов҄ѣка (Matth. 15:11—"Not that which goeth into the mouth defileth a man; but that which cometh out of the mouth, this defileth a man"); Въ не́мже злостражду̀ да́же и҆ до оу҆́зъ, ꙗ҆́кѡ злод҄ѣй: но* сло́во бж҃їе не вѧ́жетсѧ (II Tim. 2:9—"Wherein I suffer trouble, as an evildoer, even unto bonds; but the word of God is not bound"); ра́зоумъ оу҆́бо кичи́тъ, а* любы̀ созида́етъ (I Cor. 8:1—"Reason puffeth up, but charity edifieth"); Приближа́ютсѧ мн҄ѣ лю́дїе сі́и оу҆сты̀ свои́ми, и҆ оу҆стна́ми чтоу́тъ мѧ̀: се́рдце же* и҆́хъ дале́че ѿстои́тъ ѿ менѐ (Matth. 15:8—"This people draweth nigh unto me with their mouth, and honoureth me with their lips; but their heart is far from me"); жа́тва оу҆́бо* мно́га, д҄ѣлателей же* ма́лѡ (Matth. 9:37—"The harvest ruly is plentiful, but the labourers are few"); ноу́жда бо є҆́сть прїитѝ собла́знѡмъ: ѻ҆ба́че* го́ре челов҄ѣкоу томоу̀, и҆́мже собла́знъ прихо́дитъ (Matth. 18:7—"for it must needs be that offences come; but woe to that man by whom the offence cometh!"); не де́сѧть ли ѡ҆чи́стишасѧ; да* де́вѧть гд҄ѣ; (Luke 17:17—"Were not ten cleansed? but where are the nine?").

Adversative compound sentences may also be without a conjunction, for example: вы̀ ѿ ни́жнихъ є҆стѐ, а҆́зъ ѿ вы́шнихъ є҆́смь: вы̀ ѿ мі́ра сегѡ̀ є҆стѐ, а҆́зъ н҄ѣсмь ѿ мі́ра сегѡ̀ (John 8:23—"Ye are from beneath; I am from above: ye are of this world; I am not of this world"); и҆ сїѐ не ѿ ва́съ, бж҃їй да́ръ (Eph. 2:8—"and that not of yourselves: it is the gift of God"); ꙗ҆́кѡ ви́д҄ѣвъ мѧ̀, в҄ѣровалъ є҆сѝ: блаже́ни не ви́д҄ѣвшїи, и҆ в҄ѣровавше (John 20:29—"because thou hast seen me, thou hast believed: blessed are they that have not seen, and yet have believed").

§181. Disjunctive Coördination.

Compound [coördinate] sentences with a *disjunctive* sense are usually composed with the aid of the conjunction и́ли (and sometimes with the conjunction лю́бо [both translated "or"]), for example: и҆збери̏ себѣ̀ бы́ти: и҆ли̏ прїи́ду́тъ тебѣ̀ три̏ лѣ̑та гла́да на зе́млю твою̀: и҆ли̏ три̏ мѣ́сяцы бѣ́гати и҆ма́ши пред̾ враги̏ твои́ми, и҆ бу́ду́тъ гоня́ще тѧ̀: и҆ли̏ три̏ дни̏ бы́ти сме́рти въ земли̏ твое́й (II Kings [=Samuel] 24:13—"Choose [one of these things] to befall thee: whether there shall come upon thee for three years famine in thy land; or that thou shouldest flee three months before thine enemies, and they should pursue thee; or that there should be for three days mortality in thy land"); снѣ́стсѧ ли хлѣ́бъ без̾ со́ли; и҆ли̏ є҆́сть вку́съ во тщи́хъ словесѣ́хъ (Job 6:6—"Shall bread be eaten without salt? or again, is there taste in empty words?"); ты̀ ли є҆сѝ грѧды́й, и҆ли̏ и҆но́гѡ ча́емъ; (Matth. 11:3—"Art thou he that should come, or do we look for another?").

§182. Causative Coördination.

In *causative* coördination, some event is presented in the first clause, and its reason is given in the second. The second clause is joined to the first by means of the causative conjunctions и́бо and бо ["for, since"], for example: нѣ́сть тѝ ча́сти ни жре́бїѧ въ словесѝ се́мъ: и҆́бо се́рдце твоѐ нѣ́сть пра́во пред̾ бго́мъ (Acts 8:21—"Thou hast neither part nor lot in this matter: for thy heart is not right in the sight of God"); по дѣлѡ́мъ же и҆́хъ не твори́те: глаго́лютъ бо, и҆ не творѧ́тъ (Matth. 23:3—"but do ye not after their works: for they say, and do not").

The difference between the conjunctions и́бо and бо lies only in that и́бо is a combination of и҆ and бо. In comparing the Greek text with the Slavonic, we usually see the following corresponding forms: бо = Greek γὰρ, while и́бо = καὶ γὰρ, for example: и҆́бо бесѣ́да твоѧ̀ я҆́вѣ тѧ̀ твори́тъ, Matth. 26:73 (in place of и҆ бесѣ́да бо... "for thy speech bewrayeth thee"), in the Greek text: καὶ γὰρ ἡ λαλιά σου... The conjunction и́бѡ is placed at the beginning of a clause, while бо is put after the first word of a clause.

Causative compound sentences, too, may be joined without a conjunction, for example: ѡ҆ста́вите и҆̀хъ: вожди̑ сꙋ́ть слѣпи́ слѣпцє́мъ (Matth. 15:14—"Let them alone: they be blind leaders of the blind"); до́мъ і҆и҃левъ оу҆пова̀ на гд҃а: помо́щникъ и҆ защи́титель и҆̀мъ є҆́сть. до́мъ а҆арѡ́нь оу҆пова̀ на гд҃а: помо́щникъ и҆ защи́титель и҆̀мъ є҆́сть. Боѧ́щїисѧ гд҃а, оу҆пова́ша на гд҃а: помо́щникъ и҆ защи́титель и҆̀мъ є҆́сть (Ps. 113:17-19 [115:9-11, Hebrew numbering] —"The house of Israel hath hoped in the Lord: he is their helper and protector. The house of Aaron hath hoped in the Lord: he is their helper and protector. They that fear the Lord have hoped in the Lord: he is their helper and their protector").

§183. The Complex Sentence.

A compound sentence, consisting of two clauses, one of which is syntactically subordinated to the other by means of subordinating conjunctions or conjoining words, is called a *compound subordinate* [or in English a *complex*] sentence.

A clause that is syntactically dependant on another clause is called *subordinate*, as opposed to the *main* clause, on which it depends; for example: а҆́зъ посла́хъ вы̀ жа́ти, и҆дѣ́же вы̀ не трꙋди́стесѧ (John 4:38—"I have sent you to reap [that] in which ye did not labour"); here the first clause ["I have sent you to reap"] is the main clause; the second clause ["in which (where) ye did not labour"] is a subordinate adverbial clause of place.

A subordinate clause may relate to one of the parts of the main clause, to a group of parts, or to the main clause as a whole (when it expresses some adjunct [circumstance]: time, cause, condition &c.), for example: Ѻ҆ба́че го́ре человѣ́кꙋ* томꙋ̀, и҆́мже собла́знъ прихо́дитъ (Matth. 18:7 —"woe to that man by whom the offence cometh"); Тѧ̀ блгослови́мъ, вы́шнїй бж҃е, и҆ гд҃и мл́ти, творѧ́щаго прⷭ҇нѡ съ на́ми вели̑каѧ* же и неизслѣ́дѡванныѧ*, сла̑вныѧ* же и оу҆жа́сныѧ*, и҆́хже нѣ́сть числа̀ (Morning Prayer 6—"We bless Thee, O most high God and Lord of mercy, Who ever workest great and inscrutable things with us, glorious and wonderful, without number"); сѣди́те тꙋ̀, до́ндеже ше́дъ помолю́сѧ та́мѡ (Matth. 26:36—"Sit ye here, while I go and pray yonder").

Subordinate clauses can fulfill the same functions towards the main clause as any part of a simple sentence, and therefore they are classified in a similar fashion. Subordinate clauses can be of the following types: 1) subordinate-substantival clauses as subject, 2) subordinate predicative, 3) subordinate attributive (adjectival) clauses, 4) subordinate complement, 5) subordinate adverbial (adjunct, circumstance): *a)* of time, *b)* of place, *c)* of cause [reason], *d)* of purpose, *e)* of result [consecutive clauses], *f)* of manner [figurative], *g)* of condition, *h)* of concession.

In Church Slavonic there are no complex sentences without a conjunction, except for certain subordinate clauses of complement.

§184. Subordinate Subject Clauses.

A subordinate *subject* clause is one that clarifies the subject of the main clause, expressed by a pronoun (demonstrative, negative or determinant) or fulfills the function of a subject omitted in the main clause. A subject subordinate clause answers the question of the nominative case, Who? What? For example: И҆́же мѧ̀ сотворѝ цѣ́ла, то́й мѝ речѐ: возьмѝ о҆́дръ тво́й и҆ ходѝ (John 5:11—"He that made me whole, the same said unto me: Take up thy bed and walk"); Ничто́же бо є҆́сть покрове́но, є҆́же не ѿкры́етсѧ, и҆ та́йно, є҆́же не оу҆вѣ́дено бꙋ́детъ (Matth. 10:26—"For there is nothing covered, that shall not be revealed: and hid, that shall not be known"); всѧ̑, є҆ли̑ка и҆́мать О҆ц҃ъ, моѧ̑ сꙋ́ть (John 16:15—"All things that the Father hath, are mine").

A pronoun is often omitted in the main clause; however, it is easily understood: а́ще въ ва́съ пребꙋ́детъ, е́же испе́рва слы́шасте (I John 2:24—"If that shall remain in you, which ye have heard from the beginning"); и е́же а́ще свꙗ́жеши на земли̂, бꙋ́детъ свꙗ́зано на нб҃ес҆̀хъ (Matth. 16:19—"and whatsoever thou shalt bind on earth shall be bound in heaven"); и́же а́ще хо́щетъ въ ва́съ ва́щїй бы́ти, да бꙋ́детъ ва́мъ слꙋга̀ (Matth. 20:26—"whosoever will be chief among you, let him be your servant").

The absence of a subject pronoun is especially characteristic in those cases where the predicate of the main clause approaches an impersonal sense, nevertheless one could insert the pronoun то̀ into the such a clause, for example: или мни́тса тѝ, ꙗ́кw не могꙋ̀ ны́н҆ꙉ ꙋмоли́ти о҆ц҃а̀ моегѡ̀ (Matth. 26:53—"or does [it] seem to thee, that I cannot now pray to my Father"); довл҆́етъ ꙋ҆ченикꙋ̀, да бꙋ́детъ, ꙗ́кw ꙋ҆чи́тель е҆гѡ̀ (Matth. 10:25—"[It] is enough for the disciple that he be as his master"); н҆́сть бо та́йно, е́же не ꙗ҆вле́но бꙋ́детъ: ниже́ ꙋ҆таено, е́же не позна́етса и҆ въ ꙗ҆вле́нїе прїи́детъ (Luke 8:17—"For nothing is secret, that shall not be made manifest; neither any thing hid, that shall not be known and come abroad"); ѿ в҆́ка н҆́сть слы́шано, ꙗ́кw кто̀ ѿве́рзе о҆́чи сл҆́пꙋ рожде́нꙋ (John 9:32—"Since the world began was it not heard that any man opened the eyes of one that was born blind"); и҆ рече́тса тѝ, что̀ тѝ подоба́етъ твори́ти (Acts 9:6—"and it shall be told thee, what thou must do"); добр҆́е бы́ло бы е҆мꙋ̀, а́ще не бы̀ роди́лса челов҆́къ то́й (Mark 14:21—"better were it for that man, if he had never been born").

Subordinate subject-clauses are joined to the main clause by means of the following linking words and conjunctions: и́же, ꙗ́же, е́же, что̀, е҆ли́цы, е҆ли̂ка, ꙗ́кw, да, а́ще and the like (see the preceding examples).

A main clause consisting of a comparative such as лꙋ́чше е́сть, ꙋ҆до́б҆е е́сть, добр҆́е е́сть and the like, usually has a subordinate subject clause with the conjunction нѐже or нѐжели ["than"]. Such a subordinate clause is liable to have a truncated predicate, for example: лꙋ́чше є҆́сть оу҆бо́гъ ходѧ́й въ простотѣ̀ свое́й, нѐже [є҆́сть] бога́тый стропти́въ оу҆сты̀ свои́ми и҆ несмы́сленъ (Prov. 19:1—"Better is the poor that walketh in his integrity, than the rich man that is perverse in his lips, and is a fool"); лꙋ́чше части́ца ма́лаѧ со стра́хомъ гд҃нимъ, нѐжели сокрѡ́вища вє́лїѧ без̾ боѧ́зни (Prov. 15:16—"Better is a small portion with the fear of the Lord, than great treasures without the fear [of God]); Оу҆до́бѣе же є҆́сть нб҃ꙋ и҆ землѝ прейтѝ, не́же ѿ зако́на є҆ди́ной чертѣ̀ [оу҆до́бно є҆́сть] поги́бнꙋти (Luke 16:17—"And it is easier for heaven and earth to pass, than [it is] for one tittle of the law to fail").

§185. Subordinate Predicative Clauses.

A subordinate *predicate* clause is one that is used to elucidate the nominal [noun/adjective] part of the main clause predicate, expressed by a demonstrative pronoun which is often omitted. A subordinate predicate clause answers the question, *What kind of?* For example: Ꙗ҆ко́въ пе́рстный, таковѝ и҆ пе́рстнїи: и҆ ꙗ҆ко́въ нбс҃ный, та́цы же нбс҃нїи (I Cor. 15:48—"As is the earthy, such are they also that are earthy: and as is the heavenly, such are they also that are heavenly"); Моѐ бра́шно є҆́сть, да сотворю̀ во́лю посла́вшагѡ мѧ̀ (John 4:34—"My meat is ['this:—'] to do the will of him that sent me"); Что̀ є҆́сть, є҆́же и҆́маши возвѣсти́ти мѝ (Acts 23:19—"What is that thou hast to tell me?"); се́й бѣ̀, є҆го́же рѣ́хъ (John 1:15—"This was he, of whom I spake"); то́й є҆́сть, є҆мꙋ́же а҆́зъ ѡ҆мочи́въ хлѣ́бъ пода́мъ (John 13:26—"He it is, to whom, having dipped bread, I shall give it").

Suobordinate predicative clauses are joined to the main clause by means of the linking words or conjunctions и҆́же, ꙗ҆́же, є҆́же, ꙗ҆ко́въ, -а, -о, да and the like.

384

§186. Subordinate Adjectival [Attributive] Clauses.

A subordinate adjectival clause is one that limits or defines some member of the main clause, expressed by a noun, for example: сѐ бо бл҃говѣств́ю вамъ радость велїю, ꙗже б́детъ всѣмъ людемъ (Luke 2:10—"behold, I bring you good tidings of great joy, which shall be to all people").

Adjectival subordinate clauses answer the question, *Which?*

Adjectival subordinate clauses are joined to the main clause by means of the following linking words and conjunctions: и́же, ꙗже, ѐже, ꙗков́ъ, _а, _о, идѣже [where], ѐгда [when], да, ꙗкѡ &c.

The most characteristic forms of expression of an adjectival relationship are the relative pronouns и́же, ꙗже, ѐже: и помaн́ша приᲥᲥниќмъ, и́же бѣх́ во др́зѣмъ корaбли (Luke 5:7—"And they beckoned unto [their] partners, which were in the other ship"); а́зъ бо дамъ вамъ устa и премудрость, ѐйже не возмоѓтъ проᲥᲥивитиᲥᲥ или ѡвѣщати вᲥᲥ противлᲥᲥющıиᲥᲥ вамъ (Luke 21:15—"For I will give you a mouth and wisdom, which all your adversaries shall not be able to gainsay or resist").

Other examples of the use of linking words and conjunctions: б́детъ бо тогда скорбь велıа, ꙗковa же не былa ѿ начaла мıра досᲥᲥлѣ (Matth. 24:21—"For then shall be great tribulation, such as was not since the beginning of the world to this time"); и разгн́въ книѓ, ѡбрѣте мѣсто, идѣже бѣ напиᲥᲥно (Luke 4:17—"And when he had opened the book, he found the place where it was written"); прıид́тъ же днıе, ѐгда ѿиметᲥᲥ ѿ нихъ женихъ (Matth. 9:15—"but the days will come, when the bridegroom shall be taken from them"); и сıa ѐᲥᲥь любы, да ходимъ по зaповѣдемъ ѐгѡ (II John 1:6—"And this is love, that we walk after his commandments"); Какѡ ́бо сб́д́тᲥᲥ писaнıа, ꙗкѡ тaкѡ подобaетъ быти (Matth. 26:54—"But how then shall the scriptures be fulfilled, that thus it must be?"). The linking word ꙗков́ъ in the main clause may have a corresponding demonstrative pronoun таков́ъ (referring to the modified word), for example: вѣмъ, ꙗкѡ предста́виши грѣхѝ моѧ̀ предо мно́ю таковы̀, ꙗковы́ же мно́ю содѣ́яшаса (Prayer before Communion—"I know that Thou wilt place my sins before me, such as have been committed by me").

A subordinate adjectival clause may sometimes precede the word to which it refers, for example: носѧще, ꙗже оу҆гото́ваша а҆рѡма́ты (Luke 24:1—"bringing the spices which they had prepared").

§187. Subordinate Clauses of Complement.

A *complementary* subordinate clause is one that fulfills the role of an object [complement] of the predicate in the main clause, or which elucidates an object expressed by a pronoun (demonstrative or determinant).

Complementary subordinate clauses answer the questions posed by the oblique cases.

For example: Ѻ҆ни́ же тѧжа́тел€ рѣша къ себѣ̀, ꙗкѡ се́й є́сть наслѣ́дникъ (Mark 12:7—"But those husbandmen said among themselves, This is the heir"). A complementary subordinate clause that clarifies a pronoun object: Но сїе́* па́че су҆ди́те, є́же не полага́ти претыка́нїѧ бра́ту и҆лѝ собла́зна (Rom. 14:13—"But judge this rather, that no man put a stumblingblock or an occasion to fall in his brother's way"); и҆ возвѣсти́ша є҆му̀ всѧ̑*, и҆ є҆ли̑ка сотвори́ша, и҆ є҆ли̑ка научи́ша (Mark 6:30—"and they told him all they had done, and what they had taught"); и҆ всѧ̑*, є҆ли̑ка воспро́сите въ моли́твѣ, вѣ́ру́юще, прїи́мете (Matth. 21:22—"And all [things], whatsoever ye shall ask in prayer, believing, ye shall receive").

If the main clause follows after the subordinate, then a demonstrative pronoun in the main clause may have a sense of emphasis, for example: но є҆́же а́ще да́стса ва́мъ въ то́й ча́съ, сѐ глаго́лите (Mark 13:11—"but whatsoever shall be given you in that hour, that speak ye").

In Church Slavonic complex sentence constructions, an object pronoun that is correlative to a complementary subordinate clause is very rarely used, almost as an exception, so that a complementary subordinate clause may even come directly after a preposition, for example: ѡ ꙗ́кѡ да гдⷭ҇ь бг҃ъ на́шъ оу҆чннⷮ дꙊ́шы и҆́хъ въ мѣ́стѣ свѣ́тлѣ…, гдꙋ̀ помо́лнмсѧ (from the Pannikhida—"that the Lord our God will establish their souls in a place of light…, let us pray to the Lord" [the exact construction cannot be reproduced in English]); according to the construction of sentences in Russian, in this case it one would have insert the demonstrative pronoun: *о томъ, чтобы…*

Subordinate clauses of complement are joined to the main clause by means of the following conjunctions and linking words: ꙗ́кѡ, что̀, да, дабы̀, ꙗ́кѡ дабы̀, да не ка́кѡ, да не когда̀, ка́кѡ, кі́й, ка́ѧ, ко́е, и́же, ꙗ́же, е҆́же, е҆ли́къ, _а, _о, до́ндеже, когда̀, ка́мѡ [whither], ѿкꙋ́дꙋ [whence], а҆́може [to the place where], and the like, for exmple: са́мъ бо вѣ́даше, что̀* хо́щетъ сотворн́тн (John 6:6—"for he himself knew what he would do"); просн̀ оу҆ менѐ, е҆гѡ́же* а҆́ще хо́щешн (Mark 6:22—"Ask of me whatsoever thou wilt"); ты́ же пребыва́й, въ ни́хже наꙋ́ченъ е҆сн̀ (II Tim. 3:14—"But continue thou in [the things] which thou hast learned"); тѣ́мже са́мн свндѣ́тельствꙋете себѣ̀, ꙗ́кѡ* сы́нове е҆стѐ и҆збн́вшнхъ прⷪро́кн (Matth. 23:31—"Wherefore ye be witnesses unto yourselves, that ye are the sons of them which killed the prophets"); ꙗ́кѡ не вѣ́сте, въ кі́й* ча́съ гдⷭ҇ь ва́шъ прїн́детъ (Matth. 24:42—"For ye know not what hour your Lord doth come").

The conjunctions да, дабы̀, ꙗ́кѡ дабы̀ [so that, in order that], да не ка́кѡ, да не когда̀ [lest in any way, lest ever] introduce a shade of desire or purpose into the subordinate clause: блюдн́те, да* никто́же ва́съ прельстн́тъ (Matth. 24:4—"Take heed that no man deceive you"); н видѣ́вше е҆го̀, молн́ша, ꙗ́кѡ дабы̀* прешѐлъ ѿ предѣ́лъ и҆́хъ (Matth. 8:34—"and when they saw him, they besought him that he would depart out of their coasts"); бо́ѧщесѧ же, да не ка́кѡ* въ пр҃ѹднаѧ мѣ́ста впадѹ́тъ (Acts 27:29—"then fearing, lest they should have fallen upon rough [rocky, shallow] places...").

Linking words, depending on their meaning, add various nuances to the subordinate clauses they connect to the main clause, for example: до́ндеже, когда̀ — give an extra sense of time: и не оу҆вѣ́дѣша, до́ндеже* прїи́де вода̀ и взѧ́тъ всѧ̑ (Matth. 24:39—"And [they] knew not until the flood came, and took all [with it]"); рцы̀ на́мъ, когда̀* сїѧ̑ бѹ́дѹтъ (Mark 13:4—"Tell us, when shall these things be?"); ка́мѡ, ѿкѹ́дѹ, а́може contribute an additional spatial sense: вы́ же не вѣ́сте, ѿкѹ́дѹ* прихождѹ̀ и ка́мѡ* грѧдѹ̀ (John 8:14—"but ye know not whence I come and whither I go"); а́може* а҆́зъ и҆дѹ̀, вѣ́сте (John 14:4—"whither I go, ye know"); ка́кѡ, ка́кѡ бы, є҆да̀ ка́кѡ point to the character of the action: повѣ́даша же и҆мъ ви́дѣвшїи, ка́кѡ* бы́сть бѣсно́мѹ, и ѡ свинїа́хъ (Mark 5:16—"And they that saw it told them how it befell to him that was possessed with the devil, and also concerning the swine"); и҆ иска́хѹ а҆рхїере́є и҆ кни́жницы, ка́кѡ бы* оу҆би́ли є҆го̀ (Luke 22:2—"And the chief priests and scribes sought how they might kill him"); бою́сѧ же, є҆да̀ ка́кѡ* пришє́дъ, не ꙗ҆цѣ́хъ же хощѹ̀, ѡ҆брѧ́щѹ ва́съ (II Cor. 12:20—"For I fear, lest, when I come, I shall not find you such as I would"); какова̀ introduces a qualitative overtone: да оу҆вѣ́сть, какова̀* кѹ́плю сѹ́ть сотвори́ли (Luke 19:15—"that he might know, how much every man had gained by trading [lit., 'what sort of purchase they had made']").

Subordinate clauses of complement can be without a conjunction, for example: молю̀ же ва́съ, подо́бни мнѣ̀ быва́йте (I Cor. 4:16—"Wherefore, I beseech you, be ye followers of me").

§188. Subordinate Clauses of Time.

A subordinate clause of *time* is one that indicates the time of the action of the main clause predicate, or which clarifies an adverbial modifier of time found in the main clause, e.g. а҃кѡ не и҆мать прейти ро́дъ се́й, до́ндеже вс҄ѧ сїѧ҄ бꙋ́дꙋтъ (Mark 13:30—"[Verily I say unto you] that this generation shall not pass, till all these things be done"); и҆ въ пе́рвый де́нь Ѡ҆пре́снѡкъ, є҆гда̀ па́схꙋ жра́хꙋ, глаго́лаша є҆мꙋ оу҆ченицы̀ є҆гѡ̀ (Mark 14:12—"And the first day of unleavened bread, when they killed the passover, his disciples said unto him...").

Subordinate clauses of time answer the questions: *When? Since when? Until when? How long?*

To join subordinate clauses of time with the main clause, the following conjunctions are used: є҆гда̀, до́ндеже, ѿне́лѣже, доне́лѣже, пре́жде да́же ("before", always used with не), пре́жде не́же, а҆́коже, а҆́кѡ, for example: и҆ є҆гда̀ сконча́вашасѧ дни́е пѧтьдесѧ́тницы, бѣ́ша вси а҆п҃толи є҆динодꙋ́шнѡ вкꙋ́пѣ (Acts 2:1—"And when the days of Pentecost were accomplished, all the Apostles were in one accord together"); Мнѣ̀ подоба́етъ дѣ́лати дѣла̀ посла́вшагѡ мѧ̀, до́ндеже де́нь є҆́сть (John 9:4—"I must work the works of him that sent me, while it is day"); ѿне́лѣже бо Ѻ҆ц҃ы̀ оу҆спо́ша, вс҄ѧ та́кѡ пребыва́ютъ ѿ нача́ла созда́нїѧ (II Peter 3:4—"for since the fathers fell asleep, all things continue as they were from the beginning of the creation"); доне́лѣже бо їꙋ́да жи́въ є҆́сть, невозмо́жно ми́ра полꙋчи́ти веще́мъ (II Macc. 14:10—"For as long as Judas liveth, it is not possible that the state should be quiet"); Г҃и, сни́ди, пре́жде да́же не оу҆́мретъ Ѻ҆троча̀ моѐ (John 4:49—"Lord, come down ere my child die"); а҆́коже пла́кашесѧ, прини́че во гро́бъ (John 20:11—"and as she wept, she stooped down [and looked] into the sepulchre"); а҆́коже преста̀ глаго́лѧ, речѐ къ сі́мѡнꙋ (Luke 5:4—"Now when he had left speaking, he said unto Simon..."); и҆ а҆́кѡ прибли́жисѧ, ви́дѣвъ гра́дъ, пла́касѧ ѡ҆ не́мъ (Luke 19:41—"And when he was come near, he beheld the city, and wept over it").

Subordinate clauses of time may indicate an action that:

a) takes place at the same time as the action of the main clause: нє сѐрдцє ли на́ю горѧ̀ бѣ̀ въ на́ю, є҆гда̀ гла́шє на́ма на пꙋти́, и҆ є҆гда̀ ска́зоваше на́ма писа̑нїѧ (Luke 24:32—"Did not our heart burn within us, while he talked with us by the way, and while he opened [*lit.*, 'said'] to us the scriptures?"); бѣ̀ же но́щь, є҆гда̀ и҆зы́дє (John 13:30—"and it was night, when he went out"); Сѣди́тє тꙋ̀, до́ндєжє шє́дъ помолю́сѧ та́мѡ (Matth. 26:36—"Sit ye here, while I go and pray yonder"); Коли́кѡ лѣ́тъ є҆́сть, ѿнє́лѣжє сїѐ бы́сть є҆мꙋ̀; (Mark 9:21—"How long is it ago since this came unto him?");

b) precedes in time the action of the main clause: Є҆гда̀ же прозѧбѐ трава̀ и҆ пло́дъ сотвори́, тогда̀ ꙗ҆ви́шасѧ и҆ плѣ́вєлїѐ (Matth. 13:26—"But when the blade was sprung up and brought forth fruit, then appeared the tares also");

c) follows the time of the main clause's action: Є҆гда̀ же прихождꙋ̀ а҆́зъ, и҆́нъ прє́ждє менє̀ сла́зитъ (John 5:7—"but when I come, another steppeth down [here the Slavonic uses the future: ='shall step down', 'shall have stepped down'] before me"); прє́ждє да́жє а҆лє́кторъ не возгласи́тъ, трѝ кра̑ты ѿвє́ржешисѧ менє̀ Matth. 26:34—"before the cock crow, thou shalt deny me thrice"); проси́, что̀ сотворю̀ ти, прє́ждє нє́же взѧ́тъ бꙋ́дꙋ ѿ тебє̀ (IV Kings 2:9—"Ask what I shall do for thee, before I be taken away from thee").

§189. Subordinate Clauses of Place.

A subordinate clause of *place* is one that indicates the location where the action of the main clause is performed, or which clarifies an adverbial modifier [adjunct, circumstance] of place, found in the main clause, for example: и҆дꙋ̀ по тебѣ̀, а҆́можє а҆́щє и҆́деши (Matth. 8:19—"I will follow thee, whithersoever thou goest"); и҆дѣ́же бо а҆́щє бꙋ́детъ трꙋ́пъ, та́мѡ собєрꙋ́тсѧ ѻ҆рли́ (Matth. 24:28—"For wheresoever the carcase is, there will the eagles be gathered [together]"); Є҆ди́нїи же надєсѧти оу҆чєници́ и҆до́ша въ галїлє́ю, въ гóрꙋ, а́може повелѣ̀ и́мъ і҆и҃съ (Matth. 28:16—"Then the eleven disciples went away into Galilee, into a mountain where Jesus had appointed them").

Subordinate clauses of place answer the questions: *Where? Whither? From whence?* They are joined to the main clause by means of the following conjunctions: и҆дѣ́же, и҆дѣ́же а́ще, а́може, а́може а́ще, ѿню́дꙋже [ѿѻнꙋ́дꙋже], for example: а́може а́зъ и҆дꙋ̀, вы̀ не мо́жете прїитѝ (John 13:33—"Whither I go, ye cannot come"); сїѧ̑ въ виѳова́рѣ бы́ша ѡ҆б ѻ҆́нъ по́лъ і҆ѻрда́на, и҆дѣ́же бѣ̀ і҆ѡа́ннъ крестѧ̀ (John 1:28—"These things were done in Bethabara beyond Jordan, where John was baptizing"); возведо́хъ ѻ҆́чи моѝ въ го́ры, ѿню́дꙋже прїи́детъ по́мощь моѧ̀ (Ps. 120:1—"I have lifted up mine eyes to the mountains, from whence shall come my help"). Sometimes a subordinate clause of place may be joined by means of an oblique case of the pronoun и́же, for example: и҆ во́ньже до́мъ вни́дете, тꙋ̀ пребыва́йте (Luke 9:4—"And whatsoever house ye enter into, there abide").

In the main clause there may be adverbs corresponding to the conjunctions of relative clauses: та́мѡ, тꙋ̀.

§190. Subordinate Clauses of Reason.

A subordinate clause of *reason* is one that indicates the reason or cause for the action of the main clause predicate.

Subordinate clauses of reason answer the questions: *Why? Due to what? For what reason?*

To connect subordinate clauses of reason with the main clause, the following conjunctions are used: ꙗ҆́кѡ, поне́же, занѐ, зане́же, for example: бди́те ѹ҆̀бо, ꙗ҆́кѡ не вѣ́сте днѐ ни часа̀... (Matth. 25:13—"Watch therefore, for ye know neither the day nor the hour..."); дади́те на́мъ ѿ є҆ле́а ва́шегѡ, ꙗ҆́кѡ свѣти́льницы на́ши ѹ҆гаса́ютъ (Matth. 25:8—"Give us of your oil; for our lamps are going out"); и҆ и҆щꙋ́ще є҆го̀ ꙗ҆́ти, ѹ҆боѧ́шасѧ наро́да, поне́же ꙗ҆́кѡ прро́ка е҆го̀ и҆мѣ́ахꙋ (Matth. 21:46—"But when they sought to lay hands on him, they feared the multitude, because they took him as a prophet"); и҆ а҆́бїе прозѧбо́ша, занѐ не и҆мѣ́ахꙋ глꙋбины̀ землѝ (Matth. 13:5—"and at once they withered, for they had no deepness of earth"); житїѐ же и҆́хъ оу҆ѧзвлѧ́емо а҆́гг҃лы: зане́же ѡ҆скорби́ша недꙋ́жна и҆ не́мощна (Job. 36:14-15—"their life is wounded by angels: because they afflicted the weak and helpless").

§191. Subordinate Clauses of Purpose.

A subordinate clause of *purpose* is one that indicates the aim or goal of the action spoken of in the main clause.

Subordinate clauses of purpose answer the questions: *To what end? For what? With what purpose?* They are joined to the main clause by the following conjunctions: да, ꙗ҆́кѡ да, дабы̀, да не когда̀, да не ка́кѡ, е҆да̀ ка́кѡ, да понѐ (so that, lest, lest ever, lest in any way, so that at least), for example: Се́ же всѐ бы́сть, да сбꙋ́дꙋтсѧ писа̑нїѧ прⷪ҇ро́ческаѧ (Matth. 26:56—"But all this came to pass, that the writings of the Prophets might be fulfilled"); бди́те оу҆́бо на всѧ́ко вре́мѧ молѧ́щесѧ, да сподо́битесѧ оу҆бѣжа́ти всѣ́хъ си́хъ хотѧ́щихъ бы́ти (Luke 21:36—"Watch ye therefore, and pray always, that ye may be accounted worthy to escape all these things that shall come to pass"); да прише́дъ возложи́ши на ню̀ рꙋ́цѣ, ꙗ҆́кѡ да спасе́тсѧ и҆ жива̀ бꙋ́детъ (Mark 5:23—"come and lay thy hands on her, that she may be healed; and she shall live"); Просвѣти́ ѻ҆́чи моѝ, хрⷭ҇тѐ бж҃е, да не когда̀ оу҆снꙋ̀ въ сме́рть, да не когда̀ рече́тъ вра́гъ мо́й... (Prayers before Sleep—"Enlighten my eyes, O Christ God, lest I sleep the sleep of death; lest mine enemy ever say..."); послю̀ сн҃а моего̀ возлю́бленнаго, е҆да̀ ка́кѡ, е҆го̀ ви́дѣвше, оу҆срамѧ́тсѧ (Luke 20:13—"I will send my beloved son; it may be they will reverence him when they see him"); ше́дше да взы́щꙋтъ господи́на твоегѡ̀, е҆да̀ ка́кѡ дх҃ъ гдⷭ҇ень взѧ̀, и҆ пове́рже е҆го̀ на і҆ѻрда́нѣ (IV Kings 2:16—"let them go and seek thy master: lest peradventure the Spirit of the Lord hath taken him up, and cast him into Jordan"); Тѣ́мже сопроти́вное па́че вы̀ да дарꙋ́ете и оу҆тѣ́шите, да не ка́кѡ мно́гою ско́рбїю пожре́тъ бꙋ́детъ таковы́й (II Cor. 2:7—"So that contrariwise ye ought rather to forgive him, and comfort him, lest perhaps such a one should be swallowed up with overmuch sorrow"); Взыска́ти гда̀, да понѐ ѡ҆сѧ́жꙋтъ є҆го̀ и҆ ѡ҆брѧ́щꙋтъ (Acts 17:27—"To seek the Lord, if haply they might feel after him, and find him"). The subordinate clause predicate (with the conjunction да) may be expressed by the subjunctive mood, for example: и҆ ведо́ша є҆го̀ до верхꙋ̀ горы̀, на не́йже гра́дъ и҆́хъ со́зданъ бѧ́ше, да бы́ша* є҆го̀ низри́нꙋли* (Luke 4:29—"and [they] led him unto the brow of the hill whereon their city was built, that they might cast him down headlong"); Бы́сть же належа́щꙋ є҆мꙋ̀ наро́дꙋ, да бы́ша* слы́шали* сло́во бж҃їе (Luke 5:1—"And it came to pass, that, as the people pressed upon him to hear the word of God..."); и҆ ѡ҆удержива́хꙋ є҆го̀, дабы̀ не ѡ҆шелъ ѿ ни́хъ (Luke 4:42—"and [they] stayed him, that he should not depart from them").

§192. Subordinate Clauses of Result.

A subordinate clause of *result* or *consequence* is one that indicates an outcome, following from the content of the main clause.

Subordinate clauses of result are joined tothe main clause by means of the conjunction ꙗ҆́кѡ и҆ ["so that"], to which corresponds та́кѡ ["thus"] in the main clause, for example: Та́кѡ бо возлюбѝ бг҃ъ мі́ръ, ꙗ҆́кѡ и҆ сн҃а своего̀ є҆диноро́днаго да́лъ є҆́сть (John 3:16—"For God so loved the world, that he gave his only begotten Son").

However, constructions using the infinitive are characteristic and usual as subordinate clauses of result; see §143, 9.

In the books of the Holy Scriptures, a particular turn of speech is sometimes to be met with, in which subordinate clauses of purpose with the conjunctions да, да не когда̀, да не ка́кѡ are used in the sense of *result*, so as to emphasize its inescapability, for example:

кám̃ъ є́сть дано̀ вѣ́дати та́йны ца́рствїѧ бж҃їѧ: про́чымъ же въ при́тчахъ, да ви́дѧще не ви́дѧтъ, и слы́шаще не разꙋмѣ́ютъ, compare with the Russian version: *такъ-что они видя не видятъ...* (Luke 8:10—"Unto you it is given to know the mysteries of the kingdom of God: but to others in parables, that seeing they might not see, and hearing they might not understand"); и́ о́чи свои смѣ́жиша, да не когда̀ оу̓зрѧ́тъ о́чима (Matth. 13:15—"their eyes they have closed, lest at any time they see with their eyes"); see also Mark 4:12; John 12:40; Acts 28:27.

§193. Subordinate Clauses of Manner.

A subordinate clause of *manner* is one that reveals the means or character of an action, or else the extent to which the characteristic of the main clause is manifest. Subordinate clauses of manner answer the questions: *How? In what manner? To what extent? How many times?*

The connection of clauses of manner with the main clause is by means of the following conjunctions: ꙗ́коже, и́мже о́бразомъ, а́ки бы, є́ли́жды. To the conjunctions given, the following adverbs may correspond in the main clause: та́кѡ, та́ко́жде, си́це ["thus, likewise, as follows"]. For example: Ѻ̓ни́ же прїе́мше сре́бренники, сотвори́ша, ꙗ́коже наꙋче́ни бы́ша (Matth. 28:15—"So they, taking the money, did as they had been instructed"); и нача́ша глаго́лати ꙗ̓зы́ки, ꙗ́коже дх҃ъ даа́ше и̓мъ провѣщава́ти (Acts 2:4—"and they began to speak in other tongues, as the Spirit gave them to utter"); показа́вый оу̓ченикѡ́мъ твои́мъ сла́вꙋ твою̀, ꙗ́коже можа́хꙋ (Tropar of the Transfiguration—"shewing to Thy disciples Thy glory, insofar as they could bear"); ꙗ́коже вмѣща́хꙋ оу̓ченицы̀ твои́, сла́вꙋ твою̀, хр҃тѐ бж҃е, ви́дѣша (Kondak of the Transfiguration—"as far as they were able, Thy disciples, O Christ God, saw Thy glory"); ꙗ́коже бо бы́сть во дни̑ нѡ́евы: та́кѡ бꙋ́детъ и въ прише́ствїе сн҃а чл҃вѣ́ческагѡ (Matth. 24:37—"But as it was in the days of Noë, so

shall it be also at the coming of the Son of Man"); се́й і҆и҃съ
вознесы́йсѧ ѿ ва́съ на нб҃о, та́кожде прїи́детъ, и҆́мже ѻ҆́бразомъ
ви́дѣстѣ є҆го̀ и҆ду́ща на нб҃о (Acts 1:11—"this same Jesus, which is
taken up from you into heaven, shall so come in like manner as ye
have seen him go into heaven"); и҆́мже ѻ҆́бразомъ жела́етъ є҆ле́нь на
и҆сто́чники водны̑ѧ, си́це жела́етъ дꙋша̀ моѧ̀ къ тебѣ̀ бж҃е (Ps.
41:2—"As the hart desireth after the fountains of water, so doth my
soul desire Thee, O God"); є҆ли́жды бо а҆́ще ꙗ҆́сте хлѣ́бъ се́й, и҆ ча́шꙋ
сїю̀ пїе́те, сме́рть гд҃ню возвѣща́ете (I Cor. 11:26 —"For as often as
ye eat this bread, and drink this cup, ye do shew the Lord's death"");
что̀ ꙗ҆́кѡ посла́лъ є҆сѝ послы̀ вопроша́ти ваа́ла скве́рнаго бо́га во
а҆ккарѡ́нѣ, а҆ки бы не бы́лъ бг҃ъ во і҆и҃ли; (IV Kings 1:16—"Wherefore
hast thou sent messengers to enquire of Baal the foul god of Accaron,
as though there were no God in Israel?").

§194. Subordinate Clauses of Condition.

A *conditional* subordinate clause is one that contains an
indication of a condition upon which depends the realization of that
which is spoken of in the main clause. Subordinate conditional
clauses answer the questions: *In what case? Under what condition?*

Clauses of condition are subordinated to the main clause by
means of the conjunction а҆́ще ["if"], for example: а҆́ще кто̀ хо́дитъ въ
нощѝ, по́ткнетсѧ (John 11:10—"if one walk in the night, he
stumbleth").

In the main clause there may sometimes be the conjunction
то̀ ["then, in that case"], for example: а҆́ще бо съ ни́мъ оу҆мро́хомъ, то̀
съ ни́мъ и҆ ѡ҆живе́мъ (II Tim. 2:11—"For if we have died with him,
[then] we shall also come to life with him").

Complex sentences with subordinate clauses of condition may
be divided into two types: 1) clauses showing a real condition and 2)
clauses showing a desirable, possible or conjectural condition. The
predicates in clauses of the first type are expressed by the indicative

mood, while those of the second type are in the subjunctive mood, for example:

Type 1) а҆ще нога̀ твоѧ̀ соблажнѧ́етъ тѧ̀, ѿсѣцы̀ ю̀ (Mark 9:45—"If thy foot offend thee, cut if off"); а҆ще вы̀ пребꙋ́дете во словесѝ мое́мъ, вои́стинну ѹ҆ченицы̀ мои́ бꙋ́дете (John 8:31—"If ye continue in my word, then ye are my disciples indeed"); а҆ще и҆ вси̑ соблазнѧ́тсѧ ѡ҆ тебѣ̀, а҆́зъ никогда́же соблажню́сѧ (Matth. 26:33—"Even if all shall be offended at thee, yet will I never be offended"); а҆ще ли ни̑, понѐ ꙗ҆́кѡ безꙋ́мна, прїими́те мѧ̀ (II Cor. 11:16—"if otherwise, yet [at least] as a fool receive me").

Type 2) и҆ а҆ще не бы́ша прекрати́лисѧ дні́е ѻ҆́ны, не бы̀ ѹ҆́бо спасла́сѧ всѧ́ка пло́ть (Matth. 24:22—"And except those days should be shortened, there should no flesh be saved"); а҆ще бо бы́хомъ себѐ разсꙋжда́ли, не бы́хомъ ѡ҆сꙋжде́ни бы́ли (I Cor. 11:31—"For if we would judge ourselves, we should not be judged"); а҆ще не бы̀ бы́лъ се́й ѿ бг҃а, не мо́глъ бы̀ твори́ти ничесо́же (John 9:33—"If this man were not of God, he could do nothing").

§195. Subordinate Clauses of Concession.

A subordinate clause of *concession* is one that indicates a condition, despite which there takes place that which is spoken of in the main clause.

Subordinate clauses of concession are joined to the main clause by means of the conjunction а҆ще и҆ [even if, although], to which in the main clause correspond the conjunctions но [but], ѻ҆ба́че [yet, nevertheless], for example: а҆ще бо и҆ пло́тїю ѿстою̀, но дꙋ́хомъ съ ва́ми є҆́смь (Col. 2:5 — "For though I be absent in the flesh, yet am I with you in the spirit"); а҆ще и҆ сн҃ъ бѧ́ше, ѻ҆ба́че навы́че ѿ си́хъ, ꙗ҆́же пострада̀, послꙋша́нїю (Heb. 5:8—"Though he were a Son, yet learned he obedience by the things which he suffered"). а҆ще и҆ во гро́бъ снизше́лъ є҆сѝ, безсме́ртне, но а҆́довꙋ разрꙋши́лъ є҆сѝ си́лꙋ (Kondak of Pascha—"Even if Thou didst descend into the tomb, O

Immortal One, yet Thou didst destroy the power of Hades"); а́ще бо и мно́ги пѣсту́ны и́мате ѡ хрⷭ҇тѣ̀, но не мно́ги ѻ҆ц҃ы (I Cor. 4:15—"For though ye have many instructors in Christ, yet have ye not many fathers").

In a compound sentence joined by the composite conjunction ѹ̑бо — же (which is in fact a coordinating conjunction, see §180), the sense of opposition and contrast can develop into one of concession, and in this way a sentence containing an indication of a condition despite which something takes place, may be considered as a conditional sentence, for example: Не вѣ́сте ли, ꙗ́кѡ теку́щїи въ позо́рищи, вси̑ ѹ̑бо теку́тъ, є̑ди́нъ же прїе́млетъ по́честь (I Cor. 9:24—"Know ye not that they which run in a race run all, but one receiveth the prize?").

§196. Short Subordinate Clauses.

Certain turns of syntax, consisting of participles or adjectives with dependent words, have a sense close to that of subordinate clauses, and therefore they can be regarded as *short subordinate clauses*, for example: и̑ жела́ше насы́титися ѿ крупи́цъ па́дающихъ* ѿ трапе́зы бога́тагѡ (Luke 16:21—"And he desired to be filled with the crumbs which fell from the rich man's table"); и̑ дана̀ ми бы́сть тро́сть подо́бна* жезлу̀ (Rev. 11:1—"And there was given me a reed like unto a rod").

Short subordinate clauses may be adjectival or adverbial.

I. *Adjectival* short subordinate clauses fulfill a function similar to that of "full" adjectival subordinate clauses, for example: и̑ а̑бїе і̑и҃съ разумѣ̀ въ себѣ̀ си́лу и̑зше́дшую* ѿ негѡ̀ (Mark 5:30—"And Jesus immediately knew in himself that virtue had gone out of him"); Сотвори́те ѹ̑бо пло́дъ досто́инъ* покаѧ́нїѧ (Matth. 3:8—"Bring forth therefore fruits meet for repentance"). In the examples given, the short subordinate clauses have the same meaning as "long": и̑зше́дшую ѿ негѡ̀ = ꙗ́же и̑зы́де ѿ негѡ̀: досто́инъ покаѧ́нїа = и҆́же є҆́сть досто́инъ покаѧ́нїа.

This closeness of short subordinate clauses to "long" makes it possible to replace one construction with the other without changing the meaning. The "full" subordinate clauses may be replaced by short ones only in cases where they are joined to the main clause by means of the linking words и҆́же, ѧ́же, є҆́же, in the nominative or accusative [without a preposition]. Such a substitution may occur not only in adjectival clauses, but also in subordinate clauses used as a subject or predicate (сѣ́ай скꙋ́достїю, скꙋ́достїю и҆ по́жнетъ, II Cor. 9:6—"He which soweth sparingly shall reap also sparingly"). To replace a "full" subordinate clause with a short one, the linking word must be removed, and the predicate replaced with the corresponding participle form, for example:

и҆́же — in the nominative case: возлю́бленнїи, молю̀ ꙗ҆́кw пришє́льцєвъ и҆ стра́нникwвъ, w҆гребáтисѧ w҆ плотски́хъ похоте́й, ꙗ҆́же вою́ютъ на дꙋ́шꙋ (I Peter 2:11—"Dearly beloved, I beseech [you] as strangers and pilgrims, to abstain from fleshly lusts, which war against the soul"); here the short form would be: вою́ющихъ на дꙋ́шꙋ.

и҆́же — in the accusative case; the predicate is replaced by the passive participle: и҆ ви́димъ глаго́лъ се́й бы́вшїй, є҆го́же гд҃ь сказа̀ на́мъ (Luke 2:15—"and [let us] see this thing which is come to pass, which the Lord hath made known to us"); the short form would be: рече́нный на́мъ w҆ гд҃а.

By analogy with the "full" constructions that have a composite nominal predicate, short subordinate clauses may have the copula-participle сы́й, бы́вый, to which an adjective, passive participle or noun refer as a predicate member. In comparing full constructions to short ones, the following peculiarities can be noted:

a) If a noun or passive participle, *with dependant words*, is included in the subordinate clause predicate, then a short subordinate clause does not have copula-participles; for example: и҆ w҆блещи́сѧ въ но́ваго человѣ́ка, созда́ннаго* по бг҃ꙋ въ пра́вдѣ (Ephes. 4:24—"And that ye put on the new man, which after God is created in righteousness and true holiness"); Сотворите оу̀бо плоды̀ досто́йны* покаѧ́нїѧ (Luke 3:8—"Bring forth therefore fruits worthy of repentance"). However, if the short subordinate clause refers to the subject, then there may be a copula-participle: і̓ꙋде́анинъ же нѣ́кто а̓поллѡ́съ и́менемъ... си́ленъ сы́й* въ сло́вѣ, Acts. 18:24—"a certain Jew named Apollos... an eloquent man" (=и́же бѣ̀ си́ленъ въ сло́вѣ).

b) If the subordinate clause predicate includes an adjective or passive participle *without dependant words*, or a noun, then a short subordinate clause does have the copula-participle, for example: Сїю̀ дще́рь а̓враа́млю су́щꙋ, Luke 13:16—"this woman, being a daughter of Abraham" (=ѧ́же є́сть а̓враа́млѧ); see also Luke 2:5; Вручаю же ва́мъ фі́вꙋ сестру́ на́шꙋ, су́щꙋ слꙋжи́тельницꙋ цр҃кве ꙗ́же въ кегхрее́хъ, Rom. 16:1—"I commend unto you Phebe our sister, which is a servant of the church which is at Cenchrea" (=ꙗ́же є́сть слꙋжи́тельница...); и̓ сѐ мꙋ́жъ и́менемъ і̓ѡ́сифъ, совѣ́тникъ сы́й, Luke 23:50—"And behold, a man named Joseph, a counseller" (=и́же совѣ́тникъ бѣ̀). In short constructions with a noun, the copula-participle may be left out, and then the noun goes into apposition, for example: Цѣлꙋ́йте оу̓рва́на споспѣ́шника на́шего ѡ̓ хр҃тѣ̀, Rom. 16:9 — "Salute Urbane, our helper in Christ" (=су́ща споспѣ́шника на́шего...).

Given the alterations mentioned above, the tense of the participle depends on whether the predicate of the subordinate clause indicates the same time as that of the main clause, or a time preceding it, for example: и̓ желаше насы́титисѧ ѿ крꙋпи́цъ па́дающихъ ѿ трапе́зы бога́тагѡ (Luke 16:21—"And he desired to be fed with the crumbs which fell from the rich man's table"); here the full construction would be: и́же па́дахꙋ ѿ трапе́зы бога́тагѡ: па́дахꙋ and жела́ше show actions taking place at the same time, and therefore the short construction has the participle in the present tense.

In short subordinate clauses with the participles глаго́лемый, нарицае́мый a proper noun is usually put in the nominative case, for example: Приближа́шеся же пра́здникъ ѡпрѣснѡ́къ, глаго́лемый па́сха (Luke 22:1—"Now the feast of unleavened bread drew nigh, which is called the Passover"); и пришѐдъ вселѝся во гра́дѣ нарицае́мѣмъ назаре́тъ (Matth. 2:23—"And he came and dwelt in a city called Nazareth"); but not always: и поста́виша два̀, і҆ѡсифа нарица́емаго варса́вꙋ... (Acts 1:23—"And they appointed two, Joseph called Barsabas...").

A participle in a short subordinate clause has a definite sense (cf. человѣ́къ, сотвори́вый сїѧ̀ = человѣ́къ, и́же сотвори сїѧ̀ — "*the* man who has done these things"), and therefore in theory it ought to have the long ending, however (in order to match the Greek text) alongside of forms with the long ending, not infrequently the short endings are also used (where the Greek text has no article), for example: long forms— Вся́ческаѧ же ѿ бг҃а, примири́вшагѡ* на́съ себѣ̀ і҆и҃съ хр҃то́мъ, и да́вшагѡ* на́мъ слꙋже́нїе примире́нїѧ (II Cor. 5:18—"And all things are of God, who hath reconciled us to himself by Jesus Christ, and hath given to us the ministry of reconciliation"); и ѡблещи́ся въ но́ваго человѣ́ка созда́ннаго* по бг҃ꙋ въ пра́вдѣ (Ephes. 4:24—"And that ye put on the new man, which after God is created in righteousness"); short forms— Подо́бенъ е҆́сть человѣ́кꙋ зи́ждꙋщꙋ* хра́минꙋ, Luke 6:48—"He is like a man which built an house" (cf. v. 49: созда́вшемꙋ хра́минꙋ — "like a man that... built an house..."); Къ немꙋ́же приходѧ́ще, ка́мени жи́вꙋ, ѿ человѣ́къ ᲂу҆ничиже́нꙋ* (I Peter 2:4—"To whom coming, as unto a living stone, disallowed [indeed] of men...").

The definite character of the participle in such cases is sometimes emphasized by the use of a pronoun-article (see §170, 5), for example: и кни́жницы, и́же* ѿ і҆ерꙋсали́ма низше́дшїи*, глаго́лахꙋ... (Mark 3:22—"And the scribes which came down from Jerusalem said..."); compare: и нѣ́цыи ѿ кни́жникъ, прише́дшїи* ѿ і҆ерꙋсали́ма (Mark 7:1—"and certain of the scribes, which came from Jerusalem").

Sometimes the pronoun-article is also encountered with adjectives (in a short subordinate clause), for example: Й҆же бога́тый въ ми́лости, во́лею погре́блсѧ є҆сѝ (Sunday Octoechos, T. 2, Ode 8—"Thou Who art great in mercy, wast of Thine own will buried"); и҆́же ѡ҆ всѣ́хъ благі́й гдⷵнь, сла́ва тебѣ̀ (Tropar of Holy Thursday—"O Lord, Who art good towards all, glory to Thee").

An adjective in a short subordinate clause, whether with dependant words (but without an article, see the examples above), or with the participles сы́й, бы́вый is usually in the short form, for example: Сотвори́те ѹ҆́бо плоды̀ досто́йны* покаѧ́нїѧ (Luke 3:8—"Bring forth therefore fruits worthy of repentance"); и҆́же возда́дѧтъ сло́во гото́вꙋ* сꙋ́щемꙋ сꙋди́ти живы̑мъ и҆ ме́ртвымъ (I Peter 4:5—"Who shall give account to him that is ready to judge the quick and the dead").

II. *Adverbial* short subordinate clauses are expressed by adverbial participles (equivalent to gerunds) with dependant words (see §146). Short subordinate adverbial clauses may be of the following types:

1) of time: Слы́шавъ* же ю҆́ноша сло́во, ѿи́де скорбѧ̀ (Matth. 19:22—"But when the young man heard that saying, he went away sorrowful"), = є҆гда́ же ѹ҆слы́ша ю҆́ноша сло́во:

2) of reason: і҆ѡ́сифъ же мꙋ́жъ є҆ѧ̀, пра́веденъ* сы́й*, и҆ не хотѧ̀* є҆ѧ̀ ѡ҆бличи́ти, восхотѣ̀ та́й пꙋсти́ти ю҆̀ (Matth. 1:19—"Then Joseph her husband, being a just man, and not willing to make her a public example, was minded to put her away privily"), = ꙗ҆́кw (because) пра́веденъ бѣ̀ и҆ не хотѧ̀...

3) of condition: Что́ бо по́льзы и҆́мать человѣ́къ, прїѡбрѣ́тъ* мі́ръ ве́сь (Luke 9:25—"For what is a man advantaged, if he gain the whole world"), = а҆́ще мі́ръ ве́сь прїѡбрѧ́щетъ (Matth. 16:26—"if he shall gain the whole world");

4) of concession: а́ще ѹ҆́бо вы̀ лꙋка́ви* сꙋ́ще*, оу҆мѣ́ете
даѧ̑нїѧ бла̑га даѧ́ти ча̑дѡмъ ва́шымъ (Matth. 7:11—"If ye then,
being evil, know how to give good gifts unto your children..."), = а́ще
и҆ лꙋка́ви* є̑стѐ...

5) of manner: Ше́дше ѹ҆́бо наꙋчи́те всѧ̑ ꙗ҆зы́ки, крестѧ́ще*
и҆̀хъ во и҆́мѧ Ѻ҆ц҃а̀ и҆ сн҃а и҆ ст҃а́гѡ дх҃а (Matth. 28:19—"Go ye therefore,
and teach all nations, baptizing them in the name of the Father, and
of the Son, and of the Holy Ghost"), where there is no corresponding
full constructon. A short construction may have the conjunction а́ки
бы *(as if)*: Ны́нѣ ѹ҆́бо вы̀ скажи́те ты́сѧщникꙋ съ собо́ромъ, ꙗ҆кѡ
да оу҆́трѣ све́детъ є҆го̀ къ ва́мъ, а́ки бы хотѧ́ще* разꙋмѣ́ти
и҆звѣ́стнѣе, ꙗ҆́же ѡ҆ не́мъ (Acts 23:15—"Now therefore ye with the
council signify to the chief captain that he bring him down unto you
tomorrow, as though ye would inquire something more perfectly
concerning him").

As can be seen from the examples given above, the short
constructions (except for that of manner), correspond to the full, and
one can be replaced by the other.

III. To the short subordinate clauses should be assigned those
also, in which the action is expressed by an infinitive, in view of the
fact that the infinitive cannot have a meaning by itself, and
consequently cannot give the clause a full predication. Concerning
short subordinate clauses with an infinitive, see §143, 8), 9), 10) and
11).

§197. The Dative Absolute.

The *dative absolute* is the name for a particular turn of syntax,
consisting of an active participle [usually in the short form] and a
noun or pronoun (the subject of the action of the participle), which
together are put in the dative case, agreeing in gender and number.
This syntactical structure is not a part of either the subject or the
predicate, and therefore it is called [in Russian] "the independant

dative"; it has the sense of a *short subordinate clause*. The dative absolute is used in cases where the subjects of the main and subordinate clauses are different, for example: и сѣющꙋ* Ꙗмꙋ*, ѻва падоша при пꙋти (Matth. 13:4—"And when he sowed, some [seeds] fell by the wayside"); the short construction corresponds to a full one: и Ꙗгда ѻнъ сѣꙗше, ѻва падоша при пꙋти. Сшедшꙋ* же Ꙗмꙋ* съ горы, вслѣдъ Ꙗгѡ идꙗхꙋ народи мнози (Matth. 8:1—"When he was come down from the mountain, great multitudes followed him"), = Ꙗгда же ѻнъ сниде съ горы, вслѣдъ...

If the action of the subordinate and the main clause take place at the same time, the participle in the dative absolute is put in the present tense; but if the action of the subordinate clause precedes that of the main, then the participle in the dative absolute is put in the past tense; see the preceding examples.

Subordinate clauses with a dative absolute can have the following adverbial senses:

1) Of time: Собравшымсꙗ* же имъ*, рече имъ пилатъ (Matth. 27:17—"Therefore when they were gathered together, Pilate said unto them..."); и абїе, Ꙗще глаголющꙋ* Ꙗмꙋ*, возгласи пѣтель (Luke 22:60—"And immediately, while he yet spake, the cock crew"); идꙋщымъ* же имъ* кꙋпити, прїиде женихъ (Matth. 25:10—"And while they went to buy, the bridegroom came").

2) Of reason: Коснꙗщꙋ* же женихꙋ*, воздремашасꙗ всꙗ, и спахꙋ (Matth. 25:5—"While the bridegroom tarried, they all slumbered, and slept"); Восхищенꙋ* же бывшꙋ* кораблю*, и не могꙋщꙋ* сопротивитисꙗ вѣтрꙋ, вдавшесꙗ волнамъ носими бѣхомъ (Acts 27:15—"And when the ship was caught, and could not bear up into the wind, having given [ourselves] up to the waves, we were driven"); Не добрꙋ* же пристанищꙋ* сꙋщꙋ* ко ѡзимѣнїю, мнози совѣтъ даахꙋ ѿвезтисꙗ ѿтꙋдꙋ (Acts 27:12—"And because the haven was not commodious to winter in, the more part advised to depart thence").

3) Of concession: Толи́ка зна́менїа сотво́рш҄* є҆м҄* пред
ни́ми, не вѣ́ровах҄ въ него̀ (John 12:37—"But though he had done so
many miracles before them, yet they believed not on him"); и҆
толи́кꙋ сꙋ́щымъ*, не прото́ржеса мре́жа (John 21:11—"and for all
there were so many, yet was not the net broken"); Ка́мени*
запеча́тан҄* ѿ і҆ꙋде́й, и҆ во́ннwмъ* стрегꙋ́щымъ* пре́чтое тѣ́ло
твоѐ, воскре́сла є҆сѝ, тридне́вный спсе (Octoechos, Sunday Tropar of
the 1st Tone—"When the Jews had sealed the down the stone, and
while the guards were watching over Thine immaculate body, Thou
didst rise again on the third day, O Saviour").

The dative absolute may have composite forms as well, i.e.
with the copula-participles сꙋ́щꙋ, бы́вшꙋ, there can be a predicate
member, an adjective or a passive participle, which like the copula-
participle are put in the dative case, and in the short form at that.

Concerning the use of the passive participle in the dative
absolute, the following should be noted: with a passive participle (be
it of the present or past tense), the copula-participle сꙋ́щꙋ is not used,
but only the copula-participle бы́вшꙋ, that is, when the action of the
passive participle takes place at the same time as that of the main
clause, the copula is not used[1]); cf. the following examples: Ка́мени*
запеча́танꙋ*... (as above) and Восхище́нꙋ* же бы́вшꙋ*... (above,
Acts. 27:15); also: Ве́льми же ѡ҆бꙋрева́емымъ* на́мъ*, наꙋ́трїе
и҆зме́та́нїе творѧ́хꙋ (Acts 27:18—"And we being exceedingly tossed
with a tempest, the next day they lightened [the ship]"); Ска́занꙋ* же
бы́вшꙋ* мн ко́вꙋ* хотѧ́щꙋ бы́ти ѿ і҆ꙋде́й на мꙋ́жа сего̀, а҆́бїе
посла́хъ є҆го̀ къ тебѣ̀ (Acts 23:30—"And when it was told me how
that the Jews laid wait for this man, I sent straightway to thee").

---

[1]) One might regard the following example as an exception:
є҆мꙋ̀* мно́гажды пꙋ́ты и҆ ѹ҆́жы [желѣ́зны] свѧ́занꙋ* сꙋ́щꙋ*
(Mark 5:4—"Because that he had been often bound with fetters and
chains").

The dative absolute may consist of a participle with an adverb and then takes on an "impersonal" character (there is no subject of the action), for example: Сꙋщꙋ же поздѣ, ... прїиде і҃исъ (John 20:19—"when it was evening, ... Jesus came"); Поздѣ же бы́вшꙋ, ... приношахꙋ къ немꙋ всѧ̑ недꙋжныѧ и̑ бѣсны́ѧ (Mark 1:32—"And at even, ... they brought unto him all that were diseased, and them that were possessed with devils").

Sometimes the dative absolute is encountered with an omission of the noun or pronoun, if the subject of the action of the participle is easily understood from the context, for example: и̑ вы̀ подобни чл҃вѣ́кѡмъ чаю́щымъ г҃да своегѡ̀, когда̀ возврати́тсѧ ѿ бра́ка, да пришéдшꙋ* и̑ толькнꙋ́вшꙋ*, а́бїе ѿвéрзꙋтъ е҆мꙋ̀ (Luke 12:36—"And ye yourselves are like unto men that wait for their lord, when he will return from the wedding; that when he cometh and knocketh, they may open unto him immediately").

The main clause may begin with the introductory-demonstrative particle сѐ ("behold"), which gives a certain independence to the subordinate clause/dative absolute, for example: Ѿшéдшымъ же и̑мъ, сѐ а́гглъ г҃день во снѣ̀ ꙗ҆ви́сѧ і҆ѡ́сифꙋ (Matth. 2:13—"And when they [the Magi] were departed, behold, the angel of the Lord appeared to Joseph in a dream"); see also Matth. 2:1 and 19.

Although constructions with the dative absolute, as a rule, occur when there are different subjects in the main and subordinate clauses, nevertheless, by way of exception, a breach of this "rule" is sometimes met with, that is, one encounters the use of constructions with the dative absolute where there is one and the same subject in both the main and subordinate clause, for example: Не и̑мѣ́хъ поко́ѧ д҃хꙋ моемꙋ̀, не ѡ̑брѣ́тшꙋ* мнѣ* ті́та бра́та моегѡ̀ (II Cor. 2:13—"I had no rest in my spirit, because I found not Titus my brother"—used here rather than a construction with an adverbial participle: не ѡ̑брѣ́тъ ті́та бра́та моегѡ̀); ѡ̑брꙋчéнѣй* бо бы́вши* мⷶрн* є҆гѡ̀ мр҃і́н і҆ѡ́снфовн, пре́жде да́же не сни́тнса и҆́ма, ѡ҆бр'ѣ́теса и҆м8́цін во чре́в'ѣ ѿ дх҃а ст҃а (Matth. 1:18—"When as his mother Mary was espoused to Joseph, before they came together, she was found with child of the Holy Ghost"); in this example, the oneness of the subject in the main and subordinate clauses, nevertheless, is somewhat broken up by a short subordinate clause with an infinitive, which brings in a new subject (и҆́ма); similarly so in Exodus 4:21 and Jeremiah 31:32.

In the following examples, the rule of "different subjects" only appears to be broken: и҆ бы́сть и҆д8́цьнмⷱ и҆́мⷱ, ѡ҆чн́стншаса (Luke 17:14—"And it came to pass, that, as they went, they were cleansed"); Бы́сть же возвратн́вш8мнса во і҆ер8́салнⷨⷱ, и҆ мола́ці8мнса вⷱ цр҃квн, бы́тн во и҆зст8пле́нïн (Acts 22:17—"And it came to pass, that, when I was come again to Jerusalem, even while I prayed in the temple, I was in a trance"). In these examples it is бы́сть ["it came to pass"] that is the main clause, to which the following clauses are subordinated:

и҆ бы́сть	*when?* и҆д8́цьнмⷱ и҆́мⷱ
	what? ѡ҆чн́стншаса.
бы́сть же	*when?* возвратн́вш8мнса во і҆ер8́салнⷨⷱ, и҆
мола́ці8мнса	
	what? бы́тн во и҆зст8пле́нïн.

The above could be translated in the following manner: "And as they went, it happened, that they were cleansed; And when I returned to Jerusalem, and prayed in the temple, it happened to me, that I was in a trance".

The dative absolute serves to convey the Greek construction called the "genitive absolute" *(genitivus absolutus).*

§198. Compound-Complex Sentences.

Complex sentences may be of either the simple type, or of a more complicated type: co-ordinate clauses may be extended by subordinate clauses, and subordinate by further subordinate clauses.

A subordinate clause, in turn, can have one or more subordinates, to which it stands in the relationship of a main clause. For example:

1) Й поманꙋша причáстникѡмъ, *a)* и̂же бáхꙋ во дрꙋзѣ́мъ корабли, *b)* да пришéдше помóгꙋтъ и̂ма: 2) и̂ прїидóша, и̂ и̂спóлниша ѻ̂ба корабля̂, *c)* ꙗ̂кѡ погрꙋжáтися и̂ма (Luke 5:7—"And they beckoned unto their partners, which were in the other ship, that they should come and help them. And they came, and filled both the ships, so that they began to sink"). Here clauses 1) and 2) are coordinate; clauses *a)* which is a adjectival, and *b)* which is an adverbial clause of purpose, are subordinates of clause 1); clause *c)* which is an adverbial clause of result, is subordinate to clause 2); пришéдше is a short subordinate clause of manner, referring to clause *b)*.

1) Ѻ̂бáче враги моа̀ ѻ̂ны, *a)* и̂же не восхотѣ́ша менè, *b)* да цáрь бы́хъ над ни́ми, 2) приве- ди́те сѣ́мѡ, 3) и̂ и̂зсѣцы́те предо мнóю (Luke 19:27—"But those mine enemies, which would not that I should reign over them, bring [them] hither, and slay [them] before me"). Clause 1) is the main clause; clause *a)* is an adjectival subordinate clause referring to main clause 1); clause *b)* is an adverbial clause of purpose subordinate to clause *a)*.

Several subordinate clauses of the same type, referring to one and the same sentence member or to an entire clause as a whole, are known as *clauses of the same kind*, and in terms of their mutual relationship, as *coordinative*, for example: Блажéнни, и̂хже ѿпꙋсти́шася беззакѡ́нїА, и̂ и̂хже прикры́шася грѣси̂ (Rom. 4:7—"Blessed are they whose iniquities are forgiven, and whose sins are covered"); вдови́ца же да причитáетсА не мéньши лѣ́тъ шести́десАтихъ..., въ дѣ́лѣхъ дóбрыхъ свидѣ́тельствꙋема, áще чáда воспитáла є̂́сть, áще сты́хъ нóзѣ оу̂мы̀, áще стрáннаА прїА́тъ, áще скѡ́рбнымъ оу̂тѣшéнїе бы́сть, áще всА́комꙋ дѣлꙋ блгꙋ послѣ́довала є̂́сть (I Tim. 5:9-10—"Let not a widow be taken into the number under threescore years old..., [if she be] well reported of for good works; if she have brought up children, if she have lodged strangers, if she have washed the Saints' feet, if she have relieved the afflicted, if she have diligently followed every good work"); и та̂ повѣ́даста, ꙗ́же бы́ша на пꙋтѝ, и ꙗ́кѡ позна́сѧ и́ма въ преломле́нїи хлѣ́ба (Luke 24:35—"And they told what things were done in the way, and how he was known of them in breaking of bread").

Clauses belonging to various types, or of one type but referring to different sentence parts, are known as clauses *of different kinds,* for example: є҆гда̀ ви́дите сїѧ̀ всѧ̑, вѣ́дите, ꙗ́кѡ бли́зъ є҆́сть при две́рехъ (Matth. 24:33—"when ye shall see all these things, know that it [the Second Coming] is near, [even] at the doors").

Subordinate clauses may form a consecutive chain of subordination: the first subordinate clause refers to the main clause, the second subordinate to the first, the third to the second, and so on; these are called: a subordinate clause of the 2nd degree, of the third degree, &c., for example: Ны́нѣ повелѣва́етъ [бг҃ъ] человѣ́кѡмъ всѣ̑мъ всю́дꙋ пока́ѧтисѧ: (1st degree) зане́ ѹ҆ста́вилъ є҆́сть де́нь, (2nd degree) во́ньже хо́щетъ сꙋди́ти вселе́ннѣй въ пра́вдꙋ, ѡ҆ мꙋ́жи, (3rd degree) є҆го́же предꙋ́стави (Acts 17:30-31—"but now [God] commandeth all men everywhere to repent: because he hath appointed a day, in the which he will judge the world in righteousness by [that] man whom he hath ordained").

§199. The Period.

A *period* is what we call a compound (compound coordinate or compound subordinate [complex]) extended sentence, consisting of two parts: the first part presents a series of increasingly significant elements of a given event or phenomenon, while the second part gives the conclusion or deduction.

Ecclesiastical hymnody usually contains periods of various sorts, for example: Кр҃то́мъ твои́мъ ѹ҆праздни́лъ є҆сѝ, ю́же ѿ дре́ва

408

клѧ́ткꙋ, погребе́нїемъ тво́имъ оу҆мертви́лъ є҆сѝ сме́рти держа́вꙋ, воста́нїемъ же тво́имъ просвѣти́лъ є҆сѝ ро́дъ человѣ́ческїй. || сегѡ̀ ра́ди вопїе́мъ тѝ: бл҃годѣ́телю хрⷭ҇тѐ бж҃е на́шъ, сла́ва тебѣ̀ (Sunday Octoechos, T. 2, at "Lord I have cried"—"By Thy Cross Thou hast abolished the curse of the tree, by Thy burial Thou hast mortified death's dominion, while by Thy rising Thou hast enlightened the human race. Therefore we cry out unto Thee: O Benefactor, Christ our God, glory to Thee").

Note: Concerning the rising and falling of the intonation in the Church Slavonic period, one can scarcely speak, since the Slavonic text is either read on a recitative note or else sung, and in view of this manner of delivery the intonational elements of the period are not evident.

Sometimes one meets with a particular type of period, consisting of several (usually coordinate) clauses, similar in form and content and giving a kind of parallel; such a construction might be called a *period with parallelism,* for example: є҆гда̀ грѣ́шница приноша́ше мѵ́ро, тогда̀ оу҆чени́къ соглаша́шесѧ со беззако́нными. || Ѻ҆́ваѧ оу҆́бо ра́довашесѧ, и҆стоща́ющи мѵ́ро драгоцѣ́нное: се́й же тща́шесѧ прода́ти безцѣ́ннаго. || сїѧ̀ влⷣкꙋ познава́ше, а҆ се́й ѿ влⷣки разлꙋча́шесѧ. || сїѧ̀ свобожда́шесѧ, а҆ і҆ꙋ́да ра́бъ быва́ше врагꙋ̀. || лю́то є҆́сть лѣ́ность, ве́лїе покаѧ́нїе! || є҆́же мнѣ̀ да́рꙋй сп҃се, пострада́вый за на́съ, и҆ спаси́ на́съ (Wednesday in Holy Week, at "Lord I have cried"—"While the sinful woman brought oil of myrrh, the disciple came to an agreement with the transgressors. She rejoiced to pour out that what was most precious; he made haste to sell Him that is above all price. She recognized the Master; he separated himself from the Master. She was made free, but Judas became a slave to the enemy. Grievous is indifference, but great is repentance! Which, do Thou grant unto me O Saviour, Who didst suffer for us; and save us!").

Punctuation Marks in the Compound Sentence.

§200. *In subordinate clauses.* 1) Subordinate clauses, as in Russian, are set off by a comma, for example: кꙋ́плю дѣ́йте, до́ндеже прїидꙋ̀ (Luke 19:13—"Be occupied in trading, until I come").

2) There is no strict consistency in the use of commas in subordinate clauses; one can only note the general characteristics that underlie the placing of commas:

Short adjectival subordinate clauses with a participle in the full form are for the most part set off by commas (but sometimes they are encountered without a comma), for example: и̇ дивла́хꙋсѧ ѡ̇ словесѣ́хъ благода́ти, и̇сходѧ́щихъ* и̇з оу̇́стъ є̇гѡ̀ (Luke 4:22—"and they wondered at the words of grace which proceeded out of his mouth"); всѧ́ческаѧ же ѿ бга, примири́вшагѡ* на́съ себѣ̀ і̇и̇съ хрⷭто́мъ (II Cor. 5:18—"And all things are of God, who hath reconciled us to himself by Jesus Christ"); but also sometimes: благодарѧ́ще бга и̇ ѻ̇̀ца призва́вшагѡ ва́съ въ прича́стїе наслѣ́дїѧ ст҃ы́хъ во свѣ́тѣ (Col. 1:12—"Giving thanks unto God the Father, who hath made you worthy to be partakers of the inheritance of the Saints in the light").

Short subordinate clauses with a short participle or adjective are usually not set off by commas, although they may also be, for example: подо́бенъ є̇́сть человѣ́кꙋ зи́ждꙋщꙋ* хра́минꙋ (Luke 6:48—"He is like to a man building a house"); Па́ки подо́бно є̇́сть црⷭтвїе нбⷭное не́водꙋ вве́рженꙋ* въ мо́ре, и̇ ѿ всѧ́кагѡ ро́да собра́вшꙋ* (Matth. 13:47—"Again, the kingdom of heaven is like unto a net, that was cast into the sea, and gathered of every kind"); Па́ки подо́бно є̇́сть црⷭтвїе нбⷭное человѣ́кꙋ кꙋпцꙋ̀, и̇́щꙋщꙋ* до́брыхъ би́серей (Matth. 13:45—"Again, the kingdom of heaven is like unto a merchant man, seeking goodly pearls").

Short adverbial subordinate clauses are usually set off by a comma, for example: воздви́же ю̇̀, є̇́мъ за рꙋ́кꙋ є̇ѧ̀ (Mark 1:43—"he lifted her up, taking her by the hand"); и҆ запре́щꙸ є҆мꙋ̀, а҆́бїе и҆згна̀ є҆го̀ (Mark 1:43—"And straightly charging him, forthwith [he] sent him away"); и҆ прише́дше въ хра́минꙋ, ви́дѣша Ѻ҆троча̀ съ марі́ею мт҃рїю є҆гѡ̀ (Matth. 2:11—"And when they were come into the house, they saw the young child with Mary his mother").

3) Short subordinate clauses with an infinitive are always set off by a comma, for example: Ко гдꙋ҃, внегда̀ скорбѣ́ти мѝ, воззва́хъ (Ps. 119:1—"To the Lord, when I was troubled, I cried out"); Да и҆сче́знꙋтъ грѣ́шницы ѿ землѝ, и҆ беззакѡ́нницы, ꙗ҆́коже не бы́ти и҆́мъ (Ps. 103:35—"Let sinners be consumed out of the earth, and the unjust, so as to be no more").

4) Short subordinate clauses with the dative absolute are usually set off by commas, but on rare occasions they can be found without commas too, for example: и҆ влѣ́зшꙋ є҆мꙋ̀ въ кора́бль, по не́мъ и҆до́ша ѹ҆чени́цы є҆гѡ̀ (Matth. 8:23—"And when he entered into the boat, his disciples followed him"); По́здѣ же бы́вшꙋ, приведо́ша къ немꙋ̀ бѣ́сны мно́ги (Matth. 8:16—"And when evening was come, they brought to him many that were possessed with devils"); but rarely: Со́лнцꙋ же возсїа́вшꙋ присва́нꙋша (Matth. 13:6—"And when the sun was come up, they were scorched").

§201. *In compound coordinate sentences.* 1) Coordinate clauses, if they are not extended by members of the same kind, or by subordinate clauses, are set apart from each other by commas, for example: є҆ди́но дѣ́ло сотвори́хъ, и҆ всѝ дивите́сѧ (John 7:21—"I have done one work, and ye all marvel"); ра́зꙋмъ ѹ҆́бо кичи́тъ, а҆ любы̀ созида́етъ (I Cor. 8:1—"Knowledge puffeth up, but charity edifieth").

2) Sometimes, however, unextended coordinate clauses, so as to point out the apartness or independence of actions, are separated by a colon, for example: и҆ и҆зы́де во́нъ на придво́рїе: и҆ а҆ле́ктѡръ возгласѝ (Mark 14:68—"And he went out into the porch: and the cock crew"); и҆ диви́стасѧ роди́телѧ є҆ѧ̀: Ѻ҆́нъ же повелѣ̀ и҆́ма

нникомꙋже повѣдати бывшаго (Luke 8:56—"And her parents were astonished: but he charged them that they should tell no man what was done").

3) Coordinate clauses that have been extended by means of sentence members of the same kind or by subordinate clauses, and which, consequently, already have commas in them, are separated from each other by a colon, for example: и хождаше їисъ по сихъ въ галїлеи: не хотꙗше бо во їꙋдеи ходити, ꙗкw искахꙋ его їꙋдее ꙋбити (John 7:1—"After these things Jesus walked in Galilee: for he would not walk in Jewry, because the Jews sought to kill him"); Они же изшедше идоша въ стадо свиное: и се, [абїе] ꙋстремиса стадо все по брегꙋ въ море, и ꙋтопоша въ водахъ (Matth. 8:32—"And when they were come out, they went into the herd of swine: and, behold, the whole herd of swine ran violently down a bank into the sea, and perished in the waters"); и паки начатъ ꙋчити при мори: и собраса къ немꙋ народъ многъ, ꙗкоже самомꙋ, влѣзшꙋ въ корабль, сѣдѣти въ мори: и весь народъ при мори на земли баше (Mark 4:1—"And he began again to teach by the sea side: and there was gathered unto him a great multitude, so that he entered into a ship, and sat in the sea; and the whole multitude was by the sea on the land").

4) A compound coordinate sentence, consisting of several coordinate pairs (with or without conjunctions), usually has the following punctuation marks: in each pair, the clauses are set apart by a comma, and the pairs are separated from each other by colons, for example: взалкахса бо, и дасте ми ꙗсти: возжадахса, и напоисте ма: странень быхъ, и введосте мене: нагъ, и wдѣасте ма: болень, и посѣтисте мене: въ темницѣ бѣхъ, и прїидосте ко мнѣ (Matth. 25:35-36—"For I was an hungred, and ye gave me to eat: I was thirsty, and ye gave me to drink: I was a stranger, and ye took me in: naked, and ye clothed me: sick, and ye visited me: in prison, and ye came unto me"); аще бо во плоти живете, имате ꙋмрети: аще ли дꙋхомъ дѣанїа плотскаа ꙋмерщвлаете, живи бꙋдете (Rom.

8:13—"For if ye live after the flesh, ye shall die: but if ye through the Spirit do mortify the deeds of the body, ye shall live"); вы̀ ѿ ни́жнихъ є҆стѐ, а҆́зъ ѿ вы́шнихъ є҆́смь: вы̀ ѿ мі́ра сегѡ̀ є҆стѐ, а҆́зъ нѣ́смь ѿ мі́ра сегѡ̀ (John 8:23—"Ye are from beneath; I am from above: ye are of this world; I am not of this world").

5) Coordinate clauses that already contain a colon in their structure, are separated from each other by a "lesser period" (малой точкой), for example: дрꙋзі́и глаго́лахꙋ: се́й є҆́сть хрⷭ҇то́съ. ѻ҆́вїи же глаго́лахꙋ: є҆да̀ ѿ галїле́и хрⷭ҇то́съ прихо́дитъ; (John 7:41—"Others said, This is the Christ. But some said, Shall Christ come out of Galilee?"); глаго́ла и҆̀мъ сі́мѡнъ пе́тръ: и҆дꙋ̀ ры́бы лови́ти. глаго́лаша є҆мꙋ̀: и҆де́мъ и҆ мы̀ съ тобо́ю. и҆зыдо́ша же, и҆ всѣ́доша а҆́бїе въ кора́бль, и҆ въ тꙋ̀ но́щь не ꙗ҆́ша ничесо́же (John 21:3—"Simon Peter said unto them, I go a fishing. They said unto him, We also go with thee. They went forth, and intered into a ship immediately; and that night they caught nothing").

6) Coordinate clauses that do not have a conjunction are for the most part separated from each other by a colon, especially if the second clause is a clarification of the first one; for example: и҆ вве́ргꙋтъ и҆̀хъ въ пе́щь ѻ҆́гненнꙋю: тꙋ̀ бꙋ́детъ пла́чь и҆ скре́жетъ зꙋбѡ́мъ (Matth. 13:50—"And [they] shall cast them into the fiery furnace: there shall be wailing and gnashing of teeth"); ѡ҆ста́вите и҆̀хъ: вожди̑ сꙋ́ть слѣпи́ слѣпцє́мъ (Matth. 15:14—"Let them alone: they be blind leaders of the blind").

§202. *In the period.* 1) If the members of the first (or second) part of the period are only set off from one another by commas, then between the first and second parts of the period there usually is placed a colon; but sometimes a "lesser period" is used; for example: воскрⷭ҇лъ є҆сѝ ꙗ҆́кѡ безсме́ртный ѿ гро́ба, сп҃се, совоздви́глъ є҆сѝ мі́ръ тво́й си́лою твое́ю, хрⷭ҇тѐ бж҃е на́шъ, сокрꙋши́лъ є҆сѝ въ крѣ́пости сме́рти держа́вꙋ, показа́лъ є҆сѝ ми́лостиве, воскресе́нїе всѣ́мъ: || тѣ́мже тѧ̀ и҆ сла́вимъ, є҆ди́не человѣколю́бче (Sunday Octoechos, T. 4, Sessional

Hymn [Sedalen]—"Thou art risen O Saviour, from the dead as One immortal; Thou hast raised up with Thyself the world by Thy power, O Christ our God. Thou hast shattered in [Thy] might the dominion of death; Thou hast shown, O Merciful One, resurrection unto all: and for this cause we glorify Thee, O Thou Who alone lovest mankind").

Sometimes, however, if the period is not too extended, between its first and second parts there may instead be a comma; for example: а́ще не ви́жꙋ на рꙋкꙋ є҆гѡ̀ ꙗ҆́звы гвозди́нныꙗ, и҆ вложꙋ̀ пе́рста моегѡ̀ въ ꙗ҆́звы гвозди́нныꙗ, и҆ вложꙋ̀ рꙋкꙋ̀ мою̀ въ ре́бра є҆гѡ̀, не и҆мꙋ̀ ве́ры (John 20:25—"Except I shall see in his hands the print of the nails, and put my finger into the print of the nails, and thrust my hand into his side, I will not believe").

2) If in the first (or the second) part of the period, besides commas, there is already a colon, a question mark (;) or an exclamation point (!), then between the first and second parts of the period there usually is placed a "lesser period" (sometimes also a colon); for example: Съ нб҃сѐ блгⷣть прїе́мъ, є҆гда̀ вопроше́нїе оу҆ченникѡ́мъ сп҃съ двана́десѧточи́сленнымъ речѐ а҆пⷵлѡмъ: когѡ́ мѧ глаго́лютъ челове́цы бы́ти; тогда̀ оу҆́бо лꙋ́чшїй а҆пⷵлѡвъ пе́тръ, бг҃ослови́твꙋѧ ѿве́ща, ꙗ҆́снѡ возопи́въ: ты̀ є҆сѝ хрⷵто́съ, жива́гѡ бг҃а сн҃ъ. ‖ те́мже досто́йнѡ оу҆блажа́етсѧ, ꙗ҆́кѡ свы́ше прїе́мъ ѿкрове́нїе, вѧза́ти же и҆ ре́шити пра́веднѡ прїе́мъ (June 29, Ss. Peter and Paul, at the Praises—"Having received Grace from heaven, when the Saviour asked the rank of the twelve Apostles, Who do men say that I am?, then indeed the best of Apostles, Peter, proclaiming Thy Divinity answered, in crying out for all to hear: Thou art Christ the Son of the Living God. Wherefore it is meet to beatify him, since he received the revelation from above, and the gift to bind and loose in righteousness").

3) In a period with parallelism, the following punctuation marks occur: the coordinate clauses in each "row" (рядъ) are set apart

by a colon, and parallel rows are divided by a "lesser period" (see §201, 4); for example: Въ чермнѣмъ мо́ри, неискѸсобра́чныѧ невѣ́сты Ѡ́бразъ написа́сѧ иногда̀: та́мѡ мѡѵ́сей, разда̀лѝтель воды̀: здѐ же гаврі́илъ, слѸжѝтель чѸде́съ. ‖ тогда̀ глѸбинѸ̀ ше́ствова немо́креннѡ і͂иль: нынѣ́ же хр͂та̀ родѝ безсѣ́меннѡ дв͂а. ‖ мо́ре по проше́ствїи і͂илевѣ, пребы́сть непрохо́дно: непоро́чнаѧ по рождествѣ́ е͂мманѸ́илевѣ, пребы́сть нетлѣ́нна. ‖ сы́й, ѝ пре́жде сы́й, ꙗвле́йсѧ ꙗ҆́кѡ челов҄ѣ́къ, бж͂е, помѝлѸ́й на́съ (Sunday Octoechos, Dogmatic of T. 5— "In the Red Sea, the Unwedded Bride's image was once inscribed: there [was] Moses, the parter of the waters; here Gabriel, the servant of the wonder. Then, Israel rode dry-shod across the deep; and now, the Virgin hath without seed given birth to Christ. After the passing of Israel, the sea was as ever impassable. After the birth of Emmanuel, the Virgin without reproach, remains uncorrupt. Thou, O God, Who art now, hast forever been, and hast appeared as man, have mercy upon us"). See the examples in §199.

§203. Direct and Indirect Discourse.

The words of another, in Church Slavonic as in other languages, may be conveyed in two ways: by direct or indirect quotation.

Someone else's words, conveyed literally, are known as *direct discourse,* for example: Глаго́ла и̑мъ пе́тръ: идѸ̀ ры́бы ловѝти. глаго́лаша е̑мѸ̀: и̑демъ ѝ мы̀ съ тобо́ю (John 21:3—"Peter said to them: I go a fishing; they said to him: We too go with thee").

A quotation conveyed by the author in the form of a subordinate clause with the conjunction ꙗ҆́кѡ ["that"], is called *indirect discourse;* for example: Повѣ́даша же е̑мѸ̀, ꙗ҆́кѡ і͂исъ назара́нинъ мимохо́дитъ (Luke 18:37—"And they told him, that Jesus of Nazareth passeth by"); Ѻ̑на̀ же реко́ста, ꙗ҆́кѡ гд͂ь е̑гѡ̀ тре́бѸетъ (Luke 19:34—"And they said, [that] the Lord hath need of him"); ѝ вѝдѣвше всѝ ропта́хѸ, глаго́люще, ꙗ҆́кѡ ко грѣ́шнѸ мѸ́жѸ вни́де вита́ти (Luke 19:7—"And having seen, they all murmured, saying, That he was gone to be guest with a sinful man").

Both direct and indirect discourse usually are preceded by the following words: глаго́лати, рещѝ, вопроси́ти, ѿвѣща́ти, повѣ́дати, вопїа́ти and the like; the aforementioned words are also frequently met with in the midst of a quotation, for example: Ѻна́ же наважде́на ма́терїю своє́ю, да́ждь мѝ, речѐ, здѣ̀ на блю́дѣ главꙋ̀ їѡа́нна крⷭти́теля (Matth. 14:8—"And she, instructed of her mother, said, Give me here John Baptist's head in a charger").

In the books of the Scriptures (based on the Greek text) quotations usually are introduced by the conjunction ꙗ́кѡ, i.e. beginning like indirect discourse and continuing as direct discourse; for example: Тогда̀ нача́тъ роти́тися и̇ кля́тися, ꙗ́кѡ не зна́ю человѣ́ка (Matth. 26:74—"Then he began to curse and to swear, [saying] that I know not the man"), cf. in Greek: τότε ἤρξατο καταθεματίζειν καὶ ὀμνύειν ὅτι Οὐκ οἶδα τὸν ἄνθρωπον: one might say that in such constructions in Greek, the word ὅτι takes the place of quotation marks: "ὅτι recitativum". So also: и̇ кля́тся є́й (3rd person), ꙗ́кѡ є̇гѡ́же а́ще попро́сиши (2nd person) ѹ̇ менѐ, да́мъ тѝ, и̇ до полцⷬтвїѧ моегѡ̀ (Mark 6:23—"And he sware unto her, Whatsoever thou shalt ask of me, I will give thee, unto the half of my kingdom"); see also Mark 6:16; 14:57-58; 14:71; Luke 4:41; John 4:39; I John 4:20.

A rarer mixture of oblique and direct discourse is sometimes met with: the words of the author, without warning and without the conjunction ꙗ́кѡ, turn into a direct quote: и̇ то́й заповѣ́да є̇мꙋ̀ (3rd p.) никомꙋ́же повѣ́дати: но ше́дъ покажи́сѧ (2nd p.) їере́ови, и̇ принесѝ (2nd) ѡ̇ ѡ̇чище́нїи твое́мъ... (Luke 5:14—"and he charged him to tell no man: but go, and shew thyself to the priest, and offer for thy cleansing..."); Съ ни́миже и̇ ꙗ̇ды́й повелѣ̀ (3rd p.) и̇мъ (3rd p.) ѿ їерꙋса́лима не ѿлꙋча́тися, но жда́ти ѡ̇бѣтова́нїѧ Ѻ̇́ча, є̇́же слы́шасте (2nd p.) ѿ менѐ (1st p.). Acts 1:4—"And eating with them, commanded them not to depart from Jerusalem, but wait for the promise of the Father, which ye have heard of me"); see also: Acts 17:3; Acts 23:22.

From the preceding examples one may conclude that indirect discourse remains only where it conveys remarks on a 3rd party (or object), e.g. и роптаху фарїсее и книжницы, глаго́лющє, ꙗ́кѡ се́й грѣшники прїе́млетъ, и съ ни́ми ꙗ́стъ (Luke 15:2—"And the Pharisees and scribes murmured, saying, This man receiveth sinners, and eateth with them"). Were one to remove the conjunction ꙗ́кѡ, the indirect quotation, changing to a direct one, would remain unchanged.

—

APPENDIX.

Certain orthographical differences between the Moscow and Kiev editions.

Moscow:

ѡ҆́бразъ

Always with ѡ҆:

ѡ҆́бразъ, и҆зѡбраже́нїе

Kiev:

ѻ҆́бразъ

In noun roots, use ѻ҆:

ѻ҆́бразъ, пе́рвоѻбра́зный, кре́стоѻбра́знѡ:

In verb roots, use ѡ҆:

и҆зѡбрази́ти, и҆зѡбраже́нїе, воѡбраже́нїе and so on.

usually: с҆ѵ҆поста́тъ
бг҃оду́хнове́нный
де́монъ (from the root: δαίμων— δαίμον-ος)

Genitive: менѐ, тебѐ, себѐ
Before ѡ:
прї_ [прїѡбра́цꙋ]

usually: сопоста́тъ
бг҃одохнове́нный
де́мѡнъ (δαίμων)

Gen.: мене̂, тебе̂, себе̂
Before ѡ:
при_ [прїѡбра́цꙋ]

When Greek words are written in Church Slavonic, usually their root is the form taken, rather than the nominative case, for example: дра́контъ, and not *дра́кѡнъ (δράκων — gen. δράκοντ-ος [dragon]), ри́торъ (ῥήτωρ, ῥήτορ-ος [orator]), и҆ге́мѡнъ (ἡγεμών — ἡγεμών-ος [leader, commander]).

The Structure of Liturgical Chants.

The chants sung in divine services—Sticheras, Tropars, Kondaks and the like—are intended for singing, as is shown by the inscriptions they bear, indicating one or another Tone [Mode].

Just as the melodies have their own system, so too do the texts.

Ecclesiastical chants are arrranged according to 8 Tones (ἦχος), which make up the system known as "osmoglasie"). At the present time we perceive these 8 Tones as being 8 special melodies; but in the beginning they had a somewhat different significance: a "Tone" was a particular harmony, or otherwise put, it was a range of notes, a scale with intervals of various sizes (the modern scale is called a gamma). The melodies of chants were constructed in these 8 scales, as they are now constructed in two scales: the major or minor gamma, when it is a question of the borrowing or imitation of "general music". Each harmony or Tone, besides having its underlying scale, was further involved, in terms of having certain melodic peculiarities.

Originally, every chant had its own melody. The ancient hymnographers were also singers, and they composed both the words and the music at the same time. At a later time, texts began to be composed without their own melodies, with the design that they would be performed to the melody of another chant, one already known to the singers. In this way there came to be two types of chants: a chant with its own melody came to be called a *samoglasen* (ἰδιόμελον), while one with a borrowed melody was designated a *podoben* (προσόμιον). To facilitate singing, the "podobens" must reproduce exactly the syllabic structure of their model, i.e. the pattern and number of accented vs. unaccented syllables in the text whose melody they borrow; this last is referred to in such cases as the *samopodoben* (αὐτόμελον). Such an interrelationship between the podobens and samopodobens is preserved only in the original Greek texts, since, in translation to another language, including Church Slavonic, the exact syllable count is lost. The chants sung to a given podoben are identified by the first words of the original samopodoben, set over them.

Here is an example of the syllabic structure of the prosomia (podobens) in the Greek text:

T. 2: Podoben "House of Euphrates".

Πρὸς τὸ Οἶκος τοῦ Εὐφραθᾶ. Подо́бенъ: До́ме є҆нфра́дꙋовъ:

1) Πάντες τὴν τῶν σεπτῶν (6 syllables)	всн честны́хъ
2) νῦν Προπατόρων μνήμην (7)	ны́нѣ пра́о́тецъ па́мать
3) τελέσωμεν, ὑμνοῦντες (7)	совершае́мъ пою́ще
4) τὴν τούτων πολιτείαν (7)	бгоꙋго́дное житїе̇,
5) δι᾿ ἧς ἐμεγαλύνθησαν. (8)	є҆гѡ́же ра́ди возвели́чншаса.

1) Ἔσβεσαν τοῦ πυρὸς, (6)	оу́гасн́ша о́гненнꙋ́ю
2) τὴν δύναμιν οἱ Παῖδες, (7)	сн́лꙋ о́троцы,
3) χορεύοντες ἐν μέσῳ, (7)	лнкꙋ́юще посреде́
4) καμίνου καὶ ὑμνοῦντες, (7)	пе́щн, н̇ пою́ще
5) Θεόν τὸν παντοδύναμον. (8)	бга всесн́льнаго.

1) Λάκκῳ κατακλεισθείς, (6)	въ ро́вѣ заключе́нъ,
2) θηρσὶ συνῳκισμένος, (7)	звѣре́мъ со́обнта́тель,
3) Δανιὴλ ὁ Προφήτης, (7)	данїн́лъ прро́къ,
4) ἀμέτοχος τῆς τούτων, (7)	непрнча́стенъ сн́хъ
5) ἐδείκνυτο κακώσεως. (8)	показа́са ѡ̇злобле́нїа.

The syllabic scheme of this podoben is as follows:
1) ^ - - - - ^
2) - ^ - - - ^ -
3) - - ^ - - ^ -
4) - ^ - - - ^ -
5) - ^ - - - ^ - -

(Sunday of the Holy Forefathers, at the Praises).

As can be seen from the examples provided, the pattern of accented vs. unaccented syllables within one and the same podoben have no particular measure; their significance lies only in comparison with other texts modelled on the same prototype, i.e. the first line of one text has the same syllabic pattern as the first line of the following text, and each of the ensuing numbered lines corresponds to the lines with the same number in the other texts. The main accented syllables are those that have a fixed place in all of the texts sung to the same model, while the remaining accented syllables are equivalent to unaccented. Such a syllabic system in podobens might be called *syllabo- tonic parallelism,* since the lines of the podobens are parallel to the corresponding lines of the samopodoben. The advantage of such a system is especially evident where the melody is complicated— as, for the most part, the ancient melodies are.

Early Russian singing was constructed on one scale, and the difference between the various tones consisted in certain melodic characteristics (the final and next-to-last notes, melodic phrases, and the like).

In view of the fact that, in the Church Slavonic text, the syllabic structure of the prototype (samopodoben) and text modelled on it (podoben) do not match, it becomes necessary to adapt the basic melody to a somewhat different syllabic picture in each text, i.e. if there are too few syllables, then one syllable bears more notes, and when there are extra syllables, they are monotoned on the same "reciting note".

In Russian singing, the melodies of some podobens require a specific number of lines, as otherwise the concluding melodic phrase would not come out, for example, in order to chant a text to the melody of the podoben Ѽ преслáвнагѡ чꙋдесѐ: as printed in the *Sputnik Psalomschika* [1]), one must first break up the text to be sung into 9 lines. But there are other podoben-melodies that are flexible, permitting one to use the closing melodic line with any number of musical phrases. Hence the terms "devyatistrochen" ("9-liner"), "bezstrochen" ("without [limit of] lines") and the like.

---

[1]) "The Chanter's Vade-Mecum", printed with the blessing of Archbishop Arseny of Novgorod and Staraya Russa in 1916, and reprinted in Holy Trinity Monastery, Jordanville, N.Y. in 1959 and subsequently.

The example on the next page shows how syllabo-tonic parallelism is used in Church Slavonic texts.

Самоподо́бенъ: Ѿ ди́вное чу́до: (Dormition, 1st Stichera at "Lord I have cried") and the стїхи́ра подо́бна for St. Alypy (at "Lord I have cried" in the service to St. Alypy the Iconographer of the Kievo-Pechersky Monastery, Aug. 17, written by the author of this book).

From these examples of the system of samopodobens and podobens it can be seen that this is a certain simplification of singing, and therefore found mostly in services for weekdays; the expression "if there be a Samoglasen" in the rubrics gives an indication of some festivity. The services for Sundays and greater feasts contain, for the most part, "samoglasen" texts [texts which had their own special melodies].

The present-day tonal melodies in Russian church singing represent the fruits of further simplification of the music. These melodies might be called "podobens" of their own sort, which can be used with texts of any syllabic structure and any number of lines, and therefore these tones are very convenient for singers who do not know the actual melodies of the "samoglasens" and "podobens".

The canons (in the Greek text) are also composed according to this syllabic system. The Eirmos is like a "samopodoben", and the tropars of the canon copy the syllabic pattern of the Eirmos.

The Akathist Hymn to the Mother of God, which is sung on the feast of her Praises (5th Saturday in Lent), is composed in a

similar fashion[2]. The syllabic model of the 1st Oikos and the 2nd Kontakion are followed by all those that follow. The 1st Kontakion stands by itself, as a "samoglasen".

The classical metrical measure was not adopted in the composition of liturgical texts, as it would appear, because the distinction between long and short syllables had almost been lost by Byzantine times[3]), besides which such versification is hardly convenient for singing.

Be that as it may, there are several examples of the use of classical meter. An alexandrine (iambic) meter is used for the 2nd canon on the Nativity of Christ, the 2nd canon on the Epiphany, and the 2nd canon on Pentecost. A trochaic tonic tetrameter is used in the Prayer before Communion of Simeon the New Theologian, Ἀπὸ ῥυπαρῶν χειλέων (ѿ скве́рныхъ оу҆сте́нъ).

—

[2]) In the Greek service books, this Akathist alone is included.

[3]) *A Greek Grammar of NT...* by W. Funk, see §22.

CHRESTOMATHY:
The Book of Acts, Chapters 1-3.

Дѣѧ́нїѧ

ст҃ы́хъ а҆пⷭ҇тѡ́лъ.

Глава̀ а҃.

а҃. Пе́рвое ѹ҆́бѡ сло́во сотвори́хъ ѡ҆ всѣ́хъ, ѽ Ѳео́фі́ле, ꙗ҆́же нача́тъ і҆и҃съ твори́ти же и҆ ѹ҆чи́ти,

в҃. Да́же до днѐ, въ о҆́ньже заповѣ́давъ а҆пⷭ҇толѡмъ дх҃омъ ст҃ы́мъ, и҆̀хже и҆збра̀, вознесе́ся:

г҃. Пред ни́миже и҆ поста́ви себѐ жи́ва по страда́нїи свое́мъ, во мно́зѣхъ и҆́стинныхъ зна́менїихъ, де́нми четы́редесѧ́тми ꙗ҆вла́ася и҆̀мъ, и҆ глаго́лѧ, ꙗ҆́же ѡ҆ ца́рствїи бж҃їи:

д҃. Съ ни́миже и҆ ꙗ҆ды́й повелѣ̀ и҆̀мъ ѿ і҆ерⷭ҇али́ма не ѿлꙋча́тисѧ, но жда́ти ѡ҆бѣтова́нїѧ о҆́ч҃а, є҆́же слы́шасте ѿ менє̀:

є҃. Ꙗ҆́кѡ і҆ѡа́ннъ ѹ҆́бѡ крⷭ҇ти́лъ є҆́сть водо́ю, вы̀ же и҆́мате крⷭ҇ти́тисѧ дх҃омъ ст҃ы́мъ, не по мно́зѣхъ си́хъ дне́хъ.

ѕ҃. Ѻ҆ни́ же ѹ҆́бо соше́дшесѧ вопроша́хꙋ є҆го̀, глаго́люще: гдⷭ҇и, а҆́ще въ лѣ́то сїѐ ѹ҆строѧ́еши црⷭ҇твїе і҆и҃лево;

з҃. Рече́ же къ ни́мъ: нѣ́сть ва́ше разꙋмѣ́ти времена̀ и҆ лѣ́та, ꙗ҆́же ѻ҆ц҃ъ положѝ во свое́й вла́сти:

и҃. Но прїи́мете си́лꙋ, наше́дшꙋ ст҃о́мꙋ дх҃ꙋ на вы̀, и҆ бꙋ́дете мѝ свидѣ́тели во і҆ерⷭ҇али́мѣ же и҆ во все́й і҆ꙋде́и и҆ самарі́и и҆ да́же до послѣ́днихъ землѝ.

ѳ҃. И҆ сїѧ̑ ре́къ, зрѧ́щымъ и҆̀мъ взѧ́тсѧ, и҆ ѻ҆́блакъ подѧ́тъ є҆го̀ ѿ о҆́чїю и҆́хъ.

і҃. И҆ є҆гда̀ взира́юще бѧ́хꙋ на не́бо, и҆дꙋ́щꙋ є҆мꙋ̀, и҆ сѐ мꙋ́жа два̀ ста́ста пред ни́ми во ѻ҆де́жди бѣлѣ̀, а҃і. И҆же и҆ реко́ста: мꙋ́жїе Галїле́йстїи, что стоитѐ зра́ще на нб҃о; се́й Іи҃съ вознесы́йса ѿ ва́съ на нб҃о, та́кожде прїи́детъ, и҆мже ѻ҆́бразомъ ви́дѣсте е҆го̀ и҆дꙋ́ща на нб҃о.

в҃і. Тогда̀ возврати́шаса во І҆ерлⷭ҇мъ ѿ горы̀ нарица́емыа Е҆леѡ́нъ, ꙗ҆́же е҆́сть близъ І҆ерлⷭ҇ма, сꙋббѡ́ты и҆мꙋ́щїа пꙋ́ть.

г҃і. И҆ е҆гда̀ внидо́ша, взыдо́ша на го́рницꙋ, и҆дѣ́же бѧ́хꙋ пребыва́юще, Пе́тръ же и҆ І҆а́кѡвъ и҆ І҆ѡа́ннъ и҆ А҆ндре́й, Фїлі́ппъ и҆ Ѳѡма̀, Варѳоломе́й и҆ Матѳе́й, І҆а́кѡвъ А҆лфе́овъ и҆ Сі́мѡнъ Ѕило́тъ, и҆ І҆ꙋ́да І҆а́кѡвль.

д҃і. Сі́и всѝ бѧ́хꙋ терпѧ́ще е҆динодꙋ́шнѡ въ моли́твѣ и҆ моле́нїи, съ жена́ми и҆ Мр҃і́ею Мт҃рїю І҆и҃совою, и҆ съ бра́тїею е҆гѡ̀.

е҃і. И҆ во дни̑ ты̑а воста́въ Пе́тръ посредѣ̀ оу҆чени́къ речѐ: (бѣ́ же и҆ме́нъ наро́да вкꙋ́пѣ ꙗ҆́кѡ сто̀ и҆ два́десать:)

ѕ҃і. Мꙋ́жїе бра́тїе, подоба́ше сконча́тиса писа́нїю семꙋ̀, е҆́же предречѐ Дх҃ъ свѧты́й оу҆сты̀ Дв҃довыми, ѡ҆ І҆ꙋ́дѣ бы́вшемъ вождѝ е҆́мшымъ І҆и҃са:

з҃і. Ꙗ҆́кѡ причте́нъ бѣ̀ съ на́ми, и҆ прїа́лъ бѧ́ше жре́бїй слꙋ́жбы сеѧ̀.

и҃і. Се́й оу҆́бо стѧжа̀ село̀ ѿ мзды̀ непра́ведныа, и҆ ни́цъ бы́въ просѣ́деса посредѣ̀, и҆ и҆злїа́са всѧ̀ оу҆тро́ба е҆гѡ̀:

ѳ҃і. И҆ разꙋ́мно бы́сть всѣ́мъ живꙋ́щымъ во І҆ерлⷭ҇мѣ, ꙗ҆́кѡ нарещи́са селꙋ̀ томꙋ̀ свои́мъ и҆́хъ а҆зы́комъ а҆келдама̀, е҆́же е҆́сть село̀ кро́ве.

к҃. Пи́шетса бо въ кни́зѣ ѱало́мстѣй: да бꙋ́детъ дво́ръ е҆гѡ̀ пꙋ́стъ, и҆ да не бꙋ́детъ живꙋ́щагѡ въ не́мъ, и҆ е҆пі́скопство е҆гѡ̀ да прїи́метъ и҆́нъ.

к҃а. Подоба́етъ оу҆́бо ѿ сходи́вшихса съ на́ми мꙋже́й во всѧ́ко лѣ́то, въ не́же вни́де и҆ и҆зы́де въ на́съ Гдⷭ҇ь Іи҃съ,

к҃в. Наче́нъ ѿ креще́нїа І҆ѡа́ннова да́же до днѐ, въ ѻ҆́ньже вознесе́сѧ (на нб҃о) ѿ на́съ, свидѣ́телю воскрⷭнїѧ є҆гѡ̀ бы́ти съ на́ми є҆ди́номъ ѿ си́хъ.

к҃г. И҆ поста́виша два̀, І҆ѡ́сифа нарица́емаго Варса́вꙋ, и҆́же нарече́нъ бы́сть І҆ꙋ́стъ, и҆ Матѳі́а.

к҃д. И҆ помоли́вшесѧ рѣ́ша: ты̀ Гдⷭи сердцевѣ́дче всѣ́хъ, покажѝ є҆го́же. и҆збра́лъ є҆сѝ ѿ сею̀ двою̀ є҆ди́наго,

к҃є. Прїѧ́ти жре́бїй слꙋже́нїѧ сегѡ̀ и҆ а҆пⷭтолства, и҆з̾ негѡ́же и҆спадѐ І҆ꙋ́да, и҆тѝ въ мѣ́сто своѐ.

к҃ѕ. И҆ да́ша жре́бїѧ и҆́ма, и҆ падѐ жре́бїй на Матѳі́а, и҆ причте́нъ бы́сть ко є҆динона́десѧти А҆пⷭтолѡмъ.

ГЛАВА̀ в҃.

а҃. И҆ є҆гда̀ скончава́шасѧ дні́е пѧтьдесѧ́тницы, бѣ́ша всѝ А҆пⷭтоли є҆динодꙋ́шнѡ вкꙋ́пѣ.

в҃. И҆ бы́сть внеза́пꙋ съ нб҃сѐ шꙋ́мъ ꙗ҆́кѡ носи́мꙋ дыха́нїю бꙋ́рнꙋ, и҆ и҆спо́лни ве́сь до́мъ, и҆дѣ́же бѧ́хꙋ сѣдѧ́ще:

г҃. И҆ ꙗ҆ви́шасѧ и҆́мъ раздѣле́ни ѧ҆зы́цы ꙗ҆́кѡ о҆́гненни, сѣ́де же на є҆ди́номъ ко́емждо и҆́хъ,

д҃. И҆ и҆спо́лнишасѧ всѝ Дх҃а ст҃а, и҆ нача́ша глаго́лати и҆ны́ми ѧ҆зы́ки, ꙗ҆́коже Дх҃ъ даѧ́ше и҆̀мъ провѣщава́ти.

є҃. Бѧ́хꙋ же во І҆ерⷭли́мѣ живꙋ́щїи І҆ꙋде́и, мꙋ́жїе благоговѣ́йнїи ѿ всегѡ̀ ѧ҆зы́ка, и҆́же под̾ нб҃се́мъ.

ѕ҃. Бы́вшꙋ же гла́сꙋ семꙋ̀, сни́десѧ наро́дъ и҆ смѧте́сѧ: ꙗ҆́кѡ слы́шахꙋ є҆ди́нъ кі́йждо и҆́хъ свои́мъ ѧ҆зы́комъ глаго́лющихъ и҆́хъ.

з҃. Дивлѧ́хꙋсѧ же всѝ и҆ чꙋдѧ́хꙋсѧ, глаго́люще дрꙋ́гъ ко дрꙋ́гꙋ: не се́ ли всѝ сі́и сꙋ́ть глаго́лющїи Галїле́ане;

и҃. И҆ ка́кѡ мы̀ слы́шимъ кі́йждо сво́й ѧ҆зы́къ на́шъ въ не́мже роди́хомсѧ.

ѳ҃. Па́рѳѧне и҆ Ми́дѧне и҆ Є҆ламі́те, и҆ живꙋ́щїи въ Месопота́мїи, во І҆ꙋде́и же и҆ Каппадокі́и, въ По́нтѣ и҆ во А҆сі́и,

і҃. ВофРѵгі́и же и҆ Памфѵлі́и; во Е҆гѵ́птѣ и҆ страна́хъ Лїві́и, ꙗ҆̀же при Кѵрині́и, и҆ приходѧ́щїи Ри́млѧне, І҆ꙋде́и же и҆ пришелⷭцы, а҃і. Кри́тане и҆ а҆ра́влане, слы́шимъ глаго́лющихъ и҆́хъ на́шими а҆зы́ки величі́ѧ бж҃їѧ;

в҃і. Оу҆жаса́хꙋсѧ же вси̑ и҆ недоꙋмѣва́хꙋсѧ, дрꙋ́гъ ко дрꙋ́гꙋ глаго́люще: что̀ оу҆́бѡ хо́щетъ сі́е бы́ти;

г҃і. И҆ні́и же рꙋга́ющесѧ глаго́лахꙋ: ꙗ҆́кѡ вїно́мъ и҆спо́лнени сꙋ́ть.

д҃і. Ста́въ же Пе́тръ со є҆динона́десѧтми, воздви́же гла́съ сво́й, и҆ речѐ и҆̀мъ: Мꙋ́жїе І҆ꙋде́йстїи и҆ живꙋ́щїи во І҆ерⷭли́мѣ вси̑, сі́е ва́мъ разꙋ́мно да бꙋ́детъ, и҆ внꙋши́те глаго́лы моѧ̑.

е҃і. Не бо̀, ꙗ҆́коже вы̀ непщꙋ́ете, сі́и пїѧ́ни сꙋ́ть: є҆́сть бо ча́съ тре́тїй днѐ:

ѕ҃і. Но сі́е є҆́сть рече́нное прⷪро́комъ І҆ѡи́лемъ:

з҃і. И҆ бꙋ́детъ въ послѣ́днїѧ дни̑, глаго́летъ Гдⷭь, и҆злїю̀ ѿ Дх҃а моегѡ̀ на всѧ́кꙋ пло́ть, и҆ прорекꙋ́тъ сы́нове ва́ши, и҆ дще́ри ва́ша: и҆ ю҆́нѡши ва́ши видѣ́нїѧ оу҆́зратъ, и҆ ста́рцы ва́ши сѡ́нїѧ ви́дѧтъ:

и҃і. И҆́бо на рабы̑ моѧ̑ и҆ на рабы̑ни моѧ̑, во дни̑ ѡ҆́ны и҆злїю̀ ѿ Дх҃а моегѡ̀, и҆ прорекꙋ́тъ.

ѳ҃і. И҆ да́мъ чꙋдеса̀ на небсѝ горѣ̀, и҆ зна́менїѧ на землѝ ни́зꙋ, кро́вь и҆ ѻ҆́гнь и҆ кꙋре́нїе ды́ма.

к҃. Со́лнце преложи́тсѧ во тмꙋ̀, и҆ лꙋна̀ въ кро́вь, пре́жде да́же не прїити́ дню̀ Гдⷭню вели́комꙋ и҆ просвѣще́нномꙋ.

к҃а. И҆ бꙋ́детъ, всѧ́къ, и҆́же а҆́ще призове́тъ и҆́мѧ Гдⷭне, спасе́тсѧ.

к҃в. Мꙋ́жїе І҆иⷭлстїи, послꙋ́шайте слове́съ си́хъ: І҆и҃са Назѡре́а, мꙋ́жа ѿ Бг҃а и҆звѣ́ствованна въ ва́съ си́лами и҆ чꙋдесы̀ и҆ зна́менїи, ꙗ҆̀же сотворѝ тѣ́мъ Бг҃ъ посредѣ̀ ва́съ, ꙗ҆́коже и҆ са́ми вѣ́сте,

к҃г. Сего̀ нарекова́ннымъ совѣ́томъ и҆ проразꙋмѣ́нїемъ Бж҃їимъ пре́дана прїе́мше, рꙋка́ми беззако́нныхъ пригвожди́вше оу҆би́сте:

к҃д. Є҆го́же Бг҃ъ воскресѝ, разрѣши́въ бѡлѣ́зни сме́ртныѧ, ꙗ҆́коже не бѧ́ше мо́щно держи́мꙋ бы́ти є҆мꙋ̀ ѿ неѧ̀.

к҃є. Дв҃дъ бо глаго́летъ ѿ не́мъ: предзрѣ́хъ Гд҃а предо мно́ю вы́нꙋ: ꙗ́кw ѡдесно́ю менѐ є҆́сть, да не подви́жꙋсѧ.

к҃ѕ. Сегẁ ра́ди возвесели́сѧ ср҃це моѐ, и҆ возра́довасѧ ѧ҆зы́къ мо́й: є҆щѐ же и҆ пло́ть моѧ̀ всели́тсѧ на оу҆пова́нїи.

к҃з. Ꙗ́кw не ѡста́виши дꙋши̑ моеѧ̀ во а҆́дѣ, нижѐ да́си преподо́бномꙋ твоемꙋ̀ ви́дѣти и҆стлѣ́нїѧ.

к҃и. Сказа́лъ ми́ є҆сѝ пꙋти̑ живота̀: и҆спо́лниши мѧ̀ весе́лїѧ съ лице́мъ твои́мъ.

к҃ѳ. Мꙋжїе бра́тїе, досто́итъ рещѝ съ дерзнове́нїемъ къ ва́мъ ѿ патрїа́рсѣ Дв҃дѣ, ꙗ́кw и҆ оу҆́мре и҆ погребе́нъ бы́сть, и҆ гро́бъ є҆гẁ є҆́сть въ на́съ да́же до днѐ сегẁ.

л҃. Прⷪ҇ро́къ оу҆́бо сы́й, и҆ вѣ́дый, ꙗ́кw кла́твою клѧ́тсѧ є҆мꙋ̀ Бг҃ъ, ѿ плода̀ чре́слъ є҆гẁ по пло́ти воздви́гнꙋти Хрⷭ҇та̀, и҆ посади́ти є҆го̀ на прⷭ҇то́лѣ є҆гẁ,

л҃а. Предви́дѣвъ глаго́ла ѿ воскрⷭ҇нїи Хрⷭ҇то́вѣ, ꙗ́кw не ѡста́висѧ дш҃а̀ є҆гẁ во а҆́дѣ, ни пло́ть є҆гẁ ви́дѣ и҆стлѣ́нїѧ.

л҃в. Сего̀ Іи҃са воскрⷭ҇и́ Бг҃ъ, є҆мꙋ́же всѝ мы̀ є҆смы̀ свидѣ́тели.

л҃г. Десни́цею оу҆́бо Бж҃їею вознесе́сѧ, и҆ ѡбѣтова́нїе ст҃а́гw Дх҃а прїе́мъ ѿ Ѻц҃а̀, и҆злїѧ̀ сїѐ, є҆́же вы̀ нынѣ̀ ви́дите и҆ слы́шите.

л҃д. Не бо̀ Дв҃дъ взы́де на нб҃са̀, глаго́летъ бо са́мъ: речѐ Гдⷭ҇ь Гдⷭ҇ви моемꙋ̀, сѣди́ ѡдесно́ю менѐ:

л҃є. До́ндеже положꙋ̀ врагѝ твоѧ̀ подно́жїе но́гъ твои́хъ.

л҃ѕ. Тве́рдw оу҆́бо да разꙋмѣ́етъ ве́сь до́мъ Іи҃левъ ꙗ́кw и҆ Гдⷭ҇а и҆ Хрⷭ҇та̀ є҆го̀ Бг҃ъ сотвори́лъ є҆́сть, сего̀ Іи҃са, є҆го́же вы̀ распѧ́сте.

л҃з. Слы́шавше же оу҆мили́шасѧ се́рдцемъ, и҆ рѣ́ша къ Петрꙋ̀ и҆ про́чымъ Ап҃столwмъ: что̀ сотвори́мъ, мꙋжїе бра́тїе;

л҃и. Пе́тръ же речѐ къ ни̑мъ: пока́йтесѧ, и҆ да крⷭ҇ти́тсѧ кі́йждо ва́съ во и҆́мѧ Іи҃са Хрⷭ҇та̀ во ѡставле́нїе грѣхẃвъ: и҆ прїи́мете да́ръ ст҃а́гw Дх҃а.

л҃ѳ. Ва́мъ бо є҆́сть ѡ҆бѣтова́нїе и҆ ча́дѡмъ ва́шымъ, и҆ всѣ̑мъ да́льнимъ, є҆ли́ки а҆́ще призове́тъ Гдⷭ҇ь Бг҃ъ на́шъ.

м҃. И҆ и҆ны́ми словесы̀ мно́жайшими засвидѣ́тельствоваше, и҆ мола́ше и҆̀хъ, глаго́ла : спаси́теса ѿ ро́да стропти́вагѡ сегѡ̀.

м҃а. И҆̀же оу҆́бо любе́знѡ прїа́ша сло́во є҆гѡ̀, кр҃ти́шаса : и҆ приложи́шаса въ де́нь то́й дꙋ́шъ ꙗ҆́кѡ три́ ты́сащи.

м҃в. Ба́хꙋ же терпа́ще во оу҆че́нїи А҆п҃лъ, и҆ во ѡ҆бще́нїи и҆ въ преломле́нїи хлѣ́ба и҆ въ моли́твахъ.

м҃г. Бы́сть же на всѧ́кой дꙋшѝ стра́хъ, мнѡ́га бо чꙋдеса̀ и҆ зна́менїа А҆п҃толы бы́ша во І҆ерꙋсали́мѣ.

м҃д. Стра́хъ же ве́лїй ба́ше на всѣ́хъ и҆̀хъ. вси́ же вѣ́ровавшїи ба́хꙋ вкꙋ́пѣ, и҆ и҆ма́хꙋ всѧ̑ ѻ҆́бща.

м҃є. И҆ стажа̑нїа и҆ и҆мѣ́нїа продаа́хꙋ, и҆ раздаа́хꙋ всѣ̑мъ, є҆гѡ́же а҆́ще кто̀ тре́боваше :

м҃ѕ. По всѧ̑ же дни̑ терпа́ще є҆динодꙋ́шнѡ въ цр҃кви, и҆ лома́ще по домѡ́мъ хлѣ́бъ, прїима́хꙋ пи́щꙋ въ ра́дости и҆ въ простотѣ́ се́рдца,

м҃з. Хвала́ще Бг҃а и҆ и҆мꙋ́ще бл҃года́ть оу҆ всѣ́хъ люде́й. Гдⷭ҇ь же прилага́ше по всѧ̀ дни̑ цр҃кви спаса́ющыѧса.

—

A List of Books Cited

The Slavonic Scriptures (Old and New Testament),
The Liturgical Menaion (12 vols.),
The Octoechos (Book of 8 Tones),
The Lenten Triodion and the Pentecostarion
The Horologion (Chasoslov),
The Hieraticon (Sluzhebnik): Matins, Vespers, Divine Liturgy (of St.
Basil the Great, St. John Chrysostom and the Presanctified Liturgy
of St. Gregory the Dialogist),
The Trebnik (Euchologion or Book of Occasional Services),
The Pravilnik (containing the Preparation for Holy Communion),
The Prologue (Martyrology or Synaxarion— daily lives of the Saints
for reading in church).

Bibliography

F. I. Buslaev. *Istoricheskaya Grammatika.* Moscow, 1881.

Fr. Vassili Krylov. *Sokraschennaya prakticheskaya slavianskaya grammatika,* Moscow 1898.

P. Smirnovskii. *Grammatika drevniago tserkovno-slavianskago yazyka.* Moscow 1911.

A. M. Selischev. *Staroslavianskii yazyk.* Parts I and II. Moscow, 1951-52.

A. I. Gorshkov. *Staroslavianskii yazyk.* Moscow 1963.

V. P. Besedina-Nevzorova. *Staroslavianskii yazyk.* Khar'kov 1962.

L. V. Matveeva-Isaieva. *Lektsii po staroslavianskomu yazyku,* L. 1958.

V. V. Vinogradov. *Grammatika russkago yazyka.* Parts I and II. Moscow 1960.

Horace G. Lunt. *Old Church Slavonic Grammar.* Mouton & Co., The Hague, Netherlands, 1955.

C. H. van Schooneveld. *A Semantic Analysis of the Old Russian Finite Preterite System.* The Hague, 1959.

F. Blass and A. Debrunner. *A Greek Grammar of the New Testament and Other Early Christian Literature.* Translated and edited by Robert W. Funk. University of Chicago Press, 1960.

—

CONTENTS.